Cold War Germany, the Third World, and the Global Humanitarian Regime

This book examines competition and collaboration among Western powers, the socialist bloc, and the Third World for control over humanitarian aid programs during the Cold War. Young-sun Hong's analysis reevaluates the established parameters of German history. On the one hand, global humanitarian efforts functioned as an arena for a three-way political power struggle. On the other hand, they gave rise to transnational spaces that allowed for multidimensional social and cultural encounters. Hong paints an unexpected view of the global humanitarian regime: Algerian insurgents flown to East Germany for medical care, barefoot Chinese doctors in Tanzania, and West and East German doctors working together in the Congo. She also provides a rich analysis of the experiences of African trainees and Asian nurses in the two Germanys. This book brings an urgently needed historical perspective to contemporary debates on global governance, which largely concern humanitarianism, global health, South–North relationships, and global migration.

Young-sun Hong is Associate Professor of History at the State University of New York at Stony Brook and the author of *Welfare, Modernity and the Weimar State, 1919–1933* (1998). She has been a Fellow at the Woodrow Wilson International Center for Scholars, the Harvard Center for European Studies, and New York University's International Center for Advanced Studies. She has also received fellowships from the German Marshall Fund, the Max Planck Institute, the German Academic Exchange Service, and the Social Science Research Council. Hong has contributed to debates on modernity and transnationalism as part of the H-German Forum on Transnationalism (2006) and the German History Forum on Asia, Germany, and the Transnational Turn (2010). In 2008, she organized a session on Asian-German studies at the German Studies Association meeting. Currently, she serves on the editorial board of *Social History*.

For my mentors and friends,
Geoff Eley and Michael Geyer,
and
In memory of my parents

Human Rights in History

Edited by

Stefan-Ludwig Hoffmann, *University of California, Berkeley*
Samuel Moyn, *Harvard University*

This series showcases new scholarship exploring the backgrounds of human rights today. With an open-ended chronology and international perspective, the series seeks works attentive to the surprises and contingencies in the historical origins and legacies of human rights ideals and interventions. Books in the series will focus not only on the intellectual antecedents and foundations of human rights but also on the incorporation of the concept by movements, nation-states, international governance, and transnational law.

Also in the Series

Cold War Germany, the Third World, and the Global Humanitarian Regime

YOUNG-SUN HONG
State University of New York at Stony Brook

CAMBRIDGE
UNIVERSITY PRESS

CAMBRIDGE
UNIVERSITY PRESS

University Printing House, Cambridge CB2 8BS, United Kingdom

One Liberty Plaza, 20th Floor, New York, NY 10006, USA

477 Williamstown Road, Port Melbourne, VIC 3207, Australia

4843/24, 2nd Floor, Ansari Road, Daryaganj, Delhi - 110002, India

79 Anson Road, #06-04/06, Singapore 079906

Cambridge University Press is part of the University of Cambridge.

It furthers the University's mission by disseminating knowledge in the pursuit of education, learning and research at the highest international levels of excellence.

www.cambridge.org
Information on this title: www.cambridge.org/9781107479425

First published 2015
First paperback edition 2017

A catalogue record for this publication is available from the British Library

Library of Congress Cataloging in Publication data
Hong, Young-Sun, 1955–
Cold War Germany, the Third World, and the global humanitarian regime /
Young-sun Hong (State University of New York at Stony Brook).
pages   cm. – (Human rights in history)
Includes bibliographical references and index.
ISBN 978-1-107-09557-1 (Hardback : alkaline paper)
1. Humanitarian assistance, German–Developing countries–History–20th century. 2. Medical assistance, German–Developing countries–History–20th century. 3. Germany (West)–Relations–Developing countries. 4. Developing countries– Relations–Germany (West) 5. Germany (East)–Relations–Developing countries. 6. Developing countries–Relations–Germany (East) 7. Germany (West)–Relations–Germany (East) 8. Germany (East)–Relations–Germany (West) 9. Cold War. 10. Balance of power–History–20th century. I. Title.
HV555.G3H66 2015
361.2′6094309045–dc23   2014050305

ISBN 978-1-107-09557-1 Hardback
ISBN 978-1-107-47942-5 Paperback

Contents

Abbreviations

Archives, Organizations, and Acronyms

AA	Auswärtiges Amt (Foreign Ministry, FRG)
AdCV	Archiv des Deutschen Caritasverbandes (Freiburg)
ADHM	Archiv des Deutschen Hygiene-Museums
ADKGRP	Archiv des Deutschen Krankenhausgesellschaft, Rheinland-Pfalz (Mainz)
ADRK	Archiv des Deutschen Roten Kreuzes
AfZ	Archiv für Zeitgeschichte Zürich (Nachlass Dr. Samuel Teitler)
AK	Arbeitskreis
ARC	Algerian Red Crescent
ARCL	Archive of the League of Red Cross Societies (International Federation of Red Cross and Red Crescent Societies, Geneva)
AWHO	Archive of the World Health Organization (Geneva)
BAA	Bundesanstalt für Arbeitsvermittlung und Arbeitslosenversicherung (until 1969); Bundesanstalt für Arbeit (since 1969)
BAB	Bundesarchiv Berlin (Federal Archive, Berlin)
BAK	Bundesarchiv Koblenz (Federal Archive, Koblenz)
BDC	Berlin Document Center
BFM	Bundesfinanzministerium
BGL	Betriebsgewerkschaftsleitung
BMAS	Bundesministerium für Arbeit und Sozialordnung
BMI	Bundesministerium des Innern
BMW	Bundesministerium für Wirtschaft
BMZ	Bundesministerium für wirtschaftliche Zusammenarbeit
CDU	Christlich-Demokratische Union (Christian Democratic Union)
CWIHP	Cold War International History Project
DAG	Deutsche Arbeitsgruppe

DEFA	Deutsche Film-AG (German Film Company)
DGB	Deutscher Gewerkschaftsbund
DHM	Deutsches Hygiene-Museum (German Hygiene Museum, Dresden)
DKG	Deutsche Krankenhausgesellschaft
DPA	Deutsche Presse-Agentur
DPRK	Democratic Peoples' Republic of Korea (North Korea)
DRK	Deutsches Rotes Kreuz (German Red Cross)
DRV	Democratic Republic of Vietnam
FDGB	Freier Deutscher Gewerkschaftsbund (Free German Trade Union Association)
FDJ	Freie Deutsche Jugend (Free German Youth)
FLN	National Liberation Front (Front de Libération Nationale)
FRG	Federal Republic of Germany (West Germany)
GDR	German Democratic Republic (East Germany)
GPRA	Provisional Government of Algeria
HAdStFM	Historisches Archiv der Stadt Frankfurt am Main
HHStA	Hessisches Hauptstaatsarchiv (Wiesbaden)
ICRC	International Committee of the Red Cross
KFG	Koreanische Frauengruppe in Deutschland
KODCO	Korean Overseas Development Corporation
LA	Landesarbeitsamt
LRC	League of Red Cross Societies
MfAA	Ministerium für Auswärtige Angelegenheiten (Ministry for Foreign Affairs, GDR)
MfG	Ministerium für Gesundheitswesen
NARA	National Archives and Records Administration
PAAA	Politisches Archiv des Auswärtigen Amtes
ROK	Republic of Korea (South Korea)
SBZ	Sowjetische Besatzungszone (Soviet Occupation Zone)
SED	Sozialistische Einheitspartei Deutschlands (Socialist Unity Party of Germany)
SMAD	Soviet Military Administration of Germany
SPD	Sozialdemokratische Partei Deutschlands (Social Democratic Party of Germany)
Sten. Ber.	Stenographische Berichte der Verhandlungen des Deutschen Bundestages
UGTA	General Union of Algerian Workers (Union Générale des Travailleurs Algériens
UNEPTA	United Nations Expanded Technical Assistance Program
UNESCO	UN Economic and Social Council
UNHCR	United Nations High Commissioner for Refugees
UNKRA	UN Korean Reconstruction Agency
USOM	U.S. Operations Mission
VEB	Volkseigener Betrieb (People's Own Enterprise)
WWIC	Woodrow Wilson International Center for Scholars
ZK	Zentralkomitee (Central Committee)

Journals and Newspapers

ADG	*Alles für Deine Gesundheit*
AHR	*American Historical Review*
AJPH	*American Journal of Public Health*
AM	*Ärztliche Mitteilungen*
Bulletin	*Bulletin des Presse-und Informationsamtes der Bundesregierung*
CEH	*Central European History*
CSSH	*Comparative Studies in Society and History*
CWH	*Cold War History*
DÄ	*Deutsches Ärzteblatt*
DG	*Deine Gesundheit*
DH	*Diplomatic History*
FAZ	*Frankfurter Allgemeine Zeitung*
FCH	*French Colonial History*
FHS	*French Historical Studies*
GH	*German History*
GSR	*German Studies Review*
HRQ	*Human Rights Quarterly*
HWJ	*History Workshop Journal*
GG	*Geschichte und Gesellschaft*
IA	*International Affairs*
IO	*International Organization*
IRRC	*International Review of the Red Cross*
JAS	*The Journal of Asian Studies*
JCH	*Journal of Contemporary History*
JMEH	*Journal of Modern European History*
JMH	*Journal of Modern History*
JSEAS	*Journal of Southeast Asian Studies*
JWH	*Journal of World History*
MEJ	*The Middle East Journal*
ND	*Neues Deutschland*
NYT	*New York Times*
ORWHO	*Official Records of the World Health Organization*
PHR	*Public Health Review*
SH	*Social History*
SZ	*Süddeutsche Zeitung*
TWQ	*Third World Quarterly*
VJZ	*Vierteljahrshefte für Zeitgeschichte*
ZfG	*Zeitschrift für Geschichtswissenschaft*

Acknowledgments

This book has been a long time in the making. I feel fortunate to have many friends and colleagues who have had faith in my project and given me moral and professional support for many years. I am immensely grateful to the institutions whose generous financial support contributed to the completion of this work. It was a privilege to be a year-long residence Fellow at the Woodrow Wilson International Center for Scholars, the Harvard Center for European Studies, and the International Center for Advanced Studies at New York University. It was the supportive environments offered, both within and outside the seminar room, by all of these institutions that enabled me to expand my project conceptually so that it could take the form that it has today. I also thank the German Academic Exchange Service (DAAD), the Center for Contemporary Historical Research at Potsdam, the Max Planck Institute for the Study of Religious and Ethnic Diversity, and the (former) Max Planck Institute for History for financial support and sustained intellectual stimulation at various stages of the project. Their fellowships were indispensable in enabling me to rummage through archives, libraries, and used bookstores across Germany.

As anyone who has worked on a project of comparable scope well knows, it could not have been completed without the support of many archives and archivists. My deep thanks go to the Federal Archives in Berlin and Koblenz, the Political Archive of the Foreign Office, the Archive of the German Hygiene Museum, the German Red Cross Archive, the archives of the World Health Organization and the International Federation of Red Cross and Red Crescent Societies in Geneva, the SPD Archive of the Friedrich Ebert Foundation, the Berlin Document Center, and the U.S. National Archives. The archivists and librarians at the Deutscher Caritasverband went way out to make me feel welcome, and I am very grateful for their incredible support.

This book is the product of collaboration. At its inception, the members of the German Women's History Study Group helped me sharpen my ideas. My thanks go to Bonnie Anderson, Dolores Augustine, Marion Berghahn, Renate Bridenthal, Belinda Davis, Atina Grossmann, Amy Hackett, Maria Hoehn, Marion Kaplan, Jan Lambertz, Molly Nolan, Molly O'Donnell, Kathy Pence, Nancy Reagin, and Julia Sneeringer. My project also benefited from thought-provoking questions, comments, and discussions at the many conferences I attended over the years. I thank the conference organizers for inviting me to present my research at the German Modernities Workshops, the German Historical Institute in London and Washington, the University of Chicago Human Rights Program, the DEFA Summer Film Institute, the Black European Studies conference, the Research Institute of Comparative History and Culture at Hanyang University, and the universities of Bonn, Freiburg, Gießen, Hamburg, Heidelberg, Vienna, and Zürich. Over the years, my research project benefited immensely from suggestions made by many scholars, including David Blackbourn, Hubertus Büschel, Sebastian Conrad, Geoff Eley, Michael Geyer, Jennifer Hosek, Konrad Jarausch, Jennifer Jenkins, Sara Lennox, Jie-hyun Lim, Alf Lüdtke, Bob Moeller, Molly Nolan, Johannes Paulmann, Carola Sachse, Adelheid von Saldern, Quinn Slobodian, Bonnie Smith, Daniel Speich, Heidrun Suhr, Dennis Sweeney, Barbara Weinstein, Dorothee Wierling, Marilyn Young, and Andrew Zimmerman. The late Keith Nield, co-editor of *Social History*, deserves special thanks here; his numerous transatlantic trips always came with bundles of insights and, ideas on the future of politics and the academy, all topped with good humor and good drink. He is already dearly missed.

In Berlin, Bonn, and Vienna, my friends always welcomed me, shared their cozy domestic spaces, and on more than one occasion partied with me. For their hospitality, I would like to give my warm thanks to Anna Gyorgy, the Kuchenmüllers (Young-hee, Wilfried, and Tanja), Ina Merkel, Heidrun Suhr, and especially Carola Sachse and her extended family. Thanks are also due closer to home. This book has consumed more than one sabbatical, and I thank the State University of New York at Stony Brook for both this research time and for allowing me leave to take up fellowships offered by the aforementioned institutions. I also owe debts of different kinds – personal, professional, culinary – to my friends and colleagues in the Stony Brook History Department: Eric Beverley, Ned Landsman, Brooke Larson, Iona Man-Cheong, Gary Marker, Nancy Tomes, and Kathleen Wilson, as well as more department chairs than any of us would like to remember.

Larry Frohman deserves special thanks. The job of reading the countless versions of the book manuscript was, I am sure, more than what he bargained for as husband. Larry and I have been together for long enough that my former advisors know him like a former student of their own. Speaking thereof, Geoff Eley and Michael Geyer never failed to inspire me, and they have been supportive in every way possible. It is to Geoff and Michael that this book is dedicated.

* * * *

Part of Chapter 6 was first published as "'The benefits of health must spread among all:' International solidarity, health, and race in the East German encounter with the Third World," in *Socialist Modern: East German Everyday Culture and Politics* (Ann Arbor, MI, 2008, pp. 183–210), edited by Paul Betts and Kathy Pence. Part of Chapter 8 was published as "Gender, race, and utopias of development," in *Women and Gender in Postwar Europe: From Cold War to European Union* (London: Routledge, 2012, pp. 156–175), edited by Joanna Regulska and Bonnie G. Smith.

Introduction

One of my favorite documents of the Cold War is the 1958 book by William J. Lederer and Eugene Burdick entitled *The Ugly American*.[1] This work of middlebrow fiction depicted a motley assortment of Americans – diplomats, aid workers, soldiers, and even chicken farmers – serving in the fictional southeast Asian state of Sarkhan, where they were competing with their Soviet counterparts for the hearts and minds of the citizens of the new nation. These Americans were supposed to represent the best of the United States in its Cold War struggle against the menace of communism. But the Sarkhanites did not always hold them in such high esteem. In one passage, a fictional Sarkhanite journalist contrasted the arrogance and pretentiousness of the Americans with the professionalism of their Russian counterparts. The Russians, he noted, did not display any of this American ostentatiousness. They were far more sensitive to local culture and customs; they spoke the local language; and they did not comport themselves like colonial rulers by living in large houses and keeping a retinue of servants. Moreover, while large-scale projects favored by American experts showed off America's wealth and know-how, the Sarkhanite journalist could not refrain from noting that they were far less successful in meeting the needs of the local people, whose pride they often offended.

It would probably be possible to devote an entire volume to the analysis of the Cold War imaginary at work in this novel and to the visions of development around which it is organized. But I would like to begin by asking a simple question. What would happen if we introduced "ugly Germans" into the plot? How would the histories of the two German states read if they were narrated as the provincial object of a tale told by the Sarkhanites?[2] Such a story would caricature East and West German doctors competing with one another in Southeast Asia, gleefully pointing out the failings of the social system and developmental model espoused by the "other" German state. However, it is unlikely that the Sarkhanites would see much difference between the visions of modernity and development advocated by the representatives of the two countries.

We could go one step further by introducing into the story barefoot doctors and aid workers from China and Cuba. This would make the plot far more complicated because Chinese and Cuban strategies for improving the health and educational level of the Sarkhanites represented just as much of a challenge to the Russians and the East Germans as they did to the Americans and West Germans. In what ways would we have to alter our conceptual apparatus to make sense of such a world? Last, how would the narrative change if we were to imagine *The Ugly American* as the middle volume in a trilogy standing between a colonial past and an essentially open postcolonial future? This would introduce into the narrative a number of new social groups, including the national bourgeoisie, landed elites, and the communally minded peasantry, each vying with the others to shape the country's future. It would also have to take account of the constraints and opportunities presented by the ideological affinities of these groups with the superpowers and their allies.

The moral of this story is twofold. First, decolonization was a complex process. It antedated the Cold War and involved regional conflicts that cannot be explained as epiphenomena of superpower ideological and geopolitical rivalry. Once we free ourselves from the idea that all aid was manipulated by Moscow or by Washington and subordinated in a monomaniacal manner to the superpower quest for world domination, it becomes possible to identify a whole host of actors, analytical levels, and narratives that could not be made visible through the Cold War–centered perspectives. This book explores the methodological and conceptual implications of this shift. Second, the Cold War was, in the felicitous words of Heonik Kwon, "a globally staged but locally diverse regime of ideas and practices."[3] When seen from such a perspective, the Cold War – its chronology, spatiality, and topography – will assume a very different shape. My aim here is to narrate the history of a space where, as Walter Mignolo has observed, "*local* histories inventing and implementing global designs meet *local* histories, the space in which global designs have to be adapted, adopted, rejected, integrated, or ignored."[4] Accordingly, I have chosen to narrate topics that cut across the scalar divisions of the global and the local and the hierarchies implicit in them.

Although many of the local episodes that gave the Cold War its dynamic have remained untold, this does not mean, Kwon argues, that they are either "an insignificant part of local histories or an irrelevant aspect of international history."[5] The challenge is to identify which of these stories signifies something beyond itself and is thus capable of mediating between the global logic of superpower rivalry and local conflicts, which are implicated in this rivalry, but which cannot be reduced to it.

One of the central mechanisms through which the global North defined its relation to the global South were the humanitarian, development, and medical aid programs established in the 1950s and 1960s. These programs, the discourses through which they were structured, the institutions in which they were embodied, and the modes of governance that they made possible collectively constituted what I am calling here the global humanitarian regime. This regime formed the bridge by which the asymmetries between the global North and South, which had been constructed in the age of imperialism and colonial mandates, were re-articulated and reproduced across the 1945 divide. It was grounded, I argue, in notions of racial and civilizational difference, which were articulated most clearly in relation to public health, hygiene, and human rights.

However, these conceptions of difference generated specific forms of political power and authorized specific forms of global governance. In the overdetermined context of decolonization and the Cold War, the political effects of these discourses and practices of difference made it impossible to neatly separate emergency *humanitarian* relief to meliorate the human costs of decolonization and national liberation struggles from more overtly politicized *development* and *medical* aid, whose goal was to shape long-term postcolonial state-building projects in accordance with the ideology of one party or another. In this book, I will use the humanitarian, development, and medical aid programs of the two German states for the newly independent countries of Asia and Africa to explore their intertwined postwar histories, the refiguration of European modernity in its relation to the extra-European world during the era of decolonization, and the theoretical problems involved in writing a global history of the Cold War.

The individual chapters examine in detail the concrete workings of the humanitarian regime in different places and at different historical moments. They explore those transnational spaces in Korea, Vietnam, the Congo, and Tanzania, where a bevy of Cold Warriors from the North – engineers, architects, doctors, and nurses – interacted with each other and with the local inhabitants. Situating multiple actors in a polycentric transnational field will enable us not only to look at metropolitan intent but also to see how the reactions and perceptions of non-European peoples influenced the self-perception and the policies of the metropolitan powers.[6]

In Chapter 1, I trace the formation of the postwar humanitarian regime from the end of World War II through the mid-1950s. I begin by analyzing the notions of civilizational difference on which this regime rested and then show how they were encoded in the institutional and legal DNA of the United Nations, the World Health Organization, and the UN High Commissioner for Refugees. In theory, the postwar global order was structured in terms of the rights of formally equal, sovereign states. However, these discourses of difference led the Western powers to argue that the sovereignty and right to self-determination of the peoples of the Third World could only be proportionate to their level of civilization and development. Aid programs were then structured in ways that permitted these powers to govern the Third World beneficiaries of their assistance. As a result, the rights of the developing states that had to depend on humanitarian relief during the Cold War were only a pale reflection of Western norms. The formation of the postwar humanitarian regime was facilitated by the Soviet boycott at the turn of the 1950s of many of the global organizations through which this regime operated. This created a space in which France, Belgium, Britain, and the United States were able to define humanitarian and development problems as matters of security, both domestic and global, and then to instrumentalize such aid to contain communism, delegitimate national liberation movements, and reproduce neocolonial rule.

A new global constellation, which emerged in the mid-1950s, created the opportunity for multiple challenges to the Western dominance of the postwar humanitarian regime. Although it has often been assumed that communism has little to do with humanitarian and other types of aid, I show that – for reasons I detail in Chapter 1 – the Soviet Union, East Germany, and other East European countries became quite active in this domain beginning in 1955/1956. All of these countries expected that their extensive aid programs would serve as effective practical advertisements for socialism. Their conception of solidarity was based on the assumption that the countries of the Third World could only achieve their ultimate goal of self-determined development by collaborating with the Soviet bloc against capitalism and (neo)colonial rule and by emulating their model of socialist modernity. Socialist fraternal aid, however, also had a seamy underside. While it would be wrong to dismiss the rhetoric of socialist internationalism as a fig leaf for Soviet imperial ambitions, I show that the Soviet humanitarian regime was also based on conceptions of civilizational difference similar to those employed by the West, that it also represented a strategy for integrating the global South into a socialist version of the capitalist world system, and that, as a result, it reproduced the structures of domination and exploitation characteristic of its capitalist counterpart.

At the same time, the Western-dominated humanitarian regime was also challenged from a second direction by the Third World movement, which was founded at the 1955 Bandung conference. In the postwar years, the discourses of difference upon which the global humanitarian regime were based had also forced the countries of Asia and Africa into a subaltern position. The importance of the Third World movement lay in the increasingly self-conscious and assertive way that it used the language of sovereignty, self-determination, and human rights to contest both the asymmetries of the postwar humanitarian regime and the discourses on which it rested.

There was potential for both collaboration and conflict between the socialist bloc and the Third World movement. However, not all socialist countries were the same. The Chinese approach to development aid, their conception of socialist solidarity, and their response to the use of military force by settler governments and colonial powers to reassert white power in southeast Africa were quite different from those of the Soviet Union and East Germany. The growing rivalry between the Soviet Union and China for leadership of the socialist bloc thus added another dimension to an already complex account of socialist aid to the region, a story that was further complicated by the efforts of Egypt, Ghana, Guinea, and even Cuba to position themselves as champions of Third World liberation.

The two German states, both founded in 1949, played an important role in shaping the postwar humanitarian regime. The outbreak of the Korean War in 1950 accelerated the integration of both East and West Germany into their respective alliance systems. It also provided the stimulus for their participation in the bloc-wide humanitarian and development aid programs for North and South Korea. Chapter 2 examines East Germany's first development aid project in North Korea, while Chapter 3 focuses on the misbegotten history of West Germany's first major humanitarian aid program, the operation of a hospital in Pusan, South Korea. These chapters chart the initial intermeshing of the histories of the two Germanys and their East Asian partners, a development that has been virtually invisible in the dominant historical narratives of *all* of these countries. On the other hand, I argue that these programs backfired in ways that reveal as much about aims of the two German states as about the impact of their respective conceptions of racial and civilizational difference on proletarian internationalism and Western humanitarianism.

Chapter 4 examines international medical aid to both South and North Vietnam in the 1950s. Here, I argue that the securitization of U.S.-led medical aid programs to South Vietnam blurred beyond all recognition humanitarian relief, propaganda, and covert activity. In the north, a number of countries, including the Soviet Union, China, Bulgaria, Czechoslovakia, and East Germany, provided aid to the socialist government under the rubric of international socialist solidarity. While this "friendly socialist competition" between the Eastern bloc countries for political support shows that the Cold War in the Third World was, indeed, a multipolar process, I argue that such solidarity gestures were also intertwined with the desire to obtain tangible material benefits and that the East Germans endangered their own efforts to win the support of the North Vietnamese by couching their offers of assistance in the language of civilizational difference.

East Germany was one of the major supporters of a number of militant, often pro-socialist national liberation struggles, and Chapter 5 shifts from Asia to the liberation struggles in Algeria and the Congo, which together represent a watershed in the history of the postwar humanitarian regime. Picking up on questions raised in Chapter 1, I argue that the initial success of the French in defining the Algerian conflict as a matter of domestic security enabled them to securitize international humanitarian aid to Algeria and ensure that such aid could only be provided through channels and in ways that supported French military efforts to pacify the country. However, I argue that West European attitudes toward Africa and the national liberation struggles there cannot be understood apart from contemporary debates over European identity and West European integration, and I show how East German aid supported Algerian efforts to use the language of human rights and national self-determination to challenge both the parameters of the postwar humanitarian regime and French efforts to contain the conflict as a matter of domestic security. The last part of the chapter focuses on international medical aid, especially that provided by the two German states, during the 1960–1961 Congo crisis. While the story of the Congo crisis has often been told from political and military perspectives, the literature has largely ignored the topic of medical and humanitarian assistance to the Congolese and the associated controversies over the provision of this aid. I use the Congo as a case study to show how the subaltern position of Third World countries within postwar humanitarian regime prevented them from upholding their claims to sovereignty and self-determination.

The Cold War was an ideological hothouse in which each of the two blocs was constrained to insist upon the universal validity of its respective vision of modernity. On the other hand, each was ready to pounce upon the most minor failings of the other and interpret them as an indisputable sign of the moral and theoretical limitations of the liberal capitalist or the state socialist project. In this process, I argue, both West and East Germany were whipsawed by their mutual rivalry, by their relations to the superpower with which they were aligned, by other bloc members, and by the Third World countries they were supposedly trying to help. West Germany, for example, suffered from guilt by association with both the United States and the ongoing colonial wars of France, Belgium, and Portugal, and it was forced to negotiate a path between affirming its membership in the Western bloc and distancing itself from these conflicts. In a similar manner, East Germany found itself forced to compete with other Eastern European countries in Vietnam before it was caught in the downdraft of the Sino-Soviet conflict.

The Third World was also present in the two German states in the histories of their own postwar state-building projects. During these years, both East and West Germany were searching intensely for ways to legitimize their own existence, while at the same time distinguishing themselves from their ideological competitors across the inner-German border and from their shared Nazi past. The Third World was the global stage on which this Teutonic drama played out. It was also the global judge who would be swayed by the force of the better argument. The articulation of master narratives of the German past and global modernity was part of this process. While these narratives objectified the Third World in specific ways and, thereby, located them in specific discursive positions, the problem, as the two countries quickly discovered, was that their policies did not always correspond to these narratives. Not only were the Germans unable to control the ideas and expectations of these Third World publics, who were free to choose the course of their post-independence development. These countries were also themselves internally divided over where this course should take them.

In Chapters 6 and 7, I argue that European and German attitudes toward Africa and the national liberation struggles there cannot be understood apart from contemporary debates over European identity. Health and hygiene were central to the master narrative of East German socialist modernity, and Chapter 6 shows how the East German government used medical assistance programs to enhance its political legitimacy at home and gain recognition abroad. Once it became clear that the two German states were not going to be reunited in the foreseeable future and that it would have to go head to head with the Federal Republic to prove the superiority of its own system, East Germany embraced this new policy with particular verve, and medical assistance programs quickly became one of the most important tools of East German cultural diplomacy. The East Germans expected that hygiene exhibitions, along with the trade fairs with which they were often connected, would demonstrate to the Third World how science and socialism together had the potential to master nature, overcome underdevelopment, and, ultimately, transform the human condition itself. However, I argue that East Germany's attempts to sell its vision of socialist modernity were often cast in a language of civilizational difference, which limited their appeal in the Third World.

In Chapter 7, I analyze the evolution of West German development aid policy. West German policies toward Africa were inseparably bound up with the process of European integration, and they were based on the hope that the two continents could be joined in a shared Eurafrican space, in which White Europeans would take the lead in developing the human and natural resources of the underdeveloped South. The problem was that Africa and the Africans never fit without symbolic remainder into the geopolitical worldview of the West Germans, and from the mid-1950s through the early 1960s West German debates over development aid and humanitarian assistance were driven by the need to manage this discursive slippage and limit its consequences for the country's position as a stalwart member of the Western Alliance. Although West Germany sought to counter East German initiatives in Africa through propaganda safaris and exhibitions of its own, these exhibitions quickly proved to be a public relations disaster and were quietly discontinued. More important, while East Germany used humanitarian, medical, and development aid programs to circumvent and undermine the Hallstein doctrine, the West Germans sought to use development aid to enforce it. The fact that Third World countries could accept development aid from East Germany without running afoul of the Hallstein doctrine, which was narrowly focused on formal diplomatic recognition, involved West Germany in an elaborate dance with both East Germany and nonaligned beneficiary countries.

While the reputation of West Germans suffered as a result of their failure to distance themselves from white minority governments in the South, the establishment of closer relations – bordering on the verge of formal diplomatic recognition – between Egypt and East Germany set in motion a far-reaching reconsideration of both the Hallstein doctrine and the use of development aid to enforce its policy of nonrecognition.

Long before 1968, the Third World was physically present in the two German states, and in the final part of Chapter 6 and again in Chapter 8 I examine the experiences of those people from Asia and Africa who went to East and West Germany for study, training, and work. Chapter 8 focuses on those women from South Korea, India, and the Philippines who migrated to West Germany to provide the caring labor required by the country's expanding welfare system. I argue here that the employment arrangements under which these women worked, and thus the terms under which they were integrated into the global labor market, were jointly determined by forces at both ends of this global care chain. I also argue that, in addition to the economic interests of both the West German and South Korean states, global flows of female migrant labor in the postwar decades were also shaped by discourses of race and gender, which helped naturalize and legitimize the unequal power relations that were condensed in the conditions under which these women were forced to labor.

The problems encountered by people of color in East Germany were not dissimilar to those faced by Korean nurses in West Germany. Although East German programs for foreign students and trainees of color were touted as models of international anticolonial solidarity, in Chapter 6 I argue that they often proved to be counterproductive. The training provided to these persons was frequently impaired by both the problems of state socialism and the coded racism that they encountered. These trainees were further alienated by the pervasive state oversight and political education to which they, like the East German population, were subjected.

In southeast Africa, decolonization set in motion a dynamic in which the use of military force to preserve white minority governments in Angola, Mozambique, South Africa, and Rhodesia led to increasingly radical responses, both political and military, by national liberation movements. The intensity of these conflicts reached a new peak in the mid-1960s. When the revolution broke out in Zanzibar in January 1964, East Germany saw Zanzibar as a potential laboratory of German socialist modernity, while the West saw the specter of another Cuba in East Africa.

In this context, both the conception of South–South solidarity set out by the Chinese, who were becoming increasingly active in the region, and their doctrine of permanent revolution had greater appeal to the more radical leaders of revolutionary movements in the region than did the more stodgy, bureaucratic approach of the Soviets and the East Germans. As a result, by 1970 the Chinese had displaced the East Germans from the field of medical aid both on Zanzibar island and in mainland Tanganyika.

PART I

RACE, SECURITY, AND COLD WAR HUMANITARIANISM

Bipolar (Dis)Order

INTRODUCTION: THE COLD WAR AND THE POSTWAR HUMANITARIAN REGIME

In the aftermath of World War II, the Western powers responded to the absolutization of national-ethnic exclusivity – and the crimes that were perpetrated in its name – by establishing a new global political regime, which they hoped would prevent similar crises in the future. This regime was discursively grounded in what were declared to be the inalienable rights of all individuals, and it was institutionally embodied in the Universal Declaration of Human Rights, which was adopted by the United Nations (UN) on December 10, 1948. Despite the universalist rhetoric of the Declaration, however, the architecture of the new institutions of world governance was determined by both the geopolitical needs of the great powers and the discourses of difference through which these countries viewed the global South. The resulting unevenness and structural asymmetries of this global regime will be the focus of this chapter. My goal here is to use the postwar humanitarian regime to make visible the mechanisms through which these (neo)colonial relations between the global North and South were reproduced by both the Western and Eastern blocs across the 1945 divide.

The first section explores how the imagination of the global South as a domain of colonial difference shaped international law and humanitarian politics from 19th-century colonialism to the 1950s. Here, I argue that the three-world paradigm played a pivotal role in rearticulating older notions of colonial difference across the postcolonial divide, and I show how the construction of the Third World as the "Other" of Western modernity justified the continued subordination of the peoples of these regions to the European metropolitan powers. In the second section, I attempt to unearth what might be called the biopolitical underpinnings of the postwar humanitarian regime. In the eyes of Western development theory, a chain of metaphorical linkages equated poverty with disease, underdevelopment, race, and communism. I argue that, during the period under study, this biopolitical coupling led the West to view both poverty and the humanitarian crises in the global South that followed in the wake of national liberation conflicts primarily as security problems. In the third section, I look specifically at the work of the World Health Organization (WHO). Although the idea of global health was inspired by the wartime and postwar spirit of internationalism, the WHO was immediately drawn into the vortex of Cold War rivalries and national liberation struggles. I argue that the 1949/50 Soviet decision to boycott the organization made it possible for the Western powers to transform the WHO, along with other UN specialized agencies, into instruments of an American-led global strategy for containing communism.

In the fourth section, I examine in detail Western – that is, U.S. and UN – technical assistance programs, which were designed to help Third World countries break out of the poverty trap and set themselves on the path to development through broader participation in a global market economy. The fifth section focuses on the birth of Third World internationalism. In staking their claim to participate on an equal footing with the great powers of the global North, I argue, the nonaligned countries put themselves in a position to collectively challenge both Western development discourse and its global imaginary and thereby escape from the subaltern position into which this discourse had forced them. By contrast to the Western model of market-led modernization, the Soviet Union promoted an alternate development strategy. Although these socialist aid programs did present some real advantages to Third World beneficiary countries, in the sixth section I show that they suffered from many of the same disabilities as Western programs. Not only did they seek to advance the interests of the donor countries by integrating the recipients of such aid into what might be characterized as an alternate, socialist version of the capitalist world system. Like the West, they also framed their aid offers in a language of civilizational difference that may well have blunted the appeal of such offers.

I. POLITICAL VIOLENCE, WAR, AND THE FORMATION
OF THE GLOBAL HUMANITARIAN REGIME

Since the dawn of the modern era, the global South has been imagined by the Europeans as a domain of colonial difference. As Walter Mignolo has argued, in the process of its own self-constitution, Europe – as a project – had denied that the cultures of the non-European world were truly historical, that is, that they had participated in that dynamic process of continuous, revolutionary transformation that was one of the distinguishing characteristics of modernity. This logic of coloniality, which was at once temporal and spatial, dictated that these non-European peoples and cultures be relegated to a barbarian space outside of the history of reason, law, and civilization; lacking their own proper historicity, they could never do more than vegetate in an unchanging state of nature, where they would forever lag behind the more "developed" West. This originary difference created what Frantz Fanon has called the Manichean bipolarity of the human species and masked the political violence inherent in colonial rule.[7]

Although colonial empires were the product of state-organized violence, European rule over its colonies in Asia and Africa was justified in terms of a civilizational gradient and a corresponding civilizing mission.[8] These asymmetrical relations between the global North and South were institutionalized first in the rules established to legitimize claims to overseas territories in the 1880s. Consequently, as Anthony Anghie has argued, international law must be understood "in terms of the problem of cultural difference – the difference that international jurists through the centuries understood to separate civilized, European states from uncivilized, non-European states."[9]

In the first half of the 20th century, however, the imperial, colonial order that had taken its modern form across the long 19th century was disrupted by a quickening stream of events. As Donald Bloxham has argued, "the cradle of modernity, which gave the world its state system, and [which] had until the early twentieth century been a net exporter of violence, exploded at its heart, and brought its advanced capacity for military and administrative violence to bear upon itself."[10] The industrialized mass violence of World War I called into question the self-evidence of Western ideas of humanity, civilization, and law. The proliferation of discourses on Europe and the fate of white Occidental civilization after the war reflected the depth of this crisis.[11] The global hegemony of

Western Europe was also challenged from within by the Bolshevik revolution and from the periphery by pan-Asian and pan-Islamic movements.[12] In the eyes of many Westerners, these events conjured up the specter of a global race war.

After 1919, colonial rule was reproduced in neocolonial form by the mandate system set up under the auspices of the League of Nations. Article 22 of the League Covenant entrusted European colonial empires with the "well-being and development" of the indigenous populations, whom the Covenant characterized as "peoples not yet able to stand by themselves under the strenuous conditions of the modern world."[13] In this legal doctrine of trusteeship, the continued domination and exploitation of the non-European world was apostrophized as a sacred trust of civilization in which the European metropolitan powers were asked to assume the burden of setting backward cultures with their surplus lives on the path to the civilized world of work, discipline, and hygiene.

In the 1930s and 1940s, however, this liberal global order was challenged at the two ends of the Eurasian land mass by signal, and savage, attempts to restructure the globe in accordance with the principles of racist biopolitics. The crisis of European colonialism was further accelerated by such events as the forced retreat from colonial empires in Asia; the metropolitan dependence on colonial manpower and resources to survive the combined onslaught of Nazi Germany and Japan; and, in the immediate postwar years, an arc of nationalist, anti-imperialist struggles that stretched from the Chinese civil war via communist insurgencies in Malaya, Indochina, and Indonesia to the Mau-Mau uprising in Kenya.

Collectively, these events threatened to shake old Europe – the professed cradle of Western civilization – out of that "geopolitical amnesia" that had heretofore allowed its privileged position to appear natural and self-evident.[14] This threat forced the West to engage in a complex process of ideological labor to stabilize its cultural and political hegemony. The outcome of this process was the three-world paradigm, which enabled the countries of the Northern, "White Atlantic"[15] to rescue and rearticulate their conception of the imperial, colonial world order and their place in it in relation to the socialist camp, which constituted the Second World. This spatiotemporal imaginary thereby brought the Soviet Union into the picture, but it did so in a way that relegated the socialist bloc to the "fringes" of Western modernity and thus denied the legitimacy of the socialist project.[16]

The relation between the First World and the Third was even more complex. The concept of the Third World, which was coined in 1952 by the French demographer Alfred Sauvy, represented a domain of archaism and underdevelopment – the Other whose categorical difference made it possible for the countries of the global North to define their own identities and modernities.[17] This process of othering functioned in specific ways. National liberation movements in Asia and Africa represented a direct challenge to the cultural hegemony and neocolonial proclivities of the West. The Third World was a conceptual device designed to neutralize this challenge, while at the same time legitimizing the superiority of the First World and its tutelary rights and responsibilities in the global South.[18] In the era of settler colonialism, Europeans had imagined the colonial territories as a non-place where the teeming masses of the colored peoples had eternally existed in a natural condition that could only barely be termed "human." Now, at the height of decolonization, the concept of the Third World denoted a space of underdevelopment in comparison with the developed West. The distinguishing features of this less- or underdeveloped world were mass poverty, endemic disease, low productivity, high birthrates, high mortality, and the relative absence of both civilization and its equivalent, modernity. This problem complex was attributed in undefined, circular ways to ignorance, the weight of tradition, and the lack of education, all of which were regarded as constitutional features of the Third World peoples of color.

In the final years of World War II, Anglo-American politicians sought to mobilize the world public behind a wartime crusade against the axis powers, and they based their campaign on the concept of human rights set out in Roosevelt's "four freedoms" speech and in the Atlantic Charter. In the aftermath of the war, these ideas shaped the contours of postwar liberal internationalism; they also helped define the mission of the United Nations, which was charged with the defense and promotion of the rights set out in the UN charter and the Universal Declaration of Human Rights.[19]

However, as Mark Mazower has noted, the UN "was above all a means of keeping the wartime coalition of Great Powers intact at whatever cost."[20] The resulting balance between state sovereignty and universal human rights gave the postwar humanitarian regime its peculiar shape. On the one hand, as Hannah Arendt argued in 1951, to be without a state was to be without rights and to experience a form of social death, one that had often opened the way to expulsion and extermination.[21] On the other hand, the persistent logic of coloniality reproduced the privileged position of the great powers, while denying to certain states the capacity to act as autonomous subjects in defense of the collective rights of their citizens. Although all sovereign states were theoretically equal, during the debates over the human rights covenants, Britain, France, and Belgium all maintained that the indigenous peoples of Africa and Asia "had not yet reached a high degree of development" and that, therefore, both the sovereign rights of their states and the human rights of the individual members of their populations should be proportional to their level of civilization.[22] In the deliberations leading up to the final wording of the UN Charter, the European colonial powers put forward national self-determination as "a desirable ideal," but not an inalienable right, while the Soviet Union and a group of Third World countries called for the definitive end of colonial rule.[23] In the end, the UN Charter affirmed the general principle of, but not the right to, self-determination.

Consequently, neither the idea of human rights nor formal decolonization was sufficient to shake off the colonial, imperial origins of international humanitarian law. In fact, the admission of newly independent Asian and African countries to the UN tended to obscure the continuing effects of the older discourse of colonial difference. The resulting blind spots are clearly evident in the early postwar history of human rights and humanitarian aid. The UN's understanding of its own mission left the organization unprepared to deal with the major humanitarian crises that followed the partition of the Indian subcontinent, the 1948 Arab–Israeli conflict, and subsequent national liberation conflicts.[24] The Arab–Israeli conflict scattered one million Palestinian refugees across Jordan, Lebanon, Syria, the West Bank, and the Gaza Strip. In the expectation that the Palestinian refugee crisis would be of only limited duration, the UN initially took no action. However, the fear of communist influence in the Middle East led to the creation in 1949 of an ad hoc agency, the United Nations Relief and Works Agency, to assist the Palestinian refugees on a temporary, emergency basis.[25]

Similarly, the 1951 Refugee Convention restricted the scope of the UN refugee agency's responsibility to events that had taken place before January 1, 1951, and signatory countries were given the option of further limiting its scope to events in Europe. This retrospective focus on European events had an important consequence for the staggering number of "new" refugees and displaced persons who were caught in a cycle of insurgency and counterinsurgency in Africa and Asia in the years after 1945. By denying these persons official refugee status (and the material and medical assistance that was predicated upon such recognition), the Convention had by the mid-1960s created the perverse situation in which fewer than half of the refugees actually being assisted by the UN High Commissioner for Refugees fell under the provisions of the UN Refugee Convention.[26]

The Fourth Geneva Convention of 1949, which established basic protections for civilians in war zones, limited the authority of international humanitarian agencies to the civilian and military victims of "international armed conflicts," that is, conflicts between recognized sovereign states. Although the Common Article 3 – the third article of all four Geneva Conventions – addressed "the case of armed conflicts not of an international character," its provisions dealing with humanitarian aid were limited to "persons taking no active part in the hostilities."[27] As a result, to the extent that it was framed in terms drawn from traditional conflicts between sovereign states, international humanitarian law was not applicable to insurgents fighting for national self-determination. This decision legitimized the metropolitan claim to represent and speak on behalf of subaltern peoples, freedom fighters, and refugees; it made the metropolitan powers into the mediator between the global humanitarian regime and the "dependent" peoples living under their protection; and it also put them in a position where they could limit, control, and otherwise instrumentalize humanitarian aid to the millions of refugees caught up in the web of insurgent and counterinsurgent violence.

As a result, international humanitarian law was from the very beginning intrinsically resistant to addressing the problems created by colonial war, national liberation struggles, and decolonization crises. During the early postwar years, the European colonial powers were able to privatize and contain the universalist rhetoric of human rights by declaring national liberation struggles to be matters of domestic security, and they succeeded in defining in international law what constituted a humanitarian crisis and the conditions under which other nations were permitted to provide what kinds of assistance to the different parties.

Across the mid-1950s, however, these efforts were increasingly challenged the changing global dynamics, in part due to the entry of new Asian and African states into the UN and the formation of the Third World internationalism. Not only did national liberation movements appeal to the global community in the name of their human rights; but they also appealed to this community to protect these rights *from* the metropolitan powers, who had been appointed as their virtual representatives, but who were often regarded as illegitimate and oppressive. A war for definitional power then ensued over whether anticolonial struggles were to be considered domestic or international conflicts, whether they should be considered "rebellions" against *legitimate* sovereign authority or "independence movements" against *illegitimate* colonial rule, whether those who fought in such conflicts were to be designated as "bandits" or "soldiers" deserving the protection of international law, and whether metropolitan powers should have the right to control the flow of humanitarian aid.

II. GLOBAL SECURITY AND THE BIOPOLITICS OF HEALTH AND DEVELOPMENT: THE COLD WAR AND THREE-WORLD PARADIGM

In recent years, scholars have attempted to elucidate the connections between global security and biopolitics by exploring how the security of the self and the nation was established and maintained through the discursive othering and administrative surveillance and exclusion of immigrants, the poor, the sick, and all those who could be considered racially or culturally different. Such a schema can also be applied to make sense of the attitudes of the industrialized world toward the teeming, impoverished, diseased multitudes of the Third World. As Mark Duffield has argued, at the height of the Cold War decolonization evoked in the West a fear of the global circulation of superfluous life, that is, of refugees, immigrants, communists, and terrorists. The function of this deepening "biopolitical division of the world of peoples into developed and under-developed species-life" was to "contain the circulatory and destabilizing effects of underdevelopment's non-insured surplus life."[28] It was this "new biopolitical Zeitgeist" that provided the postwar machinery of world governance with a "grid of intelligibility" for its security strategy.[29]

Development was the most important discourse deployed to describe what Foucault called a "biological-type caesura" – one that was simultaneously biological, racial, medical, and civilizational – between North and South.[30] The idea of development was a transnational project whose basic ideas had been formulated long before 1945.[31] European colonial development programs had aspired to increase the production of food and raw materials by improving the productivity of indigenous workers in plantations and mines. In the interwar years, Imperial Japan, Nazi Germany, and the Soviet Union all deployed development programs in a hybrid form to accelerate the infrastructural enclosure of "territories of production,"[32] while liberal New Dealers promoted American-style development at home and in Latin America.[33]

In the postwar Atlantic context, the master trope of development discourse was an "insidious circle" in which disease bred poverty, poverty bred ignorance and overpopulation, and the latter in turn bred more disease.[34] In a 1950 essay, for example, the American Geographical Society's director of medical studies Jacques May sought to explain the connection between climate, disease, and underdevelopment by arguing that, for much of the tropical world, "the soil produces poor food, the pathogens cause poor health, both are the cause of poor working efficiency, all operating in a vicious circle. An outsider breaking into the environment would be fed its food and inoculated with its parasites, unless he brought with him the techniques by which Western civilization has triumphed over difficulties of nature." The inability to break out of this circle meant, May explained, that the peoples of these regions

cannot develop their intelligence and culture, cannot organize agriculture profitably or develop commerce and industry or the arts of social living. They are, consequently, in no position to establish institutions by which they could raise their standard of living, organize sanitary campaigns, and achieve public health. Since they cannot get rid of their most despotic tyrants and oppressors, the intestinal worms and blood parasites, they are tied down by their physical condition to their backward status.[35]

As May made clear in this passage, development theory was predicated on the assumption that traditional societies and the indigenous peoples of the Third World were incapable of negotiating on their own the complex path of economic, social, and political modernization necessary to escape from this vicious circle; that they depended, instead, on the knowledge, technology, initiative, and guidance from the more developed world; and that the task of Western development aid was to jumpstart the process that Karl Marx famously described as the primitive accumulation of capital and thus set in motion the self-sustaining economic growth believed to be both the precondition for, and the result of, a continuous process of social, political, and cultural change.

In this way development theory, which emerged as the dominant government policy and social science in the 1950s and 1960s, transformed the Third World into what Timothy Brennan has called "zones of invisibility," where the process by which the non-European is marked as backward created the conditions for primitive accumulation, while the workers who were devalued and disempowered by this process produced profits and use-value for the global North – in both its capitalist and socialist incarnations.[36] Proponents of development theory maintained that whatever demands for change that did emanate from these countries could only be understood as immediate, instinctive reactions to deprivation. This assumption rendered the West incapable of understanding the structural causes of dependency and inequality, sympathizing with demands for political self-determination, and thus recognizing the claims and aspirations of national liberation movements. As a result, anticolonial resistance movements could only be identified – in terms that were as much psychological as sociological – with that state of complete social and political negation known at the time as "communism."

If we look at Western rhetoric of the Cold War, we are immediately struck by the extent to which it employed terminology taken from the bacteriological sciences to explain the pathological effects of communism. For example, in his famous telegram from Moscow George F. Kennan demonized communism as a "malignant parasite which feeds only on diseased tissue," and he characterized the United States as a "world doctor" that was called on to play a heroic role in the global campaign to eradicate this disease.[37] In 1955, Eisenhower himself warned that "for more than half of mankind disease and invalidity remain the common phenomena and these [constitute fertile] soil for the spread of communism."[38] And in his famous 1960 work *The Stages of Economic Growth*, Walt Rostow characterized communism as a pathological epiphenomenon of the unmastered transition from traditional to modern society; it was not for nothing that the subtitle of this work was a "non-communist manifesto."[39]

These medico-metaphorical linkages between communism and disease helped mobilize domestic support for technical assistance programs in the Third World, where public health and population control became one of the central battlegrounds in the global confrontation between capitalism and communism. In this battle, what was needed to break the vicious circle of poverty and disease and cure the disease of communism was a specific form politico-medical treatment, which relied not on revolutionary social change, but rather on technical solutions provided by Western experts.[40]

Such arguments made use of a highly militaristic yet optimistic discourse intended to appeal to both educated Third World opinion and domestic audiences in the West. However, these metaphorical linkages also ran in the other direction with the martial language of the war on communism being employed to describe global health and the multifaceted war on germs. For example, in 1951 Frank Boudreau, the former head of the Health Organization of the League of Nations, called for a "world-wide united front in the struggle for good health," and he argued that carefully organized field planning and logistics were just as essential to disease control as to the military: "[N]o gaps must be found in the front facing the enemy, every sector must be held by first-class troops armed with the best weapons that science can provide. These armies are the health services and medical and health institutions in the different countries... [The] WHO is engaged in building up this *army of health*."[41]

At times, these martial metaphors could be stretched to the point where the precise object of the campaign – bacteria, communism, national liberation movements – was completely underdetermined. As we read in a 1963 publication,

this is a story about a war. [T]he enemy is cunning and treacherous. He is an old hand at guerilla warfare. He will strike where he is least expected, and then will quickly retreat into the mysterious jungle, defying men to find him out and uncover his secrets...Time and again, when he has apparently been cut off and surrounded, he will attack from the rear with whole waves of fresh troops.[42]

Without prior knowledge, there is simply no way to know that this statement is taken from a work published to promote the work of the WHO, rather than to describe counterinsurgency warfare.

Once articulated, this logic could then be extended to the geopolitical domain and spatial imaginary of the Third World.[43] In the words of one American medical official working with the United Nations,

The Good War is being waged on the many fronts of poverty – on dry desert sands and in thick tropical forests, in teeming new shantytowns and in rural communities *static in their ancient ways*, in the urban centers of emerging nations and on the *wastelands of forgotten peoples*. It is being fought wherever hopelessness holds in bondage the untold potential of man and the earth on which he lives ... Wherever men and nations want to step from the ruts of stagnation, the task forces of the Good War stand ready to show them the way. Its advance guard is composed largely of people from those nations that have gone farthest along the road of technological and commercial progress...[44]

Here, poverty, hunger, and disease are seen as the natural state of affairs in the Third World and as the source of a seething and inexhaustible reservoir of native (anticolonial) resentment.

There was one final link in this chain of signifiers used to contain the biopolitical dangers that were perpetually threatening to leap over the discursive barriers erected to contain them and infect the West. Matthew Connelly has argued that "the worldviews of Cold War-era policymakers were shaped at a time in which concerns about demographic trends and international race war were pervasive in both Europe and the United States."[45] These assumptions also shaped the policies of Britain, France, and the Netherlands as they all sought to turn back military challenges to their control in Malaya, Indonesia, Indochina, and Kenya.[46] Still traumatized by the loss of China to the Communists in 1949, the entry of Chinese "voluntary" soldiers into the Korean War rekindled the fear of the "yellow peril" and showed that the United States was not invincible. The French portrayed their desperate attempts to hold on to Indochina as a struggle between the civilization of the white Occident and the un-culture of both the communist East and "Asiatics and African and colonial natives."[47] Thus the Western alliance increasingly defined its common interest as much in terms of "white solidarity" as anticommunism.

The West Germans also made liberal use of this racialized coding of communism as "Asiatic." For example, Chancellor Konrad Adenauer considered China the "enemy of all the white," and at the 1954 Geneva Conference, he was horrified by the equality afforded to Russian, Chinese, Vietnamese, Korean, Cambodian, and Laotian delegates. As he told the cabinet, the physiognomies of the "horde" seated around the conference table sent a shudder through him and his white colleagues.[48] This discourse on communism as a barbarian Mongol horde – which had served as a central trope in justifying the Nazi racial war against the Soviet Union and the Jews – made it easier for many West Germans to buy into European integration and the anti-Communist Western alliance.

Although such anxieties were simply the obverse of the long-standing claims for the superiority of the white race and Occidental culture, they took on a new and more concrete form in the changing global context. As a result, to the extent that communism, the "colored" peoples, their demands for independence, and their "culture" were all positioned as negations of white Occidental civilization and its achievements, all of these Others tended to bleed into one another. As Gerald Horne has argued, although anticommunism "had the advantage of being – at least formally – nonracial...[,] the tagging of anticolonialists as 'red' slowed down the movement against colonialism and – perhaps not coincidently – gave 'white supremacy' a new lease on life."[49]

If in earlier times humanitarian aid had been considered a domain of charitable engagement, it was no longer politically viable, as Kennan had once proposed, to leave the Third World to its "tragic fate"[50] because neutrality or abstinence would only create an opportunity for communist subversion. As Assistant Secretary of State for International Organization Affairs Harland Cleveland told Congress during the Congo crisis, because of the danger that chaos and disorder in Third World countries would open the door to communist influence, doing nothing was no longer an option: "[S]elf-determination obviously doesn't mean letting a situation like the Congo stew in its own juice, because that isn't really one of the options. It will be either competitive bilateral intervention or it will be some form of *more sanitary intervention* by the world community as a whole." The United States, he continued in a way that mimicked the very language of Kennan's "Sources of Soviet Conduct," would have to pay "competent, unremitting attention to the periphery" and develop a new mechanism of global governance for "this new kind of world."[51] One could hardly ask for a clearer statement of the logic of containment as it pertained to the field of humanitarian aid. However, the biopolitical coupling of underdevelopment and communism in such arguments provided the framework through which the Western countries came to see humanitarian crises in Asia and Africa primarily as security problems that, like communism itself, needed to be contained. It also underpinned the Cold War logic through which counterinsurgency programs in all of their diverse forms came to be seen just as essential as food, medicine, and development assistance to securing individual freedom, collective security, and market economy.

III. THE WORLD HEALTH ORGANIZATION AND GLOBAL HEALTH GOVERNANCE, 1945–1950

The idea of global health was inspired by advances in biomedicine and the postwar spirit of globalism.[52] Advances in bacteriology and epidemiology since the turn of the century and wartime refinements in military medicine provided the technical means for a large-scale assault on epidemic disease. World War II had also created a new sense of global interconnectedness. Many people now believed that the problem could not be contained within the boundaries of a single nation-state and, instead, had to be tackled on a planetary scale if it were to be solved at all. As the Canadian Brock Chisholm, the first director-general of the WHO, explained in 1946 to the committee charged with drafting the constitution of what was to become the WHO,

biological warfare, like that of the atomic bomb, had become a fearful menace, and unless doctors realized their responsibilities and acted immediately, the whole race risked total extinction. Such action could obviously not stop at international frontiers. The world was sick, and the ills from which it was suffering were mainly due to the perversion of man, his inability to live at peace with himself... It was in man himself that the cause of present evils should be sought. These psychological evils must be understood in order that a remedy might be prescribed. The scope of the task before the Committee, therefore, knew no bounds.[53]

Chisholm encouraged the members of the committee to "aim at universal and world-wide achievement," and he proposed that the new organization be named the "World or Universal" Health Organization to highlight the fact that the scope of its mandate had to be "even more than international."[54] Chisholm also chided countries, including the United States and Britain, that continued to insist upon a nation-state-centric approach to public health. "The world," Chisholm explained, "had drastically changed, and the time had come to aim for an ideal; this ideal should be to draw lines boldly across international boundaries and should be insisted on at whatever cost to personal or sectional interests ... [S]urely at the present time no member of the Committee could be thinking in terms of international prestige... As world citizens, all should wipe out the history of the past, formulate an ideal and try to realize it."[55]

When the United Nations Conference on International Organizations met in San Francisco in the spring of 1945, the WHO was an afterthought. As Karl Evang, the outspoken Norwegian advocate of social medicine, observed in retrospect, "who would have thought ... that health would again be 'forgotten' when the Charter of the United Nations was drafted at the end of the Second World War? However, this was exactly what happened, and the matter of world health again had to be introduced more or less ad hoc..."[56] In the end, the delegates unanimously supported the idea of a world health organization. The representatives from Brazil and China, the most vocal supporters of the proposal, then asked the United States to convene an international health conference to discuss the idea.[57]

Initially, the United States and Britain opposed the creation of a single global health organization. In a letter to President Truman, Hugh Cumming, the director of the Pan American Sanitary Bureau and former Surgeon General, expressed his contempt for those "star-gazers and political and social uplifters," who otherwise dominated these meetings, and he rejected the idea of creating one single world health organization as the fantasy of "extreme internationalists."[58] Although the British and the Americans hoped to preserve the traditional dominance of the Western powers within the organization, in the end the State Department favored a more pragmatic approach that took account of the demands of the non-European member states. The Americans, however, insisted that the principle of national sovereignty had to be upheld and that the proposed organization be "dedicated to the expansion and strengthening of *national* health services on invitation of national Governments."[59]

In March–April 1946, the members of the Technical Preparatory Committee met in Paris to begin drafting a constitution for the WHO, the International Health Conference was convened in New York in June of that year, and the first plenary meeting of the newly constituted WHO took place later that same month.[60] The preparatory committee devoted much of its time to issues of membership and representation. Along with the question of what to do about the former Axis powers and their allies, committee members wrestled with whether "non-self-governing territories" could be represented.[61] Since only sovereign states could be admitted to the United Nations, it was considered logical that only such states could be admitted to the UN-affiliated WHO (which also welcomed such states even if they did not belong to the UN). The delegates agreed that protectorates could be admitted as associate members without voting rights, but that colonies were to be represented by the relevant metropolitan powers.[62]

The question of precisely who would be chosen to represent these associate members also gave rise to an extended controversy. While the British argued that colonial health officers should represent associate members, the Liberian representative Joseph Nagbe Togba argued that the persons chosen to represent these protectorates should be natives who were familiar with the "needs and interests" of their own people. Moreover, since the metropolitan powers were likely to appoint whites to fill these positions, he maintained that the British proposal would result in the reproduction of existing colonial power relationships.[63] The preamble to the WHO constitution proclaimed "the enjoyment of the highest standard of health [to be] one of the fundamental rights of every human being without distinction of race, religion, political belief, economic or social condition."[64] However, it was far from clear how representatives of the colonial powers could be expected to work to realize this goal.

At the 1946 International Health Conference, conflicts also arose over precisely whom the proposed organization would serve and how. While the victim countries of Nazi aggression claimed that they were entitled to special assistance, the countries of Asia and Latin America insisted that they, too, had special needs.[65] Most European countries believed that each state should be able to take care of its own needs, and they wanted the new organization to assist in rebuilding public health systems that had in many cases ceased to function during the war. But the real problem with the focus on the reconstruction of national healthcare systems was that such an approach could not recognize the problems that the newly independent countries of Asia and Africa would face in the age of decolonization. Under colonial rule, the few existing healthcare institutions had been reserved for the white colonizers, and colonial rulers had frequently blocked the training of indigenous healthcare professionals. As a result, these countries had neither a healthcare infrastructure nor a system for training healthcare workers, and there was no national health system that only needed to be reconstructed. All of these problems were compounded by the exodus of European physicians and administrators at independence, the near collapse of the few existing hospitals in the wake of these departures, and the refugee crises that in many places were an unavoidable side effect of national liberation struggles. One of the top priorities for the leaders of these newly independent states was to promote the training of physicians and health workers and to expand public health facilities in rural areas.

One of the important early controversies was related to the internal organization of the WHO. For administrative purposes, the WHO divided the world into six world regions (Africa, America, Southeast Asia, Europe, the Eastern Mediterranean, and the Western Pacific). These regional divisions were based on the belief that, as the Irish representative explained, "it is easier to arrive at such general solutions where the inhabitants of a region are racially homogeneous and share the same culture."[66] However, the belief in the homogeneity of health conditions within these regions was itself an essentializing construct that empowered the WHO technocracy to introduce standardized policies and programs in the countries assigned to the individual regions.

The WHO tried to avoid the problems inherent in such schemata by arguing that their regional divisions were simply administrative fictions and did not imply any claims about the real conditions prevailing in the region. Yet these fictions were themselves inherently unstable. Although the WHO hoped to stabilize the spatial division of the world by linking representation to nature, custom, and the ostensible needs of the region, every attempt invariably created more problems than it solved. In practice, the WHO honored the wishes of member states wherever possible in the assignment of specific states to individual administrative regions. For example, in view of the hostility between India and Pakistan, the Pakistani government chose to be assigned to the Eastern Mediterranean, rather than the Southeast Asian region headquartered in New Delhi.[67]

In a similar manner, colonies and protectorates were assigned to administrative regions according to the preferences of their European governors, a practice that often yielded absurd results. For example, trusteeship over Morocco was divided between Spain and France. While the French insisted that its part of the country be assigned to the European region, Spain wanted its zone assigned to Africa. The Arab delegates argued that Morocco – together with Algeria and Tunisia – should be assigned to the Eastern Mediterranean region because of the cultural, religious, and epidemiological similarities among these territories. There was a similar, equally bitter dispute between France and Egypt over the administrative location of Algeria. In this instance, Indian and Burmese support for the Egyptian position helped to forge the connections among the Third World countries, which later formed the core of the nonaligned movement.[68] Israel, on the other hand, had no desire to be lumped together with its Arab neighbors in the Eastern Mediterranean region and argued that the whole system ought to be scrapped: "The countries in such aggregations might well be geographically distant from one another and possessed of totally different health conditions. Rather than have the regional principle distorted by the artificial creation of regions formed on the basis of political, cultural, economic, social, religious or ethnic criteria, the Government of Israel would prefer to see it abandoned altogether."[69]

IV. GLOBALIZING THE AMERICAN MODEL OF DEVELOPMENT AND DEMOCRACY

By the time the first World Health Assembly convened in June 1948, few areas of the world remained untouched by manmade disasters. The Berlin blockade, which began in June 1948, finalized the division of the continent, and the WHO itself was immediately drawn into the vortex of Cold War rivalries and national liberation struggles. The Cold War within the organization determined which regions would receive which kinds of technical assistance, the distribution of fellowships for medical researchers and specialists abroad, and the transnational exchange of biomedical and pharmaceutical technology.

The cornerstone of American development policy during these years was the Point IV program, which Truman announced in his inauguration speech on January 20, 1949. By contrast to the Marshall Plan, which had provided extensive material assistance for the reconstruction of Western Europe, the goal of the Point IV program was to help the Third World break out of the vicious circle of poverty, disease, and underdevelopment.[70] As Truman explained in terms that by now should be familiar,

more than half the people of the world are living in conditions approaching misery. Their food is inadequate. They are victims of disease. Their economic life is primitive and stagnant. Their poverty is a handicap and a threat both to them and to more prosperous areas. For the first time in history, humanity possesses the knowledge and skill to relieve the suffering of these people. The United States is preeminent among nations in the development of industrial and scientific techniques. The material resources which we can afford to use for assistance of other peoples are limited. But our imponderable resources in technical knowledge are constantly growing and are inexhaustible.[71]

In June 1949, Truman proposed the creation of the Expanded Program of Technical Assistance (EPTA) to put this commitment into practice by helping the Third World increase agricultural productivity.

Truman also created the International Development Advisory Board to serve as a consultative body for the program. The Board's March 1951 report, which reflected the tensions generated by the Korean War, gave top priority to military defense against communist "aggression and subversion." It insisted that, as "a vital part of our defense mobilization," foreign assistance to the Third World should be "brought within the necessary broad strategy of a total foreign policy." Underdeveloped regions were strategically important as sources of vital raw materials and export markets, and, as such, they had to be defended from communist "economic subversion." In spelling out its strategy here, the Board explained that "economic development means much more than merely increasing the production of food and raw materials. It also means *a relentless war on disease.*"[72]

In March 1949, the United States proposed that the UN Economic and Social Council establish a parallel program; the UN General Assembly authorized this step in November of that year; and the UN Technical Assistance Administration was established in July 1950.[73] The United States hoped that the program would make it possible to coordinate assistance from other countries and avoid the wasteful competitive duplication of programs. The program was funded through voluntary contributions from member states.[74] However, because 60 percent of the UN EPTA budget came from the United States, the Americans had a disproportionate influence on both the programs directly sponsored by EPTA and those it indirectly funded – from Point IV money – through the WHO, the Food and Agricultural Organization, UNICEF, and UNESCO. The UN EPTA began its actual field operations in mid-1950s; and by 1958, it had sent about 8,000 technical experts to the Third World. Public health was the main focus of the work of UN EPTA because experts believed that technical tools and know-how, especially insecticides such as DDT and antibiotics like penicillin, could be directly exported to the Third World to eradicate social problems at their biological source. This thinking gave a useful weapon to Cold Warriors in the West, who regarded such tools as "one of the most effective weapons against the disease, discouragement and despair that breeds communism."[75]

The early years of the Cold War were an ideological hothouse, and the success or failure of assistance programs was viewed as a metonym for the virtues and vices of entire political systems. These rivalries thus made it imperative to pursue programs that could be expected to show immediate results. As H.W. Singer at the Department of Economic Affairs of the UN put it in 1949, "the prevailing opinion appeared to be that the whole program was on trial and that it would not be allowed to expand or even to continue unless it could show rather immediate returns. Hence it was believed expedient to favor projects which were deemed most likely to show results in two or three years' time and which could then be put forth as substantial reason for continuing the program on its own merits."[76]

However, the very features that made these technical assistance programs so promising in the eyes of the Western powers were the object of criticism by the Soviet bloc and the Third World. The majority of the experts dispatched to the Third World under the auspices of UN EPTA were North Americans and West Europeans, who had learned their trade in former colonial administrations. Not surprisingly, nationalist leaders generally regarded these people as agents of neocolonial influence. In Indonesia in 1952, public health programs could only slowly progress because of "the suspicion of the Indonesians of any American or foreign interference and their consequent hesitance in accepting U.S. technical experts," and in India similar suspicions led to a substantial reduction in the number of American technicians sent in 1954.[77]

The Soviet Union and its allies were also mistrustful of both the WHO and UN EPTA. By default as much as by design, the United States and its European allies dominated the WHO's policies, personnel, and programs. Not only were virtually all of the positions in the WHO secretariat reserved for officials from the major Western powers; the U.S. government also obstructed many WHO programs that were intended to help the countries of Eastern Europe rebuild their public health services. The Eastern Europeans were angered by such petty acts as the decision by the United States to block the export to Poland of materials needed to manufacture penicillin.[78] The Soviets also challenged Western health and development programs on more substantive grounds. They argued that Western-style disease prevention could never effect real change because disease and its concomitant social problems were due primarily "to poverty and colonial oppression, as well as to the arbitrary exploitation of populations deprived of their rights, and the lack of health services in colonial and non-autonomous territories."[79] And both the Soviets and representatives of many Third World countries complained that far too much money was being spent on administrative costs, rather than on the actual provision of public health services.

Shortly after Truman's announcement of the Point IV program, the Soviet Union and its Eastern European allies withdrew from active involvement in the WHO.[80] The Americans and the British were not at all unhappy to see them go. However, because the presence of the Soviet Union and its socialist allies had provided at least a modicum of support for the WHO's claim that its humanitarian work stood above politics, the departure of the socialist bloc impaired the organization's credibility in this respect. A group of peace activists tried to mend political fences with the Soviets, but to no avail, and the outbreak of the Korean War in June 1950 rendered the issue moot.[81]

This boycott enabled the United States to quickly instrumentalize the organization, along with the other UN specialized agencies, as part of its struggle to contain what they perceived as the global forces of disorder, a development that dampened the globalism of people like Chisholm. However, the WHO was never just a handmaid for the major Western powers; and in the 1950s, it reemerged as part of a global public sphere, where the competing visions of humanitarianism and internationalism clashed with each other.

V. THE RETURN OF THE DAMNED: THE BANDUNG SPIRIT AND THIRD WORLD INTERNATIONALISM

In April 1955, representatives from twenty-nine newly independent states attended the First Asian-African Conference, which was held in Bandung, Indonesia. Together, these countries were home to more than half of the world's population; as Jawaharlal Nehru noted, the Conference marked an important historical milestone for "a new Asia and Africa" as a global force.[82] The political formation of the Bandung movement – also called the nonaligned movement – represented the first systematic challenge to the idea of Europe and the geopolitical institutions established to govern the global South in the postwar world.

The roots of the nonaligned movement reach back to the March–April 1947 Asian Relations Conference, which was organized by Nehru. The conference brought together representatives from thirty Asian countries to foster mutual understanding and discuss the common problems they were facing, especially those involved in gaining independence. In 1949,

Nehru forged an alliance of fifteen Asian and African countries to support Indonesian resistance to Dutch attempts to reassert their control over the Indonesian archipelago. He hoped to establish an Asian model of internationalism based on the "five principles of peaceful coexistence."[83] These principles, which Nehru regarded as an alternative to the imperialist world order, were first set out in an agreement signed with the Chinese in April 1954, one year before the Bandung Conference.[84]

Even before the Conference, John Humphrey, the first director of the Human Rights Division in the UN Secretariat, noted that membership in the UN would give "backward countries in revolt" a forum in which to advance "their own ideas about rights."[85] Together, the entry of new Asian and African states into the UN, the Bandung movement, and the national liberation movements constituted the birth of Third World internationalism. The aim of Third World internationalism was to assert the right to participate on an equal footing with the great powers and thereby to escape from the subalternity into which it had been positioned by the security discourse described earlier.

The main political challenge was to overturn the asymmetrical understanding of the rights of Third World countries and their people, especially the right to national self-determination. The Lebanese representative made precisely this point at the eleventh session of the UN General Assembly in November 1956, when he contrasted the response of the international community to the Hungarian refugee crisis with its actions in Algeria. "When the rights of a European or a Westerner are affected," he observed,

the whole world becomes indignant. But when the rights of an African or an Asian are at stake, the United Nations conception of man becomes so different that one is led to believe that contrary to the provisions of the Charter, man is not the same everywhere and the human personality is not the same everywhere. Then again, we ask the question: why is nationalism a good thing for Europeans and an evil thing when preached and practiced by Asians and Africans?[86]

The final communiqué of the Bandung Conference raised this observation to the level of a general political principle when it insisted that the "rights of peoples and nations to self-determination" was "a pre-requisite of the full enjoyment of all fundamental Human Rights."[87] The final resolution on cultural cooperation pointed out that "Afro-Asia" had once been the "cradle of great religions and civilizations" and insisted that the countries of this vast region could again become so once freed from the fetters of colonialism and its debilitating legacies. Yet the real challenge was less to cut what Mignolo has called the "Gordian knot with the empire" through the formal, juridical declaration of independence than to decolonize the mind.[88]

The representatives gathered at Bandung set out a counternarrative that explained underdevelopment not as a quasi-natural condition, but as a legacy of colonial rule, an evil "arising from the subjection of peoples to alien subjugation, domination and exploitation."[89] The Bandung countries also had their own vision and strategy for modernization.[90] For these countries, development was the path to the collective dream of giving the substantive meaning – independence, progress, and nationhood – to their formally sovereign states. Convinced that they shared common interests different from those of the capitalist or communist blocs, they wanted to secure the globally equal conditions for national development and to do so without being drawn into the orbit of either superpower or succumbing to their tutelary pretensions. As one Indian asked rhetorically: "Are we copies of Europeans or Americans or Russians? (...) [F]or anybody to tell us that we have to be camp-followers of Russia or America or any country of Europe is, if I may say so, not very creditable to our new dignity, our new independence, our new freedom and our new spirit and our new self-reliance."[91]

To help achieve this goal, the Bandung Conference proposed that the UN establish a special development fund for the Third World. Nonalignment, that is, the refusal to be incorporated in all forms of neocolonial rule, thus represented the negative condition under which these countries could reclaim their own past – and thereby realize their own future. While Nehru characterized their project as "a practical Utopia,"[92] an Indian delegate to the 1957/58 conference of the Afro-Asian Peoples' Solidarity Organisation explained that "[Asian and African peoples] do not propose to be exploited as mere pawns on the larger chess-board of power politics. And they will no longer be helpless spectators of their fates that were at one time shaped by outsiders for their own ends. To-day, they shall mould their own destinies in their own way."[93]

There were, however, both economic and political obstacles to the realization of this goal. The Western powers reacted in various ways – mostly negative – to the Bandung conference. A number of them explicitly characterized the Bandung bloc as a global alliance of the colored peoples against White Occidental culture.[94] American Secretary of State John Foster Dulles condemned neutralism – that is, nonalignment in the Cold War – as "immoral" in a world that was divided between good and evil.[95] However, Indonesian president Sukarno insisted that refusing to take sides in the Cold War was not the same as political or moral neutralism, which he maintained was impossible "as long as tyranny exists in any part of the world."[96] Moreover, the Western powers could not accept the idea that small, poor, backward countries should have an equal voice in world affairs. These concerns had arisen in debates over the extent to which these countries should be granted full voting rights within the UN. Later, at the height of decolonization, Winston Churchill described their equal voting rights as an anomaly.[97] And all of the Western leaders feared that the Soviets would be able to ally themselves with the growing number of newly independent states to outvote the West.

Even though "Afro-Asia" was an incomplete project, these nations did not expect that their goals would be achieved in the immediate future. The decision to invite only representatives of independent, sovereign states to the Bandung conference was the correlate of their pragmatic strategy of working within the UN. However, Third World liberation movements became increasingly radical in the aftermath of the Suez crisis and the Algerian war, and they pushed back against Western efforts to contain their struggles as matters of national and global security.

This new attitude was already evident at the First Afro-Asian Peoples' Solidarity Conference, which met in Cairo from December 26, 1957, to January 1, 1958. In contrast to the Bandung Conference, the organizers of this meeting wanted to stage a "people's Bandung" that would be open to all peoples who "are still suffering under the yoke of imperialism in one form or another."[98] The address by Egyptian president Gamal Abdel Nasser, entitled "From Port Said to the World," can be read as an attempt to "de-provincialize" Africa. As Egyptian minister of state (and later president) Anwar El Sadat proclaimed in his address to the conference, "gone forever is the time when the destinies of war and peace were decided in few European capitals. It is we who decide this today. *Our world* [emphasis added] has great weight in the international field. We have only to remember our great numbers, our resources, our vast area and our strategic positions to see that war will be impossible if we are determined to maintain peace. But our determination must not be passive. It must be turned into positive action for peace."[99]

By the end of the 1950s, the Bandung movement had coalesced into a self-conscious Third World movement, whose alternative narrative of global modernity and whose institutionalized counter-public had put it in a position to challenge Western discourses of difference and under-development, the asymmetrical conception of sovereignty and rights that underlay the postwar humanitarian regime, and the forms of global governance that they authorized.

VI. SOCIALIST GLOBALIZATION AND THE SOVIET MODEL OF DEVELOPMENT

The broad reorientation of Soviet foreign policy after Stalin's death in March 1953 led to the creation of a new global constellation. Moscow's new engagement in the Third World followed upon the political formation of Third World internationalism, and the Suez Crisis (October/November 1956) created yet another opening to the Third World. The socialist countries tried to capitalize on the anticolonial sentiments that were stirred up around the world by the crisis, although their own credibility was somewhat diminished by their repression of the Hungarian uprising.

The real turning point came in 1955. Not only was that the year of the Bandung Conference. In that year, the Soviet Union also granted sovereignty to East Germany, at least to the extent possible within the Warsaw Pact. In response, the West German government proclaimed the Hallstein doctrine. This doctrine maintained that the Federal Republic was the sole legitimate state on German soil, and it stipulated that Bonn would not maintain diplomatic relations with any country (other than the Soviet Union) that recognized the sovereignty of East Germany, or what the West Germans insisted upon calling the Soviet Occupation Zone. The resulting international isolation forced the East Germans to use other, nondiplomatic means – especially humanitarian, medical, and development aid – to build bridges to the newly independent countries of the Third World in hopes of gaining *de facto*, and eventually *de jure*, recognition. The East German government eagerly took up this challenge in the hope that recognition abroad would lead to greater legitimacy at home. Soviet bloc, and especially East German, engagement in the Third World would not have been so urgent had it not been for the formation of the Third World internationalism. And it would not have been possible had Nikita Khrushchev not abandoned Stalin's confrontational approach in favor of a policy of peaceful coexistence and scientific and economic competition.[100]

Since the mid-1940s, Soviet foreign policy had been based on the "two camps" doctrine, which postulated that a global war between the two blocs was likely, if not imminent, because the winding down of the war economy would inevitably force the capitalist powers into yet another wave of imperialist warfare in order to stave off economic collapse.[101]

This retreat from both Leninist internationalism and the interwar popular front strategy reinforced the isolationist, xenophobic, and autarchic trends of late Stalinism and made it impossible for the Soviets to collaborate with the national liberation movements in Asia and Africa, whose bourgeois leaders they disparaged as pawns of the West.[102] For example, in 1949 the leading Soviet Indologist A.M. Diakov had denounced Gandhi as "the principal traitor of the mass national-liberation movement" and as an ideologue of "the counter-revolutionary bourgeoisie of India."[103] These ideological blinders took their toll on both Soviet policy in Asia and Africa and on those regional affairs experts whose views deviated from the party line.

The Soviet leadership recognized that greater knowledge of Asia and Africa was crucial to the new strategy. During the middle of the decade, the Soviets undertook a number of initiatives, including bilateral cultural agreements, the founding of friendship societies, and the exchange of athletic teams, theater troupes, and delegations, to increase its own knowledge of Third World countries and cultivate their goodwill. The Soviet Union held its first Indian film festival in September 1954. Nehru himself visited Moscow shortly after the Bandung Conference, and this was followed by Khrushchev's highly publicized trip to Southeast Asia in late 1955 and by Nasser's visit to Moscow in 1956.[104]

At the twentieth Communist Party Congress, Politburo member Anastas Mikoyan scolded the Soviet Academy of Sciences for dozing while the "whole East has awakened."[105] Soon thereafter, the Academy began to strengthen its Asian and African area studies programs, publish scholarly works dealing with these regions, and sponsor film festivals and other exhibitions.[106] In 1956, Ivan Potekhin – president of the Soviet-African Friendship Society and chairman of the African Section of the Soviet Afro-Asian Solidarity Committee – organized a Soviet congress of Africanists to discuss national liberation movements. Three years later, institutes of African and Asian Studies were established within the Soviet Academy of Sciences (with Potekhin as the director of the former). In June 1957, the first All-Union Conference of Orientalists convened in Tashkent to discuss the issues raised by the collapse of colonialism, the Bandung Conference, and national liberation movements, as well as the revelations and resolutions from the 1956 party congress.[107]

Under Khrushchev, the Soviet Union abandoned its earlier insistence that all countries had to follow an identical revolutionary path to socialism in favor of a more minimal position, which emphasized the possibilities of collaboration with Third World nationalists in their common struggle against capitalist imperialism.[108] In 1957, the World Congress of Workers' and Communist Parties endorsed the Soviet revisionist thesis while insisting that fraternal solidarity with the more advanced proletariat constituted the "core of still greater solidarity" with national liberation movements in Asia and Africa.[109]

A similar shift took place in the involvement of the socialist countries in the field of global health and development. In July 1953, the Soviet Union reversed its earlier decision to boycott UN-sponsored development programs and agreed to contribute four million rubles to the UN EPTA fund. In January 1956, the Soviet Union resumed its active membership in the WHO, and the socialist countries of Eastern Europe quickly followed suit.[110] Beginning in 1956, the health ministers of Asian and European socialist countries also met regularly to both discuss domestic health policy and coordinate medical aid policies toward the Third World.[111]

Working from a different understanding of the relation between economic development and public health than that which guided Western aid programs, the socialist countries blamed endemic and epidemic disease in the Third World on imperialism and decades of colonial rule. They pointed to the successes in eradicating malaria in the Soviet Union, and then in China and North Korea, as evidence of the superiority of socialist public health; they also argued that the lack of progress elsewhere was due to the "lack of economic development, poor health services and political instability" produced by American-led intervention. For example, in South Vietnam, Cambodia, and Laos, it was noted that colonial rulers had made no effort to check the spread of malaria. The first steps had only been taken after successful wars of liberation had created the political preconditions for the widespread use of DDT.[112]

This renewed involvement in the field enabled the WHO serve as a forum to promote a socialist vision of public health. Not surprisingly, these programs led to friction with the Western powers. In 1958, the Soviet Union proposed that the WHO undertake a campaign to eradicate smallpox around the globe. The Soviets and their allies offered to send medicine and medical experts to India, Pakistan, Burma, Indonesia, Cambodia, Ghana, Guinea, and Iraq – all countries with which they had close relations – at no cost if these countries would pay for the lodging and travel costs of their aid workers in country. However, the Soviet Union also wanted to create a special United Nations fund to extend this program to other countries. Although estimated to cost $98 million, between 1959 and 1966 only $300,000 was collected to support this

Soviet initiative – in contrast to the $29 million collected and spent on an American-led malaria eradication program during the same period.[113]

The Soviet proposal represented a clear challenge to American leadership within the WHO. But while the Soviets complained that their smallpox eradication program was being treated in such a niggardly manner by the international community,[114] the Americans disparaged the Soviet initiative as part of a broader plan for world domination. As one American expert explained,

the ultimate political objectives of the US and the Soviet Union are diametrically opposed. The US wishes to preserve the traditional Western system of free and independent nations. The USSR seeks world domination. Yet, through the WHO, both nations can advance in a number of ways their competing foreign policy objectives, even though, ironically, the WHO, like other UN agencies, was founded on premises completely inimical to avowed Soviet objectives.[115]

In 1960, amidst the Algerian war and the Congo conflict, the Soviets insisted that the principles laid down in the WHO constitution would remain empty promises until the (neo)colonial grip on the developing world had been broken by cooperation between the socialist countries and national liberation movements. At the December 1960 meeting of the WHO, an alliance of socialist and Third World countries secured the passage of a "Declaration on the Granting of Independence to Colonial Nations and Peoples and the Immediate Task of the WHO," which reasserted the importance of national self-determination and committed the organization to take steps to secure this goal.[116] This alliance came together again in 1964 in a vote to suspend South Africa from the WHO because of its policy of apartheid.[117]

Despite the money and energy devoted to cultural exchange and medical aid programs, trade and technical aid was the primary vehicle for Soviet policy in the global South. Although the Soviet Union had provided some assistance to Afghanistan in 1953, Moscow did not launch a systematic development aid program until 1955.[118] The Soviet Union signed agreements with India, Egypt, and Indonesia to fund the construction, respectively, of the Bhilai steel plant, the Aswan dam, and an enormous stadium in Jakarta to host the Asian Games. All of these projects were symbols of national independence, and they were central to nationalist efforts to overcome both the structural weaknesses of their economies and their dependent position within the global economy.[119]

The Soviet Union's opening to the Third World in the mid-1950s coincided with Egypt's search for a counterweight to Israeli power and

British and French influence in the region.[120] Although the United States (together with the British and the World Bank) offered a loan to construct the Aswan dam, the preconditions they imposed would have given them de facto control of Egypt's economic and foreign policies and blocked the purchase of arms from the Soviet bloc. These conditions were unacceptable to the Egyptians, who regarded them as a form of neocolonial rule. In 1955, the Egyptians agreed to buy arms from the Soviet Union (with Czechoslovakia serving as a front for the deal). Nasser's attempt to play off the Soviets against the Americans angered the latter. The Western powers were further antagonized by the Egyptian decision to recognize the People's Republic of China. At that point, the Soviet Union stepped in and offered the Egyptians $100 million in credits at half the rate demanded by Western banks. Shortly thereafter, the United States withdrew its loan offer in order to both punish and pressure the Egyptians, whom the Americans deemed incapable of planning and executing the Aswan project without foreign assistance.

At the time, West Germany was under attack from the Pan-Arab League for its restitution agreement with Israel. When the Egyptians asked West Germany for assistance in planning the Aswan dam, the Adenauer administration eagerly seized the opportunity to smooth over relations with the Egyptians. A consortium of West German firms then worked on the preliminary hydraulic, geologic, and structural engineering plans for the dam. The nationalization of the Suez Canal in July 1956 was quickly followed by the withdrawal of the French and British engineers involved in preliminary work on the dam, a ban on urgently needed spare parts for the construction equipment on the site, and then the Suez Crisis later that fall.[121]

The Soviet bloc countries hoped that technical aid programs would serve as effective advertisements for socialist modernity in the nonaligned world. Even with regard to projects that were smaller and less politicized than the Suez Canal, the Western powers were opposed in principle to extending loans for building public sector industries. By contrast, leaders of postcolonial states believed that long-term, central planning was necessary for fast and efficient development. When Ghanaian president Kwame Nkrumah visited Washington in 1958, Eisenhower told him that the Ghanaians should look for private sector financing, rather than American aid, for the $850 million Volta River project. Nkrumah replied that "Africa has no choice. We have to modernize. Either we shall do so with your interest and support – or we shall be compelled to turn elsewhere. This is not a warning or threat, but a straight statement of political reality."[122] Nkrumah did not need to name this "elsewhere."

The Soviets and the East Germans often cited the construction of the Bhilai plant as evidence of the superiority of Soviet engineering over that of West Germany and Britain, which were building steel plants in Rourkela and Durgapur at the same time. In the course of the construction of the Bhilai plant, the Soviets also trained more than 5,000 technicians and workers. Although a large number of Soviet engineers worked in Bhilai between 1958 to 1961, fewer than fifty Soviet experts were needed to stay on after the project was completed. Indian engineers and technicians trained by the Soviets later formed the backbone of the Hindustan Steel Works Construction Ltd, which was established in 1964.[123]

In a speech delivered when the Bhilai plant began operation in 1959, V.K. Krishna Menon – India's defense minister, former ambassador to the Soviet Union, and a delegate to the Bandung Conference – argued that the plant represented a landmark in relations between both Asia and Europe, and East and West: "For centuries... Asians and Africans had been treated as hewers of wood and drawers of water. Their role was to produce raw materials and to sell them cheap to the nations of the West, which grew rich and still richer by turning them into manufactured goods and selling them at fabulous profits... Bhilai was the first big dent into this system."[124] By contrast, West Germany's Rourkela project turned out to be an "unhappy and embarrassing experience."[125] From the moment the Germans arrived in 1957, the Indians resented the fact that the Germans behaved in a "colonial style of racial segregation on the construction site," and the Germans alienated their Indian co-workers by displaying what the latter characterized as "master race attitudes."[126]

Soviet bloc development aid was attractive for other reasons as well. As a rule, the Soviet Union extended to developing countries credits that could be used to purchase plant, capital goods, and technical services; these credits were offered at rates far lower than those offered by the World Bank or private banks in the West; and financing was structured in ways that would make it easier to repay these credits. In contrast to the aid offered by capitalist countries, which sought to turn a profit on financing, unequal terms of trade, and the exploitative transfer of technology, the Soviet bloc countries portrayed the terms of their aid as a gesture of solidarity toward the Third World.[127] The Soviet Union sometimes permitted credits to be used to obtain goods and services from other Council for Mutual Economic Assistance (COMECON) countries. For example, the Soviet Union effectively subcontracted out part of the work on the Aswan Dam to East Germany in order to elevate that country's profile in the Middle East. To coordinate such work, COMECON created permanent committees on foreign trade and the delivery of turnkey plants.

The Soviets were quite adept at exploiting technical aid projects for propaganda purposes. A Soviet camera team, headed by the famous documentary filmmaker Roman Karmen, spent six months in India filming *Morning of India* (1958). The film depicted ordinary Indians laboring to build a new nation by constructing irrigation canals, power stations, and so on. By showing the Soviets teaching Indians engineering and Russian, the film served to document the solidarity between the more advanced Soviet Union and the Indian people in their efforts to build a better future.[128]

The Soviets were no less eager to show off their accomplishments at home. They invited visitors from abroad to tour dams and hydroelectric power plants. In 1959/60, a team of Egyptian engineers and hydrologists working on the Aswan dam visited the Soviet Union, where the Ministry of Electric Power Station Construction sought to impress them with Soviet manpower, machinery, and construction techniques.[129] Likewise, when a Guinean delegation arrived in 1959 to sign an economic and technical cooperation treaty, they were given a tour of Azerbaijan, which was presented as a model of how rapidly backward areas could be developed through state-sponsored economic planning. The visitors were duly impressed, and one of them told his hosts that "this is how I imagine Guinea when it becomes truly independent."[130]

These programs also offered certain advantages to the donor countries. By the late 1950s, the countries belonging to the COMECON found it increasingly necessary to establish links to the wider world because their level of industrialization had reached the point where they needed to import primary products from the Third World and to export manufactures in return. But the governments of these states were perennially short of hard currency with which to pay for the raw materials and agricultural products needed to fulfill the economic promises they made to their own citizens. By permitting Third World countries to repay their debt in primary product exports (or in nonconvertible local currencies, which could then be used to purchase such products), they were able to improve the domestic living standard and consumption, while partially integrating these Third World countries into something resembling a socialist alternative to the capitalist world economy. By 1960, for example, 86 percent of Soviet finished goods that were sold outside its own bloc were exported to the Third World, an increase of more than 1,340 percent over pre-1945 levels.[131] Although such trade helped both reduce Third World debt obligations and improve consumption and living standards within the socialist bloc, one might legitimately ask whether such arrangements amounted to a specifically socialist form of neocolonial rule. Whatever the ulterior motives of the socialist donors, however, these aid programs did present a meaningful alternative for developing countries. And the possibility of seeking assistance from the socialist bloc gave these countries a degree of leverage in negotiating for better terms with Western countries (as will be seen in greater detail in Chapter 7).

The Americans, despite their continued opposition to the economic policies pursued by many newly independent countries, recognized the attractiveness of Soviet aid and the corresponding need to develop new aid programs to contain the growing Soviet influence in Asia and Africa.[132] These concerns were reflected in the message that John F. Kennedy sent to Congress in support of the Trade Expansion Act of 1962, where he noted that "the Communist aid and trade offensive has also become more apparent in recent years. Soviet bloc trade with 41 non-Communist countries in the less-developed areas of the globe has more than tripled in recent years; and bloc trade missions are busy in nearly every continent attempting to penetrate, encircle, and divide the free world."[133] However, this problem was not easily solved. In 1965, Lyndon Johnson again warned that "if we default on our [development aid] obligations, Communism will expand its ambitions. That is the stern equation which dominates our age, and from which there can be no escape in logic or in honor."[134]

As long as the central institutions of the postwar humanitarian regime were dominated by the Western powers, however, there were limits to the ability of the Soviet Union to work through them to achieve their policy goals. Consequently, they, like the Western countries before them, soon came to rely on bilateral agreements to promote their policies in these parts of the world, rather than working through international agencies dominated by the Western powers. Between 1954 and the end of 1965, they provided a total of $5 billion in credits to nonaligned countries (in addition to $4 billion in military aid).[135]

Many of the development projects sponsored by Eastern bloc countries were complex undertakings, such as the construction of the Aswan Dam and the East German regional reconstruction project to be described in Chapter 2. In the execution of these projects, technical experts were responsible for such things as surveys, project planning and design, construction supervision, the training of local technicians and workers, and the initial operation and management of the completed projects.[136] Between 1955 and 1965, more than 49,000 economic (i.e., nonmilitary) technicians from the Soviet bloc served in Third World countries. As can be seen in Table 1.1, in the mid-1950s the Soviet Union sent only a relatively small number of

TABLE 1.1 *Soviet Economic Technicians in Less Developed Countries, 1956–1967*

Area and Country	1956	1957	1958	1959	1960	1961	1962	1963	1964	1965	1966	1967
Total	680	830	1,965	3,310	4,580	5,595	7,095	9,005	9,700	10,735	11,780	11,054
Near East and South Asia	665	755	1,470	3,040	4,095	4,090	5,415	6,865	6,635	7,415	7,195	6,990
Afghanistan	335	420	530	905	1,535	1,800	2,200	1,825	1,860	1,890	1,340	1,000
Ceylon		5	25	15	10	25	20	35	40	40	85	85
India	220	250	495	1,120	1,000	580	550	735	745	1,275	1,500	1,500
Iran		5	5	5	5	0	20	5	160	160	375	1,000
Iraq	10	0	0	240	295	465	750	1,000	500	500	500	500
Nepal				25	25	45	40	65	70	75	270	100
Pakistan						25	80	100	110	155	150	140
Syria	20	0	165	350	365	365	260	160	150	150	350	545
United Arab Republic	55	50	145	290	410	595	115	2,115	2,500	2,600	2,030	1,600
(Dissolved 1962)												
Yemen	15	20	100	80	400	150	300	825	500	550	595	480
Other	10	5	5	10	40	40	40	0	0	20	0	40
Far East	10	75	470	235	180	375	475	525	530	405	400	230
Burma		50	120	65	55	25	25	245	50	45	40	40
Cambodia		15	20	20	30	50	50	50	75	85	85	90
Indonesia	10	10	330	150	95	300	400	430	405	275	275	100

44

Table 1.1 (cont.)

Area and Country	1956	1957	1958	1959	1960	1961	1962	1963	1964	1965	1966	1967
Africa	5	0	25	35	300	1,125	1,200	1,615	2,530	2,905	4,180	3,810
Algeria								25	525	820	1,150	1,480
Congo (Brazzaville)										65	125	160
Ethiopia			25	25	35	100	60	120	170	215	575	380
Ghana				5	120	200	275	235	460	465	735	
Guinea				5	145	695	495	500	500	380	510	40
Mali						85	180	285	300	270	335	355
Morocco						5	25	0	0	0	10	70
Somalia						15	70	330	355	395	370	370
Sudan	5	0	0	0	0	15	45	80	120	70	55	100
Tanzania						10	50	40	40	35	25	15
Tunisia									45	90	175	315
Other									15	100	115	1165

Note: Highlighted cells indicate that no data are available.

technicians to Afghanistan, India, Indonesia, and Egypt. After 1960, however, large numbers served in the Middle East (Egypt, Iraq, Syria, Yemen)
and southeast Africa (Ghana, Guinea, Mali) as these countries gained
independence.[137]

In addition to plant, machinery, and technical services, a substantial
amount of Soviet credits and grants was used to fund the study of Third
World students in the Soviet Union. Each year, some 600 students were
admitted from Asia, Africa, and Latin America, the majority of whom
studied engineering and medicine.[138] Most of these students studied at the
Peoples' Friendship University in Moscow. This school had been founded
in November 1960; and in February 1961, it was renamed the Patrice
Lumumba University of Peoples' Friendship in honor of the murdered
Congolese leader. Third World students also studied at other universities
and at technical, agricultural, and medical schools throughout the country.[139] Tables 1.2 and 1.3 show the number of students and technical
trainees, respectively, who studied in the Soviet Union between 1956 and
1964. In 1967, 5,710 African students were studying in the Soviet Union,
while 2,230 more were studying in Eastern Europe.[140] The growing
number of African students and trainees after 1960 mirrored the dramatic
increase in economic and military aid to the region.

Students were nominated for study abroad by both the government
and nongovernment organizations, including trade unions and youth
groups. This policy reflected the Soviet desire to balance between maintaining good relations with the governments of nonaligned states and
supporting communist parties in those countries. Fear of alienating the
governments of nonaligned countries also underlay the Soviet decision to
cease overt political indoctrination at the university. The hope that the
institution would help build bridges to the Third World was also reflected
in the fact that the university accepted students who did not possess the

TABLE 1.2 *Number of Students Beginning Academic Study in the Soviet
Union, 1956–64*[141]

	1956–59*	1960	1961	1962	1963	1964	Total
Middle East	845	175	1,255	985	440	140	3,840
Africa	75	360	470	1,835	1,510	865	5,115
Asia	60	405	335	370	345	230	1,745
Latin America	15	80	140	265	195	140	835
Total	995	1,020	2,200	3,455	2,490	1,375	11,353

*Total number of students during 1956–59

TABLE 1.3 *Number of Technical Trainees from Third World Countries Present in the Soviet Union, 1956–64*[142]

	1956–59*	1960	1961	1962	1963	1964
Middle East	180	280	200	465	140	1,610
Africa	0	10	290	155	255	410
Asia	1,020	95	225	190	635	675
Latin America	0	0	0	0	5	0
Total	1,200	385	715	810	1,035	2,695

*Total number of technical trainees receiving training during 1956–59

TABLE 1.4 *Subject of Study of Students Enrolled in Peoples' Friendship University, 1963–64*[143]

	Number of Students	%
Preparatory language courses	848	34
Engineering	500	20
Medicine	397	16
Economics and law	311	13
Mathematics and physics	171	7
History and philology	143	6
Agriculture	99	4
Total	2,469	100

academic credentials needed to secure admission to universities in Western countries. A substantial number of these students studied Russian and other languages, with most of the remainder pursuing professional study in technical subjects, as can be seen in Table 1.4.

* * * *

Scholars have long recognized that East-West stalemate on the European continent led to the displacement of Cold War competition into the Third World, where it much more frequently degenerated into actual military conflict. However, the Third World was not merely a proxy in the ongoing struggle between the First World and the Second Worlds, where inhabitants had neither subjectivity nor agency. Rather, it was the battlefield on which the Cold War culture wars were fought. In the tragic drama played out here, the peoples of the Third World were both audience and choir. Just as Cold War empires – both capitalist and communist – harbored expansionist global designs based on their claims to be the privileged agents of a secular and universalistic modernity, the categories through which the cold warriors of the global North understood themselves were culturally constructed through their imagined relationship to the South. In the following chapters, we will follow the diverse permutations of this process of competitive self-definition.

Moreover, the state-socialist aid described above represented a strategy for integrating the Third World into a Soviet-led global network of trade and aid. Such aid was based on the assumption that these countries could only achieve their ultimate goal of self-determined development by making common cause with the Soviet bloc in their joint struggle against capitalism and (neo)colonial rule and by emulating their model of socialist modernity. This assistance was beneficial to the developing countries to which it was offered. However, socialist bloc aid programs also reflected – in a postcolonial context – many of the parasitic, exploitive features of neocolonial rule that the socialist countries had considered characteristic of their capitalist foe. Last, Soviet bloc aid, including that provided by East Germany, was, like that of its Western counterparts, based on a narrative of specious notions of civilizational difference, and, as we shall see in later chapters, it unwittingly reproduced many of the problematic features of the Western-dominated humanitarian regime and thereby blunted its appeal to its would-be recipients.

In the 1960s, the nascent rivalry between the Soviet Union and China for leadership of the socialist bloc gradually spilled over into Asia and Africa, where, as we shall see in Chapter 9, the Chinese – and soon the Cubans – challenged the Soviet Union and East Germany for leadership in this domain of anti-imperialist solidarity and "mutually beneficial" aid. By the mid-1960s, however, Khrushchev was out of power; Nehru was dead; and Nkrumah, who had been one of the main voices of pan-Africanism, had been overthrown, as was the case with the leaders of Indonesia and Algeria, Sukarno and Ahmed Ben Bella. These events collectively marked the passing of the first Bandung generation, and from 1965 onward relations between the two blocs and the Third World were increasingly dominated by the Vietnam War.

PART II

THE GLOBAL HUMANITARIAN REGIME AT ARMS

2

Through a Glass Darkly

INTRODUCTION: THE KOREAN WAR, NORTH KOREA,
AND EAST GERMANY

The Korean War is a standard set piece in any account of the Cold War. The primary points of reference in the story of the Cold War's first hot conflict are the North Korean invasion in June 1950, the dramatic U.S. landing at Incheon in September, the equally dramatic entry of the Chinese in the fall of 1950, and a bloody stalemate that ended in July 1953 with a surly, unstable armistice that has lasted until the present day. Less well known are the story of the reconstruction of North Korea and the role of East Germany in the rebuilding of the industrial city of Hamhung, which, I argue, sheds unexpected light on the nature of socialist aid programs in the years after Stalin's death.

The East German government, as well as the architects, engineers, and planners involved in the project, hoped to make Hamhung a showcase for their vision of socialism. However, their urbanist vision and architectural style differed from those of the North Korean leader Kim Il Sung, and conflicting priorities over the allocation of resources gave rise to persistent conflicts, which led to a definitive parting of the ways at the beginning of the 1960s. Nevertheless, the people directly employed on the project continued to interact on a personal level in ways that were not completely defined by the policies of their respective governments. In the conclusion, I briefly explore the afterlife of the personal connections between East German and North Korean workers forged in Hamhung in the 1950s.

I. THE TEARS OF WAR AND THE SOCIALIST KISS: THE WORLD COMMUNITY OF FRATERNAL PEOPLES BUILDS A NEW KOREA

The war in the North was devastating. In addition to the immense loss of life and the displacement and separation of millions of families, U.S. bombing destroyed most of the country's infrastructure; 75 to 100 percent of the factories, schools, and hospitals in the North were destroyed; about 75 percent of residential dwellings lay in ashes; and the land was virtually denuded of livestock.[144] In early 1951, Kim Il Sung ordered the construction of a large underground theater at the foot of the Moranbong Hill. In August 1951 – on the eve of the sixth anniversary of independence from the Japanese – the theater was dedicated as U.S. bombs rained down on the city above. This act of defiance made the theater, in the words of a Polish diplomat, "a symbol of the invincibility of the fraternal people and of their victory" over U.S. imperialism.[145] Immediately after the armistice, the reconstruction of Pyongyang began with the help of Soviet and Hungarian architects and engineers. The well-known Soviet screenwriter Arkadi Perventsev produced a color film on the rebuilding of the capital city.[146]

The Korean War presented governments in both East and West with the opportunity to accelerate rearmament and marginalize political opponents. In Hungary, the communist party used the war as the pretext to further centralize power in the hands of the extraordinary Defense Committee, which was created in late 1950. Shortly after the outbreak of the war, the Hungarians spontaneously held a "Hands off Korea!" rally in Budapest and raised funds to send a medical team and supplies to North Korea. Soon, however, the authorities began to organize a variety of Korean solidarity campaigns to mobilize the population behind the official ideology of proletarian internationalism.[147]

In East Germany, there were also many demonstrations of solidarity with North Korea. Workers' collectives in the pharmaceutical industry volunteered for overtime work to produce medicine for the North Koreans. Such demonstrations represented the thing that the Stalinist governments of Eastern Europe feared most: political activity that was not under their control and guidance. Like their Hungarian counterparts, the members of the East German Communist Party (the Socialist Unity Party, SED) Secretariat debated "whether such a call for donations is politically defensible and whether the monies collected in response to this appeal should be forwarded" to their intended beneficiaries.[148] In response to North Korea's constant appeals for assistance, however, East

FIGURE 2.1 "Contribute to the heroically fighting Korean people. Korea for the Koreans! Germany for the Germans!"
Source: Korea-Hilfsausschuß beim Nationalrat der Nationalen Front des demokratischen Deutschland. Courtesy of Bundesarchiv, B 285 Plak-033-004.

German officials ultimately decided to favor solidarity donations (such as that represented in Figure 2.1), rather than direct government loans, although they also concluded that it would be better if such initiatives were controlled by the state.[149]

A few weeks later, the National Front of Democratic Germany – an umbrella organization of the country's political parties and state-sponsored mass organizations – declared its solidarity with the people of Korea, and in September 1950 a Korea Aid Committee (*Korea-Hilfsausschuss*), composed of representatives from the political parties, the mass organizations, and the Ministries of Foreign Affairs and Labor and Health, was established. In 1951, the committee sponsored documentary films, slide shows, and exhibitions on the situation in Korea, and it collected over 18.5 million marks to aid the war-torn country.[150] In May 1951, the Council of the Women's International Democratic Federation sent an International Commission of Women to investigate the atrocities committed by U.S. and South Korean forces against civilians in North Korea. Hilde Cahn and Lilly Wächter represented Germany in this Commission.[151] The decided antipathy of East German official opinion toward the Western powers and their policies in Korea is clearly illustrated in

FIGURE 2.2 "Vermin infestation. Korea Warns! Fight for peace against the criminals of humanity" (1952). In this poster, the East Germans turned against the West the same equation of political ideology with disease and its vectors that the West used in its campaign to contain communism. The fleas are adorned with the faces of Truman, Churchill, and Adenauer.
Source: Amt für Information der Regierung der DDR. Courtesy of Bundesarchiv, Plak 102-027-001.

Figure 2.2, which turns the rhetoric of political disease and containment back against the primary vectors for the spread of neocolonialism in the region.

During the war, the socialist countries admitted a large number of North Korean children, students, and workers for education and vocational training.[152] In East Germany, the first groups of students arrived in September and December 1952 (Figure 2.3); by 1955, a total of 334 North Koreans were studying at East German technical colleges and universities. East Germany also took in children orphaned by the war. In January 1953, a group of 205 orphans arrived in East Germany; a second group followed in November of that year; and ultimately a total of 600 Korean children lived and went to school in Dresden and Moritzburg.[153]

The Korean Armistice Agreement was signed on July 27, 1953. Stalin's death several months earlier made possible a reorientation of Soviet foreign policy, which allowed economic and technical aid to become the

FIGURE 2.3 Fifty Koreans arriving in East Berlin on Christmas Day 1952 for study and training.
Source: Erich O. Krueger. Courtesy of Bundesarchiv, B 183-17762-0001.

main vehicle through which the Soviet Union and the countries of Eastern Europe put into practice the principles of fraternal help and proletarian internationalism. On the day the armistice was signed, Georgi Malenkov, the chairman of the Soviet Council of Ministers, telegrammed Kim that Moscow would help in any way possible with the reconstruction of the country. The following day, the Polish government announced its own aid to North Korea, and a week later the Hungarian government followed suit. On August 8, 1953, Moscow offered a grant of one billion rubles, and the following month Kim Il Sung visited Moscow, where he signed a bilateral aid agreement.[154] For its part, China agreed to provide cotton, coal, and food, as well as 295 technicians and 10,000 People's Volunteers, who were to work in the rice fields, repair bridges and railways, and build dikes and factories. In 1953, East Germany agreed to convert the 30-million-ruble credit that it had offered North Korea the previous year into an outright grant and provide an additional 30 million rubles.[155] In September 1953, Hungary agreed to send architects to design a housing complex in Pyongyang; and by the end of the year, the other Eastern European countries had signed similar agreements to help the North Koreans with their 1954–6 Three-Year Plan.[156]

In December 1954, the renamed Solidarity Committee for Korea and Vietnam sent to Pyongyang a delegation headed by well-known writer Max Zimmering. Zimmering proclaimed that North Korea was the symbol of "fraternal love" that united the peoples of the socialist camp. "Korea," he continued, "is an example of proletarian internationalism. The freedom of Korea is the freedom of the entire working people, its struggle is the struggle of peace-loving youth across the world. Hence the development of Korea constitutes the common cause of the people who want to live on their own and who hate war."[157]

These ties appeared to be growing tighter by the day. Soviet bloc engineers, agronomists, and journalists were surprised to see so many foreign specialists on the same planes and trains heading toward Pyongyang and to hear so many different languages being spoken in the newly built International Hotel. Even where such mutual affection might not have been completely spontaneous, the illusion was maintained by a constant stream of films, broadcasts, publications, and public rituals. Yet beneath the surface of genuine goodwill and official ideology, there were real differences both within and between countries as to the best path to building socialism at home. These differences became increasingly clear over the years as the focus of fraternal aid to the North Koreans shifted from the overcoming of wartime destruction to the formulation of longer-term programs for the construction of socialism.

In the 1950s, Kim was first and foremost an anticolonial nationalist whose highest priorities were territorial sovereignty and economic independence. Like many first-generation leaders of postcolonial states, he pursued an authoritarian approach to national development that borrowed selectively from both the Soviet and Chinese models.[158] National independence and the building of socialism were two facets of a single, convulsive process in North Korea. Like Ho Chi Minh, Kim believed that neither of these goals could be achieved without first securing the unification of the peninsula. The North Korean development plans resonated with the North Vietnamese. When Ho launched the first Three-Year Plan, Kim visited Hanoi. More than 70,000 Vietnamese gathered at Ba Dinh Square, where Kim spoke to them on economic development in North Korea. After Kim's speech, Ho rallied the crowd by asking "Workers, peasants, armymen, intellectuals and youth, are you resolved to launch a friendly emulation with the Korean people?" The crowd responded with a resounding "Yes!" and then sang "Solidarity Is Might."[159]

Khrushchev envisioned an international division of labor within the socialist camp in which the countries of Asia would serve as producers of primary products and as markets for the manufactures produced by the Soviet Union and the more industrially advanced economies of Eastern Europe, and Moscow provided development aid in forms intended to promote this vision. For example, in the case of the aid offered to North Korea, 40 percent was to be provided in the form of industrial equipment, machines, and spare parts for hydroelectric power, steel, and fertilizer plants, as well as canneries and the renovation of a large hospital in Pyongyang. In turn, the Soviet Union imported most of the production from these factories to relieve food shortages at home. As a result, Korean food exports to the Soviet Union jumped by 1,600 percent between 1956 and 1959. Similarly, the East Germans valued North Korea as a source for a variety of primary products, such as nonferrous metals, minerals, tobacco, peanuts, and honey, and they pressured the North Koreans to devote their limited resources to the extraction of these resources.[160] However, the terms of trade contained in these agreements invariably favored the donor country.[161]

In the immediate postwar years, the countries of Eastern Europe had followed a two-pronged Stalinist strategy, which combined the forced development of heavy industry with agricultural collectivization. However, after Stalin's death domestic opposition and pressure from Moscow forced them to retreat, at least temporarily, from this strategy. They criticized Kim because they felt that the diversion of resources toward heavy industry was preventing the Korean government from taking steps to improve the standard of living at home and playing its proper role in the international division of socialist labor. Although these economic arguments were not without merit, they also represented an attempt to rationalize a policy that would have integrated North Korea into the socialist bloc world economy in ways that would have – and eventually did to a certain degree – benefited the more industrialized countries at the cost of their less developed socialist brethren.

In North Korea, these policies evoked memories of colonial rule by the Japanese, who had promoted the one-sided development of the mining industry in order to better exploit Korea as a source of minerals and other raw materials.[162] In his speech at the Third Party Congress held in April 1956, Kim explained that the goal of the 1957–61 Five-Year Plan was to liquidate "the colonial lopsidedness left by the prolonged heinous rule of the Japanese imperialists," and thereby to lay the "foundations for socialist industrialization of our country."[163] When Kim traveled to Eastern

FIGURE 2.4 East German President Wilhelm Pieck greets Kim Il Sung during Kim's visit to East Berlin in 1956.
Source: Walter Heilig. Courtesy of Deutsches Historisches Museum, Berlin BA 90/4359.

Europe in 1956 (Figure 2.4), he stressed that North Korea had to follow a special economic path that was different from that of his hosts. During this trip, he told the East German Politburo that he had to focus on the rapid development of heavy industry and machine manufacturing because his top priority was building "an economic foundation for Korean reunification," which, he insisted, was the precondition for the construction of socialism on the peninsula.[164] Although Kim's doctrine of autarchy and self-reliance (*juche*) was originally a central policy goal, it later degenerated into a rhetorical compensation for the failure to achieve economic self-sufficiency.[165]

In 1955, these colonial memories pushed North Korea to declare its solidarity with the peoples of the Bandung camp. During the Suez Crisis, the North Korean Afro-Asian Solidarity Committee provided aid to Egypt, and in the fall of 1958 Pyongyang established diplomatic relations both with the provisional Algerian government and newly independent Guinea.[166] Pyongyang also established diplomatic and trade relations with socialist-oriented African states and, after the 1965 revolution, sent aid specialists to Congo-Brazzaville. In the second half of the 1950s, the North Korean economy grew much faster than that of the South, and Kim even suggested that South Korea emulate the "brilliant achievements" of his own country.[167] The remarkable speed and scale of North Korea's postwar development led *Neues Deutschland* – the official publication of the East German state – to characterize North Korea's success as the "economic miracle in the Far East."[168]

II. EAST GERMANY'S GIFT TO NORTH KOREA: METROPOLIS BERLIN IN THE LAND OF RUINS

Hamhung and Hungnam, which are located on the northeast coast of the peninsula, were North Korea's second and third largest cities after the capital Pyongyang. The Hamhung region was the center of the country's nitrogen chemical and hydroelectric power industries. The Japanese corporate Noguchi had first developed these industries in the late 1920s, and they had later been expanded with the support of the Japanese military. Not surprisingly, this heavily industrialized area became a stronghold of the Korean nationalist and labor movements. The region was also the scene of intense fighting during the Korean War. As the U.S. Tenth Army Corps retreated from the Chinese border across Hamhung to the port of Hungnam, the area was subject to intense air and naval bombardment to slow the Chinese advance toward the coast. Military engineers then destroyed every factory, building, and piece of infrastructure that might have been of any use to the North Korean and Chinese armies.[169]

The Korean War had destroyed more than 90 percent of the houses and industrial plants in the Hamhung region. As a result, reconstructing this industrial center was no less important to building socialism than the rebuilding of the capital.[170] During the 1954 Geneva conference on Korea and Indochina, East German minister president Otto Grotewohl told a North Korean delegate that his country would be willing to help rebuild one of the cities destroyed in the war. The East German Politburo approved Grotewohl's proposal in July 1954, and Kim chose Hamhung to be the beneficiary of this East German largesse.[171] The Construction Staff Korea (*Baustab Korea*) in Berlin, established to manage the Hamhung project, reported directly to Deputy Premier Heinrich Rau, who was also Minister for Construction (and later Minister of Trade).

In late 1954, a preparatory team arrived in North Korea to gather information on the city, its history, culture, and population, as well as on the state of the North Korean economy and ongoing reconstruction efforts. In January 1955, the Construction Staff completed its initial planning work. In March 1955, the German Council of Ministers approved 204 million marks to fund the project from 1955 to its planned completion in 1964.[172] The same month North Korea created a Commission for the Reconstruction of the City of Hamhung, which was headed by vice premier and chairman of the state construction committee Bak Uiwan.[173] In 1955, the technicians and workers who made up the German Work Group (*Deutsche Arbeitsgruppe*, DAG) arrived in Hamhung.

A bilateral agreement set out the guidelines for the Hamhung project. Each year, the Korean state planning commission prepared both a budget for the Hamhung project and a detailed list of items to be purchased from East Germany so that the planning processes of the two countries became intermeshed with each other. The East German remit here was vast as they agreed to rebuild the entire city, including housing, office buildings, streets, and all other necessary infrastructure.[174] The scale became bigger after 1956, when the East Germans agreed to expand their project to include the reconstruction of industrial plant and infrastructure of Hungnam and the nearby city of Bongun, a major center of the chemical industry.

It became clear almost immediately, however, that the success of this showcase project depended on overcoming the limitations of the planned economy at both ends of this global linkage. Horst Präßler, the second director of the DAG, explained that "the effectiveness of German aid depends on specific investments by the government of North Korea."[175] Yet the East Germans were not always able to deliver on the goods that they had promised, and what the East Germans *were* willing and able to supply did not always correspond to what the North Korean government wanted to receive.[176] This was especially so when Korea looked beyond the requirements of the Hamhung project to take into account the needs of other regions and sectors of the economy. In 1955/56, for example, North Korean officials asked the East Germans if they could send round steel bars and irrigation pipes, both of which were in very short supply in North Korea, instead of the equipment for a hydraulic lime factory called for in the original agreement. The North Koreans explained that they could do without such a factory because they were already capable of producing lime and cement. East Germany rejected the request, in part because the iron bars and piping were in short supply in Germany and in part because they believed that the lime factory in Hamhung was necessary to ensure an adequate supply of cement for the Hamhung project.[177]

The intensity of these disputes rose precipitously after 1957, when the decline in fraternal aid and the launching of the Five-Year Plan led to a sharp reduction in the North Korean investment in the Hamhung project. As part of spending cuts, Korean officials decided not to build all of the new factories called for by the agreement with the East Germans and, instead, to make repairs and modifications to existing plant. For example, while the agreement called for the construction of a new fiberglass plant, the North Koreans proposed that the Germans set up the equipment in a vacant factory building in the western part of the country, rather than building an entirely new structure. Money saved in that way, they argued, could be used to build more housing in Hamhung. The Germans, however, rejected the proposal. The full "political effects" of their showcase project could only be realized, they insisted, if all of the new German enterprises being constructed in the country were concentrated in the Hamhung region.[178]

While the East Germans focused all of their attention on the Hamhung–Hungnam region, the Korean government had to balance between the requirements of the Hamhung project and the needs of the larger national economy, especially with regard to such key materials as iron and steel.[179] Spending cuts and shortages led to the underutilization of the machinery, equipment, and credits, which were provided by East Germany, but which were only to be used for the Hamhung project. An increasing quantity of East German credits for the project remained unspent, and the North Koreans asked if 10 million rubles in credits that had not been drawn upon could be used instead to cover the trade deficit resulting from their failure to meet their raw material export quota. Although the East Germans agreed to this request, they also feared that the failure of the North Koreans to provide the raw materials and agricultural products – including millions of cigarettes – would seriously harm the economy of their own country.[180] In view of the relatively high proportion of the costs that they had to bear, the North Koreans increasingly came to see the Hamhung project less as a contribution to their national development plan than as a burden on it.[181] Their desire to shift resources to other projects increasingly clashed with the East German desire to complete the project as originally planned. Thus, in reality fraternal aid among socialist countries was neither a means of Soviet manipulation nor selfless aid from the developed to the less developed world. Rather, individual aid programs were always the result of give and take among nations whose interests never fully coincided.

III. THE PLAN: ...WHILE VISIONS OF SOCIALISM DANCED IN THEIR HEADS

The second pillar of East German aid to North Korea was technical aid, which included the employment of experts in a variety of fields, such as architecture and engineering, public health, and mineral geology. One of Kim's priorities was to use the reconstruction of Hamhung as a vast training shop to help North Korea make the transition from artisanal to mechanized construction, and he asked the East Germans to send urban planners, engineers and master artisans organized in a self-contained work brigade equipped with modern machines and tools so that they could transfer to Korean workers their organizational and work methods.[182] In his view, a group equipped in such a manner would contrast favorably with the volunteer construction brigades sent by the Chinese, most of which lacked such tools.

In view of the political, economic, and ideological significance of the Hamhung project, German officials put much emphasis on the professional and personal qualifications of these technicians. The recruitment guidelines specified that they had to have the imagination and organizational skills needed to independently solve problems in a foreign land, the leadership skills needed to motivate their foreign colleagues, rather than simply to command them, and the intelligence needed to communicate to the Koreans "the basic, routine activities of his specialized area *without an interpreter.*" Most important of all, they should not be inclined to arrogance or expressions of "racial superiority."[183] As goodwill ambassadors, they could help repair the country's damaged reputation abroad by showing that Germany, or at least its eastern part, could no longer be associated with National Socialism. In the words of Erich Selbmann, the first director of the DAG, "it is to be expected that, after a very long period, in which the name of Germany was associated with destruction and annihilation, and a brief intermediate period, in which Germany could only passively participate in the international field, the German Democratic Republic can participate in this worldwide process of establishing peace."[184] Similarly, the chairman of the executive board of the construction union *IG Bau-Holz* challenged the DAG to show the North Koreans "through your work and initiative in the application of the most progressive and exemplary work methods and through a high work morale that you are fighting as the representatives of the new, peaceful and democratic Germany to realize the goal of the working class."[185]

Across 1955, several waves of East Germans arrived in Hamhung. The original plan called for 188 East Germans (including 65 specialists, such as architects, urban planners, and engineers, and 103 master artisans, machinists, and craftsmen). However, already before the end of that year, the number of craftsmen was cut in half when Pyongyang reduced its investment in the project.[186] Although most of the original 132 short-term contracts expired at the end of 1955, the Berlin-based Construction Staff Korea did not send timely replacements for these departing workers. By early 1956, only 48 East Germans – mostly administrators – remained in the city. The acute shortage of planners and construction supervisors resulted in delays in construction work.[187] Recruitment was a constant cause of friction between the DAG and the Construction Staff Korea. The DAG leadership complained that they had not been consulted regarding the technical and character qualifications required for the job and that the Construction Staff Korea had sent too many unqualified and immature persons to Korea. Some simply dropped their work and flew home, while many others were sent home for a variety of reasons, including ill health, incompetence, "moral misconduct," and other actions that were considered harmful to East Germany's reputation.[188]

To judge from the list of people who worked there, employment on the Hamhung project was a prestigious position. Selbmann was the brother of Heavy Industry Minister Fritz Selbmann. The chief architect and deputy director Hans Grotewohl was the son of the minister president, and the wife of the younger Grotewohl worked as an architect on the project. Several of the other architects were also prominent in their field. Hartmut Colden and Peter Doehler together won the 1952 competition to design the new headquarters for *Neues Deutschland*.[189] Landscape architects Hugo Namslauer and Hubert Matthes played an important role in

"Architektencollektiv Buchenwald," the group commissioned by the Ministry of Culture to design the memorials for the former concentration camps at Buchenwald, Ravensbrueck, and Sachsenhausen.[190] Konrad Püschel would later become a professor at the Bauhaus in Dessau. Präßler later became a high-ranking official at the Ministry of Construction.[191] Many of the Germans who returned from North Korea in 1956 and 1957 acknowledged that they had learned a great deal from their work in Hamhung; these people would later direct East German development programs in North Vietnam, Zanzibar, and Yemen.[192]

In October 1955, East Germany decided to allow certain specialists to bring their wives and children to Hamhung and to give these women jobs doing secretarial and bookkeeping work, teaching at the school for the German children, supervising the Korean service personnel, and organizing social and cultural events.[193] Many of the DAG specialists resented the fact that only a few experts were allowed to bring their family members to Korea, and this initial restriction was soon lifted.[194] At the end of 1956, a total of 125 Germans were living in Hamhung, including 20 children and 26 women (Figure 2.5).[195]

FIGURE 2.5 The members of German Work Group (DAG) in Hamhung in front of their living quarters (c. 1956). Horst Präßler is fourth from the right in the front row. Courtesy of Renate.

Some members of the DAG were represented by the East German construction workers' union, *IG Bau-Holz,* an affiliate of the FDGB.[196] At the local level, the DAG established a union to improve the living and working conditions, discuss work-related grievances, and resolve conflicts among team members. The fact that both Selbmann and Grotewohl were related to high-level politicians created the impression among craftsmen that the DAG management was immune to criticism and that their own grievances would not be looked on favorably. However, the union also saw itself as a representative of the German workers and their fraternal solidarity, and its members prided themselves for fighting together with "our Korean friends" for the common good of the working classes and contributing to "strengthening international friendship and peace."[197]

The first year was primarily devoted to the advance work that had to be done for the project: setting up depots in preparation for the arrival of construction equipment, vehicles, and machines from Germany; building onsite shops to produce bricks made from locally available clay; and improving the quality of the communal living quarters for the Germans. Architects and engineers also began surveying building sites. The project leaders had to get acquainted with their Korean counterparts and learn how to secure the machines, materials, and workers that they would need. To facilitate this work, the Korean government temporarily recalled Korean students from East Germany to work as interpreters.[198]

The actual construction work was carried out by the North Korean "Construction Trust No. 18," which in January 1957 consisted of some 3,300 primarily female workers. These women did masonry work, cleared rubble, and operated machines and transport vehicles.[199] Initially, the Germans had to figure out how to teach Korean workers the mechanized construction techniques to be employed at Hamhung. In May 1955, the DAG set up an eleven-member committee to organize the training of Korean technicians and skilled workers.[200] German machinists and craftsmen gave the Koreans on-the-job training in precision work, while other workers were taught how to operate machines and construction vehicles.[201] In less than six months, Construction Trust No. 18 was capable of taking over many tasks; by the end of 1956, more than 200 Koreans had qualified as skilled workers; and in two years, the Germans trained thirty Korean engineers and technicians.[202]

The responsibilities of the East Germans themselves became both more extensive and more complex as the DAG moved to the execution of large-scale infrastructure projects, such as the central heating plant, streets, and the installation of underground utility lines and piping, as well as the

FIGURE 2.6 Apartment building under construction in Hamhung. Courtesy of Rainer Ressel.

construction of high-profile public buildings, such as a hotel, a hospital, and a technical college. These projects were so complex that they challenged the expertise of the German engineers who had come in the first wave of specialists. For example, the engineers working on the piping plant were unable to properly insulate the furnace foundation, and the DAG repeatedly asked – in vain – the Construction Staff Korea to send a special engineer to solve the problem.[203]

While the surface area of the East German projects increased fivefold in 1956, the size of the German team could remain more or less unchanged because by that time the Korean workers and technicians of Construction Trust No. 18 were capable of taking over less complicated tasks, such as the construction of apartment buildings (Figure 2.6).[204] By 1958, the DAG would decline to approximately 35 persons, primarily architects and engineers employed in the declining number of industrial projects still underway at that point.[205] Moreover, as the Korean workers acquired more and more knowledge, they were increasingly able and willing to criticize the work of the East Germans. As one German working in Hamhung noted, the German specialists could no longer get by giving simple instructions like "the machines must be placed over there and the stones must be placed here...." The DAG wrote to Berlin that, if the East

Germans were to be able to continue fulfilling their mission of transferring technical knowledge, the Construction Staff needed to send over "really qualified" regional planners and civil engineers.[206]

IV. A VIEW FROM THE GROUND: BECOMING "HAMHUNGER"

Because of the sheer size of the DAG and its seven-year presence in North Korea, the Hamhung project offers an unusual opportunity to examine Korean and German understandings of socialist fraternal help, patterns of conflict and cooperation between the East German and North Korean teams, and differences between the lived experiences of the team members and official state pronouncements.

On the whole, the Germans seemed to have enjoyed their experience in North Korea. They traveled freely and extensively in the country, something that would be unimaginable in present-day North Korea. There were beach resorts near Hamhung as well as mountains with ancient temples and pavilions. The DAG organized excursions outside the province, and the high point for many of the East Germans was a tour of Beijing on their way back to Berlin. The group also organized many social and cultural gatherings with Soviet, Czech, and Polish aid workers, although the East Germans preferred to socialize with the Czechs more than either the Soviets or the Poles, whom they considered to be too conservative. The Germans also paraded together with the local population in major celebrations such as May Day, the anniversary of the Bolshevik revolution, and the celebration of Korean independence (Figure 2.7).[207]

The DAG did not live in a ghetto. The members interacted with the North Koreans on a regular basis and at a number of different levels. At the leadership level, the Germans and Koreans – including architects and urban planners – consulted with each other through the entire construction process. Figure 2.8 captures the formal instruction and planning sessions associated with any project of comparable size. Below them were the craftsmen responsible for training Koreans in their respective specialties. It was contacts at this level that the North Korean and East German authorities packaged as the embodiment of solidarity and fraternal help. But there was also another, informal level that was less amenable to state regimentation, at least initially. In comparison with the two states' focus on work, technology, and socialist modernity in their official representations of the program, DAG members tended to highlight their personal contacts with Koreans, so much so that both the Korean and German

FIGURE 2.7 "Long live international solidarity" (September 1957). Courtesy of Rainer Ressel.

FIGURE 2.8 Präßler speaking to a planning meeting with Korean translator and bilingual instructions. Courtesy of Renate Präßler.

authorities sometimes warned against becoming "too friendly" with their foreign co-workers, both male and female.[208]

To improve living conditions for the Germans, the Korean authorities provided cleaners, cooks, maids, barbers, and seamstresses, and the canteen offered many opportunities for more personal contacts between the North Koreans and the East Germans. In *Hamhunger Heimatreportage*, the DAG newsletter distributed to its former members to keep them abreast of the development of "our child Hamhung," there are many references to familiar Korean faces in the canteen as well as to the Korean food, alcohol, and cigarettes that the East Germans enjoyed in Hamhung: "The cook 'Müller' is still at his job along with the sweet comrade Pak-dongmu ["dongmu" is the Korean word for comrade] and Kim-dongmu – the sweet Korean women who always took care of our needs in a friendly manner. When we are thirsty and pour ourselves a Chinese beer, then everything tastes better. We decide to eat Korean food. There is Omreis [fried rice with an omlet on top] and other delicacies as well."[209]

The East Germans developed a sense of transnational identity based on their living and working experiences in Hamhung, and they constructed their own collective identity as the "Tokils" ("Tokil" is the Korean word for Germany) and "Hamhunger." Neither the North Koreans nor the members of the DAG emphasized that they were from the German Democratic Republic.[210] The DAG also constructed an orphanage for the local community (Figure 2.9). For many of the Germans, it was often these informal contacts and daily experiences that helped them appreciate the local culture and customs that they remembered with fondness for years to come. While our knowledge of international aid programs is often pre- or overdetermined by state-enforced, ritualized ideology and practice, we need to be sensitive to those experiences that escaped and exceeded the more rigid intentions of the states that sponsored these programs.

Although the project managers emphasized the importance of German-Korean cooperation in every aspect of the work, neither the collaboration nor the training always went as smoothly as the East Germans had hoped.[211] There was a pervasive problem with excessive drinking, verbal altercations, fist fights, absenteeism, and instances of sexual abuse of Korean women – some of which resulted in pregnancy. Sometimes, these dangerous liaisons had to be resolved politically. In one instance, a German man wanted to marry his North Korean lover; when his request was turned down by the German authorities, he tried – in vain – to become a North Korean citizen. Racial tensions surfaced regularly in the earlier years. Some of the Germans were so arrogant and authoritarian that, as one member of their team reported, the North Koreans complained that Germans made the former Japanese rulers pale in comparison.[212] Some Koreans drew embarrassing

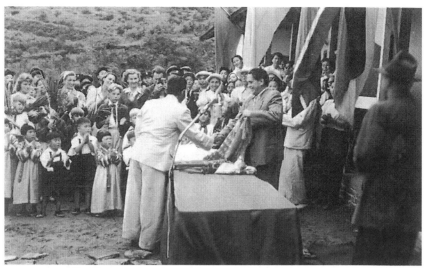

FIGURE 2.9 Präßler opening the orphanage built by the Germans in 1957. Courtesy of Renate Präßler.

parallels between the autocratic comportment of the Germans and "Hitler's fascism."[213]

At a different level, the simple act of asking their North Korean co-workers how well they themselves were being fed was problematic because the question itself was seen as an affront to the country's leadership. North Korea was heavily dependent on food imports from China. The food shortage was particularly acute in 1955 because of the poor harvest the year before, the acceleration of collectivization, and excessive requisitioning.[214] Selbmann explained to the Germans that their task was to teach their hosts "the newest technical and economic knowledge" in the construction field, and he warned them not to attempt to change the existing local conditions "through any measures of help that do not concern us."[215] The Germans, however, enjoyed an ample supply of food, cigarettes, alcohol, and other consumer goods. Some of the East Germans gave leftovers from the canteen or parties to the Koreans, and some of them even invited their Korean friends to parties at the DAG compound, where they could enjoy the food and drink.

The issue became more pressing in 1957, when Korean officials began to discourage unofficial contacts with foreigners and issued a more or less formal prohibition on visits by the Koreans to the DAG compound.[216] The Germans had long been uncertain just how friendly they could be with their counterparts without arousing the suspicion or ire of Korean authorities. The Koreans became more cautious and reserved in their personal interaction with the Germans than they had been in the previous years. The DAG leadership began to require that all invitations of Koreans to private gatherings be approved in advance by the director. Both Korean and German officials also sought to discourage the Germans from giving their Korean co-workers small gifts, such as food, clothing, and items purchased in the canteen. Korean authorities told the DAG that such practices would favor only those few Koreans acquainted with the Germans and create enmity among those Koreans who did not enjoy access to such East German favors.[217]

V. BUILD FASTER AND CHEAPER!

The Hamhung project had great symbolic importance for East Germany. The construction of a vast urban-industrial complex was an opportunity to showcase its technological achievements for all the world to see. The SED leadership also hoped that the project would become a mirror in which the East Germans could see their own future reflected.

From the very beginning, what the East Germans were proposing to do in Hamhung was measured against what the Soviets had already accomplished in Pyongyang. In addition to the obvious question of whether buildings in the second city of Hamhung should be higher or in any way superior to those already erected in the capital, there was also the more pragmatic question of why, for example, a school in Hamhung should have steam heating if this had not been deemed necessary for a school in Pyongyang?[218] In a 1957 report to Rau, the DAG described the ways in which the houses that were being built in Hamhung were superior to those in Pyongyang. The report emphasized the superior quality of the buildings and their interior fixtures, as well as the uniform design of the entire housing complex, whose impressive exterior appearance magnified the political symbolism of the project.[219]

The reconstruction of Hamhung was as much a sociocultural as a civil engineering project. The Germans complained that the Koreans were culturally challenged by modern urban life, especially the idea of living in multistory apartment buildings. Although the Koreans had been critical of the apartment buildings that the Hungarians had built in Pyongyang, like the leftist Bauhaus architects of the Weimar years, the DAG leaders believed that living in more modern, functional housing would educate the residents to a socialist way of life, and they tried to persuade the Koreans of the virtues of their vision of the socialist city.

Debates over architectural style and construction technology were central to the socialist transformation of Moscow and Berlin in the mid-1950s. The major points of contention in the rebuilding of East Berlin were whether the real needs of the laboring classes could be best satisfied – and the identity of the new socialist state best represented – by historicism, Stalinist-era socialist realism, or Bauhaus modernism and how these different architectural styles would help mold the new socialist personality.[220] Initially, the East Germans had opted for a combination of socialist realism and historicism, but the atmosphere shifted perceptibly after Stalin's death. In his December 1954 speech to the All Union Conference of Builders and Architects, Khrushchev denounced Stalinist style and instead called for the industrialization or mechanization of construction, that is, the use of prefabricated modules and other construction materials and methods to maximize labor productivity and minimize costs and materials.[221] These principles were carried over to Hamhung. For example, not only did the Central Train Station reflect the new socialist architecture and construction methods. The group of public buildings clustered around the train station was also meant to give tangible expression to the leading role of the party and the state in North Korean socialism.

Khrushchev's proposal quickly became the dominant post-Stalinist paradigm of architecture and urban planning in the Soviet bloc, and from Moscow to Berlin the fortunes of architects and bureaucrats rose and fell depending on their position on this crucial question. In April 1955, East German authorities took over Khrushchev's call to build "better, faster, and cheaper" as their own motto.[222] These same issues also led to controversy at the first North Korean conference of architects and builders, which met in January 1956.[223] The discussions there clearly echoed recent debates in Eastern Europe. Following the conference, the Construction Ministry was sharply criticized for failing to widely employ the mechanized construction of prefabricated buildings, and it was ordered to adopt these modern methods on a large scale.[224] However, North Korea lacked the infrastructure, machinery, and skilled workers needed to emulate Soviet and East German construction methods on such a scale, and the increased reliance on the ideological mobilization of unskilled labor could not make up for these shortcomings.

The leaders of the DAG had long argued that their advanced construction technologies would yield enough efficiencies to enable them to escape the political and budgetary constraints that were tightening around them. Their confidence seemed justified in light of productivity on the Hungnam project, where they recorded a 130 percent increase in productivity in the first quarter of 1956.[225] As Präßler noted, "with the help from the DAG, the Hamhung project is not only in terms of form, architectural picture... but also in the question of the application of norms, standards, and mechanization quite exceptional."[226]

In 1957, the construction of these public buildings had advanced to the stage where the DAG was ready to begin installing the heating, electrical, and plumbing systems (including such things as showers and toilets). It was at this point – at the latest – when the latent differences between the Germans and the Koreans came out into the open. When the DAG leaders met with the Korean state planning commission to finalize the materials to be shipped from Germany in 1958, the latter objected to a number of interior fixtures that the East Germans considered indispensable to preserving the distinctly East German character of the buildings. For example, although the DAG insisted on installing automatic light switches in corridors and stairwells and on putting electrical outlets in every room in the residential buildings, the Korean authorities objected to the proposal, arguing that such items cost too much (₩170 in comparison to the ₩100 that they had paid for similar items in Pyongyang) and that they would encourage the unnecessary use of electricity. They also objected to East German standards for the size and ceiling height of the apartments. And whereas deputy premier Bak had originally asked the Germans to install toilets in each flat, this idea was scrapped as a luxury later in 1958.[227]

Präßler feared that changes demanded by the North Koreans were undermining the viability of the East German plan for the reconstruction of Hamhung. If the North Koreans did not live up to their original financial commitments, he argued, the Hamhung project would cease to be politically tenable for East Germany, and the North Koreans would lose face with the "socialist camp as a whole."[228] In addition, the DAG had long assumed that the use of East German furniture and fixtures in cultural clubs, department stores, and theaters would encourage the North Koreans to desire more goods made in East Germany, and they worried that cutting corners would also damage the future value of of North Korea as a trading partner.[229] By that point, the onsite cement plant was producing prefabricated concrete slabs that sped up construction, as did the widespread mobilization of "volunteer" workers to clear rubble for street construction and do pick-and-shovel work for the water and sewage systems. As the DAG management reported back to Berlin, "underground work is lagging, but we are now catching up, above all through the patriotic mobilization [of workers] comparable to that employed in the construction of the Berlin Stalinallee, so that by the end of the year most housing can be connected to water and sewage."[230]

VI. GREAT LEAP FORWARD AT PYONGYANG SPEED

The first Korean Five-Year Plan, which was to run from 1957 to 1961, involved the all-out mobilization of the population for the construction of the heavy industrial foundations of economic independence. This was known as the Chollima movement, which the Central Committee of the Korean Workers' Party introduced in December 1956. The movement was named after a legendary winged horse that could travel 1000 li (a bit more than 300 miles) in a day; the name was chosen to describe the frenetic pace at which the country was to be rebuilt.

The Korean plan bore many similarities to the contemporary Chinese Great Leap Forward, and it reflected a growing distance from the Soviet model of socialist transformation. However, North Korea suffered from an acute labor shortage due to the loss of life during the war and the migration of so many people to the south. To compensate for this shortage, the authorities mobilized every able-bodied person – officials, skilled and unskilled workers, farmers, housewives, and schoolchildren – for construction work.[231] The people had to live in an environment of fear and insecurity as the government resorted to punitive measures to sustain the ideological mobilization of the populace. Moreover, although the party leadership increased wages and lowered the prices of some consumer goods, any benefits of these measures were offset by the overall rise in the cost of living.

In every socialist country, plans for rapid socialist transformation led to conflicts within the ruling party and purges of those left holding the short end of the political stick. In North Korea, construction policy quickly became one of the main ideological battlefields both within the regime and between the North Koreans and the East Germans. During the Japanese colonial era, many Koreans had moved to China and the Soviet Union, and Stalin had then forcibly relocated them to Central Asia. Many of these ethnic Koreans and their descendants, who had studied in the Soviet Union and worked there as technicians, teachers, and party functionaries, returned to Korea after 1945. Initially, this pro-Soviet group occupied many top-level positions in industry, construction, and education. These people had been schooled in the same planning tradition as the East Germans; they shared European enthusiasm for modern construction methods and the productivity gains they promised; and they feared that the unrealistic production goals contained in the Five-Year Plan would disrupt the balanced growth of the economy and ultimately do more harm than good.

As the country geared up for the Five-Year Plan, however, they became the object of suspicion because Kim regarded their Soviet connection as a threat to his power. Kim's doubts about their loyalty led to a wave of political repression across the second half of 1957. Three-quarters of the officials in charge of coordinating the Hamhung project and Construction Trust No. 18 were caught up in these purges, which cost the DAG many of the connections that it had carefully built up at both the central and provincial levels. The purges culminated in the removal of deputy premier Bak, one of the most powerful members of this pro-Soviet faction, in December of that year. Bak was the DAG's "last and the most significant of the leading Korean comrades with whom a close contact and a good cooperation existed," and the Germans lamented that his removal left the DAG without a reliable partner on the North Korean side. Eventually, many of those who had been purged were allowed to return to their former jobs, but a pervasive atmosphere of suspicion and fear persisted.[232]

Now, with the institution of the Chollima movement, increased speed and decreased costs became the sole criteria by which the success of the project was measured. The North Koreans gave up any pretext of achieving European construction standards. While the original reconstruction plan had been based on the construction of new factories, the North Korean government abandoned this plan and, instead, focused increasingly on refurbishing existing plants and repairing older machines and equipment. These growing divergences became clear at the annual planning meetings held to determine precisely what items would be supplied by each side during the coming calendar year. In November 1957, the East Germans had agreed to build a clay-piping factory and to equip a furniture factory. Although the Koreans doubled their planned investment in Hamhung for 1958 and wanted the DAG to construct a gas works, a thermal power plant, and a broadcasting station for the city, they themselves were not meeting their export requirements under the trade agreement. The Germans were unwilling to provide such complex and expensive items so long as the Koreans were failing to hold up their end of the deal – even if these shortfalls were due, at least in part, to Kim's efforts to improve the country's living standards by limiting food exports.[233]

Moreover, as construction targets were raised, capital and construction materials became correspondingly scarce. The response of the North Korean government was to devolve responsibility for plan fulfillment down onto provincial authorities. The latter were suddenly faced with the task of ensuring adequate supplies of consumer goods, financing construction, and procuring the necessary material, machines, and people. Because all important construction materials, especially steel and cement, were in short supply, all major production projects were forced to build their own cement kilns, foundries, and electrical generating stations to meet their own needs for producer goods. Similar tendencies toward economic autarchy could also be observed in consumer goods industries. This was hugely inefficient and wasteful process.[234]

The East Germans were becoming increasingly exasperated with the chronic shortages of basic construction materials and skilled workers. While these shortages were due to a number of factors, the DAG blamed the problems on the devolution of project management responsibility onto provincial officials, whom the Germans regarded as incompetent and whom they accused of siphoning off scarce material and equipment that was earmarked for German projects. In early 1958, Pyongyang created a new agency to manage the Hamhung–Hungnam project; the head of this group held the rank of vice minister; and he reported directly to the Council of Ministers. However, the DAG still complained that the agency was not independent enough. In the fall of 1958, the Korean Communist Party Central Committee – at least in part at the instigation of the DAG – held hearings into work speed and methods in Hamhung. The ensuing trials led to the removal of the director and several other Korean officials responsible for the Hamhung project, and the director of Construction Trust No. 18 was also later removed in response to German pressure.

The Germans in Hamhung feared that this highly ideologized productivity campaign would disrupt the logic of central planning. At the end of 1957, the DAG asked provincial party officials not to approve any hurried resolutions regarding construction methods that would impact its work because Koreans at every level were afraid that anything they said would conflict with the party line. The situation was "especially bad for those lower-level cadres who work with us, because we give them technical instructions and advice that appear to go against the party line and other higher authorities."[235] Although the DAG felt that they "should refuse to collaborate in making technical and economic mistakes,"[236] such purism would have required them to abandon the

Hamhung project. In practice, the subsequent history of their work became one of halting, unsatisfactory compromises between modernist ideology and North Korean realities.

VII. *PYONGYANG HOUR*: COMPETING VISIONS OF SOCIALIST MODERNITY IN NORTH KOREA

In October 1958, when the Five-Year Plan had only been underway for 18 months, Pyongyang announced an ambitious plan to complete the Five-Year Plan in only three and a half years. The intense, chaotic, and ideologically charged atmosphere of the time is nicely captured in the novel *Pyongyang Hour* by Choi Hak Su, who was later awarded the Kim Il Sung Prize for his literary labors.[237] The novel, which opened in November 1957, provided a fictionalized and highly idealized account of real developments in the construction field in 1957/58. The main characters were three young men, who arrived in Pyongyang after completing their military service to help with the reconstruction of the fatherland. One of the men, Rhee Sang Chul, was a native of Pyongyang, where he had spent a miserable, impoverished childhood under Japanese rule. His brother-in-law Mun Ha Rin was the director of urban planning for the city. However, Mun had become politically suspect because he had been trained in a European architectural tradition, which, it was claimed, prevented him from grasping the importance of the Five-Year Plan and the Chollima movement. In the novel and in reality, Kim had denounced such people as reactionaries, claiming that their blind adherence to foreign doctrines betrayed both a secret loyalty to other powers and a lack of confidence in "our own power, wisdom, and ability." Mun and his superiors were in due course denounced for their architectural and political failings. Mun's rehabilitation depended on his ideological conversion.

In the novel, Kim delivered a rousing fictionalized speech in which he called on architects to build more housing at lower cost and to abandon foreign aesthetic values for a revolutionary emphasis on efficiently meeting the basic needs of the laboring masses. Mun saw the light and recognized the virtues of traditional building practices. He became a convert to the traditional ondol (subfloor heating, which had been rejected by Western builders, even though it was cheaper than European electrical heating) and asked himself why anyone would conceivably wish to introduce Western-style beds, which wasted precious iron without being superior in any way to sleeping on futons on ondol-heated floors. Mun even criticized the adoption of Western dimensions in housing design because they seemed to thoughtlessly take over foreign standards without giving any thought to the traditional norms that were best suited for the needs of the Korean people:

The ceilings are also high like the houses in foreign countries. They lack style and coziness. In the past, our ancestors knew just how high ceilings should be...[Now] ceilings are so high that the space appears empty. Was it really necessary to make them so high?...How high was the ceiling in traditional Choson [Korean] homes? What is the average height of the Choson people? What is the optimal height for temperature, ventilation and light? When he was trying to find the right number, he was shocked to realize that he was ignorant of the average height of the Choson people. Without knowing such a thing, how could he have designed a house for them?...In the past he had imitated what others had done, and he had not succeeded in truly designing anything, which would be appropriate for our country and its people.

After reflecting on these questions, Mun threw himself back into his work and designed a prototype standardized apartment building, which he regarded as the "most solid path" to the construction of mass housing at minimal cost. He continued the culture war against foreign influence by claiming that the methods used to prefabricate and mechanically assemble standardized housing units on a mass basis were Korean inventions.[238]

In real life, Kim had predicted in January 1958 that the coming year would mark a turning point in the construction campaign, and in the novel one of the other characters exclaimed "isn't it such a source of pride and joy to be an architect? ...Construction! Something truly worthwhile. Soon there will be a fierce battle in that field."[239] The reader is given a detailed account of the construction of onsite plants to produce the building materials needed for the housing project. The novel follows the emergence of new construction specialists, such as assemblers and welders, who became the heroic protagonists in the struggle for self-reliance. The assembly brigade in which Rhee is employed developed new techniques for assembling buildings, and the brigade ultimately succeeded in reducing the amount of time it took to put up the walls of a simple flat to a mere sixteen minutes. This new assembly method was sixty-one times faster than conventional methods, and the application of this new method to all of the new housing in the fictional Pyongyang led to the overfulfillment of the construction quota for 1958. The rapid pace of this furious transfiguration of tradition as the construction of socialism came to be known as "Pyongyang speed."

At the end of January 1958, in realtime, Kim asked the DAG project directors to meet with him and the other high officials responsible for the

Hamhung–Hungnam project.[240] At the meeting, Kim demonstrated a surprisingly detailed command of costs and construction methods. According to Kim, the cost per square meter for residential construction had increased from ₩3,580 in 1957 to ₩4,500–4,800 in 1958. Although construction teams in Pyongyang had managed to push the cost down to ₩3,100 in response to a party decree issued in October of the previous year, this was not enough, and the advisory teams dispatched by the party pushed the figure down to ₩1,685.

These savings had been achieved, Kim explained, by reducing the size of the apartments, eliminating individual bathrooms in favor of communal toilets and showers, reducing kitchen space by 50 percent (to 5 m²), and lowering the ceiling height to 2.2 meters. These alterations resulted in a reduction of 50 percent of the amount of cement and steel, 70 percent of the piping, and 38 percent of the labor that would have been required by the original plan. These savings made it possible to increase the 1958 plan target from 2,750 to 5,100 housing units, and Kim hoped to increase this to 10,000 units through the use of volunteer labor. He then asked the DAG to apply these same standards to the housing project in Hamhung. The East Germans were naturally reluctant to go along with this proposal. After all, they had not come halfway around the world just to build cheap housing that could hardly serve as a model of socialist modernity. Kim made a partial concession on this point. The Korean government would establish a single cost per unit for housing construction in both cities, but Hamhung provincial officials would be allowed to include the German amenities if they wished to pay for them. It is not clear whether these provincial officials availed themselves of this option.

In mid-1958, the North Korean party leadership set new and even higher plan targets for the Five-Year Plan. The Korean Council of Ministers decreed that 65 percent of all housing constructed would have to use prefabricated materials – with the figure rising to 80 percent for the following year.[241] Korean planners and architects were hard pressed to meet these goals, and it was increasingly doubtful whether there was any constructive role left for the DAG. For example, when Korean architects designed a 48-unit apartment building for Hamhung in 1958, they included 16 communal lavatories and one communal washing area with two showers. While the Koreans could not ignore state construction guidelines, the East Germans could not in good conscience consent to a plan that deviated in such essential respects from their own mandate "to build a modern socialist city" in Korea.[242] The Germans were also becoming increasingly exasperated with the chronic shortages of basic construction materials and skilled workers.

The persistence of so many problems of such magnitude made it clear that it was not a problem of bureaucracy or of individuals, but of fundamentally conflicting priorities as the two countries pursued their own paths to communism. In 1960, the East German government decided to sharply reduce its aid to North Korea.[243] In a letter to Kim, Grotewohl blamed this decision to cut back their commitments in Hamhung on West German militarism, although this was probably only a fig leaf for a decision that was taken on very different grounds. Kim replied in equally empty language that "we are firmly convinced that the fraternal friendship and cooperation between the Korean and German peoples on the foundation of the principles of proletarian internationalism will continue to be further strengthened."[244] The project officially ended on September 15, 1962, with a ceremony in which a high-ranking East German delegation officially turned over to the Koreans the "Ten Thousand Hurrahs Bridge" in Hamhung. In the end, East Germany only spent 63 percent of the money originally budgeted for the project.[245]

CONCLUSION

In 2005, the 75-year-old Wilfried Lübke reminisced about his time in Hamhung nearly a half-century earlier: "I was elated ... I could travel. In my mid-20s I escaped from the East German prison."[246] In 1956, he arrived in Hamhung to help with the construction of the city's water works. His wife Helga joined him a year later. In 1960, shortly after their return to East Germany, they fled to West Berlin. They felt that everywhere they went in East Germany they were being mistrustfully watched, and, after their experience of the wider world during their stay in Korea, they could no longer bear the "narrowness" of East Germany. But despite his antipathy toward East Germany, he remembered the enthusiasm with which he had originally gone to North Korea to build a better, communist society: "In Hamhung I thought for the first time that communism could actually work....Here, far away from my homeland, an almost American spirit prevailed among the East Germans, few party bigwigs, flat hierarchies. Many East German citizens worked here with genuine idealism. We wanted to build up after Germany had brought so much destruction to the world."

During their time in Korea, the Lübkes also made friends with two Koreans, a female graphic designer named Park and a translator named

Zang. We get glimpses of the two Koreans in Helga's diary, which reports how, on one icy winter evening at the home of Park's parents, four Koreans and three Germans had no difficulty carrying on "a lively conversation" in broken Korean and German. Although the general deprivation was evident in the fact that old newspapers served as wallpaper, there were still "many small, delicious, but spicy foods" that she tried – for the first time in her life – to eat with chopsticks. Wilfried Lübke fondly remembered "the exquisite supply of foodstuffs and first-class construction materials" that were available in North Korea. But these casual, everyday contacts were partially overshadowed by his encounters with Kim Il Sung, "who frequently sat together with the Germans in their living quarters and debated for hours with the leader of the DAG. The personality cult that we have today didn't exist then. One time he shook my hand and said 'Keep it up, comrade!'."[247] The Lübkes often related their Korean experiences to their daughter Britta-Susann, who grew up with these stories as well as photos of Buddhist temples, Eight-Dragon-Mountain, and Thousand-Moon-River. In 2002, she accompanied her father on a trip back to North Korea, which she carefully documented for Radio Bremen. Their former Korean acquaintances Park and Zang were no longer alive, and the country did not have the same dynamism that Lübke remembered. It was like "returning to an empty house."[248] The story of the "Hamhungers" and the "Tokils" had become a chapter in the history of two countries that no longer existed.[249]

The history of East Germany's brief presence in Hamhung has recently been in the news again as a reminder of the pain caused by the Cold War division of the world. The same year that the first team of East Germans arrived in Hamhung, a 20-year-old North Korean student named Hong Ok Geun arrived in East Germany. While studying chemistry at Friedrich Schiller University in Jena, Hong met 18-year-old Renate Kleinle. The two were married in February 1960; their first child was born in June of that year; and a second pregnancy soon followed. However, in April 1961, Hong and 350 other Korean students were recalled – with only two days' notice – to North Korea. The couple corresponded until early 1963, when he was no longer allowed to write. Renate's repeated efforts to maintain contact with her husband went nowhere until early 2007, when the North Korean government finally informed the German embassy in Pyongyang that her husband was still alive and living in Hamhung.

Although the North Korean government initially refused to allow the couple to meet, in August 2007 Renate Hong traveled to Seoul, hoping that the couple's case would be discussed at the second summit between the North and the South, which was to be held in Pyongyang in October 2007. She asked the president of South Korea to deliver her letter to Kim Jong Il. In the letter, she pleaded with Premier Kim: "I wish my husband, Hong Ok-gun, would have a chance to see his two sons, who are now grown-ups. ... If it is impossible for my husband to come to Germany, I would be more than happy to visit to meet him. Can I expect support from you, Mr. Chairman?"[250] Finally, in July 2008 – after a separation of 47 years – Renate Hong, then 71, arrived with her two sons in Pyongyang to meet 74-year-old Hong Ok Geun.

It is astonishing to see the many different levels – the local, the national, the global, and the human – intersected in this story of East German assistance to Hamhung, of the two divided countries, and of the global Cold War. The history of this one couple is part of a much larger story. In this case, it is the story of the Sino-Soviet split that ended this initial phase or dimension of the relationship between North Korea and East Germany. It is also the story – almost a half-century later – of the efforts of the two Koreas to overcome the legacy of the Cold War and of the two Hongs to heal the wounds it left.

3

Mission Impossible

INTRODUCTION: WEST GERMANY JOINS THE GOOD WAR
IN SOUTH KOREA

Aid programs for refugees fleeing the 1956 Soviet invasion of Hungary have generally been regarded as the first postwar international humanitarian mission. However, the picture changes dramatically as soon as we look beyond the relief programs undertaken in direct response to the consequences of World War II in Europe. In fact, during the two decades following the partition of the Indian subcontinent, a number of international aid actions were undertaken in response to humanitarian crises caused by wars of national liberation and postcolonial nation-building conflicts that were politicized around the East–West axis. While most histories of the Federal Republic note the role of the Korean War in priming the pump for two decades of postwar economic growth and facilitating rearmament, it has never been noted that the Korean War also led the West German government to undertake its first international humanitarian mission: the operation of a hospital in the port city of Pusan, located on the southeastern tip of the peninsula.

In the first section, I will argue that the soft power of humanitarian aid was inextricably entangled with hard military and political efforts to contain the spread of communism around the world and that the transformation of these aid programs into a mechanism for U.S.-led global governance resulted in the systematic subordination of aid to geopolitics in Korea, Indochina, and elsewhere. The second section will focus on the establishment and operation of the Pusan hospital. Here, I will show that the West German government made singularly poor choices in selecting the staff to run the institution. Many of these doctors and nurses were unregenerate Nazis, who had more antipathy toward, than sympathy for, the Koreans, and their record in Pusan was one of medical malpractice, administrative incompetence, sexual abuse, ceaseless internal strife, and public scandal, all of which precipitated the closing of the hospital in 1959. Although it would be wrong to suggest that the misanthropy and misdoings of the Pusan staff were representative of all West German aid programs, they were not entirely accidental either. Their ingrained racism led many of the staff to take a rather jaundiced view of the humanitarian undertaking in which they were ostensibly participating. In the third section, I will argue that, as a result, they ultimately viewed themselves in rather masochistic terms as the victims of what might be called a postcolonial version of the White Man's Burden, rather than as agents of development or humanitarian aid. The concluding section will reflect briefly on the afterlife of these medical misadventures in Pusan.

I. RED KOREA, YELLOW PERIL, AND THE GLOBAL HUMANITARIAN REGIME

The Korean War was the first hot war of the Cold War era, and the most deadly one, even though it was in theory a police action carried out by the United Nations, rather than a formally declared war. More important in the present context is the fact that the Korean peninsula remained the site of intense Cold War ideological competition among the superpowers and their allies even after the ceasefire was signed on July 27, 1953. The weapons employed in this conflict were not only guns but also humanitarian aid programs and propaganda campaigns. The war was also a proving ground for a system of postwar global governance, which was nominally led by the UN, but which in reality was shaped by the United States, whose influence within the UN was magnified by the Soviet boycott.

UN military engagement in Korea was authorized by the Security Council on June 27, 1953, two days after the outbreak of hostilities. At this meeting, the U.S. ambassador to the UN, Warren R. Austin, declared that the North Korean attack was "an attack on the United Nations itself" and that, as a result, the UN itself was now facing "the gravest crisis in its existence."[251] Since the UN itself did not possess an army of its own, the June 27 resolution asked member countries to provide military assistance to the South Korean government in order to restore international peace and security. President Harry Truman relied on this appeal to dispatch U.S. forces to Korea without waiting for Congressional approval. A Security Council resolution passed on July 7, 1950, recommended the establishment of a Unified Command under U.S. authority; on July 15, South Korean president Rhee Syngman gave General Douglas MacArthur operational control over the South Korean armed forces; and on July 25, 1950, the United Nations Command was established with MacArthur as commander-in-chief. That same day, the U.S. military and the South Korean government agreed on measures to control the movement of refugees.[252]

The UN did not take up the question of relief for the civilian population until July 31, 1950, when the Security Council adopted a resolution sponsored by Britain, France, and Norway. The resolution asked the commander of the UN forces "to exercise responsibility for determining the requirements for the relief and support of the civilian population of Korea, and for establishing in the field the procedures for providing such relief and support."[253] It also asked the Secretary General, UN organs and specialized agencies, and "appropriate" NGOs to "provide such assistance *as the Unified Command may request* [emphasis added] for the relief and support of the civilian population of Korea."[254] Thus, the effect of the July 7 and 31 resolutions was to give the Unified Command – in practice, the U.S. military – control over military operations and relief programs carried out by both military and civilian authorities. UN Secretary General Trygve Lie was expected to act as a passive liaison whose job was simply to accept requests for assistance coming from the Unified Command, transmit these requests to individual member countries and UN specialized agencies, and then pass their responses back to the Unified Command.[255]

Austin praised the July 31 resolution as an "historic step in the total mobilization of the world peace machinery."[256] On the same day the resolution was passed, the U.S. Senate reminded those European countries that had benefited from Marshall Plan aid of their duty to help the United States "fight the United Nations battle in Korea."[257] The priority given to the global containment of communism allowed no space for the neutrality and impartiality that had long made it possible to describe humanitarian aid as nonpolitical. In Austin's words, even "moral support" for North Korea could be "regarded as giving aid and comfort to the enemy of the United Nations."[258] One could hardly ask for a clearer restatement of the logic of containment as it pertained to the field of humanitarian aid. Sharp lines were drawn, eliminating any space for medical and refugee aid that did not reinforce the UN crusade against communism. Similar beliefs informed the August 14 resolution of the UN Economic and Social Council, which proclaimed its willingness to provide "such assistance as the Unified Command may request," but which also called on member countries and NGOs to "assist in developing among the peoples of the world the fullest possible understanding of and support for the action of the United Nations in Korea."[259]

Given the parameters imposed by such policies, was it possible for UN agencies and NGOs to play any constructive role?[260] Although further research needs to be done, anecdotal evidence suggests that efforts to send humanitarian aid to North Korea were stifled. For example, the Indian government attempted to send – by means of a Norwegian freighter – medical personnel and supplies to Manchuria to benefit Chinese troops who had been wounded in Korea. However, the shipment was hijacked with the assistance of the nationalist government in Taiwan.[261] Similarly, although the ICRC worked out a plan to send medical supplies to the civilian population in North Korea via the Hungarian Red Cross, the plan was never implemented, and the British Red Cross Society never found a way to deliver what it described as "a small donation for medical supplies in North Korea."[262]

On August 5, 1950, the Unified Command sent the Secretary General its first request for assistance. It asked for twenty specialists in public health and civil relief, who would serve as liaisons between the UN Command and the Korean government and assist them in the "distribution and efficient utilization of relief supplies."[263] This group operated as an army unit, and its goal was to further the military objectives by ensuring that "minimum humanitarian requirements" were met.[264] The WHO and the International Refugee Organization promptly agreed to second their staff to the UN Command. However, communist countries and prosocialist international NGOs charged that the subordination of relief policies to U.S.-led containment strategy violated the spirit of the UN charter. For example, Poland criticized the WHO for violating the principle of neutrality, and, in announcing the country's withdrawal from the organization, the Poles condemned the organization as politically bankrupt.[265]

International humanitarian aid to South Korea was in part a response to past failures. As Frank Boudreau, the former head of the Health Organization of the League of Nations, noted, "we failed to act in 1920 and the most devastating war in history followed. Now that a third world war [in Korea] threatens, we must act before we become involved in that final catastrophe. Our neighbors in the other world must be given sound reason to believe that help is on the way or they will embrace any doctrine, no matter how destructive to our society, that promises them relief."[266] While seeking to blunt the ideological appeal of communism, one of the main goals of civilian relief was to create the optimal conditions for military success by ensuring that hunger and disease behind the lines did not lead to unrest or facilitate the infiltration of guerrillas.

Military concerns and the desire to prevent the formation of any parallel channels also influenced operational procedures for civilian relief in Korea. The U.S. Eighth Army had control over every aspect of such programs, including determining needs and then procuring, warehousing, allocating, and distributing supplies. The U.S. military forbade what it called "out-of-channel" shipments of supplies and equipment to South Korea. The Unified Command issued lists of urgently needed relief supplies, while private aid agencies in the United States worked through a State Department coordinating committee, which asked them to "submit a definitive offer to the United Nations, specifying, as far as possible, the approximate amount of this request that they will be able to supply."[267] Any offers that did not come through these channels were not accepted. The decision to channel all donations into a common pool posed a problem for NGOs and other private aid agencies, which had long used charity as a vehicle to extend their influence in non-Western countries, because it prevented religious and nondenominational aid groups from targeting their aid to specific groups. This made it difficult for these groups to maintain their identities. In the United States, aid organizations such as the Red Cross and Church World Services lobbied to get this policy changed, and they formed American Relief for Korea in 1951.[268]

Early in the war, when the military was desperate to defend the Taegu-Pusan perimeter, access to food, medical care, and transportation remained under close military control, and civilian relief operations focused on controlling the movement of refugees and screening them for communists and other internal enemies. All able-bodied men had been drafted, and refugees were almost exclusively women, children, the elderly, and the disabled, whom the military still considered as a potential source of disease and subversion. The first military-run civilian relief program, which was limited to the Pusan perimeter, did not begin its work until September 1950.[269] In the Pusan area alone, there were an estimated 300,000 refugees, and after the Inchon landings there were approximately 1.5 million refugees in the area controlled by UN forces. The UN Command in Tokyo sent five medical officers to establish a mechanism for coordinating the relief work of the Eighth Army and the

Korean government, to survey the prevailing health and refugee relief conditions, and to determine which supplies were most urgently needed.

At the very moment when these relief organizations were being set up, the fortunes of war shifted – briefly – in favor of the UN–U.S. forces. On October 1, 1950, South Korean troops crossed the 38th parallel; and on October 7, the UN General Assembly's resolution on an independent and unified Korea established a Commission for the Unification and Rehabilitation of Korea. The ambiguous wording of the resolution appeared to implicitly approve of the occupation of North Korea, which was to lead to unification. Right after this resolution, on October 9, UN forces crossed the 38th parallel, and ten days later Pyongyang fell, leaving all of North Korea temporarily under military government. In the fall of 1950, at the moment when UN forces had advanced far to the north, the U.S. military command created the Economic Cooperation Agency in Korea in the optimistic hope that it would soon be possible to turn to economic stabilization and reconstruction of a reunified peninsula. However, the entry of the Chinese into the conflict at the end of October and the retreat of UN forces created one of the worst humanitarian crises since World War II. Almost one million refugees moved south from Seoul alone. It was estimated that as of May 1951, there were 5.8 million refugees in South Korea and that another 6.2 million persons had been displaced by the destruction of their homes and livelihoods. This meant that approximately 60 percent of the entire population in South Korea was in need of relief.[270]

In December 1950, the Eighth Army created a civilian relief field organization, whose final designation was the United Nations Civil Assistance Command, Korea (UNCACK), which was attached to the Army's Civil Affairs Section. Most UNCACK staff were recruited from the WHO, the International Relief Organization, and, beginning in early 1951, from the League of Red Cross Societies. This subordination to the military ensured that relief operations would ultimately support military efforts.[271] By July 1951, the area south of the 38th parallel had been more or less stabilized, although skirmishes continued along the front during the lengthy armistice negotiations. After the stabilization of the front line, UNCACK took over relief responsibilities for the southern part of the country, while Civil Affairs Sections of the different groups of the Eighth Army were in charge of relief operations in combat zones. The military thrust of civilian assistance programs was also obvious in the rear areas, where UNCACK, in close cooperation with the U.S. Military Advisory Group and the U.S. Information Service, engaged in anti-guerrilla and pacification programs.

UNCACK's functions were expanded far beyond the civilian relief and public health. Part of its mission was to "maintain continuous surveillance over all information media"; and beginning in 1951, it monitored and screened Korean political, social, and cultural organizations and their leaders.[272] Organizations deemed unfriendly to "United Nations objectives" were banned. In cooperation with the U.S. Information Service, UNCACK dropped propaganda leaflets over the areas where guerrillas were believed to be hiding, and identification cards were issued to facilitate the monitoring of the civilian population and identify potential spies and subversives.[273] Radical nationalist, anti-communist paramilitary organizations, such as the voluntary fire corps, the police corps, and Korean Youth Defense organization, were also mobilized to combat guerrillas, sympathizers, and other perceived internal enemies. Local relief committees also set up their own policing and screening mechanisms and worked closely with police and para-military groups. Many of these humanitarian counterinsurgency programs had first been developed in the Philippines, and it would be interesting to follow their development around the Pacific in the early 1950s, although this is beyond the scope of the present chapter.

Determinations of need and the allocation of relief were influenced by considerations of how to secure the loyalties of the population.[274] However, UNCACK never succeeded in meeting even the minimal needs of the refugee population. Although central authorities were supposed to supply rice to local offices, these deliveries were often delayed because the military had first claim on available transportation. Even when rice was delivered, the destruction of local mills meant that there was no way to process it. At the same time, the use of relief to control the movement of refugees worsened the provisioning situation. The military wanted to divert refugees away from the relatively safe zone around Pusan and channel them instead into those areas known to harbor guerrillas, and relief was withheld from those who refused to go where they were directed.[275] In one instance, UNCACK ordered the mayor of the city of Taejon not to provide emergency food to refugees who refused to comply with the order to move south on foot, even though it was the dead of winter; ultimately, officials refused to feed some 12,000 refugees, who were too weak to make the trek on foot.[276]

Ever since the founding of Republic of Korea in August 1948, U.S. forces had influenced the government of the new country through foreign aid and economic and military advisory missions. During the war itself, U.S. control was near total. The South Korean government was obligated to make available for military purposes as much labor and raw material as possible, and the country's army increased from a prewar size of 90,000 men to 380,000 in mid-1951 and ultimately to 600,000. However, the only way for a poor country to pay the cost of war was through inflationary deficit spending. The counterpart funds requirement, and control over foreign exchange, offered UNCACK two mechanisms through which to combat inflation. The commander-in-chief of the UN forces was responsible for providing the Korean government with supplies, equipment, and services needed to ensure adequate relief for the civilian refugee population. In turn, the Korean government was responsible for the storage and transportation of these materials within the country. The Korean government was also expected to deposit into a special counterpart fund an amount in local currency equal to the dollar costs of the supplies and services provided by the military in order to defray the local cost of relief and economic assistance programs. The U.S. military preferred using these so-called counterpart funds over dollars to pay for local programs because the obligation to maintain these funds gave the U.S. military control over the South Korean government, constrained South Korean government spending, and thus forced it to pursue anti-inflationary policies.[277]

It was, therefore, only logical that aid negotiations in the winter of 1951–2 brought to the surface tensions over the impact of the counterpart fund requirement on South Korean sovereignty. At the time, Rhee told the commander of UNCACK that, while he did not object to consulting with the United States on economic and fiscal matters, it would be "politically inexpedient and inadvisable" for him to "authorize or sign a document indicating the UN or US would have control or supervision over the use of this money." Such an agreement, he insisted, would give the communists even more reasons to denounce him as a puppet of the United States.[278]

UNCACK also retained primary responsibility for planning and implementing short-term projects in agriculture, mining, and small industry that were expected to directly bear on the war effort. However, the purpose of such reconstruction programs was less to aid the Korean people or help them determine their own future than to "assist in preventing the development of economic conditions in the area that would prejudice the success of the military operations now in progress." To ensure the attainment of this goal, in April 1951 the head of the United Nations Command was given "complete and overall responsibility for all economic aid to the Korean people, including but not limited to immediate relief, short-range rehabilitation and reconstruction, long-range planning and technical assistance to the officials of the ROK [Republic of Korea] government."[279] Precisely because such projects were designed to meet the immediate needs of the military, their contribution to long-term modernization and nation-building was minimal.[280] The problem was that the UN had already created an organization – the United Nations Korean Reconstruction Agency (UNKRA) – for that purpose. But the United States decided that UNKRA would remain inoperative "until such time as the military operations will permit the transfer of this responsibility" to the UN organization, a determination that was itself to be made by the commander of the UN forces.[281] As a result, UNKRA led a stunted existence under the tutelage of the military organization.[282]

II. THE NAZI PAST IN THE KOREAN PRESENT

Adenauer's Gift to the United States: The German Red Cross Hospital in Pusan

In West Germany, the Korean War raised the specter of a localized war of Soviet expansionism in the heart of Europe. This, in turn, led to a more open discussion of national security and rearmament and accelerated the country's rearmament, which more than anything else symbolized the normalization of the country's status.[283] One of West Germany's first steps toward rearmament was in the area of wartime civil defense. The sanitary and welfare work of the German Red Cross had long been closely coordinated with that of the military, and the Fourth Geneva Convention had added civil defense to the responsibilities of national Red Cross societies. Less than two weeks after the outbreak of the Korean War, Otto Geßler, the president of the (West) German Red Cross, met with Interior Minister Gustav Heinemann and his State Secretary Hans Ritter von Lex (who was to become president of the German Red Cross in 1961) to discuss the need for civil defense preparation. Shortly thereafter, Adenauer approved the creation of a civil defense committee headed by Geßler.[284] In August 1950, Heinemann asked Otto Lummitzsch, a civil engineer who had acquired extensive experience in the civil defense area during the Weimar and Nazi years, to organize a corps of technicians and engineers who could be deployed for civil defense in case of catastrophe or in times of national emergency. This was the origin of the national emergency management agency, which was officially established in 1953 as the *Bundesanstalt für Technisches Hilfswerk*.[285]

The West German government had already begun making plans to deploy military hospitals to Korea in 1951, and in early 1952 the Interior Ministry asked Geßler to help staff ten army hospitals, which were to be shipped to Korea in March 1953 to care for wounded soldiers. During his visit to the United States in April of that year, Adenauer offered to send the hospitals to the Asian theater of war.[286] These efforts to mobilize the army medical auxiliary were made at a time when substantial numbers of West Germans opposed rearmament because they feared that the heightening of tensions in Europe might trigger another major war.[287] In view of this broad anti-war sentiment, the government felt it was important to emphasize the peaceful, humanitarian aims of civil defense programs.

For the same reason, the government did not publicly acknowledge its plan to dispatch army hospitals to South Korea, even though Adenauer's offer had been covered in the press.[288] Even as late as November 1953, the Foreign Office was still trying to keep the mission secret. The administration did not decide to announce its plan until the media reported that the technicians and nurses who had applied to work for the German Red Cross overseas had begun to receive call-up letters.[289] The Foreign Office portrayed the mission as a contribution to world peace and as an example of practical humanitarianism. The media promoted the mission as an opportunity to prove one's value in the domain of "practical charity in the Far East" side-by-side with British, Swiss, Swedish, and American aid workers.[290] The German public embraced the mission, as it embraced Ottmar Kohler, the "Doctor of Stalingrad," who had chosen to remain in a Soviet POW camp to treat the soldiers remaining there and who received a hero's greeting when he finally returned home at the end of 1953.[291]

German medicine had not always been used for humanitarian ends. The Nuremberg Doctors Trial, which was held in 1946–7, had led to the conviction of a number of physicians for their roles in the Holocaust and for medical experiments on camp inmates. These trials had severely damaged the reputation of the German medical profession, at least abroad if not at home.[292] An important step toward normalizing the country's identity would be to rehabilitate German medicine abroad, and the members of the medical profession employed a number of strategies, both individual and collective, to achieve this goal.[293]

The German Red Cross faced a similar challenge when it was re-established in early 1950. During World War II, the German Red Cross had been deeply involved in the racial policies at home and in the occupied territories. In recognition of the indispensable service that the Red Cross provided to the military, the army had agreed – immediately after the invasion of Poland – to pay the salaries of Red Cross personnel, and, two years later, the German Red Cross, which was in theory a voluntary organization, had been elevated to quasi-public status.[294] Although the German Red Cross had been one of the most thoroughly Nazified organizations during the Third Reich, after 1945 its leadership denied any link to the Nazi regime and its crimes. The organization then made a smooth transition to the postwar period by identifying itself with the humanitarian spirit of the 1949 Geneva Conventions, and in 1952, it was admitted to the League of National Red Cross Societies. The West Germans hoped that medical aid programs such as the Pusan hospital project would also help rehabilitate the reputations of the medical profession and the country.

With Friends Like These, Who Needs Enemies?

From the beginning, Adenauer and his government were interested more in the "political effect" of the proposed medical mission than in any benefits to the Koreans themselves.[295] As a tangible sign of its investment in regaining control over the country's fate, Adenauer's administration committed itself to the mission as long as the U.S. military remained in Korea. The United States had originally wanted West Germany to build a 400-bed hospital for the U.S. army, and this wish persisted even after the armistice was signed in July 1953. At the beginning of 1954, however, the U.S. military changed its position. The hospital that Adenauer had offered would be repurposed to provide medical care to the civilian population, although it would remain under the overall authority of the Far East Command of the U.S. military.[296] Within these broad parameters, overall responsibility for the new German Red Cross Hospital in South Korea lay with the West German Foreign Office, while the director, Günther Huwer, who is shown in Figure 3.1 with State Secretary Walter Hallstein, would be in charge of its internal administration.[297]

The South Korean government was plagued by social and economic crises, which, along with pervasive corruption, nepotism, and political oppression, seriously weakened its popular legitimacy. Despite – or perhaps because of – this weakness, the government was especially sensitive about its claims to sovereignty and its desire to be recognized as a sovereign state by the major powers. Although this was a common concern for all of the newly independent countries of Asia and Africa, in South Korea the rapid succession of colonialism, liberation, and U.S. military occupation further heightened this anxiety.[298]

FIGURE 3.1 State Secretary Walter Hallstein (right) shaking hands with Huwer as the first group of West German doctors and nurses leave for Pusan. Copyright Deutsches Rotes Kreuz.

The United States provided large amounts of military and economic aid to the Rhee government, which presented itself as a bulwark against communism in the region. But this aid also served as a vehicle for extensive intervention in the country's political, economic, and military affairs.[299] After the armistice, the military civilian affairs office continued its work under the name of the Korea Civil Assistance Command, whose programs overlapped in complex ways with those of foreign humanitarian and development aid agencies. While aid had been provided directly to the Korean government during the war, the Eisenhower administration shifted from direct aid to active support of American private aid organizations, which were granted public subsidies, material support, and free transportation across the Pacific for people and supplies. The influence of private aid groups and advisory teams was further enhanced in strategically important countries like South Korea and South Vietnam by the creation of corporatist structures to coordinate the work of state and nonstate aid groups.[300] The membership of the Korea Association of Voluntary Agencies, which was created in 1952, grew steadily, and by 1956 forty-five voluntary agencies, including Save the Children Foundation, CARE, the Red Cross societies, the American-Korean Foundation, Church World Services, the National Catholic Welfare Conference, the Northern Presbyterian Mission, and the Methodist Mission, belonged to the organization.[301]

The United States was not the only country whose aid appeared to undermine South Korean sovereignty. From the very beginning of its five-year operation in Korea, the German Red Cross Hospital in Korea stood at the center of a similar conflict. During the war, the South Korean government had allowed the U.S. military to use the building, which had previously housed the Pusan Girls Junior High and High School, as an army hospital. However, after the ceasefire the Americans refused to vacate the building and, instead, handed it over to the Germans. Figure 3.2 shows president Rhee visiting the hospital. As a result, 2,600 pupils remained crowded into temporary, makeshift classrooms. Both the national and provincial government proposed that the hospital be relocated to the hospital annex of the new Pusan Medical College, where it could better serve the needs of the country. The parents of the displaced children argued that the hospital's mission of helping the poor could be better achieved in the countryside, where there were no doctors or medical services. As they wrote to Huwer, "please continue your fine work, but help the education of our little girls, please."[302] Huwer, however, opposed relocating the hospital and dismissed the plea as presumptuous.[303]

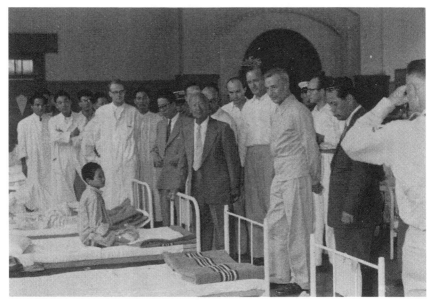

FIGURE 3.2 President Rhee Syngman visiting the Red Cross Hospital in Pusan. Copyright Deutsches Rotes Kreuz.

FIGURE 3.3 The German Red Cross Hospital complex. Copyright Deutsches Rotes Kreuz.

The Pusan hospital opened its doors to Korean patients in May 1954 (Figure 3.3). The staff of eighty-five included eleven German doctors and thirty-two German nurses. The German staff led a relatively privileged existence in Pusan. Some of the doctors had Korean houseboys, and all of the Germans enjoyed the same privileges and benefits as U.S. military personnel, including access to the U.S. military post, the PX, and U.S. rest and relaxation facilities in Japan.[304] The German nurses were surprised that they were welcomed warmly by the Americans and the other Europeans, who also operated hospitals in the city. The German nurses felt "a genuine friendship among nations" in their encounters with other Westerners, whom they thanked for showing them "such a sense of fraternity." On evenings when films were shown in the Swedish hospital, the German nurses were thrilled to be in the company of "Americans, Negroes, a couple of Brits, and the Swedes." Such comradeship, they noted, would have been unimaginable only a few short years before.[305] This was their first opportunity to socialize with people from these nations. The head nurse was pleasantly surprised to learn that Korea had such an international scene, and she noted that Germany's reputation would have suffered if the country had not been represented there.[306]

Many of the German doctors working in Korea had been closely connected to the Nazi Party. They had served in the military during World War II, and since 1945 a number of them had worked in Asia and Africa. Many of them also appear to have been unreconstructed Nazis. For example, Huwer (1899–1992), who joined the Nazi Party in 1933, had worked his way up through the ranks at the University of Jena at the time when the notorious Karl Astel served as professor for "human breeding" and as rector of the university. Huwer worked at various hospitals in China from 1935 to 1952, displacing a Jewish physician in 1939 to become the director of the German Hospital in Peking.[307] Huwer was both an authoritarian manager and a racist, who looked down not only on the Koreans but also on many of his staff, and he limited his contacts to a small clique of physicians, who were former Nazis or sympathizers.[308] The staff members closest to Huwer were Walter Drescher (1921–?), Harald Edmund Friedrichs (1917–?), Wolf-Dietrich Germer (1911–1996), and Eberhard Daerr (1912–2005).[309] Germer and Daerr were directors of internal medicine and surgery at various stages of the hospital's existence, and together with Huwer they shaped the atmosphere and the social life of the hospital.

Germer, who joined the Nazi party in 1938, had built his career as bacteriologist and hygienist at the time when Nazi Germany was vastly expanding its control over bacteriological institutes working on typhus and tropical medicine.[310] He conducted research in Spain, at the institute of racial biology in Würzburg, and at the Pasteur Institute in Paris. During the final years of the war, he directed a bacteriological station in the Balkans. These research credentials, which were also valued by the Americans and the British, helped him make a smooth transition to the postwar period, and he worked as professor, senior physician, and director of the bacteriological laboratory at the university hospital in Tübingen.[311] Ludwig Pfannemüller (1915–2008), a bacteriologist and specialist in tropical medicine, had served as a military doctor on the Eastern front. After the war, he worked in Afghanistan and Iraq before going to Korea in 1954. Drescher had conducted research on yellow fever in Brazil from 1939–1941; he served as a military doctor in Greece from 1941 to 1945; and he worked as a surgeon in Iran from 1951 to 1954.[312] Friedrichs joined the Hitler Youth in 1929, and in 1934, he applied to join the SS, but his application stalled because he was unable to provide the required information on one of his great-grandfathers. After passing his medical exam in 1943, he served as an assistant doctor at an air force hospital in Bavaria, and the following year he became an assistant surgeon on the Russian front. He worked in Iran for several years in the 1950s.[313] Daerr, who would later (1969–1972) serve as Inspector General of the Army Medical and Sanitary Service, trained in surgery in Schleswig-Holstein before working from 1951 to 1953 as a surgeon for the Public Health Service of Liberia.[314]

During its five-year existence, a total of eighty-five German Red Cross nurses worked at the hospital.[315] Their professional histories were similar to those of the doctors under whom they served. Like the German Red Cross itself, the Red Cross nursing order (*Verband Deutscher Mutterhäuser vom Roten Kreuz*) was deeply entangled with the Nazi regime. During World War II, the number of nurse aides and "voluntary" nurses grew dramatically, with the latter rising from 14,000 in 1933 to 313,000 in 1945.[316] The order was re-established at the end of 1948, and it rejoined the German Red Cross when that organization was re-established in 1950.[317]

Since its founding, the German Red Cross had been closely linked to Germany's conservative establishment, and many of the nurses who served in Korea came from prominent conservative families. For example, Isa Gräfin von der Goltz (1922–2007), who came to Pusan with her younger sister Renate,[318] had fled the family estate at the end of the war and moved to Schleswig-Holstein. One of her grandfathers had been the head of the military medical service under Kaiser Wilhelm II. Similarly, the father of Ingeborg Napp, the last head nurse in Pusan (1958–59), had served as the acting head of the voluntary medical service during the Third Reich.[319] Many of the other nurses who served in Pusan were former party members, some of whom had joined before 1933, and a number of them had worked in field hospitals or sanatoria on the Eastern front.[320] For example, the first head nurse, Imelda Wieners, had several years of experience working immediately behind the French and Russian fronts. Hertha Ernst had many years of military nursing experience in occupied Russia. And Lotte Hartog (1904–?) had served as the head nurse at a military hospital on the Eastern front. Luise von Oertzen, the mother-superior of the Red Cross nursing order through the Third Reich and the postwar years, had specifically asked her colleagues to select women with wartime experience in the East because she believed that such experience had accustomed them to the kind of grueling work they could expect in Korea. It comforted her to compare Korea with previous colonial service, when German women had gone to German East Africa for work that had "enriched" their lives.[321]

Many of the West German doctors who chose to go to South Korea did so less from a commitment to aiding the Koreans than because they hoped to gain the knowledge of tropical diseases that would advance their careers. Soon after his arrival, Huwer told U.S. officers that German doctors were primarily interested in exotic diseases and pathogens whose study could further their careers,[322] and doctors like Germer valued a tour in South Korea because it offered them the chance to conduct research they could not do at home. In fact, some nurses complained that the physicians spent too much time on their own research.[323] Although the new work regulations issued in 1955 did not state that the physicians were expected to engage in research, many of them continued to do so, and work with U.S. sanitation officers on malaria helped at least one of the Germans obtain a visiting fellowship at the Walter Reed Medical Center.[324] Others saw a tour in Korea as an opportunity to gain surgical experience more quickly than would have been possible at home.[325] As Drescher explained, "a doctor can learn more about diagnosis, surgery, and prognosis in six months [here in Korea] than he could in a lifetime back in Germany."[326] Friedrichs openly admitted that he was going to pack up and leave Korea as soon as he had gained enough experience.[327]

The size of the German staff declined from eighty-five in 1954 to seventy-five the following year and fifty in 1958 (with the number of surgeons dropping from five to only two in 1957).[328] The number of

German doctors also declined from twelve in 1954 to nine in 1955 and seven in 1958. At the same time, the number of Korean doctors working in the hospital increased from twenty-three in 1954 to thirty-one in 1956 and forty in 1958.[329] There were many reasons for this trend. Huwer's preferred way of dealing with internal criticisms – and there were many – was to fire the critic. While we will return to this issue below, here it is important simply to note that physicians who left or were fired were often not replaced. In 1956, Huwer was already recommending that the German government reduce the number of doctors and nurses serving there, and experienced Korean doctors, who earned only a fraction of what was paid to their German counterparts, were increasingly hired to fill the gap.[330]

Although the Korean doctors working at the hospital were supposed to receive advanced training in various specialties, the shortage of German doctors meant that the Korean physicians had to take up the slack and, consequently, had less time for such training. The Germans, however, were unable or unwilling to recognize that the Koreans were indispensable for the daily operation of the hospital. Huwer told his superiors in Bonn that the reason the hospital needed so many Korean doctors was that, since these men could never be as skilled and productive as their German counterparts, a disproportionate number of Koreans was needed to make up for the loss of every German.[331] Although the value of the clinic was often measured in the German press by outpatient care provided by German doctors and nurses, Huwer only allowed patients to be seen for a few hours in the morning. The number was capped at 150 outpatients per day, and by 1956 all were being treated by Korean doctors.[332]

As of mid-1957, the hospital had 250 patients and 290 Korean personnel, including doctors, nursing students, and unskilled workers, such as guards, cleaning staff, laundresses, and other support workers.[333] Inside the hospital compound, living and dining arrangements were segregated. Korean doctors were forbidden to eat together with their German colleagues, and the budget for feeding the Germans was twice as much per person as for Koreans. While each German doctor had a room to himself, three to five Korean doctors were forced to share a small room, and they were made to feel subordinate in other ways as well. Many German doctors thought highly of their Korean colleagues, their surgical skills, and their grasp of U.S. and German medical literature.[334] However, whenever Koreans asked for better pay and living conditions or for the opportunity to treat more challenging cases, Huwer rejected their requests with what a witness described as "colonial methods."[335]

The situation was similar with regard to the training of Korean nurses. Beginning in May 1954, twenty student nurses were selected each year to take part in a three-year training program. The students in the first class, some of whom were refugees from the north, were all aged between 17 and 20 years.[336] The curriculum was a minimally modified version of that followed by German nursing students, although at the time nursing certification in Korea was more rigorous than that in Germany itself.[337] The instruction offered by the Germans was compromised in other ways as well. German nurses did not have the qualifications and credentials required to teach the material. To cover this up, Huwer submitted falsified records showing that the German nurses had lectured at German universities. One German instructor, Inge Wegener, criticized her senior colleagues, who maintained that the hospital's program need not involve more than the simple demonstration of practical work and skills, and she warned that such a substandard training program "could hardly be sustained over the long term."[338] Huwer, however, dismissed a call by the Korean authorities for a more rigorous curriculum as "burdensome and meaningless."[339]

Not all the German physicians shared Huwer's beliefs, and there was infighting among the staff from the very beginning. For example, Hans-Werner Graumann (1911–2001),[340] the director of the radiology department, felt that it was his responsibility to restore Germany's good name abroad.[341] He maintained that the hospital could never fulfill its humanitarian mission so long as it was run by people like Huwer, and he sent several reports to the German Red Cross and the German legation in Seoul detailing the situation in the hospital. However, Graumann never received a response and, instead, was fired by Huwer.[342] Huwer also fired a female physician who had complained about her colleagues, including the homosexual activity of one physician. Once back in Germany, the two fired doctors – separately – sued their employer, the German Red Cross, for wrongful termination. By that point, the organization was in possession of substantial evidence documenting the racism and mismanagement at the hospital. The Red Cross managed to keep the affair quiet (in part by reaching a financial settlement with the woman doctor), but it was only a matter of time before the problems in Pusan became public knowledge.[343]

III. FIRST, DO NO HARM: ALBERT SCHWEITZER AND "CONCENTRATION CAMP KOREA"[344]

The surgery department and its director, Friedrichs, were the source of many serious complaints. As later reported in *Der Spiegel* and other major newspapers, Friedrichs frequently hit his patients, including children.[345] Moreover, although Friedrichs had only minimal training and experience, Huwer promoted him to department head, and on one occasion he served for several months as acting director when Huwer was away on vacation. Friedrichs was accused of a number of cases of malpractice that resulted in the death of the patient. Two German surgeons became alarmed by the frequency of such mistakes, which Friedrichs covered up by filing false reports. In early 1958, one of these surgeons finally brought the matter to Huwer's attention. Huwer took no action. The two surgeons then sent reports to the German legation in Seoul, to the German Red Cross in Bonn, and to the Chamber of German Physicians. Finally, all eight of the other German doctors in Pusan – excluding Huwer and Friedrichs himself – sent a report to the general secretary of the German Red Cross, who brushed off the charges and, instead, chided the surgeons for applying German medical standards to Koreans, both doctors and patients. Otto Buurman, one of the top officials of the German Red Cross, who had himself been a high-ranking health official in Nazi-occupied Poland, even disciplined the surgeons for criticizing their superior.[346] At the time, it appeared that things at the hospital would remain unchanged.[347]

In September 1958, Franz Josef Rosenbaum, the newly appointed director of internal medicine, arrived in Pusan. By that time, the overall atmosphere at the hospital had perceptibly worsened, and Rosenbaum was appalled by conditions. Huwer's desire to keep tight control over the staff had gone so far that he did not allow any of the staff to go outside of the hospital compound by themselves. At the same time, it was widely known, even among Koreans, that German doctors and nurses were more interested in ministering to the needs of their own flesh than to the physical ills of the Koreans. Huwer himself encouraged the German staff to "amuse themselves," and the hospital soon acquired greater fame as a brothel than as a medical facility.[348] The hospital had virtually ceased functioning in such key areas as surgery because of poor hygienic conditions. Rosenbaum believed that a combination of racism and mismanagement accounted for the deplorable conditions at the hospital and its overall atmosphere. In his view, the Pusan hospital had become a waste of taxpayer money, and he urged German authorities to immediately close the hospital, which he described as "an island to which unreconstructed, dyed-in-the-wool Nazis have withdrawn and where they do not shy away from giving expression – sometimes with brute force – to their opinions."[349]

All of the physicians on the staff – except Friedrichs – supported Rosenbaum.[350] Huwer, however, attributed the poor conditions in the hospital to the Korean mentality and way of life, and he scorned Rosenbaum for his naiveté.[351] In November 1958, the German Red Cross finally responded to the steady stream of complaints by sending – at the request of the Foreign Office – a delegation to Pusan. However, the delegation spent less time investigating the accusations, which they believed to be true, than in trying to persuade Rosenbaum not to make them public, especially those relating to sexual misconduct by the staff. Buurman, who headed the delegation, sent a telegram back to the Foreign Office urging that the hospital be immediately closed, not so much because of the hospital's failure to perform its humanitarian mission as to protect West Germany's reputation.[352]

Although news of the problems in Pusan had gradually filtered back to Germany during 1957, it was not until the fall of 1958 that politicians in Bonn and the West German media began paying attention.[353] In September of that year, a Catholic clergyman, who was a friend of Adenauer's son, Paul, was traveling in Korea, and he met Rosenbaum at the residence of the bishop of Pusan. At their meeting, Rosenbaum described to this clergyman the conditions at the hospital. The clergyman passed the information along to Paul Adenauer, who, in turn, relayed the unsavory news to his father, who then ordered an investigation, which finally led to the closing of the hospital at the end of March 1959.[354]

IV. MISSION IMPOSSIBLE: THE WHITE MAN'S BURDEN AND THE THEORY OF ANTI-HUMANITARIANISM

The term *emergency* denotes a temporary condition, and it implies or presupposes the existence of a more normal state of affairs, one which existed prior to the emergency and to which the system will return after a disruption. However, the comments made by the Pusan medical staff raise the question of how to define normality in 1950s Korea. How did the Germans who served there understand Korean conditions and their relation to what they considered to be the norms of Western civilization? The failures of the German mission to Pusan and the misdeeds of its staff can best be understood not merely as administrative failures, but rather as the logical consequence of a racial worldview, held over from the Nazi years and then modified for the Far East, where for a few years the medical staff had relatively free reign to live out their misanthropic fantasies under the guise of humanitarian aid. These views, however, cannot be read out of the history of the hospital itself. Instead, we must turn to later writings by the medical staff to learn how they understood Koreans, Korea, and the West German mission there.

This worldview was based on the representation of Asian people and culture, and especially that of Korea, as the irreconcilable and potentially threatening antithesis of Occidental civilization. For example, in a piece published in a West German newspaper in 1957, Drescher argued that traditional Christian humanitarianism was fundamentally impossible in places like Korea because concepts such as individuality, foresight, and personal responsibility were alien to the "Asian mentality." At the hospital, he argued in a curiously incongruous manner, it was the Korean patients, employees, and doctors who "pocketed the wages for the voluntary labor of the Germans" while remaining indifferent to human suffering.[355] According to Drescher, Koreans felt uneasy with the "virtuousness of the German character" precisely because thievery was an integral element of their national or racial character.[356]

Behind such reasoning lay a series of discursive displacements in which Germans were depicted as making great sacrifices to aid the poorest, most underdeveloped people, whose innate inferiority was invoked to explain both the need for such sacrifice and its inevitable failure.[357] For example, the Germans failed to equip the wards with bathing facilities, toilets, and running water for patients; nor did the hospital have an intensive care unit or isolation units to prevent patients with contagious diseases from being crammed together in the corridor.[358] When followed to its logical conclusion, Drescher's reasoning implied that, by being forced to make hopeless sacrifices for an ungrateful and incorrigible people, the German medical staff were victims of an inferior civilization, rather than its benefactors.

Drescher expanded on these ideas in a book he published in 1959, after the hospital had come under public scrutiny. In this book, Drescher described what he regarded as the "rigorous automatism of a [Korean] termite state," whose vertical organization did not permit its citizens any horizontal space in which to cultivate individuality, creativity, and charity.[359] These immutable mental strictures, he maintained, meant that any attempt to elevate the people of Asia to the same cultural level of those of the Occident was bound to fail. At best, Asians would only be able to imitate the West, while harboring a secret resentment against the bearers of superior civilization. Moreover, because they would never be capable of standing on their own feet, they would remain forever dependent on foreign assistance. Similarly, Drescher told the German Red Cross that Germans should avoid all cultural contact with Koreans, whom he regarded as knife-wielding criminals, murders, and thieves. He proudly added that he had no problem being known as a person who was "mad and filled with indignation" toward Koreans.[360]

These racializing representations of Koreans underlay the securitization of humanitarian aid, which was embodied most often in the insistence that true charity for such persons consisted in teaching them to accept such virtues as order, discipline, punctuality, thoroughness, and, more generally, self-effacing submission to the Germans. The allegedly innate inability of the Koreans to work their way up the cultural gradient from East to West led the Germans to depict their hospital complex as an island of Western culture that was under siege and constantly in danger of being submerged in an ocean of barbarism and unculture. It was, they wrote, an "island of salvation in the midst of a sea of rats"[361] and "an island of Western thought and sensibility in a stormy sea of a brutal mentality."[362] This racial reasoning turned the situation inside out and culminated in the perverse, masochistic claim that in Pusan – and, by implication, throughout the Third World – the Germans were being held captive, for their own security, in a concentration camp identical in kind to those they had constructed for Jews and other community aliens during World War II.[363] In such a situation, they asked themselves, did it make any sense to engage in Christian charity or struggle to preserve the lives of beings who were not fully human?[364] And even when Koreans were admitted to the hospital, they were treated capriciously and subjected to surprise inspections by the staff.[365]

The German medical staff in Pusan drew a sharp contrast between its approach to charity and that of the Americans, whose "pure humanitarianism" they regarded as naïve.[366] The Americans, they argued, were attuned to respecting the beliefs of people of other cultures, and they were willing to give freely, if not indiscriminately, to achieve political and economic gain. However, their commitment to working in partnership with Third World peoples was bound to fail when their ostensible partners lacked the character traits needed to make the arrangement work. By contrast, the German approach was, Drescher explained, instrumental, functional, and free of any extraneous or, in view of the circumstances, inappropriate considerations of political or economic gain, colonial rule, or religious mission:

We administer, channel, and carefully measure out aid and wealth against the naked misery out there. That's why we are here. And to insure that the aid is targeted, robust, and effective, we have to keep an eye out that no leaks are sprung through which our stores – and by no means only our material aid – will wastefully seep away. Here outside a hundred eyes are on the lookout for such leaks... On the inside, we... must comport ourselves in a more upright manner than is good for human nature. Those on the outside persist in the attitude of the eternal supplicant, which is far less healthy. Behind the walls, the pressure is too strong and too high.[367]

By the end of 1958, both the German Red Cross and the Foreign Office had admitted internally that Rosenbaum's accusations were largely true, but they also agreed that it was important to protect Germany's reputation abroad. The Foreign Office found itself in a delicate situation because the conflict between the hospital leadership and the staff pitted "old and incorrigible Nazis" against physicians from the very groups that had been persecuted during the Third Reich.[368] For this reason, the Foreign Office decided to keep a low profile and work closely with the Red Cross to manage the political fallout from the scandal, which was first reported in January 1959 by *Der Spiegel* and then by other publications.[369]

In response to this negative publicity, Huwer asked current and former employees of the hospital to send their own accounts of the hospital and its work to the press.[370] Drescher and two other physicians close to Huwer published a piece in *Frankfurter Allgemeine Zeitung* in which they praised Huwer as a role model and described the exceptional difficulties involved in doing "medical work in a foreign, 'underdeveloped' country."[371] This was soon followed by other racially charged reports about the lack of gratefulness on the part of the Koreans and their supposed anti-white sentiments.[372] Buurmann defended the humanitarian work of the Pusan hospital as an attempt "to make something out of nothing." He compared their work to that of Albert Schweitzer in Africa, but he did so in a way that emphasized the impossibility of transcending the civilizational divide separating the Europeans from the peoples of the Third World.[373] One of the hospital administrators explained that even the greatest degree of cooperation and understanding would not have been enough to "bridge the thousand-year-old barrier between races and religions."[374] Drescher pointed to the insuperable barrier to progress represented by "the indifference of an Asiatic environment, which was empty of all thought and which day after day weakened everything that had been achieved."[375] While one Christian Democratic politician suggested that the staff be publicly honored,[376] the press had begun to report on Huwer's Nazi past. One article even compared the proposed honors to Adenauer's defense of his close advisor Hans Globke, who co-authored the official commentary on the Nuremberg race laws. This article also called into question the character and qualifications of the International

Red Cross, noting that this was the same organization that had found conditions in Buchenwald and Auschwitz to be "in order."[377]

The scandal was further fueled by a lawsuit by Huwer, who sought – unsuccessfully – to prevent Rosenbaum and the *Rheinische Merkur* from making public statements about the poor conditions at the hospital.[378] Rosenbaum, in turn, sued Huwer for wrongful termination,[379] while Huwer and Friedrichs filed suit to protect their own reputations. In early 1960, the president of the German Red Cross wrote to Huwer saying that, while Rosenbaum's accusations were factually correct, he thanked God the organization had not been required to make public in court all of the embarrassing correspondence relating to the Pusan hospital.[380]

For its part, in 1959 the German Red Cross published a commemorative volume in which it explained that the mission of the hospital had been to help transform a Confucian agrarian state into a modern nation-state by educating the Koreans in the principles of modernity: "Only one who understands how fundamental a change we are demanding in the thinking of the Orientals can measure the success of our humanitarian and pedagogical labor, and I mean that this success has been real."[381] However, this was a transparent attempt to whitewash the failings of a humanitarian mission that from start to finish had operated according to very different principles.

V. THE AFTERLIFE

The closing of the Pusan hospital in 1959 did not mark the end of its history, which lived on in the subsequent history of humanitarian aid in West Germany. One reason why the Pussan affair became so highly politicized was that it occurred at the moment when questions were being raised about the proper role of the state and the churches in international humanitarian aid. Some people in the German Red Cross speculated that it was not by chance that Catholics played such a key role in bringing conditions in the Pusan hospital to the public's attention. The scandal coincided with a shift in policy that in the early 1960s led to the creation of an arrangement whereby church charities received substantial government subsidies to support their humanitarian and development programs in the Third World.

To raise world awareness about global problems, the UN declared 1959 World Refugee Year, and the UN Food and Agricultural Organization also proclaimed it the Freedom from Hunger year. In West Germany, many politicians recognized that the country, which had itself been the recipient of substantial humanitarian and Marshall Plan aid, had a duty to assist nations that were less well off. In hopes of persuading the country's citizens to give generously to charitable causes, President Heinrich Lübke delivered an address to the Bundestag in which he emphasized both the moral obligation to help the less fortunate and the practical benefits that would accrue to the country from helping to diminish the appeal of communism in the underdeveloped world.[382] Although Lübke characterized state-sponsored humanitarian aid as an expression of Christian charity, the churches felt that such programs were infringing upon their privileged domain. To meet the challenge of expanding state involvement, the Catholic and Protestant churches each launched major collection programs to aid the underdeveloped world. The Catholic Bishops' Organization Misereor organized its first Easter Appeal in early 1959, and the German Evangelical Church started its Bread for the World program at Christmas of that year. Although both were originally supposed to be one-time actions, the unexpected success of these programs led to their permanent institutionalization.[383]

Many conservative politicians in West Germany maintained that Christian charity should be the foundation for the country's development policy. Adenauer's personal intervention in 1960 to secure public subsidies for the work of church charities overseas laid the foundation for the subsequent state–church partnership in humanitarian and development aid.[384] In 1962, this corporatist arrangement was formalized when the two Christian churches each founded a Central Bureau for Development Aid, which was responsible for deciding which projects would receive support, managing state subsidies, and for serving as the intermediary between the state and the churches. Although West German humanitarian and development aid to the Third World continued to draw on precisely those Christian traditions that were the object of such scorn by the Pusan medical staff, such charity did not supplant U.S. and Soviet development programs and, instead, provided a rationale for supporting those efforts. It also helped compensate for the psychological costs resulting from the disappointments and resentments inevitably experienced by everyone who sought to bear the postcolonial version of the White Man's Burden.

Second, the decision to close the Pusan hospital raised the question of how West Germany could continue to fulfill the promise to the United States that had originally led to the establishment of the hospital. Even before the decision to close the Pusan hospital had been made, the West Germans were in contact with the Americans about the situation. The Americans, having already turned their eyes to Vietnam, were worried about the increasing intensity of anti-American sentiment, and they proposed that the West Germans assume responsibility for modernizing the curriculum and instruction at the medical school in the Vietnamese city of Hué. This would allow the Americans to keep their promises to the South Vietnamese government without provoking further opposition by the students there, many of whom were particularly hostile to the Americans.[385] In 1960, the West German Foreign Office dispatched Professor H. O. Krainick to head the medical faculty at the University of Hué, and over the following two years a number of doctors from the University of Freiburg were assigned to teach there and provide medical care to civilians from the surrounding area – just as had been the case in Pusan. However, in Hué the politics of humanitarian assistance played out quite differently. One of the German doctors, Erich Wulff, became an important channel through which radical students communicated to the outside world and fueled opposition to the war.[386]

Third, when the Pusan hospital closed in 1959, forty nursing students were still studying in the hospital, where an estimated twenty-five to thirty recent graduates also worked.[387] These students were able to continue their studies at the Presbyterian hospital and polyclinic, which were run (with financial support from Misereor) by the German Benedictine Sisters in the nearby city of Taegu. Most of the nurses who completed their studies in Taegu would eventually leave for West Germany in search of higher pay and advanced training. In addition, while some of the licensed nurses found jobs at the newly established Scandinavian National Medical Center in Seoul, during the 1960s others were recruited by the Red Cross nursing order, which was having problems finding enough qualified nurses to staff its clinics and nursing homes in Germany (see Chapter 8).[388]

4

Back to the Future in Indochina

Since the 1950s, both aid organizations and academics have often attempted to draw clear distinctions between the supposedly apolitical, purely humanitarian emergency relief programs that proliferated during the era of decolonization and more explicitly political development programs that were intended to contribute to long-term postcolonial nation-building. However, such distinctions are problematic. In the overdetermined context of the period, national liberation struggles against (neo)colonial powers were inextricably intertwined with both indigenous struggles to determine the future shape of the nation and the geopolitical maneuverings of the two superpowers and their respective allies. In such a world, humanitarian aid always bore traces of both global and local conflicts, and the ability to determine who received such assistance (and under what conditions) invariably strengthened the position of one side or another and thus implicitly furthered their specific vision of the postcolonial nation. As we have already seen with regard to both North and South Korea, the highly charged, often paranoid environment of the Cold War inevitably led to the politicization of all forms of humanitarian, development, and medical aid and thereby turned them into tools for the pursuit of that ever-elusive goal: security. In this chapter, I will focus on the specific ways in which such aid was used by both sides for military and ideological ends in Vietnam.

A century ago, the Viennese critic Karl Kraus described psychoanalysis as a disease that believed itself to be its own cure. In the first section, I will argue in a similar way that U.S. aid programs to Vietnam in the 1950s produced the very refugee crises that enabled the humanitarian doctor hero to emerge as a medico-political savior for the victims of these crises, although only if the underlying political causes could be successfully hidden in the murky realm of covert action and displaced onto more visible ideological opponents. In the second section, I will focus specifically on Soviet and Eastern European medical aid programs to North Vietnam. While the influence of the Chinese and the French on the Vietnamese health system may be obvious, the medical aid programs sponsored by the Soviet Union and the socialist countries of Eastern Europe are much less well known.

Here, I will make two loosely related arguments. First, to the extent that East German medical aid influenced the outcome of the Vietnamese conflict and the shape of the postcolonial nation, and to the extent that these initiatives in turn mobilized the East German populace behind the socialist project at the global level, then the study of these aid programs will lead us to reconceptualize the space of East German history and to situate it on a much larger global canvas. Second, the inclusion of these fraternal solidarity programs adds additional layers to the already complex history of health and hygiene in Vietnam, which both straddles the colonial/postcolonial divide and bears traces of Indochina's many pasts. Although these programs did provide meaningful assistance to the North Vietnamese and did so in ways that demonstrated the potency of the alliance of science and socialism, I will argue in the third section that, by couching their claims to leadership in the language of civilizational difference, East German doctor heroes endangered their larger goal of gaining the political loyalty of the North Vietnamese.

I. DOCTORS, SPIES, AND COLD WARRIORS: THE *DRAMATIS PERSONAE* OF THE COLD WAR IN ASIA

Doctor Ton That Tung, the Vietminh's Jungle Doctor

In Indochina, the French legacy in the field of public health was one of discrimination and malign neglect. During the colonial era, hospitals had only been constructed in politically sensitive cities, such as Hanoi, Haiphong, and Saigon, and in regions of particular economic importance, such as coal mining and rubber-producing areas. No substantive measures were taken until after the turn of the century to improve the health of the general population and thus enhance the productivity of the rich delta regions. These problems were compounded by the absence of native physicians. The French were unwilling to offer full training in Western medicine to the Vietnamese themselves because they feared that such an education would undermine the racial superiority that they claimed for themselves. The only way for a Vietnamese to become a fully trained physician was to study in France, but only a very small number of individuals were able to do so.[389] As a result, in 1939 there were only 102 physicians – all Western – in Indochina, and at the end of World War II, there was only one doctor for every 180,000 persons.[390] Vietnamese and Chinese natives could study to become para-physicians (or assistant doctors, *médicins auxiliaires*) at the Hanoi Medical School. The school had only admitted its first class of thirteen students in 1902, and the number of such assistant doctors remained quite small. At the end of the 1930s, there were 968 Vietnamese assistant doctors to treat the indigenous population, although their work did not so much amplify the care provided by Western physicians as enable these doctors to devote more time to their lucrative private practices for fee-paying whites.

In the 1920s, colonial authorities finally took the first steps toward improving the medical care available to Vietnamese population.[391] In 1935, the Hanoi Medical School was recognized as a branch of the Paris Medical University, and its faculty and curriculum were correspondingly upgraded. The following year, Jacques May arrived in Hanoi to head both the medical school and the Phu Doan Hospital, the teaching hospital associated with the school. However, the motives for these reforms were substantially less noble than the country's self-proclaimed civilizing mission. As the colonial governor informed May, "you should discourage among your students any desire to go to France for their studies. The reason we have brought you here is precisely to prevent any such tendency. We want Paris to come to them but don't want them to go to Paris where usually they squander our money and learn to despise us for our weaknesses, rather than admire us for our virtues."[392]

Officials feared that the colonial racial hierarchy would be upset if local students competed successfully with Frenchmen for internships or, later, in private practice, so they closed off this avenue of social mobility by refusing to admit Vietnamese applicants to the internship program. One of the individuals who were affected by this arbitrary decision was Ton That Tung (1912–1982), who would later become director of the Phu Doan Hospital, deputy health minister of North Vietnam, and one of the doctor heroes of the Vietminh. In 1937, Tung wrote to May protesting the arbitrary closing of the internship program: "I want to become an intern..., and every year I will come and renew my request."[393] As a compromise, the French agreed to hold an internship competition the following year, but to only admit Tung.

During the tumultuous years of Vichy and then Japanese rule, May and Tung went their separate ways. May, who was being watched by the Vichy police, sneaked out of Vietnam aboard a British ship in 1940. He then spent the next several years fighting on the Allied side. After the war, he became the leading expert on medical geography in the United States, and he later served as advisor to U.S. medical aid programs in South Vietnam. Tung continued to work at Phu Doan Hospital during the war. When the uprising against French colonial rule began in August 1945, Tung and other Vietminh activists took control of the hospital and removed both the Japanese director and Vietnamese collaborators.[394]

Ho Chi Minh proclaimed the independent Democratic Republic of Vietnam on September 2, 1945.[395] A year later, the French Expeditionary Forces attacked Haiphong, marking the beginning of the First Indochina War, which was to last for eight years.[396] In December 1946, when the French forced the Vietminh People's Army to retreat from Hanoi, Tung organized a team to collect medicine and medical supplies and send them to secret bases outside Hanoi. Then Tung, together with two other doctors and a large group of medical students, followed the People's Army into the forests and mountains. There, he served in the Viet Bac Mobile Surgical Team and trained medical students at the Health Cadres School of the Resistance.[397]

Eisenhower's *Dr. America* and the French *Angel of Dien Bien Phu*

In January 1950, China and the Soviet Union recognized the new Democratic Republic of Vietnam, and the following month the United States recognized the State of Vietnam (that is, the government of the southern part of the country that until 1955 was ruled by former emperor Bao Dai).[398] Soon thereafter, the Eisenhower administration sent Special Technical and Economic Mission (STEM) teams to Indochina to help the government become strong and stable enough to withstand the perceived communist menace. Although the French controlled the major cities in the North, much of the countryside was under the control of the Vietminh, and in the North U.S. STEM teams were only able to operate freely in those parts of the Red River delta region that were under French control. As a result, most of them worked in the South.[399] These teams focused on short-term rural pacification programs, and public health played a central role in their work. Their goal was to awaken among the villagers a consciousness of the importance of good health and hygiene and then teach them that the best way to achieve good health was to mobilize the community and its resources under the guidance of health professionals. They hoped that such health education would overcome the resistance of the peasantry and lead to changes in "basic life habits in individuals and the modification of community attitudes and mores in societies."[400]

Initially, the STEM teams expected that they would be able to provide a quick solution to the problems of underdevelopment. They set up first-aid stations in hamlets, recruited village first aiders, whom they hoped would be the foundation of the nation's healthcare system, and launched programs to saturate villages with educational materials. They also distributed generous quantities of basic drugs and medical supplies, such as bandages, in the hope of winning the local inhabitants over to the democratic cause. However, it quickly became clear that such a grassroots approach would not work because the country lacked the civil society needed to support such programs, and the mission began instead to work through existing notables while continuing to complain about their corruption and ineffectiveness.[401] The Eisenhower administration also hoped that the STEM personnel would dispel fears of racial discrimination on the part of the Americans. As one U.S. congressman pointed out after an inspection trip to Southeast Asia in 1955, "I was especially pleased to see some Negro doctors at work for the U.S. government out there in an area where anti-colonialism has gotten to a fever pitch." Another Congressman on the trip noted in similar terms that "the presence of this fine, dignified, and effective young Negro, alone, accomplished very much to allay the misunderstandings that the Indochinese people had as a result of all the insidious information they were actively being fed by Communist interests."[402]

Although donors regarded both humanitarian and development aid as matters of national security and geopolitical import, they sought to mask the political nature of these programs by embedding them in narratives that portrayed such assistance as a manifestation of either an elemental human solidarity with the less fortunate or, in the East, of anti-imperialist solidarity with the exploited peasantry. On both sides of the Bamboo Curtain, the protagonists of these Cold War political romances were the heroic doctors – and, to a lesser degree, nurses – who were struggling out of the purest of motives to bring better health, modern ideas, security, and greater prosperity to the peoples of the underdeveloped world. In fact, the figure of heroic doctor was one of the most enduring cultural icons of the Cold War, one whose popularity reached its height in the 1950s and 1960s.

The first of these heroic figures to achieve widespread fame in the 1950s was a French nurse, Geneviève de Galard, the "Angel of Dien Bien Phu." Hoping to capitalize on her popularity at the time of the 1954 Geneva Conference, the Eisenhower administration invited Galard to visit the United States. In New York, a ticker-tape parade was held in her honor, and, when Eisenhower awarded her the Medal of Freedom in Washington, where he praised Galard's courageous fight against communism at Dien Bien Phu as being "in accordance with the finest traditions of humanity."[403] If Galard was the embodiment of heroic nurse, then her Mephistophelian counterpart was Colonel Edward G. Lansdale, who arrived in Saigon in June 1954 to head the U.S. military mission there. Lansdale had learned his trade in the Philippines, where he played a key role in putting down the Huk rebellion and securing the election of Ramon Magsaysay as president.[404]

The Geneva conference had been convened on April 26, 1954, to discuss both Korea and Indochina. On May 7, the French surrendered at Dien Bien Phu. The following day the Geneva conference turned its attention to Indochina. As Ilya Gaiduk has shown, however, the leaders of the great powers were less concerned with Indochina than "European and national security."[405] The Geneva Accords, which were signed on July 21, 1954, allowed for the free movement of people between the North and the South until May 1955, when the partition of the country was to become final.[406] This was Lansdale's window of opportunity, and in the months leading up to the partition of the country, he directed an elaborate covert program to discredit Ho and his government and encourage mass migration to the South. The U.S. government believed that settling refugees from the north, many of whom were Catholic, in "traditionally unfriendly areas," that is, in areas in the south that had supported the Vietminh, would build a human bulwark against communist influence and increase support for South Vietnamese prime minister Ngô Dinh Diêm.[407]

Ultimately the American, French, and British helped some 900,000 persons move to the south. The codeword for the naval operation to transport these people was "Passage to Freedom." U.S. propaganda depicted the flight of these persons, which had been directly encouraged by U.S. covert operations, as a desperate search for political and religious freedom by people who had been tortured and terrorized by communists.

This U.S.-engineered humanitarian crisis was instrumentalized for two related purposes. The sheer scale of the crisis was used as evidence of the illegitimacy of the socialist regime. At the same time, the misery and disease suffered by these refugees – caused by the absence of facilities to adequately feed, house, and care for them – was then used as proof of the backwardness of the Vietnamese and of the need for Western aid, which then flowed into the South in copious quantities.

This refugee crisis also created America's own iconic figure of anti-communist medical internationalism: Dr. America! The real-life individual behind this icon of America's commitment to health, development, and freedom everywhere in the Third World was Thomas A. Dooley, a navy officer assigned to a Haiphong refugee camp that served as a transit station for Vietnamese fleeing to the south. Dooley's account of his experiences in Vietnam was published in 1956 under the revealing title *Deliver Us from Evil*. It became an instant bestseller, which the U.S. government distributed around the world.[408] Dooley described communism as a "ghoulish thing which had conquered most of the Orient and with it nearly half of all mankind." He attributed the refugee crisis to communist depredations and portrayed the U.S. humanitarian mission as the embodiment of all that was good about America. "Rival ideologies," Dooley wrote, "are fighting this war now and *not* with guns and hydrogen bombs either. They are competing for the souls of those who are rising in search of a better life. So we have to demonstrate that *our* way of life has qualities that are good."[409] In turn, a massive publicity campaign aimed at both U.S. readers and the South Vietnamese public portrayed him as a doctor crusading for freedom and hailed his humanitarian work as another example of America's willingness to protect the world from communism.[410]

After leaving Vietnam, Dooley went on to serve as co-founder of Medical International Cooperation (MEDICO), which was funded by the International Refugee Committee. The authors of *The Ugly American* rewarded Dooley for his work with this organization by bestowing upon him the title "Doctor of Democracy." They praised the MEDICO staff, who worked "quietly and without fanfare" throughout Asia, as America's answer to communism.[411] But what neither Dooley nor those who extolled his achievements said out loud was that his original mission in North Vietnam also included a secret assignment to collect intelligence on indigenous parasites and bacteria "so if and when we have to fight here the men will know exactly what to expect in the way of disease."[412] It was through such rhetoric that global health, U.S. medical internationalism, and security were conflated.

Operation Brotherhood

While France was becoming entangled in another colonial war in Algeria, the United States intensified its rural pacification program in South Vietnam and sponsored a number of bilateral and multilateral aid programs to undermine local support for the communists.[413] As chief of the National Security Program of the Military Assistance Advisory Group, Lansdale was in command of all U.S. military and civilian pacification programs in South Vietnam, where he secured international support for the counterinsurgency program in the South and gave these programs a humanitarian façade. For example, his connections in the Philippines enabled him to persuade the Philippine Junior Chamber of Commerce to serve as the "benign 'front organization'" for what came to be known as Operation Brotherhood.[414]

Operation Brotherhood had a bevy of high-profile sponsors ranging from Magsaysay to Eleanor Roosevelt, theologian Reinhold Niebuhr, Eisenhower, Richard Nixon, and John Foster Dulles. Most of its funding came from the U.S. Operations Mission in Saigon and the International Red Cross. Given the prominence of its supporters, the organization also received extensive media coverage.[415] A full-page advertisement for Operation Brotherhood, which appeared in *The New York Times* on May 10, 1955, showed a large photograph of Vietnamese refugees streaming into Haiphong in search of transportation to the South. The caption read: "They are voting with their feet." Underneath was a brief account of the organization's work, an endorsement by Eisenhower, and a coupon that read "Here is my contribution of $___ to help the men, women and children who chose to live in freedom in South Viet-Nam."[416]

Operation Brotherhood arranged for Filipino doctors and nurses to fly to Vietnam to provide medical relief in refugee settlement areas. The first team arrived in Saigon in October 1954. Despite the connections to the U.S. pacification program, every effort was made to give their work the appearance of a humanitarian action by Asians for Asians. Although the team left from a U.S. air force base in the Philippines aboard a military aircraft, the plane was clearly marked with the Red Cross emblem. The team of seven doctors and three nurses were accompanied by the Philippine Red Cross representative to Vietnam, and on its return flight to Manila, the plane carried Vietnamese soldiers who had been selected for counterinsurgency training in the Philippines. A second Filipino team arrived in February 1955, and by October of that year there were more than 100 Filipinos – including twenty-five doctors, fifty nurses, ten social workers – working in South Vietnam.[417] The staff of Operation Brotherhood also collected information for the security services and provided paramilitary training for selected villagers.

The composition of the Filipino mission changed once the closing of the border made it possible to focus on community development in the South. While the initial Filipino teams were made up exclusively of medical personnel, by late 1955 incoming teams also included both technical experts to educate the local population on such matters as livestock, agriculture, fisheries, canning, and food preservation and social workers charged with organizing health and hygiene campaigns. In addition to routine clean-up weeks and sewing and cooking classes, as part of its community development program, Operation Brotherhood staff also organized contests for the cleanest school, home, and neighborhood. The winner of one of the contests to come up with a slogan for these campaigns was "Though poor, we can be clean."[418] To ensure that as many people as possible showed up for the award ceremony, Operation Brotherhood workers set up a hygiene exhibition that permitted the locals to look through a microscope and see the germs carried by the flies and mosquitoes that they were being urged to eradicate. Filipina nurses also provided first aid training to villagers and organized demonstrations on proper childcare for local women.

Medical aid and military aims were inseparably conjoined in pacification programs in both the central highlands and the tropical lowlands of the South. As one U.S. Operations Mission official explained with regard to the latter region, "with the evacuation of Vietminh from the Soctrang–Camau area it becomes a responsibility of the National Security Program to assume responsibility for reestablishing security and civil services. Health is of vital importance in the rehabilitation of the people of that area. In this endeavor it is of vital importance that the medical team entering this area have in their possession certain vitamins essential in the medical care of the people."[419] Such assistance was just as important for Lansdale, who regarded medical supplies as a tangible complement to political propaganda: "The 13 cases [i.e. first aid kits] were given to mobile psychological warfare teams of the First Region Armed Propaganda Company, each of which was accompanied by a trained first aid man. These teams have reached areas entirely inaccessible either to the JCI medical teams or to the limited number of Vietnamese Army medical personnel with their limited stock of medicine. It is recommended that these 13 cases be turned over to the village first aid school once sufficient students have been trained to reach the villages which are presently being covered only by the propaganda teams."[420]

In addition to those U.S.-operated programs, the U.S. government both mobilized the international community to provide technical aid to South Vietnam and sponsored many multilateral health programs in cooperation with WHO, UNICEF, and the FAO, as well as NGOs such as Catholic Relief Services and the Mennonite Central Committee.[421] In September 1954, the Western Pacific Regional Conference of the WHO adopted a resolution demanding that health programs be given priority in those regions that were most directly threatened by communism, including South Vietnam, Laos, and Cambodia.[422] This intertwinement of UN organizations and U.S. counterinsurgency efforts exposed the former to sharp criticism from many quarters. According to Arthur E. Brown, the WHO representative in the region, "delicate situations have arisen because of the acknowledged political aims behind US Aid which are of no concern to WHO as a specialized technical agency of the UN." Brown, however, brushed off such criticism, arguing that by their very nature medical and humanitarian aid were apolitical.[423]

II. THE SOCIALIST FRACTURING OF THE COLONIAL IMAGINARY

Ho's Guerilla War, Oriental Medicine, and Maoist Health Campaigns

In contrast to the South, not only was North Vietnam excluded from most international organizations.[424] In the late 1940s and early 1950s, the Soviet Union had not shown any interest in aiding its ostensible allies in the North. Stalin distrusted and disparaged Ho, calling him "a communist troglodyte," and he kept his distance from the Vietminh.[425] In fact, during the struggle against the French, the People's Republic of China provided more aid to the Vietminh than did the Soviet Union. After 1950, when the Chinese had finally succeeded in driving the remnants of Chiang Kai-shek's Nationalist army from the Chinese-Vietnamese border, Mao was in a position to regularly send food and military supplies, as well as military advisors, to the Vietminh.[426]

While Chinese military assistance was crucial to the success of the Vietminh war effort, the Chinese also influenced the wartime health policy of the Vietnamese. At the First National Health Congress (1950), Chinese officials had launched the First Patriotic Health Campaign.[427] In North Vietnam, mass health and hygiene campaigns were essential elements of the government's efforts to create a productive population.[428] For their own campaigns, the Vietminh freely borrowed Chinese slogans, such as "Triple Cleanliness" (of food, water, and housing) and "Death times 4" (i.e., the extermination of flies, bed bugs, rats, and insects). Troops of medical workers traveled to the countryside to promote modern hygienic awareness and mobilize the peasantry in support of the new nation. Between 1950 and 1952, over 150,000 brochures were produced in order to mobilize civilians in liberated zones to build latrines and eliminate flies, mosquitoes, and rats.[429]

Waging a guerrilla war against the well-equipped French Expeditionary Force for eight years was no small feat.[430] As military commanders have known for ages, disease can often be more important than the enemy in degrading the fighting capacity of an army. The Vietminh gave high priority to sanitary policing programs in rural areas whose public health systems had been neglected under French rule. In combat areas, such programs played a crucial role in winning the loyalty of those villagers whom they relied on for food and shelter. And in those zones under their control, the Vietminh established military and civil health committees at the village and district levels, opened maternity homes in hamlets, and built clinics and other healthcare facilities in larger towns and cities. Together, the Health Ministry, the health section of the People's Army, and the Hanoi School of Medicine and Pharmacy offered expedited training to a much larger number of doctors, pharmacists, and auxiliary health workers than were being trained at the time in the South.

Vietminh authorities also took a number of steps to alleviate the acute shortage of medicine and medical supplies. For example, to increase production, the government sought to persuade workers at pharmaceutical plants of the patriotic importance of their labor (the slogan was "Self-Confidence and Self-Help"). While the French had disparaged oriental medicine and native medicinal herbs and plants, Vietminh health authorities aggressively promoted their use. Vietminh pharmacologists conducted research on Sino-Vietnamese herbal medicine in hopes of relieving these shortages without expending precious foreign exchange on imported medicine.[431]

After the signing of the Geneva Accords, the North Vietnamese government declared 1954 the "Year of Peace" and set up healthcare clinics for those "patriotic" Vietminh returning from the South. French bombing during the war had destroyed many hospitals in the North, including the largest tuberculosis sanatorium and the only leprosarium in the country. As part of its reconstruction plan, the government emphasized the need to both renovate and expand existing hospitals in Hanoi and Haiphong and build new healthcare facilities, including veterans' hospitals.[432] The government also sought to provide additional training to those doctors and assistant doctors who had studied at the "jungle university."

Building Soviet-Style Hospitals in North Vietnam

The parameters of international medical aid to North Vietnam were influenced by developments within the socialist bloc. In the first half of the 1950s, Moscow continued to move at glacial speed in fulfilling a verbal pledge to provide economic aid to North Vietnam, and Khrushchev did not sign a formal aid agreement until Ho visited Moscow in June 1955. Three months later, the first Soviet medical team of twenty-six doctors and nurses arrived in Hanoi; within a month, the team moved to the country's main mining and rice-producing regions to collect epidemiological data on malaria, trachoma, and venereal diseases. The next year, a second Soviet team began work on reforming the country's medical curriculum, modernizing its research centers, and promoting prophylactic measures.[433] As part of a campaign to transcend the country's colonial past, Soviet specialists also began renovating a hospital that would later be named the Vietnamese-Soviet Friendship Hospital. This was to serve as a teaching hospital where Vietnamese doctors would learn to apply the "progressive medical science of the USSR."[434]

This process, however, did not go as smoothly as both sides would have liked. In 1957, the North Vietnamese established an Institute of Oriental Medicine to conduct research on indigenous medicinal plants and acupuncture.[435] The Vietnamese insisted on incorporating both traditional Sino-Vietnamese medicine and Western biomedicine into their public health system. However, Soviet advisors insisted that it be based solely on Western biomedicine and Soviet-style social hygiene. The Vietnamese desire to reappropriate older traditions and make them part of the country's postcolonial modernity was just as foreign to these Europeans as the language and customs of Vietnamese. These Westerners worried that, whatever the potential practical benefits of such an approach, it could become a Trojan horse for Chinese political influence.

The Vietnamese-German Friendship Hospital

The East German and North Vietnamese governments had recognized each other in February 1950, but East Germany showed little interest in the region until Soviet policy shifted after Stalin's death. In 1955, the East Germans organized a flurry of solidarity activities and propaganda

ÜBER DIE FREUNDSCHAFT
ZU DEN MENSCHEN
KOREAS UND VIETNAMS

SO
FERN
UND
DOCH
SO
NAH

FIGURE 4.1 "So far and yet so close." Solidarity poster soliciting funds to help North Korea and North Vietnam (1954).
Source: Nationalrat der Nationalen Front des demokratischen Deutschland. Courtesy of Deutsches Historisches Museum, Berlin DG 60/12.

campaigns (such as that shown in Figure 4.1). The Democratic Farmers' Party raised money to equip a dispensary in North Vietnam; the Potsdam Thälmann Pioneers donated a tractor and a printing press to their Vietnamese counterparts; and the Solidarity Committee for Korea and Vietnam sponsored a medical aid team to Hanoi.[436]

The East German medical team, which consisted of thirty-two surgeons, nurses, and technicians, arrived in February 1956.[437] Ho welcomed them with a reception at his residence to celebrate the lunar new year. The guests responded positively to Ho's reminiscences of the time that he had spent in Berlin in the 1920s. In the spring of 1956, other medical teams from Bulgaria, Czechoslovakia, Hungary, and Romania arrived in Hanoi. These teams generally included thirty to forty persons, and they usually stayed for a year. The Bulgarians worked on a project to expand the Hanoi Army Hospital and construct a blood transfusion center.[438] The Czech and Hungarian teams worked in the provinces outside Hanoi to train medical cadres and provide healthcare to the rural population.[439] In January 1957, the Czech government also agreed to renovate a Haiphong hospital dating from the French colonial era and to staff it for two years with a forty-person team. And Soviet, Czech, Hungarian, and Rumanian medical teams collaborated with the Vietnamese on a campaign to eradicate malaria and trachoma.[440]

In the 1950s, the showcase for East German aid for North Vietnam was the Phu Doan Hospital, the only surgical hospital in the country. The East German Solidarity Committee for Korea and Vietnam raised money to equip the surgical and radiological departments, outfit a prosthetic workshop, and furnish the wards. It also provided the hospital with washing machines, beds, and other furniture, while the Vietnamese provided the materials and labor to renovate the building. For the East German government, it was culturally and economically important to transform the Phu Doan Hospital into a modern, well-equipped hospital staffed with physicians committed to building the medical correlate of socialism. Not only would the East Germans thereby neutralize one of the most potent symbols of the colonial past; they would also make it into a symbol of the solidarity and partnership of the two countries. Economically, the hospital also served as a "small industrial fair" where East German medical technology was on display.[441] The East German Foreign Ministry sought to publicize its role in modernizing the North Vietnamese public health system, and the East Gemrans provided tours to delegations from India, Indonesia, and Cambodia so that representatives of these countries could compare the achievements of East German socialist medicine in the Third World with those of their Eastern European allies and competitors.

As was the case in North Korea, cultural differences sometimes led to friction between the East Germans and the North Vietnamese. Traditional forms of opera and theater had deep roots in Chinese-Vietnamese popular culture. Because literacy rates were low in rural areas, the Vietnamese government sought to repurpose these age-old media to communicate its message to the unlettered masses. The East Germans, however, believed that part of their mission was to communicate the values of punctuality and order. When a Vietnamese lab assistant repeatedly missed work or showed up late, German technicians were disturbed and asked Richard Kirsch, the head of the team, to inquire into the matter. As it turned out, the Vietnamese medical staff had been preparing to stage a play to teach hospital employees about the importance of health and reinforce their work and social norms, and the ostensible slacker had missed work because he had been busy writing and revising the script, while other workers had been involved in building the set.[442]

The Europeans soon learned that they had to acquire a more systematic knowledge of the epidemiology of local, tropical diseases before they could even think about proffering biomedical solutions to the Vietnamese. However, even then, the assistance they provided often reflected as much their own preferences, resources, and needs as it did those of the recipient country. When a Vietnamese official approached the Czech team with a proposal to establish a medical school in Haiphong, the Czechs explained that a project of such magnitude would require many of the socialist states to pool their resources. However, at their April 1956 meeting, the conference of socialist health ministers opted instead to create a research institute for tropical medicine. Because the European socialist countries had temperate climates, Vietnam came to serve – quite literally – as an important colonial laboratory for the Soviet bloc. As the East German health minister explained, because the East Germans were establishing relations with Third World countries with tropical climates, they had to be able to protect their own citizens before they could hope to improve the health of the citizens of those countries, and the research center would offer German doctors an ideal location for studying tropical disease.[443]

III. BERLIN, HANOI, AND THE ALTERNATIVE SPATIALITY OF GERMAN HISTORY

Transparent Woman Goes to Hanoi

Cultural differences also arose in conjunction with East German medical exhibitions in the country too. The exhibit *Man* (see Chapter 6) opened in Hanoi in 1958. Available sources allow for a relatively textured reading of how these exhibitions represented East Germany's socialist hygienic modernity and national identity. The timing of the exhibition was auspicious because it coincided with the launch of Vietnam's Three Year Plan (see below). The exhibition included the Transparent Woman. Both the German Hygiene Museum and the Foreign Ministry were initially concerned that the display of the female reproductive organs might offend local moeurs. If Vietnamese officials insisted on covering all or part of the body of the transparent woman, the Germans feared, this would severely diminish the educational value of the exhibition. Although these fears quickly proved to be unfounded, Vietnamese officials did warn their German counterparts that the exhibition should not promote hygienic ideals (such as modern housing or improved nutrition) that were unrealizable under existing local conditions. Instead, they asked that the exhibit focus on "the constitution and functions of the human body and on particular hygiene measures (dental care, the elimination of germ-carrying insects)."[444]

When the exhibition opened in Hanoi on October 7, 1958, 10,000 tickets were sold in three hours; reportedly, the exhibition had to be temporarily closed to give the police the opportunity to gain control of the throng of visitors trying to get in. An average of 13,000 people attended the exhibit on weekdays and 18,000 on Sundays. A total of 290,000 persons ultimately visited the exhibition, including many seventh- and eighth-grade students, and more than 125,000 additional persons saw the exhibition when it toured several major provincial cities.[445] Both Ho and Premier Pham Van Dong toured the exhibition. Ho suggested that the East Germans add a special section on tropical diseases to include charts and diagrams showing the incidence and costs of mosquito-borne illnesses, as well as microscopes to give visitors the chance to get an up-close view of disease-causing micro-organisms.[446] When the exhibition opened in Thai Nguyen, the capital of the autonomous Viet Bac region in the mountainous North, the East German embassy reported that people had walked sixty kilometers and slept outside overnight just to see the show.

The exhibition was also important because the accompanying public pronouncements provide a window into the self-understanding of the East Germans in the field of medical aid – and of their attitudes toward the Third World. At a press conference, Wolfgang Bethmann – a surgeon who headed the Leipzig University Hospital and who succeeded Kirsch as head of the medical mission at the Phu Doan Hospital – took the exhibition as an opportunity to expound the principles of German socialist hygienic modernity to both the press and his Vietnamese counterparts. As Bethmann explained, the most basic principle was prophylaxis for the working masses, the "builders of socialism." Preventive medicine, he argued, could only be fully effective if coupled with the systematic enlightenment of the population regarding the central elements of a healthy lifestyle, and he described the set of exhibitions, educational materials, lectures, slide shows, and films produced in East Germany as teaching tools. But enlightenment could only be effective if it were engaging and intelligible to the intended audience, and Bethmann described the various teaching aids that the hygiene museum had created to make the principles of modern hygiene more accessible to the general public.[447]

In a radio address, Bethmann drew a stark contrast between the primitive era of unscientific medicine and the modern age. In this new era, Bethmann explained, scientific knowledge of the natural world had been extended to the human body itself, thereby removing health from the domain of superstition and making it an object of rational control. The most tangible sign of this march toward modernity was the success of medical science in discovering the causes of, as well as the means of treating, most diseases. He believed that scientific research was on the verge of conquering the remaining epidemic diseases. Bethmann concluded by reminding the audience that the exhibition represented a genuine act of international solidarity between the two countries and that it marked the first step toward bringing such scientific enlightenment to the people of North Vietnam.[448]

The intended audience of Bethmann's lectures and talks varied, and, depending on the audience, his focus shifted as well. When he delivered a lecture at Hanoi University, his audience included leading functionaries from the health, education, and culture ministries, the army, the Vietnamese Red Cross, and representatives from a variety of mass organizations. He began by explaining what the exhibition was *not* about. Judging from the questions, as he explained, many Vietnamese people entertained "totally wrong ideas about the meaning and aim" of the exhibition and its relation to socialist medicine. Bethmann emphasized that biomedicine was the cornerstone of East German public health and that the exhibition was not a panacea for the challenges facing North Vietnam. Rather, the purpose of the exhibition was to make knowledge of the human body – its constitution, functions, ailments, and treatments – available to the entire population and thus to lay the foundation for a long-term process of popular hygienic enlightenment.

Although little in what Bethmann said – beyond the rhetorical flourishes – was specifically socialist, speaking before this group he made clear what he believed to be the logical connection between socialism and health. Ignorance, he claimed, was little different from slavery and colonial rule. "The political independence of the people alone is not enough," he insisted, "if the people are not also emancipated mentally – emancipated from ignorance, superstition and prejudices. Enlightenment is the logical sequel to the armed resistance struggle."[449] He criticized the narrowness of the North Vietnamese hygienic enlightenment campaign and argued that it should focus on promoting preventive medicine, especially that targeted at the productive population, rather than simply on disease control. However, when he left the country, Bethmann seemed convinced that his official audience had understood his message: "People in responsible positions in Vietnam understood what the issue was and what 'protecting the nation's health' entailed."[450]

Mosquitos, Bamboo, and Bananas: An Orientalist Tale for East German Children

The East German government often published memoirs of physicians who led aid missions to Asia and Africa. While the East Germans may not have produced a direct counterpart to Dr. America, their accounts of their work in North Vietnam were still informed by a logic of colonial difference that transformed them into a distinctive form of socialist Orientalism. Kirsch's memoirs – originally entitled *A Doctor in Southeast Asia* – are a good example of such an account. In this volume, Kirsch followed the well-established colonial narrative of the white doctor bringing medical succor to the ignorant, diseased, and impoverished people of the non-European world. He portrayed the Vietnamese as primitives marveling at the baubles offered by the West. He likened the unbounded joy felt by the Vietnamese as they unpacked the first shipment of medical equipment and supplies from East Germany to the experience of a child tearing into a stack of presents: "No child has ever played more devotedly with his toys underneath a Christmas tree than did this young [Vietnamese] doctor when he examined his new instruments. [With these instruments] he undoubtedly carried out in his mind many new examinations and operations that until this point he could only dream." For Kirsch, the arrival of this equipment marked the true beginning of Vietnamese history. It was "a blissful day on which the difference between the past and the future again became clear."[451]

The book also contained numerous Orientalizing passages that described his experience of the lush, exotic East. Vietnam was portrayed as a fairytale land of bananas, oranges, and other tropical products that were rarities in East Germany. "My mouth waters," Kirsch wrote, "when I think of the wonderful, juicy fruit that one can buy there for a few pennies." However, Kirsch also gave the exotic a particular ideological flavor. In the book, which included many examples of aid provided by the European socialist countries, Kirsch described how, thanks to fraternal aid from Eastern Europe, the mechanization of rice farming was finally replacing practices that had been handed down "for a thousand years...from father to son." He wove these passages into an account of how East German machinery and engineering expertise were helping to shake the country out of its tropical lethargy and set it moving down the path to modernity. The book also described how technical aid from the Soviet bloc was transforming the traditional, exploitive system of coffee plantations with more modern socialist collectives.[452]

The civilizational gradient that underlay Kirsch's narrative was important in legitimating international medical aid in the eyes of the East

German public and in helping stabilize the Ulbricht regime. In the late 1950s, however, other East German officials found these representations problematic, and Kirsch's account of the contributions of the heroic socialist doctor in Southeast Asia ran afoul of these censors. Both the publisher and the Foreign Ministry disapproved of both the pervasive tone of "arrogance" running through the book. They objected to Kirsch's depictions of the "superiority" of "European, German intellectuals" as infantilizing the North Vietnamese, rather than treating them as equal comrades, to his offensive and disparaging descriptions of Vietnamese culture and customs, and to his denomination of the facility as the Wilhelm Pieck Hospital, rather than the Viet-Duc Hospital, thus erasing the agency of the Vietnamese themselves.[453] In the end, the censors advised against the publication of the book, although it did appear five years later in altered form as a children's book under the title *Mosquitoes, Bamboo, and Bananas.*[454]

FIGURE 4.2 A group of Vietnamese trainees from the Electrochemical Combine Bitterfeld depart on a Baltic cruise sponsored by the Free German Youth on the ship *Völkerfreundschaft* (1970).
Source: Eva Brüggmann. Courtesy of Bundesarchiv, Bild 183-74690-0007.

IV. DIVIDED WE FALL?

The network of friendship hospitals that were built by the Soviet bloc countries in Vietnam were not the product of a one-way transfer of knowledge. Not only were they laboratories of colonial modernity. They were also the main site of collaboration both among the socialist countries and between the Second and Third Worlds. Because of the opportunity it afforded for the study of tropical disease, in the late 1950s North Vietnam became a favorite country for visits by East European scientists and doctors. For example, in 1958, a Hungarian neurosurgeon, a Soviet cardiopulmonary specialist, an East German radiologist, a French anesthesiologist, and a Cuban urologist were all working side by side in the Phu Doan Hospital. At the same time, because the basic medical training that most physicians had received during the war had produced a generation of doctors with little knowledge in specialized fields, medical internationalism gave Vietnamese health officials the opportunity to learn from these visiting experts. This confluence of factors made the hospital the primary site for transnational, medico-cultural exchange in North Vietnam and a symbol of the multiple medical traditions that were shaping the country's public health system across the postcolonial divide.[455]

Nor did France completely sever connections to its former colony. The Saint Paul Hospital, which was jointly operated by the North Vietnamese and French governments, opened its doors in April 1957. Although the Clinique St. Paul had previously been reserved for European patients, after independence Vietnamese and French doctors worked together in the new hospital, thus providing "concrete proof for the possibility of cultural cooperation."[456] Moreover, foreign doctors also helped shape medical practice in the new socialist state. The public health "system" that ultimately emerged from these interactions resembled a palimpsest with each of the many powers that successively dominated or assisted the region adding its own layer of medical knowledge and practice – without ever being able to either fully erase what had been written before or to keep its own medico-political language from bleeding into the layers above and below it.

Vietnam was also an important site for what was known as "fraternal (socialist) competition" in which the different national missions competed with one another to be the first to complete its renovation project or to provide the Vietnamese with the best-equipped hospital.[457] Despite repeated assurances of the friendly nature of this competition, these endeavors always had an edge because these teams were all aware that the success or failure of their work in Vietnam and elsewhere would serve as a measure of the legitimacy of the socialist government at home and its standing in the wider world. As we have seen, staffing and equipping these institutions was a highly visible way of showcasing the achievements of socialist medicine, not to mention a great way to create export markets for Eastern bloc pharmaceuticals and medical equipment. This was not an inconsequential matter for the East Europeans. Although they were genuinely interested in training North Vietnamese medical personnel at these friendship hospitals, they also hoped that these local physicians would continue to use the products with which they had become familiar. According to the East Germans, the Czechs excelled in this regard. The Czech staff working at the Vietnamese-Czechoslovak Friendship Hospital were well trained, and their medicine and equipment were "excellent" in both "quantity and quality." Czech doctors were always available to guide native and foreign visitors through the hospital, and they never missed an opportunity to tout "the advantages of Czech products." By contrast, the East Germans felt that their own products did not hold up well in the tropics. Kirsch, however, argued that sending medical personnel to Vietnam would "eventually bring more profit, even after subtracting all the costs." "Based on my good knowledge of the health system here in Vietnam," he continued, "we have a good development possibility here [with our products].[458]

The dynamic of East German medical aid programs to North Vietnam – and those of the Eastern bloc countries more generally – was also shaped by the growing rivalry between the Soviet Union and China for leadership in the socialist bloc.[459] Mao rejected both peaceful coexistence and the possibility of a nonrevolutionary transition to socialism, and he portrayed the Chinese Great Leap Forward (1958–60) as the best route to rapid socialist transformation under the specific socioeconomic conditions (overpopulation, the scarcity of both land and capital, and industrial underdevelopment) in China and throughout much of Asia.[460] In 1958, the North Vietnamese announced a Three Year Plan closely modeled on the Great Leap Forward; construction of the Ho Chi Minh Trail began in May 1959; and in December 1960 the National Liberation Front was founded to wage military and political struggle against the Diệm government in the south.[461] However, in 1959/60 the North Vietnamese began to distance themselves from Chinese-style agricultural collectivization. In 1960, the Soviet Union sent scientific and technical advisors to North Vietnam and provided substantial credits to help finance agricultural and industrial development. In addition, the emphasis in the country's first Five Year Plan (1961–5) on the role of heavy industry, rather than agriculture, reflected the renewed influence of the Soviet bloc.[462] Although the decision to pursue a Maoist strategy of armed conflict with the South opened up an ideological divide with the Soviet Union, Khrushchev's fall in October 1964, together with the Sino-Soviet split, led to a sharp increase in the Soviet economic and military aid to North Vietnam.

By the time the North Vietnamese began to build the Ho Chi Minh Trail, they had made great progress in the field of public health. At the end of World War II, there had been only seventy-eight hospitals, clinics, dispensaries, and other healthcare facilities in the entire country. By 1959, the number had increased to 185 such facilities in the North alone, where they served a population of approximately fifteen million. The number of healthcare workers also increased rapidly. In 1959, there were 600 fully trained doctors in the country, some 1,900 para-physicians, several thousand practitioners of Oriental medicine, and over 10,000 mid-level medical cadres, such as midwives, assistant pharmacists, and nurses.[463] Nevertheless, when the second East German medical team left in November 1957, it was not replaced.[464] This was due in part to the flight of so many doctors and nurses to West Germany, in part to a recognition of growing Chinese hegemony in the region, and in part to a decision by the Soviet bloc countries to focus their international aid programs on the nonaligned world.

The East German legacy in North Vietnam was mixed. On the one hand, their medical and technological expertise undoubtedly helped the North Vietnamese construct their own version of a socialist public health system, although it was one that bore clear traces of both Maoist ideology and traditional Chinese medicine. On the other hand, the impact of East German medical aid was blunted by the fact that, as we saw with Kirsch, the superiority of East Germany's hygienic modernity could only be established by means of an invidious comparison with the Vietnamese themselves. As the censors recognized, this rhetorical move would undoubtedly have weakened their protestations of solidarity, and we will explore these contradictions at greater length in our analysis of the problems involved in representing East Germanness in the nonaligned world in Chapter 6. One thing is certain, though: Without the knowledge of tropical disease gained in North Vietnam, the East Germans would not have been able to mount such extensive medical aid programs in sub-Saharan Africa after 1960.

5

"Solidarity Is Might!"[465]

Even though the global humanitarian regime had only assumed its definitive form at the turn of the 1950s, across the middle of the decade the Soviet invasion of Hungary, the Suez Crisis, the radicalization of the Algerian conflict, and, at the beginning of the 1960s, the Congo crisis all combined to reveal the asymmetries that had lain hidden behind the universalist rhetoric of international humanitarian aid. These last two conflicts were two of the most protracted, violent, and politically significant conflicts to arise out of the struggle to win independence and shape the postcolonial nation. In this chapter, I will use the Algerian and Congo conflicts to analyze the formulation of East and West German policy toward the Third World and then show how the socialist country worked together with national liberation movements to contest neocolonial rule on a global scale.

As noted in Chapter 1, the postwar humanitarian regime enabled the major Western powers to define what constituted a humanitarian crisis and the conditions under which aid could be provided to the different parties. The French were initially on firm legal ground when they declared the Algerian conflict to be a matter of internal security, and in the first section I will show how the French sought to leverage this doctrine and contain the Algerian conflict by ensuring that humanitarian aid could only be provided in ways that supported their efforts to pacify the country. However, by the end of the 1950s this position became harder to maintain as the National Liberation Front (FLN) and its supporters in the Third World began to use the language of sovereignty and human rights to contest French efforts to preserve the asymmetrical structure of the global humanitarian regime.

The Algerian conflict was also politicized in both West and East Germany. In the Federal Republic, the Adenauer administration carefully avoided challenging the French claim that the Algerian conflict was a matter of internal security. However, by 1958 the growing probability of Algerian independence led Bonn to cautiously build bridges to the FLN. In the second section, I will describe the pro-independence activities of Algerian expatriates in West Germany and then show how the Algerian conflict radicalized a segment of the West German youth and helped shape the consciousness of the New Left.

In the third section, I will look at the broad palette of East German policies and programs relating to the Algerian conflict. While Bonn regarded the Algerian conflict as a political hot potato, the East Germans saw it as an opportunity. Assistance to the Algerians was the first large-scale humanitarian action undertaken by the East Germans in a nonsocialist country. Yet these programs, like those in Zanzibar (Chapter 9), exemplify the permanent tensions between Third World liberation movements and socialist internationalism. While East German aid played an important role in helping the Algerians contest the global humanitarian regime, it also served East German interests, and I will show that the SED leadership used humanitarian aid to the FLN as a means of gaining recognition abroad and solidarity initiatives at home to build political support for the socialist state.

The fourth section focuses on the humanitarian crisis in the Congo in 1960–1. Although the postwar global order was, at least in theory, structured in terms of the rights of formally equal, sovereign states, in this section, I will use the humanitarian aid provided by the two German states to show how Western-dominated humanitarian regimes often operated in such a way as to circumscribe and hollow out this sovereignty.

I. SECURITY, HUMAN RIGHTS, AND THE ALGERIAN WAR: COLONIAL STATE OF EMERGENCY OR WAR OF NATIONAL LIBERATION?

The Algerian War of Independence began on November 1, 1954. While the French insisted that the dispute was an internal matter, the strategy of the FLN was to "make the Algerian problem a reality for the entire world."[466] This internationalization of the Algerian conflict developed in step with the radicalization of both the war itself and the political claims of the Third World movement. Initially, even other Third World countries had treaded lightly around the Algerian question. The FLN failed to persuade a December 1954 meeting of the Colombo group of neutral Asian countries to mention Algeria in their final communiqué. The following year, the Bandung Conference's declaration of the right of peoples and nations to self-determination did not explicitly mention Algeria.

In 1955, the French government had already created the Specialized Administrative Sections as a counterinsurgency unit to fight against the FLN. In response to the intensification of the conflict, the French also introduced a national identity card to better monitor and control the general population, whom they believed were providing cover and support for the armed wing of the liberation movement.[467] After their embarrassment at Suez, the French redoubled their efforts to hold on to Algeria. Regular military and Foreign Legion units employed the same tactics that they had used in Indochina, and the use of napalm and aerial bombardment inevitably created large numbers of casualties, both civilian and military.[468]

Counterinsurgency warfare blurred the line dividing civilians from the military. The French feared that any assistance to the indigenous population would directly or indirectly strengthen the fighting capacity of the FLN, and they were determined to leverage their channel over borders, infrastructure, and the movement of people to channel the flow of aid. In addition, the requirement that doctors and hospitals verify the identities of their patients and report suspicious injuries gave the French authorities an effective means of denying medical care to Algerian soldiers, partisans, and sympathizers. Many doctors were imprisoned or, in some cases, sentenced to death for violating the law.[469] The French also banned the sale of medicine and medical supplies to the Algerians, and French-owned firms in Tunisia and Morocco refused to make prosthetic limbs for Algerians. In this way, food, clothing, medical care, and other aid were discursively repositioned as potential weapons, whose flow into the region and subsequent distribution had to be closely controlled. One of the great challenges for the FLN was to clandestinely procure medicine, surgical instruments, and other medical supplies and smuggle them past the French military.

As in Southeast Asia, French counterinsurgency measures were complemented by pacification programs aimed, at least rhetorically, at building a "New Algeria" by means of a "war on underdevelopment."[470] Medical teams and social workers traveled to rural areas – often accompanied by propaganda teams – to demonstrate the benevolent, progressive nature of French rule. The French also attempted to claim the moral high ground by flooding other Western countries with leaflets, radio broadcasts, and documentaries depicting themselves as the chief defender of the Caucasian West in the global war against both Communism and "Asiatics and African and colonial natives."[471]

Cracks in the Postwar Humanitarian Regime: Hungary, the Suez Crisis, and the Algerian War

The chief political goal of the FLN was to overturn both the French claim that the Algerian conflict was a purely domestic affair and the humanitarian aid policies that flowed from this assertion, and in 1957 it launched its own campaign to counteract the French propaganda offensive.[472] The FLN focused much of its energy on the UN itself. In its *Answer to Mr. Guy Mollet, Prime Minister of France*, the FLN contrasted the Algerian people's quest for self-determination with France's "colonial fanaticism." The organization also argued that the misguided attempts by the French to tar the liberation movement with the brushes of Moslem fanaticism and communism were "the traditional battle cry of colonialists destined to frighten the western world." "A people fighting for its independence," the FLN proclaimed, "inspires a natural sympathy throughout the world. This was true for Europe. Why should it be less true for Asia and Africa?" The FLN also reminded the French of the help they had received to free themselves from Nazi occupation and of their own duty "to concern themselves with the unfortunate situations of the peoples of Africa."[473]

In this campaign, the FLN used Western aid to Hungarian refugees to highlight the difference between the standard applied to human rights in the Third World and that employed within the global North. When, for example, 180,000 Hungarians fled their country in the wake of the October 1956 Soviet invasion, Western governments and private aid organizations, as well as the International Red Cross and the UNHCR, were more than willing to stretch the letter of the 1951 Refugee Convention. This outpouring of humanitarian action gave the Western countries the opportunity to trumpet their commitment to human rights in the face of the totalitarian challenge.[474] This response stood in stark contrast to initial indifference of the Western powers to the plight of Algerian refugees.

Nor were these governments and international NGOs any more prompt in responding to the refugee crisis precipitated by the Suez crisis.[475] French and British air attacks drove more than 15,000 civilians from their homes, and conditions were particularly bad in Port Said, the site of the main fighting. Although ICRC convoys bound for Port Said arrived in Cairo in mid-November with aid and medical supplies for Egyptian prisoners of war and displaced civilians, the Israelis did not permit the convoys to continue on to the city until the following February. The unwillingness of the major Western powers to overrule the Israelis, together with the political fallout resulting from their own role in the crisis, seriously undermined their claim to the moral high ground with regard to Algeria.[476]

This French stranglehold over foreign aid was the catalyst behind the 1956 FLN decision to establish the Algerian Red Crescent (ARC) in Tangier, Morocco, as a conduit for international humanitarian assistance that would not be beholden to the Western powers.[477] The very founding of the organization explicitly challenged the global humanitarian regime. As Bensmaine Hadj Boumediene, the Deputy Secretary-General of the ARC, explained, as long as the Red Cross societies of the "free world" – which had provided help to Hungary, but which remained indifferent to "tragic fate of the Algerian martyrs" – continued to comply with the conditions laid down by the (former) colonial powers after 1945, they would be complicit in supporting counter-revolutionary movements.[478] Although the ICRC was willing to work with the ARC informally, the League of National Red Cross Societies refused to recognize the organization, and only a few of its member organizations – mostly from Arab countries – were willing to alienate the French by responding to ARC appeals.[479] In the West, Norway, Switzerland, and Spain were among the few exceptions.

The General Union of Algerian Workers (*Union Générale des Travailleurs Algériens,* UGTA) also tried to mobilize the world public. However, while the pro-Western International Confederation of Free Trade Unions had provided a substantial amount of aid to Hungarian workers, its response to the Algerian appeal was only lukewarm. The UGTA had better luck with the pro-socialist World Federation of Trade Unions, which at its 1957 conference established the International Trade Union Committee for Solidarity with Algerian Workers and Algerian People.[480]

Third World Internationalism and Global Humanitarianism

Millions of Algerian civilians were affected by French counterinsurgency campaigns (Figure 5.1). By October 1957, 200,000 Algerians were

FIGURE 5.1 Refugees fleeing the Algerian conflict (undated).
Source: Gouvernement provisoire de la République Algérienne, Ministère de l'Information. Courtesy of Bundesarchiv, Bild Y2-1583/00.

camped along the eastern border with Tunis, while another 100,000, primarily children, women, and the elderly, found shelter along the western border with Morocco.[481] Because both Tunisia and eastern Morocco were still French protectorates, aid could only be channeled into this humanitarian borderland through the French Red Cross. Even after these territories gained their independence in March 1956, the French Red Cross continued to control aid flowing into the region because the League of the National Red Cross Societies had not yet recognized the Tunisian and Moroccan Red Crescent Societies.[482] French control over aid to these Algerian refugees was reinforced by the League's refusal to recognize organizations, such as the Algerian Red Crescent, which were established by "elements hostile to the legal government."[483] The French Red Cross was only willing to provide minimal assistance to Algerian refugees and to do so only if these persons had registered with the French consulate. But many Algerians rightly feared that making themselves visible in this way would render them susceptible to French reprisals.[484]

In April 1957, France terminated its aid to Tunisia in retaliation for the decision by the Tunisian government to allow the FLN to establish bases in the country. The following month, Tunisian president Habib

Bourguiba asked the UN to extend the protections guaranteed by the Refugee Convention to Algerian refugees within its borders. Despite the limits imposed by the UN Refugee Convention, the fear of the political side-effects of the looming humanitarian crisis, rather than a change of heart as to the legitimacy of anti-colonial struggles, led High Commissioner Auguste Lindt to use his good offices to begin providing relief to Algerian refugees in Tunisia in 1958. This was UNHCR's first humanitarian action related to decolonization and national liberation struggles in the Third World. However, the program was organized in such a way as to comply with the French demand that such aid not be considered as implying official UN recognition that the Algerian refugee crisis fell within the purview of international aid organizations.[485] The actual relief was provided by the League of Red Cross Societies. The Eisenhower administration supported the operation in Tunisia, primarily because it feared that the failure to do so would encourage the spread of communism in northern Africa, and in the fall of 1958 the American Food for Peace Program contributed a large quantity of surplus wheat and powdered milk to Algerian refugees in Tunisia.[486]

By the winter of 1957–8, world opinion had begun to shift away from the French and their humanitarian policies in Algeria. The FLN scored a major symbolic victory at the nineteenth International Red Cross Conference, which unanimously adopted a revolution condemning the French instrumentalization of humanitarian aid in Algeria. The resolution appealed to all governments to refrain from discriminating in the treatment of the wounded and persecuting physicians who cared for specific groups of patients, to respect the principle of doctor–patient confidentiality, and to guarantee the free circulation of medicine.[487] The passage of this resolution represented an important step toward reclaiming for the Third World the discourse on human rights and employing this symbolic capital to overturn the asymmetries that had shaped the postwar humanitarian regime.[488] Following up on the resolution, in December 1957 the ICRC and the League jointly issued the appeal to the world on behalf of Algerian refugees.

At the same time, the Algerian armed struggle also received strong support at the first Afro-Asian Peoples' Solidarity Conference.[489] In a report to the conference, the Algerian delegate Aiah Hasan denounced the French use of humanitarian aid as a weapon in a war of "genocide" against the Algerian people. He described how the French systematically denied medicine and medical care to the Algerians, punished physicians who treated Algerian fighters, and bombed field hospitals and clinics. He concluded by asking, "shall history tell one day that the peoples of Asia and Africa left, without reacting, the coalition of imperialist powers to exterminate a people whose only wrong was their claim for freedom? The Algerian people do not think so."[490] The message clearly resonated with the audience. The conference passed a resolution recommending that every country provide material assistance to the FLN and mobilize the public to stop the French violation of human rights and the Geneva Conventions. The delegates to the conference also decided to name March 30, 1958, the day of world solidarity with the people of Algeria. Shortly thereafter, the countries that had attended the conference founded the International Aid Committee for Algeria.[491] The underlying sentiments were echoed by other Third World conferences, such as the Conference of Independent African States and the All African Peoples' Conference. On March 30, 1958, the Algerian newspaper *El Moudjahid* wrote – in an editorial probably penned by Frantz Fanon – that "on the 30th of March a very sharp line appeared dividing the world in two; on one side the western camp and on the other side the anti-colonialist camp comprising the overwhelming majority of mankind."[492]

The year 1958 was a turning point in these concerted efforts to challenge Western discourse on self-determination and human rights. On February 8, shortly after international relief operations had begun in Tunisia, the French bombarded the Tunisian town of Sakhiet Sidi Youssef, on the border of Algeria; seventy-five civilians were killed, mostly Algerian refugees, and ICRC trucks carrying relief supplies were also destroyed. The incident galvanized pro-Algerian protesters and prompted the Soviet Red Cross to establish its own relief operation for Algerian refugees in Tunisia.[493] In April, Ghanaian president Kwame Nkrumah hosted a pan-African congress, at which Fanon, the emissary of the Algerian Provisional Government, gave a passionate speech calling for armed resistance against colonial rule. "In our fight for freedom," he declared, "we should embark on plans effective enough to touch the pulse of the imperialists – by force of action and, indeed, violence." The conference, however, rejected Fanon's militant approach and, instead, endorsed the Gandhian strategy of nonviolent resistance favored by Nkrumah.[494] This defeat proved only temporary. In December 1958, delegates to the first All African Peoples' Conference endorsed Fanon's call for armed struggle.[495] That same month, the UN finally adopted the resolution, which had been repeatedly introduced by the Afro-Asian bloc countries since 1955, calling for the recognition of the Algerian right to self-determination. This resolution, in turn, cleared the way for UN recognition of the Algerian crisis and for joint UNHCR-Red Cross League relief programs for Algeria.[496]

II. THE BONN–ALGERIA CONNECTION

The Algerian war presented diplomatic opportunities for both German states. To improve their positions on the global stage, however, governments in both states had to manage both pro-Algerian popular mobilization and a slowly evolving international constellation. In West Germany, both the Adenauer administration and all the major political parties were keen to ensure that the Franco-Algerian conflict did not spill over into the country's streets and that the Algerians living there did not engage in political activity that would disrupt relations with their western neighbor.[497] This became more difficult in April 1957, when the FLN moved its European headquarters from Paris to Düsseldorf to escape surveillance and harassment by the French police. The FLN also set up an unofficial representative in the Tunisian embassy in Bonn, and FLN operatives resided in the country with full knowledge of the Bonn government. Not only was West Germany a haven from the French police; the country also provided ready access to the socialist countries of Eastern Europe, which were an early source of humanitarian aid to the FLN. West Germany was also an important conduit of arms. Although the Occupation Statute had been lifted in 1955, the Federal Republic did not pass its own arms trafficking law until 1961, and the FLN took advantage of this window of opportunity to obtain weapons from West German arms dealers.[498]

The tolerance of FLN operations by the West German government was predicated on the organization's willingness to abstain from indiscreet political activity, especially terrorist attacks against the French, and to control the Algerian community inside West Germany.[499] Moreover, as Siegfried von Nostitz, the West German consul general in Algiers, noted, the 3,000 to 4,000 Algerian refugees living in West Germany – on whom the FLN levied taxes to finance the war against the French – would be a useful bargaining chip after independence because Bonn could then argue that the country had provided asylum to Algerian freedom fighters.[500]

The West German government did not have the same degree of control over its own citizens as it did over the Algerians residing in the country. Galvanized by both the colonial war and the continued French use of Algeria as a nuclear testing ground, an older generation of pacifists and

Trotskyists, as well as others on the left, began to make contact with the Algerians. They were soon followed by the younger members of the Socialist Youth of Germany and the Socialist German Student Union. Unlike the 1968 generation, what Claus Leggewie called "the Algerian generation" (or the 1958ers) was not a homogenous group. However, it did represent the "first breath of internationalism" that assumed much larger proportions among the New Left and the extra-parliamentary opposition in the late 1960s.[501]

The political tactics and forms of practical engagement of these groups differed from those of the older generation. Hans-Jürgen Wischnewski, who at the time was national chair of the West German Young Socialists and who later served as Minister of Economic Cooperation, provided legal assistance and other forms of aid to FLN operatives in West Germany. A number of people participated in the *Kofferträger* (literally, suitcase carriers) network set up by the French philosopher Francis Jeanson in 1957 to smuggle people and aid in and out of France.[502]

Other groups focused on convincing the German soldiers, who made up 75 percent of the 30,000 to 40,000 French Foreign Legion troops fighting in Algeria, to defect.[503] In this area, the activists worked hand in hand with the FLN and its military wing, the National Liberation Army (ALN), which had set up an underground network to help these soldiers escape from Algeria. By December 1962, the organization had helped repatriate more than 4,100 legionnaires – including approximately 2,800 Germans.[504]

Other activists focused on counteracting what they considered to be bias toward France in the West German media. Following the example set by Jeanson, they engaged in the arduous labor of collecting materials to document the conflict and then disseminating this information to the West German public to prove both the brutal nature of French counterinsurgency and the significance of the Algerian war for West German democracy. In September 1958, the Cologne-based Action Group of the Friends of Algeria published the first issue of its newsletter, *Free Algeria*, in which it criticized the West German government and the mass media for refusing to take a position on the Algerian conflict, arguing that silence amounted to tacit support for France's "dirty war." The editorial likened the French use of terror, torture, and concentration camps to the tactics used by the Nazis. In its call for solidarity with the Algerian liberation movement, the group reminded readers that "all progressive people in the Federal Republic share the responsibility of paying off the blood debt of the German Legionnaires through public solidarity with the liberation movement."[505]

By contrast, the SPD distanced itself from Algerian cause and reprimanded members of its youth organization for their pro-Algerian activities.[506] Only a small number of SPD representatives to the Bundestag, including Wischnewski, Peter Blachstein, and Hellmut Kalbitzer, supported the Algerians.[507] However, engagement in the Algerian cause moved some members of the Social Democratic youth organization to attack the party's political lethargy and what they regarded as the careerist opportunism of many party members. In April 1958, the Young Socialists called on their elders to take seriously their abstract principle of solidarity with the oppressed, and the following month they smuggled a number of Algerian freedom fighters into the national party congress in order to protest party policy. The Young Socialists also formed transnational alliances with their counterparts in other countries, who also clashed with their elders over the Algerian conflict. For example, on May Day 1958 West German and Austrian Young Socialists simultaneously staged small pro-Algerian rallies in Cologne and Vienna. In August 1959, the German and Austrian groups, including Wischnewski, collaborated to stage a pro-FLN event on World Refugee Day in Vienna.[508]

Although only a small number of West Germans actively protested against the French war in Algeria, they chose their targets well. For example, when Adenauer and President Charles de Gaulle met on November 26, 1958, in the town of Bad Kreuznach, a gray Volkswagen with the banner "Freedom for Algeria" cruised through the town. It attracted the attention of the 100 reporters who had gathered there to cover the summit, and a French journalist scuffled with German FLN supporters when he tried to rip the banner from the car.[509] In 1959, the national committee of the Young Socialists urged its local affiliates to organize protests against the Algerian war on International Human Rights Day. Taking up this call, Walmot Falkenberg, who chaired the Young Socialist group in Frankfurt and who served as a *Kofferträger*, distributed to Christmas shoppers a pamphlet contrasting the West German media's outlandish attentiveness to the trivial tribulations of the Persian princess Soraya with its neglect of widespread human rights violations by the French in Algeria. He also questioned whether French tactics in Algeria were compatible with the Occidental traditions and values for which the French were ostensibly fighting.[510]

As a growing body of literature on the New Left and the events of 1968 demonstrate, the encounter with Third World national liberation movements played a catalytic role shaping the consciousness of the 1968 generation.[511] West German activism on behalf of the Algerians needs to be understood as a first step by the younger generation away from both the paternalism of the Adenauer era and the Atlantic alliance that formed the bedrock of Adenauer's foreign policy. In this respect, it represents an important neglected chapter in the prehistory of the West German New Left.[512] With the discovery of the Third World, as Leggewie noted, "the door of the Federal Republic, with its provincial consciousness, was opened a bit and its 'moral schizophrenia' revealed."[513]

III. THE BERLIN–ALGERIAN CONNECTION

"The Real Germany for Algerians Is the GDR"[514]

The French counterinsurgency measures described earlier made it very difficult for Algerian refugees and the National Liberation Army to obtain medicine and medical care. In July 1956, the French army captured three female nurses serving in the National Liberation Army. Three months later, a female pediatrician was arrested for traveling from Algiers to the Kabyle maquis to care for the sick and wounded. To compensate for the acute shortage of doctors and nurses, crash courses were set up in some refugee camps to provide emergency training for nurses and auxiliary healthcare workers. In 1956–7, a large number of young Algerian women joined the National Liberation Army, and, after completing such a course, they worked as nurses for the organization.[515] Figure 5.2 shows Algerian Red Crescent nurses giving vaccinations to ALN soldiers. However, trained professionals remained in short supply, and the care provided to soldiers was primitive. As Alistair Horne has noted, the facilities that passed for hospitals

would generally be sited deep in the interior of dense forests, well camouflaged from the air, near a clean stream. The wounded would be scattered about in rough shelters, lying on straw matting on the ground, with the rare mattresses reserved for only the most serious cases. Drugs and medicaments, more precious than gold, would be concealed in safe caches some distance from the "hospital," so as not to fall into enemy hands in the event of the whole encampment being forced to strike camp and move, dragging the wounded with them.[516]

These French restrictions gave the East Germans and other socialist countries the opportunity to demonstrate their solidarity with the Algerians. In the summer of 1957, shortly after East Germany sent its first load of medical equipment to Tangier, the vice president of the ARC asked the East German Red Cross (DRK) for a portable X-ray machine. Ten days later, the ARC Central Committee asked the East Germans to send

FIGURE 5.2 Algerian Red Crescent nurses giving vaccinations to Algerian Liberation Army soldiers (late 1950s).
Source: Gouvernement provisoire de la République Algérienne, Ministère de l'Information Courtesy of Bundesarchiv Bild Y2-1582/00.

orthopedic aid for amputees, whom French-owned prosthetic firms refused to fit. In response to these requests, the health workers' union collected money to buy an ambulance worth 25,000 marks.[517] But getting such solidarity shipments (Figure 5.3) to the right people was complicated and risky. The East Germans had to find ships that were traveling to Morocco or Tunisia without stopping in France, and there was always the chance en route that the French might seize any goods destined for the FLN or the ALN.[518] Moreover, such ships were not always available. In February 1958, for example, forty-three crates of medical supplies had to be flown from Prague, where they had arrived by truck, via Brussels to Tripoli and then from there to Tunis. In this instance, the most valuable cargo – the ambulance – had to be left behind. After a lengthy delay, the ambulance was eventually shipped on a vessel sailing under the West German flag.

East Germany, together with Yugoslavia and Czechoslovakia, agreed to provide medical treatment, prostheses, and occupational training to Algerian soldiers who had been wounded in the fighting, but who were otherwise unable to secure treatment because of the restrictions imposed

FIGURE 5.3 East German solidarity shipment for Algerian refugees in Tunisia.
Source: Gouvernement provisoire de la République Algérienne, Ministère de l'Information Courtesy of Bundesarchiv, Bild Y2-1586/00.

by the French. At least nineteen amputees and five Algerians suffering from tuberculosis had already been sent to East Germany in early 1959.[519] The biggest East German initiative in this area was the fall 1960 decision by the Free Trade Unions (FDGB) to bring fifty wounded fighters to East Germany, along with ten FLN supporters, who were suffering from tuberculosis, but who could care for the wounded men during the trip.[520]

Like many other socialist states, the East German government initially relied on the official ideology of socialist internationalism in the struggle against capitalism and imperialism to forge connections with the leaders of anticolonial movements. However, these ideas were already seriously compromised as a basis for regime legitimacy at home, and they needed to be translated into more practical policies in order to meet the immediate needs of these movements. Maimed bodies, which could function as signifiers of capitalism and imperialism, could also, thanks to the medico-scientific expertise of the East Germans, be transformed into political support abroad and then, hopefully, into greater legitimacy at home. For example, in 1959 the popular health magazine *Alles für deine Gesundheit* (Everything for Your Health) published an article entitled "Fraternal Solidarity with the People of Algeria," which detailed the medicine and medical supplies the East Germans had provided to the Algerians. The article also reproduced pictures of injured and amputated Algerian bodies, noting proudly that these victims were being treated in East German hospitals.[521]

The East Germans were eager to put a face on the stilted proclamations of solidarity that continuously circulated within the socialist bloc. In 1957, for example, the faculty, employees, and students of the Dresden Technical University, who were inspired by their own achievements and the success of Sputnik, decided to sponsor the treatment of one Algerian amputee. Asked to propose one "patriot" to receive this honor, the Algerian Red Crescent selected 27-year-old Ahmed Adaris and sent his photo and personal information to the Germans.[522] No one knows whether Adaris was a real person or how authentic this information was. However, this is beside the point. The effect was to bring the face of Algeria closer to home, at least for a while, and to give a more tangible form to the otherwise abstract idea of socialist solidarity.

These initiatives were part of a broader effort to make solidarity with Third World national liberation movements one of the central elements of East German national identity and foreign policy (see, for example, Figure 5.4). The "Ten Commandments of Socialist Morality and Ethics" included a commitment to international solidarity and a willingness to combat "revisionism, repression and exploitation of other peoples, participation in imperialist colonial politics in all of its forms."[523] The socialist country promised to support the Africans in their struggle against imperialism and racism and presented the Ghanaian government with a fully equipped mobile clinic as a token of of their solidarity with African liberation movements.[524] The FDGB also became increasingly involved in solidarity activities for the region. An FDGB delegation – headed by its chair Herbert Warnke – visited Ghana and Guinea in 1960, and in that year alone the organization transferred two million marks to the newly created Fund for Solidarity with National Movements in African States. It also regularly subsidized the East German Committee for Solidarity with the Peoples of Africa.[525] These activities permitted East Germany to build bridges to Africa without running afoul of the Hallstein doctrine or forcing the Africans to choose between Bonn and Berlin.

In December 1959, the SED Central Committee established the Working Group for the Struggle Against Neocolonialism. The group's

FIGURE 5.4 "The socialist world system is so firmly established, that the wheel of history cannot be turned back in any country ... and it is still turning [forward]" (undated).
Source: Zentralkomitee der Sozialistischen Einheitspartei Deutschlands, Abteilung Agitation und Propaganda. Courtesy of Deutsches Historisches Museum, Berlin PLI04624.

1960 guidelines declared national liberation movements to be "the most important allies of the socialist camp." On the one hand, these guidelines committed the East Germans to the struggle against neocolonialism, especially that emanating from West Germany. In the words of the working group, "the fight against West German neocolonialism in all of its forms is for the GDR a national and international duty and imperative necessity. *Without this fight can there be any effective support for the peoples fighting for national independence?* [emphasis added] Through it we help the peoples of the former colonized and national liberation movement to recognize the danger of West German neocolonialism and to protect themselves from it."[526] On the other hand, the guidelines also made it clear that the proper understanding of this global dynamic would have to culminate in the diplomatic recognition of East Germany by these countries. However, in so arguing, the East German doctrine elided the possibility that the aims of the two partners might not perfectly coincide – that is, that the East German people might not understand their support for the Algerians in the same way as the government, or that Algerians themselves might not equate the struggle against colonial rule with the struggle for socialism in the same way as the East Germans.

National liberation movements in Africa provided the occasion for a host of East German propaganda initiatives.[527] During the Suez crisis, East Germany organized a Committee for Friendly Aid for Egypt, in part to deflect public attention from its support for the Soviet invasion of Hungary. And when the French arrested Ahmed Ben Bella and other FLN leaders in October 1956, East German protesters demanded their release. The East German Red Cross also complained to the League of National Red Cross Societies about violations of the human rights of the Algerians by France and West Germany and equated these actions with the persecution of French Jews by the Nazi and Vichy regimes.

In addition to mounting their own broadsides, East Germans helped the FLN produce its own propaganda material. Not only did Algerian Red Crescent officials carry money to buy medicine when they traveled to East Germany, but they also brought photographs documenting torture by the French, aerial bombing, and the forced resettlement of Algerians into barbed-wired camps.[528] The FLN also sent Arabic-language documents and pamphlets to East Germany to be translated;[529] the East Germans trained Algerians for radio jobs – as broadcast editors, announcers, and technicians – and as cameramen; and in March 1961 Radio Berlin International, the East German international broadcast service, began to broadcast – in Maghrebi, French, and German – a special program for the people of Algeria.[530]

East Germany's *cinéma moudjahid*

The FLN relied on moving pictures to mobilize support for Algerian independence. Because France denied Algerians access to film-processing labs, the FLN depended primarily on Egypt, Czechoslovakia, and East Germany for help producing its propaganda films.[531] East German state film studio DEFA provided technical assistance on films about the Algerian resistance fighters. One good example of this *cinéma moudjahid* is the 1958 film *Algérie en flammes* (*Algeria in Flames*). For the first time, this 25-minute documentary made available to the world moving images of National Liberation Army soldiers and their struggles in the Aurès mountains. The film was produced by the French filmmaker René Vautier (who on this film worked under the alias Willi Müller) together with the Algerian film production collective that he had set up within the National

Liberation Army.[532] DEFA provided post-production assistance for the film, and it then produced 800 copies of the final print, which the FLN then distributed around the world in German, French, and Arabic.[533] Although the film contained many scenes of young Algerian women in military fatigues, the women depicted as soldiers in many propaganda films and photographs were actually nurses. The Algerians hoped that such images would reinforce the legitimacy of their cause and counteract the French propaganda, which depicted Algerian militants as a terrorist fringe group.[534]

East German films frequently focused on the baneful role of West Germans serving in the French Foreign Legion in Algeria – and on the corrupting and often fateful consequences of such service.[535] The most famous propaganda film on the service of West Germans in the French Foreign Legion in Algeria was *Escape from Hell* (*Flucht aus der Hölle*), broadcast in East Germany as a television miniseries in October 1960.[536] In the film, a young West German named Hans Röder (played by Armin Mueller-Stahl), who had served in the legion for three years, decides to desert. With help from the Algerian Liberation Army and the FLN, he escapes to Tunis, where he witnesses the assassination of his guide by the Red Hand, the anti-FLN terrorist group linked to the French intelligence services. Back home in West Germany, Röder and his fiancée are pursued by the Red Hand, and they only find lasting safety when they flee to East Germany.

When a high official of the ICRC visited East Germany in July 1957, the vice president of the East German Red Cross noted that it was "sobering" to see how many Germans were participating in the bloody suppression of the Algerian struggle for freedom, and this experience led him to insist that the East German Red Cross had a "special obligation" to aid Algerian victims. On January 2, 1958, the National Council of the National Front of Democratic Germany appealed to German legionnaires: "With the help of the Algerian national liberation movement, come to the German Democratic Republic, the fatherland of workers, the nursery of freedom, democracy and socialism in Germany."[537] The mirror image of such solidaristic reasoning is shown in Figure 5.5, which seeks to associate German legionnaires with Western imperialism.

Franco-German collaboration in the exploitation of the oil and gas fields in the Algerian Sahara was also an inviting target for East German propaganda seeking to highlight what they regarded as the continuities of capitalist imperialism in the two countries. In addition, when French

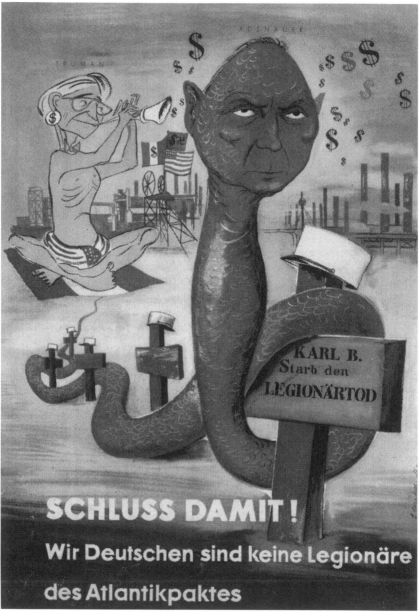

FIGURE 5.5 "Enough! We Germans are not Legionnaires of the Atlantic Pact."
This propaganda poster shows Truman, dressed as a snake charmer, trying to use
American wealth to entice West Germans – symbolized here by a snake with
Adenauer's face – into supporting American, French, and West German
capitalism.
Source: Zentralkomitee der Sozialistischen Einheitspartei Deutschlands, Abteilung
Agitation und Propaganda. Courtesy of Deutsches Historisches Museum, Berlin
P61/644.

plans to test their own atomic bomb in the Algerian Sahara came to light in the summer of 1959, the East Germans supported African protests against the plan and charged the Federal Republic with the desire to "bind the Africans to colonial dependence and to utilize the African territories to prepare for war."[538] When the erection of the Berlin Wall in August 1961 threatened to do serious damage to the country's reputation abroad, the East German government responded by intensifying its propaganda efforts. It dispatched more delegates from mass organizations to Africa and invited more Algerian freedom fighters, students, and officials to East Germany.[539] As part of this campaign, the FDGB, the German Women's Association, and the Free German Youth (FDJ) sent tools, machines, and sewing machines to train young Algerians in refugee camps.[540]

The East German documentary film *Allons enfants...pour l'Algérie,* which premiered three months after the construction of the Wall, documented both the imperialist policies of France and West Germany and their joint interest in nuclear weapons research and the exploitation of Saharan oil and gas fields, which the East Germans regarded as the bedrock of the Franco-German alliance. By making the viewer feel the threats posed by the capitalist West, the film justified the erection of the "anti-fascist protective wall." The film then foregrounded East German aid to the Algerians. The title of this middle section was named after Aïcha Bouzar, a 25-year-old National Liberation Army nurse who cared for Algerian refugees in Tunisia. The last segment, entitled *Vive L'Algérie algérienne!,* projected on the screen the unity between the Algerians living in France and the Algerians in the Maghreb in their fight for freedom.

Anti-French sentiment in East Germany rose sharply after the massacre of hundreds of Algerians by the Paris police on October 17, 1961.[541] In addition to holding rallies, the East Germans also invited Bouzar to attend the November premiere of the film in Leipzig. They also offered medical treatment to Djamila Bouhired, a female militant (shown in *The Battle of Algiers*), whom the French had tortured and sentenced to death, when she was released from prison on the eve of the Algerian independence (Figure 5.6).[542] This wave of cultural diplomacy actions crested when fifteen wounded veterans of the National Liberation Army arrived at Schönefeld airport on December 7, 1961, where they received a hero's welcome from dignitaries of the Ministries of Health and Foreign Affairs, the president of the German Red Cross, representatives of the Solidarity Committee and the Free German Youth, and a number of young Algerians studying in East Germany.[543]

FIGURE 5.6 Third World students in East Germany demonstrating for the release of Djamila Bouhired, an Algerian militant physician, who had been imprisoned and tortured for treating wounded Algerians (April 1959).
Source: Zentralbild Schmidt. Courtesy of Bundesarchiv 183-61747-0001.

"Last Stop the Soviet Zone?" German State Socialism and International Solidarity

In January 1959, an article appeared in the newspaper of the West German public service workers union under the title "Last Stop the Soviet Zone? A Young Algerian Vainly Seeking Help in the Federal Republic." This was a human interest story about two young Algerian men, who were neither terrorists nor criminals; they simply did not want to be governed by the French. However, because West German immigration officials regarded them as French citizens, they were not eligible for political asylum or social assistance, and they could be deported for political activity or poverty. The only way out of their predicament seemed to be to immigrate to East Germany.[544] In fact, in November 1958, the East German government announced its decision to grant asylum to Algerian refugees, and by the end of the year a total of eighty-seven Algerians had arrived in East Germany.[545]

While the SED controlled East German aid to Algeria, the German Red Cross, which was also responsible for the actual purchase and transportation of this aid, served as a front organization to maintain the official appearance of humanitarian neutrality. The lion's share of the financing for Algerian aid came from the FDGB.[546] However, the Algerian Red Crescent was not simply a passive recipient of aid; it also coordinated humanitarian assistance among the socialist donor countries. For example, the organization requested nonmedical supplies, such as shoes, textiles, and electric sewing machines, from Czechoslovakia.[547] Sewing machines and textiles were especially important; although European-style clothing was often donated to the Algerians, many Algerian women preferred traditional women's clothing, which then had to be fabricated on site.

The SED saw the Algerian conflict as an opportunity to pursue its goal of gaining diplomatic recognition, and its support for the FLN was a calculated wager that such a demonstration of goodwill would build relationships with the militants who could be expected to hold important positions in the future government of independent Algeria. The problem was that, at the time, the Soviet desire to settle the German question, together with its distrust of Algerian nationalists, led the Soviet Union to keep its distance from the Algerian conflict. This provided an ample opportunity for China, which had been openly supporting the FLN since 1955, to criticize Moscow for ignoring this obvious injustice and thus in effect taking "the side of French imperialism."[548] This Soviet policy also forced the East German government to keep secret its aid to the Algerians until the end of 1957, when the East German Red Cross informed the League of the Red Cross about its aid to the Algerian Red Crescent.[549]

By going public, the authorities also hoped to mobilize popular support to raise additional funds for Algerian refugees. The German Red Cross launched solidarity actions in collaboration with state-sponsored mass organizations and the media. Collection drives pitted district against district, and radio programs were larded with appeals for donations. When the popular weekly magazine *Wochenpost* announced a fundraising drive for Algeria in 1960, citizens donated more than 250,000 marks, which was used to purchase, among other things, two cars for Algerian orphanages in Morocco.[550] As a result of these actions, the amount of aid they provided increased sharply, and a consignment worth a quarter million marks was shipped to Tunis in early 1958.

Between 1957 and 1962, the radio broadcasting service, which organized solidarity concerts for Algerians, received more than 100,000 letters condemning French racism and terror in Algeria.[551] These ritualized expressions of solidarity were an important means for educating citizens of the new state to speak the language of communism, and the East German authorities hoped that this activism would also help legitimate the regime and serve its diplomatic interests. Yet they always worried that mass political activism would take on a life of its own and that the rhetoric of self-determination might boomerang and destabilize the regime. This is why the government relied on state-sponsored mass organizations, such as the Free Trade Unions, the FDJ, the Committee for Solidarity with the Peoples of Africa, and the German-Arab Society, to collect relief goods and organize protest rallies.

The East Germans may have sympathized with oppressed Algerians living far away, but relations closer to hand were not always cordial. In 1958, the local FDJ committee at the VEB Sachsenring Automobilwerke in Zwickau, the producer of the Trabant, East Germany's most widely used passenger car, raised money to donate several ambulances to the Algerians. Two years later, however, the same factory became the scene of tension. Nine Algerians and two Moroccans had been promised training for skilled jobs there, but the German workers complained that the North Africans lacked the necessary discipline and skills and, instead, assigned the men unskilled work. Although Germans and Algerians had frequent confrontations over job performance, qualifications, and payment, the complaints of the North Africans invariably fell on deaf ears.[552] Nevertheless, and despite the official character of solidarity campaigns, there was also evidence of genuine grassroots support for national liberation struggles. For example, when an Algerian youth organization called on the world's youth for humanitarian help in 1960, some 450 students at a Leipzig clothing factory (VEB Leipziger Bekleidungswerke) worked more than 3,000 hours of overtime and raised 8,000 marks to support 170 Algerian orphans.[553]

Such outpourings of sympathy also reflected the transformation of East German society in the late 1950s and early 1960s. In 1957, East Germany could not send food and clothing to the Algerian Red Crescent because the country was itself suffering from shortages of these goods. However, around the turn of the 1960s the government began to devote more resources to the production of consumer goods, and the ability to purchase basic consumer goods put East German citizens in a position where they could afford to give away used items such as shoes and clothes.[554] East Germany also began to offer its workers a way to combine humanitarianism and tourism. In 1960, the FDGB acquired its first vacation ship for worker-citizens, the *Völkerfreundschaft*, and the following year the ship sailed from Rostock to Tunis.[555] On board were more than 500 vacationing workers, as well as a film production team from DEFA and the *Deutscher Fernsehfunk*. After landing in Tunisia, the team drove to the Algerian border to film a refugee camp. Several of these films were released in 1961: *Ahmed weine nicht, Mit Kombi und Camping durch Tunesien, Sorah und Ali,* and *Allons ... enfants de l'Algerie.*[556]

The authorities tried to use mass participation in these actions as evidence of popular commitment to building socialism both at home and around the globe. The president of the East German Red Cross claimed that this participation proved that "the spirit of true humanism, the authentic love of peace, and the will to understanding among the peoples of the world" were alive and well in East Germany, and he was certain that these solidarity actions had enhanced the international reputation of the country.[557] According to one estimate, between June 1957 and December 1962, East Germany provided 11.7 million marks to the Algerians (including the cost of medical care in East Germany for forty injured and sick Algerians, technical training, subsidized university study for more than 100 Algerians, and occupational training for Algerian workers).[558] Once Algerian independence became a possibility, more attention was paid to Algerian refugees. And, in December 1960, East Germany sent aid worth 78,700 marks to the Tunisian Red Crescent (rather than to the ARC) to be used for international refugee relief.[559]

IV. LITTLE MAN, WHAT NOW? POST-INDEPENDENCE ALGERIA AND THE TWO GERMANYS

By the time Algeria gained its independence in 1962, the field of humanitarian aid to the country had become much more crowded than it had been only five years before, when East Germany had been one of the few non-Arab countries to support the FLN. When it had become clear that the French were not going to be able to maintain their position in Algeria, the Western countries that in deference to the French had blocked direct assistance to Algerian refugees began to rethink their position and provide aid through the International Red Cross.[560]

On the eve of independence, one of the top priorities for international humanitarian organizations was to repatriate Algerian refugees living in Tunisia and Morocco, along with more than two million internally displaced persons, whose homes had been burned and whose lands had lain unattended for years.[561] Immediately after the country gained its independence, a commission comprising representatives of the UNHCR, the French High Commissioner in Algeria, and the Algerian Provisional Government was established to oversee the repatriation of Algerian refugees. With the exception of one Indian, the executive staff of the commission exclusively comprised representatives from Western countries, including a West German deputy chair. The on-site personnel of the League of National Red Cross Societies, who were responsible for coordinating and distributing the relief flowing in from around the world, were also predominantly Westerners. Western influence was further reinforced by the growing presence of humanitarian organizations based in Western Europe and the United States (including the Church World Service, the London Aid Committee for Algerian Refugees, and Cimade, a French aid organization for refugees and migrants). Tunisian Red Crescent officials felt bitter about being suddenly marginalized in their own country, as did the socialist countries that had provided so much moral and material support long before the Western countries evinced any real interest in the Algerian problem.

Nor did East Germany's support for the FLN and the ALN pay off as handsomely as the SED had hoped. Colonel Houari Boumédienne, defense minister (and former ALN chief of staff), was grateful to East Germany for the aid that it had provided. In fact, his open sympathy toward the socialist state led the West German consulate general to confess that "the time is past when, as a matter of course, we could claim to be the only legitimate German state. Now we have to defend ourselves." However, Ben Bella and the FLN were more favorably inclined to the West, and the West Germans were undoubtedly relieved when the post-independence civil war in Algeria led to the purge of many of the military officers with whom the East Germans had built close ties.[562]

Another factor behind the post-independence marginalization of the East Germans was the increasing amount of moral, military, and material assistance provided by China and Cuba. China recognized the Algerian Provisional Government immediately after it was established (and two full years ahead of the Soviet Union), and it opened a consulate in Oujda, Morocco in 1959. The first shipment of Chinese aid landed at Casablanca in April 1959, and Mao also agreed to train Algerian officers.[563] Cuba was not far behind. In December 1961, a Cuban ship unloaded a first shipment of military supplies at Casablanca; on the return trip to Havana, it carried seventy-six war-wounded and twenty refugee children, who were to attend school in Cuba. Aid from Cuba and China, the practical embodiment of South–South solidarity, diminished the importance of East German aid. However, these conflicts of interest did not become manifest until the end of the 1960s, and we will return to this question in the course of our discussion of aid to Zanzibar and Tanganyika in Chapter 9.

The scope and nature of Algeria's humanitarian problems changed with independence. The country's medical infrastructure had been already weakened during the war. Now Algeria faced a catastrophic shortage of general practitioners and specialists, especially in rural areas, as all but 400 of the 2,000 French doctors who had been practicing in the country joined the more than one million *pieds-noirs* who returned to France at independence. The subsequent departure of 200 French military doctors then left the country with only 200 physicians.[564] A brand new, fully equipped 130-bed hospital in Rouiba, near Algiers, had no surgeons; much of the high-tech medical equipment imported from the United States and West Germany remained unused; and, despite the staggering number of handicapped veterans who needed orthopedic limbs and rehabilitation, the only prosthetic workshop in the country was at a clinic in the town of Tixeraine that was owned by a West German oil company.[565]

The dire state of the country's healthcare system posed a serious challenge to the administration of President Ben Bella, who had pledged to take care of the veterans who had fought for the country's independence. On Christmas day in 1962, the Algerian government made an urgent appeal to foreign doctors to come work in Algeria. Even before this appeal, however, the United States and the socialist countries of Eastern Europe, as well as Egypt and Saudi Arabia, dispatched physicians and other healthcare workers to the country. In July 1962, before formal diplomatic relations had been established, twenty-six Yugoslav doctors and nurses arrived in Algeria. They worked at hospitals in Tizi Ouzou and Algiers and set up an orthopedic workshop. A Bulgarian team arrived soon thereafter to work with Russian doctors at the tuberculosis hospital and sanatorium in Tizi Ouzou. In addition, Lebanese and Egyptian doctors also came to help.[566] The Castro government dispatched its first overseas medical mission after Ben Bella's visit to Cuba at the time of the 1962 Cuban missile crisis. Despite the exodus of doctors from Cuba itself, in May 1963, Castro sent a medical team of fifty-five men and women to Algeria, along with his minister of health, and a second team of sixty-one Cubans arrived the following year. Relations between the two countries grew even closer when Che Guevera traveled to Algeria for the first celebration of Algerian independence.[567] Meanwhile, the Chinese had sent fourteen physicians in May 1963, while the Soviets financed the construction of a hospital and agreed to pay the salaries of the medical staff for six months.[568]

These developments, together with the growing presence of the Third World medical missions, brought to the surface latent conflicts over the future shape of the Algerian healthcare system. The French system was organized around the provision of clinical care in hospitals. However, the Algerian Health Ministry wanted to move away from the French system, reduce the number of hospital beds, and expand ambulatory care. The Algerian Red Crescent was particularly interested in obtaining mobile dispensaries that could be attached to policlinics outside the larger towns.

Soviet bloc doctors working in Algeria were concerned about competition from the West, as well as from Cuba and China, and they feared that the individualist materialism prevailing in hospitals run by Western-dominated, international humanitarian organizations, combined with the inflow of aid money from Western governments, would thwart such progressive reform plans. They also worried about the growing number of Western pharmaceutical firms trying to gain a foothold in the Algerian market. In one display of goodwill, the West German Bayer Corporation donated 100,000 marks worth of medicine to the health ministry. To signal the importance of the gift, a number of high-level Algerian officials were on hand to receive the medicine, and the actual transfer was covered by public relations personnel from the West German embassy.[569] To counter these trends, the Czech Red Cross and the East European doctors working in Algeria all argued that the Soviet bloc should send more physicians and healthcare workers to the country.[570]

These tensions were also reflected in the competition between East and West Germany in Algeria. In December 1962, Algerian officials asked both the East and West German governments for medical assistance. As the Algerian Red Crescent wrote to the East German Red Cross, "since our country has inherited from rotten colonialism nothing but misery and tears...we are forced to send a new SOS for more help..., especially because of an alarming situation of our population."[571] East Germany promptly sent a large shipment of aid, including medicine and soap. To make sure that the gift was repaid with the proper political loyalty, officials of the East German trade mission in Algiers personally handed it over to the Algerian government.

The West German ambassador to Algeria also encouraged the Foreign Office to act: "We should most definitely take advantage of the opportunity, which presents itself here, to take over a humanitarian task that will most certainly have a positive impact on our efforts to improve our international reputation."[572] Although the Adenauer government presented the Algerians with a mobile clinic to commemorate the first anniversary of independence and agreed to pay a German physician to operate it, this gift quickly became a public relations disaster. As the ambassador reported to Bonn, this represented the "most unpleasant episode in the history of German development aid for Algeria." To begin with, the company that manufactured the mobile clinic cheated the government by sending a used vehicle, rather than a new one. Then the physician hired to staff the vehicle was fired for embezzling development aid funds and other misbehavior. The doctor who replaced him turned out to be even more disastrous.[573] An unrepentant Nazi, he spent more time in bed drunk or reading porn than practicing medicine, and he, too, embezzled funds to pay for his vices. Even when he was sober enough to work, many patients would have been better off if he had stayed home. Not only did he misdiagnose many cases and provide treatment that fell well below the standard of care. He was also homosexual, and he used his position to abuse some of his male patients, while many others simply refused to see the "pervert," as they called him.[574] Despite all of this, the West German government was able to avoid a scandal because German marks and medical supplies were an offer that the Algerians could not refuse; the West Germans sweetened the deal with an offer to equip a hospital in Tizi Ouzou and to staff it with West German medical personnel, half of whose salaries would be paid by the West German government.

In an attempt to upstage the West Germans, the East German government made an even more lavish offer to construct a policlinic, fully equip its departments of internal medicine, gynecology, pediatrics, and surgery, and pay (for at least the first few years) the salaries of ten East German medical professionals to work there. Recognizing that the critical condition of the public health system in Algeria made medical aid all the more valuable, the SED leadership hoped that such a generous offer would nudge the Algerian government toward formal diplomatic recognition.

But the East Germans faced an uphill battle to persuade the Algerians to accept this offer.[575] In May 1963, an East German Red Cross delegation traveled to Algeria to undertake further negotiations on this politically and symbolically important project. The proposed hospital was to be outfitted only with East German equipment; medicine was to come only from East Germany; the hospital would be staffed (at least initially) only with East German medical personnel; and the specifically East German character of the hospital was to be clearly reflected in its name. The German delegates were directed to emphasize the official "character of East Germany as a socialist, anti-imperialist state" and its desire to strengthen its "fraternal solidarity and friendship to all young and anti-imperialist nation states."[576] The delegation was also to seize every opportunity to express the East German outrage over the recent French nuclear test in the Sahara and their opposition to the "neo-colonialist endeavors of West Germany and Bonn's complicity in this explosion through a war pact with de Gaulle."[577]

Although the delegation met with the health minister, months passed without a response from the Algerian government. In a last attempt to move things forward, the East German health ministry drafted a bilateral agreement and sent it to the Algerians. In January 1964, however, the Algerian government finally rejected the offer, in all likelihood due to West German pressure.[578] After two years of negotiations, the East Germans finally gave up. Fortuitously, a socialist revolution took place in Zanzibar that same month, and, as we shall see in Chapter 9, the East Germans decided to present their fully equipped policlinic to the Zanzibaris instead.[579]

V. THE CONGO CONFLICT: HUMANITARIAN AID, GLOBAL GOVERNANCE, AND NATIONAL SOVEREIGNTY

Patrice Lumumba, the United Nations, and the Global Cold War

The final stage of the Algerian war, the entanglement of the two German states with national liberation movements, and the dynamics of the global humanitarian regime cannot be fully understood without taking into consideration both the decolonization crisis and humanitarian intervention in the Congo from 1960 to 1961. On the eve of independence, about 95,000 Europeans were living in the Congo, including approximately 20,000 whose safety and needs were guaranteed by the secessionist regime in the mineral-rich Katanga province. Many of these Europeans fled to neighboring Angola and Rwanda-Burundi, and the original goal of international humanitarian operations in the Congo was to assist these Europeans. Leading officials of the international aid organizations working in Algeria, including Jean-Pierre Robert-Tissot, the director of the Relief Bureau of the League of Red Cross Societies, and Edward Reinhard, of the League's Algerian refugee relief group in Morocco, were promptly reassigned to "European refugee" relief operation in the Congo. However, this refugee crisis was over almost before it began, and most of the Europeans had returned to the Congo by the middle of 1961. It was the military intervention by Belgium and the United States to protect European, especially Belgian, nationals, who feared reprisals from the native population, that fundamentally transformed both the nature of the crisis and the goals of the international humanitarian organizations operating in the country.

Humanitarian aid programs in the Congo were subject to conflicting political forces, which operated at different levels and pushed the UN, the League of Red Cross Societies, its member states, and the various factions fighting for control of the Congolese government in different directions. The centrifugal forces resulting from the breakdown of the central government were strengthened by the regional distribution of political loyalties, and Moïse Tshombe, the leader of Katanga province, alternated between bids for national power and threats of secession. These political conflicts were overlaid by ethnic conflicts both within the country (between the Luluas and the Balubas) and across the border (between the Hutus and Tutsis in neighboring Rwanda-Burundi). They were further complicated by the influx of refugees and guerrillas from neighboring Angola, which was in the midst of its own fight for independence from Portugal; they were given a peculiar intensity by the desire – particularly on the part of Western mining interests – to control the country's vast mineral resources; and each of these conflicts was inflected in specific ways by its position in the Cold War geopolitical rivalries that, like underground aquifers, flowed through the region.

Conflicts of interest and perspective were no less complex within the aid community itself. Reflecting the political divisions among its members, the UN was divided along multiple axes: between its military and civilian operations, between the New York headquarters and the headquarters of the Congo operation in Léopoldville (now Kinshasa), and between the UN aid officials in Léopoldville and the multinational teams operating in the field. As we shall see, there were also important policy differences between the UN specialized agencies, which, in contrast to Algeria, were deeply involved in the Congo from the very beginning, and the major international humanitarian organizations, especially the League of Red Cross Societies. Here, as in Algeria, the concrete meaning of humanitarian assistance was the product not of universal declarations, but rather of complex political calculations.

Ignoring the root causes, politicians and the media in the West portrayed the Congo crisis as the result of a Soviet conspiracy to take over the world. To accentuate the danger, many observers likened the conflict to a second Korean War in the heart of Africa, and Belgian Minister of State Camille Gutt expressed the hope that the U.S. response would "be as firm as [it had been] in the Korean case."[580] The United States felt that blocking such bilateral assistance was the key to preventing the communists from infiltrating the Congo.[581] This new strategy would make the United Nations a clearinghouse for all international assistance to the Congo. In Cleveland's words, such measures would constitute "intervention by the world community in the name of nonintervention for the purpose of preventing intervention by individual [i.e. communist] countries."[582]

The Security Council resolution of July 1960 prohibited bilateral aid to the Congo and stipulated that all aid go directly to the UN representative in the Congo, not to the Lumumba government or the people of the Congo.[583] Because this policy could not have been enforced without the ability to impose a logistical *cordon sanitaire* on all surface and air routes into the country, the de facto dependence of the UN on the U.S. military to airlift troops, civilian employees, and material assistance from all corners of the world to Léopoldville turned out to be an advantage for the United States. The blockade was further tightened as UN forces closed the airports in Léopoldville and Stanleyville. UN aid restrictions applied to the transfer of knowledge and technology, as well as to scholarships for Congolese students, no matter whether sponsored by governments or NGOs. Citing this policy, the U.S. government voided an agreement between the Lumumba government and the Phelps Stokes Fund, an American philanthropic institution, to bring young African Americans to fill mid-level technical and managerial positions left empty by the departure of the Belgians.[584]

The U.S. policy was unpopular not only among the Lumumbists, who saw it as an affront to national sovereignty. The Soviet Union and many nonaligned states also considered it tantamount to the reintroduction of a UN protectorate over the Congo. Although the Soviets had initially agreed to work through the United Nations, they were soon marginalized by Western-dominated UN programs and organizations. For example, in August 1960 not one of the sixty-five civilians working in the UN Congo administration was from Eastern Europe, and none of the leading positions were held by Africans, who were restricted to subordinate roles.[585]

As a result, the Soviet Union decided to ignore UN policy and deliver food, medicine, vehicles, and other assistance directly to the Congolese central government. As Khrushchev wrote to Lumumba in August, unlike colonial powers past and present, the Soviet Union was providing aid to enable the people of the Congo to appropriate their natural resources for "their own national interests, improve its [sic] well-being, and strengthen the political and economic independence of their homeland."[586] In

August 1960, a Soviet merchant ship arrived in Léopoldville carrying – in addition to 9,000 tons of wheat, 1,000 tons of sugar, and 270,000 cans of condensed milk – twenty doctors and nurses, who were to work directly for the Congolese provincial authorities in Stanleyville, not the United Nations. A Czech team of fifteen doctors and ten nurses arrived at the same time; and within a week, a second Soviet ship arrived carrying 100 trucks, spare parts, a repair shop, and a group of instructors and mechanics.[587]

Although the U.S.–UN policy on international humanitarian aid clearly infringed upon the national sovereignty that the United Nations so vigorously upheld in other contexts, UN Secretary General Dag Hammarskjöld explained in response to Congolese complaints that states dependent on assistance were not fully sovereign:

In this situation spokesmen of the Central Government speak about the assistance rendered by the international community through the UN as if it were an imposition and treat the Organization as if they had all rights and no obligations. They seem to believe that the independence of the Republic of Congo, in the sense of international sovereignty of the state which everybody respects, means independence also in a substantive sense of the word which, in our interdependent world of today, is unreal even for a country living by its own means and able to provide for its own security and administration. A government without financial means is dependent on those who help it to meet its needs...[588]

On September 20, 1960, the UN General Assembly finally voted in favor of a U.S. proposal to create a special fund to serve as the official channel for all aid to the Congo. Belgium, however, immediately violated the spirit of this resolution by agreeing, with U.S. support, to dispatch back to the Congo the personnel it deemed essential to the security and economic life of the country. Many of these Belgian technicians were former military officers who had no sympathy for either Congolese self-rule or UN intervention. They believed that the UN was providing assistance to the communists in the region, and they obstructed UN operations by stealing or hijacking UN vehicles, arresting UN personnel, and denying the UN access to the river transportation vital to transporting troops around the country.[589]

In September 1960, the political situation became more volatile. On September 5, President Kasavubu dismissed Premier Patrice Lumumba and put him under house arrest. Nine days later, with U.S. and Belgian support, Colonel Mobutu Sese Seko, the commander-in-chief of the new Congolese National Army, launched a coup. The mineral-rich provinces of South Kasai and Katanga also declared their secession from the central government in Léopoldville. While the Western powers and the UN supported Mobutu as a bulwark against communism, the Lumumbists set up a rival government in Stanleyville (the capital of Orientale province in the northeast), which was headed by Antoine Gizenga, Lumumba's deputy prime minister. It is beyond the scope of the present study to follow the twists and turns of the Congolese civil war across from the end of 1960 to Mobutu's takeover in 1965, which was supported by the Western powers. Instead, I would like to return to the summer of 1960 to examine in detail the work of German medical assistance missions in the Congo.

Doctors Who Came in from the Cold: The Two Germanys and International Medical Aid to the Congo

Widespread starvation, epidemics, combat-related injuries to both the military and civilian population, torture, and rape were depressingly common motifs in the tangled story of decolonization in Africa. But there was another aspect of this crisis: the collapse of healthcare systems caused by the departure of Western medical professionals at independence. The resulting problems were so severe that even the most outspoken nationalist leaders were forced to retreat from their goal of immediately Africanizing their medical systems. Although events followed such a course in Algeria, Malawi, and Ghana, the largest and most publicized of these crises occurred in the Congo.

In the weeks following independence in the Congo, 560 of the 760 Belgian physicians working in the country departed, and the remaining doctors were either clustered in the larger, safer cities or worked in the clinics operated by the mining firms in Katanga province. That left only one physician for every 50,000 to 100,000 persons in the countryside, depending on location. There was only one native Congolese physician, and he had just returned from his training abroad. Belgian physicians continued to stream out of the country, provincial and district hospitals were deserted, and vaccination and disease prevention programs ground to a halt.[590] The near collapse of the country's public health system also endangered the lives of UN peacekeeping forces and civilian aid workers.

On July 22, 1960, Lumumba asked UN Secretary General Hammarskjöld for emergency medical relief, and WHO Director-General Marcolino Candau immediately relayed this appeal to the ICRC and the Red Cross League.[591] Although the original plan was to provide emergency relief for a three-month period, conditions were so bad that within a week the

International Red Cross issued a second appeal to eighteen additional member countries, including the two German states, Czechoslovakia, and Rumania. Over the course of the following year, some fifty-seven medical teams comprising 168 persons from twenty-three nations served in twenty-six Congolese hospitals.[592] The main goal of the operation was to provide a skeleton staff to fill the gap created by the departure of the Belgians and to keep the Congolese medical system from total collapse. As a rule, a team assigned to a district or provincial hospital was responsible for anywhere from 100,000 to 250,000 persons, and racial tensions often flared between Western physicians and the native Congolese, who had been hired to run these hospitals after the departure of the Belgians.[593]

The two German states and Austria saw the humanitarian crisis in the Congo as an opportunity to burnish international reputations that had been so badly tarnished by World War II. In the words of Austrian Defense Minister Ferdinand Graf, participation in the mission was essential to avoid endangering "the laboriously acquired prestige of our fatherland abroad," and a total of 166 Austrians served in the eastern Congo between 1960 and 1963.[594] Although East Germany remained hobbled by the Hallstein Doctrine, membership in the League of Red Cross Societies allowed the country to participate for the first time in a major international aid action. The departure of the East German team was widely reported by the domestic media, and the minister of health and other dignitaries saw them off at Berlin's Schönefeld airport. The total number of East German healthcare professionals serving in the Congo in 1960–1 was second in size only to that of the Danes. Its size – six medical teams comprising a total of twenty persons – was even more impressive considering that most participating Red Cross societies sent only one team.

Headed by Wolf Weitbrecht, deputy president of the German Red Cross, the first East German medical team consisted of twelve persons, and they brought with them medicine purchased with funds raised through solidarity drives. When they arrived in Léopoldville, East German officials, including Weitbrecht, made a symbolic gesture toward Congolese sovereignty by presenting State Secretary Lumbala with a certificate that formally transferred title to the medicine to the Lumumba government.[595] In this way, the East Germans also made sure the Congolese saw these medical supplies as coming from the socialist part of a divided country, rather than being pooled together with the other donations that were being channeled through the UN.

The East and West German emergency medical teams were assigned to the eastern province of Kivu, whose capital Bukavu was located at the southern tip of Lake Kivu. A Yugoslav medical team was assigned to the Bukavu provincial hospital, and a Swedish team was posted 100 miles further south in Uvira, on the northern end of Lake Tanganyika. After they arrived in Bukavu, however, the East Germans were not allowed to proceed to their destination because the area had not yet been secured by UN troops. Weitbrecht saw this as a blatant attempt to exclude the socialist physicians and diminish their influence, and he complained that "the request for emergency medical relief came from the Congolese central government and from Patrice Lumumba personally, and nowhere was an order for such dependence on the UN troops issued to us."[596]

The West German team was headed by Margaret Hasselmann, a 62-year-old pediatrician with twenty-six years' experience in the Philippines. All three West German doctors had originally been assigned to a hospital in Lubero. However, when they arrived in Goma, on the Congolese-Urundi border, they learned of a plague outbreak in Lubero, and they were forced to remain in Goma until vaccines could be delivered from Léopoldville.[597] The Lubero team finally began work in late September. Just north of Lubero, there was an excellent laboratory for studying plague and leprosy; to judge from his request to extend his tour for an additional year or two, the West German doctor with a strong interest in tropical disease must have enjoyed his work.[598]

The West German team was surprised to see how much better their East German counterparts were prepared. The West German team had been assembled in such a hurry that they had not had time to get their vaccinations, and they had been sent off from Bonn by a Red Cross official with a hope and a prayer. As the West Germans complained, their uniforms looked "tattered and filthy," and they all wished that they had been outfitted as smartly as the East Germans in their blue pants, jackets, and linen shirts: "Even the East German orderlies are better equipped than we are." And once they reached Kivu, they did not have any medicine: "Although we West Germans could still travel into the mountains and diagnose problems, we could not care for the patient."[599]

Much to the chagrin of the West Germans, the East German mission brought with them four tons of medicine and medical supplies that had been donated by the Solidarity Committee with the Peoples of Africa. The West Germans were particularly impressed by the organization of the East Germans. Every crate of medicine was numbered, and its contents carefully inventoried, so that, whenever the West Germans requested a particular drug, the East Germans could simply consult their master list, locate the proper crate, and retrieve the drug. As West Germans complained to the German Red Cross in Bonn, "we have no medicine… Do like the people from the eastern zone and put at least a portion of your aid at our disposal."[600]

Participation in a UN-sponsored mission such as the one in the Congo yielded valuable cultural capital that helped boost the legitimacy of the regime at home. Weitbrecht tried to familiarize the East German public with the mission through a popular account of the team's work, *The Congo: As a Doctor under the Burning Sun.* The book highlighted the country's role in the international aid community by describing the constant interaction with leading officials of the WHO, the International Red Cross, the Congolese government, doctors, and UN peacekeepers from across the world.[601] The book also described the technological achievements of the socialist bloc and the enthusiasm that the passengers all felt flying on a Soviet-designed, Czech-operated Ilyushin II-18, which had won Grand Prix at the Brussels World Expo in 1958. When the "silver bird" crossed the equator, they made a toast "to the equator, to Africa, to Lumumba, to our friendship, to international solidarity!" In such socialist travel literature, the achievements of socialist modernity were often juxtaposed with the poverty resulting from imperialist exploitation, and the team's mood was darkened by the contrast between the shanties, where poor Congolese children played, and the luxurious mansions inhabited by the Belgians.

Weitbrecht's account explained how capitalism and imperialism had brought the Congo, a country that was richly endowed with natural resources, nothing but exploitation, slavery, and "a level of misery that is unimaginable for us."[602] He explained that the Deutsche Bank was a member of the Western mining consortium that played a central role in the country's political conflicts, and he argued that West German imperialism was deeply implicated in the Congo's misfortunes. By way of authentication, Weitbrecht spoke not in his own voice, but in those of UN and International Red Cross officials, foreign doctors working in the region, and Congolese officials, nurses, and workers, as well as European expatriates. Throughout the book such explicitly ideological passages were mixed with lively, colorful portrayals of the landscape, the indigenous people, and their customs.

The West Germans were well aware of recent East German aid and propaganda offensives in Africa. Just prior to independence, the Foreign Office had warned the newly appointed ambassador to the Congo that the entire Eastern bloc was making a major effort to win over the newly independent states in Africa in order to "serve its political and ideological goals."[603] However, mutual suspicion and ideological rivalries notwithstanding, the medical missions from the two German states in Kivu soon found that they could collaborate without undue friction and that mutual assistance was not only mutually beneficial but also necessary for them to achieve their goals in this isolated province on the far eastern border of the country. The two German teams worked closely together until they parted ways to work in different hospitals, and a degree of German–German solidarity developed on the ground.[604]

While the Germans may have found unexpected solidarity, not all of the Congolese greeted their East German benefactors with open arms. For example, the Congolese minister of finance, a devout Catholic, did not hide his antipathy toward communism. On the other hand, Weitbrecht insisted that medicine was independent of politics: "There is no communist or capitalist treatment for malaria; it must be combatted medically according to the most recent advances in medical science." However, he went on to point out that the number of persons who were sick and in need of treatment "depends to be sure on the particular social system, and this choice belongs to the Congolese themselves." The East Germans were also offended by a poster, which showed a world map with the entire socialist bloc encircled in barbed wire, hanging over the main entrance to a Catholic church in Bukavu. Outside the circle, a priest blessed a kneeling female figure, while accompanying text exhorted the viewer to follow God even in need. Weitbrecht asked sarcastically whether the poster was a welcome gift for the team.[605]

In December 1960, three East German replacement teams arrived to work at the hospitals in Kindu, Schabunda, and Mwenga, all in the southern Kivu province.[606] Their arrival coincided with a period of unrest in the region. In late November, Lumumba escaped from house arrest. However, within days Mobutu's forces had recaptured Lumumba, who was tortured and murdered on January 17, 1961. In the brief period between Lumumba's escape and his execution, Antoine Gizenga declared himself the head of the legitimate central government.

With the support of the United States and Belgium, troops under the command of Mobutu and the UN imposed a blockade on Orientale and Kivu provinces, the stronghold of the Gizenga government. Air, land, and river transportation to the region was suspended, communications cut off, and shipments of food and medicine halted; these measures brought the economy of these provinces to the verge of collapse. The United States also bribed the Sudanese into denying overflight and landing rights for

flights to Stanleyville, and the Sudanese government even refused to grant
visas to officials of the Gizenga government, thereby preventing them
from traveling to Cairo.[607] Claire H. Timberlake, the American ambassador to the Congo, was pleased with the effect of blockade: "[B]arring
substantial airborne assistance from Bloc and UAR [United Arab Repub-
lic], which would be most difficult from standpoint of logistics, a solution
in Stanleyville seems fairly near. Economic collapse is predictable in two
to four weeks. There will be a potential violent reaction when the population becomes hungry and out of work."[608]

As Timberlake predicted, these measures led to mass hunger in Kivu
and Orientale provinces; hospitals ran out of medicine and other supplies
by the end of January; and there were outbreaks of sleeping sickness,
rabies, and yellow fever.[609] The deteriorating conditions led to the evacuation of all Red Cross medical teams – except for the East German teams –
from the eastern Congo, although there were still nineteen medical teams
operating elsewhere in the country.[610] In January 1961, special envoys
from Egypt, Ghana, the Soviet Union, and Czechoslovakia visited the
president of Sudan, General Ibrahim Abboud, hoping – vainly – to open
land and air routes to Stanleyville.[611] Egyptian President Nasser even
toyed with the idea of parachuting supplies to the province or organizing
clandestine convoys through the Sudan. However, the Soviet Union did
not want to risk the consequences of such steps, and the Sudan also
blocked a Czech proposal to begin regular air flights along the route from
Prague to Cairo, Khartoum, and Stanleyville. Prevented from establishing
its own air connections to the outside world, one official of the Gizenga
government exclaimed in frustration: "[I]f the UN objects to the establishment [of a commercial airline] let it take the responsibility for aiding
Stanleyville. We can't understand the UN position... If some Western
airlines serve Tshombe and Mobutu, why does the UN and Sudan object
to delivering consignments to Stanleyville?"[612]

The Red Cross societies of the Soviet bloc pressured the League of
National Red Cross Societies to take action. Although the League recognized that something had to be done, the organization was reluctant to
deliver aid directly to the eastern Congo, rather than to the central
government, and, in any case, its logistical dependence on the United
Nations and the United States left it little room to maneuver.[613] Nor
was the UN civilian operations division interested in intervening.[614]
Finally, in late April 1961, the League managed to send a barge of
emergency relief food up the Congo River from Léopoldville to Stanleyville, and the next month the four Nordic Red Cross Societies airlifted five
tons of medical supplies to the region.[615]

The Radicalization of Third World Liberation Movements

The growing involvement of the Western powers in the Congo galvanized Third World interest in developments there. There was a marked change of sentiment within the UN as well. On December 14, 1960, the UN adopted the "Declaration on the Granting of Independence to Colonial Countries and Peoples," which had been submitted by the Soviet Union, and a related resolution the following day recognized the sovereign right of states to dispose of their own wealth and natural resources.[616] In early January, the heads of the more radical nonaligned states (including Ghana, Guinea, Mali, Morocco, the United Arab Republic, and the Provisional Government of Algeria, as well as Libya and Ceylon) convened in Casablanca, where they declared that any assistance to France in the Algerian war would be considered an "act of hostility directed against Africa as a whole."[617]

Two weeks later, an extraordinary session of the Secretariat of the Afro-Asian Peoples' Solidarity Conference called on the UN and the world public to protest against the interference of imperial powers in the internal affairs of the Congo, Algeria, and Laos. The organization also recommended that the world community send aid to the Stanleyville Government, and it expanded the scope of the existing International Committee for Aid to Algeria to include the Congo. In addition, to protest Western influence over UN operations in the country, Egypt, Morocco, Guinea, and Indonesia all decided to withdraw their contingents from UN peacekeeping forces operating in the Congo.[618]

In November 1960, the radicalization of Third World internationalism came together with the intensification of the Sino-Soviet conflict to convince the Soviet bloc countries to collectively pledge material and moral support for national liberation struggles in Asia and Africa. In January 1961, Khrushchev himself proclaimed that armed liberation struggles were "not only admissible but inevitable," and he called on the world's communist parties to "fully support such just wars and march in the front rank with the peoples waging liberation struggles." Moscow also announced that the Soviet Union was "ready to provide all possible assistance and support for the Congolese people and their legitimate Government in their just struggle against the colonizers."[619]

News of Lumumba's death further radicalized the Third World liberation struggle and sparked protests around the world. In Cairo, Arab and African students organized a funeral procession for Lumumba, and protesters rallied in front of both the Belgian, U.S., and British embassies and

UN buildings. As Radio Cairo noted on February 14, "today we do not weep for Lumumba. We weep for the UN, its Charter and its honor."[620] The same day, Khrushchev and Nasser both recognized the Gizenga government as the sole legitimate government of the Congo. The more radical group of nonaligned states that had just met in Casablanca convened again in Accra, and they, too, urged other countries to recognize the Gizenga government. The mood at the third All African Peoples' Conference, which was held in Cairo in March 1961, reflected growing antipathy toward the West. The conference specifically named the Congo crisis as an exemplary case of "international imperialism in the face of the development of revolutionary movements in Africa;" it denounced "the balkanization of new independent states through the UN-led intervention;" and it decided to establish a Permanent Aid Committee to assist those peoples who were fighting for their independence.[621]

There was also renewed protest in the Soviet bloc. In February 1961, the Soviet Union renamed the Peoples' Friendship University the Patrice Lumumba Peoples' Friendship University.[622] In Berlin and Leipzig, local authorities and mass organizations organized protest rallies, which were addressed by a Congolese student and a physician who had recently returned from Red Cross medical relief work in the Congo. The Politburo decided to give the Gizenga government 300,000 marks in emergency relief, two-thirds of which was to be used to purchase medicine and medical instruments, and to send military, security, and economic advisors to Stanleyville to help the Congolese build an efficient state apparatus and implement the basic elements of economic planning.[623] The East German Red Cross and the Committee for the Solidarity with the Peoples of Africa also collected money and supplies for Congo relief, and the consignment was ready for shipment on January 31, 1961.[624] However, the Western blockade prevented those countries that wished send food, medicine, arms, or even advisors to the Congo from doing so. In this way, the people of the eastern Congo were held hostage to the U.S. crusade to contain communism.

By the middle of 1961, the government in Léopoldville, backed by the United States and the United Nations, succeeded in defeating the Lumumbists. A large number of Belgians returned to Stanleyville, which was now protected by Ethiopian troops and an Austrian sanitary force, both of which were operating under UN auspices. In August of that year, a new central government was established under Prime Minister Adoula, who in a gesture of national unity gave cabinet posts to a few leaders of the former Gizenga government in Stanleyville. Shortly thereafter, the East German diplomatic mission, which had originally been accredited by the Gizenga government, was expelled from the country.

When the international medical relief operation to the Congo ended in June 1961, the International Red Cross celebrated the completion of the operation by publishing *Congo Medical Relief*. In this celebratory volume, the organization wrote that, "for the first time, Red Cross personnel from all six continents worked together in the Congo, with teams from Africa, Asia, Oceania and South America working side by side with teams from Europe and North America."[625] The book praised these medical teams for arriving in Léopoldville so promptly once the political and military crisis had turned into a humanitarian one.

The Red Cross adopted a similarly self-congratulatory tone with regard to its work in Algeria. In 1963, the League of National Red Cross and Red Crescent Societies celebrated its centenary, and that year the organization won the Nobel Peace Prize for this work. In his Nobel lecture, entitled "The Red Cross in a Changing World," League chairman John Alexander MacAulay expounded on Red Cross heroics in Africa: "The largest relief operation ever undertaken by the League remains without doubt the one from which 285,000 Algerian refugees benefited. These refugees, installed in Tunisia and Morocco from 1958 to 1962, received regular care from medical teams and were provided with foodstuffs and clothing." MacAulay then listed a number of other crisis areas, including the Congo, Angola, Rwanda–Burundi. These places were unimportant, perhaps even unknown, to many people in the audience.

The world, however, was rapidly changing. Around the time of MacAulay's lecture, the Congo crisis was moving into its second phase. Lumumbist leaders, some just back from exile in People's Republic of China, were mobilizing young soldiers from the Congolese National Army for war against what they regarded as puppet regime of the Americans and Belgians in Léopoldville. This crisis ended violently in the winter of 1963–4 when the Americans and Belgians bombarded Stanleyville, while an army of mercenaries from South Africa, Rhodesia, and Western Europe invaded soon thereafter.

The Red Cross' Congo volume addressed none of these obstacles to its humanitarian aid mission. It did not mention that Belgian obstruction and sabotage had aggravated the logistical problems caused by the breakdown of transportation and communication systems or the fact that Mobutu's blockade of the eastern part of the country had caused catastrophic shortages of food and medicine and endangered medical teams working in the region. Most importantly, the International Red Cross did not even attempt to make sense of the political assumptions that underlay its supposed policy of neutrality or to reflect on its human consequences. To call this an oversight would be to misunderstand the issue because the self-evidence of this decision represented the constitutive blindness of the policy of containment. However, this inbuilt bias did not escape the representatives of the Third World. During a UN debate on the Congo in December 1960, the Indian representative Krishna Menon called upon the organization to live up to its policy of neutrality, rather than to use it as a fig leaf for Western hegemony. The failure to do so, he argued, poses a "challenge to the authority and prestige of the UN which, if it is lost in Africa, would be one of the greatest calamities of our time, reflected in the rest of the world." "It is now necessary," he insisted, "for the UN to govern or get out."[626]

* * * * *

In the preceding pages, I have shown how the structure of the postwar humanitarian regime made it possible to instrumentalize aid as part of a broad campaign to contain communism. In Algeria, success was predicated on the idea that colonial conflict was a problem of internal security and that, therefore, the rules of democratic government and national self-determination did not apply. In the Congo, it was a question of controlling humanitarian aid in ways that rendered sovereignty – something that was theoretically indivisible – partible and differentially structured.

I have also shown how the efforts of the Soviet bloc countries reinforced the demands set forth by an increasingly self-conscious and self-assertive Third World movement, whose national liberation program often coincided to a substantial degree with the socialist critique of neocolonialism without ever being fully absorbed by it. Conversely, the postwar humanitarian regime also limited the ability of East Germany to provide humanitarian aid in ways that would support national liberation movements. As a result, East Germany had only limited succes in leveraging its aid in order to achieve its main foreign policy objective: diplomatic recognition from those Third World countries with which it theoretically enjoyed a natural solidarity. However, the diplomatic failure of the East Germans in Africa was also due in part to the growing influence of China and Cuba in the region. Although the Sino-Soviet conflict remained latent in both Algeria and the Congo, in Chapter 9 I will show how aid from these countries undercut the appeal of assistance provided by the Soviet bloc.

PART III

GLOBAL HEALTH, DEVELOPMENT, AND LABOR MIGRATION

6

Know Your Body and Build Socialism

INTRODUCTION: EAST GERMAN HEALTH EXHIBITIONS
IN THE THIRD WORLD

The Hallstein doctrine was the cornerstone of West German foreign policy from its proclamation in 1955 to 1972, when the Federal Republic normalized relations with German Democratic Republic. During much of this time, the Hallstein doctrine severely constrained East Germany's ability to secure diplomatic recognition outside the socialist camp. However, the East German government was never content to be dictated to by the West, and in response East Germany developed a broad palette of non-state, quasi-state, and official programs that operated below the level of formal diplomatic relations and that enabled the country to circumvent and compensate in part for the restrictions imposed by the Hallstein doctrine. In the words of one former East German diplomat, these programs laid a "solid foundation for the ambitious political plans of later years."[627]

From the 1950s to the early 1960s, medical aid programs, and especially the traveling hygiene exhibitions, were one of the most important tools of this cultural diplomacy and one of the most effective means through which the East German government sought to gain *de facto* – and eventually *de jure* – recognition by Third World countries. Here, the term "medical aid" is used to denote a wide variety of initiatives, both large and small, including hygiene exhibitions, the construction of clinics, the service of German medical professionals, the provision of hospital equipment and medicine, the training of Asian and African health workers in East Germany, and humanitarian medical relief for those injured or displaced by national liberation struggles.

Much of the recent scholarship on the Cold War has approached the period from a cultural perspective and focused on such topics as films, cultural exchanges, and industrial fairs, including the famous 1959 kitchen debate between Nixon and Khrushchev.[628] This approach makes it possible to explore not only the images of modernity and the good life set out by each of the blocs and their member countries but also how they chose to represent themselves abroad. In addition, it also makes it possible to inquire into "what sense of themselves was produced in response to the image the 'other' projected of itself and to the image of *them* it presupposed?"[629] Medical assistance programs provide an ideal medium for studying the representations of East Germanness by a state that was desperately seeking recognition both by its own people and the international community.

In the first section, I will analyze East German public health policy from the 1940s to the early 1960s, the role of health and hygiene in molding the new socialist person, and the complex relations between health, citizenship, and socialist modernity.[630] The East Germans argued that ill health, disease, and premature disability were essentially social problems that could only be definitively solved in a socialist society. However, the consciousness and subjectivity of the citizenry still had to be revolutionized, and the Dresden Hygiene Museum was responsible for hygienic enlightenment programs both at home and abroad. In the second section, I will recount the history of the Hygiene Museum from the turn of the century through the 1950s. Focusing on its most famous exhibit, the Transparent Man, I will analyze the sociomedical vision that inspired its exhibitions and explain how the museum maintained its leading role in the field from the Empire to the Weimar Republic and the Nazi era and then into the postwar socialist state.

In the third section, I will turn to overseas health and hygiene exhibitions. In many respects, these exhibitions succeeded in communicating to a Third World audience the potential health benefits of modern hygiene and medical science. However, representing Germanness abroad was a complicated undertaking, and I argue that the exhibitions were less successful in establishing the specifically socialist nature of the country's achievements in medicine and hygiene.

In the fourth section, I will switch perspectives and examine the experiences of those young men and women who in the 1950s and early 1960s came to East Germany from Africa for study and training – primarily in the fields of medicine and nursing. Here, I will argue that the success of these programs was limited by the chasm separating what the Africans desired to learn from what the East Germans could teach them. Shunted into menial tasks, these students were rapidly alienated by the persistent, institutionalized racism they encountered. I will conclude by using the experiences of a South African nursing student as a window into the coercively collectivist sociality characteristic of socialist bloc countries.

I. HEALTH, CITIZENSHIP, AND THE MAKING OF *HOMO SOVIETICUS-GERMANICUS*

From the very beginning, East Germany was a state in search of a society. As part of this search, the government sought to make the ideal of healthy, productive living into a source of popular legitimacy and national identity. Their belief that good health, well-being, sustained productivity, and the pleasures that they brought could only be fully realized under socialism was reflected in such official slogans as "Socialism is the best prevention" and "Socialism is the path to health."[631] Such ideas were often just as important to the new regime as the more widely studied rhetorics of antifascism and productivism. To achieve this goal, however, the East Germans had to distinguish their own conception of socialist medicine and hygiene not only from the racial policies of the Nazis but also from what they regarded as the individualist, materialist approach to public health in the Federal Republic.

The Soviet public health system had long given priority – at least in theory – to preventive care, and this principle was institutionally anchored in a network of policlinics, ambulatories, and outpatient clinics. Although the top priority of the Soviet military administration in the summer of 1945 was to prevent the flare-up of contagious diseases, with the establishment of the German Central Public Health Administration the Soviets began dismantling the apparatus created to administer Nazi Germany's racial policy and reconstructing the German public health system in their own image. In the Western-occupied zones, both the allies and the Germans regarded this Soviet decision as the imposition of a foreign system by a nascently totalitarian power. However, Germany had a long tradition of social hygiene, which reached back to the 1890s, but which had been interrupted by twelve years of Nazi rule.[632] After 1945, the reliance on returning socialist physicians to staff this postwar public health system made it possible to represent the new system as a return to an older German tradition, while glossing over the fact that it corresponded with Soviet ideals and was backed up by Soviet power. As one of these returning communists noted, the German defeat made it possible to "put into practice old Social Democratic ideas in the artificial environment (*Käseglocke*) created by Soviet occupation."[633]

In the communist party's plan for building socialism in the eastern part of divided Germany, health was linked in complex ways with work, industrial policy, and social governance. After the founding of the German Democratic Republic in October 1949, the government passed various labor and social laws that granted its citizens the right to work and social security, and in November 1950, a national health ministry was established for the first time in German history.[634] One aspect of the East German social contract was a social right to health. However, this right was closely tied to the social obligation to labor in a productive, disciplined manner for the good of the community.[635] To help achieve this goal, the Council of Ministers named the Hygiene Museum in Dresden the Central Institute for Health Education. Its mission was to transform individual consciousness and create "an informed population," who both understood the interrelationship between work, health, and socialism and were committed to self-transformation on this basis.[636]

The point at which all of these ideas converged was the new socialist person. According to official pronouncements, individual character and morality had been pervasively deformed by a social order based on private property. By the second half of the 1950s, however, party theorists argued that nationalization, collectivization, and the implementation of state economic planning had created the material basis for a new kind of post-bourgeois person, who was finally in a position to internalize the collectivist principles of socialist morality and who was personally committed to the construction of socialism. According to the Ten Commandments of Socialist Morality and Ethics promulgated by the party in 1958, a genuinely socialist person would strive to improve his or her achievement and productivity, adhere to socialist work discipline, love the socialist homeland, and live in a "clean and upright" manner.[637]

The conscious commitment to a healthy lifestyle was presented not as an onerous obligation, but rather as a means of individual self-realization through which the new person would come to identify with the socialist order. As Health Minister Max Sefrin explained in 1961, "the socialist state is the foundation and precondition for effective and many-sided work in the service of man. Our social order makes possible an active, healthy, happy and fulfilled life for every citizen. What men create belongs to them; how they live, they alone determine; they are free people. The noblest task of the public health system is to show these citizens how they can properly use this freedom to preserve and maintain their creativity and happiness in life."[638] Hygienic enlightenment programs were one of the cornerstones of East German efforts to cultivate a new socialist personality and teach the individual to govern him- or herself in accordance with the principles outlined above. In the words of Rolf Thränhardt, a leading East German health official, "through a patient process of enlightenment and education we must steer the needs of the population along a path which corresponds to a healthy way of living."[639]

But this was not just civic or political education. East German socialism claimed to be nothing if not scientific. The public health community believed that, by yielding objectively valid truths, advances in medical science, no less than those in Marxism–Leninism, would provide an unshakable foundation for the management of the health of the entire population. As one public health official explained in 1962, the goal was "to guide our population in a *uniform* manner according to the most recent advances in medical science and to educate the people to a rationally healthy lifestyle."[640] This policy raised all sorts of conflicts regarding the respective contributions of science, education, and coercion in the realization of this goal. But the policy also depended on striking the proper balance between the rights of the individual – including the right to engage in activities (such as smoking), which were pleasurable, but potentially harmful to both the individual and the community – and his or her obligations to the community.[641] Such conundrums, however, did not shake the confidence that these political problems could be solved without the need for coercion. The optimism associated with this marriage of science and socialism is nicely captured in a popular book that was distributed to all 14-year-olds on the occasion of their civic initiation (*Jugendweihe*):

By the end of this century...medical research will understand how to overcome all natural illnesses... In the same manner that they will eliminate vices, socialist societies will prevent the unhealthy misuse of the rich possibilities of consumption... The result will be persons who are healthy through and through, who are productive enough for their ambitious tasks, but who are also in a position to make the proper use of the abundance of their world. They will have no fear of disease or premature death.[642]

Having bestowed such great political importance upon improved health and longevity, it was incumbent upon the state to define the norms of individual and public health, enlighten the public on how to apply medical and hygienic knowledge to prevent disease and maintain productivity, and convince the population to adopt its vision of the new socialist personality.[643] In January 1957, Health Ministry officials met with representatives of the country's major media outlets to discuss ways in which they could promote greater awareness of such public health issues as cancer, smoking, women's reproductive health, and healthy eating.[644] Popular medical magazines, such as *Deine Gesundheit* (Your Health), used eye-catching titles and humorous illustrations and cartoons, including the cartoon series "Nurse Monika," to reach a wide readership. During the post-Sputnik years, in particular, popular medical literature regularly featured stories on the latest Soviet advances in medical research and technology. Photographs of new surgical instruments and diagnostic technology were widely used to help readers identify with "Sputnik in surgery" and "medicine in space."[645] The East German press also displayed a similar faith in the future of the country's own medicine. For example, a 1962 cartoon rendition of the state of East German medicine in the year 2000 showed stylish young men and women taking advantage of hyper-modern, space-age medicine to select high-tech organs and body parts. In this vision, social – and socialist – medicine was transformed into bionic consumerism.[646]

In addition to propaganda directed at the general population, the government also began to target the medical intelligentsia (as producers of medical knowledge) and its cadres (as healthcare administrators). This new focus reflected an awareness of the fact that many medical professionals had been strong supporters of Nazism and that they remained among the strongest opponents of socialist transformation in East Germany. As this transformation reached more deeply into the public health system, a growing number of physicians, dentists, and pharmacists fled to West Germany. The 511 medical professionals who fled west in 1956 represented a 28 percent increase over the previous year, and they made up nearly half of that year's medical and dental school graduates. However, the construction of the Berlin Wall finally put the government in a position where it could pursue more aggressive public health reforms without having to worry about accelerating the flight of medical and scientific professionals.[647]

In early 1960, the Social and Medical Commission of the SED Central Committee approved a master plan that declared a "healthy way of life" to be the guiding principle for the future development of medicine and public health in the country.[648] As the Commission explained, "the education [of the people] to healthy habits is a social task…It is necessary that doctors and all those employed in the health sector actively work to develop a broad propaganda effort on behalf of public health and insure that the public is provided with effective education in matters of health."[649] In February of that year, the SED, the FDGB, and the Health Ministry jointly sponsored a national conference on the theme "Health, Productivity, and the Joy of Life for the Victory of Socialism."[650] This high-profile conference was attended by 500 medical professionals, 300 mid-level healthcare workers (such as nurses), and hundreds of other officials and functionaries.[651]

Building on the momentum generated by this conference, the government created the National Committee for a Healthy Lifestyle and Health Education in September 1961 – immediately after the building of the Berlin Wall. The Committee comprised representatives from the Ministries of Health, Education, and Commerce and Consumption, as well as the German Red Cross and the mass organizations of workers, women, and youth. The Committee's charge was to become the driving force behind the effort to make a healthy lifestyle a reality for all East Germans.[652] The organization responsible for putting this program into practice was the Dresden Hygiene Museum, whose history and work will be the focus of the next section.

II. "HYGIENE EYE" ON WATCH: THE GERMAN HYGIENE MUSEUM UNDER THREE REGIMES

All of the itinerant hygiene exhibitions that the East German government dispatched to Asia and Africa in the 1950s and 1960s were designed by the German Hygiene Museum, whose history illuminates both the socialist vision of hygienic modernity and the connections between global health and socialist internationalism. To understand all of this, we need to understand the vision of hygienic modernity that informed the museum's most famous and enduring creation: the Transparent Man (*Der gläserne Mann*).

The Hygiene Museum grew out of the First International Hygiene Exhibition, which was held in Dresden in 1911.[653] The organizer of the exhibition, which attracted over five million visitors, was the industrialist Karl August Lingner, who had made his fortune from the mouthwash Odol.[654] The theme of the German exhibit at the Exhibition was *Man* (*Der Mensch*), which was to remain the basic theme for subsequent exhibits sponsored by the museum. The meta-narrative of *Man* was the perfectibility of human beings through progress in biomedicine.[655] In the entrance hall stood a giant statue of Hercules with the words "Oh Health, no riches can equal you" chiseled into its base. Lingner regarded the human being as both a machine and a prototype of the organizational forms of industrial modernity, and he viewed the human body as a mechanism whose individual parts meshed so perfectly that it brought to life the classical ideals of human beauty.

A year later, *Man* found a permanent home in the newly opened Dresden Hygiene Museum. The goal of the museum was to make advances in medicine and hygiene accessible to the general public, including the unlettered laboring classes, by employing a wide variety of technologies and display techniques to communicate its message of better living and human perfection through scientific knowledge. Visitors were expected to look not only at the exhibits but also through microscopes, press buttons, and touch the items on display in order to learn how their health and well-being were influenced by nutrition, housing, consumption, work, and leisure and how they could apply this knowledge in their everyday lives.[656]

The crowning achievement of this early period of pedagogical innovation was the Transparent Man, which – after three years of labor by museum technicians – was unveiled in 1930 at the Second International Hygiene Exhibition. The Transparent Man was modeled on a classical Greek statue, and, like the 1911 exhibit *Man*, it symbolized the possibility of fusing Greek ideals of physical and spiritual harmony with modern technology.[657] As the exhibition catalogue put it, the Transparent Man presented the human being as both "a technical and an aesthetic masterpiece."[658] What attracted so many visitors and what made the exhibition so successful were the methods employed to render visible the invisible skeleton and organs. The Transparent Man was more effective than recent discoveries, such as X-rays, which could also make the invisible visible, but whose low-quality, two-dimensional images limited their effectiveness as a teaching tool.[659]

After 1933, the museum became deeply involved in popularizing Nazi views on eugenics and racial hygiene. Georg Seiring, the president of the museum, collaborated with the Nazi leadership; party representatives served on the museum's board; and a State Academy for the Cultivation of Race and Health was established within the museum in April 1934. During the 1930s, the museum also organized a number of exhibitions on themes that reflected Nazi ideology, including *Volk und Rasse* (1934) and *Das Wunder des Lebens* (1935). In 1937 alone, the museum organized seven traveling exhibitions, including *Know Thyself*, *Blood and Race*, and *Eternal Volk*. That same year, the Transparent Man served as the centerpiece of the German pavilion at the Paris World Exhibition. While the initial exhibits had emphasized the unity emerging out of the functional interaction of the body's different organs and systems (each equal in value and importance), in the 1930s this egalitarianism was replaced by the "biological Führer principle" as the master biopolitical metaphor. Between 1930 and 1945, the museum produced a total of four transparent men and one transparent woman. They were shown around the world. However, all of the copies in Europe were either lost or destroyed during the war, and about 80 percent of the museum, its workshops, the library, and collections – including the original Transparent Man – were destroyed by the allied bombing of Dresden in February 1945.[660]

In the first months after the end of the war, the threat of epidemic disease, especially venereal disease and tuberculosis, prompted the Soviet military administration to organize popular health campaigns.[661] Despite the support – and prodding – of Soviet officials, the museum was unable to quickly resume its work. Most of the museum's collections remained buried in the rubble, and there was no plan to restart its workshops. It was not until the spring of 1949 that workers began refurbishing the displays that had been salvaged from the wreckage of the building.[662]

Despite this close association with the Nazi regime, the museum would go on to play a prominent role in the Soviet Occupation Zone and then in the German Democratic Republic. In the first years after the war, its earlier achievements enabled the museum to present the public health policies imposed by the Soviets as the resumption of an authentically German tradition of preventive social medicine, rather than as something imposed by foreign occupiers, while its international renown gave the museum a degree of leverage with Soviet medical authorities, who themselves hoped to capitalize on this reputation. All of this enabled the museum and its staff to conveniently gloss over their work during the Nazi years.

The reconstruction of the museum quickly became bogged down in debates over whether it should remain independent, be incorporated into the zonal health administration, or be administered in some other manner.[663] The status of the museum within the Soviet Occupation Zone was further complicated in 1947, when Seiring and the museum's chief technician, who had been involved in the creation of the Transparent Man, fled to West Germany. In 1949, they established German Health Museum in Cologne, which claimed to be the legitimate heir to the Dresden Hygiene Museum.[664] The East Germans alleged that they took with them the blueprints for many of the museum's most famous displays. Although this claim was disputed by the Dresden museum,[665] the existence of a competing institution put the East Germans in a difficult position because the Soviet plan to nationalize the Dresden museum would have weakened its credibility in the western zones. Instead, the museum was transformed into a public corporation that reported directly to the Health Ministry.[666]

In the early 1950s, the two institutions competed with one another in the areas of technology and design. Initially, the Cologne museum fell behind because of financial problems and conflicts among its leaders. However, the Dresden museum suffered from severe shortages of displays, charts, and other educational materials. As a result, in many instances the museum had to use materials produced during the Nazi era, while slightly modifying their tone to make them compatible with the values of the East German state.

East Germany hoped to capitalize on the reputation of the museum and its transparent figures, and one of the top priorities of the Dresden museum was to produce new copies of the Transparent Man.[667] The first postwar Transparent Man and Transparent Woman were displayed at the 1948 international industrial fair in Stockholm, where visitors were enchanted by this "Eighth Wonder of the World."[668] The Saxon state government then gave the transparent couple to Stalin as a present on his 70th birthday. In 1949, the East German government also gave a copy of the Transparent Man to Mao to celebrate the founding of the People's Republic of China.[669] The transparent figures were also displayed at the 1953 industrial exhibition in Peking, which reportedly drew over 1.5 million visitors.[670] Thus, within a few years the Transparent Man and the Transparent Woman had been transformed from a symbol of Nazi racial imperialism into a symbol of socialist hygienic modernity, and the museum itself became a standing attraction on the itinerary of foreign dignitaries, including Ho, who visited the museum in 1957. Ultimately, the museum produced a total of forty-three transparent figures between 1949 and 1961, twenty-seven of which would be displayed at international fairs, mostly in Asia and Africa.[671]

The year 1961 marked the fiftieth anniversary of the first international hygiene exhibition. This provided an ideal opportunity to review the legacy of German medicine and emphasize its integral role in building socialism in East Germany. The Council of Ministers organized an exhibit to showcase East German achievements in the fields of medicine and hygiene. The core of the 1961 exhibition was *Man*, and East German health experts added a new section that portrayed the East German health system as the culminating achievement of humankind in this domain.

The accompanying text linked the pleasures of a healthy lifestyle not with the individualist hedonism of the West, but with socialist conceptions of collective well-being.

But the exhibition was directed not only at a domestic audience. At the opening ceremony, director Walter Friedeberger praised the museum's success in establishing relationships with fifty-three countries around the world, "from the Soviet Union to the African nation states of Ghana and Guinea." This global reach, he noted, was due to the quality and precision of the educational materials produced by the museum, the success of these exhibits in communicating the fundamental values of the socialist state – "awe before human life, protection of health, and not least of all struggle for peace, happiness and well-being for all men" – and the role of medicine and hygiene in making these ideals a reality.[672]

III. THE TRANSPARENT MAN IN THE THIRD WORLD

Bilateral trade agreements were one way of establishing relations with nonaligned countries that did not violate the threshold established by the Hallstein doctrine; and in many cases, hygiene exhibitions were held in conjunction with, or grew out of, commercial and industrial fairs held to promote such agreements. In March 1953, Egypt became the first nonaligned country to sign a trade agreement with East Germany. Similar agreements soon followed with other nonaligned countries, including Libya (1953), India and Indonesia (both 1954), and Burma (1955). The 1954 industrial and hygienic exhibition in Cairo was the first attempt by the East Germans to use industrial and cultural policy to establish de facto relations with a non-aligned country.[673] Figure 6.1 shows Trade Minister Heinrich Rau with Indian dignitaries at the 1955 commercial exhibition in New Delhi, and Figures 6.2 and 6.3 show the Transparent Woman and Man on display at trade fairs in Ceylon and Cairo.

The idea of a German trade fair had originally been proposed in 1952 by the West German–Egyptian Chamber of Commerce. However, this plan quickly went nowhere due to Arab displeasure with West Germany's decision to sign a treaty with Israel compensating the Jewish state for the Holocaust. The Egyptians then responded positively to an East German proposal that they mount an exhibition in Cairo.[674] This exhibition displayed East German machinery, motors, vehicles, and consumer goods. It also became the scene of high drama when the two Germanys fought in the Egyptian courts for the right to use the trademark of the Carl Zeiss company, which was internationally known for its

FIGURE 6.1 Indian President Rajendra Prasad and Health Minister Amrit Kaur with trade Minister Heinrich Rau in the East German pavilion (November 1955). *Source*: Courtesy of Deutsches Historisches Museum, Berlin BA90/1101.

optical products, but which the East Germans had nationalized in 1948. After the West German Carl Zeiss company won the case, the Egyptian police confiscated the many Zeiss products displayed at the exhibition.[675]

This fair also included a hygiene exhibition, whose centerpiece was a Transparent Man. This exhibition, which also included numerous human anatomical models, moulages, preparations, and instructional charts,

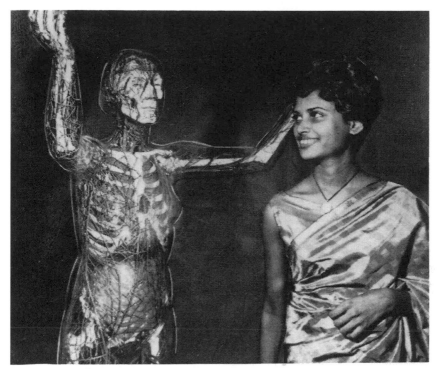

FIGURE 6.2 The Transparent Woman in Ceylon (1950s). Courtesy of Deutsches Hygiene-Museum Dresden.

reportedly attracted more than 200,000 visitors in three weeks. Despite East German efforts to market the exhibition as a display of the new socialist state's achievements, the West German ambassador in Cairo noted with satisfaction that enthusiastic Egyptian visitors simply regarded it as an example of "German" industry, which would not directly harm West German interests.[676] Such failures to distinguish between the two German states were quite common in the Third World, and they bring a note of slapstick levity to the otherwise deadly earnest competition between the two states.

Nevertheless, the East German government used the trade fair to document for its own citizens the country's growing role on the international stage. The DEFA film *Under the Egyptian Sun* (Unter der Sonne Ägyptens, 1956) showed the first models of the Trabant and the Wartburg being test-driven in Egypt against the backdrop of the country's exotic landscapes. Similarly, *Damascus Fair* (Messe in Damaskus, 1958) gave the East Germans the pleasure of seeing many East German

FIGURE 6.3 The Transparent Man on display in Cairo (1950s). Courtesy of Deutsches Hygiene-Museum Dresden.

products, ranging from passenger cars to Radeberger beer, displayed at the Damascus trade fair next to those of the Soviet Union and Czechoslovakia. It drove home the message of how the socialist countries were contributing to the modernization of the Syrian economy, which, according to the narrator, had in the recent past been little more than an "oriental bazaar."

The hygiene exhibition also led to closer relations between East Germany and Egypt in the medical field. The Egyptian authorities wanted to purchase all of the items on display in the 1954 exhibition for the Cairo Hygiene Museum, and they ordered a transparent pregnant woman from the Dresden Hygiene Museum.[677] In 1956, Egypt asked Health Minister Luitpold Steidle to send a team of experienced nurses as part of a technical assistance program to help build a national health system.[678] Although no action had been taken on this request when the Suez Crisis broke out in July of that year, the East Germans acted quickly when the Egyptians asked them to send eleven qualified nurses – young and unmarried – to train Egyptian nurses at hospitals in Cairo and Port Said. This was East Germany's first medical aid mission to a nonaligned country, and German officials approached it with high hopes. Steidle made it clear that "it depends very much on the ability of these nurses to prove themselves in every respect and thus to become forerunners of a much broader collaboration with our Egyptian friends."[679]

In January 1957, one supervisor and ten nurses, who were mostly in their twenties and thirties, arrived in Cairo. However, this Egyptian medical aid program quickly proved to be an unhappy undertaking for all involved. The team was supposed to work at a newly built hospital and divide its time between patient care and teaching.[680] But the nurses did not speak any English, and – because of the peculiarities of the German nurse training system (see Chapter 8) – they were not as well educated as the Egyptian women whom they were supposed to train. Moreover, both the Egyptians and the East Germans were exasperated by the continuous requests by the German nurses for a variety of petty privileges.[681] In hopes of transforming this failure into an argument for closer relations, the East Germans pressed for a bilateral agreement to facilitate the exchange of students, doctors, and nurses.[682]

The second East German industrial exhibition, which was held in Cairo in October/November 1957, gave Rau the opportunity to calm the waters by donating to the Egyptians – with much fanfare – all of the materials that had been displayed at the first exhibition.[683] Although the initial medical aid program ended in a fiasco, it also served as a learning experience. The East Germans recognized that, in the future, special care would have to be taken to ensure that aid specialists had the necessary maturity, the awareness that they were going as representatives of the socialist state, and the language skills needed to successfully complete their missions.[684]

Holy Cow, Comrade Ulbricht!

In October 1957, the Soviet Union launched Sputnik, the first artificial satellite to orbit the earth. In so doing, the country staked its claim to global leadership in science and technology.[685] Although this feat came as an extremely unpleasant and unsettling shock to the West, many people around the world saw it as a symbol of the rapid technological progress possible under socialism and of the potential of the socialist path to modernity. Two years later, East Germany proudly introduced its own technological wonder at the World Agricultural Fair in New Delhi, India: a transparent cow named Heidi (Figure 6.4).

Heidi, too, was regarded as a "miracle of human ability and perseverance" whose construction required 15,000 man hours and 60,000 meters

FIGURE 6.4 Indian Prime Minister Jawaharlal Nehru (far right) looking circumspectly at Heidi, the Holy Cow of East Germany's socialist modernity. Courtesy of Deutsches Hygiene-Museum Dresden.

of copper wire and plastic tubing. She was an exact replica of a real bovine that the Hygiene Museum had secretly selected, impregnated, and, finally, shot and preserved so that she could fulfill her dharma and be reincarnated in celluloid form along with her five-month embryo.[686] Heidi made her first pilgrimage to New Delhi as a symbol of the achievements of East Germany, and the many visitors to the German pavilion paid symbolic homage to this holy cow, which held the promise of social rebirth through socialist modernity.

Heidi could speak twenty Indian languages, and Prime Minister Jawaharlal Nehru sat through an entire lecture that Heidi delivered in Hindi.[687] In all likelihood, few of the visitors to the New Delhi exhibition knew (or cared) much about the division of Germany. Much to the consternation of the East German representatives, many of these visitors explained in the guest book that Heidi had convinced them of the advanced level of German – not *East* German – science and technology. Some wrote that Heidi was the only attraction in an otherwise "boring" pavilion.[688] However, an East German report on an ignorant Indian farmer who traveled for days just to present an offering to the transparent cow reflected the contradictions that underlay the East German exhibitionary program.[689]

While the backwardness, ignorance, and epidemic disease of the tropical world provided the dark backdrop against which East German hygienic modernity could shine all the more brightly, the exhibition raised questions about the newly independent state's capacity for self-guidance and whether the Indians would ever be able to transcend the civilizational difference that presumably lay at the root of their current problems.

Socialist Hygienic Modernity on Display

But even if the East Germans did not problematize civilizational difference in such a way, this does not mean that their message could be directly communicated by these exhibitions, which could just as easily be instrumentalized by the host countries. For example, *Man* opened in Pyongyang on June 15, 1957. By that time, German engineers had already been working for two years in Hamhung. The health exhibition, which was later shown in the city of Kae Sung, was reportedly a huge success, drawing a total of 369,546 visitors. This was the largest number of persons to ever attend an international exhibition in North Korea.[690] A number of the Koreans who attended the exhibition – a soldier, students, medical specialists, and a housewife – wrote, undoubtedly at the direction of the government, enthusiastic letters to the East German embassy in Pyongyang. "When I saw the 'transparent man,'" wrote one correspondent, "I thought I was dreaming everything." An employee of the state central bank in Kae Sung wrote that ill-health meant "a great offense against nation and people. Therefore, we must strengthen our health for the sake of building socialism and a happy future. In the future, I will uphold the norms of personal hygienic behavior." Other letter writers pledged to observe hygienic norms in daily life so that they could better serve their country. One woman wrote with unbelievable openness, "as a housewife I have learned an especially great amount concerning the norms of sexual activity within the family and why hygienic norms must be observed from conception to delivery."[691]

The dozen letters that were translated and sent back to the Hygiene Museum were undoubtedly selected because they expressed exactly the ideas that both the East German and North Korean governments hoped visitors would take away from the exhibit, and they read as if their writers had memorized the text accompanying the displays. That did not bother the East Germans, who could use the flattering letters at home to demonstrate the esteem in which East German socialism was held abroad. However, the North Korean authorities seem to have hoped that these

letters would convince the East Germans to provide more tangible material aid, rather than just educational materials. Many letters expressed the
hope that the Germans would offer scholarships to Korean students. One
student at the Medical Institute in Pyongyang praised the advanced state
of medicine in East Germany and expressed his conviction that, "considering the present situation in our country, more students should be sent
to Germany in the future so that they can contribute to the development
of our medical science." Similarly, a mason voiced his hope that the East
German government would donate the exhibition materials "as a gift to
our medical workers for further scientific work."[692] However, the East
Germans did not give in to these entreaties, and the North Koreans
eventually agreed to purchase the materials.

The decision to display *Man* and the Transparent Man in the Third
World presented other difficulties for the Hygiene Museum and for the East
Germans more generally. Since its first showing, *Man* had not been changed
in any significant respect, and until the mid-1950s *Man* had only been
exhibited in other industrialized countries. However, these materials were
not appropriate for audiences in Asia and Africa, whose people were less
conversant with modern medicine and less literate. East German health
officials had little knowledge of either the epidemiological profile of such
countries or the modes of hygienic intervention available to these lands, and
they quickly realized that they would have to rethink the popular hygienic
enlightenment strategies that they had successfully employed at home.

Compared to such countries as North Korea and North Vietnam, the
East Germans faced tough challenges from the West in convincing the
nonaligned countries of the superiority of socialist modernity. In Cambodia, Indonesia, and India, East Germany had to compete fiercely with both
Western nations and pro-Western international organizations. As Arthur
Brown, a WHO representative in Southeast Asia, noted in 1954 regarding
the situation in Cambodia,

everyone is running after this country like young men after a pretty girl – with the
same result – she is absolutely spoiled. There is USAID, 700 millions; ... French
aid, 800 millions; ... Chinese aid, 800 millions... and now there is talk of Russian
aid. Aid from the UN agencies is minuscule in comparison and, apart from
UNICEF, is technical. The need and importance of a technical input is not
understood. For one genuine counterpart trainee, there are three foreigners advising and helping him. They surely have a good laugh watching us all going round in
circles, competing with one another![693]

In such circumstances, it was no longer possible to stage an exhibition
simply by sending abroad whatever materials the Hygiene Museum

happened to have on hand. To compete successfully in these lands, it would be necessary to create new materials that corresponded more closely to the social and cultural conditions of the host country. After the closing of the 1957 exhibition in Jakarta, the final report remarked that in those countries, one should not and could not "improvise. Not even when the country itself still has achieved only a relatively low degree of development. The exhibition is the public face of the German Democratic Republic."[694]

In Cambodia, for example, the Sihanouk regime had received medical aid from both of the superpowers and its former colonial ruler. Assistance from both the United States and the WHO made possible the founding of the Health Center in Takhmau in February 1960, and a combination of U.S. and French support funded the new medical school in Phnom Penh in 1962. The Soviet Union built the large Soviet–Khmer Friendship Hospital, which opened in 1960 with a staff of Soviet doctors.[695] The East Germans also hoped to establish a humanitarian toehold in Cambodia. Already in 1961, the East German Foreign Ministry had entertained the idea of sending a hygiene exhibition with a Transparent Woman to Cambodia to "propagandize for the role of East Germany as the first German state of peace. Also there is the hope that the relationship between East Germany and Cambodia will be normalized by that time."[696] After all, since Cambodia had allowed East Germany to open a consulate there – despite opposition from the West Germans – in September 1962, there was all the more reason to push for such an exhibition.[697] The other socialist diplomats in the region warned the East Germans that, in view of the health exhibitions from the major powers that had already been shown in the country, they should only send a high-quality exhibition to Cambodia so as not to endanger these diplomatic successes.[698] Negotiations were also complicated by questions of cost and financing. The Cambodian health minister insisted that the East Germans foot the entire bill. Moreover, when the Hygiene Museum delegation asked whether Cambodia would pick up the costs for a week-long stay by the German health minister, the Cambodians responded that the relatively low value of the exhibition (approximately 100,000 marks) did not justify a visit by the minister.[699] Despite these frictions, the exhibition "Health – The Supreme Good of Man" opened there in 1964 in time to commemorate the fifteenth anniversary of the founding of East Germany.

A recurring problem for the East Germans was their inability to meet certain requests from host governments. For example, although Burma, which hosted *Man*, together with the Transparent Man, from December 1959 through January 1960, the Burmese wanted the exhibit to include a special section on malaria, a tropical disease on which the Hygiene Museum had no expertise. In addition, while the Burmese wanted the East Germans to include educational films, the museum could offer only color slides, an embarrassing omission from a country claiming to be among the most modern in the world.[700] Nor could the East Germans comply with the request that the Transparent Man speak Burmese or that the text accompanying the exhibit be translated into the local language.[701]

Despite these problems, the Burmese mission ultimately proved to be a success. Richard Kirsch, professor of surgery at the Humboldt University, traveled to Burma for the opening of the exhibition. However, by this time the relationship between the two states had cooled somewhat, and Kirsch's real task was to reverse the country's flagging political fortunes in Burma. Although the East German government was planning to send a high-level delegation to Southeast Asia, including Burma, the Burmese government was not at all receptive and even denied the East German delegation a transit visa through the country. When Kirsch was giving the Burmese foreign minister a tour of the hygiene exhibition, the minister complained about a stomach tumor that needed an operation and then invited Kirsch to observe the operation that a Burmese surgeon was supposed to perform on him. On the day of surgery, with everyone scrubbed and ready for the first incision, the Burmese surgeon offered the scalpel to Kirsch – a gesture that was presumably prearranged. Kirsch ended up performing the operation, and, as an expression of gratitude, the minister issued the visa that the East Germans had sought in vain to obtain through regular channels. But things didn't stop here. Kirsch challenged the opinion of a U.S. physician, who had been treating another important military officer, and he eventually took over treatment of that dignitary as well. These personal accomplishments earned Kirsch an invitation to a dinner party thrown by Prime Minister General Ne Win, where he was able to secure approval for a visit by the top-level East German delegation. In 1960, a delegation headed by Health Minister Sefrin arrived in Rangoon, where he was able to persuade the Burmese government to allow the East Germans to open a consulate general.

Displaying East Germanness in nonsocialist countries became even more complicated after the construction of the Berlin Wall in 1961. Many countries refused to invite the East Germans or issue the appropriate visas. Even when they were invited, they found themselves engaged in their own struggle for "equal treatment" because of West German pressure to prevent the "Soviet Occupation Zone" from using the name "German" Democratic Republic or displaying its flag or other insignia.[702] Other than Guinea and Ghana, however, only a small number of the newly independent countries in sub-Saharan Africa initially dared to defy the West Germans.[703]

The need to close the knowledge gap on tropical disease and local hygiene problems gained new urgency by decolonization in sub-Saharan Africa. Once the East Germans had a foot in the diplomatic door to the region, the government tried to use health and hygiene exhibitions to force the door open even wider.[704] In view of the importance attributed to them, the Ministries of Health and Foreign Affairs insisted that future exhibitions should be of high quality so that they would more clearly demonstrate the "superiority the socialist health system vis-à-vis capitalist states." However, to speak directly to the needs of these African countries, the Germans would need greater first-hand knowledge of public health systems and hygienic conditions in the region.[705] In 1960, the scientific and technical directors of the Hygiene Museum visited Ghana and Guinea to gather information for an anti-malaria exhibit.[706] Upon their return, the museum staff laboriously designed new materials geared to low literacy levels. More than fifty colored illustrations and charts described the vectors by which malaria was transmitted; the exhibit also used photographs to show how the landscape bred mosquitoes, to illustrate the hygienic hazards of houses and marketplaces, and to propagandize for the use of DDT.

The timing of the exhibition could not have been better. The WHO had declared 1960 malaria eradication year, and in 1962 the World Health Assembly launched a malaria eradication postage stamp campaign under the slogan "The World United Against Malaria" to raise both global awareness of malaria and funds to fight the disease.[707] As part of this campaign, 101 countries issued postage stamps with anti-malaria themes. One of the anti-malaria stamps produced in East Germany showed a disinfector standing on the axis connecting central Europe with the spine of Africa and demonstratively pointing his spray gun at North America.

The new anti-malaria exhibition opened in Conakry, Guinea, in 1962. The Foreign Ministry considered it "the most important East German cultural-political measure" in Africa in recent years.[708] This two-week exhibition was held in the state publishing house "Patrice Lumumba," which East Germany built and then donated to the Guinean government. It drew more than 7,000 visitors, including a large number of women and schoolgirls, who proved especially interested in a model of the female anatomy.[709] The delegation was headed by Herbert Landmann, a researcher at the Tuberculosis Research Institute in Berlin and a member of both the East German legislature and the Berlin municipal government.[710] In the many lectures, he delivered during the course of the exhibition, Landmann described East Germany's advanced socialist medical system and explained the role of its popular hygienic enlightenment campaign, pre- and postnatal care, and its efforts to prevent tuberculosis and venereal disease. To judge from the fact that the Guinean government decided to show the exhibition in four more areas at its own expense, the exhibition must have been a success. As Sefrin reported to Willi Stoph, the First Deputy of the Council of Ministers, "in this way our goal of securing *the lasting political effect* of the exhibition and providing genuine support for Guinean experts was achieved."[711] After the exhibit closed, the East Germans donated the materials to the Guinean government and invited a number of Guinean doctors and mid-level health workers to come to Germany for advanced training.[712] The exhibition also traveled to neighboring Mali and to Cuba.

East German authorities also tried to capitalize on the malaria exhibit at home. *Neues Deutschland* praised it as East Germany's "friendship bridge to Africa." In their commentaries on the exhibition, the East German press described it as an exemplary contribution to the struggle against malaria, which they characterized as a legacy of colonialism.[713] To reinforce this idea, the media portrayed the Africans in positive, but obviously exaggerated terms as "true fanatics regarding cleanliness, who frequently wash themselves with great thoroughness and clean their dishes with equal assiduousness." This was then followed by examples of various indigenous customs that the East Germans interpreted as evidence of the lack of "a conscious sense of hygiene." In this way, Africans were represented as people who possessed the basic capacity to live in a hygienic manner, but who still needed to be guided along the proper path by their socialist big brothers.

This narrative misrepresented the role of the Guineans in the construction of the exhibit. From the beginning the Guinean health authorities had insisted on playing an active role in planning the exhibition, and their ideas had been incorporated into the displays. In addition, the East German preparatory work could not have been accomplished without the local knowledge of the Guineans themselves. As Sefrin explained at a 1963 planning meeting, East Germany could not hope to match the knowledge of tropical medicine possessed by the long-time colonial powers "since we seldom see cases of malaria and thus do not have sufficient experience in treating the disease."[714] Nevertheless, East German health officials continued to insist on the superiority of European biomedicine and its hygienic norms.

The East German press frequently portrayed the country as the medical liberator and doctor hero of the Third World, a perception that was widely shared among the leadership and the population. For example, when the East German government was planning an exhibition in Cuba, the technical director of the Hygiene Museum remarked that "the socialist countries themselves already possess ample possibilities and experiences for health education," but that Cuba could use help from East Germany to improve "the general educational level."[715] Despite the challenges, they faced in matching the knowledge of tropical medicine possessed by the long-time colonial powers, East German health officials continued to complain that their Asian and African counterparts had no clue about either hygiene or the organization of hygiene exhibitions. However, in voicing these complaints, they had to guard against offending the sensibilities of the newly independent states and their peoples. For example, in designing a health museum for Rangoon, museum officials wanted to present health as a secular, scientific concern: "No supernatural force, no God as cause and guardian, was necessary for this." However, Health Ministry officials asked that this sentence be deleted to avoid offending the Burmese.[716]

In East German theory, national liberation and the end of backwardness in the global South went hand in hand with the construction of socialism and the defeat of capitalism in the global North. Nevertheless, despite the efforts to adapt the Weimar-era social hygiene to meet the needs of developing countries, these hygiene exhibitions never quite fulfilled the high hopes placed in them by the East German government. Although the exhibitions were well attended and positively received, they tended to limit their own impact by making explicit racialized constructions of cultural difference on which the promise of socialist modernity rested. Last, there was the question of West Germany. In the Third World – with the exception of a narrow intellectual and political stratum – the division of Germany did not have any of the significance that it had for those living in the two halves of the divided country.

On October 6, 1967, after a year of planning and preparation by the Dresden Hygiene Museum, the exhibition "You and Your Health" opened in Rangoon. Sefrin and his Burmese counterpart, Colonel Hla Han of the Revolutionary Council, opened the exhibition to great fanfare. Like many other Third World countries, Burma was the object – and beneficiary – of ideological competition between the two Germanys, and the opening was timed to coincide with a visit to Burma by West German Chancellor Kurt Kiesinger. Not surprisingly, the East German delegation loaded the exhibition with symbols of East German sovereignty. The entrance to the exhibition hall was capped by an arch inscribed with the name of the German Democratic Republic written in Burmese, and no one could miss the large East German flag hanging at the entrance. Inside the hall hung a large map of East Germany, and a special section on the German question presented the perspective of the peace-loving socialist state. Films were shown twice daily to enlighten the Burmese about the East German health system and the country's hygiene programs. West German television crews were allowed to film the exhibition on the condition that the East German state name and its flag be prominently featured. To the great relief of the East Germans, West German diplomats in Rangoon kept a low profile and did not protest the presumptive display of sovereignty by what they still regarded as the Soviet Occupation Zone. Instead, the West German ambassador explained – undoubtedly to the consternation of the East Germans – that, just as there was only one German state and one German culture, this was a *German* exhibition mounted by the world famous *German* Hygiene Museum established in 1911.[717] This matter-of-fact statement was probably well-attuned to the attitudes of his Burmese audience – and well calculated to infuriate the East Germans.

IV. THROUGH AFRICAN EYES: "ACTUALLY EXISTING SOCIALISM" IN BLACK AND WHITE

The East German public first encountered the Third World within the borders of the socialist state in the form of the students and trainees who arrived in the 1950s and 1960s. This group long antedated state contract workers who came from Cuba, Mozambique, Vietnam, and Angola in the late 1970s and 1980s. In contrast to the vast amount of research on foreign migrant workers in West Germany, the question of foreigners and racism in East Germany has only recently begun to attract scholarly attention.[718] Despite the importance of such students and trainees to the East German government, the persistence of long-standing racial prejudices in the socialist state undermined the effectiveness of these aid programs in building solidarity across the color line, and this and other problems led to constant friction between Third World students and trainees and both their immediate supervisors and higher levels of the

East German government. The voluminous correspondence, complaints, and petitions relating to these matters provide an opportunity to study how East German officials and citizens interacted with these foreigners.[719]

As we have already seen, North Korean orphans and students were the first large group of non-Europeans to come to East Germany. They were followed in 1955/56 by 348 children from North Vietnam, although a small number of Vietnamese doctors and pharmacists also came to East Germany for training in orthopedics and other medical specialties during these years.[720] Across the remainder of the 1950s, a small but steady flow of young people came to East Germany from Third World countries to study medicine, agriculture, and engineering and to acquire experience in newly mechanized trades.[721] Ultimately, a total of about 44,000 foreigners studied at East German universities and technical schools over the course of the country's forty-year existence.[722] During the first half of the 1960s, most such trainees came from the West African countries of Ghana, Guinea, and Mali, although the increasing priority given to Zanzibar and Cuba after 1964 reflected the changing geopolitical situation in those regions. All told between 1961 and 1973 about 450 men and women from the nonaligned countries of the Third World completed their training in nursing, midwifery, radiology, and orthopedics in East Germany.[723]

Almost all non-European trainees in these fields completed their studies and subsequent practica at the Dorothea Christiane Erxleben hospital in Quedlinburg.[724] Quedlinburg was an idyllic, medieval town that had largely remained untouched by the great wars of the twentieth century. It was located about sixty miles from Halle. In the 1960s, this was a rather isolated location not far from the western border of East Germany. Although the Quedlinburg hospital served as a teaching hospital for East German nursing programs, it is not clear why East German authorities chose it as the school for these trainees, unless for its relative isolation. Despite this virtual ghettoization of non-European students in Quedlinburg, elsewhere ordinary East Germans were more likely to be exposed to these trainees by media coverage of cultural exchange programs. The pictures that accompanied these stories showed exotic images of young African women dressed in colorful African outfits, leisurely strolling together down streets lined with medieval timber-framed houses (Figure 6.5).[725]

The presence of the people of color in East Germany was also publicized in the popular media on other occasions, such as May Day and Women's Day. Under the title "Medicine Knows No Borders,"

FIGURE 6.5 African nursing students in Quedlinburg (1963).
Source: Zentralbild Schmidt. Courtesy of Bundesarchiv, 183-B0503-0008-006.

Deine Gesundheit published interviews with physicians from Vietnam, Sudan, and Iran, who had recently completed their internships at the Berlin Charité. In October 1962, East Germany hosted an international congress of medical and healthcare workers. Participants came from Zambia, Cameroon, India, Ghana, and Nigeria. Both the East German representative and foreign guests praised East Germany for providing aid to Algeria, Cuba, and other African and Asian countries and for the role it played in helping these countries reconstruct their national health systems.[726]

Many of non-European trainees were sponsored by the quasi-official mass organizations. The FDGB and its member organizations played a particularly prominent role in funding training and study visits for Third World students, journalists, and union functionaries. In 1961, for example, the FDGB funded seven Togolese women and ten Nigerians to travel to East Germany for healthcare training.[727] The following year the FDGB and the medical workers' union extended a similar offer to the Nigerian Trade Union Congress.[728]

These visitors were not left to their own devices in East Germany. The purpose of these solidarity programs was to mold them into socialist citizens, who would propagandize on behalf of East Germany and who, as their influence grew in their home countries, would eventually help East Germany gain diplomatic recognition and break out of the diplomatic stranglehold of the Hallstein doctrine. This meant that, in addition to the transfer of knowledge and skills, organizations such as the FDGB and the FDJ were expected to monitor these visitors to ensure that they developed the attitudes and personality traits deemed appropriate for socialist citizens. The FDGB required its local branches to regularly report whether the trainees they were mentoring could be expected to become "highly qualified and class-conscious medical cadres and friends of the German Democratic Republic."[729] East German officials worked diligently to convince their international audience that political freedom, economic development, and social progress depended on the solidarity between the Third World and the socialist camp in their common struggle against imperialism, racism, and all forms of exploitation and oppression. However, this fusion of vocational education and political indoctrination was not necessarily greeted with any greater enthusiasm by Third World students and trainees than by the East German populace itself. While the ritualistic proclamations of solidarity that were the target of East European dissent may have rolled off the back of many of these visitors, others chafed under the continuous political education that was forced upon them. The resulting conflicts generated much of the documentation of the experiences of students and trainees from the Third World in East Germany.

Because training physicians was a long and costly undertaking, the East German government was only able to fund medical study or provide advanced medical training in specialized fields to a limited number of doctors from selected countries of "special political interest." In 1961, for example, seventeen physicians from India, Iraq, Sudan, Syria, Tunisia, and Egypt traveled to East Germany for one-year study visits, while thirty-two mid-level medical administrators came from Africa.[730] Conversely, although many developing countries asked the East German government to send them physicians for extended periods,[731] the health ministry could not comply with such requests because so many qualified medical personnel had fled for the West.[732] Between 1954 and the construction of the Wall, some 3,371 physicians had fled to West Germany.[733] In fact, the shortage was so severe that the East German government was forced to recruit doctors from elsewhere in Eastern Europe, with the first group of seventy Bulgarian doctors arriving in 1957.[734] The East Germans also tried to exploit doctors from the Third World and other European countries, who, they reasoned, could help care for the population while acquiring advanced training in a medical specialty.[735]

Mali was the first sub-Saharan African state to send auxiliary medical workers to East Germany for advanced training on the basis of a bilateral agreement between the two countries. In September 1961 eighteen Malinese men between the ages of 17 and 34 arrived in East Berlin.[736] They came from privileged families, had graduated from high school and/ or college, and had worked in French colonial hospitals before independence, some even as head nurses.[737] According to the terms of the agreement, fourteen of them would be trained as physician assistants, and the rest would study anesthesiology, dentistry, sanitary inspection, medical laboratory techniques, or some combination thereof. When the terms were first being worked out, Malinese Health Minister Sominé Dolo had emphasized that, after returning to Mali, many of these trainees would work as directors and administrators in rural dispensaries, that their training should prepare them for a wide range of responsibilities, that the program should focus on tropical medicine, and that German language instruction should be kept to a minimum in order to maximize the time available for professional study.[738] The minister assumed – mistakenly, as it turned out – that this last request could be easily met because many East German doctors were fluent in French.[739]

Whatever faith Malinese health officials originally placed in the East German system, they were soon disappointed by a training system ill-suited to their needs and a bureaucracy unresponsive to their concerns. Despite years of healthcare experience in Mali, the trainees were required to clean rooms and make beds for several months as an ostensible part of their basic training. The lack of expertise in tropical medicine created a serious disconnect – one that was never bridged – between the educational needs of the trainees and a German curriculum that was designed to train nurses to work in urban hospitals.[740] As one official wrote in a different context, "it will not be easy for us to provide the training desired by the Africans in a way that our friends will be able to meet all of the challenges they will face when they return home…We hardly have even a theoretical knowledge of many of the most prevalent diseases there, and our friends already know more about these than we do…Only now do we really see how different our ideas are from the realities there."[741]

The gap between expectation and reality dismayed the Malinese government. In a note to the German trade mission in Bamako, the Malinese Foreign Ministry pointedly asked whether the responsible officials would provide the students with the previously agreed-upon course of study and ensure training in the relevant medical specialties.[742] These complaints led to a series of meetings between state officials, the school, and the trainees themselves, who asked why they were placed in a class below their level and kept apart from the German students. However, to judge from an interview with the Malinese trainees on Radio Berlin International, these meetings did not yield any substantial improvements. As the interviewer reported to the Foreign Ministry, "the students had gradually come to the belief that it would be better to return to Mali."[743]

Many of these problems recurred when a second group of medical trainees arrived from sub-Saharan Africa. In August 1962, four men and women arrived in Dessau from Niger for training sponsored by the Committee for Solidarity with the Peoples of Africa. At the welcoming ceremony held in their honor, the secretary of the Committee told the Nigeriens that they were now among friends "among whom openness and honesty rule in all questions." Representatives from the local branches of the party, FDGB, and the FDJ, as well as health officials, promised to be attentive to the needs of the visitors and to help them understand the significance of the division of Germany. They wanted the Nigeriens to understand that "imperialism is our common enemy so that they will find in this knowledge sustenance for their struggle at home."[744]

The problems that would plague all such training programs soon became visible. The physicians shunted responsibility for their training to the head nurse, and for their first six months in Quedlinburg the Nigeriens, including their group leader Ide Mamoudou, who had already worked for eight years as a nurse, were required to perform unskilled cleaning work. Unhappy with being treated in this manner, the Nigeriens began showing up late for work and leaving early. Soon the medical staff, including the head doctor, refused to work with the most defiant of the group and asked the Health Ministry to deport him. The other trainees asked to return home ahead of schedule.[745] On top of all this, Touré Hama, one of the four Nigeriens, had been mistakenly assigned to metal work training, and it took authorities six months to correct the problem. Although Hama wanted to become an assistant physician, the German insistence that he first complete two years of basic training in nursing delayed the start of his desired training until May 1965. Moreover, once his training finally began, he was neglected by the physician who was supposed to be training him. In a letter to the authorities he pleaded to be transferred to another city, where he hoped to receive better training. This request was denied.[746] After the Nigeriens left the country in January 1965, Deputy Health

Minister Michael Gehring wrote to the hospital praising the administration and staff for "contributing through your untiring labor to strengthening international solidarity and friendship with the peoples of Africa."[747]

In November 1960, East Germany signed a technical exchange treaty with Cuba. Under the provisions of the treaty, 180 Cubans were to travel to East Germany for training. According to this agreement, the Committee for Solidarity with the People of Cuba, which had been established in January 1961, was supposed to fly wounded Cuban veterans to East Germany for medical treatment and rehabilitation and provide the Cubans with the equipment and blueprints for an orthopedic workshop and assistance in getting the shop up and running.[748] In the spring of 1964, ten Cuban women traveled to Quedlinburg to study nursing.[749] They do not appear to have fared any better than the Africans. When the Cuban education minister visited East Germany in 1965, these women complained that they were not being taught how to give intravenous injections or receiving training in midwifery, postnatal care, or psychiatry, all of which were shortage fields in Cuba itself. Many of them already had basic training in nursing, and they did not see why they should repeat this part of the curriculum, as the Germans demanded.[750]

We must look to systemic causes, rather than individual failings, to explain why these training programs yielded neither the practical benefits expected by the trainees nor the political benefits expected by the East German government. Because most of the population in Africa lived in rural areas far from the few existing hospitals, these countries had a pressing need for medical officers, midwives, physician assistants (*Arzthelfer*), and sanitary inspectors. Work in the rural healthcare centers where most of these trainees would be employed required a much broader body of knowledge and skills than those taught by European schools.[751] Nor were the East Germans able to integrate into their curricula indigenous medical knowledge and practice, which they regarded as little more than witchcraft. These trainees often had substantial education and experience in their home countries and had high hopes for what they might learn in East Germany. However, the absence of a clear program for meeting their needs, together with the housekeeping tasks and basic patient care into which they were shunted, quickly alienated these visitors.

The goals of these programs were also compromised by essentially racist views of the Africans. During their time in East Germany, African students routinely encountered racial prejudice, which most often manifested itself in the conviction that Africans had to be taught the basic virtues of work, discipline, and order before they could hope to acquire skills or technical knowledge of any kind. Most of these trainees were well-educated individuals who had grown up in urban centers. For example, most British physicians and medical officers left Zanzibar soon after the 1964 socialist revolution (Chapter 9). As part of a plan to fill the gap created by their departure, the government selected a group of healthcare workers for additional training in East Germany. This group of fifteen men and five women from Zanzibar were comparatively well-educated and experienced. Most of them had graduated from Lumumba College or Nasser Technical School; they had already passed their nursing exams; and they generally had five to ten years of healthcare work behind them. However, in the eyes of many East Germans they were bushmen and -women, who were assigned to filthy, demeaning jobs that no German workers would accept. Such views were still current in the 1980s, when an unprecedented number of people of color were employed as contract workers in East Germany.[752]

Although their efforts were not always successful, the people who administered training programs went to substantial lengths to prevent African trainees from having close personal – and sexual – relations with the East Germans. Within a few months of their arrival in Quedlinburg, the school reported to the Health Ministry that the Malinese men had entered into "undesirable" relationships with German students and that these relationships had led to pregnancies.[753] School officials in Quedlinburg and elsewhere were extremely sensitive about such relationships between East Germans and African students. The director of the medical school in Potsdam, for example, panicked when he realized that four men from Zanzibar, who had just completed their training, had some free time before they were scheduled to return home. He was worried that these Africans had "an increasingly strong need for a variety of female acquaintances." Although he blamed the German women involved with these African men, he nevertheless asked the Health Ministry to transfer the Zanzibaris from Potsdam to Quedlinburg, where they would have fewer opportunities to socialize with German women.[754]

The problem of interracial relations was compounded by the fact that racism could not be publicly discussed in a socialist country where it was not supposed to exist. However, the issue could not be avoided completely, as can be seen in the story of Antoinette Diarra, a 16-year-old Malinese who, along with two other girls, came to East Germany in 1960. One of girls was the daughter of a Malinese minister. She had graduated from high school and wished to study medicine in East Germany, while Diarra expected to become a midwife or physician assistant. Instead, all three girls were assigned jobs as nurse aides at the Hufeland Hospital in Berlin-Buch, where they had to perform unskilled manual work for first few months.[755] The hospital staff had no idea what to do with these African girls. Out of frustration, they started not showing up for work. Luckily, officials from the Health Ministry, who visited the girls on International Women's Day to demonstrate solidarity with the peoples of Africa, saw how unhappy the girls were and took steps to improve their training.

Eventually, Diarra was sent to Quedlinburg to join the eighteen Malinese men. She completed her basic training and then moved to Leipzig to study midwifery at Karl Marx University. However, the head teacher of the midwifery program wrote a damning evaluation, saying Diarra "is not in a condition to succeed either in training in midwifery or any other vocation in the German Democratic Republic. She does not show either energy or willpower. She can not think logically. In addition, she is extremely unreliable and dishonest."[756] Diarra felt the director had treated her unfairly, and in a letter to the Health Ministry she challenged her supervisor's evaluation. "You," she wrote to the ministry,

can judge for yourselves whether someone could make it all the way from Africa to the GDR without doing anything. That is very curious. If I wanted to play around, I could stay at home. But I have come here to learn a profession and then return home. What the director says is pure silliness, and the people back in Mali will never believe it. Since I've been here, the director has not given me any money…If the people in Mali knew that, they would be very unhappy… The director is not very honest. If the director does not want to have me in her school, she should say the truth rather than insisting that I do not want to work. The director has really taken away my spirit. If she were a student in Mali, no one would treat her the same way that I have been treated here in the GDR.[757]

Nor were African trainees any less sensitive to hardships caused by the persistent shortages of consumer goods. Health Ministry officials were aware that the country's widespread housing shortage and the poor condition of the available housing could damage the "reputation of the German Democratic Republic in the developing countries."[758] But there was no easy remedy. Some of the women were forced to live in a room next to the hospital morgue, and even they were better off than those who still had no permanent lodgings long after the semester had begun. Nor were conditions any better for one South African woman. She worked as a midwife in Erfurt before becoming pregnant herself. With her due date approaching and her boyfriend about to begin his university studies in Berlin, she repeatedly asked the Health Ministry to help her find a job and an apartment for both of them. Ministry officials, however, replied only rarely and always in the negative.[759]

Although many East Germans imagined that these students from presumably primitive cultures and underdeveloped lands would see the socialist country as a land of plenty, these African trainees also faced a number of other hardships directly related to the nature of the East German *Mangelgesellschaft*. Although the tropical fruits they routinely ate were unavailable, the African students could at least tell themselves that the East German population fared no better. However, pervasive food and material shortages affected Africans differently than the Germans themselves. While ordinary Germans were happy with whatever pork products the regime provided, African Muslims found their diet somewhat restricted, especially because other kinds of meat were in short supply.[760]

Foreign trainees reacted against their daily difficulties in a variety of ways, from absenteeism to direct confrontation with the authorities. Some left a trail of petitions documenting their efforts to work things out. The Zanzibari men wrote to the Health Ministry that "we are of the firm conviction that a decline of our health and a decrease in the ability to concentrate – both of which are dependent on nutrition – will be the unavoidable consequences" of the poor quality and low nutritional value of their food in East Germany. While many East German teachers and health officials blamed the poor performance of the African students on a lack of discipline, language problems, and laziness, the Zanzibaris pointed to the poor living conditions. They offered to let the ministry deduct extra money from their monthly stipends in order to procure better-quality food, a request to which the ministry acceded.[761]

Conditions were not much better with the actual learning environment. Given the predictable difficulties with separable prefixes and armies of umlauts, the Zanzibari students believed their studies would proceed more smoothly if they could get their hands on medical books and dictionaries written in French or English. They were even willing to use their own money to buy English texts on anatomy, anesthesiology, and tropical dietetics. However, the Health Ministry admonished the students that the Zanzibari government "would certainly not look kindly upon it if, in questions of training and continuing education, the citizens of its country were to rely on English-language literature."[762]

Curricular problems also continued to hinder Zanzibari trainees. In 1967, two Zanzibari men were supposed to study anesthesiology at the Robert-Koch hospital in Dessau. According to the head nurse, they were both "very clever, open-minded, eager to learn and extremely disciplined."[763] The problem was that the faculty in Dessau had no idea what to teach them.[764] Knowledge of anesthesiology was important for African healthcare workers because they often had to administer anesthesia until patients could be brought from remote rural areas to an urban clinic. But in East Germany, anesthesiology was a specialty for physicians, and the hospital staff in Dessau was unprepared to provide appropriate instruction to these men. Nor were the Germans particularly adept at building upon the traditional medical and healing practices of these peoples. The two students eventually wrote to the East German health ministry complaining – politely – that in Dessau they hadn't learned "anything useful" and asking to be transferred to another place "where we could learn something." "We would like to inform you," they wrote a little later, "that it would be like a punishment for us if we have to remain in Dessau."[765] Their request was denied.

Volumes of correspondence between the Health Ministry and medical schools, instructions from the top, and reports of inspection visits from the Health Ministry to local teaching hospitals testify both to the extent of their efforts to keep foreigners under tight control and the concern, which often verged on paranoia, that neglected students might become saboteurs.[766] As a result, many of the trainees were alienated by the overt politicization of these development and exchange programs.

There was one final aspect of state-socialist modernity from which these non-Western trainees could not escape. Like all East German citizens, these trainees were enmeshed in a tight network of surveillance and political education, which Konrad Jarausch has characterized as "coercive care."[767] The Health Ministry required written evaluations of foreign students from a variety of individuals and institutions: the school director, department chair, advisor, head nurse, station nurse, chief doctor, and station doctor. Trainees were evaluated for work discipline, order, and punctuality, as well as personal hygiene and appearance.[768] Character and comportment counted just as much, and even excellent academic and work performances would not offset a bad evaluation if a trainee's personal behavior did not live up to expectations with regard to political and ideological standards.

Over the years, the practice of writing evaluations became increasingly ritualized, and it functioned in two important ways to promote stability. First, this enforced record-keeping made individuals and local institutions complicit in the disciplinary complex of state socialism. Second, it was through this practice that the authors of these evaluations articulated and enacted the basic principles of socialist citizenship. The standardized evaluation form emphasized the development of the socialist self over the course of the training period. Evaluators took this category seriously, and they were particularly sensitive to a student's failure to develop confidence and a sense of self-awareness. Especially among foreign students, traits such as shyness, passivity, and sensitivity were regarded as childish, backward, and even something innate to non-European peoples. The ideal person was not private and self-centered in the way that the acquisitive individuals of the capitalist world were imagined to be, but rather worked in harmony with the overlapping network of social collectivities in which all citizens were embedded. Theorists of socialist society believed that participation in these groups was essential to transforming individuals into collective beings.[769] Written evaluations usually followed a standard structure, beginning with a description of individual character, then rating of academic and work performance, and finally a measure of his or her interaction with the collective. Disproportionate importance was assigned to this last element.

The nursing or hospital station collective was the primary collective responsible for socializing foreign trainees, who were expected to interact successfully within it.[770] However, African and Asian trainees – like many East Germans – found mandatory socialization onerous, and they preferred to spend their time with the African Student Union or other students from their home country. In addition, cultural differences, language barriers, and traditional German attitudes toward foreigners made it next to impossible for these visitors to perform the desired self-fashioning of the socialist citizen in a German context; as a result, many of them were marked down for their insufficiently enthusiastic participation.

A case in point was the experience of Cora B. N., a 17-year-old South African, who came to East Germany in September 1969 to study nursing. She was pregnant – a circumstance that caused some concern among high-ranking state officials. This "pressing and complicated" situation became even more so when Cora sought an abortion against the wishes of both her doctor and school authorities. Cora was ultimately unable to procure the abortion.[771] However, her case went all the way to the SED Central Committee, which sought to make Cora into an example of the power of the socialist state to remold the character of this obstinate young woman and bring her around to a proper understanding of her social obligations. In the words of a leading Health Ministry official, "the best help for her would be, in my opinion, if we helped her arrive at a socialist understanding of the problem...I will see to it that careful medical and social support is provided."[772]

The government granted Cora all available medical and welfare benefits. She was admitted to a maternity home, where she delivered a girl named Rita; she was granted a paid postnatal leave; and her daughter was admitted to a nursery, where Cora was expected to visit her regularly. In September 1970, Cora resumed her training in a German-only class in Quedlinburg, and two-and-a-half years later she received her state nursing certificate. Cora wanted to become a nursing instructor.[773] She first worked as a nurse at a district hospital in Potsdam for a semester, where she needed to get good evaluations in order to enroll in the medical pedagogy program at the Polytechnic College for Medicine and Social Welfare in Potsdam. She received high marks in every area – academics, work, and relation to the collective – except for lack of work discipline and her supposed neglect of maternal duties. Reportedly, Cora failed to visit Rita every weekend, as her collective had suggested, and her responses to questions about Rita's well-being ranged "from exaggerated foolishness to defiance." Based on their evaluation of Cora's "total self-development," school officials had serious doubts about whether she should be allowed to continue with her studies in medical pedagogy.[774] Perhaps because of the symbolic significance of her case, this evaluation was overruled, and in September 1973 Cora was allowed to begin her studies.

Two years later, however, the school asked the Health Ministry for permission to expel her. Although Cora was very smart and spoke fluent German, she had, as the director of the college put it, an "attitude problem," meaning that she was unwilling to participate in collective activities and other politico-ideological group projects. Cora traveled to West Berlin, slept during indoctrination, participated only passively in student activities, and invited outsiders to the dorm in the evening. She also failed to demonstrate a "sufficient sense of obligation" toward her daughter, despite urgings from teachers, colleagues, and members of the FDJ. In the end, they were unable to bring about a "decisive reorientation in Cora's behavior."[775] The FDJ branch at the Potsdam college also wrote its own evaluation of Cora's development. Under the category of "Position and Comportment in the Collective," the evaluation cited all the important political and ideological meetings and mass ceremonies in which she did not participate or where she played only a passive role. The evaluation also emphasized that Cora did not respond to many initiatives from the collective and the study group intended to help her.

For example, hoping to correct Cora's alleged neglect of her motherly duty, one student took it upon herself to act as sort of a godmother for Cora and Rita, and she invited them to her house "in order to create [for Cora] a familial atmosphere and a place that she can call home." As the FDJ leadership at the Potsdam college put it, despite numerous "tough confrontations and discussions," Cora did not show "tact, courtesy, comradeship and responsibility" for the collective and its members. Based on this assessment, they concluded that Cora lacked the character necessary to become a teacher.[776]

Although Cora came close to being expelled from the school, she was given one more chance to prove herself by working for a year as a nurse in a district hospital in Dresden-Friedrichstadt. Now it was the staff and colleagues there who had a chance to evaluate her, and Cora seemed to pull it off this time. She received positive marks on her interaction with the hospital collective.[777] Unfortunately, Cora's South African mentor was displeased because she refused to break up with her politically questionable African boyfriend, and he asked the school director and the SED Central Committee to not allow her to continue her studies. Although the African Student Association supported Cora, this man was determined to expel her.[778] In July 1976 the Central Committee ordered her to leave the country within six weeks.[779] The last document of Cora's misadventures in the land of actually existing socialism is a letter from July 1977. At that point, Cora and her daughter were living in Lusaka, Zambia. In the letter, Cora asked for copies of her transcripts so that she could resume her studies. She concluded with a comment on how much she had learned in Zambia where, in contrast to East Germany, she had been entrusted with many important responsibilities.[780]

While the East Germans hoped that this political education would solidify support for East Germany in the Third World, these programs – like the hygiene expositions – never fully succeeded. Not only were the East Germans unable in many cases to provide the promised instruction. East German physicians, nurses, and officials also seemed unable to consistently display solidarity toward the real people from Asia and Africa with whom they interacted on their home soil, despite the constant, ritualized proclamations of international solidarity against oppression. These problems were exacerbated by material shortages that affected foreign trainees in specific ways and by a persistent core of essentially racist attitudes toward people of color and their cultures. Instead of forging closer bonds, the pervasive institutional discrimination faced by these trainees often alienated these trainees and their home governments from East German socialism.

Last, by the end of the 1960s, the ideological energies that had initially inspired the socialist project in East Germany flagged, and in the 1970s the government adopted a more pragmatic, consumerist approach to maintaining stability. The new political economy of late socialism also affected attitudes and policies toward young people from the Third World, who were increasingly seen as a source of cheap labor, rather than as comrades in arms. Beginning with the Algerian contract workers who arrived in East Germany in 1974, technical exchange programs ceased to be a vehicle of cultural diplomacy and became, instead, one more means of propping up a tottering socialist economy.

7

The Time Machine "Development"

INTRODUCTION: FROM EURAFRICA TO THE COMMON MARKET

As we have seen in previous chapters, East Germany began its medical and development aid programs to the Third World after 1956 in conjunction with shifts in Soviet policy and as a means of circumventing the constraints imposed by the Hallstein doctrine. West Germany did not systematically engage with the question of Third World development until several years later. This new sensitivity to the Third World was due to several factors: (1) the radicalization of national liberation movements, (2) East Germany's expanding initiatives in the nonaligned world, and (3) the reconfiguration of the relationship between the European powers and their (former) colonies and protectorates associated with the formation of the Common Market. In this chapter, I will analyze West German medical and development aid programs from the early 1950s through the mid-1960s.

Germany had a long tradition of overseas medical charity work. Since the turn of the century German missionaries, colonizers, and settlers had established and operated a number of hospitals in Asia, Africa, and South America, and in the early 1950s the West Germans sought to reestablish ties with these institutions. However, after 1945 it was impossible for the German imperial imagination to go home again in any simple sense. The world war and decolonization made it much more difficult to speak of these institutions in any direct or simple sense as "German," and in the first section I will examine the tortuous and ultimately less-than-successful efforts to negotiate this minefield of political memory in order to construct a viable postwar national identity.

West German development policy was not simply a response to decolonization, but also a reaction to the reconfiguration of the economic and geopolitical space of Europe. In the second section, I will attempt to tease out the connections between decolonization, European integration, and the reimagination of Europe's relation to the non-European world. Despite the formal process of decolonization, European influence in Africa remained integral to Europe's self-perception and helped shape the idea of the Common Market, and I will argue that the West Germans held to a modernized, postcolonial idea of the White Man's Burden to justify their privileged position in this Eurafrican space. Moreover, like the East Germans, the West Germans also sponsored traveling exhibitions in Africa. However, their propaganda safaris fared little better than their mission in South Korea for many of the same reasons that underlay the fiasco in Pusan.

As we have seen, East Germany was first off the mark with regard to constructive cultural-political engagement with the nonaligned world. However, at the turn of the 1960s West Germany began a concerted effort to catch up, both with regard to promoting its image in the Third World and formulating its own development aid policy. The third section will examine both West Germany's propaganda and public relations campaign in Africa and East Germany's response as each country sought to disparage the other in the eyes of the African audience by burdening them with the more unsavory aspects of their shared past.

The Hallstein doctrine also provided the basis for West Germany's response to both decolonization and East Germany's foreign policy initiatives in the Third World. Just as East Germany used humanitarian, medical, and development aid to circumvent the constraints of the Hallstein doctrine, so West Germany used aid to enforce it. As West Germany became more active in international development aid, the promise of aid represented, as the West German Finance Minister put it in 1964, a "premium for good behavior in regard to the German question."[781] While the Hallstein temptation is mocked in Figure 7.1, the threat to withhold such assistance represented a form of soft power that could be deployed throughout the Third Word to blunt East German initiatives.

However, as the last section will show, this effort involved West Germany in an elaborate dance with both East Germany and the nonaligned countries. While the East Germans were constantly seeking to outmaneuver Bonn to gain the loyalty of the nonaligned world, the Africans constantly played the two German states against each other,

FIGURE 7.1 This East German cartoon parodied West Germany's effort to gain support for the Hallstein Doctrine in northern Africa (1961). The signs mounted on the camels are hawking the Hallstein doctrine – like a political patent medicine – to the accompaniment of Hallstein playing a flute and music blaring from the gramophone mounted on the last camel in the caravan.
Source: Louis Rauwolf. Courtesy of Zeitgeschichtliches Forum, Leipzig, Haus der Geschichte, Bonn.

hoping to maximize the amount of aid available to pursue nation-building agendas that did not necessarily coincide with the preferences of either German state. At the same time, the increasing self-assertiveness of national liberation movements and their willingness to use force to challenge white rule were gradually depriving the Hallstein doctrine of much of its potency and making it increasingly difficult to discursively contain the dangers emanating from the Third World. Once the West Germans realized that the financial sacrifices they made to promote development in Africa were only going to be repaid with inconsistent gratitude, they reacted acerbically to every attempt by Third World countries to play the two blocs against each other in the aid game and blamed the steadily decreasing political leverage of their aid programs on the flawed character of the Africans, rather than on the growing desire for self-determination in these former colonies.

I. ME AND MY SHADOW

In October 1957, a 36-year-old Iranian doctor named Sadj-djād Sādjadi visited the West German embassy in Tehran. He was from a family of large landowners in Azerbaijan, and he presented an elaborate plan for building a German hospital in Tabriz, a city in the northwestern part of the country. The mission officer was impressed by Sādjadi's plans, and it did not hurt that Sādjadi had specialized in surgery at Hamburg University or that, since 1951, he had been working there as a surgeon. Sādjadi had already recruited some West German medical professionals for the proposed facility; he had secured the property for the hospital and funding for its construction; and he was promising to purchase all of the medical equipment and supplies from West German companies. In other words, he was not asking so much for financial assistance to build the hospital as for the blessing of the German government and the right to call it the "German Hospital." What he offered in return was a precious commodity: goodwill. As he explained, not only would the hospital strive to "preserve the prestige of German medical sciences," the project would also help cement relations between Germany and Iran. "In my opinion," Sādjadi wrote, "the construction of this hospital in Iran, and, in particular, in the province of Azerbaijan, which desperately needs such assistance, will contribute, like an intense fire, to strengthening cultural relations between the two countries. Together with my brothers and the energetic people of Tabriz, we will work to insure that these relations become closer and more beautiful with every passing day."[782]

The mission officer forwarded the plans for the project to his superiors in Bonn with a favorable recommendation. Unfortunately, the people back in Bonn were not swayed by Sādjadi's rhetoric because they didn't think that German Hospital was "German" enough. At the German Chamber of Physicians, Werner Röken voiced "substantial reservations in principle" regarding the proposal. In order to protect the reputation of Germandom and German medicine in the wider world, Röken argued, the right to call an institution a German hospital should be subject to stringent standards, which could only be met if German authorities were given a degree of oversight and control over the operation of the hospital, something an Iranian private enterprise was unlikely to permit.[783] The Foreign Office agreed and wrote to Sādjadi that, if he wanted to call the hospital German and thus serve a flag-bearer for German medicine in that part of the world, he would have to find ways to institutionalize German influence on its staffing and operation.[784]

This story leads back to a very simple question: Just what did the term "German" mean to West German authorities in the 1950s and 1960s? During these years, the West Germans devoted considerable energy to reactivating and, if necessary, re-Germanizing hospitals and clinics founded by German individuals and organizations in the decades before 1933, but that in the intervening years had lost their original connections to the European metropole. The reconstruction of (West) German national identity required a great deal of complex cultural labor that involved reaching back to the heroic age of German medical science, reknotting the ties binding overseas medical charities to the Germans who had founded them, striking a balance between the Germanness of these organizations and their loyalties to the nations (both old and new) where they were located, and mastering the Nazi past or, in some instances, simply shipping it overseas.

For many Germans, advances in medicine, physics, and chemistry were the crowning achievement of German science and the legitimizing force for German colonialism.[785] The symbolic value of these accomplishments was embodied in the Nobel Prize awarded in 1905 to Robert Koch for his work in bacteriology. Bacteriology became the springboard for a series of German advances in tropical medicine, and in the first decades of the 20th century each innovation served as tangible proof of the beneficent role of German medicine in the colonial world. In the 1960s, this legacy of German colonialism was rearticulated to provide the ideological underpinnings of West German aid to the Third World.[786]

Because German medicine had played such a sinister role in the Nazi regime, many physicians had a difficult time either opening private practices or finding employment after the war. These men eagerly welcomed offers to work in Asia and the Middle East, where new governments were building national health systems and looking for foreign doctors to staff hospitals and train native physicians. Beginning in 1949, the German Chamber of Physicians recruited German doctors to work in Iran, and in September 1950 alone more than 600 German doctors applied for forty positions in the country. German doctors, male and female, were soon employed in Saudi Arabia, Ethiopia, Liberia, and Indonesia.[787] Inge Schubart, who was "so sick and tired of postwar poverty" in Munich, concluded that working in Indonesia as a state-employed physician was the only way to save enough money to open a private practice.[788] Third World countries also hired physicians who had been forbidden to practice medicine at home because they had been implicated in more egregious Nazi crimes. For example, Horst Schumann, who had conducted experiments on the use of radiation to sterilize inmates at Auschwitz and Ravensbrück, worked as the medical director of a hospital in Khartoum, Sudan, for some years after the war.[789]

During the interwar years, German flagship hospitals in major cities – Istanbul, Shanghai, Teheran, London, Rome, and Madrid – had solidified the international reputation of German medicine. However, during the war Allied forces or host governments confiscated these facilities, and many of them had lost any meaningful connections to the European metropole.[790] After the founding of the Federal Republic, Adenauer, who concurrently served as Foreign Minister until mid-1955, decided that reestablishing hospitals and schools abroad would enhance the new state's international reputation. In 1952, the Foreign Office instructed all of its missions to identify German hospitals in their areas and provide information on the number of German doctors and nurses working in these facilities, their ownership and legal status, whether they needed to be renovated, and, if so, the estimated cost of this work.[791] In response, overseas mission officers sent details about these institutions, their characteristics, their historical background, and even patient profiles. They enjoyed great latitude in defining what constituted a "German" institution. For some diplomats, it was enough if the director of the hospital director was German, even if a non-German entity owned it.

In Africa, most German hospitals and dispensaries had been established by Christian missionaries during the colonial era. However, this coupling of medical care with religious proselytizing led to popular resentment, especially after 1945.[792] Because all of these institutions were financially strapped, the prospect of aid from Bonn tempted them to emphasize their Germanness, no matter how attenuated. For example, writing on behalf of a brand new hospital in India, the director of the Institute for Medical Missions explained that the hospital embodied "German thoroughness, cleanness and solidness" and that the German physician and nurses working there, as well as the German medicines they used, enjoyed exceptional trust among the Indian people.[793] A letter written on behalf of a maternal clinic in Windhoek, Namibia (former German Southwest Africa) tacked in precisely the opposite direction, boasting that the clinic, founded by the German Colonial Society, had exclusively served "for all the white women of the country since 1908 and also through the two World Wars."[794] Such positive representations of the German colonial tradition, which were widespread among both private aid agencies and foreign missionaries, reflected not only a willful blindness to the ways these institutions reproduced colonial power relations but also to West Germany's criminal past. In this sense, they reflected the policy of the Adenauer administration, which was to remain as silent as possible about the past while integrating the perpetrators into West German society.

German hospitals abroad took on a hybrid character, either as the result of confiscation during World War II or from the influx of local staff after independence. As a result, it became increasingly difficult to speak of these institutions without qualification as German. For example, the German consulate in Porto Alegre in southern Brazil reported that it was now impossible to categorize the many German hospitals that had existed in the area before World War II as "officially as German or predominantly German," and he blamed the "excessive nationalism" of the Brazilians for the virtual disappearance of the German character of those facilities.[795] In some instances, the prospect of German aid led hospital administrations to reduce the number of non-German staff to make their facilities appear more German. For example, a hospital that had originally been built by German immigrants to Brazil had been nationalized by the Brazilian authorities, and Polish women were now in charge of the nursing staff. However, the hospital director, a German descendent, told the German embassy in Rio de Janeiro that "in the interest of Germandom" he was going to replace Polish nurses with Germans: "In this way cultural interests can be better maintained, especially since these German nurses should devote themselves to German language instruction and the education of the young." Although this may not have been a straight *quid pro quo*, the hospital did receive funding from Bonn.[796]

In March 1958, the Foreign Ministry decided to compile a list of German hospitals abroad that might be eligible for aid to modernize their buildings and equipment so that they could maintain the standards expected of "German" facilities. Foreign missions were instructed to enumerate all the German hospitals and similar institutions (old age homes, infant homes, and maternal homes) in the country. Whereas an earlier request had simply asked for a list of German institutions, this time the requirement that such institutions be only "predominantly" German rendered the definition substantially more elastic, perhaps to accommodate the murky realities on the periphery. The diplomats were asked to elaborate in their responses on the "German" character of the hospitals, that is, whether the legal ownership was a German hospital association or missionary society, whether the medical director was a German doctor, whether the nursing staff were German, and so on[797]

Many of these institutions had links to the two Christian churches, and in 1960 Adenauer decided to offer subsidies to the churches and their affiliated organizations working in the Third World. At the end of that year, the Foreign Office asked diplomatic representatives to report on German missionary work "in the broader sense," including the educational and social-charitable activities of the churches, as well as their plans in the field of technical aid. In the case of programs run by non-Germans, consular officials were instructed to explain if their predominantly German character was due to the staffing of the key administrative positions or "*the perception of the local population,*" a possibility that stretched the concept of Germanness to its limit.[798]

The meaning of such elastic characterizations was never clearly defined. Most Catholic missionary organizations in Africa, such as the White Fathers, were operated by nationally mixed groups, and a growing number of Africans served as priests and nuns. In response to an interrogatory, the Foreign Office ruled that, to qualify for assistance, "*at least* the responsible director of the project for which an assistance was requested should be German."[799] In one such project in Ghana, the Metropolitan Archdiocese of Cape Coast and the local authorities were jointly funding the construction of a new mission hospital. However, there was a question of how to pay for furniture and medical equipment. In a request for support from the Foreign Office, the new medical director knew exactly which notes to hit. Although German doctors enjoyed high esteem in Africa, where they were the "representative of the German Federal Republic," the director wrote, "the reputation of a hospital rises and falls with" the quality of the medical equipment. An endorsement from the German embassy in Ghana added that "in every instance a hospital that is under the direction of a German physician fulfills a German mission."[800]

The Foreign Office reminded the diplomatic missions to be discreet about emphasizing their German character in order to minimize the danger of a nationalist backlash. The German consul in southern Brazil, who was clearly aware of "the remaining nationalist tendency" of local authorities, decided not to gather the required information from the Brazilian director and administrators of the hospital in order to avoid giving the impression that "German authorities were trying to exert influence on this institution." Any hint of undue German influence, he continued, could lead to "unfriendly political discussions." Nevertheless, he asserted that the hospital had only survived due to "constant willingness of the ethnic German population to make the necessary sacrifices" and that, for this very reason, it deserved state subsidies.[801]

Such stories received wide coverage in the West German media, which eagerly recounted how German settlers abroad had created their own German hospital association, built their own hospital to care for their compatriots, lost it all to the allies or postwar nationalization, and now, thanks to aid from Bonn, were rebuilding. The German Hospital in Buenos Aires was the object of one such romanticizing, nationalist narrative in the *Süddeutsche Zeitung*: "When all of the signs bearing the word 'German' were taken down in Buenos Aires during the last war, only the two words *Hospital Alemán*, which for almost eighty years had marked the entrance to the complex of the German hospital, remained unchanged." After the war, the hospital faced imminent demise, and the question was "whether one could dare to make the great leap, build a bridge to the future, and remain among the leading hospitals in Argentina and South America?" The newspaper reported that the Bundestag had approved two million marks for the hospital and that German industry also pledged its aid. Such institutionalized support was essential, explained the chair of the hospital association, because "the hospital can no longer exist as a local association, but only as one example of generous German cultural labor abroad. That we have found a willing ear for this idea from Bonn gratifies us even more than the financial support."[802]

Such constructions of Germanness sometimes repressed or veiled the rich history of local institutions, whose existence and survival was due not just to the sacrifice of Germans alone, but to the multiethnic pooling of local and national resources. For example, a Chilean hospital, which had been founded by German immigrants in 1907, but that had burned down in 1948, was rebuilt with substantial financial support from the Chilean government. However, the subsequent reinvention of the institution as a German hospital left no trace of the Chilean role in its rebuilding.[803]

II. GERMANY AND THE EURAFRICAN IMAGINATION

The external borders of West Germany, and of Western Europe more generally, were definitively stabilized by the mid-1950s. In 1955, the two German states were granted sovereignty within the overarching frameworks of NATO and the Warsaw Pact.[804] All hopes of rolling back communism and undoing the Yalta settlement were dashed for the foreseeable future by the Soviet acquisition of nuclear weapons and by the inability of the United States to halt the Soviet invasion of Hungary in 1956.[805] Ultimately, the two superpowers reached a tacit agreement that the Cold War in Europe would remain cold and "that neither side would do anything to change boundaries."[806] The Treaty of Rome was signed in 1957, and the European Economic Community came into existence the following year.[807]

While the two superpowers opposed formal colonial rule, the continuation in one form or another of imperial rule in Africa was central to the conception of Europe that informed debates over European integration and the Common Market in the 1950s.[808] These debates were shaped by three main concerns. The first was the desire to institutionalize those forms of economic cooperation that were considered the key to overcoming the nationalism that had played such a baneful role in European history over the previous century.[809] Second, the Soviet threat and the search for security, together with the recognition that the only geopolitical option for West Germany was integration into the Atlantic alliance, had a "disciplining and solidarizing" effect on the countries of Western Europe.[810] The third set of concerns revolved around empire, decolonization, and the relation of colonies to the future continental community.

By the mid-1950s, the control of the European powers over their respective overseas empires had grown more tenuous than ever before. The decision to pursue a greater degree of political and economic integration by means of the Common Market represented, as Peo Hansen has argued, a way of displacing and compensating for the rapid deterioration of their position overseas in the aftermath of the Suez debacle. However, in the minds of many of its architects, the success of the undertaking was premised, as Hansen has argued, on the "hidden enlargement" of the European Economic Community into Africa.[811]

Although the Versailles Treaty had stripped Germany of its colonies, Africa remained important to West Germany's European identity, and the country's relations to both Africa and the Common Market were conceptualized in terms of the economic and geopolitical concept of Eurafrica.[812] During the Weimar years, many intellectuals and politicians had used the concept to theorize a form of informal rule.[813] Conservative thinkers in France, Germany, and Italy regarded the integration of Europe and Africa into a single economic and geopolitical space as the key to the survival of white, occidental civilization. Eurafricanists argued that Africa had remained underdeveloped due to the inferior mentality and physique of the natives, and they envisioned a global division of labor in which the Europeans would provide the technology, creativity, and discipline needed to exploit the vast resources that the Africans were incapable of developing on their own – with the Africans ostensibly benefiting from both the initiative and the sacrifice of White Europeans. This vision of

Eurafrica was then coupled with the vision of a global struggle between the white, the black, and the yellow races, a trope that figured prominently in the work of a number of German and French writers from Oswald Spengler down to a host of lesser-known figures.[814]

After 1933, the idea of Eurafrica was taken up from a more specifically ethno-racial perspective in which scientific and technological expertise, a rigid work ethic, and moral discipline were associated more with the German master race than with white Europe, while the exploitation of Africa's resources was seen as the material foundation for the new *Volksgemeinschaft*.[815] Although German planners spent the early part of the war devising plans for the exploitation of Africa and its integration into the Nazi empire that they anticipated would be the ultimate fruit of German conquest, by the early 1940s Hitler put an end to these discussions in order to concentrate all available resources on the conquest of *Lebensraum* in the East.[816]

The Eurafrican idea was revived in the immediate postwar years. Africa's vast agricultural potential and mineral resources held a strong attraction for a country that had lost its agricultural heartland to the Soviet Union, Poland, and the Soviet Occupation Zone. German Eurafricanists maintained that the Europeans had both a moral obligation and an economic rationale to exploit Africa's wealth, that this could be done to the benefit of people on both continents, and that the formation of an integrated Eurafrican economic space was necessary if Europe were to represent a viable third way beyond that of the two superpowers.[817] In the postwar years, the Austro-German journalist Anton Zischka, who had gained prominence during the Nazi years by promoting the technocratic exploitation of nature as the scientific foundation for a peaceful *Volksgemeinschaft*, extended these ideas to justify a leading role for West Germany in African development. Zischka described the African warehouse of raw materials as the natural complement to European industrialism (what he called "*Fabrik Europa*"), and he argued that Europeans should take the initiative in exploiting this natural wealth because the Africans themselves lacked the intellectual qualities needed to do so. "Negroes can't plan or organize," Zischka wrote. In contrast, the white man "does what he alone can do. He colonizes and organizes the great tasks of the community. The black man, however, simply goes about his life."[818]

West Germany's renewed interest in overseas market was a product of its defeat in World War II and its still-subordinate position in relation to Britain and France and their economic interests. Once the wartime damage to its infrastructure had been repaired, the West Germans hoped that the export of manufactured goods would again become the engine driving the country's economic growth. Because Britain and France both took steps to limit the penetration of West German manufactures into their domestic markets and their overseas possessions after 1945, West German economic initiatives in Africa had focused primarily on South Africa, Liberia, Ethiopia, Libya, and other countries outside the economic space of its European neighbors.[819]

In their quest to open up export markets without alienating the Western powers, German government and industry followed a policy of restraint.[820] Because the Federal Republic did not have full control over its foreign and economic policy until 1955, the Adenauer government relied on major firms and the Federation of German Industry to serve as "private economic diplomats" in building economic relations with other countries.[821] On the other hand, in 1953 the government set aside a portion of its Marshall Plan funds to "secure in a timely manner a position – which, in view of the dependence of German industry on exports, was particularly important – in the markets of the less-developed world, especially Latin America and Asia."[822] This was the origin of West Germany's "technical assistance for less developed countries," a program that subsidized the cost of sending West German technicians to developing countries in the expectation that, once people were trained to operate German machinery and equipment, they would become customers for the companies that had manufactured these products.[823]

Across the mid-1950s, a number of organizations were created to promote greater West German involvement in Africa. The Europe–Africa Union was founded in 1954 with the express goal of securing African raw materials and markets for West Germany, and the members of the organization hoped this Eurafrican entity would be a bulwark against communism in the region. In May 1956, the German Africa Society was founded to educate the general public about the potential economic value of Africa. Its members included such prominent figures as Alfred Müller-Armack, the leading theorist of the social market economy, Foreign Minister Heinrich von Brentano, Bundestag president Eugen Gerstenmaier, future minister for Economic Cooperation and Development Walter Scheel, and sociologists Helmut Schelsky and René König.[824] In January 1957, the Imperial Colonial School was rechristened the German Institute for Tropical and Subtropical Agriculture, which continued the work of its predecessor in the same building and under the same leadership. The Hamburg Institute for Tropical Studies also resumed work during these years.

West German industrial groups launched a public relations campaign to assuage the fears of the French and the British. For example, Fritz Berg, the president of the Federation of German Industry and a confidant of Adenauer, argued that the presence of German industry in the Third World served all the allied powers because its exports incorporated developing countries into the global market economy and thereby helped prevent the poverty and social unrest that made these countries a fertile breeding ground for communism. In a similar vein, during a 1956 visit to Washington, the chief executive of Krupp proposed that Western firms form consortia to undertake large-scale capital investment and infrastructure projects in the Near East and Asia and that the American government provide long-term, low-interest credits for the venture. Although the Krupp program was known as the Point Four and a Half Program because of the expectation that such aid would help contain communism, Krupp and other major firms also hoped that joint ventures such as these would enable German industry compete in the European colonies and protectorates from which it was otherwise excluded while at the same time dispelling fears of German economic dominance.[825]

III. SAHARAN OIL, FRANCO-GERMAN RAPPROCHEMENT, AND NEOCOLONIAL DEVELOPMENT

West German interest in the Middle East and North Africa sharpened after the discovery of oil in Syria and Libya in the second half of the 1950s, the precise moment when the Arab League countries sought to distance themselves from the former colonial powers.[826] British and French companies had long dominated oil production in the Middle East and North Africa, and after 1945 they succeeded in excluding German firms. However, Syria, which had gained its independence from France in 1946, was particularly eager to exclude Britain and France, and in 1958 the country offered exploration rights to the *Deutsche Erdöl Aktiengesellschaft* (DEA), the leading West German oil company.[827] In view of Syria's increasingly close relations with the Soviet Union following the Suez crisis, France and Britain began to welcome West German firms as partners and to form the multinational consortia the West Germans had been advocating. In the process, the DEA came to view itself as "Europe's oil supplier" and as the representative of Western interests "in a region that closed its door to French and British companies at the moment."[828]

The Saharan oil boom also attracted West German producers. In 1957, the Federation of German Industry created a special group to compete for contracts to build the infrastructure needed to exploit Saharan oil. That same year German and French banks formed a number of joint ventures to fund oil exploration and production companies.[829] However, this was not the first time that German petroleum engineers had been involved in the region. Already in the 1930s, German industry had financed scientific expeditions to the Sahara, and in 1942 special scientific groups attached to the Africa Corps had prospected for oil in the North African desert. This wartime experience gave German engineers and geologists a leg up on competitors from other countries. The West Germans discovered the largest gas field in the Algerian Sahara in 1956, and by early 1960 thirty-five of the forty-six producing wells in the Algerian Sahara were operated by German and Italian companies.[830]

The French were ambivalent about foreign investment in Algeria. Although such activity ran counter to their traditional protectionism, the French also hoped that the presence of foreign firms would encourage the other Western powers to support their continued control over the region. As part of the ceremony held in December 1959 to mark the opening of the 400-mile pipeline from the Saharan Hassi-Messaoud oilfields to Boughie on the Atlantic coast, the French gave Western dignitaries a tour of the Saharan oil fields. Nor did the French miss any opportunity to extoll the benefits of oil exploitation for the Algerians themselves.

By the end of the 1950s, however, the prospect that the French would retain control over Algeria was becoming increasingly remote, and the Saharan oil business was becoming correspondingly risky. The Provisional Government of Algeria was established in Tunis in September 1958, and minister president Ferhat Abbas declared that, when the country gained its independence, the new government would not honor oil deals made with France during the war. As illustrated in Figure 7.2, the high profile of the West Germans in the Algerian oil industry made it easy for the East Germans and the Soviets to portray the Saharan oil boom as an imperialist venture.[831] In response, the West German oil and gas industry produced propaganda films that portrayed its work in Algeria as a form of development aid that ultimately benefited the Algerian people. This was the context for the debate over the role of colonies in the proposed Western European Economic Eommunity – and the catalyst behind the Franco-British attempt to reconsolidate European power after Suez.[832]

By 1956, negotiations over the European Common Market were already well advanced. However, the process of integration forced the countries of Western Europe, and West Germany in particular, to rethink their relation to both their colonies and the wider Third World; they had to do this at a moment when the continued existence of formal

FIGURE 7.2 The SED hoped that this piece of propaganda would convince the East German people to reject the foul-smelling geopolitical soup being cooked up by Adenauer out of a mixture of dollars and bayonets over the heat collectively provided by *Mein Kampf*, West German revanchism, and the European Defense Community.

Source: Zentralkomitee der SED, Abt. Agitation und Propaganda. Courtesy of Stiftung Haus der Geschichte der Bundesrepublik, Bonn.

colonialism seemed increasingly unlikely, especially in the face of militant national liberation movements in Algeria and elsewhere in Africa; and they had to make it possible to integrate the Third World into the economic and geopolitical structures of the Western bloc while at the same time marking the difference between West and South in ways that would enable the former to define the terms on which this integration took place.

The French wanted overseas-dependent territories of member states be considered as "associate" members of the community, who would be allowed to trade with the community on a tariff-free basis.[833] In addition to the formal colonies of the member states, this policy of association would have also applied to UN trust territories, including Belgian Ruanda-Urundi, the French Cameroon and Togo, and Somalia. However, it would not have applied to Algeria, which was regarded as an integral part of France, rather than as a colony. This proposal would have simultaneously cemented French power in Africa, France's influence within the Common Market, and the country's status as a global power.

In many ways, the policy of association embodied the interwar idea of Eurafrica, and the integration of the colonies of the member states into the continental economic community tended to perpetuate colonial rule, rather than bring it to an end.[834] The West Germans were ambivalent about the policy. A number of politicians (especially in the SPD) expressed reservations about being drawn into the controversial colonial policies of their European allies, especially those of France, because they worried that West German foreign policy would be tarred with the brush of colonial rule. Others supported the idea of association. For example, Christian Democrat Hans Furler called on his colleagues to ratify the treaty because he feared that otherwise competition among the superpowers for influence in Africa would deprive Europe of that "natural" supplementary space that was crucial for its economy.[835] However, virtually everyone involved believed that the Europeans exerted a positive influence on Africa and that they had a moral obligation to help the Africans by promoting development. As Carlo Schmid (SPD), a longtime member of the Parliamentary Assembly of the Council of Europe, explained to his colleagues, the French were taking important steps to promote development in Algeria, but they alone could not bear the costs of "transforming Algeria...in such a manner that its inhabitants can achieve a humane standard of living and thus be freed from the communist temptation." He also argued that the increase in private sector investment in the region made possible by the policy of association represented an indirect way of investing in the defense of free Europe.[836]

These beliefs regarding the beneficent influence of Europe in Africa were shaped by a misunderstanding of the nature of the Algerian conflict. Many West Germans regarded the Algerian war as a conflict between European civilization and extra-European barbarism. The vice president of the Bundestag publicly announced that his own moral conviction about the superiority of white European civilization meant there was a natural solidarity between West Germany and France with regard to the Algerian conflict.[837] This belief in the superiority of white Occidental civilization helped smooth over many of the everyday conflicts that arose as the European powers jockeyed for position in Africa. Virtually the only person to criticize association was Willi Birkelbach (SPD). He argued that the community had to rest on solidarity among genuinely equal countries and that it should not become "a kind of compensation at the cost of those developing countries seeking their independence."[838]

One purpose of the Treaty of Rome was to reaffirm the solidarity "which binds Europe and the overseas colonies" and "ensure the development of their prosperity."[839] As a tangible sign of this commitment to the well-being of the extra-European world, the Common Market development fund was established in 1958, with a third of its budget coming from the Federal Republic. It is important to bear in mind that these programs and the benefits they promised were intended to contain communism as much as to serve humanitarian ends. However, their ability to function in this manner was predicated on a subtle reconfiguration of the logic of civilizational difference, which allowed the peoples of Asia and Africa, whose backwardness was often seen as an opportunity for communist subversion, to reemerge as potential allies of the West in the struggle against the ideological enemy.[840] As Adenauer explained in his presentation of the party program in 1957, his fellow Germans had to be willing to make sacrifices to assist all of those countries that were capable of modernizing and that had a genuine will to freedom.[841] Furler echoed these sentiments and argued that European involvement promised to spare the Africans from the evils of communism, which he insisted would be much worse than colonial rule.[842]

Although politicians and the Western media praised the policy of association as a "Eurafrican Monroe doctrine" and a "New Deal" for Africa,[843] many Africans regarded it as a form of neocolonial rule. In 1957, the First Afro-Asian Peoples' Solidarity Conference declared that the arrangement served as a means of subverting and rolling back decolonization.[844] Guinean president Ahmed Sékou Touré criticized the community in more sophisticated terms, arguing that the logic of Western geopolitics invariably reduced Africa and the Africans to the means for the realization of ends that were defined by the Europeans and that ultimately benefited only them: "For Africans it concerns people, not Europe or America, Asia or the Orient, not a '*Großraum*'. Our natural *Großraum* is Africa, not Eurafrica or Afro-Asia."[845] In contrast to Western-educated *evolué* nationalist leaders, many younger Africans felt that the policy of association would solidify the structural dependence of their countries on the European economy and that the benefits of metropolitan trade would accrue primarily to the urban elites who profited from cheaper imports. For its part, the Soviet Union argued that the Common Market represented a last desperate attempt to preserve the "colonial system of exploitation and oppression," while the East Germans took the opportunity to argue that West German membership in the organization transformed it into a de facto colonial power.[846]

Even after the signing of the Treaty of Rome, the West German government had to tread lightly in Africa to avoid offending its allies.[847] Businessmen and diplomats were asked to be discreet in their dealings with African countries. For example, when Germany's former colony Togo gained its independence from France, Foreign Minister Brentano advised against doing anything that could "evoke in France the impression…that the Federal Republic might want to act in a disloyal manner and exploit the sense of friendship, which the Togolese still felt toward Germany, to the disadvantage of the French, or that it might take advantage of the new situation created by Togo's independence in order to contain the influence of the French."[848] To escape from this dilemma, the Foreign Office tried to position West Germany as a mediator between the countries of Africa, the (former) colonial powers in Europe, and the United States, by constructing a positive version of a German *Sonderweg*, according to which the country's economic strength and the absence of a colonial burden of its own made it perfectly suited for such a role.[849]

West Germany could have earned substantial political capital from the "colored world" by condemning South African apartheid. Although Adenauer insisted on preserving the special relationship between the two countries, diplomats were cautioned not to make any "demonstrative assertion" of friendship.[850] On the other hand, any offended sensibilities among the Africans themselves could be salved by pointing – as did Gerstenmaier and Erhard at the first "Africa Week," which was held in

1960 – to the 17 million Germans living under "communist dictatorship and slavery" and by reminding the African audience that "the worst colonialism is imperialism in communist-totalitarian form."[851]

It is difficult to know precisely what the African public made of these claims or of the lofty rhetoric of humanity, development, and progress spouted by West German diplomats and aid workers. It seems certain, though, that after 1960 it became difficult to balance loyalty to the country's European allies with the need to gain support from those people who were involved in increasingly militant struggles for national liberation.

IV. PROPAGANDA SAFARIS, PUBLIC RELATIONS WARS, AND COMPETING NARRATIVES OF THE GERMAN PAST

As the West Germans became increasingly involved in the nonaligned world, they found themselves forced to go head to head with the East Germans in their efforts to persuade the nonaligned countries of the superiority of their social and economic system. The importance of these competitive representations was evident to contemporaries. As the *Stuttgarter Nachrichten* noted in 1960, commercial and trade fairs have "of necessity become an instrument of politics and the visiting card of the free West." West Germany had been unpleasantly surprised by the sophistication of the East German exhibit at the 1955 international exhibition in New Delhi. However, by the end of the decade West Germans were determined not to be outdone again.[852]

The establishment of the Common Market was quickly followed by rapid decolonization in Africa, beginning with Ghana and Guinea, which gained their independence in 1957 and 1958, respectively. While Bonn had upgraded its consulate to a full-fledged embassy in Accra in June 1957, Ghanaian president Nkrumah did not allow East Germany to open a trade mission with consular rights until early 1959.[853] However, roles were reversed in Guinea.

When the French approved the constitution of the Fifth Republic in 1958, the country's colonies were given the choice between maintaining a political association with France or full independence. In a referendum held in September 1958, all of France's colonies supported continuing association with the metropolitan power – with the exception of Guinea, where the population voted overwhelmingly in favor of full independence.[854] When Touré declared Guinea's independence on October 2 of that year, none of the Western powers immediately recognized the new country for fear of offending the French, who themselves threw a temper tantrum and "ripped out telephones, smashed light bulbs and stripped the police of uniforms and weapons" as they decamped in anger and insult.[855] As a result, the new republic of Guinea was economically weakened and diplomatically isolated, while the French smuggled arms into the country in hopes of reversing the course of events. In contrast, the day after its declaration of independence, Guinea was recognized by East Germany, which was also the first state to sign trade and cultural agreements with the newly independent country.[856] The East Germans also sent a delegation to the first All African Peoples' Conference, which met in Ghana in December 1958.

Lothar Killmer, East Germany's first overseas correspondent for *Neues Deutschland*, recounted his experiences at this conference in *Beating the Drums of Freedom in Accra*. Throughout the book, Killmer drew parallels between the *presence* of American imperialism and the *past* of German colonialism, while arguing that the German Democratic Republic bore no responsibility for Germany's colonial past, which remained inscribed on the country in the form of the border separating Ghana from neighboring Togo. What enabled Killmer to perform this rhetorical sleight-of-hand was the claim that the postwar socialist transformation had brought about a spiritual rebirth that had cleansed the eastern part of the German lands of the country's colonial sins. As Killmer proudly explained, "I am not responsible for the imperialist policies of the German empire or of any other era. My country, the German Democratic Republic, is anti-imperialist and anti-colonial. Moreover, Wilhelm's proconsuls had already been driven out of Africa when I was born in 1919." In this way, Killmer reenacted the founding myth of East German antifascism in his encounters with the Ghanaians. This sense of moral superiority was also reflected in his invidious comparison between neocolonial investments, which sucked the wealth out of the Third World, and the development aid provided by the socialist bloc. Thanks to such assistance, Killmer asserted, the Volta River had been harnessed to power the development of the land. "The current of the Volta," he exclaimed, "sings no longer of the past, but of the future."[857]

Part of the reason why relations with the small country of Guinea garnered inordinate diplomatic attention from the Western powers was that, in the words of John Morrow, the first U.S. ambassador to the country, "the Communist bloc nations were using this new republic as a laboratory for determining the best methods of winning over the developing nations of Africa and striving desperately to make it their showplace."[858] Regardless of the veracity of this claim, in the late 1950s the

East Germans made a concerted effort to convince the Africans of their support for independence and development.

This pro-African campaign went hand in hand with a number of academic and cultural exchange programs designed to strengthen ties between East Germany and the countries of sub-Saharan Africa and to give the Germans a more solidly grounded knowledge of the society, culture, and language of the region.[859] Walter Markov, the leading Africanist, established a research project on colonial history and national liberation movements at Karl Marx University. In April 1959, he organized an international conference, attended by over 200 scholars from Africa and Europe, on the history of modern Africa.[860] In 1960, the university established an institute for African studies, where students could prepare for careers in diplomacy and development work by studying the languages (Hausa and Swahili), history, and culture of the African peoples.[861] Markov believed that the history of Africa had been thoroughly deformed by racism and colonialism, and he hoped that the institute would free the African past from the distortions of older colonial narratives and convince the Africans of the superiority of socialism as a path to modernity.[862] The East Germans also made a symbolic attempt to help the Africans recover their own history by giving Ghana copies of some 400 documents, dating back to the 17th and 18th centuries, relating to slave trading by Brandenburg-Prussia.[863]

Bonn could not afford to abandon the field entirely to the East Germans, and, as part of its own cultural offensive in Africa, the government organized several mobile exhibitions to give Africans a firsthand look at life in the Federal Republic. The Foreign Office and the Ministry of Economics hoped that these exhibitions would have as great an impact on the African public as the Marshall Plan Exhibitions had on the European public more than a decade before.[864] Although the West Germans also hoped that these exhibitions would persuade the peoples of Africa of the justness of their position with regard to the German question, the main question was, in the words of one Foreign Office official, "can a hungry, sick, unemployed and barely-clothed African from the bush learn to appreciate the tragedy of our Berlin problem?"[865]

Between November 1961 and June 1962, Bonn's "propaganda safari" toured nine west African states; a second exhibition ran from May to November 1963 in seven countries in Eastern Africa.[866] Unfortunately, the exhibitions proved as much an advertisement for the good old days of the Third Reich and for West German diplomatic incompetence as for the country's achievements since the war. Much of the responsibility for staffing and operating the exhibition was delegated to the conservative Christian Association of Youth Villages. The first director of the West Africa exhibition, a former senior SA officer and a Holocaust denier, was fired soon after the exhibition arrived in Africa. He was replaced by Werner Lott, a former senior SS officer whose idea of relaxing in the evening was to sit around singing Nazi songs.[867] Lott was no better suited for the job. Lott believed Germany's colonial rule had been beneficial to the Africans, who, he insisted, did not harbor any resentment against the Germans. What the exhibition most needed to communicate, he argued, were the traditional German virtues of organization, order, and discipline.[868] The military music that blared from loudspeakers as the West German exhibition pulled into town, the Nazi proclivities of the exhibition staff, and the intrusive displays of other military rituals, such as flag-raising ceremonies, parades, and fireworks, cannot have won the West Germans much support in Africa.[869]

The messages communicated by the exhibition materials were little more appropriate than the staffing decisions; they oscillated between ambivalence and insult. While West Germany portrayed itself as a big brother who would provide the peoples of Africa with the advice and support that they needed to "participate more and more in the technological and economic progress in the world as free and equal partners," the accompanying visual images made it clear that the West Germans were the moving force in this partnership and that aid programs "must be first developed by the people of the Federal Republic."[870] The Africans were not happy with this paternalism, as some West Germans realized (Figure 7.3). The Ugandan minister of economics nicely captured the attitude of the Africans themselves toward the exhibition when he explained that "how we should live, what we should accomplish – these are things that we ourselves already know; this isn't something that needs to be explained to us. It is much more important to lend a helping hand to reach this goal. This kind of an exhibition is pointless if its goal is simply to demonstrate the willingness to help without taking any actions."[871]

The exhibits themselves were equally problematic. A local newspaper complained that many of the exhibits "were almost insultingly naïve," noting that "a photograph of a man in a field with some naive caption like 'plants need plenty of water' does not move a Kampala crowd to enthusiasm."[872] A West German agronomist criticized the exhibition for failing to recognize that German agricultural methods could not be directly transferred to tropical conditions. He noted that, in comparison to the

FIGURE 7.3 "In the end we have to show them in what direction we are guiding their development, right?" Courtesy of Volker Ernsting.

knowledge of the agricultural faculty at Makerere College in Kampala, Uganda, "we Germans do not have anything of equivalent value to offer and in Africa we should ourselves learn rather than teach, especially in the area of agronomy."[873]

One of the most controversial exhibits was a paper maché model of an African child with a motorized arm that moved a toothbrush across his teeth. Visitors to the exhibition complained that the model looked like a pygmy with an oversized head, and they felt insulted by the imperialist hubris of suggesting that Africans needed to be instructed in the basic principles of dental hygiene. The model had to be removed temporarily, although its replacement did not prove any better.[874] Stereotypical views of Africans as uncivilized bushmen also colored West German media coverage of the exhibitions, and the African press wondered aloud the West Germans' intentions.[875] As a major Tanganyikan newspaper noted, "it would be unnatural if the Africans did not regard [the exhibition] with suspicion. These days there is a certain apprehension among the poorer nations that the flag might follow aid."[876]

In 1959, the Foreign Office began a public relations campaign to enlighten the new African countries about the division of Germany and the "red" colonialism in the eastern part of the country. Even before the actual construction of the Wall, the West German government had wanted foreign visitors to travel to West Berlin to see for themselves the line drawn through the country by the communist "colonial" rulers of the East. However, it is not clear just how effective this program was. As the Nigerian *West African Pilot* tartly observed, "for a few Marks worth of economic aid Africa is expected to take sides in the east-west tug-of-war" among the Germans.[877] The Foreign Office, the German Africa Society, and the German Foundation for Developing Countries also sponsored events intended to inform the public of the Federal Republic's longstanding, beneficent commitment to Africa. Many non-European students who attended these events complained about the negative stereotyping of Africans in the media.[878] Such stereotypes were also reinforced by West Germany's first "Africa Week," which opened at the height of the Congo crisis.[879]

The two German states also sought to tar each other in the eyes of the African public with the brush of Nazism. In the East, the SED based its right to govern on the claim to have transformed East German society and thus eliminated the social foundations of militarism, fascism, and capitalist imperialism. This enabled them to deny that their country bore any responsibility for the German past and to foist all blame onto the Federal Republic, which they portrayed as the illegitimate successor to the Kaiserreich and the Third Reich.[880] In the West, while the corpulent, cigar-chomping Erhard resembled nothing so much as the malevolent overweight magnates of Georg Grosz' paintings from the 1920s, Erhard's girth, along with his glib advocacy of the free market, made him an ideal symbol of the country's economic success in the 1950s and 1960s. The fact that gluttony and what was known at the time as "prosperity alcoholism" were perceived by many as signs of the tangible benefits of a democratic society and free market economy led König to exclaim in the early 1960s, "a thin Erhard? Never. Why, people wouldn't believe in West Germany's prosperity."[881] Whatever the virtues and vices of these beer-guzzling survivors of World War II and their consumerist Biedermeier, it was easy for the Western media to positively compare them to the jackbooted members of the Nazi war machine, the East German secret police, and the political pallor of the people living on the other side of the Iron Curtain. As *Time* magazine reported in 1963, the "East Germans are barely getting enough to eat. Their faces tend to look grey because of the lack of citrus and other fresh fruits," and the diminishing waistlines and pallid complexion of the East German people were read both as a sign of the failures of economic planning and politically as a measure of the lifelessness and lack of freedom in a totalitarian state.[882]

V. THE TWIN CRISES OF DEVELOPMENT POLICY AND THE HALLSTEIN DOCTRINE

When the Hallstein doctrine was set out in 1955, it was self-evident to the West Germans that any aid granted to other countries would have to be predicated on their recognition of the claim that the Federal Republic represented the sole legitimate German state. However, the East German medical assistance, development aid, and public relations initiatives that began in earnest in 1956 made it increasingly difficult to maintain this hard-line position. At the turn of the 1960s, West Germany began to formulate its own development aid program, which it hoped would turn back the East German challenge and shore up the Hallstein doctrine. Things did not work out quite as the West Germans expected. By 1960, almost before the Federal Republic had articulated its own development aid policy, the underlying logic of containment began to unravel, forcing Bonn to reevaluate both the country's aid policy and the Hallstein doctrine to which it was lashed.

The issue that most vexed West German policymakers was the growing sense that East German aid had so improved the bargaining position of Third World countries that now West Germany itself was being exploited and manipulated, rather than the other way around. As Erhard noted in December 1957, the underdeveloped countries had learned to "manipulate the two fronts in order to suck out as much as honey as they can from the flowers."[883] The West Germans may have overstated their claim to be the sole legitimate German state, but their concerns were not unwarranted.

West German concerns about East Germany's success in gaining a degree of international recognition and the impact of such contacts on its ability to enforce the Hallstein doctrine crystallized around developments in East Germany's most important partner in Africa, Egypt. Relations between the two countries grew closer across the late 1950s. In 1958, East Germany extended to Egypt substantial long-term credits to purchase the factories, machinery, and technical services needed to modernize such industries as textiles and the manufacture of bicycles and photographic film.[884] Nasser's counter-gesture – the decision to allow Premier Otto

Grotewohl to make a state visit in January 1959 – represented a major symbolic victory for East Germany. During the visit, Nasser honored Grotewohl with the Nile Order and announced his intention to establish a consulate general in East Berlin. To exploit this newfound international recognition, DEFA produced a film, *Friendship Is the Basis of Peace* (1959), which documented Grotewohl's goodwill visits to the United Arab Republic, Iraq, and India, as well as China, North Vietnam, and North Korea.[885] In December 1958, Egypt finally accepted the Soviet offer to finance and oversee the first phase of building the Aswan dam. This decision, which came as a distinctly unpleasant surprise to the West German consortium that had been involved in the project since 1953, also benefited East Germany, to whom the Soviets contracted out some of the work.

In an article published January 1959, *Der Spiegel* concluded that in this area "the Federal Republic, the most promising suitor in the West, was completely outplayed,"[886] and the story went on to describe the competition between East and West Germany to curry favor with the Egyptians. The accompanying cartoon depicted Nasser as a six-armed, scorpion-like figure basking in the heat of the two economic suns. With three of his arms, he reached out greedily to grasp the money and military aid proffered from the East and to present a medal to Grotewohl; with two of his other three arms, he was reaching toward the dollars and marks being extended to him from the West; the sixth arm, which might have otherwise taken hold of the lire being held out to him, appears instead to be throttling a character intended to symbolize Israel.[887] Adenauer was absolutely livid about the Egypt's nationalization of the Suez Canal; he was furious that a small, impoverished country like Egypt could – with Soviet support – cut one of main commercial arteries of the European economy; and he easily lapsed into racial insults to express his feelings. Nasser's decision deepened Adenauer's own convictions about the "inability of colored peoples, especially Africans, to responsibly govern themselves." Adenauer complained that Nasser's actions endangered "the reputation of the White peoples" because "the unbridled self-confidence of the colored peoples is enhanced in such a way that it could give rise to very bad effects and consequences."[888]

If this cartoon captures the attitude of Adenauer and of the West German public toward Nasser, it also shows how the mere possibility of aid from East Germany was changing the balance of power between West Germany and the global South. West German sensitivities were nicely captured in a second story, published in *Der Spiegel* in 1960, which described East German's use of development aid to curry favor with

Sékou Touré in Guinea. A cartoon (Figure 7.4) that accompanied the article showed a dour-looking Adenauer being boiled in the cauldron of his Africa policy – cooked from below by a smoking fire from the Hallstein doctrine and baked from above by the tropical heat of East Germany's incursion with the region. This caricature of the tribulations of West Germany's hapless political Mr. Magoo was captioned "Some like it hot!"[889]

In view of these developments, West Germany felt increasingly constrained to articulate a more coherent policy toward Africa. Up to this point, in the field of development aid West Germany had piggybacked on the Common Market's European Development Fund. However, such funds were limited to the (former) colonies of member states and did not meet West Germany's need for a more broadly focused policy. The

Manche mögen's heiß!

Frankfurter Rundschau

FIGURE 7.4 "Some like it hot" (1960).
Source: *Frankfurter Rundschau*. Courtesy of the *Frankfurter Allgemeine Zeitung*.

question of development aid to those countries that did not have the special relations with the Common Market became more urgent when seventeen African states gained their independence in 1960.[890] In the second half of the 1950s, West Germany's own aid programs were, at best, a misnomer. The country's technical aid had grown out of programs that were originally intended to increase West German exports, and their rebaptism as development aid was based on the belief that integrating the country into the global market economy represented the best way of eliminating the main sources of political and social discontent and thus containing the spread of communism.[891] Such an approach left little room for the divergent interests of developing countries themselves.

West German health officials often diagnosed ailments of migrant workers from the Mediterranean as manifestations of the psychic dislocation they experienced upon arriving in the industrialized world. The same basic schema also informed the West German understanding of its development programs.[892] For example, Scheel himself was concerned about the socially and psychologically disruptive consequences of rapid modernization and any attempt "to transfer the civilizational achievements, which are the fulfillment of a particular culture, to another space and the cultures that occupy it without these cultures having passed through the centuries-long process of development that first gave rise to them." It was, he suggested, "simply impossible to transfer the technical achievements of our civilization to other countries, whose entire social order still belongs to the Middle Ages."[893]

Similarly, the free market liberals who shaped the economic policies of the early Federal Republic argued that the country's first development programs, which they disparaged as a "Marshall Plan for the Third World," suffered from the defects inherent in all forms of state economic planning. They maintained that these programs were bound to fail because the intrinsic differences in culture and mentality between North and South would undermine the intended impact of the transfer of technology and know-how. Although public health was the only domain where these liberals felt that development programs might yield any sustained benefits, they worried about their unintended consequences and argued that over the short run improvements in public health would simply worsen the food and population crises of the Third World and render these regions even more susceptible to the temptations of communism. They also argued that the rapid expansion of development aid as a result of the competition between the two superpower blocs was leading to the breakdown of traditional tribal bonds and the creation of undernourished, uprooted, and proletarianized masses, a process that they feared would issue in a global race and class war between North and South.[894]

In September 1958, the ministers of finance, commerce, and foreign affairs formulated initial guidelines for the distribution of foreign aid.[895] They felt that it was necessary to improve both the quality and quantity of development aid in order to demonstrate the superiority of the West German free market economy, that a greater emphasis should be placed upon technical aid to develop the human capital of beneficiary countries, rather than on large-scale infrastructure or industrial development projects that tended to disrupt the country's economy and social structure, and that development aid should also promote "German interests," especially the Hallstein doctrine and the country's policy of reunification.[896] At the same time, the government took a number of steps to systematize development aid and bring it under central political control. In the fall of 1960, the cabinet decided to regularize funding by integrating development aid into the federal budget. From that point onward, aid spending sharply increased, with much of this money being redirected from Asia to Africa.[897] In December 1960, an informal body was set up to coordinate development policies and programs among the concerned federal ministries.[898] And in 1961 the Ministry for Economic Cooperation – headed by Scheel – was created with an aid budget of approximately 5 billion marks.[899]

The second main factor driving this systematization of development policy was changes in U.S. foreign policy.[900] By the early 1960s, the U.S. economy was beginning to suffer from the effects of the continued balance of payments deficit that was essential to the country's role as Western hegemon, and the U.S. government was looking for ways to reduce the cost of its presence in Europe. To achieve this goal, the Kennedy administration asked the Western allies to develop a priority list of countries, regions, and programs so that they could coordinate their aid and maximize its impact. This proposal would have entailed a fundamental shift in West European, especially West German, aid policies. At the time, the overwhelming majority of French and British aid continued to go to their own former colonies.[901] Although West Germany spent only half as much on foreign aid as France and Britain (and only one-eighth as much as the United States), these funds were distributed among a far larger number of countries, thereby diminishing its political leverage over individual recipients.[902] The rationale behind this "watering can" strategy (Figure 7.5) was that, in view of its rivalry with the other half of the divided nation, West Germany had to provide some money to *every* developing country to ensure that there were no gaps in the underdeveloped world that could be exploited diplomatically by the East Germans.

Improved coordination of Western development aid presumed a shared understanding of the Sino-Soviet split and Soviet-U.S. détente. However, it soon became clear that the West Germans and the Americans held substantially different views on these questions.[903] The Germans were much more skeptical about the potential benefits of détente, and their reserve undoubtedly reflected fear that the policy could weaken the U.S. commitment to the defense of Western Europe and lead to the de facto recognition of Germany's postwar division.[904] As a compromise

Der Entwicklungsengel

Rheinischer Merkur

FIGURE 7.5 "The Development Angel" (1964). Source: *Rheinischer Merkur*. Courtesy of Michael Rutz.

solution that would relieve U.S. finances without diminishing the number of U.S. forces in Europe, the United States asked the West Germans to contribute a battalion of soldiers for service in the Congo.[905] However, the West Germans feared that such a step would damage its relations with the other countries of Africa, and the United States ultimately agreed to a West German counterproposal to provide planes and pilot training to the Tanganyikan air force.[906]

In 1964/65, West Germany faced two important diplomatic crises that brought about a far-reaching reconsideration of both the Hallstein doctrine and the aims of the country's development policy. First, as we shall see in greater detail in Chapter 9, revolutionary Zanzibar recognized East Germany in early 1964. Although this infuriated the West Germans, the merger with more moderate Tanganyika in April of that year held out the possibility that the decision might be reversed. A year later, the Nyerere administration finally announced that united Tanzania would not formally recognize East Germany, which would have to close its embassy in Zanzibar, but which would be permitted to open a consulate in Dar es Salaam.[907] The West Germans were not satisfied by this compromise, and they retaliated by canceling all major development programs and ordering the immediate withdrawal of the military advisors serving in the country.

Second, in October 1964 the press revealed that the West German government had agreed to sell 150 tanks to Israel. The news outraged Egypt and the Arab League. This revelation forced the Erhard administration to do a volte face on the arms deal and to reaffirm existing policies against the sale of arms to areas of tension. Two weeks later, in a gesture of defiance Nasser invited East German head of the state Walter Ulbricht to visit Cairo, which he did from late February to early March 1965.[908] In response, West Germany decided to cut off almost all development aid to Egypt, although it did agree to fulfill existing contractual obligations. In May of that year, Erhard went a step further and extended diplomatic recognition to Israel, a momentous step that led most Arab countries to suspend diplomatic relations with the Federal Republic.

Together, the decisions by Erhard to recognize Israel and by Nasser to host Ulbricht revealed the weaknesses in the elaborate web of strategic calculations that had been woven over the preceding decade by the two German states and that had up to that point – much like the Bismarckian alliance system in the run-up to World War I – both enframed and constrained their room for diplomatic maneuvering. In West Germany, this diplomatic crisis sparked a sustained debate over the country's reunification policy, its development policies, and their relations to one another. After all, if the purpose of development aid was to discourage recognition of the "Soviet Occupation Zone" as an independent state on German soil, then the failure to prevent Egypt from taking that step called into question the very *raison d'être* of such programs.[909]

For most West German politicians, and especially the members of the diplomatic corps, it went without saying that development aid served to encourage support for the Hallstein doctrine – and that the threat of withholding aid was intended to discourage second thoughts on the matter. The problem was, as we have seen, that such external rewards and punishments encouraged Third World countries to "extort" or "blackmail" the West Germans by playing the two German states, and the two blocs more generally, against each other. A cartoon published in *Der Spiegel* in 1964 provides a crude but effective illustration of West German perceptions of the problem. The picture shows an emissary from an African state preparing to leave for West Germany. As he repeats the directions, he has received from his chief to confirm that he has understood them, the caption reads: "'I repeat, my lord: Don't mention money right off the bat. Rather, first visit the Wall and show deep concern. But then play hardball'."[910] This game was doubly complicated in the field of development aid where there was little difference between *de jure* and *de facto* recognition of East Germany. This allowed beneficiary countries to proclaim their support for West Germany by refusing diplomatic recognition to East Germany while promiscuously accepting gifts from their socialist suitor.

As a result, the preservation of the Hallstein doctrine was increasingly regarded as a political illusion (Figure 7.6). The dual crises of 1965 made it clear to the West Germans that the only way they could escape from this situation was to rethink their carrot-and-stick approach to development aid. The broad, complicated public debate that ensued pitted two main groups against one another: those who wished to make development aid into a more effective instrument for enforcing the Hallstein doctrine, and those who wished to more clearly separate development aid from the vagaries of day-to-day foreign politics so that it could more effectively promote economic development, social progress, and political stability in the Third World.

The most cogent statement of the first position came from Rolf Pauls, deputy director of the trade and development department of the Foreign Office.[911] Pauls argued that the Hallstein doctrine was simply the logical extension of the basic principle that the Federal Republic was the sole

FIGURE 7.6 "Fata Morgana." In the aftermath of the dual diplomatic crises of 1964, West Germany's hope that the Hallstein doctrine would enable it to maintain its claim to be the sole German state was proving to be a political mirage. *Source*: Peter Leger. Courtesy of Stiftung Haus der Geschichte der Bundesrepublik Deutschland, 1998/03/0010.00537.

legitimate representative of all Germans, and he insisted that the country had the obligation to ensure that this right was recognized by nonaligned countries. Any line of reasoning that separated development aid from reunification was, Pauls insisted, "an...idle intellectual game that is harmful to German interests." "No German administration," he maintained, "can justify making available funds raised by the German people to anyone who opposes the German interest in this most important matter."[912]

The opposing argument had already been advanced a few years earlier in the debates over the creation of the Ministry for Economic Cooperation, and it was restated by Scheel in 1965. Scheel criticized the use of such aid as a weapon for short-term "political punitive expeditions," and he rejected the claim that the crisis of the Hallstein doctrine entailed a corresponding crisis of development policy.[913] Instead, Scheel proposed to "objectify" (*versachlichen*) development policy by emancipating it from the constraints of the Hallstein doctrine. He coupled this argument with the suggestion that, instead of being drawn into an aid race with East Germany at every point around the world, West Germany should concentrate its assistance on those countries where aid would have the greatest political and economic impact.[914]

The Finance Ministry echoed Scheel's call for the objectification of development aid, but spun it in a different direction. Officials there believed that economic and social development would almost always result in positive political development, and they argued in a quasi-Hegelian manner that, no matter what the motives of a foreign country, over the long term well-designed development programs would, so to speak, bring about desirable changes in the country's politics behind the back of whatever administration happened to be in power, regardless of its politics.[915]

While such a separation of intent and effect was anathema to the Foreign Office,[916] others sought to combine different aspects of the two main positions. For example, one memorandum – presumably authored by Bundestag representative Gerhard Fritz (CDU) – argued that Hallstein doctrine should be abandoned because the policy of nonrecognition had become a distinction without a difference. However, the memorandum also argued that the categorical distinction between friends and others drawn by Scheel had to be supplanted by a more finely modulated set of incentives and sanctions that could be applied in a more measured way to different countries. It also proposed a strategy for counterattacking against the Achilles' heel of East German development aid: the limited wealth of the country and its inability to support a lavish aid program across the board. While the Western states spread their aid over eighty to ninety developing countries, socialist bloc aid was limited to less than thirty countries. The consequence was that "Eastern block development policy can always act in a targeted manner, while the Western powers are damned to react in a punctiform way. In the field of development policy, the East operates according to the principle of political selectivity. The West cannot be selective." Rather than abandoning parts of the field to focus on selected friends, the memorandum argued that West Germany should turn the tables on the Eastern bloc countries and force them to pursue their own watering-can strategy and thus ultimately commit themselves to foreign aid programs that their economies could not sustain.[917]

This debate over the Hallstein doctrine was not resolved at the time. One thing, however, is clear: By the mid-1960s, the East German medical and development aid programs described in this and the previous chapter had stripped the Hallstein doctrine of much of its substance even before Social Democratic *Ostpolitik* definitively deprived it of its *raison d'être*.[918]

8

Far Away, but Yet So Close

INTRODUCTION: THE EURASIAN GLOBAL CARE REGIME

In the late 1960s and early 1970s, West Germany was embroiled in a number of international scandals involving the trafficking of young Asian women. The Indian public was outraged to learn that 240 young girls, many of them minors, had been forced into virtual indentured servitude in West German healthcare institutions. Lured to Germany by the promise of a high-quality nursing education, the girls spent most of their time cleaning toilets and mopping floors, and many were forced to work in psychiatric institutions avoided by German nurses. The Indian parliament asked the government to investigate, and the affair was covered by the press in Germany and elsewhere in Western Europe.[919]

It turned out that many religious orders, faced with an unprecedented shortage of novices, were recruiting young women from the South Indian state of Kerala to perform necessary menial labor in their clinics and nursing homes. West Germany would have been lucky if India had been the only nation to complain, but the Hong Kong *China Mail* also reported that Chinese girls were being "sold" to West Germany.[920] As with the Indians, these Chinese girls had been promised nursing training in West Germany, but were instead exploited as housekeepers. Despite the gravity of these scandals, none of them led to a serious public discussion in West Germany about the plight of these Asian women or the role of the country in driving the global migration of female care workers.

This chapter focuses on the Asian nurses who came to West Germany in the 1960s and 1970s – with a special emphasis on the South Korean women who made up the majority of these migrants. The terms under which they were to be integrated into the global labor market were jointly determined by the governments on both ends of this global care chain, and I argue that the experiences of these women cannot be fully understood unless we also understand how the expanding need for low-wage healthcare workers in the West dovetailed with both the developmental strategies of the Third World nations from which these women emigrated and the evolution of the West German welfare state.

Second, in addition to the political and economic interests of both the West German and South Korean states, we need to examine the conceptions of race, gender, and class that helped naturalize and legitimate the conditions under which these women labored. In South Korea, these nurses occupied a specific position in the country's development strategy. In the words of Lee Su-kil, a Korean-born physician who worked at the university hospital in Mainz and who functioned as one of the chief recruiters of caring labor, "the export of nurses requires no capital, but instead brings our country even more foreign exchange."[921] The Korean government was more interested in pursuing its own development strategies than in the welfare of the individual women who were to be the agents of these policies, and, as we shall see, the West German understanding of underdevelopment examined in previous chapters also helped shape this global care regime.

Third, labor is always performed by living individuals. Many of these Korean nurses ventured to the far side of the world in hopes of a better life for themselves and their families. However, their dreams ran counter – in ways that only gradually became clear – to state policies that reflected very different priorities. These women found themselves in a no-man's land between skilled nursing work, unskilled work in basic patient care, and menial housekeeping labor with no connection to their training or aspirations. The disappointment and discrimination Korean women experienced in West Germany raise important questions of agency and identity. As I will show, changes in their employment conditions resulting from the economic downturn of the 1970s led these women to develop a cosmopolitan political subjectivity and a new form of transnational social action through which they resisted the forces that placed them in a subaltern position in both South Korea and West Germany. These women were alienated by the lowly work and grim way of life they encountered abroad, and their dreams of returning "home" with the education and property commensurate to their professional aspirations were often disappointed. However, they also learned that, as much as their home was nowhere, through conscious struggle they could make their home everywhere. In the end, many of these women, whom West German contemporaries condescendingly called "girls from overseas" or "lotus girls," fashioned themselves into genuine cosmopolitans, citizens of the world.

I. THE RECRUITMENT OF ASIAN NURSES: STATES, NGOS, AND THE POLITICAL ECONOMY OF THE GLOBAL CARE CHAIN

In August 1961, two weeks after construction had begun on the Berlin Wall, *Der Spiegel* published the first installment of a four-part series entitled "The Federal Republic – an Underdeveloped Country." Due to the acute shortage of space in the country's hospitals and the sorry state of their buildings, the magazine reported, many patients had to make do with emergency clinics that had been set up during the war for soldiers and refugees. According to the magazine, in Bavaria 42 percent of those seeking admission to a hospital – 300 persons on any given day – were turned away due to lack of space. There was an equally severe shortage of physicians and – of special concern here – nurses, and the article concluded that "the Federal Republic itself is – in aspects of its public life – an underdeveloped land. Those monuments to civilization that are being constructed for colored tribes in desert and jungle are also badly needed here in West Germany."[922]

By the end of the 1950s, rising affluence and advances in medical science had nearly eliminated epidemic disease. At the same time, however, a growing number of people were suffering from such chronic ailments as cardiovascular disease, cancer, and diabetes, which required sustained, intensive care and far more hospital beds and nurses.[923] In 1964, another 35,000 women were still needed to staff the country's hospitals.[924] Unfortunately, demand for nurses was rising at the very moment when sociodemographic trends were reducing the number of women interested in such jobs. The expanding economy was creating jobs with better pay and higher social status in industry and commerce, while those religious orders, which had traditionally supplied a substantial proportion of the nurses employed in the nation's hospitals, found themselves hard pressed to recruit a new generation of nuns and deaconesses.[925]

In addition to skilled patient care, nurses in Germany were responsible for a variety of housekeeping tasks, including cleaning floors and hallways, transporting patient meals, and doing hospital laundry, as well as bathing patients and providing other personal care. These activities consumed 30 to 40 percent of their time. In hopes of relieving this shortage of skilled labor, the German Hospital Association introduced a new category of healthcare worker: the nurse aide, who was supposed to take over unskilled ancillary responsibilities and allow licensed nurses to concentrate on patient care.[926] Between January 1962 and March 1966, the Federal Employment Agency recruited nearly 3,800 such workers – nearly all women – from Spain, Greece, and Turkey. In view of the availability of such women, German officials saw no reason to deviate from their policy of not issuing work permits for unskilled workers from beyond Europe and its traditional Mediterranean recruiting countries. Nevertheless, in May 1966, more than 5,000 cleaning and housekeeping positions remained unfilled. Nursing was the only sector in which demand for foreign workers did not decline during the 1966/67 recession.[927]

Virtually, all of the problems faced by the Asian women hired to fill this gap arose because the training and career expectations of nurses in Germany differed from those of nurses elsewhere in the world. Korean and Filipino training and licensing requirements were modeled on those of the United States and Britain. There, nurses were regarded as medical assistants to doctors, whom they accompanied on daily rounds; basic patient care was provided by family members, who often stayed with the patient in the hospital. By contrast, nursing qualifications in Germany were lower than in much of the world. The nursing curriculum in Germany was more practical than academic, and students were required to serve a two-year apprenticeship in housekeeping work and basic patient care tasks before moving on to more professional training. As a result, foreign nurses who were trained in Germany often did not meet the licensing requirements of their own countries, to which most expected to return.

While the substantial overlap between skilled and unskilled work greased the wheels of the global labor market, it also created a great deal of confusion as to the precise role of these Asian nurses in the German healthcare system. Licensed nurses from Asia felt their qualifications were being ignored by employers, and nursing students wondered if their education would ever advance beyond housekeeping and basic patient care. This overlap, together with the urgent need for caring labor of all kinds and the inability to either employ nurses in a skilled capacity or provide students with the promised training until they had attained a degree of linguistic proficiency, meant that for substantial periods of time these women were regularly channeled into housekeeping and basic patient care duties at odds with their training, career expectations, and social status.

Given how much time even skilled nurses were expected to spend on housekeeping and basic patient care, it was difficult to separate the shortage of trained nurses from that of aides and housekeepers. The temptation for employers to use Asian nurses and nursing students to meet their needs for unskilled labor was reinforced by a pervasive racism, which viewed these Asian women as representatives of essentially backward peoples, who needed to be taught the classic German virtues of work, punctuality, order, and cleanliness before advancing to training in nursing. The intractability of this problem ultimately convinced federal officials to approve large-scale recruitment of nurses from Asia, thus opening the history of the West German welfare state out into that of the wider world. However, the unavoidable gap between the expectations of these women and the realities they faced on the job gave rise to friction and frustration with their work, while the German state had to manage all of the ensuing conflicts.

One of the key factors in explaining recruitment patterns is state strength. While West Germany recruited large numbers of Asian nurses from strong states and weak ones, state strength in the country of origin determined both the shape of the recruiting mechanisms and the specific ways in which the citizens of these states were positioned in the global labor market. Into the mid-1960s, South Korea, the Philippines, and India all had weak states, which showed neither interest in making the export of migrant labor serve a larger development strategy nor the ability to impose their will on either their citizens or other state-level negotiating partners. Such weak states created a persistent problem for German authorities because inadequate political and administrative capacity opened the door to unregulated recruitment by both clerical entrepreneurs and for-profit agencies. This led to the exploitation of both women wanting to work in the West and the German healthcare institutions seeking to employ them, while at the same time making it more difficult to verify the women's nursing credentials. It also meant that nurses came to Germany without any knowledge of the conditions under which they would be working, the kinds of work that they would be expected to do, or the protections offered to them under German labor law. The scandals that broke at the end of the 1960s brought all these problems to light.

Women from India, the Philippines, and Korea first came to West Germany for nursing training in the late 1950s. Initially, nearly all were recruited by individual ecclesiastical entrepreneurs, the country's major nursing orders, healthcare institutions, and socially minded Catholics, such as Karl Tacke. Tacke was the owner of a textile mill in Wuppertal, and the founder of the Association for the Promotion and Supervision of Asian Students. Working with the Catholic priest Franz Eichinger, who served for many years as a missionary in China, Tacke brought roughly 500 Koreans to train and work in West Germany. Approximately 200 of these persons were nursing students, while most of the others – primarily women – were employed in the textile industry.[928] The first group of Indian women, also recruited by an ecclesiastical entrepreneur, arrived in German hospitals in 1960. By 1968, about 500 to 600 young Indian women were working in Catholic healthcare institutions.[929]

This early labor import strategy offered a number of advantages. Reliance on societal actors allowed the companies and institutions that employed these foreign workers to benefit from government development aid subsidies and enabled the government to quietly help the country's healthcare institutions meet their labor shortages without violating its own rules against employing unskilled workers from outside Europe.[930] In addition, the religious orders and institutions that employed these women and supervised their private lives promised to shelter them from culture shock and other social dangers. In fact, one high-ranking Interior Ministry official proposed restricting Asian nurses and nursing students to confessional schools and hospitals because "previous experience had shown that only confessional relationships with constant supervision and care appear broadly capable of preventing mistakes by Korean women, who would otherwise be isolated and on their own."[931] Nevertheless, these recruiting and employment strategies generated their own problems – problems that taught the West German government to appreciate the value of a strong, developmental state as a negotiating partner.

The Philippines

The recruitment of Filipina nurses to West Germany in the second half of the 1960s illustrates the problems of unregulated recruitment from a country with a weak state. As early as 1962, the Foreign Office, the Labor Ministry, and the German Hospital Association had begun negotiating with the Filipino government to recruit a substantial number of nurses. However, these negotiations had progressed only slowly. The decision to recruit from the Philippines was based on the widespread belief that these islands had a surplus of highly educated nurses. However, it soon became clear that the reason why so many Filipina nurses were leaving for the United States and Canada was not so much a surplus of nurses as a desire to emigrate to more affluent lands.[932] Moreover, from the beginning there were doubts as to whether German hospitals could compete with the wages and working conditions in North America, where nurses were certain to be engaged in a professional capacity, rather than being burdened with unskilled tasks. On the other hand, the president of the Filipino Nurses Association had widely publicized what she regarded as the poor working conditions in German hospitals. She warned that Filipina nurses might end up spending a substantial amount of their time doing laundry and cleaning in some of the older, overfilled hospitals, which were most likely to suffer from staff shortages. She also cautioned that diminutive Filipina women would have problems bathing and caring for stocky, oversized Germans. Recruiting was further complicated by the fact that the training of registered nurses from the Philippines was substantially more rigorous than that of German nurses.[933]

Negotiations between the West Germans and the Philippines were complicated by both the availability of other options to the Filipina nurses and the inability of the Germans to compete on equal terms in the world market, as well as a number of issues on the Philippine end.[934] To forestall any accusations of discrimination, the West Germans wanted to negotiate a single model contract that would spell out the minimum wages and working conditions for foreign nurses from all countries working at hospitals and other healthcare institutions throughout the country. Moreover, in view of the ambivalence of the Filipino public and the Filipino Nurses Association, German officials were keen to have the Philippine government involved in selecting qualified women for work in West Germany. However, recruiting arrangements at the Philippine end virtually encouraged abuse. The for-profit Catholic Travel Center, which was under the jurisdiction of the archbishopric of Manila, had a quasi-official semi-monopoly on recruiting nurses for work overseas. The West Germans were unhappy with this situation. They felt that the agency was charging German hospitals exorbitantly high prices for its recruiting and travel services, and charging applicants high fees, all without being in a position to guarantee the qualifications of applicants for nursing positions in Germany.[935]

All of these factors combined to delay an agreement between the two countries. In the spring of 1965, the federal government and the German Hospital Association agreed to recruit 150 Filipina nurses on a trial basis, hoping to eventually hire as many as 1,500. This figure quickly proved wildly optimistic, although small groups of Filipina nurses did receive permits to work in West Germany in the second half of the 1960s. In a February 1966 letter to the Labor Ministry, the executive director of the

German Hospital Association complained about the incomprehensibly slow pace of negotiations, especially when 120 licensed, well-trained Korean nurses "could be recruited in the shortest time" and "could already be deployed in Frankfurt hospitals at the beginning of February."[936] In mid-1967, the German government temporarily broke off negotiations, although it did not oppose continued recruiting by individual hospitals.[937] In late 1968, the Philippine government finally agreed to a model contract.[938] However, this only resulted in a marginal and temporary increase in the transparency of the recruiting process because the Philippine government had decided to grant licenses to a total of eight firms to recruit workers for overseas employment.[939] The West Germans, who had long been pressuring the Philippine government to establish an official agency responsible for managing overseas labor recruitment, were hugely frustrated by this decision, which seemed to them to be a step in the wrong direction.[940]

The story of the recruitment of nurses from the Philippines is that of a weak state unable to shape the terms under which its population would be integrated into the global labor market and that sought instead to profit from the growing number of agencies it licensed to act as labor recruiters. This decision forced the Federal Republic to give up – at least temporarily – its efforts to persuade Philippine officials to establish an official labor recruitment agency. Instead, the West Germans decided to allow hospitals and hospital associations to directly recruit Filipina nurses on their own. The number of Filipina nurses traveling to Germany increased from 54 in 1969 to 1,090 in 1970, 980 in 1971, 901 in 1972, and 400 in the first four months of 1973.[941] Under President Ferdinand Marcos, the Philippines were becoming an increasingly authoritarian country; the imposition of martial law in September 1972 strengthened the grip of the Philippine state over civil society; and by the mid-1970s, the Marcos regime had begun to control the freedom of its citizens to travel and work abroad. The 1974 signing of an agreement between the German Hospital Association and the Philippine Labor Ministry regulating the recruitment of nurses was the most visible sign of the changing nature of the Philippine state in this domain.[942]

India

The recruitment of Indian nurses proved even more chaotic and problematic than was the case with the Philippines.[943] In December 1964, forty-eight Indian women arrived in West Germany; they were followed by a second group in February 1965; and by 1972 there were approximately 2,500 Indian women – 700 of whom belonged to Catholic religious orders – working in the country's hospitals and healthcare institutions.[944] Until the end of the 1960s, almost all of these women came from the Christian communities of the south Indian state of Kerala, where they had been recruited by the Catholic clergyman Hubert Debatin.

Debatin worked in collaboration with the Keralan church, and he envisioned this work as a combination of Christian service for the sick and moral uplift and selective Westernization for the Indians themselves. Almost all of these young women (mostly aged 16–18 at the time they left for Germany) were interested in learning nursing, rather than in pursuing a religious vocation. However, their work and everyday life in Germany were organized through the religious association Nirmala Seva Dalam ("To Serve in Joy"). The status of this organization in ecclesiastical law was murky. However, as the spiritual advisor of the group, Debatin made the young women take an oath of personal obedience to him, and he imposed a number of severe restrictions on their personal freedom in order, so he argued, to protect these simple village girls from the temptations of Western hedonism and individualism. They had to live together in a dorm according to the rules of the Nirmala community. These included, in addition to daily prayer, the promise not to venture out on their own without the permission of their religious superiors, not to socialize with or marry German men, and to wear the traditional Indian sari during their off-duty hours. Any woman who did not follow these rules could be sent back to India.[945]

Many of these women were assigned to psychiatric hospitals, which were shunned by German nurses because of the working conditions.[946] When these Indians arrived at their places of employment, they were put to work doing menial jobs – and there many remained for six to seven years. They did not sign individual contracts with the institutions where they worked. Rather, these institutions signed a contract under which the religious community agreed to provide a certain number of workers in return for payment to the community. Each month the hospitals paid 570 marks directly to Nirmala for the services of each woman. From this amount, 115 were deducted for room and board; the women themselves received 50 to 80 marks as pocket money; some of their earnings were to be remitted to their families; some seems to have made its way into the hands of Indian church authorities; and the remainder was to be deposited in savings accounts to enable these women to pay for their flight home and to provide them with a nest egg upon their return.

Although such group contracts with religious orders were not unusual, the failure to spell out the conditions under which the promised training was to take place could be read as a violation of the immigration law provisions under which they had been brought to the country. In addition, the failure to clearly state the pay, benefits, and other conditions pertaining to each woman clearly violated German labor law, while Debatin's semi-feudal, semi-pastoral authority, combined with the absence of supervision by either the Indian state, Indian church authorities, or the Baden-Württemberg hospitals that employed most of these women, brought him into perilous proximity to the child trafficking scandal referenced at the beginning of this chapter. Ultimately, his refusal to work with the Catholic charities responsible for the welfare of foreign workers led the German church to shut down his operation in 1970.

Although German officials were not without sympathy for the plight of these Asian women, they were torn between their need for workers and their promise to provide training and skilled employment. And no matter what their sympathies, they had to deal with the personal and political consequences of unregulated recruiting, so it should come as no surprise that they placed a high premium on having an official partner in the sending land.

South Korea

The decision by the West German government to rely on Korea for caring labor was not an obvious choice. The immigration of a large number of Germans to Central and South America during the 19th century made these Latin American countries potentially attractive places to recruit nurses. In fact, German businessmen in South America frequently noted the existence of many nurses and nursing students, who could be recruited to help alleviate Germany's nursing shortage. But the German federal government remained cool toward such suggestions because it did not feel that these countries had strong, centralized governments that could serve as reliable partners in organizing the migration of nurses.

German officials initially thought that their best opportunity in Asia was the Philippines because the country's Catholic culture, the familiarity with Western lifestyle, and the general fluency in English would make it easier for Filipina women to adapt to German society and communicate with other hospital staff. However, these potential advantages were more than offset by the problems described earlier. South Korea was one of the first Asian countries to make labor export into a central pillar of its development policy, and the 1965 decision by the South Korean government to establish such an agency created an unexpected opportunity to provide the largest contingent of Asian nurses in West Germany.

Large-scale export of Korean labor became a central element of South Korea's development strategy under the regime of Park Chung-hee, who came to power after a 1961 coup that ushered in almost two decades of political repression. Park staked his right to rule on economic development, and he single-mindedly pursued a wide-ranging program of state-sponsored modernization.[947] At the same time, he tried to move away from excessive economic and military dependence on the United States, and he hoped to compensate for this loss, at least in part, by forging closer relations with West Germany. Park's idea of exporting Korean workers to West Germany represented a way of building on the nascent commercial ties between the two countries in order to meliorate the problems of high population growth rates, economic stagnation, and industrial unrest, while generating the foreign capital needed to finance the country's own development.

Park deeply admired Germany, and he believed there was a strong affinity between the two countries.[948] His 1963 *The Country, the Revolution, and I* even included a chapter entitled, "The Miracle on the Rhine and the German People." Although Park attributed West Germany's economic miracle to an unsurpassed "love for order and work," he also pointed to a German legacy of strong leaders: "It is a fact that Bismarck and even Hitler were men, who achieved important things for their people. Therefore, it is no exaggeration to claim that the postwar miracle rests on good leadership."[949]

In 1961, Korean officials asked the West German government to accept 2,400 trainees in various occupations. Although they emphasized the importance of the technical training that the Koreans would acquire through working in West Germany, German authorities regarded this request as a transparent attempt to bypass German restrictions on Asian guest workers, and they rejected the proposal outright.[950] On the other hand, German officials were not insensitive to the needs of German employers. The Ruhr mining industry, which was in desperate need of workers, wanted to hire 400 Korean men, and in April 1963 the Labor Ministry agreed to allow 250 Korean men to travel to Germany to work for three years. The first contingent of Korean miners arrived soon thereafter.[951]

Many of the Koreans who were selected for work in the Ruhr had either attended or completed college, and they often regarded their three-year work commitments as a stepping-stone to further study in Germany. However, their lack of experience in mining, misinformation about pay and working conditions, and widespread discrimination led to job-related accidents, labor conflict, and general discontent. By the fall of 1964, the International Human Rights League of Korea had become involved in these Ruhr labor conflicts, and the organization sent Chancellor Erhard a letter expressing concern over the deaths of Korean miners.[952] Communist countries pounced on these developments for propaganda purposes. The official Chinese news agency characterized the employment of Korean men in German mines as a form of human trafficking.[953] Soon after these reports, 150 Korean miners in Castrop-Rauxel staged a four-day strike for better wages and health benefits. However, fearing that such conflicts would foil the government's plan to send even more workers abroad, the Korean ambassador in Bonn intervened to end the strike.[954]

Despite these problems, Korean officials took advantage of this crack in German policy to ask whether it might also be possible to send a number of women to work and train as nurses.[955] The Labor Ministry suggested that, despite this impasse at the governmental level, Catholic and Protestant social service organizations might be interested in such a program.[956] In the medium term, the introduction of nurses into the discussion would lead to a displacement of the primary agents of international labor exchange onto the level of non-state actors. In fact, in the first half of the 1960s many of the Korean nurses who came to work in Germany had been recruited by Eichinger. However, in 1965/66 both church and government officials began to realize that the lack of transparency and accountability was responsible for many of the problems encountered by the nurses in Germany, and church officials began to more closely supervise the recruiting and employment of Asian nurses.

At the same time, the government and the German Hospital Association were working to make the nursing association more attractive. In 1965, the Bundestag revised the regulations governing the training of nurses. While this law increased the amount of theoretical instruction in medical care included in the nursing curriculum, it also sought to relieve licensed nurses of many of the unskilled tasks that they had traditionally been expected to perform by creating the new job category of nurse aide.[957] The law also prohibited hospitals from using nursing students to fill the gap in unskilled manpower. Although the German Hospital Association had long been lobbying for such reforms, the law exacerbated the existing shortage of un- and semi-skilled healthcare labor, and it prompted the president of the German Hospital Association to urge the government to make an exception to its immigration policies and permit Asian women to fill these jobs.[958]

At the same time, the Korean government also began to exert more direct control over the process. During these years, two Korean physicians working in Germany, Lee Su-kil and Lee Jong-soo, acted as intermediaries between the German hospitals and the Korean government. In April 1965, the first Lee contacted hospitals in the Frankfurt area to see if they were interested in hiring Korean nurses. The terms he proposed were quite favorable for the Germans: Korean nurses would sign contracts obligating them to work for three years at the same hospital; airfare from Seoul to Frankfurt would be advanced by the hospitals and then repaid through deductions from the monthly paychecks of the nurses; and the hospitals would be allowed to select desirable candidates from a list proposed by the Koreans.[959] In August 1965, the director of the Hofacker-Verband, which represented a number of hospitals in the Frankfurt region, sent an urgent request to the Hessian Labor Ministry asking for work permits for 143 South Koreans, including sixty licensed nurses, thirty-six nursing students, eight nurse aides, and thirty-nine housekeepers. The letter explained that "extraordinary situations require extraordinary measures," and the association warned the Ministry that, "if the lack of personnel were to lead to the closing of nursing stations or even entire clinics," then its member hospitals in Frankfurt "would not want to have to reproach themselves for contributing to the situation by failing to take the initiative."[960]

The very success of this quasi-official labor export program led the Korean government to become more directly involved in the recruiting process. In October 1965, it established the Korea Overseas Development Corporation (KODCO) as the official agency responsible for promoting and regulating overseas labor migration; this brought the overseas migration of caring labor under the direct control of the Korean state. In the future, interested West German hospitals would have to obtain the necessary work permits from the German government and then forward all of their requests to the Korean embassy in Bonn, which, in turn, would forward the requests to KODCO in Seoul.[961] The two governments also drafted a standardized contract to govern such employment.

In signing this agreement, the South Korean government had a very specific vision of the position of these women in Korean society, how they would meet the labor needs of the West German healthcare system, and how their work in West Germany would contribute to the economic development of South Korea. In the eyes of the Korean officials and recruitment intermediaries, these women were commodities that could be exported like any other. What remained invisible were power relations in Germany and Korea that determined how and why these women entered the global labor market.

The year 1966 marked a turning point in the recruitment of Korean nurses for work in Germany. In the first half of the year, Lee Su-kil recruited 434 nurses to work in Frankfurt area; later that year, Lee Jong-soo in Bonn brought another 638 women; and by June 1967, there were about 2,000 Korean nurses working in Germany.[962] In fact, in 1966 one out of every five nurses working in South Korea departed for Germany.[963] The success of the Frankfurt hospitals in tapping this new source of labor encouraged hospitals elsewhere in the country to begin recruiting nurses from Korea.[964] According to a German embassy report, the speed with which the Korean women were recruited and delivered gave German recruiters the impression that Korea represented "an inexhaustible reservoir of nurses."[965]

The accelerating exodus of Korean nurses raised important questions in both countries. The export of so many nurses threatened to denude Korean hospitals of a substantial proportion of their own nursing staffs. For example, out of the thirty-five licensed nurses originally employed by the Fatima Hospital in Taegu, five left for Germany in early 1966, and fifteen more submitted their resignations in the expectation of departing for the West. The hospital director feared, if this trend continued, many Korean hospitals would have to close their doors, and she urged the German government to stop this recruitment, which she characterized as development aid policy in reverse.[966]

The reform of U.S. immigration law in the 1960s also prompted a growing number of Korean physicians to leave. Almost 2,000 Korean doctors left for the United States between 1962 and the end of 1968, and in the second half of the decade approximately half of the graduates of Korea's eleven medical schools followed the same path. The American physician Paul S. Crane, the director of Presbyterian Medical Center in Kwangju, deplored the morality of both U.S. and German policy: "Good grief! Who cares, let the people of rural Korea die, seems to be the attitude of the people running this human export business, as they clasp hands with the smiling bureaucrats in the U.S. and German Embassies who chop their visas for the considerable benefit of their own affluent societies." He criticized the entire trend:

This is getting pretty ridiculous! Some fellow from a Podunk town in Georgia shows up in Seoul to recruit 14 Korean interns for his hospital. Next week we can expect a fellow from the Ozarks wanting to recruit members of the Economic Planning Board no doubt... It seems that the economists have taken over the land encouraged by the whiz kids of the American Aid Program. Their "Let-the-People-Be-Damned" approach values a dollar target for exports higher than human health and life. They seemed to have never left their air-conditioned offices in Seoul to see the real health situation in Korea as they spin their grandiose schemes for building superhighways, factories, and tall buildings in Seoul.[967]

Both the South Korean and West German governments were widely criticized for their role in these developments. Particularly critical of these state-sponsored programs were those international organizations that had given substantial amounts of aid to train doctors and nurses. WHO officials argued that it was pointless to spend so much money to improve the Korean health system when this work was undone by the immigration of Korean nurses to Germany.[968]

German officials were also divided over the program. While the Development Ministry complained that the development aid subsidies provided to the program were being used more to solve the labor problems of the German hospital system than to aid either Korean nurses or the Korean people, the mayor of Mainz wrote to the Labor Ministry, explaining that the new 600-bed university hospital was almost complete and that they were depending on 130 additional Korean nurses to staff the facility. The Interior Ministry of Rhineland-Pfalz also wrote to the federal Interior Ministry warning that a third of the hospital beds in the state would have to be closed if nurses could not be recruited from Korea.[969] And Bundestag President Gerstenmaier insisted in rather mercenary terms that German financial contributions to various United Nations organizations were "so large that I would not have any objection if these UN organizations [such as WHO and UNICEF] for once did something that benefitted us."[970]

Korean officials repeatedly denied that the migration of so many nurses had any deleterious impact on Korea's own healthcare system. They painted a rosy picture of the state of Korean hospitals and reiterated the claim that Korea had plenty of nurses to spare to help ensure the proper staffing of the German welfare state. The German government, seeking to avoid blame for the Korean brain drain, disingenuously accepted this assurance at face value, despite abundant evidence to the contrary.[971] Although some Koreans complained about the pay and working conditions in Germany and questioned the impact of the policy on Korea itself, the Korean Central Intelligence Agency (KCIA) quickly squelched this domestic opposition.[972]

In early 1967, however, mutual plans to expand the recruitment program were temporarily derailed by a kickback scandal, which led to exactly the kind of bad publicity the German government had hoped to avoid by working through the Korean government.[973] In response, the German government decided to halt, at least temporarily, the recruitment of nurses from Korea.[974] Relations between West Germany and South Korea were further clouded in June of that year, when fifty KCIA agents stole into West Germany; kidnapped seventeen Korean students, coal miners, nurses, and scientists residing there; and spirited them back to Seoul to stand trial for spying for North Korea. The world-renowned composer Yun I-sang and his wife were kidnapped, leaving their two young children behind; and in Seoul a German citizen, Heidrun Kang, who worked for the German Academic Exchange Service, was arrested along with her Korean husband.[975] This affair reminded the German public of the South Korean presence in their country – and of the reach of the South Korean security services. It also generated a substantial amount of support from German students and academics, many of whom signed petitions demanding the release of the Koreans kidnapped from Germany. The German president sent a letter to Park asking for their release, and Bonn suspended discussions on further development aid to Korea.[976]

Despite strained relations between the two countries, in October 1967 the German government lifted the suspension of the nurse recruiting program, which then continued at its high level through the end of the decade. From November 1968 to December 1969, the German government issued 1,195 work permits to non-European nurses; almost three-quarters of these went to South Koreans.[977] By the early 1970s, there were 5,000 Koreans, 3,000 Filipinos, and 1,500 Indians worked in German healthcare institutions.[978]

Nevertheless, these public discussions did force the Korean and German governments to alter their policies. In 1969, the three-year contracts for the first large group of nurses who had gone to Germany were set to expire, and it was predicted that many of these women would return to Korea (just over 40 percent of them did). In April 1970, both KODCO and the German Hospital Association agreed that until Korea had enough licensed nurses to meet its own needs, only up to 500 licensed nurses could be recruited annually; the ceiling for nurse aides was set much higher.[979] This agreement represented a reaction to West German fears that it was draining South Korea of its trained nurses. However, it did not mean that the South Korean government had abandoned its commitment to the mass export of caring labor. Instead, in November 1969 the government began a program to train nurse aides for export to Germany. These women would be jointly trained by KODCO and the Korean Health Ministry specifically to meet the needs of West German hospitals, and their level of training would not be so high that the agreement limiting the migration of trained nurses would apply to them.[980] In February 1971, KODCO and the German Hospital Association reached an agreement, which specified that, between 1971 and 1974, up to 4,500 licensed nurses and 11,000 nurse aides could be recruited for work in Germany. In practice, such aides accounted for more than 80 percent of the Korean nursing force recruited for work in Germany.[981]

As we shall see in the following section, many of the Korean nurses who had come to Germany in the second half of the 1960s suffered both from adjustment problems and discrimination because they had little knowledge of what to expect when they arrived in the country and could not speak the language. To prevent this problem from recurring, the 1971 agreement also required the Korean government to provide the recruits with three months of training in the German language, additional instruction in those German healthcare practices that were not included in their Korean training as nurse aides, and a general introduction to German society and its hospital system.[982]

Despite this agreement, German hospitals remained unable to meet their needs for unskilled housekeeping labor, and there was growing pressure on the government to drop its prohibition on the employment of unskilled workers from the global South. One newspaper neatly summed up the prevailing sentiment when it noted that "[The] Last Hope for [German] Hospitals are Asians and the Third World." The article cited the president of the North Rhine-Westphalia state labor office as saying that "in many countries of the world people are starving. Not only can we feed them. We also have a pressing need for them as workers if we can manage to overcome the negative attitude towards people from other parts of the world." The people he had in mind were "girls and women from Korea, India and Latin America," whose employment in domestic and caring work would relieve educated and qualified German women from such menial tasks.[983]

In March 1970, the West German government finally gave in and allowed the recruitment of un- or semi-skilled hospital workers from outside Europe, although only from the same countries (Korea, the Philippines, India, and Jordan) from which it already recruited nurses. At that point, approximately half of all non-German healthcare workers working in the Federal Republic came from Asia, and the absence of additional reserves in the European labor market meant that the number of Asian healthcare workers would continue to grow in the coming years.

The 1971 agreement was renewed in 1974.[984] By that point, KODCO possessed the ability to train 2,000 nurses and 2,000 aides annually, and the target recruiting figure for 1975 was 2,000 nurses and 1,000 aides. The 1974 agreement placed greater emphasis on helping these women reintegrate into Korean society at the end of their stay in Germany. The problem with the program was that, while it met a German need, training for semi-skilled work in German hospitals did not qualify the women to work as nurses in Korea any more than did German nursing certification. It was clear from the beginning that these women would be at a significant disadvantage on the job market both in Germany and when they returned home. The Korean government, however, did not see this as a problem. Having originally embarked on its labor export program to relieve the pressure of surplus population and accumulate foreign exchange, the Korean authorities still regarded these women as "dispensable," to quote the director of the Korean Labor Office.[985]

II. GERMANY'S FORGOTTEN GUEST WORKERS

Angels from Land of Morning Calm: The First Wave

On January 30, 1966, the first group of 128 South Korean nurses left for West Germany. They were seen off by the prime minister and the minister of health and social affairs. When they arrived in Frankfurt, they were greeted at the Römerberg by the mayor and other dignitaries. The Korean ambassador told the audience that this was the "beginning of a necessary friendship between two peoples, who are forced to suffer a common fate by their divided homelands," and he explained that these nurses, all dressed in traditional silk hanbok, were motivated solely by familial love, rather than by any hopes of personal enrichment.[986] The major dailies ran orientalizing stories about their tender hands, black hair, and "almond eyes" and about their unlimited spirit of sacrifice.[987] Once the reception was over, the nurses were separated into smaller groups to be distributed to nine hospitals and six nursing homes in the Frankfurt area. Each nurse wore a color-coded ribbon: Those with red ribbons were assigned to municipal hospitals and homes; those with blue ribbons were to be taken to the Markus Hospital; and the others were to work at the municipal mental asylum and old-age homes.[988]

The importance the Korean government placed on the export of nurses was reflected in many ways. Job openings in Germany were announced by the Korean Ministry of Health and Social Affairs in September 1965.[989] The interviews were conducted by a Korean Health Ministry official, the president of the Korean Nurses Association, and Lee, and the entire application and interview process was completed in only a month. The women selected were more highly educated than their German counterparts; they were highly motivated; and they were also privileged.

These initial groups of Korean nurses were – with the exception of nursing students – graduates of universities and nursing schools. In a country where higher education was both highly valued and reserved for a minority of the population, many of these women came from privileged social backgrounds, as reflected in the fact that a number of them had arrived for their interviews in Seoul in chauffer-driven cars. Age and physical appearance obviously mattered to the people involved in the selection process, and many applicants perceived the selection process to be in large part a beauty contest. One Korean newspaper reported that Lee Su-kil had turned down eight applicants in their thirties because he considered them too old and unattractive.[990] The final selection was based on university grades, work experience, and recommendations from supervisors and/or the Korean Nurses Association. The women selected had work experience in one of the country's twenty-one major hospitals. A large majority of the women selected to work in Germany (66–76 percent) were single, and at least two-thirds of them were under age 27.[991] There was great excitement among those who were selected. K. Chang-Ja, a classical music aficionada who spent her spare time singing in Yonsei University's Oratorio Choir, was overjoyed to be selected because she also hoped to study music in a country famous for its classical tradition while she was working.[992]

Even after the first three groups of Korean nurses had begun to report back, the Korean media continued to disseminate a highly idealized image of the life and work of these women in the Frankfurt region. The major dailies reported that Korean nurses were very popular among German patients because they had a special, painless technique for giving shots, that these Korean nurses worked eight hours per day, five days a week, that they enjoyed free time on the weekends, that for their first year these women would only be working half-days, and that they were spending their remaining time learning German. There were hints that these women were tasting the temptations of Western consumer culture as, for example, when the papers reported that each woman had her own dorm room furnished with a bed, a phone, and a living-room set. However, the papers reassured their readers that these women were not impressed by the more open style of relationships between German men and women and that they preferred a traditional arranged marriage to a Korean man. Many parents feared that their daughters' sojourn in Germany would diminish their marriage chances, especially if tarred by the charges of loose morality that also circulated in the Korean press, and reports such as those about the women already working in the Frankfurt region helped reassure families who were worried about the corrosive influence of Western moeurs.

The subaltern position that these first groups nurses occupied in the global labor market was at odds with their education and their aspirations, and the problems growing out of this conflict were amplified at the German end by a distinct sense – sometimes explicit, sometimes not – of racial and/or civilizational difference that equated the underdevelopment of their homeland with the absence of education and culture and with the need for discipline, a stronger work ethic, and other Western virtues. All of these motifs are condensed in the description of the attitudes of her German supervisor penned by one Korean nurse:

Our head nurse is extremely arrogant and intolerant. She treats us as if we should be thankful for a piece of bread because we come from a poor country. Her racial discrimination is unbelievable. When a new nurse is assigned to our unit, she only introduces her to the other German nurses. She is really an ill-mannered person. One time, she asked me what I did in my free time. I told her that at home I sometimes listened to classical music or play tennis. She responded by saying sarcastically that I am leading such a wonderful life here in Germany. We came here to earn money, not to lead such a luxurious life.[993]

From very early on, it was clear that nurses and aides from Korea, India, and the Philippines faced a number of problems in adapting to both their new jobs and their living conditions in West Germany. The failure either to anticipate these problems or respond to them in a timely manner ensured that for a large proportion of these women their much-anticipated stay in Germany would be frustrating and often bitterly disappointing. In many instances, the most basic terms of their employment were not explained to these women before they left their home countries, especially those who were recruited by for-profit agencies and ecclesiastical entrepreneurs such as Debatin. But there were other issues of equal importance.

The first had to do with the relationship between work and training. Licensed nurses from both South Korea and the Philippines were overeducated for their actual duties; conversely, German nursing licenses were not recognized by the countries to which most expected to return. These hard truths often came as a shock to the Asian nurses. Young women who came to Germany not as licensed nurses but as nursing students found themselves in the same boat. As one West German warned, "these Asian women must not be brought on false premises. Someone needs to explain to them that what is expected of them here is first of all work, not training, and that German nurses do not enjoy an elevated status, but – in contrast to the situation in hospitals in most other countries – also do the work of nurses."[994] While immigration and labor officials focused on enforcing the prohibition on the import of unskilled labor from outside Europe, welfare organizations such as the Caritasverband were more sensitive to the impossibility of reconciling learning with labor and to the fact that invariably it was the former that lost out. As one Caritasverband official explained, "the many difficulties caused by the presence of these girls from overseas result from, among other things, the fact that the hospitals want above all to solve their labor shortage, while the girls are expecting a good education."[995]

Both nurses and nursing students did, as we shall see, more than their fair share of strenuous work. However, there was a widely shared feeling among the Germans that these nurses and nursing students were being dragged into a form of debt servitude by the need to pay for their travel costs. In the words of one participant at a Caritasverband meeting on the topic, "it is not fair that, after their training course, during which they have had to pay off in installments the cost of their flight here, they then have to add on another year or two to pay for their flight home. This means that, during the couple of years they spend in Germany, they have simply labored to pay off their travel costs and that they maybe pass a couple of examinations here that are of no use at all for them at home." The speaker characterized these problems not only as difficulties but also as "outright injustices."[996]

A second cluster of problems grew out of the fact that Korean nurses seldom had any knowledge of the German language before they arrived in the country. Even licensed nurses could not be assigned to skilled patient care duties until they were able to communicate with both patients and staff, and the language barrier contributed substantially to the sense among the Korean nurses that they were regarded only as a source of menial labor. One German nurse said, "a Korean nurse, who comes to Germany without any knowledge of the language, is immediately put to work washing patients and dishes because little explanation is required for such work."[997] Young-ja Kim Peters, the Caritasverband social worker responsible for working with Koreans in the Frankfurt area, said that almost all Korean nurses had, at least occasionally, the sense that they were little more than slaves. These feelings were, she noted, aggravated by communication problems, much more so with nurses and doctors than with patients. She said hospital staff showed little understanding for the problems facing Korean nurses and only criticized them for the mistakes they made, rather than explaining the problem.[998] The language barrier tended to set in motion a cascade of additional problems, as women who did not feel comfortable interacting with Germans tended to remain isolated and become depressed. On top of all this, because many Asian nurses were employed in small groups at widely dispersed institutions, it was difficult for them to maintain a sense of community and for the institutions that employed to provide the language instruction that was so important to their integration into German society. It was not until the early 1970s that Korean nurses chosen to work in German hospitals began receiving better preparation prior to their arrival in Germany.

Finally, a whole complex of problems arose from these women's feelings that they were suspended between two cultures. The three-year separation from family, and sometimes from spouses and children, weighed heavily upon women, and efforts to establish romantic relationships with either Koreans or Germans brought complications. On the other hand, the very things they did in the hope of better fitting into German society made their future reintegration into Korean society all the more challenging. Moreover, many of these women did not want to return to Korea because of the lack of jobs, because their German nursing certification was not recognized at home, because they feared that they had missed the window of opportunity for marriage, and/or because of their ambivalence about the subordinate position of women in Korean society.[999]

Go West, Young Girl, Go West: Motives for Nurse Migration

Until well into the 1960s, the idea of traveling abroad, especially to the West, was unthinkable for most of the South Korean population. Quite apart from the high price of airfare, the government imposed strict limits on the amount of currency people could take abroad; this limited the ability of even the most affluent Koreans to travel to foreign countries. In addition to the very opportunity for such travel, these nurses were drawn to Germany for a combination of factors.[1000]

Although the Korean media downplayed the importance of pecuniary motives, many of the women who signed on as nurses or aides were willing to spend three years apart from their families in exchange for the chance to earn more money than they could possibly earn in Korea. For example, two sisters who were selected for the program resigned their positions as military nurses to go to Germany. Not only were they proud to bring their professional experience to the job, but they also hoped to save enough to open their own hospital in Korea with their younger brother, who was a medical student.[1001] Such financial motivations easily blurred into a more general desire for upward mobility. For example, one newly married couple agreed in 1970 that the wife would work for three years in Germany in the hope they could buy a house with her earnings when she returned home.[1002]

Some of the nurses expected work in Germany to advance their careers when they returned to Korea. For one 29-year-old nurse, the main reason to work in Germany was to "deepen her professional experience," and she hoped to open a practice with her uncle, a surgeon at a state hospital, when she returned.[1003] Another nurse explained that "people often speak of the highly advanced medical technologies in the Federal Republic. I found that highly attractive. I hoped that, when I go to Germany and work in a highly modern hospital, I will acquire a lot of knowledge about new technologies, which my friends in Korea do not have." Unfortunately, her hopes and expectations meshed poorly with her actual experience.[1004]

Other women saw nursing as a stepping stone to higher education in fields such as medicine, music, and the arts, fields that would have been closed to them had they remained in Korea. During the years, the average Korean couple had six children, and many families were hard-pressed to send all of their children to high school, much less college. Families with limited means reserved their precious resources for sons. Women, including many of those who went to Germany, were expected to contribute to the family income and help finance the education of their brothers. For example, one aide, an eldest daughter born in 1947, felt a "special responsibility" to her family, and she decided to go to Germany when her brother passed university entrance exam because otherwise the family would not have been able to afford to pay for his education.[1005] The willingness of these women to sacrifice for the welfare of their family and its male offspring did not mean they themselves did not harbor dreams of continuing their education. Many of these nurses planned to save for three years so they could attend university afterward.

FIGURE 8.1 South Korean nurses arriving in Frankfurt in May 1969.
Source: Pressebild-Verlag Schirner. Courtesy of Deutsches Historisches Museum, Schirn 94178/31a.

Nearly half of the women who traveled to Germany said that one reason for their decision was the desire to experience other cultures.[1006] As more and more women left for Germany, friends who remained behind began to receive letters encouraging them to jump on the bandwagon. For example, Kook-Nam Cho-Ruwwe wrote that, while she was supporting her family as a school nurse, she received a letter from a friend who was working in Germany, and soon thereafter another friend returned from a three-year stint in a German hospital. "I was enchanted by travel reports from Europe," she recalled. "What a privilege! My youthful spirit, my curiosity about an unknown world and culture, and the consolation that I would be home in three years with opportunities to earn a better living, and above all the unprecedented opportunity to travel abroad."[1007]

As the Park regime became dictatorial after 1970, contract work abroad became one of the few ways to escape punishing conditions at home.[1008] As one nurse aide explained at the time, "I hate the social structure of contemporary Korea. The rich and prosperous can do everything while the poor remain poor forever. I found that unbearable." Although she was offered a civil service position after she graduated, she did not take it "because the corrupt system disturbed me. I felt alienated from society." When she decided to leave for Germany in 1973, she had the feeling that she would never return to her homeland.[1009] Financial motives, the opportunity for additional education, the desire to broaden one's cultural horizons, and a growing distaste for various aspects of Korean society could seldom be neatly separated from one another. This complex might be said to define the developmental ideal of these women, one that was at odds with that of the Park regime.

III. DREAMLAND DEUTSCHLAND: WORKING AND LIVING CONDITIONS

Although most Koreans had vaguely positive notions about Germany, they had very little concrete knowledge of the country and its customs, and neither the German nor the Korean government did much to smooth the path for the first contingents of Korean nurses. The women signed contracts written in German either on board the plane or after they arrived in Germany; they were given no explanation of where they fit in the German division of healthcare labor; and they were put off by the way they were treated on their arrival. In the words of one nurse,

we were shoved around like cows that have new owners. After we arrived at the airport, we went in a large bus with many other Korean women who arrived at the same time. Each time, when the bus stopped, a few of them climbed out, and each time, I thought, it would be my turn to go. We were completely exhausted from a flight that lasted more than 20 hours and then from the long bus ride... [The next morning] we were in the hospital administrative offices to take care of the formalities. None of us could understand what they wanted us to do. We all understood everything differently, but the main thing was that we all signed and, no matter what, said yes... Despite our anxiety and complete overexhaustion, because our sleep had been interrupted so often, we all had to be at our stations the next morning at six.[1010]

When these nurses were asked to clean toilets and bathe patients, they were deeply shocked. When Hessian state radio interviewed three Korean nurses who had come to Germany in 1967, these women left no doubt how traumatic their experiences had been. They recalled how painful and humiliating it had been to encounter white-coated doctors while they were cleaning the toilet and taking care of basic patient needs. One nurse recalled that she had turned red as a beet and had felt so ashamed that she hid in the toilet until the doctor had left the room. Another nurse hid behind a curtain holding a bedpan until the doctor had finished his morning rounds. These women complained that the nursing skills that they had acquired in Korea were deteriorating from lack of use, and they feared that when they returned home they would be less skilled than nurses who had remained in Korea.[1011]

According to one survey, 32 percent of these Korean nurses performed only cleaning work, 25 percent bathed patients, and 31 percent accompanied them to the toilet and cleaned bedpans. Not surprisingly, more than half of these women were dissatisfied with their work during their first year, although this number tailed off to approximately 20 percent for those who had been working in Germany longer than three years; over this same time period, the number of those satisfied with their work rose from an abysmal 13.5 percent to a still-anemic 24.2 percent, with the remainder being partly satisfied.[1012]

Regardless of their qualifications, these women shared a common experience of mistreatment and discrimination. Many Korean nurses felt traumatized and degraded. In the words of a nurse who came to Germany in 1970,

I am sometimes confused because I don't know whether I am a cleaning lady or a kitchen assistant. Every day, the work is the same. I remember my time in Korea, when I was responsible for medications and injections. When I applied to come to Germany, I thought about the highly developed treatment techniques that I hoped would allow me to expand my own knowledge. This has proven to be a delusion. The way things actually are now, they would be better advised to bring cleaning ladies and maids from Korea... The result is that I am even forgetting the techniques that I learned at the university and the hospital in South Korea.[1013]

Working conditions were worst in confessional institutions, where the rate of dissatisfaction was several times higher. But everywhere, Korean nurses had to struggle to wash patients who were unable to move, and one nurse who was employed in a nursing home complained that her work

consists solely of bathing the elderly patients, emptying bedpans, making beds, and making the people comfortable in bed. When I go back to my room at lunchtime, I often don't feel like eating. Sometimes it is difficult to get to bed because I am so exhausted. It is almost impossible to do anything with my spare time because by the time I get off work it is generally too late to do anything.[1014]

There were also constant conflicts over scheduling and the distribution of tasks among Korean and German nurses. As one Korean nurse complained, her supervisor intentionally assigned more professional tasks to German nurses while relegating Korean nurses to bathing patients and housekeeping: "Up until now I alone have done almost all of the cleaning work for which our station is responsible."[1015] Other Koreans complained that their wishes were ignored when weekly schedules were made up and that they always got stuck with the worst shifts. As one Korean recalled, "for once I wanted to have time off this year at Easter. And do you want to know what the nurse in charge of our station said to me – that I didn't need to have Easter free because I didn't have anyone with whom to spend the holidays."[1016] Korean nurses were also expected to respond whenever a patient rang during the morning breakfast break. One aide recalled that she began to smoke during the break "just so that, like the other [smokers], I would not have to get up when the bell rang."[1017] Another woman said, "for the past two years I have worked almost only in the kitchen. My hope that in Germany I would be able to expand my professional experience has proven to be a false one. The inequality in the way they treat us is so great... I want not only to work in the kitchen or bathing patients, but also to work at the bedside of the patients like my German colleagues...I don't want to do the same thing all the time, but the Germans don't want to understand that."[1018]

There was also friction over symbols of social status, especially the right to wear a nurse's cap. One Korean nurse had been assigned to a small Catholic nursing home in Berlin for mostly elderly, bed-ridden persons. On her first day at the new job, she got up early to get ready, and she wore a white gown, white socks and shoes, her nurse's pin on her chest: and " – what was most important – my hair was carefully combed underneath my nurse's cap. Everything was perfect and precisely done, and I looked just like a Korean nurse should have looked." However, when she arrived, she found a supervisor waiting for her with a bucket and mop. The supervisor pointed her in the direction of the toilets, put the bucket and mop in her hands, and, without even saying good morning, she disappeared back to her breakfast table: "At that moment, it was very difficult for me to maintain my composure. I took my cap, which was the symbol of our profession and our education, from my head, and began to clean the toilets."[1019]

Few of these women had what we might term a support network. Some attempted to commit suicide; many more suffered from depression; others protested and sought to protect their sense of dignity; and many women fought individually for their rights at work. One woman later recalled how her work as a housekeeper in a German hospital made her look back on the good old days in Korea, where nurses enjoyed professional status and respect. One day she, too, appeared at the hospital wearing a nurse's cap, which she wasn't supposed to wear because she wasn't working as a nurse. For her, this cap was a symbol of her self-esteem and dignity. The station nurse went over to her and yanked it off her head without saying a word. When she put the cap back on, the head nurse reported her to a doctor, who then came over and pulled it off her head again. The Korean woman sat down and cried for a long time because she was so humiliated.[1020]

Korean nurses complained that whenever something went wrong at their station, German nurses blamed the Koreans because they could not defend themselves in fluent German.[1021] Two-thirds of all Korean nurses claimed that they had been discriminated against by their German colleagues, and one-third of Korean nurses characterized their relationships with the German staff as bad.[1022] Korean nurses seem to have had better relations with other foreign women working in Germany.[1023] This was not, however, an unalloyed good. One nurse told of a German woman, who passed by a table where Korean, Filipino, and Indian nurses were dining together, and muttered "you tableful of crap."[1024]

This discrimination reflected an ignorance of Korean culture that easily bred contempt. Intentionally or not, many Germans equated "Korean nurse" with "primitiveness and poverty."[1025] If German colleagues asked about Korean culture, it was often simply to confirm their suspicion of how backward Korea was; such conversations often led Koreans to lose interest in building closer relations with the Germans. One aide reported that she found breakfast time unpleasant because she was peppered with such questions as whether there were cars and televisions in Korea and "what I was going to do with all of the German money that I am earning here and how many Korean families I was supporting. This primitiveness makes me speechless. But when I don't answer, they all start laughing."[1026] Another woman recalled that with the passage of time she actually grew more distant toward her German colleagues. She told of a colleague who had been ridiculed for sleeping on the floor by Germans. After that, the woman always had pat answers ready-to-hand.[1027]

Turnover patterns were a good barometer of job satisfaction. A small number of women simply quit their jobs in frustration, even though this meant that they had to reimburse their employer for their flight to Germany – and pay for their flight home. One woman wrote to the Korean embassy, KODCO, and Lee Su-kil, in February 1967, desperately seeking to escape from the monotonous job she had been doing for a full year. "Not even for one day have I ever felt comfortable and happy in this hospital," she wrote. Ultimately, she decided to leave her job after the first year of a three-year contract.[1028] Other women tried to find better conditions at different hospitals. In 1969, the Hessian state labor office reported that, of 357 women who had been hired in 1966, 121 changed jobs within Germany or left for third countries.[1029]

Most Koreans lived in dormitories attached to the hospitals where they worked, so there was no separation between their workplace and their private space. Over and over again, these women recalled that, when they felt that they had been discriminated against or suffered an injustice, their only recourse was to lock themselves in their rooms. However, this did not automatically make them feel better. As one woman explained, when she went to her room, "I feel abandoned. Sometimes I am even afraid when I think that I am going to have to meet these people at the station in the morning, and I become even more upset."[1030]

Korean nurses sometimes had an entire dorm floor to themselves, while at other hospitals they shared space with German nurses. In the latter case, there were often conflicts over the use of the kitchen and common areas. Like writing letters, cooking Korean food was a form of therapy and a way of relieving homesickness. Cafeteria meals were automatically deducted from the nurses' paychecks, even though they complained about the constant diet of potatoes, bread, and meat covered with thick sauces. During their free time, Korean nurses relaxed by cooking with spices that they had brought from home. Over time, they became more creative and found ways to make a hybrid kimchi from German cabbage. They also identified a plant (*namul*) that was a popular green in Korean salads. Although they picked the plants regularly from nearby fields, this was not an unmixed blessing. One day, a German passer-by asked what they were doing. When they explained that they were going to use the plants as a salad, he roared in laughter, "here, only rabbits eat those weeds." The Koreans responded that "the poor Germans, who otherwise only eat bread and meat, don't know how delicate and aromatic *namul* tastes." In addition, someone apparently reported the story to the hospital administration, who told them that it was forbidden to pick the plants.[1031]

On occasion, though, the farmyard tables were turned on the Germans. Jung-Ja Peters related the story – still vivid in her memory – of the first meal that she ate after she arrived in Germany, a yellow bean stew. The meal stuck in her memory "because at home the yellow bean hulls were only used as cattle fodder. At this point, at the very latest, I realized that I was living in an entirely different world... And the shock was repeated at dinner, when we were served salted herring in cream sauce. With its slimy skin, the fish looked like a snake and smelled very, very alien!"[1032]

Both kimchi and Korean miso soup have a very strong smell, and the German residents in one dorm, who had to share a refrigerator with the Koreans, made a huge fuss about the smell. One day, one of the Korean nurses found that a German colleague had thrown away a jar of her precious kimchi, and the German warned her not to put anything in the refrigerator that stank so abominably. "I cried in anger," the woman later explained, "because I already have such strained relations with people at work. I have eaten kimchi all of my life, and it helps to keep me from being estranged from my culture."[1033] In another case, when several Korean nurses cooked some fish using a traditional Korean recipe, the Germans opened all the windows and protested about the smell. The dorm supervisor then warned the women that "they weren't allowed to stink up the entire house and could not cook anything like that again in the future." This incident infuriated the Koreans, especially since the Germans also ate smelly foods: "We never said that the Germans eat smelly cheese or that they don't have a culture of food. But we are reluctant to cook our own kind of food because the Germans are so insulting toward us. That is why we generally have a hot plate in our rooms."[1034]

Romantic relationships between Korean nurses and Korean men working in the Ruhr caused great concern in West Germany. Between 1964 and 1966, approximately 2,500 Korean miners had been brought to West Germany. An additional 2,000 arrived from 1970 through 1971.[1035] Although these Korean miners often wanted to remain in Germany for the same reasons as Korean nurses, they were expected to leave the country when their contracts expired, and they could remain in the country if the mining companies themselves wished to retain these workers (which was often the case), if they had been admitted to a German university, or if they married a Korean nurse.[1036]

According to one sample, nearly 90 percent of the Korean healthcare workers in Germany were single with the vast majority being in their twenties and thirties. Of this sample, fewer than 10 percent married while in Germany, two-thirds to Korean men. However, a substantial number of these Korean women had German boyfriends and said that they would consider marrying a German.[1037] Negotiating the boundaries of love and sex in Germany was tricky, in part because German men and Korean women entered into romantic relationships with different expectations and frames of reference, in part because the sexual moeurs of the Korean women were changing. These Korean women sought out contacts with German men for a variety of reasons: to improve their German, to escape from their loneliness, to broaden their exposure to the society in which they were living, and, of course, for love and lust. Many met their boyfriends in the hospital as patients, medical students, or university students doing civilian rather than military service.

The question of marriage and sexuality was linked to broader changes in gender norms. The Korean nurses feared that if they married, and especially if they then returned to Korea, they would be forced back into traditional female roles. If they returned to Korea unmarried, they might be rejected as unchaste, either in reality or by association. These fears were reflected in this confession by one nurse that "I am positively inclined toward getting married to my German boyfriend. However, when I think of what my mother said to me when I left Korea, I can't go through with it. She said that I should never forget that she did not want to have grand-children with a big nose and that, if this happened, she would be so ashamed that she could not live in our homeland."[1038] According to a 1968 survey, only 10 percent of the Korean nurses working in Germany wanted to return to Korea when their contracts expired; half wanted to continue working in Germany; and 30 percent wanted either to pursue further education or move on to a different Western country. Many did not want to return to Korea, the survey noted, because they feared that their chances of finding employment or a spouse were low.[1039]

IV. SUBALTERNITY AND BEYOND: BECOMING A TRANSNATIONAL SUBJECT

West Germany had long regarded foreign migrant workers as guest workers, who would eventually return to their home countries. However, by the early 1970s it was becoming clear that many of the first generation of postwar migrant workers intended to settle permanently in the country. This development unleashed a long debate over immigration policy and Germany's emergent status as a society of in-migration. The debate was just taking shape when the 1973 oil crisis and the ensuing recession led the West German government to halt the recruitment of foreign workers and take steps to encourage (or force) those already in the country to return "home."[1040]

As the crisis deepened, individual hospitals began cutting back on foreign nursing staff, and individual states began taking measures to restrict the recruiting of Asian nurses. By early 1975, these local actions had coalesced into a national policy that limited the number of nurses recruited from Asia.[1041] An additional reason for the tighter job market was that more German women were studying nursing, and some women who had stopped working for family reasons were finding it necessary to take up nursing work again. In response to this trend, federal officials revised their recruiting policy in July 1975. The new policy stipulated that, henceforth, (1) nurses were only to be recruited outside Europe from those countries (Korea and the Philippines) with which formal agreements had been concluded; (2) married women would no longer be recruited; and (3) in the future only licensed nurses, rather than nursing students or aides, would be recruited.[1042]

Taken together, the decision not to renew expiring residence permits and not to recruit additional nurses from Asia led to a precipitous decline in the number of Asian women working in Germany. The number of Koreans coming to Germany dropped from over 1,000 per year through the first half of the 1970s to 320 in 1975 and only thirty-seven in the first four months of 1976.[1043] These reductions were soon reflected in the statistics on the number of Asians living and working in Germany. Between the beginning of 1975 and the end of 1977, the number of Koreans working in Bavaria declined from 1,044 to 436 and the number in Baden-Württemburg, from 607 to 385. At the national level, the number of Koreans in West Germany, which peaked at around 8,000 in 1970–5, declined to approximately 5,500 by 1979.[1044] The number of Indians working in hospitals in southern Germany declined from 1,999 in July 1975 to 988 in March 1977. And the number of Filipinas working in North Rhine-Westphalia dropped from 1,870 at the beginning of 1976 to 1,200 two years later.[1045]

A tough job market and tougher immigration policy represented a real threat to many of these Asian nurses. They found themselves forced to regularly work night shifts, to move to different cities in search of work, and to take undesirable jobs in old-age homes and psychiatric clinics. The nation-state system, with its internal and external borders, made the already vulnerable position of these transnational migrants even more precarious. Neither the diplomatic representatives of their home country nor German officials were willing to intervene on their behalf, and they had few protections against being sent back home if they protested too loudly against their mistreatment or if the labor market worsened.

Under existing immigration regulations, people who had worked for five years in West Germany had the right to continue to work in the country indefinitely. But this provision did not do them any good if local officials were unwilling to issue the necessary residence permit. Permits could only be issued if this did not injure the interests of the Federal

Republic, and most officials came to believe that the long-term presence of foreigners, especially from Asia and Africa, was intrinsically problematic. These arguments were buttressed by the country's development aid policy, which maintained that Asian nurses who came to Germany to receive "advanced training" should be required to return to their home countries with their newly acquired nursing skills.[1046]

Many nurses were angered by what they perceived to be their arbitrary treatment by immigration authorities, who recruited them to come to Germany, where they had to learn a foreign language and overcome many other obstacles, only to be told they had to leave. Awareness of their common problem motivated the nurses to take collective action.[1047] In 1974, Korean nurses in Germany established regional self-help groups to discuss common problems and to build a sense of group solidarity. Inspired by the UN declaration of 1975 as International Women's Year, they organized a workshop, held in Heidelberg in April 1976, on the Korean women's movement. Over the subsequent months, associations were founded in major cities where there were substantial numbers of Korean women, and in the fall of 1978 they came together to form the nationwide Korean Women's Group in Germany.[1048]

By the time of their next workshop in 1977, German officials had begun to enforce the return migration of Korean nurses. Those attending the workshop decided to launch a protest campaign to publicize their situation. Between summer 1977 and January 1978, they collected more than 11,000 signatures on a petition demanding fairer treatment; Westdeutscher Rundfunk broadcast a story about them in March 1978; stories were also published in the leading feminist magazines *Emma* and *Courage*; and in May 1978, there was a Bundestag hearing.[1049] These protests, together with an appeal by the German Hospital Association, ultimately seem to have swayed federal and state interior ministries. By the end of 1977, a decision had been reached in principle to extend residence permits for Korean nurses as long as they were working (and, in case of unemployment, to make them eligible for at least a year of unemployment benefits) and make all foreign workers eligible for continuing residence after they had lived in the country for five years.[1050]

The local associations of Korean nurses became increasingly vocal in demanding that their grievances be redressed. The Göttingen Korean Women's Group distributed a flier in which they complained that "the practice of blaming us for a situation that we did not cause by withholding information concerning our rights and claims and through neglect and indifference is inhumane and unjustified." They argued that, in view of how much they had contributed to West Germany, they were entirely justified in demanding that they be allowed to work in the country as long as they wished. "We believe that we are in the right," they insisted, "when we demand the right to determine ourselves when we return home so that we have the time and opportunity to prepare ourselves financially and socially for our return to Korea."[1051]

Korean officials, on the other hand, saw no reason to take vigorous action to protect the women's rights abroad. In fact, the Korean government pressured them not to provoke German officials because they feared that such actions might jeopardize the flow of foreign remittances crucial to the government's broader development strategy or to price Korean workers out of the global labor market. It was at this point that it became evident how much they had been exploited by both governments. As one of the leading members of the Korean Women's Group later wrote,

at that point it became clear to me that we were only cheap labor, almost a commodity, but not humans. On top of this, German officials introduced new residence and work regulations. To get permission to work, one had to have a residence permit. However, when we went to the immigration office to get a residence permit, they told us that we had to have a work permit in order to qualify for residence. They played the same game at the labor office, and we were bounced back and forth between the two offices. This game was set up so that we couldn't win, and we had to endlessly run the same gauntlet. They practically told us to our faces: Your contract has expired, now go home. That really opened my eyes. In their eyes, we were simply beasts of burden that could be set to work whenever one pleased and then sent away at will. The idea that people might have made friends, started families, and led a personal life in the country where they worked played no role at all [in their considerations].[1052]

Trapped between the two governments, neither of which supported them, the women decided to mobilize grassroots support from the German public, and they eventually succeeded in achieving their immediate goal. This experience was quite a revelation for these women. As one of them later wrote, "participating in this signature campaign was a turning point in my life. At that point, I was a young woman living alone, and cooperation with other Korean women was important. That opened my eyes for history and collective life." This campaign ultimately contributed in important ways to the development of both their individual character and their collective solidarity: "The signature campaign was not only a valuable experience for me; it also helped me grow. To go up to a stranger and explain my circumstances and then ask for a signature was by no means something easy."[1053]

Participation in this collective venture also helped the Koreans learn how to deal with those Germans who looked down on them and disparaged their work. When one nurse first encountered such discrimination, she wrote,

I was deeply wounded, even ashamed, so that I couldn't react at all... Later we laughed together about how afraid we had been at the beginning and how we changed in the course of the campaign, how we had become more self-conscious and-assertive. Civil disobedience and resistance were concepts that were completely alien to us at the beginning. At first, it was anything but self-evident that we should stage protests and demonstrations. But we learned what was possible and that one can and must demand one's rights.[1054]

Once these first successes had been acheived, the Korean Women's Group also encouraged its members to think in broader terms about the social, economic, and political factors that precipitated their labor migration to Germany and to focus on the gendered nature of exploitation and subordination of women in society and economy. They also raised money on behalf of female textile workers on strike in Korea.[1055] However, it is important to note that, even in West Germany, it was not easy to show support for women workers in Korea. The Korean community in Germany was under the constant surveillance of the KCIA, and they had to censor themselves for fear of being branded as communists. In fact, many Koreans in Germany referred to them as the "Red Brigands" or "Communists," and one man even threatened to divorce his wife if she did not leave the group.[1056]

CONCLUSION

In recent years, it has become fashionable to use the idea of the "global woman" or the "global care chain" to explain the commodification of the reproductive labor of Third World women. The rising rate of employment of Third World women as domestic employees in the West (as well as in parts of Asia and the Middle East) has become a potent symbol of globalization and its corrosive impact on the global South.[1057] However, as we have seen, this process was already well underway by the second half of the 1960s, long before these women became the symbol of the unevenness of contemporary globalization. In countries like Korea and the Philippines, the female labor force was mobilized in the 1960s and 1970s in a variety of ways to support national development. Women worked abroad to earn vital foreign exchange and support their families; they provided labor that functioned as form of a human collateral for

Western development loans; and they worked both as "industrial sol-diers" in what have euphemistically been called "export processing zones" and as sex workers serving U.S. soldiers and Japanese tourists.[1058] The Asian women whose stories I have examined in this chapter represent only one facet of this broader phenomenon.

The 20th century is now part of the past, and most of the founding members of the Korean Women's Group have witnessed epochal changes both in South Korea and Germany. Many of them are now in their sixties or older and work on behalf of refugees and migrants in Germany. In a collection of essays entitled *Where and What Is My Home?* (2006), a dozen members of the Korean Women's Group attempted to make sense of their own lived transnational experiences during these decades. What these women, or at least some of them, have found is that their experiences gave rise to multiple, more cosmopolitan identities. As Kook-Nam Cho-Ruwwe explained,

I belong to both places, and at the same time I belong to no place. The search for a geographical home leads me to an inner division that permanently expels a part of me. But I want to include everything within myself. My home is everything that I was, am, and will be. It is in me. Therefore, my home is everywhere where I was, am and will be. Every person possesses the wisdom to understand at some point the path through which she has become what she is. At such moments I sense how my previous paths from Korea, from Germany, flow out of the past and out of the future like rivers of time that flow together into the lake that is me. The separation between the spaces and the times where I have lived is dissolved beyond all delimitation. Nevertheless, I can distinguish the different colors and songs of these worlds without rending my soul. I often immerse myself in my deep sea and rediscover there my wonderful treasures. I want to flow even further in order to reach the sea.[1059]

As the editors of the book, who are themselves daughters of group members, note, "it is more a feeling of feeling comfortable and of having arrived and of having made a connection to a concrete place. In the end, the inner dividedness or lack of orientation that is often ascribed to migrants can't be found in any of the authors."[1060]

Korean nurses, their families, and their children have been a permanent presence in West Germany since the 1960s. However, only in the past decade have their individual experiences, as well as the social phenomenon of labor migration, become the topic of explicit public discussion. This renewed emphasis is due, on the one hand, to a wave of literary works by Korean–Germans and, on the other, to accelerating globalization, including the frenetic economic activity in Germany by major Korean corporations such as Samsung and LG.

On May 20, 2006, the Korean Nurses Association in Germany (created in 1985) organized a ceremony in Frankfurt to commemorate the fortieth anniversary of the organized migration of Korean nurses to the country. About 1,000 Koreans living in Germany attended the event, which was sponsored by Samsung, and Chancellor Angela Merkel sent congratulatory message. Speaking on behalf of the Korean government, the Minister of Health and Welfare and the ambassador to Germany praised those Korean nurses who had come to Germany in the 1960s. They embodied what the men called the "excellence" of the Korean nation, the same excellence that had helped South Korea achieve its own postwar economic miracle. On a mega-screen behind the podium appeared a poem composed by the head of Samsung's Europe division. It read: "You are our mother. Leaving behind *Heimat*...and parents... friends..., it has now been forty years."[1061]

This was myth-making on a grand scale. It ignored the fact that the women who had come in the 1960s had been regarded as disposable, rather than as heroes. In addition, it simply failed to acknowledge that the Germano-Korean social space, which had been forged in the 1960s out of the joint needs of the German welfare state and the Korean developmental state, was now being sustained by the forces of neoliberal globalization, as embodied by the central role of Samsung at both ends of the arc connecting the two countries.

9

Things Fall Apart

INTRODUCTION: A TALE OF THE TWO GERMANYS
AND CHINA IN AFRICA, 1965–70

The final major arena of East and West German involvement in the global
South that we shall examine are the development and medical aid programs for Zanzibar and the united Republic of Tanzania in the second
half of the 1960s. The aspirations and methods employed by the two
German states will by now be familiar. What is novel here is the altered
global context in which these programs played out, especially the prominence of the Chinese, who displaced not only the West Germans as the
dominant donor country in the region but also the East Germans, who
served there as a surrogate for the Soviet Union and its approach to
economic development.

This new context was characterized by four main developments. First, in
a number of sub-Saharan countries the pressure for decolonization and the
threat of black majority rule led settler governments and colonial powers to
resort to increasingly radical means to maintain white minority rule. The
key events here were U.S. and Belgian intervention in the second Congo
crisis; the November 1965 declaration of independence by Rhodesia's white
minority regime; Portugal's increasingly tenacious efforts to retain Angola,
Mozambique, and Portuguese Guinea; and the brutal enforcement of apartheid in South Africa. To legitimize white power in black Africa, all of these
movements argued that traumatic experience of modernity rendered the
African majority infantile, irrational, and bestial; they emphasized the
positive virtues of continued white minority rule for the preservation of
order; and, in turn, these tropes served to legitimate counterinsurgency

campaigns against national liberation movements that were depicted as harbingers of chaos and pawns of communist subversion.[1062]

The second element in this volatile political mixture was the Sino-Soviet split.[1063] The main point of contention was the Chinese rejection of the Soviet doctrine of peaceful coexistence. In addition, the Chinese argued that the objective solidarity among the countries of the global South made them, rather than the increasingly bureaucratized Soviet Union, the natural champion of Third World liberation. This solidarity, they argued, was based on a shared history of racial and colonial subjection and an affinity between the frugal, peasant mentality of the Chinese and that of the Africans, and it gave rise to an alternate model of development aid. The Chinese criticized Soviet technical experts for neglecting the real needs of African peoples and seeking, instead, to plunder poor countries for their individual and collective profit.[1064]

This focus on South–South friendship was a reaction to the 1960 Soviet decision to suspend economic and technical aid to China.[1065] Zhou En-lai encapsulated the difference between Chinese aid and that provided by both the West and the Soviet Union when he declared that such assistance had to be premised on the equality of the two parties "who share joys and sorrows without the least intention of maltreating the small and weak countries by the big and strong."[1066] In January 1964 – in the midst of a tour of ten nonaligned African states – Zhou proclaimed the "Eight Principles on Foreign Economic and Technical Aid," which read like a point-by-point critique of what many Third World countries regarded as the reality of development aid, no matter whether it came from the countries of the First World or the Second.[1067] These principles stated that the Chinese would respect the sovereignty and independence of recipient countries, provide free or low-cost loans for projects designed to help these countries along the path to independent economic development, and focus on projects that could be completed more quickly and with lower capital requirements. They also stated that experts would teach the residents of the recipient country how to operate the technologies they received and that these experts would not demand a standard of living that was higher or more comfortable than that of the people whom they were assisting.[1068] In 1967, the Chinese sent abroad more than 3,000 technical experts, despite the shortage of such persons at home; about two-thirds of these persons worked in Guinea, Mali, and Tanzania. Although both the United States and the Soviet Union publicly derided Chinese aid programs as backward, they were both impressed with the country's ability to sponsor such an ambitious technical aid program.[1069]

Third, the 1960s saw a radicalization and militarization of Third World revolutionary struggles, which were defined, especially by the younger generation, in increasingly explicit racial terms. The immediate catalysts for this radicalization were the increasing oppression by the apartheid government in South Africa and the growing presence of white mercenaries in the Congo. However, they were energized by the Chinese commitment to popular mobilization and their support of armed liberation struggles in such places as Vietnam and Cuba, which they regarded as a more appropriate response than peaceful coexistence to the increasingly violent attempts to preserve white minority rule in the region. They were also inspired by the Cuban revolution, by Cuban aid to the region, and by the guerrilla campaign in the Congo, which was led by Che Guevara – the cultural icon of the Cuban revolution – in 1965.[1070]

Fourth, the African states were also coming to understand the extent to which the social and economic problems that they all faced were related to the ways in which they had been incorporated into the global economic order. Their awareness of their position within the capitalist world system was driven home in the early 1960s by a sharp decline in the world market price of many primary products and by the resulting Third World debt crises. In this context, they criticized the North for instrumentalizing development aid for commercial purposes, and they called on the United Nations to create an organization to help redress the neocolonial structures of the world economic system (a demand that led to the establishment of the UN Conference on Trade and Development in 1964). These ideas were echoed by Cuban President Osvaldo Dorticós Torrado that year, when he urged the second Conference of Non-Aligned Countries to broaden the scope of liberation struggles to include the struggle against global economic inequality.[1071] All of these developments were then linked to racial violence in Africa and the United States, which the nonaligned countries regarded not just as a local issue, but rather as a threat to world peace. This new vision of antiracist solidarity found its institutional embodiment in the Organization of African Unity (OAU) . The OAU, which was founded in 1963, functioned as a counterpublic sphere – outside of the United Nations – through which the member states could contest the racist underpinnings of both the global humanitarian regime and neocolonial influence on the continent. The 1963 UN decision to impose an arms embargo on South Africa was an important, albeit incomplete, victory in African efforts to globally politicize the issue of racial oppression.

I. UGLY AMERICANS, UGLY GERMANS, AND PROPAGANDA WARS IN EAST AFRICA

In 1958, William J. Lederer and Eugene Burdick published *The Ugly American*.[1072] In the United States, *The Ugly American* was a sensation, and it went through twenty printings in only a few months. While many people have sought to reduce the Cold War to a single essence, we might better concede that it was about many things. One of these was which system produced citizens with the firmest character. Like David Riesman's *The Lonely Crowd* (1950), and Daniel Bell's *The End of Ideology* (1960), *The Ugly American* was an exploration and, in its own way, a celebration of the American national character. It helped define one small dimension of the larger Cold War: the epic struggle between the Ugly American and the Ugly Russian, in which the foibles, virtues, blunders, accomplishments, and attitudes of the protagonists became windows into the very souls of the two competing ideological systems.

Soon after its publication, the state secretary in the West German Foreign Office asked all mission chiefs to read the book and report back to Bonn.[1073] It was widely recognized within the West German diplomatic corps that many technical experts and aid workers were less than competent and that they tended to comport themselves like colonial rulers of times past. Several mission chiefs cited the book to emphasize the importance not only of training and expertise but also the need for greater sensitivity to local customs and at least rudimentary knowledge of the local language.[1074] However, we need to avoid falling into the trap of romanticizing the motives of either socialist bloc representatives – themselves the object of a counter-novel by Victor Lasky, *The Ugly Russian*[1075] – or the local population. In many instances, the line separating sensitivity to local needs, the desire to make connections with influential persons in the host government, and outright bribery and favoritism was often difficult to draw.

By 1960, these character wars and the goal of producing, both at home and in the Third World, a new type of personality had emerged as a key dimension of the competition between capitalism and communism in the age of peaceful coexistence. When John F. Kennedy pledged to create a "peace corps" during his 1960 presidential election campaign, he had in mind "the best Americans we can get to speak for our country abroad."[1076] But wherein lay the unique genius of the American character and its social system? In 1961, Riesman told a large Japanese audience that the "new type of young American" was "sensitive, not greedy or power-hungry, versatile and capable but not purse-proud about it, cooperative but not conformist, tolerant and unfanatical, not liking to throw his weight around and not liking his country to throw its weight around either." The New Americans, he explained, had "faith that they could accomplish something concrete in giving self-confidence to a local community, in showing them that they did not fatalistically have to be helpless before nature, before their own suspicions, and before the wiles or the inertia of other men."[1077]

In the new American imagination of the early Kennedy years, the moon and the Third World both represented "figurative frontiers to be explored and mysteries to be solved."[1078] Faced with decolonization abroad and racial turmoil at home, Kennedy hoped that the young men and women serving in the Peace Corps would be able to win the peoples of the Third World over to the West. As he wrote to Secretary of State Dean Rusk, "Ghana has accepted 50 to 70 Peace Corps volunteers. Guinea is asking for 40 to 60 road builders and engineers from the Peace Corps. If we can successfully crack Ghana and Guinea, Mali may even turn to the West. If so, these would be the first communist-oriented countries to turn from Moscow to us."[1079] In Ghana, Nkrumah was willing to accept Peace Corps volunteers because the country did not have enough teachers to implement his goal of universal primary education, and the first contingent of volunteers arrived in Accra in August 1961.[1080]

The Soviet Union responded to the U.S. challenge by creating its own cadre of specially trained young volunteers; they went to Ghana, Guinea, and Mali to provide the same kinds of assistance as the Peace Corps, albeit with a different ideological spin.[1081] Both West and East Germany followed suit. Under pressure from Washington,[1082] West Germany established the German Development Service (*Deutscher Entwicklungs-dienst*, DED) on June 24, 1963 (Figure 9.1). Three months later, East Germany established the Friendship Brigades of the FDJ (Figure 9.2). In August 1964, the first DED team departed for Dar-es-Salaam, Tanzania, to work on a slum-clearance program.[1083] The FDJ Friendship Brigades, which included construction engineers, masons, carpenters, doctors and nurses, as well as agronomists, veterinarians, and a sport instructor, left at the same time for Mali and Algeria.

One issue conveniently left out of *The Ugly American* was U.S. racial problems, and recent work by U.S. historians has explored the global dimensions of the civil rights movement and the mutual implication of domestic politics and the international rivalries during the Cold War.

Entwicklungshelfer in Afrika,
Asien und Lateinamerika

Deutscher
Entwicklungs-
Dienst

FIGURE 9.1 "Development Aid Workers in Africa, Asia and Latin America" (c. 1970). Promotional brochure to recruit volunteers for the West German Development Service.
Source: Deutscher Entwicklungsdienst. Courtesy of Deutsches Historisches Museum, Berlin, D02 2001/56.

As Martha Biondi has noted, "[t]he international spotlight of the Cold War and the rising challenges to colonial rule in Asia and Africa ... made the U.S. government acutely conscious of a global audience critical of American racial oppression. As this sensitivity became clear, many civil rights leaders tried to turn the Cold War to their advantage."[1084] Conversely, U.S. Jim Crow laws provide the socialist bloc with ample opportunities to play on the visceral memories of colonialism among Africans and Asians and to attack the hollowness of capitalist democracy.

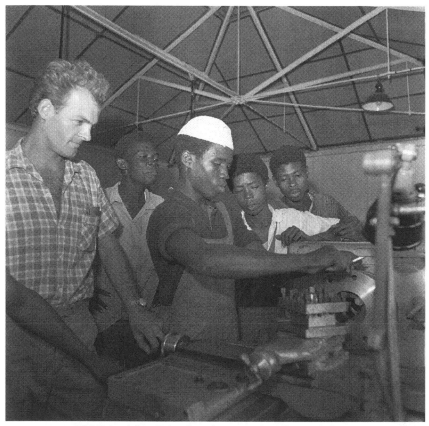

FIGURE 9.2 FDJ Friendship Brigade volunteer providing training to Zanzibari men.
Source: E. Appel. Courtesy of Bundesarchiv Bild 183-E0527-0049-001.

East German propaganda was aimed at a global audience, especially in Africa. It maintained that socialism and the international solidarity of workers and national liberation movements represented the only path to independence, progress, and racial justice.[1085] The East Germans continually harped on what they saw as the persistence of imperialist militarism and racism in West German society – and on the way that the two problems flowed together in West German support for continued colonial rule and white minority governments in the Portuguese colonies, South Africa, and the Congo. Major newspapers in East Africa reported incidents of racial discrimination in West Germany, including a much-circulated report that a Berlin restaurant refused to serve four Tanganyikan trainees.[1086] In October 1963, the German-African Society in East Germany distributed in Tanganyika and Zanzibar an English-language broadside criticizing West German support for racist regimes in neighboring countries. As the flier explained,

when Portuguese airplanes with their West German machine guns hunt down peaceful people in Angola and Mozambique and shoot them like deer, officials in West Germany do not waste a single word on the topic. We citizens of the German Democratic Republic are indignant at these events... These are the same forces that in the years before 1945 plunged our people and the whole of Europe into distress and misery by unleashing an imperialist war. We condemn colonialism and will always side like a faithful friend with peoples struggling for their freedom.[1087]

German imperialism had become a topic of intense public debate following the 1961 publication of Fritz Fischer's *Germany's Aims in the First World War*.[1088] West Germans were sensitive to East German references to the country's colonial past, and in the spring of 1964, the Foreign Office asked its African missions to survey the perception of East and West Germany by local elites. To judge from the responses, East Germany appeared to be winning the public relations war in Africa. Many sympathized with East Germany, which they described as the underdog in its competition with the Federal Republic; they praised East German aid to Zanzibar; and many of them mentioned both the persistence of racism in West Germany and the country's militarist heritage as the reasons for their views.[1089] The Africans also criticized West Germany for selling arms to Portugal for use in the war in Angola, training Portuguese soldiers in Mozambique, and providing medical care to wounded Portuguese soldiers.[1090] In 1965, East Germany launched a propaganda campaign denouncing the West German government for exporting the Holocaust to Vietnam through its support of American military efforts there.[1091]

All of these motifs came together in a book entitled *The Neo-colonialism of the West German Federal Republic*. This book, which the East German government distributed to African readers, documented the careers of many prominent West German politicians – including President Lübke – during the Third Reich, the economic interests that benefited from the country's development programs, and the influence of its military-industrial complex.[1092] The West Germans were put on the defensive, fearful that East German historians might rummage through the papers of the Colonial Office – which were held in East German archives – to document the brutality of German rule in its African colonies and impugn West Germany's development policy by tarring it with the country's unmastered colonial past.[1093]

11. "IMPERIALISM ACTS WITHOUT QUALMS."[1094]
REASSERTING WHITE SUPREMACY IN BLACK AFRICA

The 1960s were a time of rapid and often violent change in sub-Saharan Africa, and the Western powers were concerned about the spread of communism in southern Africa. The place to begin our account is the former French colony of Congo-Brazzaville, where an uprising in August 1963 led to the creation of a socialist government. The impact of these events rippled outward through the region. The Angolan liberation government in exile established its headquarters in Brazzaville, and the Congolese National Liberation Council (CNL) was founded there in October 1963.

When we last discussed developments in the Congo itself in Chapter 5, the post-independence civil war had come to a provisional conclusion with the victory of Mobutu in the summer of 1961. However, in 1963/64 armed revolutionary groups on the eastern and western borders – both of which had connections to China – challenged the Mobutu government in Léopoldville. The rebellion in the western part of the country was led by Pierre Mulele. Mulele was a Lumumba supporter, who returned from China to organize a guerrilla force in the Congo. The CNL forces in the east received financial support from both the Chinese (through their embassy in Burundi) and the OAU. Both groups attracted young Congolese, who were angered by Mobutu's pro-Western policies, which had increased social inequality, devastated small-scale agriculture, and led to the breakdown of the country's infrastructure. The forces in the eastern part of the country captured Stanleyville, the capital of Kivu privince, and on September 5, 1964, they established the People's Republic of Congo. In an editorial published in mid-1964, the Chinese communist party daily *Jenmin Jih Pao* saluted the Congolese for having created an "excellent revolutionary situation." The Chinese were hopeful that the armed insurrection would quickly consume the entire Congo, which, "like a phoenix, is bound to emerge from the flames of struggle," and they predicted that the Congolese struggle would inspire Vietminh-style armed rebellions across the region.[1095]

At the time, there was also a third site of revolutionary change in southeast Africa. On January 12, 1964, a revolution in Zanzibar led to the exile of the sultan and many Arab elites and to the establishment of a socialist-leaning government. In April of that year, Zanzibar merged with mainland Tanganyika, which was headed by the pan-Africanist Julius Nyerere, to form the new state of Tanzania. Tanzania's capital Dar es Salaam was the home of the Committee for the Liberation of Africa, which the OAU had established to coordinate military and logistical aid to liberation movements, including the CNL and the People's Republic of Congo government in Stanleyville. Nyerere also offered a safe haven to the leadership of the African National Congress and the organizations fighting for the independence of Angola, Mozambique, Namibia, and Zimbabwe (Southern Rhodesia). In June 1964, Nyerere accredited the first Cuban ambassador and celebrated the beginning of Tricontinentalism in East Africa.

All of these developments led the West to fear, as the *Daily Telegraph* reported in November of that year, that Dar es Saalam had "become the centre of subversion against white-dominated Africa, the arsenal for the Communist arms build-up in East Africa, a city obsessed with suspicion, intrigue and anti-Western hysteria."[1096] This assessment of the situation was also shared by the U.S. and Belgian governments. They feared that the instability posed a threat to Western economic interests in the country and were determined to roll back these changes. "The question, especially in the Congo," was, as historian John Kent has noted,

how best to do that. And what the contradictions between the emerging values of a decolonised African world and an essentially old socio-economic framework, if applied to the continent, would be. Independence initially indicated they would rule out any significant benefits for more than a few Africans in the Cold War Congo. It was clear by the time Johnson became president that a successful Cold War outcome for US attempts to overcome the contradiction was increasingly impossible and undesirable.[1097]

Although U.S. intelligence was clearly aware that the Soviet Union had played only a marginal role in events in the Congo, the Western powers used the Communist threat as a pretext to justify intervention.

UN peacekeepers were scheduled to withdraw from the Congo at the end of June 1964. As the date approached, U.S. intelligence and military officials began planning for what they hoped would be the endgame in the region.[1098] The United States and Belgium brought Moise Tshombe back from his exile in Spain. The U.S. government lent him military airplanes flown by exiled Cuban pilots and provided funds to recruit a force of white mercenaries from South Africa and Rhodesia. The growing involvement of the Western powers and white mercenaries in the conflict drew criticism from the UN, which feared that the credibility of its work in the region was being undermined.[1099] It also galvanized African public opinion. In August, more than 500 people gathered outside the U.S. embassy in Dar es Salaam and protested against its support of Tshombe and its military actions in Vietnam and Cuba.

The OAU established a Congo Conciliation Commission to seek a peaceful resolution of the conflict. However, while the Commission insisted that mercenaries and foreign troops be withdrawn before negotiations could begin, the U.S. and Belgian governments continued – despite the support of American civil rights leaders for the OAU initiative – to provide military assistance to Tshombe.[1100]

It was at the height of this conflict that the second Conference of Non-Aligned Countries convened in Cairo (October 1964). Mali's President Modibo Keita charged that political violence against small states in the name of peace was imperialist, illegal, and immoral, and he warned that such aggression would ultimately "hollow out" the very meaning of peace and, instead, "transform it into *a permanent war* against small countries." Keita also warned the nonaligned countries that they should be ready to defend their ideals with every means possible, rather than simply relying on a "verbal shield of resolutions and pious wishes." "Imperialism," he noted in a somber tone, "acts without qualms."[1101]

The turning point of the second Congo crisis came in November 1964. Under the pretext of protecting the white Europeans living in the country, the United States and Belgium – with British support – bombarded Stanleyville, while Belgian paratroopers and 300 South African and Rhodesian mercenaries invaded the country. Speaking on behalf of the OAU, Nyerere described this foreign aggression as an "insult to the entire continent" and charged that it had annihilated all the work of done by the organization to find a peaceful solution to the Congo conflict. Western intervention in the Congo sparked protests around the world and further radicalized African antipathy toward white minority rule on the continent. In Dar es Salaam huge protests were held outside the U.S. and Belgian embassies, and there were protests against Tshombe when he visited Rome, Paris, and Bonn.[1102] When Martin Luther King, Jr. accepted the 1964 Nobel Peace Prize, he declared that the Congo crisis was a global issue and reminded the audience that racial violence in the United States and South Africa remained an obstacle to world peace.[1103]

The Congo conflict was also the topic of UN discussions in December 1964.[1104] There, each side charged the other with racism.[1105] Western governments accused the Stanleyville government (the People's Republic of Congo) of barbarism in conjunction with the killing of hostages immediately after the landing of the Belgian paratroopers. Belgian Foreign Minister Paul-Henri Spaak compared the Stanleyville government to the Nazi regime and accused African states of "anti-white racialism," while portraying Belgian paratroopers and white mercenaries as soldiers fighting in the name of humanity. "Belgium," he insisted, "is not colonialist; Belgium is not neocolonialist; Belgium is not imperialist."[1106]

African leaders, on the other hand, denounced the Congo intervention as an example of "white racist imperialist" rule and as a threat to world peace and security. The foreign minister of Mali argued that the goal of the action was "to crush Stanleyville, the bulwark of true Africanism in the Congo where the flame of Lumumba still shines brightly." When Che Guevara made a brief stop in New York on his way to three-month tour of Africa, he admonished the UN General Assembly:

All free men of the world must be prepared to avenge the crime of the Congo. Perhaps many of those soldiers, who were turned into subhumans by imperialist machinery, believe in good faith that they are defending the rights of a superior race. In this Assembly, however, those peoples whose skins are darkened by a different sun, colored by different pigments, constitute the majority. And they fully and clearly understand that the difference between men does not lie in the color of their skin, but in the forms of ownership of the means of production, in the relations of production.[1107]

Although the UN adopted a motion calling for the withdrawal of all mercenaries from the Congo, Tshombe ignored it and continued to increase the number of white mercenaries in his employ.[1108] To help the revolutionary armed struggles in the region, in 1964/65 the Cubans offered military assistance to both neighboring Congo-Brazzaville and the Angolan liberation movement, and in mid-1965 Guevara arrived with a force of 120 Cubans.[1109] In an effort to counter the growing influence of the Chinese in the region, in early 1965 both the Soviet Union and East Germany began to provide increasing amounts of military and technical assistance to the leftist rebels who continued the struggle in the eastern part of the country.[1110]

III. METROPOLIS BERLIN IN ZANZIBAR CITY

The growing influence of China in sub-Saharan Africa had already become evident by the end of 1964, when Hessian Minister President Georg August Zinn traveled to Tanzania and met with Nyerere. He returned home with the distinct impression that the Africans were increasingly attracted to the Chinese model of development because they had a number of things in common: They both belonged to the "colored world"; they shared a history of colonial subjection; and they faced the same problems of overpopulation and underdevelopment. Zinn was also alarmed that the Chinese were beginning to send "militant" technicians to Africa "to gain the sympathy of the Africans" and showcase their model of socialist development there. Foreign Minister Gerhard Schröder agreed that the common experience of "low standards of living and economic backwardness" might produce a sense of solidarity among the peoples of Asia and Africa. However, he doubted that such an affinity could be translated into an enduring anti-white alliance because the Asians had an even more pronounced sense of racial superiority with respect to the Africans than did the Europeans themselves.[1111]

Summing up the situation, the West German ambassador to Tanzania concluded that "even though Tanganyika will certainly not become a 'second Cuba,' it is no longer that far from becoming a 'second Ghana.'"[1112] A NATO group, on the other hand, concluded that China was playing the race card against both the West and the "white, less militant Soviets."[1113] The East Germans were also concerned about the Chinese. This section will use German aid to Zanzibar and united Tanzania to document the rising appeal of the Chinese approach to national liberation and development in southern Africa.

Zanzibar, a small island country with a total population of about 300,000, had long been governed by a sultan and an Arab minority. When the revolution broke out there on January 12, 1964, both the Arab population and the 20,000 Asians of Indo-Pakistani ancestry, who dominated the trade and small business sector, were the object of reprisals by the indigenous African population. While the Western press generally ignored the autochthonous nature of the revolution and portrayed it instead as the product of communist subversion, the Zanzibari Revolutionary Council insisted that "the motives behind the revolution were simply the motives of an oppressed people rising against their oppressors and were entirely disconnected from any international motives."[1114]

The socialist countries saw the revolution as an opportunity to transform the island country into a people's republic in their own image. While the United States, Britain, West Germany, and other Western countries waited more than a month to recognize the new government, China, East Germany, and the Soviet Union immediately recognized the People's Republic of Zanzibar and coupled this recognition with promises of lavish assistance, much of which was immediately forthcoming. Moscow and Peking sent arms and military advisors to train the Zanzibar People's Liberation Army. The Chinese sent a gift of $500,000 and offered an interest-free $14 million economic development credit. East Germany also took the plunge and promised to supply an array of aid, ranging from Stasi training for a unit of the security police to an agreement to print new postage stamps.[1115]

Revolutionary Zanzibar led an independent existence for only 100 days before merging with the mainland to form the Union of Tanganyika and Zanzibar in April 1964. West German officials regarded Nyerere as more moderate than the Zanzibari revolutionaries, and they supported the political union in hopes of moderating the latter. On the other hand, both the Zanzibaris and their supporters in the socialist bloc hoped that the union would give them a broader political beachhead on the mainland. In the first years after the union of the two countries, however, the military weakness of the Nyerere government prevented it from exercising substantial control over Zanzibar, which continued to pursue an independent revolutionary course. In the narrative below, the terminological slippage between Zanzibar and Tanzania represents an attempt to accurately portray this unresolved state of affairs.[1116]

The East Germans hoped that Zanzibar would become the driving force behind the revolutionary transformation of the united republic of Tanzania, and they had a strong presence on the island.[1117] East German economic and technical aid had already begun in February 1964 with the arrival of the three-man team charged with modernizing a government information and broadcasting system; an East German served as chief advisor at the Zanzibari Ministry of Finance; and in March Deputy Foreign Minister Wolfgang Kiesewetter traveled to East Africa to meet with the presidents of Tanganyika and Zanzibar.[1118] In the course of the year, fifty to seventy-five East German advisers, technicians, and diplomats worked in Zanzibar.

East Germany offered a grant of 5 million marks, as well as a credit for more than 10 million, which could be used to purchase plant and equipment from East Germany. The bilateral trade agreement of September 1964 specified that these funds would be used to build milk processing facilities, rice mills, and a brickworks and to purchase fifteen fishing boats.[1119] East Germany also offered to equip a policlinic and a nurse training school, build apartment buildings, send doctors, nurses, and teachers to the island, and provide nearly sixty young Zanzibaris with scholarships for medical training in East Germany. A good part of East Germany's reputation in Zanzibar was due to the speed with which its promises of lavish aid were fulfilled.[1120] In June, a cargo ship arrived carrying equipment for a policlinic and a school for mid-level medical staff; in early September, a second ship arrived with the materials needed to begin construction on the first housing project that the East Germans had promised to construct; and another ship arrived several weeks later carrying much of the equipment – and the fishing boats – that had been sold to the Zanzibaris.

The East Germans also launched a major public relations campaign commemorating the fifteenth anniversary of the founding of the country. An exhibit on the "Development of the German Democratic Republic since its Founding in 1949" showcased the achievements and promise of German socialist modernity. The exhibit prominently displayed a number of images, charts, and objects – including motorcycles, typewriters, and textiles – representing the political and industrial achievements of the country.[1121] The local cinema also showed a number of East German films, including *Militant Africa – We Extend You Our Hand, Operation Teutonic Sword, The Silent Star, Türingen,* and *Beethoven.*[1122] One documentary showed the Zanzibaris unloading the construction materials and machines from an East German cargo ship, as well as joyous Asian and African guests studying in East Germany.

The centerpiece of East German aid to Zanzibar was the housing project that they promised to construct in Zanzibar City, the capital of the island (Figure 9.3). Before the revolution, the town had been divided along class

FIGURE 9.3 East German housing project in Ng'ambo (c. 1965). Courtesy of Dr. Ruth Radvanyi.

and racial lines. European, Arab, and Asian elites lived in Stone Town, a part of the city that enjoyed modern, hygienic amenities such as electricity and sewage lines. Ng'ambo (the "other side" in Swahili) was populated primarily by Africans, especially migrants from the mainland and transients from rural areas, who had squatted in the district since the 1950s. Ng'ambo youth had been the backbone of the revolution, and the Revolutionary Council needed continuous political support from the group.[1123] As a reward for his supporters, President Abeid Karume decided to clear the mud hut slums of Ng'ambo and construct modern flats in their place.

A pilot project consisting of 150 two- and three-bedroom flats in the Kikwajuni district of Ng'ambo was to be a gift from the East Germans to the Zanzibari people and a monument to their republic.[1124] The project, which was alternately known as New Berlin or Kikwajuni GDR, was to include fourteen multistory brick buildings along with a community center, a shopping center, and a garage. The flats were to be equipped with electric stoves and hot water, bathrooms with Western-style bathtubs and toilets, and separate living and sleeping rooms. As Karume explained, "the purpose is to provide each family with a flat, for a person who lives in a miserable ramshackle hut rather than a modern flat cannot truly be said to be free."[1125]

Both construction machinery and materials, including cement, bricks, prefabricated panels, and – allegedly – even sand, were shipped to Zanzibar.[1126] The first shipment arrived in July 1964, and the speed with which the East Germans moved ahead with the project led the West German ambassador to conclude that "all appearances indicate that the Soviet Occupation Zone is intent, regardless of the cost, on using Zanzibar as a model to demonstrate their potential capability in the area of development aid, something that, in view of the small size of the country, appears to be eminently achievable."[1127] When Karume was invited to lay the cornerstone for the project in August of that year, he reminded the crowd of the huge social inequalities of the colonial era and proclaimed that "today is a day that will change our lives." The director of the East German construction team, the *Baustab Sanzibar*, employed equally lofty rhetoric in portraying the "selfless help for the repressed and underdeveloped countries" as the embodiment of the solidarity between the two countries.[1128]

Such descriptions, however, glossed over the history of colonial urban planning. Parts of Ng'ambo had already been developed in the years immediately following World War II, and the original huts had been demolished and replaced by more modern, standardized structures. This urban renewal project, which had been undertaken during a period of labor unrest, had been designed to enable colonial authorities to more effectively monitor the population and impose modern sanitary standards upon the inhabitants.[1129] These accounts also glossed over the political realities of the post-revolutionary project, which involved the displacement of Zanzibaris of Arab and Indian origin, who were condemned as enemies of the revolution, the confiscation of the property of colonial elites, and "voluntary" labor by the inhabitants.

While such labor on this and other projects undoubtedly helped hold down costs, it was also meant to instill among the youth and workers employed on the project a sense of collective purpose and a commitment to the creation of a new nation. This new community could not be built without first reshaping the character of the individuals who comprised it. In the words of Minister of Education and National Culture and later (1968–72) Minister of Health and Social Insurance Ali Sultan Issa, "we wanted a New Man who could be pushed and encouraged to conform and who, without threats, would constantly desire to improve. In this way, we could build a socialist paradise in Zanzibar."[1130] The importance of this work was reinforced by the participation of the Zanzibari leadership and high-ranking foreign diplomats. A picture published in the local newspaper showed President Karume, Vice President Hanga, the Soviet and East German ambassadors, and the Chinese and the U.S. chargés d'affaires lifting their tools "in the Zanzibar 'harambee' spirit, giving voluntary labour in a nation-building project."[1131]

The first major part of the pilot project to be completed was the Zanzibar – GDR Friendship House, which served as the community center for the housing complex. When the center opened in September 1964, *Neues Deutschland* noted that the "gleaming white" of the Friendship House presented a telling contrast to the surrounding "brown mud huts" and explained to its readers that the area would soon be filled with bright residential buildings.[1132] The East German media widely publicized this pilot project and other aid programs. A number of television shows were already covering events on the island. *Neues Deutschland* printed an architectural rendering of the future apartment complex, which would later be surrounded by palm trees, well-dressed people and passenger cars, and described the complex as a gift to the "friendly island republic in East Africa." The paper used such phrases as "Beautiful Buildings Instead of Huts" and "Model Settlement of Ultra-Modern Residences" to communicate to its East German readers that the project represented "a heretofore unrealizable dream of African families."[1133]

Although this coverage was aimed at both the Zanzibaris and the East German public, the language used to describe these developments made it clear that the moving force in the modernization of Africa – even in a revolutionary socialist republic – were the Europeans. The East Germans, the newspaper explained, were on the island to lend a helping hand to the Zanzibaris "who had been condemned by the Sultan, the British colonialists, the Indian and Arab bourgeoisie and feudal class to vegetate in dirty slums." "The most visible position in this struggle," the newspaper noted, "is that assumed by the collective of construction experts from our republic, the Zanzibar Construction Group." It was, the paper continued, East German technicians who held the key to development in Africa and to teaching the Africans how to help themselves:

Unskilled Africans very quickly become skilled concrete workers, who know how to work with mixers, wheelbarrows and shovels. With good reason their eyes glow with happiness and pride. Workers, crane operators and truck drivers – inspired by the real possibility that they will be able, with the help of the German Democratic Republic, to create humane living conditions and spurred on by the readiness of their German friends to help – all set themselves in a sure-handed and fluent manner to the difficult work of unloading the [cargo ship] "Werner Seelenbinder," which is sitting at the pier.[1134]

Yet both sides found it very difficult to translate this lofty rhetoric into action. While protests by African workers seeking higher pay led to delays, to make up for the lost time the East Germans introduced overtime work (two shifts during the week plus Saturdays) without pay for Zanzibari trainees, a decision that led, in turn, to further unrest and delays.

In addition to this pilot project, two other major housing projects were started under Karume. The one at Kilimani (under construction from 1966 to 1976) included 403 flats. Construction work here provided the opportunity for on-the-job training for Zanzibari workers. The Mchenzani project was much more grandiose in conception. The plan envisioned the construction of 229 buildings with nearly 7,000 flats and the use of prefabricated concrete slabs, which were one of the hallmarks of socialist bloc housing projects. Ultimately, the complex was to provide housing for 30,000 persons. Thousands of existing, still-habitable homes were demolished to create the grand rectilinear boulevards on which the project would stand and which provided the vista required to appreciate the magnitude of the undertaking. In the end, only eight of the planned 229 buildings were actually constructed. These owed their completion in part to the enforced labor of prisoners and the ostensible idlers who had been rounded up to help with the work, and the authorities branded those who refused to volunteer as enemies of national development.[1135] Neither of these projects was substantially more successful than the pilot project. However, they did provide a stage for the political theater of the FDJ Friendship Brigades, which were called in to counter the influence of the West German Development Service and to model voluntary labor in the service of international proletarian solidarity.[1136]

The propaganda value of these housing projects was further diminished by the fact that the new flats were unpopular with the residents. While indigenous single-story, rectangular huts had attached gardens, where the occupants could grow food and keep chickens and goats, East German and Zanzibari planners hoped that modern housing would sweep away this traditional way of life. However, the people themselves were decidedly uninspired by such prospects. In the case of the New Berlin project in Ng'ambo, out of the 150 homeowners whose houses had been demolished to make way for the new project, only one-third accepted flats in the new complex, while the remainder demanded cash compensation. As of mid-1966, ninety-five flats were still vacant; most of these were subsequently given to party loyalists from outlying areas.[1137]

IV. TO ZANZIBAR WITH BULLDOZERS: THE WEST GERMAN PEACE CORPS IN DAR ES SALAAM

In mainland Tanganyika, Nyerere also made slum clearance and new housing construction the top priority of his first five-year plan (1964–9). Not only did he want to replace 1,000 slum housing units each year. Like Karume, Nyerere also wanted to use these projects to mobilize the population, encourage self-help, and teach unemployed and unskilled workers basic skills, while women and children were to learn the principles of hygienic living at the schools and community centers contained within these housing projects. While the Zanzibaris may have relied on East German aid, West Germany played a much larger role in mainland Tanganyika. As *Der Spiegel* noted in November 1964, the unification of the two regions made for strange politics: "The Cold War for Africa is being fought first of all in the individual private home. Behind German walls the residents of the United Republic of Tanzania are to decide who their true friends are: the communists from Pankow or the capitalists from Bonn."[1138]

The West German government hoped that targeted aid projects would convince the Tanzanians to push the East Germans out of the country. As an incentive, Bonn continuously increased the credits it offered for slum clearance in Dar es Salaam so that by the end of October 1964 they were offering 10 million marks.[1139] The Federal Republic also offered to complete – at its own cost – of all of the projects that the East Germans had promised to the Zanzibaris, but only if the East Germans were excluded from the United Republic of Tanzania.[1140] Tanzania's Foreign Minister Oscar Kambona told West German officials that it was "bad policy" to attach such strings. But West German officials held the line here, and, ultimately, Nyerere chose not accept the offer.[1141] Despite this rebuff, West Germans continued to provide technical and financial aid for housing construction in Dar es Salaam. The Bonn government offered the Tanzanians an interest-free credit of 10 million marks to purchase construction machinery, tools, and vehicles from West Germany; several of the federal states chipped in an additional 650,000 marks; and the West German Heinrich G. Schmidt advised Nyerere in his capacity as director of the Tanganyikan National Housing Corporation.[1142]

The West Germans were no less eager than their East German counterparts to publicize their work on the mainland. They invited leaders of African states visiting Dar es Salaam to visit the construction site. In June 1964, a week after a visit to the construction site by Liberian president Tubmann, the Germans invited Ethiopian ruler Haile Selassie to lay the cornerstone. At the ceremony, Schmidt impressed the visiting dignitaries by personally operating a West German bulldozer. The West German government also sent a group of newly trained members of the German Development Service to assist with the project. The first group arrived in Dar es Salaam in August 1964, and by early 1965 there were thirty-six volunteers working on site. In contrast to the Peace Corps volunteers in Tanzania, who were mostly college students, the West German group included four architects, thirteen nurses, and other technicians and craftsmen.[1143] Schmidt claimed that the combination of "German equipment, the German Development Service, German materials, and Tanganyikan labor would create a classic example of properly applied development aid for African countries."[1144]

The East Germans criticized the work of their West German competitors. In 1968, an East German camera team spent five months touring sub-Saharan Africa, and their labors resulted in a book and a television show. In addition to pointing out the difference between their own commitment to international solidarity and the persistent racism on the part of the West Germans, the East German team also sought to downplay West German achievements by arguing that the West German project had simply altered the façade of the buildings and substituted stone for mud, while leaving unaltered the open-air cooking places in the courtyard and the backward way of life associated with such design. The East Germans, in contrast, erected "high-rise buildings, which are not only adapted to the tropical conditions, but which also meld a modern, urban way of life with communal living. For the occupants the switch from an individual way of living to a collective existence with the neighbors under a single roof will entail," they insisted, "a new set of social attitudes."[1145] But no matter how hard the East and West Germans tried to highlight the uniqueness and superiority of their own architectural style, construction methods, and overall way of life, in the end they remained much more similar to one another than either side recognized. They both saw themselves as agents of industrial modernity, who brought scientific knowledge, technology, and initiative to the stagnant cultures of Africa. They both regarded the Africans primarily as a source of labor power and raw materials needed to realize the creative visions of industrialized countries.[1146] And, as a result, they both had a fractured relation not only to the official planners in Zanzibar and Tanzania, but also to the populations for whom they were building a better way of life.

V. BUILDING GERMAN HOSPITALS IN ZANZIBAR

The Zanzibari revolution had brought major changes to the island's medical system. For example, the largest hospital in Zanzibar City, built in 1896, had primarily served the colonial ruling class. Immediately after the revolution, the Revolutionary Council nationalized the hospital and renamed it the V.I. Lenin Hospital, and doctors there began to provide medical treatment free of cost. On March 26, 1964, the Revolutionary Council ordered all remaining British civil servants to leave the island within a month. It also banned the import of medicine, medical supplies, and medical instruments from the United Kingdom.[1147] These measures represented an understandable attempt to negate the island's colonial past, but they created a new set of problems. When an East German physician arrived in May 1964, he was the only surgeon at the hospital, and there was only one anesthesiologist, an Indian. The first Chinese medical team, which consisted of thirteen doctors and nurses, did not arrive at the Lenin Hospital until September 1, 1964.[1148]

During the first years after the revolution, the East Germans played the leading role in the reform of the nation's healthcare system. An East German was the only foreigner who served as a senior advisor in the Zanzibari Ministry of Health. In June 1964, the East Germans signed a bilateral agreement to supply a wide range of medical assistance to the island. They agreed to equip a policlinic and a medical training center; provide 120,000 marks' worth of medicine (in part to alleviate the acute shortage of medicine following the Zanzibari ban on British imports); send doctors, nurses, and nursing teachers to the island; and invite twenty Zanzibaris to East Germany for training in mid-level health professions.[1149] When the school for training mid-level health personnel opened in October 1964 in Zanzibar, the faculty entirely comprised East Germans, who also designed the curriculum. The East German government also furnished the building. The school had about eighty male and female students, and the Zanzibari government expected that the first graduates would staff the four new hospitals to be constructed as part of the nation's Three-Year Plan.

On Pemba, the second largest island of the Zanzibari archipelago, East German physicians and nurses worked at a hospital in Chake Chake, the largest town on the island, and at the attached policlinic. The staff included a surgeon; specialists in internal medicine, pediatrics, and gynecology; four nurses; a lab technician; and an administrator. The team was headed by gynecologist Ruth Radvanyi (Figure 9.6), the daughter of novelist Anna Seghers and Johann-Lorenz Schmidt, professor of economics at Humboldt University. The policlinic staff made regular visits to the larger towns in the north (Wete and Mkoani), where they provided basic care to the locals, and patients needing special care were referred to the Chake Chake hospital.[1150]

The East German medical team formed a workplace collective.[1151] However, the group never functioned in an exemplary manner. The director of the nurse training school proved to be less than competent in virtually every respect, and she was sent back to Berlin after less than three months. One of the nurses appeared to be more interested in passing time with local elites and Western experts than in contributing to the life of the collective; she, too, was recalled in January 1965.[1152] Ultimately, almost half of the team had been replaced by the end of the first year.

By the late 1960s, relations between the East Germans and the Zanzibari government were becoming strained. The Zanzibaris were disillusioned by the high cost of supporting East German doctors and technicians, and they were unhappy that six Zanzibari medical trainees (out of an original group of twenty) had returned from East Germany without having completed their training. When the bilateral agreement expired in May 1967, the Zanzibari government did not show much interest in renewing it. In 1967, the Zanzibari Ministry of Health decided not to employ East German nurses. Not only had a number of indigenous

FIGURE 9.4 Zanzibari woman and her child at a village health education meeting. Courtesy of Dr. Ruth Radvanyi.

nurses been trained in the meantime, but Karume's Africanization program had also rendered the presence of foreign experts less necessary. The East Germans saw the Africanization program as a threat to their presence in the region, and they eventually pressured the Zanzibaris to place East German nurses in Pemba.[1153] The East German Foreign Ministry and the diplomats in Zanzibar also tried hard to create a niche for medical aid field on mainland Tanzania. As they quickly learned, however, it was difficult to compete with the financial largesse offered by the West

FIGURE 9.5 Zanzibari girl looking through a microscope. Courtesy of
Dr. Ruth Radvanyi.

German government, which heavily subsidized the German church
groups that had an extensive network of clinics and dispensaries on the
mainland.[1154]

By that point, the Zanzibaris had recognized the perils of multinational
development aid, and they openly expressed their dismay with the egoism
of each of the donor countries. Competition among the foreign aid groups
working on the island and their unwillingness to work together and with
local health workers wasted resources and created administrative problems coordinating their competing demands. As one high-ranking health
official complained,

why must we have so many prima donnas? ... The East Germans wanted to work
by themselves, so the health services on Pemba Island had been turned over to
them. However, they were still aloof when it came to collaborating with the

FIGURE 9.6 Radvanyi painting signs for the hospital. The horizontal sign reads "Get rid of anemia and bilharzia by building a toilet." Courtesy of Dr. Ruth Radvanyi.

Zanzibar nurses and medical auxiliaries. The Chinese worked as a team and had asked to be given responsibility for rural health; they, too, did not integrate well with the Zanzibari staff in the village dispensaries.[1155]

Worst of all, the growing animosity between the Chinese and the Soviets forced the Zanzibaris to place military advisors and training teams from the two countries as far away from each other as they could.

Nor were the East Germans the most effective advocates for their own position. The Zanzibaris were trying to reorient their public health system away from a hospital-centered, curative medical strategy to a system that relied on district dispensaries that could better meet the healthcare needs of the largely rural population, which did not have easy access to urban hospitals. The East German vice consul clearly recognized that the newly adopted decentralized system gave East German doctors the opportunity to get a foothold in Zanzibar City and in every province "to progressively implement our treatment methods in all dispensaries and roll back the prevailing Chinese influence in the countryside."[1156] The problem was that the German physicians did not fit easily into this redesigned system. Their professional identity was centered on the hospital and its technological apparatus, rather than on popular hygienic enlightenment, and they only reluctantly embraced their new role as district medical officers.

Although the viability of this new system depended on the availability of reliable vehicles, which would have permitted individual physicians to reach the rural dispensaries among which they rotated, officials in Berlin were unable or unwilling to comply with this request. As a result, team members wasted much of their time negotiating irregular and unreliable public transportation, and their patience was tested by worn-out state vehicles, which frequently broke down, forcing doctors to change vehicles more than once as they made their rounds. It was not, therefore, uncommon for East German doctors to be met by angry villagers, who had been waiting for hours for them to arrive. In addition, German doctors were frustrated by the frequent failure of officials in Berlin to supply the medicine and supplies needed for a medical mission that was ostensibly one of great importance. As Dr. Günter Franke, the head of the medical team in the town of Wete, admonished his colleagues in Berlin, "if we place so much emphasis on enabling our experts to help the Zanzibaris with the future construction of socialism, then it is incumbent on the corresponding East German ministries to provide better support and for all involved to work and react in a substantially quicker manner."[1157]

Across the 1960s, the Zanzibari economy had been suffering from both declining prices for primary product exports and the corruption and inefficiencies resulting from state control over the distribution of basic necessities. In 1968, Karume decided to stop importing rice, sugar, and flour and to mobilize the population to plant and harvest rice. However, these measures led to widespread food shortages.[1158] As a result, the working conditions for the East Germans continued to deteriorate. Moreover, one East German physician working in Pemba defected in 1969 – much to the relief of Zanzibari officials and health workers who had been deeply troubled by his professional competence and his character flaws. To prevent the recurrence of such an event, the Zanzibaris took away the passports of the remaining team members, who were angered that the East German consulate had so willingly acquiesced to this action.[1159] The defection left the team short handed, but Berlin did not respond to their requests for additional physicians and supplies.

The austerity policy also affected the import and distribution of medicines and medical supplies and the hiring of foreign technicians in the health sector. Every request to purchase medicine from abroad had to be submitted to the Ministry of Health for approval; and in September 1969, the Health Minister Issa imposed a complete ban on the import of medicines and vaccines.[1160] When Karume heard from a WHO official that it was not feasible to completely eradicate malaria, he stopped funding the WHO malaria eradication program on the island, an action that soon led to a sharp spike in the disease.[1161] In view of the economic hardship and social discontent caused by this austerity program, Zanzibari security officers began to monitor the activity of every hospital department. Although foreign medical personnel were exempt from their surveillance, by this time it was clear that the influence of the East Germans on the Zanzibari revolution was rapidly waning.

VI. CHINA AND THE DECLINING INFLUENCE OF EUROPEAN SOCIALISM IN EAST AFRICA

By the end of the decade, the Chinese had displaced the East Germans from the field of medical assistance in Zanzibar. The primary reason for this shift was the growing disillusionment of the Zanzibari government with the Soviets, for whom the East Germans served as surrogates in the region. Many Zanzibari officials considered the Soviets haughty and selfish, as the following incident clearly illustrates. In his memoirs, Ali Sultan Issa, Zanzibari Minister of Health (1968⊠72) explained the reasons for his antipathy toward the Soviets:

I asked the Russians for some teachers, and ... [t]hey said they wanted to be paid in gold. I said, "We don't have any gold here; we have cloves." And then they told me that, if a Russian teacher were to die in Zanzibar, then we should pay for his coffin to be sent back home. I said, "Your colleagues the Chinese cremate their people here. I think if your comrades die, you should pay for their remains to be sent home yourself." ... We renamed the hospital in town "V.I.Lenin Hospital," but the Russians sent only sporadic shipments of medicine. Meanwhile, the Chinese sent us a full team of doctors, and they remain even now at two hospitals, one here and one in Pemba. We should have called the hospital "Mao Hospital." There was no comparison. Here the Chinese were backward; they wanted to develop their country first, but still they helped. Here the Russians were advanced with Sputnik and everything, yet they were stingy. They were very mean and arrogant, I can say.[1162]

These grievances were compounded by the growing dissatisfaction with the Soviet conception of scientific socialism, and the Chinese challenge to the leadership of the Soviet Union within the socialist camp muddied the ideological waters in Zanzibar even before the arrival of Cuban military and development aid. On both Zanzibar and the mainland, villagers identified more easily with the frugal, modest, and hard-working Chinese, while Nyerere, who visited the People's Republic in 1965 and 1968, believed the Chinese model of popular mobilization and militant revolutionary struggle could well serve the Tanzanians.[1163] The Chinese model of development also appealed to nationalist leaders in Africa because it involved less capital and promised more rapid returns than did the Soviet approach, an advantage that was of great importance to the Zanzibaris in view of the deteriorating economic and social conditions in the island province.

The first major Chinese development project in the region was the construction of the Tanzania-Zambia Railway, which was to run from Dar es Salaam to the copper fields of landlocked Zambia. In 1964, the World Bank had decided against funding the $415 million project. However, the following year, the Chinese offered to provide an interest-free loan to build the rail line. Because the white settler regimes in the surrounding countries posed a threat to both Zambia and Tanzania (a threat that was worsened in November 1965 by Rhodesia's declaration of independence), the railway would link Zambia to the outer world and lessen its dependence on these regimes.[1164] As the Dar es Salaam *Sunday News* editorialized when construction finally began in 1970,

the railway is important to us not just as a new link with Zambia, but also as a blow against the southern racists. It is of historic importance in that it has brought the Chinese back to Africa... We welcome the representatives of the People's Republic of China today, not just because of their timely assistance to our development efforts, but also because of the relevance which their experiences has for us... Today it is impossible for any underdeveloped country to ignore the example of China, a country which – to use Mao's graphic phrase – has "stood up," without the assistance of the World Bank, the Eximbank and other so-called development agencies... Some Western countries accuse Tanzania of being a bridgehead. We reply that we would be proud, if by this is meant that the ideas of discipline, frugality, and self-reliance, of hostility to racism and imperialism, that have characterized the Chinese government since the revolution, were to spread through Tanzania into the rest of the great continent of Africa.[1165]

Chinese involvement in the construction of the Tanzania-Zambia Railway and the growing radicalism of Nyerere's own views created an opportunity for the Chinese to become more involved on the mainland and in Zanzibar. In early 1968, a Chinese team arrived in Tanzania to tour the country's medical facilities and assess its needs. The Chinese government acted quickly on the findings of this mission. Only two months after the mission had completed its work, a large Chinese medical team of about forty physicians and nurses arrived in the country with 1,000 cases of medicine and equipment. The team was divided into groups of eight and dispatched to different rural areas, where they provided basic care to the inhabitants of the surrounding villages.[1166] The Chinese barefoot doctors in Africa adhered to the principles preached at the First National Conference on Health Care in August 1950, when Mao had urged doctors to combine both Oriental and western medicine and to "organize a solid united front to strive for the development of the people's health work."[1167]

The East Germans mocked Chinese medicine. They feared that, under the influence of the Chinese, the Zanzibari health workers, whom they had trained in "modern" medical science, would forget all that they had learned.[1168] However, the local population had a decidedly more positive attitude toward the use of medicinal herbs and acupuncture. When the Chinese were building the Tanzania-Zambia Railway, the medical team attached to the workforce also provided free medical care to the local population. When rumors about miraculous treatment by the Chinese doctors spread in the area, hundreds of villagers, including many dignitaries, reportedly rushed to the Chinese clinics for treatment.[1169] The Chinese also seemed to have a better sense of how to relate to African villagers.[1170] They seemed to be more sincerely interested in helping the Tanzanians acquire medical and other kinds of technical knowledge.[1171] In contrast, the local population felt that the East Germans acted like former colonial rulers and demanded wages and living accommodations that were noticeably superior to the local standard for physicians. In contrast, the Chinese medical team lived like Africans and were willing to share their material possessions with their Tanzanian hosts, as well as the material hardships they faced.[1172]

In May 1970, the government dismissed many Zanzibari physicians and public health administrators. Most of these doctors had studied in the Soviet Union, and they were ostensibly dismissed because of their poor training. However, they were told that they could voluntarily relinquish their licenses, resign their positions, and then be retrained by Chinese physicians. The following day, all of these physicians resigned, but – in the presence of Chinese doctors – begged to keep their titles and Soviet diplomas. The East Germans regarded the incident as an example of the growing anti-Soviet, pro-Chinese orientation of the Zanzibari leadership.[1173]

As we have seen, East Germany had provided extensive medical assistance to Zanzibar since the beginning of 1964. Government officials regretted this "loss of a framework in which the German Democratic Republic has worked in an extremely successful manner," and they attributed the Zanzibari decision to the combination of Chinese machinations and "reactionary forces in Zanzibar, which are intentionally working to undermine...the very effective relationships with the German Democratic Republic."[1174] However, as long as the East Germans remained fixated on the idea that Chinese approaches to public health and development were scientifically backward and ideologically flawed, they would be blind to deeper historical and cultural bases of the affinity that the locals felt toward the Chinese and the Cubans in the 1970s. Their claim that the Chinese had bribed Issa was an attempt to save face even as they were being pushed out of Zanzibar, which they had long regarded as a laboratory for their own vision of socialist modernity.[1175]

On July 2, 1970, Zanzibari officials held a farewell ceremony for the departing East German medical workers. Issa did not speak at the ceremony, and no one from the Zanzibari Ministry of Health showed up for the reception held that evening at the German consulate to honor the departing team.[1176] While East German involvement in Zanzibar began with a bang in early 1964, it ended with a whimper in 1971, when the last Eastern European medical workers left the country. At this point, though, the Chinese were rapidly moving in to fill the resulting vacuum.

Epilogue

Doing Transnational History in a Global Age

Globality is both the precondition and the subject of transnational history, and I would like to conclude with a few thoughts about the challenges of doing transnational history in a global age and the significance of such work for the historiography of modern Germany. It has become widely accepted that History (with a capital H) was deeply implicated in the formation of the nation-state and its naturalization as the basic unit of historical space and time, as the primary framework for the organization of social life, and as the central focus of individual meaning and human endeavor. By accepting the nation-state and its rigidly bound territorial sovereignty as self-evident and universal, historians became active agents of the emerging international system of nation-states. As a result, modern historical writing has, as Antoinette Burton has argued, been bound in "a 'narrative contract' with the territorially bounded nation-state."[1177] It is for this very reason that Joyce Appleby has appealed to historians "to stand outside of the filiation of history and the nation-state."[1178]

These insights into the limitations of state-centered historiography are the product of historians doing what they do best, that is, historicizing their subject – in this instance, their own discipline. This trend has been further accelerated by the collapse of communism and the end of the Cold War. Together, these events have put historians in the exhilarating yet slightly vertiginous position of trying to give meaning to the past at the same time that the passing of the metanarratives that they had long relied on to make sense of the modern world has forced them to confront the radical historicity of their own knowledge. The complexity of the present situation has been further compounded by the critique of Eurocentrism, which has opened the door to the return of those "traditions and ideologies that were assigned by modernization discourse to the dustbin of history."[1179] Within the narrative space created by this opening, those groups who had been literally written out of history have begun to find the conceptual voice needed to narrate their own experiences at the border of European modernity and, in this way, to speak the truth back to the Western powers.

The "transnational turn" has given rise to a search for a satisfying way to uncover, conceptualize, and narrate that which was excluded or obscured by this state-centered historical approach to the modern world. The productive power of a transnational approach to German and European history lies precisely in this ability to destabilize traditional analytic categories and thereby to make it possible to explore social formations and structures that do not coincide with the boundaries of the nation-state. For European intellectuals and politicians, the transnational turn has been most visible in the discourse on Europeanness. This interest flows in part from the reemergence of empires as an object of scholarly concern and political action. But it has also grown out of a search for new values that could help legitimate an integrated Europe. As Ulrich Beck and Edgar Grande have argued, the completion of the European project depends on moving mentally beyond the nation-state:

Whoever thinks of Europe in national terms misunderstands its reality and its future. Not only does a national perspective hinder both the self-perception of the continent and scholarship; it also blocks political action... Both within and beyond the continent, the necessary opportunities to act and shape [the future] can only be won through *negation*, that is, through the radical critique of existing concepts of politics and the state. What thus arises and what thus must be conceptualized and developed is a *nova res publica*: the *cosmopolitan empire* of Europe.[1180]

This search for a usable European identity that would subsume that of its constituent political entities is often couched in a rhetoric of "European transnationalism." However, in this discourse the terms "Europe" and "transnational" have been uneasy bedfellows. In practice, such arguments tend to stop far short of critically interrogating the ways in which Europe was constructed. Instead, by recentering Europe in a new world order, they recapitulate the shortcomings of state-centered historiography, although at the continental, rather than the national, level, and thereby recuperate that decentering of national sovereignty that Aiwha Ong rightly views as one of the essential achievements of transnational analysis.[1181]

The history of Germany's Third World outlined in the preceding pages has hinted at the alternate spatialities, temporalities, and topographies that can be made visible through a transnational history of postwar Europe. As I have shown, the global South was present in West and East Germany – both physically and in the national imaginations of the two states – since their founding, and it served as both the mirror image of their own society and as the object of humanitarian and development programs. This presence however escaped the spatial frameworks and narratives of Cold War Germany within which most histories of the period have been embedded. However, the global South and North were both pulled apart and intimately connected along multiple axes, and, as we have seen in Vietnam and Korea, the simultaneity of decolonization and Cold War makes it virtually impossible – and undesirable – to analytically separate the two processes.

An alternate understanding of spatiality is a critical strategy that is more than the sum of its parts. It enables us to open out the already intertwined histories of the two Germanys into the broader history of both postwar globalization and the global South. "Being in and of the world is the condition of modern history for all societies," as Thomas Bender has argued.[1182] A transnational approach to German history requires nothing more and nothing less than articulating the diverse ways in which the nation-state is "in and of the world." Thus, to the extent that East German aid contributed to the success of North Vietnamese state-building efforts, the study of medical and development aid to North Vietnam forces us to rethink the space of German history – and that of Eastern Europe more generally – and to situate it on a much larger global canvas. However, such a move invariably entails the provincializing and defamiliarizing of many master narratives.

In the past few years has the history of postwar Germany begun to reflect a broader understanding of the Cold War as a global phenomenon, and this broadening of perspectives has already led to several studies of German development policies in Asia and Africa in the 1960s.[1183] Although I built on these studies, in this book I attempted to go beyond them in two ways.

First, I argued – especially in Chapter 8 – that development, migration, and labor must be seen together as *related* aspects of a larger process, one that gave rise to a transnational social space that cannot be adequately grasped so long as we attempt to conceptualize these developments in terms of categories drawn from the history of the nation-state. The Cold War aid battle entangled both East and West Germany in Third World struggles for national development, and in this process, the political economies of the German welfare state and the South Korean developmental state were entwined in specific ways. The resulting dynamic shaped the terms in which these nurses were incorporated into the global market for caring labor. However, these interlinkages have seldom been seen as an integral element of any of the master narratives of German history, even though they provide a virtually paradigmatic example of the construction of a transnational socioeconomic space.

Second, this approach also enables us to explore the racial formation of postwar German society. It has been argued that – for reasons unique to the histories of the two countries – racial thinking was not a salient factor in the political life of either East or West Germany until the rise of the "new racism" of the 1980s.[1184] However, as we have seen, the ideas of under-development and the global South together functioned as a surrogate for race in the two Germanys, and in this form race continued to shape the way Germans – both East and West – looked at themselves, their nations, and the wider world in the postwar decades. This racism was not simply a vestige of earlier attitudes, but rather was continuously renewed and repro-duced in the postwar years.

In conclusion, I would like warn against romanticizing East German rhetoric of anti-imperialist solidarity. In the past few years, there has been a trend – especially among former East German aid workers – toward viewing these policies as one of the main positive legacies of East Ger-many. For example, Hans-Georg Schleicher, the former East German ambassador to Namibia, has recently claimed that "East Germany and its citizens contributed to the overcoming of colonialism and apartheid through active solidarity," and he has argued that the "legacy of East German Africa policy should become the foundation of present-day rela-tions with Africa."[1185] Similarly, Irene and Gerhard Feldbauer, who previously worked for the official East German print media, have claimed that, although East Germany may have had many dark sides, the coun-try's solidarity with Vietnam remains "an excellent chapter in the coun-try's history, which every citizen … can be proud of." However, as we have seen, there was always a slippage between the experiences of soli-darity on the part of individual citizens and aid workers, the official use of solidarity rhetoric to mobilize the citizenry behind a certain understand-ing of socialism, the policies that the state wished to pursue, and those other factors, such as material shortages and persistent racism, that marked the limits of solidarity policies. In such statements, there is little self-consciousness or critical distance, and, as a result, they exaggerate the agency and the legacy of the East Germans.[1186]

Notes

1 William J. Lederer and Eugene Burdick, *The Ugly American* (New York, 1958).
2 The term "provincializing" is taken from Dipesh Chakrabarty, *Provincialising Europe: Postcolonial Thought and Historical Difference* (Princeton, 2000).
3 Heonik Kwon, *The Other Cold War* (New York, 2010), 32.
4 Walter D. Mignolo, *Local Histories/Global Designs: Coloniality, Subaltern Knowledge, and Border Thinking* (Princeton, 2000), ix.
5 Kwon, *The Other Cold War*, 32.
6 See my comments in "Asia, Germany and the Transnational Turn," *GH* 28:4 (December, 2010), 515–536. See also Geoff Eley, "Historicizing the Global, Politicizing Capital: Giving the Present a Name," *HWJ* 63 (2007), 154–188; and Michael Geyer and Charles Bright, "World History in a Global Age," *AHR* 100:4 (October 1995), 1034–1060.
7 Frantz Fanon, *The Wretched of the Earth*. Trans. Constance Farrington (New York, 1963), 42. See also Mignolo, *Local Histories/Global Designs*; Tom Crook, Rebecca Gill, and Bertrand Taithe, eds., *Evil, Barbarism and Empire: Britain and Abroad, c. 1830–2000* (New York, 2011); Bo Stråth, ed., *Europe and the Other and Europe as the Other* (Brussels, 2000); Martin Thomas, *Violence and Colonial Order: Police, Workers and Protest in the European Colonial Empires, 1918–1940* (Cambridge, 2012); and A. Dirk Moses, ed., *Empire, Colony, Genocide: Conquest, Occupation, and Subaltern Resistance in World History* (New York, 2008).
8 Carey A. Watt and Michael Mann, eds., *Civilizing Missions in Colonial and Postcolonial South Asia: From Improvement to Development* (New York, 2011); Osama Abi-Mershed, *Apostles of Modernity: Saint-Simonians and the Civilizing Mission in Algeria* (Palo Alto, 2010); Gary Wilder, *The French Imperial Nation-State: Negritude and Colonial Humanism between the Two World Wars* (Chicago, 2005); and Harald Fischer-Tiné and Michael Mann, *Colonialism as Civilizing Mission: Cultural Ideology in British India* (New York, 2004).

9   Anthony Anghie, "Colonialism and the Birth of International Institutions: Sovereignty, Economy, and the Mandate System of the League of Nations," *International Law and Politics* 34 (2002), 513–633, citations 517, 627.

10 Donald Bloxham, *The Final Solution: A Genocide* (Oxford, 2009), 331.

11 Alan Kramer, *Dynamic of Destruction. Culture and Mass Killing in the First World War* (Oxford, 2007); Alf Lüdtke and Bernd Weisbrod, eds., *No Man's Land of Violence: Extreme Wars in the 20th Century* (Göttingen, 2006); Donald Bloxham and Robert Gerwarth, eds., *Political Violence in Twentieth-Century Europe* (Cambridge, 2010); and Luisa Passerini, *Europe in Love, Love in Europe: Imagination and Politics between the Wars* (New York, 1999). On colonial troops during World War I, Christian Koller, "The Recruitment of Colonial Troops in Africa and Asia and Their Deployment in Europe during the First World War," *Immigrants & Minorities* 26:1/2 (March/July 2008), 111–133.

12 Cemil Aydin, *The Politics of Anti-Westernism in Asia: Visions of World Order in Pan-Islamic and Pan-Asian Thought* (New York, 2007); Erez Manela, *The Wilsonian Moment: Self-Determination and the International Origins of Anticolonial Nationalism* (Oxford, 2009); Sebastian Conrad and D. Sachsenmaier, eds., *Competing Visions of World Order: Global Moments and Movements, 1880s–1930s* (New York, 2007); Michael Adas, "Contested Hegemony: The Great War and the Afro-Asian Assault on the Civilizing Mission Ideology," *JWH*, 15:1 (2004), 31–63; and Leela Gandhi, "Postcolonial Theory and the Crisis of European Man," *Postcolonial Studies* 10:1 (2007), 93–110.

13 Article 22 of the League Covenant, cited in Anghie, "Colonialism and the Birth of International Institutions," 524. See also Anghie, "Civilization and Commerce: The Concept of Governance in Historical Perspective," *Villanova Law Review* 45 (2000), 887–911.

14 David Slater, "Latin America and the Challenge to Imperial Reason," *Cultural Studies* 25:3 (May 2011), 455.

15 Victoria de Grazia, *Irresistible Empire. America's Advance through 20th-Century Europe* (Cambridge, MA, 2005), 36. Similarly, Michael Geyer and Charles Bright argue that the European-North Atlantic world reflected an "Anglo-Saxon racism" in its exclusion and subordination of the territories and peoples outside the region. Geyer and Bright, "World History in a Global Age," 1034–60, especially 1051f.; and Bright and Geyer, "Where in the World Is America? The History of the United States in the Global Age," in Thomas Bender, ed., *Rethinking American History in a Global Age* (Berkeley, CA, 2002), 63–99, especially 78.

16 Mignolo, *Local Histories/Global Designs*, 112.

17 Alfred Sauvy, "Trois mondes, une planète" in *L'Observateur* 118 (August 14, 1952), 14. Sauvy spoke of an "ignored Third World (*Tiers Monde*), exploited, scorned like the Third Estate." As Matthew Connelly shows, Sauvy used the concept to "banish forever the thought that there might be only one world, in which all humanity shared mutual obligations." Connelly, *Fatal Misconception. The Struggle to Control World Population* (Cambridge, MA, 2008), 154.

18 On the competing concepts of the Third World, Richard Saull, "Locating the Global South in the Theorisation of the Cold War: Capitalist Development, Social Revolution and Geopolitical Conflict," *TWQ* 26:2 (2005), 253–280; B.R. Tomlinson, "What Was the Third World?" *Journal of Contemporary History* 38:2 (April 2003), 307–321; and Chandra Tapande Mohanty, "Introduction: Cartographies of Struggle," in Mohanty, Ann Russo, and Lourdes Torres, eds., *Third World Women and the Politics of Feminism* (Bloomington, MN, 1991). On the theoretical debate, see Jennifer Wenzel, "Remembering the Past's Future: Anti-imperialist Nostalgia and Some Versions of the Third World," *Cultural Critique* 62 (Winter 2006), 1–32; Arif Dirlik, Vinay Bahl, and Peter Gran, eds., *History after the Three Worlds: Post-Eurocentric Historiographies* (Lanham, MD, 2000); Arturo Escobar, "Beyond the Third World: Imperial Globality, Global Coloniality and Anti-globalization Social Movements," *TWQ* 26:2 (2005), 207–230; and Gyan Prakash, "Writing Post-Orientalist Histories of the Third World: Perspectives from Indian Historiography," *CSSH* 32 (1990), 383–408.

19 Johannes Morsink, *The Universal Declaration of Human Rights: Origins, Drafting, and Intent* (Philadelphia, 1999); Akira Iriye, Petra Goedde, and William I. Hitchcock, eds., *The Human Rights Revolution: An International History* (Oxford, 2012); Stefan-Ludwig Hoffmann, ed., *Human Rights in the Twentieth Century* (New York, 2011); and Samuel Moyn, *The Last Utopia: Human Rights in History* (Cambridge, MA, 2010). On the contingencies and future possibilities that were open in immediate postwar years, see Geoff Eley, "When Europe Was New: Liberation and the Making of the Post-War Era," in Monica Riera and Gavin Schaffer, eds., *The Lasting War: Society and Identity in Britain, France and Germany after 1945* (New York, 2008), 17–43.

20 Mark Mazower. *Governing the World. The History of an Idea* (New York, 2013), 212. Stalin, like the Western powers, believed in the primacy of imperialist geopolitics and refashioned Central and Eastern Europe as the buffer zone behind Iron Curtain. On the United Nations, Mazower, *No Enchanted Palace: The End of Empire and the Ideological Origins of the United Nations* (Princeton, NJ, 2009); and Sunil Amrith and Glenda Sluga, "New Histories of the United Nations," *JWH* 19:3 (2008), 251–274.

21 Hannah Arendt, *The Origins of Totalitarianism* (New York, 1951).

22 Roland Burke, "'The Compelling Dialogue of Freedom': Human Rights at the Bandung Conference," *Human Rights Quarterly* 28 (2006), 962.

23 Elliot R. Goodman, "The Cry of National Liberation: Recent Soviet Attitudes Toward National Self-Determination," *IO* 14:1 (Winter 1960), 92–106; Harold K. Jacobson, "The United Nations and Colonialism: A Tentative Appraisal," *IO* 16:1 (Winter, 1962), 37–56; and Roland Burke, *Decolonization and the Evolution of International Human Rights* (Philadelphia, 2013). See also S. Moyn, "Imperialism, Self-Determination, and the Rise of Human Rights," *The Human Rights Revolution*, 159–78.

24 On decolonization and refugee crises in general, see Panikos Panayi and Pippa Virdee, eds., *Refugees and the End of Empire: Imperial Collapse and Forced Migration in the Twentieth Century* (Basingstoke, 2011); Peter Gatrell, *The Making of the Modern Refugee* (Oxford, 2013); and Aristide R. Zolberg, Astri

Suhrke and Sergio Aguayo, *Escape from Violence: Conflict and the Refugee Crisis in the Developing World* (New York, 1989). On Palestinian refugees, Dawn Chatty, *Displacement and Dispossession in the Modern Middle East* (Cambridge, 2011). On the partition of India and refugee crisis, Vazira Zamindar, *The Long Partition and the Making of Modern South Asia: Refugees, Boundaries, Histories* (New York, 2007).

25 A year after the adoption of the Geneva Conventions, the outbreak of the Korean War created millions of refugees and put to the test the newly minted Fourth Convention on the relief of civilian victims of war. The first instance where the UN explicitly charged the WHO with a humanitarian mission came at the beginning of the Korean War (Chapter 3), when it was asked to assist the United Nations Command with its military operations of pacifying the civilian population. The anti-communist thrust of this program was also more explicit than had been the case in the Middle East.

26 UNHCR, *The State of the World's Refugees 2000: Fifty Years of Humanitarian Action* (Oxford, 2000), 53. See also Cecilia Ruthstrom-Ruin, *Beyond Europe: The Globalization of Refugee Aid* (Lund, 1993). The International Refugee Organization, the predecessor of the UNHCR, replaced the United Nations Relief and Rehabilitation Administration, which had wound up its work on June 30, 1947. The UNHCR, created in 1949, was originally intended to operate for three years only.

27 Heather A. Wilson, *International Law and the Use of Force by National Liberation Movements* (Oxford, 1988), 42ff; and William I. Hitchcock, "Human Rights and the Laws of War: The Geneva Conventions of 1949," *The Human Rights Revolution*, 93–112.

28 Mark Duffield, *Development, Security and Unending War. Governing the World of Peoples* (Cambridge, 2007), citations 23, viii. See also Duffield, *Global Governance and the New Wars: The Merging of Development and Security* (London, 2001); and Anna Selmeczi, "'… we are being left to burn because we do not count': Biopolitics, Abandonment, and Resistance," *Global Society* 23:4 (2009), 519–38.

29 Michael Dillon and Julian Reid, *The Liberal Way of War: Killing to Make Life Live* (London, 2009), citation, 50. For example, Julian Huxley, first director-general of the UNESCO, continued to maintain that the white civilization was the highest stage of evolutionary progress, and he used his new position to promote the white civilizing mission in guiding the "biologically intrinsic inferiority of the 'less developed races.'"

30 Michel Foucault, *"Society Must Be Defended": Lecutres at the Collège de France 1975–1976*, eds., Mauro Bertani and Alessandro Fontana, and trans., David Macey (New York, 2003), 255. On Foucault's concepts of biopolitical caesura and state racism, see Michael Dillon and Andrew W. Neal. eds., *Foucault on Politics, Security and War* (New York, 2008); and Achille Mbembe, "Necropolitics," *Public Culture* 15, 1 (2003), 11–40.

31 Recent scholarship on development has taken a global, transnational approach. See Hubertus Büschel and Daniel Speich, eds., *Entwicklungswelten* (Frankfurt a.M., 2009); Andreas Eckert, Stephan Malinowski and Corinna R. Unger, eds., *Modernizing Missions. Approaches to 'Developing' the Non-*

Western World after 1945 (*JMEH* 8:1 [2010]); and Engerman and Unger, eds., *Towards a Global History of Modernization* (*DH* 33:3 [2009]). On European development policies across the 1945 divide, see Hubertus Büschel, *Hilfe zur Selbsthilfe – Deutsche Entwicklungsarbeit in Afrika 1960–1975* (Frankfurt, 2014); Daniel Maul, *Human Rights, Development and Decolonization: The International Labour Organization, 1940–70* (New York, 2012); April R. Biccum, "Theorizing Continuities between Empire and Development: Toward a New Theory of History," in Duffield and Vernon Hewitt, eds., *Empire, Development & Colonialism: The Past in the Present* (Woodbridge, 2009), 146–60; and Marc Frey, "Control, Legitimacy, and the Securing of Interests: European Development Policy in South-east Asia from the Late Colonial Period to the Early 1960s," *Contemporary European History* 12:4 (2003), 395–412.

32 Bright and Geyer, "Where in the World Is America?" 80–8. On the Soviet project of development, see Yves Cohen, "Circulatory Localities: The Examples of Stalinism in the 1930s," *Kritika* 11:1 (Winter 2010), 11–45; David L. Hoffmann, *Cultivating Masses: Modern State Practices and Soviet Socialism, 1914–1939* (Ithaca, NY, 2011); Michael David-Fox, *Showcasing the Great Experiment: Cultural Diplomacy & Western Visitors to the Soviet Union 1921–1941* (Oxford, 2012); and David C. Engerman, *Modernization from the Other Shore: American Intellectuals and the Romance of Russian Development* (Cambridge, MA., 2003). Similarly, Daniel Speich emphasizes the need to situate development within the larger context of "the global emergence of a knowledge society." Speich, "The Kenyan Style of 'African Socialism': Developmental Knowledge Claims and the Explanatory Limits of the Cold War," *DH* 33:3 (2009), 449–66, citation, 465. See also Alessandro Iandolo, "The Rise and Fall of the 'Soviet Model of Development' in West Africa, 1957–64," *CWH* 12:4 (November 2012), 683–704; and Mark T. Berger, "Decolonisation, Modernisation and Nation-Building: Political Development Theory and the Appeal of Communism in Southeast Asia, 1945–1975," *JSEAS* 34:4 (2003), 421–448.

33 On American-style development and its liberal New Deal roots, David Ekbladh, *The Great American Mission: Modernization & the Construction of an American World Order* (Princeton, NJ, 2010). On the convergence between development as a policy science and foreign policy in Cold War America, see Michael E. Latham, *The Right Kind of Revolution: Modernization, Development, and US Foreign Policy from the Cold War to the Present* (Ithaca, NY, 2011); Latham, *Modernization as Ideology: American Social Science and "Nation Building" in the Kennedy Era* (Chapel Hill, NC, 2000); and Nils Gilman, *Mandarins of the Future. Modernization Theory in Cold War America* (Baltimore, MD, 2003).

34 Nick Cullather, *The Hungry World: America's Cold War Battle Against Poverty in Asia* (Cambridge, MA, 2010). On the Third World, development, and structurally conditioned dependency, Arturo Escobar, *Encountering Development: The Making and Unmaking of the Third World* (Princeton, NJ, 1995), James Ferguson, *Antipolitics Machine: "Development," Depoliticization and Bureaucratic Power in Lesotho* (Cambridge, 1990); D. K.

Fieldhouse, *The West and the Third World: Trade, Colonialism, Dependence and Development* (Oxford, 1999); Walter Rodney, *How Europe Underdeveloped Africa* (London, 1972); and Andre Gunder Frank, *Capitalism and Underdevelopment in Latin America* (New York, 1967).

35 Jacques May, "Medical Geography: Its Methods and Objectives," *Geographical Review* 40:1 (January 1950), 9–41, citations 40. On May, see Tim Brown and Graham Moon, "From Siam to New York: Jacques May and the 'foundation' of medical geography," *Journal of Historical Geography* 30:4 (2004), 747–63. May was the former director of the Hanoi Medical School and the Phu Doan Hospital (1936–40).

36 Timothy Brennan, "The Economic Image-Function of the Periphery," in Ania Loomba, et al., eds., *Postcolonial Studies and Beyond* (Durham, NC, 2005), 111.

37 Christina Klein, *Cold War Orientalism. Asia in the Middlebrow Imagination, 1945–1961* (Berkeley, CA, 2003), 98.

38 Chris Osakwe, *The Participation of the Soviet Union in Universal International Organizations: A Political and Legal Analysis of Soviet Strategies and Aspirations inside ILO, UNESCO and WHO* (Leiden, 1972), citation 115. The same language was used in a U.S. Public Health brochure aimed at recruiting physicians, sanitary engineers, nurses, and medical technicians to join the overseas health missions attached to the U.S. Operations Missions. See *U.S. Public Health Service, Health Abroad: A Challenge to Americans. Iran: One of Many* (no place, no date; presumably 1954).

39 Walt Rostow, *The Stages of Economic Growth. A Non-Communist Manifesto* (Cambridge, 1960).

40 John J. Hanlon, "The Design of Public Health Programs for Underdeveloped Countries," *PHR* 69:11 (November 1954), 1028–32.

41 Frank George Boudreau, "International Health," *AJPH* 41 (December 1951), 1477–1482, citation 1479, emphasis added.

42 Ralph Lee Smith, *Getting to Know the World Health Organization. How U.N. Crusaders Fight for Life* (New York, 1963), 9.

43 Gearóid ó Tuathail and John Agnew, "Geopolitics and Discourse: Practical Geopolitical Reasoning in American Foreign Policy," *Political Geography* 11:2 (March 1992), 190–204; Keith Aoki, "Space Invaders: Critical Geography, the 'Third World' in International Law and Critical Race Theory," *Villanova Law Review* 45 (2000), 913–57; and William Pietz, "The 'Post-Colonialism' of Cold War Discourse," *Social Text* 19/20 (Autumn 1988), 55–75.

44 Marian Maury, *The Good War. The UN's World-Wide Fight Against Poverty, Disease and Ignorance* (New York, 1965), 16–17, emphases added.

45 Matthew Connelly, "Taking Off the Cold War Lens: Visions of North-South Conflict during the Algerian War for Independence," *AHR*, 105,3 (June 2000), 739–69, citation 753.

46 On national liberation struggles and colonial counterinsurgency in the 1940s and early 1950s, see John A. Nagl, *Learning to Eat Soup with Knife: Counterinsurgency Lessons from Malaya and Vietnam* (Chicago, 2006); Daniel Branch, *Defeating Mau Mau, Creating Kenya: Counterinsurgency, Civil War, and Decolonization* (Cambridge, 2009); Caroline Elkins, *Imperial Reckoning: The*

Untold Story of Britain's Gulag in Kenya (New York, 2005); and Pieter Lagrou, "1945–1955. The Age of Total War," in Frank Biess and Bob Moeller, eds., *Histories of the Aftermath* (New York, 2010), 287–96. See also Arthur Dommen, *The Indochinese Experience of the French and Americans: Nationalism and Communism in Cambodia, Laos, and Vietnam* (Bloomington, IN, 2001).

47 Matthew Connelly, *A Diplomatic Revolution. Algeria's Fight for Independence and the Origins of the post-Cold War Era* (Oxford, 2002), 48.

48 Cited in Alexander Troche, *"Berlin wird am Mekong verteidigt": Die Ostasienpolitik der Bundesrepublik in China, Taiwan, und Südvietnam, 1954–1966* (Düsseldorf, 2001), 59–60.

49 Gerald Horne, "Race from Power. U.S. Foreign Policy and the General Crisis of 'White Supremacy,'" *DH* 23:3 (Summer 1999), 437–61, citation 454. See also Sue Onslow, ed., *Cold War in Southern Africa: White Power, Black Liberation* (London, 2009).

50 Anders Stephanson, *George Kennan and the Art of Foreign Policy* (Cambridge, MA, 1989).

51 *United Nations Operations in the Congo. Hearing before the Subcommittee on International Organizations and Movements of the Committee on Foreign Affairs, House of Representatives, Eighty-seventh Congress, first session, April 13, 1961* (Washington, DC, 1961), 14, 22; and Kennan (Mr. X), "The Sources of Soviet Conduct," *Foreign Affairs* 25:4 (1947), 566–82, where he spoke of containing the Soviet Union by means of "the adroit and vigilant application of counter-force at a series of constantly shifting geographical and political points."

52 The most important accounts of global health governance include Sunil S. Amrith, *Decolonizing International Health: India and Southeast Asia, 1930–65* (Basingstoke, 2006); Connelly, *Fatal Misconception*; and Alison Bashford, *Global Population: History, Geopolitics, and Life on Earth* (New York, 2014).

53 Cited in John Farley, *Brock Chisholm, the World Health Organization, and the Cold War* (Vancouver, 2008), 69.

54 Technical Preparatory Committee. Summary Record of the Sixth Meeting (March 21, 1946), NARA RG59, General Records of the Department of State, 1907–50, Entry A1 5468, Box 4.

55 Technical Preparatory Committee. Seventeenth Meeting (April 1, 1946), NARA RG 59, Entry A1 5468, Box 4.

56 Cited in Freeman H. Quimby, *Science, Technology, and American Diplomacy. The Politics of Global Health.* Prepared for the Subcommittee on National Security Policy and Scientific Developments of the Committee on Foreign Affairs, U.S. House of Representatives (USGPO, 1971), 38. Evang was a leading member of the Norwegian Labor Party, and he served as Chief Medical Officer to the Norwegian exile government during World War II.

57 The United States and Britain had been discussing the formation of a single international health organization since 1944, although for reasons that were quite different from those of non-European advocates. "Introductory Remarks, Dr. Thomas Parran, Chairman," NARA RG 59, Entry A1 5468, Box 2. Department of State, Advisory Health Group (October 11, 1945).

58 Instead, Cumming insisted in a letter to Truman (June 9, 1945) that the Pan American Sanitary Bureau retain its quasi-independent status, NARA RG 59, Entry A1 5468, Box 2.

59 "Memorandum to the President": Views of Department of State regarding Letter from Dr. Hugh S. Cumming (undated), NARA RG 59, Entry A1 5468, Box 2.

60 *ORWHO*, No. 1. Minutes of the Technical Preparatory Committee for the International Health Conference (New York, 1947); *ORWHO*, No. 2. Summary Report on Proceedings Minutes and Final Acts of the International Health Conference (New York, 1948); and *ORWHO*, No. 13. First World Health Assembly (Geneva, 1948). See also WHO, *The First Ten Years of the World Health Organization* (Geneva, 1958).

61 "Report and Resolution on Health Questions Submitted for Approval to the Council by Its Drafting Committee," NARA RG 59, Entry A1 5468, Box 3. UN Economic and Social Council (June 10, 1946), and "Action taken by the Economic and Social Council on Health Matters" (June 30, 1946), NARA RG 59, Entry A1 5468, Box 4. While there was a clear consensus that Germany and Japan were to be represented through the Allied Control Commission, after some debate it was eventually agreed that Italy, Austria, Romania, Bulgaria, Hungary, and Finland, together with other countries that did not belong to the UN, were to be invited to the International Health Conference as observers.

62 Technical Preparatory Committee. Summary Record of the Thirteenth Meeting (March 27, 1946), NARA RG59, Entry A1 5468, Box 4.

63 *ORWHO*, No. 2, 73–74.

64 http://apps.who.int/gb/bd/PDF/bd47/EN/constitution-en.pdf accessed May 27, 2014.

65 Javed Siddiqi, *World Health and World Politics. The World Health Organization and the UN System* (London, 1995), 80. The International Health Conference was attended by delegations from 51 United Nations member states (20 of them in Latin America), observers from 13 non-member states, and representatives of several NGOs.

66 Letter from the Irish Government to the Director General Chisholm (December 18, 1952), AWHO, OD20.

67 Amy L.S. Staples, *The Birth of Development: How the World Bank, Food and Agriculture Organization, and World Health Organization Changed the World, 1945–1965* (Kent, OH, 2006), 147.

68 Siddiqi, *World Health and World Politics*, 74; and Farley, *Brock Chisholm*, 95–6.

69 M.P. Kidron (Director, International Organisations Division, Ministry for Foreign Affairs) to Chisholm (December 10, 1952), AWHO, OD20.

70 Nicolaus Mills, *Winning the Peace: The Marshall Plan and America's Coming of Age as a Superpower* (Hoboken, NJ, 2008).

71 "Inaugural Address of the President," in *The Department of State Bulletin* 20:500 (January 30, 1949), 125.

72 The International Development Advisory Board, "Partners in Progress. A Report to the President" (March 1951), emphasis added (www.

trumanlibrary.org/whistlestop/study_collections/pointfourprogram/documents/
index.php?documentdate=1951-03-00&documentid=3-2&pagenumber=1;
accessed July 2, 2013).

73 Technical Cooperation Administration, Department of State, "Quarterly Report for the Period Ending December 31, 1950," copy attached to letter from James Webb to Truman (May 16, 1951), (www.trumanlibrary.org/whistlestop/study_collections/pointfourprogram/documents/index.php? pagenumber=1&documentdate=1951-05-16&documentid=3-7; accessed July 5, 2013). The Department of State also created the Bureau of United Nations Affairs to coordinate bi- and multilateral assistance programs. Harry S Truman Public Library (www.trumanlibrary.org/whistlestop/study_ collections/pointfourprogram/documents/index.php?documentdate=1951-03-00&documentid=3-2&pagenumber=1; accessed July 5, 2013).

74 The following account is based on David Owen, "The United Nations Expanded Technical Assistance Program – A Multilateral Approach,"*Annals of the American Academy of Political and Social Science*, Vol. 323 (May 1959), 25–32. Owen was Executive Chairman of the UN Technical Assistance Board.

75 U.S. Public Health Service (September 18, 1952), NARA RG 469, Records of the U.S. Foreign Assistance Agencies, Box 3, Subject File 1953–57.

76 H.W. Singer, "International Approaches to Modernization Programs," *Modernization Programs in Relation to Human Resources and Population Problems* (New York, 1950), 38.

77 Louis L. Williams, Jr. to Director of Health & Sanitation Staff, Technical Cooperation Agency (November 25, 1952, and December 3, 1952), NARA RG 469, Box 3.

78 Polish minister Julian Przybos to WHO (August 15, 1950), AWHO OD 14-1.

79 At the fifth plenary meeting of the First World Health Assembly (June 26, 1948), *ORWHO*, No. 13. First World Health Assembly (Geneva, 1948), 39–43, citation 41. Even those aid organizations that nominally supported the WHO complained about the seemingly lavish salaries paid to WHO employees and about the fact that the organization spent far more on salaries and travel (43 percent of its budget in 1950 and 69 percent in 1951) than on disease control itself. Farley, *Brock Chisholm*, 70, 77, 82.

80 Circular from the WHO Director-General to the Executive Board (February 18, 1949), AWHO, EB3/52. There was no procedure for a country to withdraw from the WHO, and in the end the Soviet bloc members were denoted as "inactive." See the correspondence in AWHO, OD 14-1. By contrast, after Taiwan notified the WHO that it was withdrawing effective May 1950, the People's Republic of China sent a cable – which was promptly ignored – to the organization claiming to be the only legitimate representative of the Chinese people. Siddiqi, *World Health and World Politics*, 111.

81 Marian E. Parmoor to Chisholm (June 16, 1950), and S.S. Sokhey (Acting Director General, WHO) to Martin Hill (June 21, 1950), AWHO, OD 14-1. In a joint statement issued in May 1950, the Secretary General of UN and the executive heads of the UN specialized agencies, including the WHO,

reaffirmed commitment of the UN and its specialized agencies to the principle of universality. Martin Hill to Chisholm (May 11, 1950), AWHO, OD 14-1.

82 Cited in League of Arab States, *The First Asian-African Conference Held at Bandung, Indonesia (April 18–24, 1955). Report submitted by Mohamed Abdel Khalek Hassouna, Secretary-General of the League of Arab States to the League Council* (Cairo, 1955), 154f.

83 Samuel E. Crowl, "Indonesia's Diplomatic Revolution: Lining Up for Non-alignment, 1945–1955," in Christopher E. Goscha and Christian F. Ostermann, eds., *Connecting Histories: Decolonization and the Cold War in Southeast Asia, 1945–1962* (Washington, DC, 2009), 238–257; Sally Percival Wood, "Constructing an Alternative Regional Identity: Panchsheel and India-China Diplomacy at the Asian-African Conference 1955," in Leong Yew, ed., *Alterities in Asia: Reflections on Identity and Regionalism* (London, 2011), 46–64; and Pang Yang Huei, "The Four Faces of Bandung: Detainees, Soldiers, Revolutionaries and Statesmen," *Journal of Contemporary Asia* 39:1 (February 2009), 63–86.

84 Christopher Lee, ed., *Making a World After Empire: The Bandung Moment and Its Political Alternatives* (Athens, 2010); Prasenjit Duara, ed., *Decolonization: Perspectives from Now and Then* (London, 2004); Partha Chatterjee, "Empire and Nation Revisited: 50 Years after Bandung," and Sunil S. Amrith, "Asian Internationalism: Bandung's Echo in a Colonial Metropolis," both in *Inter-Asia Cultural Studies* 6:4 (2005), 487–96 and 557–69, respectively.

85 Roland Burke, "From Individual Rights to National Development: The First UN International Conference on Human Rights, Tehran, 1968," *JWH* 19:3 (2008), 275–96, citation 279. At the end of 1945, 13 of the 51 members of the UN were from Asia, the Middle East, and Africa. Two decades later, states from these regions made up 61 out of the 114 member states. Rupert Emerson, "Colonialism, Political Development, and the UN," *IO* 19:3 (Summer 1965), 484–503.

86 Samir N. Anabtawi, "The Afro-Asian States and the Hungarian Question," *IO* 17:4 (Autumn 1963), 872–900, citation 883.

87 "C. Human rights and self-determination," in Final Communiqué (www.cvce.eu/obj/communique_final_de_la_conference_afro_asiatique_de_bandoeng_24_avril_1955-fr-676237bd-72f7-471f-949a-88b6ae513585.html; accessed July 10, 2010). African Americans played an important role in these counter-hegemonic struggles worldwide. See Kevin K. Gaines, *American Africans in Ghana: Black Expatriates in the Civil Rights Era* (Chapel Hill, NC, 2006); Carol Anderson, *Eyes off the Prize: The United Nations and the African American Struggle for Human Rights, 1944–1955* (Cambridge, 2003); James H. Meriwether, *Proudly We Can Be Africans: Black Americans and Africa, 1935–1961* (Chapel Hill, NC, 2002); and Penny M. von Eschen, *Race Against Empire: Black Americans and Anticolonialism, 1937–1957* (Ithaca, NY, 1997).

88 Mignolo, "Delinking: The Rhetoric of Modernity, the Logic of Coloniality and the Grammar of De-coloniality," *Cultural Studies* 21:2–3 (March/May 2007), 449–514, citation 457.

89 *The First Asian-African Conference Held at Bandung, Indonesia,* 129. See also "D. Problems of Dependent Peoples," in *Final Communiqué of the Asian-African Conference of Bandung (April 24, 1955).* (www.cvce.eu/obj/ final_communique_of_the_asian_african_conference_of_bandung_24_ april_1955-en-676237bd-72f7–471f-949a-88b6ae513585.html; accessed on July 16, 2010).

90 Vijay Prashad, *The Darker Nations: A People's History of the Third World* (New York, 2006); Berger, "Decolonisation, Modernisation and Nation-Building," and Cullather, "Development? Its History," *DH* 24:4 (2000), 641–53.

91 Statement of the Indian delegation at the closing session, (www.cvce.eu/obj/ declaration_de_la_delegation_indienne_a_la_seance_de_cloture_bandoeng_ 17_au_24_avril_1955-fr-ff02a695–6b4a-4d88-ba17–7595b8715e62.html; accessed July 10, 2010).

92 In an interview with *Le Monde Diplomatique,* cited in League of Arab States, *The First Asian-African Conference Held at Bandung, Indonesia (April 18–24, 1955). Report submitted by Mohamed Abdel Khalek Hassouna, Secretary-General of the League of Arab States to the League Council* (Cairo, 1955), 151.

93 *Afro-Asian Peoples Conference (26 December 1957 – 1st January 1958). Principal Reports submitted to the Conference* (Cairo, 1958), 17.

94 Matthew Jones, "A 'Segregated' Asia?: Race, the Bandung Conference, and Pan-Asianist Fears in American Thought and Policy, 1954–1955," *DH* 29:5 (November 2005), 841–68; Jason Parker, "Cold War II: The Eisenhower Administration, The Bandung Conference, and the Reperiodization of the Postwar Era," *DH* 30:5 (2006), 867–92; Connelly, "Taking Off the Cold War Lens," 739–69; and Henry William Brands, *The Specter of Neutralism: The United States and the Emergence of the Third World, 1947–1960* (New York, 1989).

95 Cited in Immanuel Wallerstein, "What Cold War in Asia? An Interpretative Essay," in Zheng Yangwen, Hong Liu, Michael Szonyi, eds., *The Cold War in Asia: The Battle for Hearts and Minds* (Leiden, 2010), 16. See also Kathryn C. Statler and Andrew L. Johns, *The Eisenhower Administration, the Third World, and the Globalization of the Cold War* (Lanham, MD, 2006); and Roland B. Rakove, *Kennedy, Johnson, and the Nonaligned World* (Cambridge, 2012).

96 Cited in Wood, "Constructing an alternative regional identity," 58.

97 Similarly, British Foreign Secretary Lord Home blamed the system for precipitating a "crisis of confidence" in the United Nations. Ali Mazrui, "The United Nations and Some African Political Attitudes," *IO* 18:3 (1964), 499–520, here 511.

98 *Afro-Asian Peoples Conference,* 46.

99 Ibid., 48.

100 Nikita S. Khrushchev, "On Peaceful Coexistence," *Foreign Affairs* 38:1 (October 1959), 1–18. See also Rosa Magnusdottir, "'Be Careful in America, Premier Khrushchev!': Soviet Perceptions of Peaceful Coexistence with the United States in 1959," *Cahiers du monde russe* 47:1–2 (2006), 109–30;

Roger D. Markwick, "Peaceful Coexistence, Detente and Third World Struggles: The Soviet View, from Lenin to Brezhnev," *Australian Journal of International Affairs* 44:2 (1990), 171–94; and Nigel Gould-Davies, "The Logic of Soviet Cultural Diplomacy," *DH* 27:2 (April 2003), 193–214.

101 The chief Soviet ideologist Andrei Zhdanov set out the two camps doctrine at the inaugural meeting of the Communist Information Bureau in September 1947. Vladislav Zubok and Constantine Pleshakov, *Inside the Kremlin's Cold War: From Stalin to Krushchev* (Cambridge, MA, 1997). See also Dieter Heinzig, *The Soviet Union and Communist China 1945–1950: The Arduous Road to the Alliance* (Armonk, NY, 2004).

102 Silvio Pons, "Stalin and the European Communists after World War Two (1943–1948)," *Past and Present* (2011), 210 (Supplement 6), 121–138. For the reception of the Soviet Cold War orthodoxy in Asia in the late 1940s, see Karl Hack, "The Origins of the Asian Cold War: Malaya 1948" and Harry A. Poeze, "The Cold War in Indonesia, 1948," in *Journal of Southeast Asian Studies* 40:3 (October 2009), 471–96 and 497–517, respectively.

103 A.M. Diakov, *The Crisis of British Domination in India and the New Stage of the Liberation Struggle of Her Peoples* (Moscow, 1949), cited in Alvin Z. Rubinstein, "Selected Bibliography of Soviet Works on Southern Asia, 1954–56," *The Journal of Asian Studies* 17:1 (November 1957), 46.

104 Sudha Rajagopalan, *Indian Films in Soviet Cinemas: The Culture of Movie-Going after Stalin* (Bloomington, 2008), 2; and Gould-Davies, "The Logic of Soviet Cultural Diplomacy," 104.

105 Rubinstein, "Selected Bibliography of Soviet Works on Southern Asia, 1954–56," 53.

106 On the Cold War cultural struggles between the two superpowers, see David Caute, *The Dancer Defects: The Struggle for Cultural Supremacy during the Cold War* (Oxford, 2003); Yale Richmond, *Cultural Exchange and the Cold War: Raising the Iron Curtain* (University Park, PA, 2003); Nicholas J. Cull, *The Cold War and the United States Information Agency: American Propaganda and Public Diplomacy, 1945–1989* (Cambridge, 2009); Justin Hart, *Empire of Ideas: The Origins of Public Diplomacy and the Transformation of U.S. Foreign Policy* (Oxford, 2013); Kenneth A. Osgood, *Total Cold War: Eisenhower's Secret Propaganda Battle at Home and Abroad* (St. Lawrence, 2008); and Walter L. Hixson, *Parting the Curtain: Propaganda, Culture, and the Cold War, 1945–1961* (Basingstoke, 1997).

107 George Skorov, "Ivan Potekhin–Man, Scientist, and Friend of Africa," *The Journal of Modern African Studies* 2:3 (November 1964), 444–7; O. Edmund Clubb, "Soviet Oriental Studies and the Asian Revolution," *Pacific Affairs* 31:4 (December 1958), 380–9; and Geoffrey Wheeler, "Middle Eastern Studies in the USSR," *Middle Eastern Studies* 1:1 (October 1964), 84–90.

108 For more, see Hooshang Amirahmadi, "The Non-Capitalist Way of Development," *Review of Radical Political Economics* 19:1 (1987), 22–46. Several months later, the Soviet scholar Modeste Rubinstein published "A Non-capitalist Path for Underdeveloped Countries," *NYT* (July 5 and August 2, 1956) in which he explicitly endorsed Nehru's government.

109 Declaration of the World Congress of Workers' and Communist Parties of the Socialist Countries Meeting in Moscow (www.marxists.org/history/international/comintern/sino-soviet-split/other/1957declaration.htm; accessed January 8, 2012).

110 Albania, Bulgaria, Poland, and the Soviet Union attended the 10th World Health Assembly in May 1957; Czechoslovakia and Romania attended in 1958; and Hungary in 1963. Siddiqi, *World Health and World Politics*, 108.

111 See the records of the Conference of Health Ministers of the Countries of the Socialist Camp in BAB, DQ1/12552. The meeting was atended by representatives from Albania, Bulgaria, Hungary, East German, Poland, Rumania, Czechoslovakia, the Soviet Union, North Vietnam, China, North Korea, and Mongolia. See also O.P. Schepin and L.I. Vladimirova, *Cooperation between the USSR and Countries of the Socialist Community in Medical Science and Health* (Moscow, 1981), 4, 8–9.

112 A. Y. Lysenko, I. N. Semashko, "Geography of Malaria," in *Medical Geography 1966* (Moscow, 1968) (available online at www.rollbackmalaria.org/docs/lysenko).

113 B. M. Zhdanov to M. G. Candau (January 30 and March 19, 1959), AWHO, N 52/372/2 USSR.

114 Kelley Lee, *The World Health Organization (WHO)* (London, 2009), 55.

115 Maureen Gallagher, "*The World Health Organization. Promotion of US and Soviet Foreign Policy Goals,*" *JAMA* (October 5, 1963), 34.

116 Osakwe, *The Participation of the Soviet Union in Universal International Organizations*, 116–8.

117 Siddiqi, *World Health and World Politics*, 114.

118 In 1954 and 1955, Moscow extended to Afghanistan credits of $3.5 million and $100 million, respectively. Although other East European socialist states also contributed, more than three-quarters of the estimated $1.2 billion in Soviet bloc development aid for the period 1953–57 came from the Soviet Union itself. Karel Holbik, "Aid Programs Compared and Contrasted," *Intereconomics* 3:5 (1968), 134–137.

119 Guy Laron, *Origins of the Suez Crisis: Postwar Development Diplomacy and the Struggle over Third World Industrialization, 1945–1956* (Washington, DC, 2013); Srirupa Roy, *Beyond Belief: India and the Politics of Postcolonial Nationalism* (Durham, NC, 2007), Christian Strümpell, "Social Citizenship and Ethnicity around a Public Sector Steel Plant in Orissa, India," *Citizenship Studies* 15:3–4 (June 2011), 485–98; and Jonathan P. Parry, "Nehru's Dream and the Village 'Waiting Room': Long-distance Labour Migrants to a Central Indian Steel Town," *Contributions to Indian Sociology* 37:1–2 (2003), 217–49.

120 Joel Beinin, "Labor, Capital, and the State in Nasserist Egypt, 1952–1961," *International Journal of Middle East Studies* 21:1 (February 1989), 71–90; and Asha L. Datar, *India's Economic Relations with the USSR and Eastern Europe 1953 to 1969*, (Cambridge, 1972), 3.

121 Elizabeth Bishop, *Talking Shop: Egyptian Engineers and Soviet Specialists at the Aswan High Dam* (Dissertation, University of Chicago, 1997), I:14ff., 241. See also Robert W. Rycroft and Joseph S. Szyliowicz, "The

Technological Dimension of Decision Making, The Case of the Aswan High Dam," *World Politics* 33:1 (October 1980), 36–61; and Silvia Borzutzky and David Berger, "Dammed If You Do, Dammed If You Don't, The Eisenhower Administration and the Aswan Dam," *MEJ* 64:1 (Winter 2010), 84–102.

122 Cited in Sergey Mazov, *A Distant Front in the Cold War: The USSR in West Africa and the Congo, 1956–1964* (Palo Alto, CA, 2010), 53. The Volta River project involved damming the river and using hydroelectric power to produce aluminum from the abundant local bauxite deposits. The United States did offer to provide technical assistance for the project. See also Douglas G. Anglin, "Ghana, the West, and the Soviet Union," *The Canadian Journal of Economics and Political Science* 24:2 (May, 1958), 152–65. In October 1957, Ghana's Minister of Finance was refused service at a restaurant in Delaware.

123 Bernard D'Mello, "Soviet Collaboration in Indian Steel Industry, 1954–84," *Economic and Political Weekly* 23:10 (March 5, 1988), 473–86, here 475f.; and Marshall I. Goldman, "A Balance Sheet of Soviet Foreign Aid," *Foreign Affairs* 43:2 (January 1965), 349–60, here 350. At Bhilai, "686 engineers and skilled workers were trained in the USSR and 4,500 workers and 500 engineers in India by the Soviet side," Datar, *India's Economic Relations with the USSR and Eastern Europe*, 64.

124 Cited in Y. Rumyantsev, "Model of Fruitful Cooperation," *IA* 30:3 (1984), 137–40, citation, 137. Rumyantsev (139) emphasized that the Soviets were interested not only in building, but in "teach[ing] others to build." See also Andreas Hilger, "Revolutionsideologie, Systemkonkurrenz oder Entwicklungspolitik? Sowjetisch-indische Wirtschaftsbeziehungen in Chruschtschows Kaltem Krieg," *AfS* 48 (2008), 389–410; Ragna Boden, *Die Grenzen der Weltmacht: Sowjetische Indonesienpolitik von Stalin bis Breznev* (Stuttgart, 2006); and Maxim Matusevich, *No Easy Row for the Russian Hoe: Ideology and Pragmatism in Nigerian-Soviet Relations, 1960–1991* (Trenton, NJ, 2003).

125 John White, "West German Aid to Developing Countries," International Affairs 41:1 (1965), 78. See also Konrad Illgen, *Freundschaft in Aktion* (Berlin, 1961), 183–85; Jan Bodo Sperling, *The Human Dimension of Technical Assistance. The German Experience at Rourkela, India* (Ithaca, NY, 1969); and "Rourkela: Russen auf dem Dach," *Der Spiegel*, Nr. 14/1960 (March 30, 1960), 22–3. At times, there were as many as 1,800 Germans in Rourkela, and more than 250 had to stay on after the completion of the project.

126 Armin Grünbacher, "Profits and Cold War – Politically Motivated Export Finance in West Germany during the 1950s: Two Case Studies," *German Politics* 10:3 (December 2001), 141–58, citation 153. See also Amit Das Gupta, *Handel, Hilfe, Hallstein-Doktrin: Die bundesdeutsche Südasienpolitik unter Adenauer und Erhard 1949 bis 1966* (Husum, 2004); Konrad Seitz, "Indo-German Economic Co-operation: A Survey," in Vadilal Dagli, ed., *India and Germany: A Survey of Economic Relations* (Bombay, 1970), 81–92; and Corinna R. Unger, "Rourkela, ein 'Stahlwerk im Dschungel': Industrialisierung, Modernisierung und Entwicklungshilfe im Kontext von

Dekolonisation und Kaltem Krieg (1950–1970)," *AfS* 48 (2998), 367–88; and "Industrialization vs. Agrarian Reform: West German Modernization Policies in India in the 1950s and 1960s," *JMEH* 8:1 (2010), 47–65.

127 V. Rymalov, "Soviet Assistance to Underdeveloped Countries," *IA* 5:9 (1959), 23–31; V. Vershinn and V. Demidov, "Disinterested Aid," *IA* 6:1 (1960), 34–40; and G. Savin, "The Socialist States: True Friends of the Underdeveloped Countries," *IA* 8:4 (1962), 98–100.

128 A. Ivanov, "Soviet Cinerama," *Current Digest of the Russian Press* 9:4 (March 6, 1957), 41–42. See also Pia Koivunen, "The 1957 World Youth Festival: Propagating a New, Peaceful Image of the Soviet Union," in Melanie Ilič and Jeremy Smith, eds., *Soviet State and Society under Nikita Khrushchev* (London, 2009), 45–65.

129 Bishop, *Talking Shop: Egyptian Engineers and Soviet Specialists at the Aswan High Dam*, I:141–66.

130 S. Mazov, *A Distant Front in the Cold War*, 70.

131 A. Nekrasov, "Soviet Aid: Past and Present," *IA* 9:3 (1963), 78–85, here 79.

132 Eisenhower to John Foster Dulles (December 1955), cited in Borzutzky and Berger, "Dammed If You Do, Dammed If You Don't," citation 93.

133 Cited in Karel Holbik and Henry Allen Myers, *West German Foreign Aid 1956–1966* (Boston, 1968), 5, fn. 10.

134 CIA, "Foreign Aid and Foreign Policy" (January 21, 1965), S-1392.

135 *Soviet Foreign Aid to the Less Developed Countries: Retrospect and Prospect* (February 9, 1966), 2. For example, in 1960 bilateral aid to Africa amounted $1.23 billion, while multilateral aid to Africa totaled $146 million, most of which ($130 million) came from the World Bank. Paul-Marc Henry, "The United Nations and the Problem of African Development," *IO* 16:2 (Spring 1962), 362–74, citation 366.

136 For detailed accounts of Soviet aid programs, see I. Tatarovskaya, *The Developing Countries: Work for Peace* (Moscow, 1972); Nikolai Kolesnikov and Sergei Sokhin, *Soviet Aid in Education and Personnel Training* (Moscow, 1974); and CIA, Office of Research and Reports, "Soviet Bloc Technical Assistance to the Less Developed Countries," CIA/RR CB 64–46, June 1964. See also Ragna Boden, "Cold War Economics: Soviet Aid to Indonesia," *Journal of Cold War Studies* 10:3 (Summer 2008), 110–28; Jeffrey James Byrne, "Our Own Special Brand of Socialism: Algeria and the Contest of Modernities in the 1960s," *DH* 33:3 (June 2009), 427–47; and Haile Gabriel Dague, *Das entwicklungspolitische Engagement der DDR in Äthiopien* (Münster, 2004).

137 CIA, "Soviet Foreign Aid to the Less Developed Countries: Retrospect and Prospect" (February 9, 1966), 22 (www.foia.ucia.gov; accessed January 6, 2012). Between 1954 and 1963, 41,000 Soviet bloc agricultural, educational, medical, economic planning, managerial experts were sent to developing countries, while about 6,800 people from the Third World received technical training. CIA, Current Support Brief. Soviet Bloc Technical Assistance to the Less Developed Countries. CIA/ RR CB 64–46 (June 1964), 1.

138 I. Maximov, "Friendship University" *IA* 10, 2 (1964), 106.

139 Constantin Katsakioris, "Soviet Lessons for Arab Modernization: Soviet Educational Aid to Arab Countries after 1956," *JMEH* 8:1 (2010), 85–105; Maxim Matusevich, "Probing the Limits of Internationalism: African Students Confront Soviet Ritual," *Anthropology of East Europe Review* 27:2 (Fall 2009), 19–39; Matusevich, "Journeys of Hope: African Diaspora and the Soviet Society," *African Diaspora* 1 (2008), 53–85; and Julie Hessler, "Death of an African Student in Moscow: Race, Politics, and the Cold War," *Cahiers du monde russe* 47:1–2 (2006), 33–64. On the Western propaganda counteroffensive, M. Ayih, *Ein Afrikaner in Moskau* (Cologne, 1961); E. J. Hevi, *Schwarzer Student im Roten China* (Bern, 1963); Olabisi Ajala, *An African Abroad* (London, 1963); and Jan Carew, *Moscow Is Not My Mecca* (London, 1964).

140 CIA, "Soviet Foreign Aid to the Less Developed Countries: Retrospect and Prospect," 22, and CIA, Intelligence Report, "Communist Aid to Less Developed Countries of the Free World, 1974," ER IR 75–16 (June 1975), 8. CIA FOIA Electronic Reading Room (www.foia.ucia.gov). From 1956 to 1974, approximately 65,700 students from the Third World (32,660 from Africa) studied in China and Soviet bloc countries; the overwhelming majority of these students studied in the Soviet Union (37,790) and Eastern Europe (26,835), only 1,030 studied in China.

141 CIA, Soviet Academic and Technical Programs for students from the Less Developed Countries of the Free World (May 1965), 4. See also CIA, Office of Research and Reports, "Soviet bloc Technical Assistance to the Less Developed Countries," June 1964, CIA/RR CB 64–46.

142 CIA, "Soviet Academic and Technical Programs for students from the Less Developed Countries of the Free World," 14.

143 *Ibid.*, 7.

144 *Postwar Rehabilitation and Development of the National Economy of D.P.R.K.* (Pyongyang, 1957), 8.

145 Richard Deperasinski, "From My Recollections," *Korea through the Eyes of Foreigners* (Pyongyang, 1957), 12.

146 Arkadi Perventsev, "A Few Weeks' Stay in Korea," *Korea through the Eyes of Foreigners*, 42.

147 A total of 162 Hungarians served in the country's medical mission by the time of its ending in June 1956. Karoly Fendler, "The Korean War (1950–1953) in the Foreign Affairs of Hungary: Forms of Hungarian Assistance," *Korea Journal* (November–December 1990), 49–60. Romania, the Soviet Union, Poland, and Czechoslovakia also sent doctors, medicine, and medical supplies to North Korea.

148 Lehmann to Otto Grotewohl (August 2, 1950), BAB, NY/4090/481.

149 Rüdiger Frank, "Lessons from the Past: The First Wave of Developmental Assistance to North Korea and the German Reconstruction of Hamhung," *Pacific Focus* 23:1 (April 2008), 46–74. Frank's interviews revealed that many East Germans felt that "it never was the same again as in the early days of the Korea aid program," Ibid., 52, n. 16. See also Frank, *Die DDR und Nordkorea: Der Wiederaufbau der Stadt Hamhung von 1954–1962* (Aachen, 1996).

150 Korea-Hilfsausschuß, "Überblick" (June 9, 1952), BAB, NY/4090/481. In November 1954, the Koreahilfsausschuß was renamed the "Solidarity Committee for Korea and Vietnam." By the end of 1954, the Committee had collected approximately DM 40 million to aid the two countries. See the Solidarity Committee report (December 1, 1955) in the same folder.

151 Hilde Cahn and Lilly Wächter to Grotewohl (July 25, 1951), BAB, NY/4090/481. The Commission criticized UNESCO for failing to act aggressively to meet the urgent needs of Korean civilians. Wächter headed the West German division of the Democratic Women's League of Germany in the early 1950s. For more on Wächter, see Ursula Schröter, "Die DDR-Frauenorganisation im Rückblick," in Schröter, Renate Ulrich, and Rainer Ferchland, *Patriarchat in der DDR: Nachträgliche Entdeckungen in DFD-Dokumenten, DEFA-Dokumentarfilmen und soziologischen Befragungen* (Berlin, 2009), 33ff.

152 Fendler, "The Korean War (1950–1953)," 55. Approximately 900 Korean workers were sent to Czechoslovakia, and 1,000 children and students were sent to Hungary, although the latter were recalled immediately after the 1956 uprising there. North Korea also sent 3,000 people to China for training in 1955 and again in 1956. "Materialzusammenstellung" (January 24, 1956), PAAA, MfAA/A7013, and Fischer, "Aktenvermerk, betr. Visite beim ... Kim Ir Sen" (August 5, 1954), PAAA, MfAA/A5575.

153 These North Korean orphans only stayed in GDR until 1955/56. Immediately after these children returned home, their places were taken by North Vietnamese children (149 in 1955 and 199 in 1956). Mirjam Freytag, *Die "Moritzburger" in Vietnam* (Frankfurt a.M., 1997), 46.

154 Walter Ulbricht to Grotewohl (August 6, 1953), Anton Ackermann to Grotewohl (August 11, 1953), "Beschlüsse der Regierungen der UdSSR, der Volksrepublik Polen und der Ungarischen Volksrepublik zur Unterstützung des Wiederaufbaues der koreanischen Volksdemokratischen Republik" (August 13, 1953), and "Die ökonomischen Beziehungen der Koreanischen Volksdemokratischen Republik zu den Ländern des sozialistischen Lagers," all in BAB, NY/4090/481. See also Charles K. Armstrong, "'Fraternal Socialism': The International Reconstruction of North Korea, 1953–62," *CWH* 5:2 (May 2005), 161–87.

155 "Die ökonomischen Beziehungen..." BAB, NY/4090/481.

156 The following information is derived from "Hilfe der UdSSR für die KVDR im Jahre 1957," and GDR embassy in Pyongyang to MfAA (February 21, 1958), in PAAA, MfAA/A7013. In August 1953, the North Koreans had sent a delegation to Eastern Europe with a detailed list of the kinds of aid they needed. Anton Ackermann to Grotewohl (August 19, 1953) and to Gregor (August 26, 1953), Strassenberger to Gregor (September 2, 1953), and Gregor to Grotewohl (September 15, 1953), all in BAB, NY/4090/481.

157 Max Zimmering, "As a Guest to the Land of Mountains and Rivers," *Korea through the Eyes of Foreigners*, 16, 22.

158 Balázs Szalontai, *Kim Il Sung in the Khrushchev Era: Soviet-DPRK Relations and the Roots of North Korean Despotism, 1953–1964* (Palo Alto, 2005). See also Joshua Barker, "Beyond Bandung: Developmental Nationalism and

(Multi)cultural Nationalism in Indonesia," *TWQ* 29:3 (2008), 521–40; and Sumit Sarkar, "Nationalism and Poverty: discourses of development and culture in 20th century India," *TWQ* 29:3 (2008), 429–45.

159 "Hanoi Mass Rally Welcomes Korean Government Delegation" (November 28, 1955), *Everlasting Friendship Between Korean, Chinese and Vietnamese Peoples: Documents on Goodwill Visits of the D.P.R.K. Government Delegation to China and Viet-Nam* (Pyongyang, 1959), 219.

160 "Informationsmaterial über die Handelsbeziehungen" between GDR and DPRK from 1952 to 1956, BAB, NY/4090/481; "Delegationsleiter Protokoll" on foreign trade, January – February, 1956, BAB, DL2/4407; "Aktennotiz" on a meeting with Korean Handelsrat on July 15, 1957, BAB, DL2/1686; and Balázs Szalontai, "'You Have No Political Line of Your Own:' Kim Il Sung and the Soviets, 1953–1964," *CWIHP Bulletin* 14/15 (Winter 2003/Spring 2004), 93.

161 Martin Rudner, "East European Aid to Asian Developing Countries: The Legacy of the Communist Era," *Modern Asian Studies* 30:1 (February 1996), 1–28; and Jude Howell, "The End of an Era: the Rise and Fall of G.D.R. Aid," *The Journal of Modern African Studies* 32:2 (1994), 305–28. Kim refused to join COMECON because he regarded unequal terms of trade as a sign of dependency.

162 In the fall of 1950, both Stalin and Mao threatened to abandon North Korea and leave the country to face UN forces alone; this experience reinforced Kim's suspicions of foreign powers. Alexandre Y. Mansourov, "Stalin, Mao, Kim, and China's Decision to Enter the Korean War. September 16–October 15, 1950: New Evidence from the Russian Archives," *CWIHP Bulletin* 6/7 (Winter 1995/1996), 118–9; Shen Zhihua, "Sino-North Korean Conflict and Its Resolution during the Korean War," *CWIHP* Bulletin 14/15 (Winter 2003/Spring 2004), 9–24; and Kathryn Weathersby, "Stalin, Mao and the End of the Korean War" in Westad, ed., *Brothers in Arms: The Rise and Fall of the Sino-Soviet Alliance* (Palo Alto, CA, 1998), 90–116.

163 Kim, Report of the Central Committee of the Workers' Party of Korea to the Third Party Congress (held in April 1956), in *Postwar Rehabilitation and Development of the National Economy of D.P.R.K.* (Pyongyang, 1957), 10.

164 "Stichwortprotokoll" (June 8, 1956), BAB, DY30/J IV 2/2 A/500. When Ulbricht asked specifically how North Korea was going to go about achieving national unification, Foreign Minister Nam Il said that they were seeking "peaceful reunification" and that, therefore, the "first task" was economic growth and improvement in the standard of living.

165 Heonik Kwon, "North Korea's Politics of Longing," *Critical Asian Studies* 42:1 (2010), 2–25; and Kwon, *The Other Cold War*, 48–53, 90–116. See also Bernd Schaefer, "Weathering the Sino-Soviet Conflict: The GDR and North Korea, 1949–1989," and Szalontai, "'You Have No Political Line of Your Own'," both in *CWIHP Bulletin* 14/15 (Winter 2003/Spring 2004), respectively, 25–38 and 87–103.

166 See the address by Han Sul Ya, chairman of the DPRK National Peace Committee, to the DPRK National Peace Congress, in *Appeal to the Peace-Loving People of the World*, 12–3; and Charles Armstrong, "Juche and

North Korea's Global Aspirations," WWIC, North Korean International Documentation Project, Working Paper #1 (April 2009), 10.

167 Kim Il Sung, *Report on the 10th Anniversary of the 15 August Liberation of Chosun by the Glorious Soviet Army* (Pyongyang, 1955), 25; and *Appeal to the Peace-Loving People of the World* (Pyongyang, 1960), 9. For a comparison of rates of economic growth in North and South in the 1950s, see Sae-kil Park, *Rewriting Contemporary Korean History. Vol. 2: From Armistice to 10.26* (Seoul, 1989, in Korean), 50. The rapid industrialization in the north raised the proportion of industrial workers and technicians to 65 percent of working population, while in the south the corresponding figure was a mere 8.8 percent. The U.S. aid to South Korea was criticized for nothing more than a politically profitable way of ridding the country "in the guise of aid" of its excess agricultural products.

168 Radmann, "Ein Wirtschaftwunder im Fernen Osten," *ND* 27 (December 1960), cited in Armstrong, "'Fraternal Socialism,'" 180. According to Armstrong, between 1953 and 1960 total industrial output grew at an average rate of 39 percent per year.

169 Just before the bombing, 100,000 people had been evacuated from Hamhung to the Pusan area.

170 On the rebuilding of Pyongyang, see Armstrong, "'Fraternal Socialism,'" 171–6.

171 Kim to Grotewohl (July 1, 1954), BAB, NY/4090/481; and note on the meeting between Park Kil Jon and Lothar Bolz (July 7, 1954), BAB, DL2/4423. For speculation on the exact origins of East Germany's Hamhung project, see Frank, "Lessons from the Past," 55–57.

172 Hafrang to Heinrich Rau (January 14, 1955), BAB, DL2/4423; Minutes of a Baustab Korea meeting (March 28, 1955), BAB, DL2/4398; and Baustab Korea to Präsidium des Ministerrats (June 27, 1962), BAB, DL2/4408.

173 "Verordnung des Ministerkabinetts über die Bildung einer Kommission für den Wiederaufbau der Stadt Chamchyng [sic]" (March 7, 1955), PAAA, MfAA/A10211.

174 Baustab Korea, "Informationsmaterial über die Durchführung der Hilfe der Deutschen Demokratischen Republik beim Aufbau der Stadt Hamhung" (1955), BAB, NY/4090/481. In a letter to Kim, Grotewohl explained that the Hamhung reconstruction project had stretched the resources of his state "to the very limits of their capacity"; he then asked for understanding in view that East Germany itself was facing "great domestic and foreign difficulties" at that time. Grotewohl to Kim (February 19, 1955), PAAA, MfAA/A10257.

175 Präßler to Fischer (January 11, 1957), BAB, DL2/4416.

176 For example, the East Germans informed the North Koreans that they would not be able to deliver electrical and heating equipment for some buildings for at least three years. It is not clear whether this equipment was ever actually delivered. Förster, "Teilbericht" (May 25, 1959), BAB, DL2/4416.

177 Minutes of a meeting with deputy premier Dzong, ministers for construction and chemistry, and chairman of the state planning commission (May 16, 1956), BAB, DL2/4416.

178 DAG to Rau (July 10, 1957), BAB, DY/30/IV2/6.06/21.

179 The following is drawn from Präßler to Fischer (January 11, 1957), and Guhlich to Präßler (February 6, 1957), both in BAB, DL2/4416.

180 Rau to DPRK Minister of Trade (January 7, 1957), BAB, DL2/4416, "Aktennotiz über Besprechung mit dem koreanischen Handeslrat" (undated), BAB, DL2/1686; and "Delegationsleiter Protokoll über die gemeinsame Sitzung der Import-und Export-Kommission" (January–February 1956), BAB, DL2/4407.

181 Stasch and Präßler to Rau (July 10, 1957), BAB, DY/30/IV2/6.06/21.

182 Fischer, "Aktenvermerk" (August 5, 1954), PAAA, MfAA/A5575.

183 "Vorschlag für deutsche Kader: Strukturplan 'Bauindustrie...'" (January 3, 1955), BAB, DL2/1686.

184 Selbmann, "Jahresbericht der DAG Hamhung für 1955," BAB, DL2/4411.

185 Tille to Nimschke (August 1, 1955), BAB, DY36/1176. See also Tille's letter to the Korean Construction Workers' Trade Union (August 11, 1955) on the occasion of the tenth anniversary of the national independence.

186 Betriebsgewerkschaftsleitung (BGL), Bericht (July 8, 1955), BAB, DY36/1176.

187 DAG, Quarterly Report, 1. Quarter 1956 (April 1956), BAB, DY36/1176, and DAG, Quarterly Report, 2. Quarter 1956, Teil 2., in BAB, DL2/4397.

188 Among the extensive materials documenting these problems, see minutes of staff meetings on June 24 and 27 and on November 6, 1955, BAB, DL2/4398. The DAG became more stable as the East Germans working there coopted friends and relatives to take the place of departing workers.

189 "Erinnerung. Hartmut Colden (1915–1982)," BAB, Sgy30/2222. Doehler was one of the persons accused of moral misconduct. He was recalled to East Germany, but then sent back to North Korea, where he was once again accused of misconduct toward Korean women and toward Koreans in general. Minutes of staff meeting (May 26, 1955), BAB, DL2/4398; and DAG to Ambassador Fischer (May 6, 1957), BAB, DL2/4402.

190 Hubert Matthes, "Hugo Namslauer zum Gedenken," *Studienarchiv Umweltgeschichte* 5 (1999), 31–32; and www.arbeitskreis-konfrontatio nen.de/Kunst_als_Zeugnis/Erinnerungskulturen/Ravensbrueck (accessed June 12, 2012).

191 www.hermsdorf-regional.de/ehemalige/praessler-horst/start.html (accessed June 12, 2012).

192 Wolfgang Bauer, Reportage: "Die letzte Stadt der DDR. Ein Besuch in Hamhung," www.wolfgang-bauer.info/pages/reportagen/nordkorea/nordkorea. html (accessed September 12, 2007).

193 Präßler, Note (May 14, 1956), BAB, DL2/4402.

194 Minutes (October 3, 1955), BAB, DL2/4398; Baustab, Note (October 25, 1955), BAB, DL2/4422; and "Collective Resolution" (August 1, 1957), and DAG to Guhlich (August 8, 1957), both in BAB, DY/30/IV2/6.06/21.

195 "Entwicklung der DAG Hamhung," BAB, DL2/4402.

196 Minutes of a meeting of the BGL (June 8, 1955), BAB DY36/1176.

197 Georg Nimschke, the chairman of the BGL, to Tille (June 10, 1955), BAB, DY36/1176.

198 BGL to Tille (July 12, 1956), BAB, DY36/1176.

199 Chair of the Korean Democratic Women's Organization of the Construction Trust No. 18 to Frauenbund des VEB Bau-Union Hoyerswerda (January 21,

1957), and director of Ham Nam Bautrust to director of VEB Bau-Union (June 22, 1957), both in BAB, DY/30/IV2/6.06/21.

200 Minutes (May 23, 1955 and May 30, 1955), BAB, DL2/4398.

201 Präßler, Quarterly Report (April 1956), BAB, DY36/1176; Minutes of DAG staff meetings (May 12, 1955 and October 29, 1955), BAB, DL2/4398; and unidentified press clipping "Hamhung im Aufbau durch die Hilfe des deutschen Volkes," BAB, DY/30/IV2/6.06/21.

202 Secretary of the Korean Workers' Party at the construction trust No. 18 to his counterpart at the VEB Bau-Union Hoyerswerda (January 21, 1957), BAB, DY/30/IV2/6.06/21.

203 DAG Leitung-Kollektiv (Präßler, Stasch, Hessel) to Rudi Guhlich (June 24, 1957), BAB, DL2/4402.

204 Präßler, Quarterly Report (April 1956), BAB, DY36/1176.

205 Data on the makeup of the East German mission taken from annual reports, 1956–9, in BAB, DL/4397 and BAB, DL2/4416.

206 Präßler to Gulich (May 24, 1957), BAB, DL2/4402, DAG Leitung-Kollektiv to Guhlich (June 24, 1957), BAB, DY/30/IV2/6.06/21, and Guhlich to Josef Lux (Abt. Bauwesen beim ZKdSED) (June 29, 1957), BAB, DY/30/IV2/6.06/21.

207 Rechenschaftsbericht (July 8, 1955) and Report to Tille (July 12, 1956), both in BAB, DY36/1176; Stasch to Lux (July 13, 1957), BAB, DY/30/IV 2/6.06/20; and Präßler, Jahresschlußbericht für 1957 (January 20, 1958), BAB, DL2/4397.

208 DAG, "Jahresbericht für 1955," BAB, DL2/4411; Guhlich, Memo (October 25, 1955), BAB, DL2/4422; and Minutes of BLG meeting (April 3, 1957), BAB, DL2/4398.

209 *Hamhunger Heimatreportage*, No. 2 (October 26, 1959), BAB, DL2/4421.

210 *Hamhunger Heimatreportage*, No. 1 (July 1957), No. 2 (October 26, 1959), BAB, DL2/4421.

211 Minutes of DAG staff meetings (May 12 and 26, October 1 and 3, 1955, and April 3, 1957), BAB, DL2/4398; and Baustab, notes on interviews with the Germans who had just returned from Korea (October 18 and 25, 1955), BAB, DL2/4422.

212 Frank, *Die DDR und Nordkorea*, 35–36.

213 Quoted in Kim Myun, "East Germany's Hamhung Construction Project," *Minjog* 21 (June 1, 2005) (www.minjog21.com/news/read.php?idxno=1815).

214 In 1955, farmers were subjected to "excessive forced deliveries" of up to 50 percent of their harvest. Both domestic pressure and urging from Moscow forced the North Korean government to invest more in agriculture. See reports by the Hungarian embassy in Hamhung to the Hungarian Foreign Ministry (April 13, 1955, May 10, 1955, and August 17, 1955), *CWIHP Bulletin* 14/15 (Winter 2003/Spring 2004), 107–10, and Szalontai, "'You Have No Political Line of Your Own'," 90.

215 Minutes of DAG staff meeting (June 10, 1955), BAB, DL2/4398.

216 Guhlich, Note (October 25, 1955), BAB, DL2 /4422.

217 Minutes of DAG staff meeting (April 3, 1957), BAB, DL2/4398.

218 Report on the visit of Kim Il Sung and a deputy premier in Hamhung on March 21-22, 1957, BAB, DL2/4416.
219 DAG to Rau (July 10, 1957), BAB, DL2/4416.
220 Manfred Nutz, *Stadtentwicklung in Umbruchsituationen: Wiederaufbau und Wiedervereinigung* (Stuttgart, 1998), 75.
221 Christine Hannemann, *Die Platte: Industrialisierter Wohnungsbau in der DDR* (Vieweg, 1996), 61ff.
222 Nutz, *Stadtentwicklung in Umbruchsituationen*, 72.
223 Report on the First Baukonferenz (no date, but presumably February 1956), BAB, DL2/4426.
224 DAG, "Gedankenkonzeption" (December 18, 1956), BAB, DL2/4416.
225 DAG, Quarterly Report (April 1956), BAB, DY36/1176, and Präßler, "Expose" (January 10, 1956), BAB, DL2/4416. Although the Soviets had only achieved a paltry 6-percent increase in productivity in their work on the fertilizer plant that they were building in the region, these figures quietly glossed over the greater degree of complexity involved in the construction of the Soviet plant.
226 DAG to Rau (July 10, 1957), BAB, DL2/4416.
227 Präßler, "Jahresschlußbericht" (January 20, 1958), BAB, DL2/4397.
228 Präßler, "Gedankenkonzepten zum Beschluss des Zentralkomitees der Partei der Arbeit Koreas...," (December 18, 1956), BAB, DL2/4416.
229 DAG, Quarterly Report (April 1956), BAB, DY36/1176.
230 DAG to Rau (July 10, 1957), BAB, DL2/4416.
231 Szalontai, *Kim Il Sung in the Khrushchev Era*, 121–3.
232 DAG, "Protokoll über die Parteileitungssitzung" (December 28, 1957), BAB, DY/30/IV2/6.06/20.
233 Förster to Fischer (May 14, 1958), Guhlich to Förster (June 26, 1958), Förster to Fischer (July 1, 1958), and minutes of a meeting with the chair of the State Construction Committee on September 10, 1958 (September 13, 1958), all in BAB, DL2/4416. Szalontoi, *Kim Il Sung in the Khrushchev Era*, 147–8, 154.
234 Minutes of a meeting with chairman of the State Construction Committee in Pyongyang (September 10, 1958), BAB, DL2/4416. See also Szalontai, *Kim Il Sung in the Khrushchev Era*, 134f.
235 Protokoll der Parteileitungssitzung vom 3.12.1957 (December 4, 1957), and Stasch to ZKdSED (December 6, 1957), both in BAB, DY/30/IV2/6.06/20.
236 Protokoll über die Parteileitungssitzung (November 23, 1957), BAB, DY/30/IV2/6.06/20.
237 Choi Hak-Su, 평양시간 (*Pyongyang Hour*, Pyongyang, 1976).
238 *Pyongyang Hour*, 127, 156–58.
239 *Ibid.*, 179, 37.
240 Protocol of a meeting with Kim Il Sung (February 1, 1958), BAB, DL2/4416,
241 The Polish embassy, Note on the Korean Five Year Plan (June 18, 1958). WWIC, North Korea International Documentation Project. Document Reader. "New Evidence on North Korea's Chollima Movement and First Five-Year Plan (1957–1961)," ed., James Person (February 2009).

242 Förster to Fischer (July 1, 1958), BAB, DL2/4416; and Förster, Semi-annual report (July 28, 1958), BAB, DL2/4397, "New Evidence on North Korea's Chollima Movement and First Five-Year Plan."

243 Baustab Korea, IA, to Guhlich (November 8, 1960), BAB, DL2/4399.

244 Letter of November 5, 1960, cited in Schneidewind to Schwab (November 11, 1960), WWIC.

245 Baustab Korea to the Presidium of the Ministerrat (June 27, 1962), BAB, DL2/4408.

246 Bauer, Reportage: "Die letzte Stadt der DDR. Ein Besuch in Hamhung".

247 *Ibid.*

248 Britta-Susann Lübke, "Das Märchenland meiner Kindheit. Die Rückkehr meines Vaters nach Hamhung (2002)" in Christoph Moeskes, ed., *Nordkorea. Einblicke in ein rätselhaftes Land* (Berlin, 2004), citations 138, 144.

249 www.koreaverband.de/kultur/film/filmTip.html "Nordkorea – eine Wiederkehr. Der Traum vom Tausend-Mond-Fluß" broadcast on June 30, 2003 (22.10 – 23.40 on arte). Ein Film von Britta Lübke (Eine Produktion von Radio Bremen für Arte D/Nordkorea 2003).

250 The couple's story was widely covered in the press. See, for example, Jack Kim, "After 46 years, Couple Hope to Meet again in North Korea," *The Guardian* (August 24, 2007); and Cho Sang-Hun, "German Woman Seeks Reunion with North Korean Husband," *New York Times* (August 22, 2007). See also Ryu Kwon-ha, "North Korean Husband of German Woman Is Alive," *JoongAng Ilbo* (February 13, 2007); Wieland Wagner, "Eine Liebe damals in Jena," *Der Spiegel* 36 (2007), 134; "Couple Reunited in North Korea after 47 Years," *New York Times* (August 6, 2006); and "North Korea Allows a Separated Couple to Reunite after 47 years," *JoongAng Ilbo* (August 5, 2008). Hong Ok Geun was remarried and had three children in Hamhung.

251 United Nations, *Korea and the United Nations* (New York, 1950), 10.

252 On July 25, the U.S. military also issued an order to shoot anyone caught crossing defense lines. This order resulted in the July 26 massacre of civilians at No Gun Ri, an event that has been the object of much recent attention. See Charles J. Hanley, Sang-hun Choe, and Martha Mendoza, *The Bridge at No Gun Ri: A Hidden Nightmare from the Korean War* (New York, 2001); Sahr Conway-Lanz, "Beyond No Gun Ri: Refugees and the United States Military in the Korean War," *DH* 29:1 (January 2005), 49–81; and Saang-woo Lee's 2009 film *A Little Pond*.

253 "Security Council Resolution of July 31, 1950," in United Nations, *Korea and the United Nations*, 28.

254 *Ibid.*

255 "Procedures for Co-ordination in the Handling of Assistance to the Republic of Korea: Relief Measures," ARCL (uncatalogued).

256 United Nations, *Korea and the United Nations*, 27.

257 *Ibid.*, 53.

258 *Ibid.*, 27.

259 Similar sentiments can be found in the documents compiled by UN Economic and Social Council for the 11ᵗʰ Session of the Executive Board (E/1851/ Rev.1), ARCL (uncatalogued).

260 With regard to the UN Korean Reconstruction Agency (UNKRA), we know the answer was no. UNKRA was established in December 1950 as a UN operational agency responsible for relief and rehabilitation in the post-hostility period. Gene M. Lyons, "American Policy and the United Nations' Program for Korean Reconstruction," *IO* 12:2 (Spring, 1958), 180–92; and Lyons, *Military Policy and Economic Aid: the Korean Case, 1950–1953* (Columbus, OH, 1961).

261 Joseph C. Goulden, *Korea: The Untold Story of the War* (New York, 1983); and Paul Edwards, *Unusual Footnotes to the Korean War* (Oxford, 2013).

262 The British Red Cross to the LRC (July 20, 1951), ARCL (uncatalogued).

263 Public Information Office, UN Command (August 18, 1950), and Requests by the Unified Command. Nos. 1, 2, and 3, dated, respectively, August 5 and September 1, 1950, both in ARCL (uncatalogued).

264 UN Economic and Social Council, "Assistance for the Civil Population of Korea," Report by the Secretary General (October 11, 1950), and General Headquarter, UN Command, Public Information Office (August 18, 1950), all in ARCL. See also "World Health Organization. Director-General in London," *The British Medical Journal* 2:4687 (November 4, 1950), 1049; and *Korea and the United Nations*, 28.

265 Julian Przybos, Minister of Poland to WHO (August 15, 1950), AWHO, OD 14–1.

266 Boudreau, "International Health," 1477–82, citation 1477f.

267 Andrew Cordier, Executive Assistant to the Secretary General, to the LRC (September 29, 1950), ARCL (uncatalogued). The LRC worked as a clearing house for the assistance provided by those national Red Cross societies that were willing to help meet these specified needs.

268 Correspondence between the American Red Cross, the Advisory Committee on Voluntary Foreign Aid (at the State Department), the Church World Services, and the American Relief for Korea as well as General Headquarters, UN Command, Public Health and Welfare Section, all in NARA RG 331, Box 9436.

269 Directives by command of General MacArthur (September 2, 1950), ARCL (uncatalogued). The UN Command established the Public Health and Welfare Section (PHW) on September 2. This was the origin of the military civilian relief organization, whose official name was the UN Command Public Health and Welfare Section Field Organization National Level Team. In addition, in September 1950, a Central Joint Committee for Relief was founded to coordinate the relief work of the PHW and the South Korean government. Deputy Chief Pollock, "Civilian Relief Program in Korea" (November 10, 1950), NARA RG 331, Box 9436; and Public Health and Welfare, UNC, Field Organization in Korea, Semi-monthly report, "Civilian

Refugee Relief Program in Korea," Report No. 1 (Autumn 1950), NARA RG 554, Box 90.

270 ROK Ministry of Social Affairs, "Statement of General Reporting" (May 15, 1951), NARA RG 331, Box 9432. A year later, 50 percent of the country's 20 million citizens were still in need of assistance. J. N. Byler, "Report on Korea" (June 6, 1952).

271 General Headquarters, Supreme Commander for the Allied Powers, Medical Section to the Surgeon General USPHS (November 29, 1951), NARA RG 331, Box 9432. A number of military personnel also worked at UNCACK.

272 Lt. General van Fleet, Eighth U.S. Army, Appendix 1 (Civil Affairs in Korea) to Annex C (Personnel) June 25, 1951, NARA RG 554, Box 65.

273 Cheju-Do Team (7–13 February 1951), NARA RG 554, Box 90.

274 ROK Ministry of Social Affairs, Distribution List of Relief Goods Donated from the various governments and voluntary societies. May 13, 1951, NARA RG 331, Box 9432.

275 Minutes of a meeting of the Central Relief Committee (January 24, 1951), NARA RG 331, Box 9432; and Kyongsang Nam Do Team (5–11 Feb. 1951), NARA RG 554, Box 90.

276 Brindley E. Harris, "Kimchon Trip" (January 21, 1951), NARA RG554, Box 90 Entry A-1 1309.

277 Headquarters, Eighth Army to CINCUNC (July 2, 1951), and Report of the General Headquarters Survey Group, "The Economic Stabilization Program," approved by Chief of Staff, the Far East Command (December 31, 1951), both in NARA RG 554, Box 65.

278 Brigadier General Crist, Commanding General, UNCACK, to Commanding General, Eighth Army (December 28, 1951), NARA RG 554, Box 65.

279 State Department to SCAP (October 1, 1950), NARA RG 554, Box 65.

280 Allan Loren, Memorandum to Ambassador Muccio (May 26, 1951), NARA RG 554, Box 65.

281 General MacArthur, UN Command to Commanding General, Eighth U.S. Army Korea (April 2, 1951), and General Ridgway to Commanding General, Eighth Army (May 24, 1951), both in NARA RG 554, Box 65.

282 Commander in Chief, the Far East Command to the Department of Army (February 26, 1951), and John B. Coulter, Deputy Army Commander, Eighth Army to Arthur Rucker, Deputy Agent General of the UNKRA (June 28, 1951), both in NARA RG 554, Box 65. After mid-1952, voluntary aid groups were permitted to participate in small-scale community development programs.

283 Ch'oe, Hyŏng-sik, *Germany's Rearmament and the Korean War* (Seoul, 2002 [in Korean]).

284 Geßler had served as defense minister for most of the Weimar period (1920–8) and then as Reich Commissar for Voluntary Medical Service until 1933. He was the president of the German Red Cross from 1950 to 1952. The meetings were held in secret because the allies had not yet given permission for the German government to act in matters of defense and security. In

July 1951, the allies gave permission for the establishment of civilian air defense programs. See Dieter Riesenberger, *Das Deutsche Rote Kreuz: Eine Geschichte 1864–1990* (Paderborn, 2002), 400–3.

285 Rainer Schwierczinski, "Das THW im Bundesamt für Zivilschutz," in Bundesamt für Bevölkerungsschutz und Katastrophenhilfe, ed., *50 Jahre Zivil- und Bevölkerungsschutz in Deutschland* (Bonn, 2008), 38–45.

286 Correspondence (May 1951) between the German Red Cross, the Interior Ministry, and the LRC, ADRK 2216; and note (June 4, 1964), ADRK 2806. Sixteen of the men who were scheduled to serve as part of this Korea-deployment program took part in the first training course sponsored by the THW when it began operation in 1953, Akademie für Krisenmanagement, Notfallplannung und Zivilschutz des Bundesverwaltungsamtes – Zentralstelle für Zivilschutz, ed., *50 Jahre Ausbildung im Bevölkerungsschutz* (Bad Honnef, 2003), 42.

287 Michael Geyer, "Cold War Angst: The Case of West-German Opposition to Rearmament and Nuclear Weapons" in Hanna Schissler, ed., *The Miracle Years: A Cultural History of West Germany, 1949–1968* (Princeton, NJ, 2001), 376–408; Bert-Oliver Manig, *Die Politik der Ehre: Die Rehabilitierung der Berufssoldaten in der frühen Bundesrepublik* (Göttingen, 2004); and David Clay Large, *Germans to the Front: West German Rearmament in the Adenauer Era* (Chapel Hill, NC, 1996).

288 Hartmann, Secretary General of the DRK, to DRK-Landesverbände and Verband Deutscher Mutterhäuser vom Roten Kreuz (April 18, 1953), ADRK 429. The mission was originally scheduled to leave on October 1, 1953. Some of the reports criticized Adenauer's offer as a policy of imperialism. See "Deutsche nach Korea," *Nordeutsches Echo* (April 9, 1953); "Feldlazarett nach Wehrmachtmuster" *Westdeutsche Zeitung* (April 10, 1953); "Deutsches Rotes Kreuz überrascht" *SZ* (April 11, 1953); and "Das deutsche Korea-Lazarett. Aufbau nach dem Muster einer Sanitätskompanie," *Rhein-Zeitung* (April 10, 1953).

289 "'Gestellungsbefehl': Ab nach Korea," *Generalanzeiger* (November 14, 1953), and "Deutsches Lazarett für Südkorea," *Neue Zeitung* (November 20, 1953), both in PAAA, B92/281; Trützschler to Glässing (November 13, 1953) and Glässing, "Pressekonferenz DRK-Hospital Korea" (November 26, 1955), both in PAAA, B92/281; and AA to DRK (October 10, 1953 and December 21, 1953), ADRK 2806.

290 "'Gestellungsbefehl' nach Korea," *Mittag* (November 12, 1953), AA to DRK (November 16, 1955), both in PAAA, B92/281. See also "Abschied von Bonn," *Generalanzeiger* (January 30–31, 1954), "Flug zu den Witwen und Waisen," *Christ und Welt* (January 28, 1954), "Sterbende Hoffen auf das Grosse Wunder," *Lippische Landes-Zeitung* (June 19, 1954), and "Tausende standen vor dem Hospital: Die Koreaner erwarten Wunder von dem deutschen Feldlazarett in Pusan," *Mannheimer Morgen* (June 19, 1954), all in ADRK 429.

291 Adenauer personally welcomed Kohler at the train station Cologne on January 1, 1954. Bernd P. Laufs, "Der Arzt von Stalingrad: Projektionsfläche für die Suche nach dem guten Deutschen," *DÄ* 105: 25 (June 20,

2008), A 1385. Heinz G. Konsalik's *Der Arzt von Stalingrad* (1956) was modeled on Kohler and became instantly a best seller when it was published in 1956. See also Robert G. Moeller, *War Stories, The Search for a Usable Past in the Federal Republic* (Berkeley, CA, 2001); and Frank Biess, *Homecoming: Returning POWs and the Legacies of Defeat in Postwar Germany* (Princeton, NJ, 2006).

292 Paul Weindling, *Nazi Medicine and the Nuremberg Trials: From Medical War Crimes to Informed Consent* (New York, 2004).

293 Sigrid Oehler-Klein and Volker Roelcke, eds., *Vergangenheitspolitik in der universitären Medizin nach 1945: Institutionelle und individuelle Strategien im Umgang mit dem Nationalsozialismus* (Stuttgart, 2007); Norbert Frei, *Adenauer's Germany and the Nazi Past: The Politics of Amnesty and Integration* (New York, 2002); Timothy R. Vogt, *Denazification in Soviet-occupied Germany: Brandenburg, 1945–1948* (Cambridge, MA., 2000); and Ulrich Brochhagen, *Nach Nürnberg: Vergangenheitsbewältigung und Westintegration in der Ära Adenauer* (Hamburg, 1994).

294 D. Riesenberger, *Das Deutsche Rote Kreuz*, 344–6.

295 AA, "Entwurf Aufzeichnung" (May 14, 1958), PAAA, B92/293.

296 Krekeler to AA (June 4, 1953, and September 23, 1953), PAAA, B92/281.

297 West Germany and the United States signed an agreement concerning the hospital on February 12, 1954. The Foreign Office told the Red Cross that, beyond than lending its name to the hospital, the organization would play virtually no role in the operation of the mission. See also the DRK "Dienstanweisung" for the Hospital in Pusan, PAAA, B92/281.

298 "Stichworte für Bericht Korea-Hospital in der Präsidiumssitzung v. 23.03.1954," ADRK 2806.

299 Lyons, "American Policy and the United Nations' Program for Korean Reconstruction"; and David Ekbladh, *The Great American Mission*, Chapter 4.

300 Delia Pergande, *Private Voluntary Aid in Vietnam: The Humanitarian Politics of Catholic Relief Services and CARE, 1954–1965* (Dissertation, University of Kentucky, 1999).

301 Edith M. Alexander, WHO Regional advisor, "Supplementary Report of Field Visit to Korea" (WPRO/MCH/4A/56, August 20, 1956). In South Vietnam, the Voluntary Agencies Coordination Committee was created right after the signing of the 1954 Geneva Accords.

302 Pusan Girls Junior School to Huwer (May 25, 1955), PAAA, B92/281.

303 Huwer to ROK Health Minister (September 10, 1954) and to the German Interior Ministry (August 24, 1955), both in ADRK 683; and Huwer to Governor Lee (May 30, 1955) and the DRK General Secretary (June 8, 1955), both in PAAA, B92/281.

304 Kurt Witting, "Tätigkeitsbericht" (February 26, 1954), PAAA, B92/281; and Rainer Schopp, "Tätigkeitsbericht des DRK-Hospitals Korea" (February to July 1955, and July to December 1955), ADRK 429.

305 Letter from Christine Dörmer (February 5, 1954), ADRK 433.

306 Letter from Imelda Wieners (February 19, 1954), ADRK 430. They also noted that many of the Westerners had spent time in Germany and that they

all had only good things to say about the country. Letter from Hertha Ernst (March 5, 1954), ADRK 430.

307 Berlin Document Center (BDC), DS/B32/Bild Nr. 2683, "Prof. Dr. med. Günther Huwer," *DÄ* 89:40 (Oktober 2, 1992), 3253, and Norbert Jachertz, "Deutscher Arzt in China – Prof. Huwer und die deutschchinesische Medizintradition," *DÄ* 79:2 (January 15, 1982), 24–26.

308 Generaloberin Luise von Oertzen, "Bericht über das DRK-Hospital in Pusan," ADRK 429.

309 "Personalien der DRK-Mitglieder vom Hospital Korea," PAAA, B 92/289. The hospital administrator, Emilie Thürmer (1907–?), was a long-time companion of Huwer.

310 BDC, PK/D34/Bild-Nr. 343, "Berufliche Werdegang" PAAA, B 92/288; and "Varia: Personalien," *DÄ* 93:18 (1996), A-1214. Around 1941, the government had considered him for a position in the colonial administrative service.

311 Paul Weindling, *Epidemics and Genocide in Eastern Europe, 1890–1945* (Oxford, 2000), has shown how the military and the SS exploited and sponsored such research.

312 Guido Zöller, "Deutsche Ärzte in Pusan: Bemerkungen zu einem Erlebnisbericht," *Rheinischer Merkur* (May 8, 1959).

313 BDC, RS (Rasse-und Siedlungshauptamt SS) B499, Bild-Nr. 2835. See also Dr. Leo Nonn to Huwer (November 14, 1955), PAAA, B 92/288.

314 BAK, BW 24/14653; and "VARIA: Personalien," *DÄ* 102:31–32 (2005), A-2190, B-1850, and C-1750.

315 Korea-Einsatz, ADRK 429; and the contract form, ADRK 435.

316 Fritz Korte, ed., "Als Krankenschwester an der Ostfront (1941–1945). Teil I," *Neue Nettelstedter Blätter*, No. 31 (December 1997), 2.

317 Verband der Schwesternschaften vom Deutschen Roten Kreuz, ed., *Rotkreuzschwestern* (Hildesheim, 2007).

318 BDC, EWZ-Baltikum/B48/Bild Nr. 1973, "Presseinformation: Rotes Kreuz trauert um Isa Gräfin von der Goltz" (May 17, 2007), (archive.is/ZshQp; accessed December 28, 2011).

319 Oertzen to Huwer (November 21, 1957), ADRK 429.

320 Jens Eber and Sibylle Penkert, eds., *Briefe einer Rotkreuzschwester von der Ostfront* (Göttingen, 2006); Ingeborg Ochsenknecht, *"'Als ob der Schnee alles zudeckte': Eine Krankenschwester erinnert sich. Kriegseinsatz an der Ostfront"* (Munich, 2004); and Elfriede Schade-Bartkowiak, *Sag mir, wo die Blumen sind: Unter der Schwesternhaube. Kriegserinnerungen einer DRK-Schwester im II. Weltkrieg an der Ostfront* (Hamburg, 1989). See also Andreas Frewer, Bernhard Bremberger, Günther Siedbürger, eds., *Der "Ausländereinsatz" im Gesundheitswesen (1939–1945): Historische und ethische Probleme der NS-Medizin* (Stuttgart, 2009).

321 Oertzen to Margarethe Bruhn (September 10, 1953), ADRK 430.

322 Cited in Mac Hillard, "West Germany Aids U.N. Effort in Korea," *Stars and Stripes*, cited in Herzt's letter to AA (November 10, 1956), PAAA, B92/292.

323 Letter from Eva Fechthrup (June 19, 1954), ADRK 430.

324 R. Schopp, "Tätigkeitsbericht des DRK-Hospitals Korea vom Februar bis Juli 1955," ADRK (uncatalogued), and AA, "Hospital Korea" (March 23, 1955), ADRK 2806.

325 Consul General Richard Herzt to AA (November 10, 1956), PAAA, B92/292; and Bommert and Hannak to DRK-Bundesarzt Dr. Buurman (March 13, 1958 and April 13, 1958), PAAA, B92/293.

326 Herzt to AA (November 10, 1956), PAAA, B92/292.

327 Hans Bommert in "Anlage zum Protokoll vom 6.11.1959," ADRK 2222; and Bommert and Hannak to DRK-Bundesarzt Dr. Buurman (March 13, 1958 and April 13, 1958), PAAA, B92/293.

328 Semi-annual reports (1957 I & II), PAAA, B92/292; and "Entwurf Reisebericht Ritgen," ADRK 2220. See also Buurman, "Korea: Besuchsbericht," ADRK 2214.

329 Ritgen, "Reisebericht," ADRK 2220.

330 Huwer to DRK (June 21, 1955), PAAA, B92/300. There was also one refugee doctor, a former professor of epidemiology and public health at a university in North Korea. This man had seven children to support; and although his expertise and experience in the field was highly valued by German doctors at the hospital, he was asked to work at the German hospital without pay for a year.

331 Huwer to DRK (December 12, 1955), PAAA, B92/287.

332 Hertz to AA (October 31, 1956), PAAA, B92/292; "Ecclesiastical Matters and Assistance for German Hospitals, Vortrag von Dr. König am 6.10.1956 vor Vertretern der WEU im Auswärtigen Amt," PAAA, B92/292.

333 Witting, Semi-annual Report (January – June 1957), PAAA, B92/292.

334 Huwer, Report (July 1954), PAAA, B92/291.

335 Engelberg, Reports, ADRK 2217.

336 "Liste der examinierten koreanischen Schwestern" (April 1957), ADRK 429. Huwer and Oerzten did not succeed in persuading the BMI to grant German nursing certificates to the first class of Korean graduates, who had been trained at the German hospital in Pusan, and who subsequently passed the exam. BMI to Oerzten (July 13, 1957), ADRK 429.

337 ROK Health Ministry to Huwer (September 10, 1954), ADRK 435.

338 Letter from Wegener (March 12, 1956), ADRK 433.

339 Correspondence between Huwer and both the ROK health minister (September 10, 1954) and the BMI (August 24, 1955), ADRK 683.

340 BDC, PK/D151/Bild-Nr 2187.

341 Graumann to Foreign Minister Brentano (January 15, 1959), DRK to Consul Kindler in Seoul (August 6, 1957), secretary general of the DRK to AA (March 24, 1959), all in PAAA, B92/287. Although Graumann had joined the Nazi Party in 1933, he had risked his life and career by helping Jewish doctors escape to Switzerland, and he had also hidden a Jewish man during the war. Graumann to Samuel Teitler (August 11, 1946; March 15, 1950), Archiv für Zeitgeschichte Zürich, Nachlass Dr. Samuel Teitler.

342 "Erklärung" (January 9, 1956), PAAA, B92/287. In the face of such criticisms, Huwer asked the doctors to sign a form supporting his continued leadership.

343 See the interviews with the physicians conducted by the DRK Bundesarzt, Buurman (November 6, 1959), ADRK 2222.

344 Zöller, "Deutsche Ärzte in Pusan" *Rh.*

345 Hannak to Buurman (July 28, 1958), PAAA, B92/293.

346 *Ibid.*

347 Hannak to Neuffer (July 21, 1958), PAAA, B92/293.

348 For detailed first-hand accounts, see ADRK 2234.

349 Franz Josef Rosenbaum, Report to German Red Cross Secretary General (September 23, 1958), ADRK 2234.

350 Inge Napp to Oerzten (October 15, 1958), ADRK 2234.

351 Huwer to DRK General Secretary (October 13, 1958), PAAA, B92/293.

352 Buurman, Bericht (early 1959), PAAA, B92/292.

353 The German Chamber of Physicians awarded Huwer its prestigious Paracelsus Medal.

354 Paul Adenauer to the president of the DRK (October 16, 1958), ADRK 2234. In this letter, Adenauer cited a report, which described the hospital as "a gathering of former Nazis, a brother, a disgrace for Germany, the incompetence of the head doctor, including his interaction with the Koreans, disregard for local patients." The president of the DRK met with Foreign Minister Brentano, who finally agreed that keeping the hospital open would not be in the best interest of Germany's international reputation. Weitz to the vice president of the DRK, Bargatzky (October 26, 1958), ADRK 2234.

355 Drescher [under the pseudonym Stefan W. Escher], "Unterricht im Mitleiden," *Handelsblatt* (May 10/11, 1957). German nurses also echoed Huwer's charge that Koreans did not help each other or even look twice at dead bodies lying in the streets. For example, see the letter from Wegener (March 12, 1956), ADRK 433.

356 Stefan W. Escher [Drescher], *Das Jahr in Pusan: Logbuch eines Arztes* (Munich, 1959), 114.

357 Oertzen, "Bericht über das DRK-Hospital in Pusan," and Rosenbaum to DRK Secretary General (October 16, 1958), ADRK 2234.

358 Rosenbaum to DRK Secretary General (September 23, 1958), ADRK 2220.

359 *Das Jahr in Pusan*, 70.

360 *Ibid.*, 55, 70.

361 "Eine rettende Insel in der Flut des Elends," *General Anzeiger* (July 27, 1955).

362 Uli Faber, "Kindernot in Korea," *General Anzeiger* (June 15–16, 1957).

363 See the interviews with the physicians conducted by Dr. Buurman (November 6, 1959), ADRK 2222, as well as Zöller, "Deutsche Ärzte in Pusan."

364 Faber, "Kindernot in Korea."

365 Napp to Oertzen (October 25, 1958), ADRK 435.

366 *Das Jahr in Pusan*, 184.

367 *Ibid.*, 57.

368 AA, internal correspondence (February 10, 1959), PAAA, B92/301.

369 See "Nase Zukneifen: DRK-Lazarett," *Der Spiegel*, Nr. 5/1959 (January 28, 1959), 33–34; "Prügel gab's für die Patienten. Deutsche Ärzte schädigten

unseren Ruf im Ausland," *Der Stern* (February 7, 1959); and "Anfang gut –
Ende peinlich," *Die Welt* (February 1, 1959).

370 Lucie Schulz to Redaktion des Sonntagsblattes (February 6, 1959), "Notizen
von dem Telefongespräch mit dem Abteilungsleiter der Propaganda-
Abteilung der Tageseitung 'Die Welt' am 13.2.59," and Huwer to former
employees (February 7, 1959), both in ADRK 429. Oertzen's letter was
published in *Sonntagsblatt* on February 8, 1959. See also Hille, Note (February 10, 1959), PAAA, B92/301.

371 "Etwas bleibt hängen," *FAZ* (no date), ADRK 429.

372 *The Hanguk Ilbo*, a leading Korean newspaper, noted with disapproval the
sense of superiority on the part of the Germans and warned that their
contemptuous attitude toward the Koreans could harm relations between
the two anti-communist countries. See the clipping (February 16, 1959),
PAAA, B92/301.

373 Buurmann, "Leserbrief an das Sonntagsblatt" (February 3, 1959),
ADRK 429.

374 "Das deutsche Hospital war sehr gefragt," *Kieler Nachrichten* (January 22,
1959). Among the many media reports on the scandal, see "'Herrenmenschen'
blamieren uns," *Berliner Zeitung* (January 22 1959), "'Engel arbeiten nicht im
Krankenhaus'," *FAZ* (January 21, 1959), and "'In Pusan arbeiten keine
Engel'," *Die Tat* (February 3, 1959), all available in ADRK 429.

375 Escher [Drescher], "Wie war es wirklich in Pusan?" *Christ und Welt* (February 12, 1959), ADRK 429.

376 The Foreign Office, however, recognized that such action would lead to a
negative public reaction (July 21, 1959).

377 "'In Pusan arbeiten keine Engel.'"

378 "Pusan-Chefarzt Huwer abgewiesen," *FAZ* (October 28, 1959), ADRK 429;
and Zöller, "Deutsche Ärzte in Pusan."

379 See the materials in ADRK 262, 2222, and 2234.

380 Weitz to Huwer (January 7, 1960), ADRK 2234.

381 Deutsches Rotes Kreuz, *Fünf Jahre DRK-Hospital Pusan. Der Korea-Einsatz
des Deutschen Roten Kreuzes* (Bonn, 1959).

382 *Sten. Ber.*, 80. Sitzung (September 15, 1959), 4378.

383 As part of this process, in November 1959, the Catholic Church created its
Working Group for Development Aid to build "educational and social-
charitable organizations in developing countries" and to recruit and train
aid workers overseas. Hein Bastian, *Die Westdeutschen und die Dritte
Welt* (Oldenburg, 2006), 61–72. In 1962, Brot für die Welt created its own
organization, the Dienst im Übersee.

384 AA to foreign missions, "Einrichtungen und Leistungen der deutschen christlichen Missionsgesellschaften im Ausland," (December 1960), PAAA, B92/
379. See also Bastian, *Die Westdeutschen und die Dritte Welt*, 61f.; and
Ulrich Willems, *Entwicklung, Interesse und Moral: Die Entwicklungspolitik
der Evangelischen Kirche in Deutschland* (Opladen, 1998), 244.

385 Note on German aid for Vietnam (November 18, 1966), PAAA, B37/326.

386 Wulff also testified at the International War Crimes Tribunal (Bertrand
Russell Tribunal) regarding what he had witnessed during his six-year stay

in the city. See Georg W. Alsheimer [E. Wulff], *Vietnamesische Lehrjahre: Bericht eines Arztes aus Vietnam, 1961–1967* (Frankfurt a.M., 1972).

387 "Aufstellung über Einsparungen beim DRK-Hospital in Pusan" (November 25, 1958), ADRK 2220.

388 Verband Deutscher Mutterhäuser to AA (January 15, 1960), and German embassy in Seoul (Bünger) to AA (January 10, 1961), both in PAAA, B58/90.

389 Despite their training, even those who studied abroad were still discriminated against upon their return. One good example is Henriette Bui, who was born in 1906 and would become Vietnam's first female physician. In 1935, she returned to Vietnam with a medical degree and naturalized French citizenship, but she was never accepted by the French medical establishment in Indochina. Tran Thi Liên, "Heinriette Bui: The Narrative of Vietnam's First Woman Doctor," in Gisele Bousquet and Pierre Brocheux, eds., *Viet Nam Exposé. French Scholarship on Twentieth-Century Vietnamese Society* (Ann Arbor, MI, 2002), 278–309.

390 The Central Board of the Union of Healthcare Workers, a report on a study visit to North Vietnam in October 1961 (March 15, 1962), PAAA, MfAA/A8586. The East German delegates were surprised to see that Vietnamese nurses were highly experienced and able to perform basic surgical procedures.

391 Laurence Monnais, "Preventive Medicine and 'Mission Civilisatrice'. Use of the BCG Vaccine in French Colonial Vietnam between the Two World Wars," *International Journal of Asia Pacific Studies* 2:1 (May 2006), 40–66; and Monnais and Noémi Tousignant, "The Colonial Life of Pharmaceuticals: Accessibility to Healthcare, Consumption of Medicines, and Medical Pluralism in French Vietnam, 1905–1945," *Journal of Vietnamese Studies* 1:1 (2005), 131–68.

392 Jacques M. May, *Siam Doctor* (Garden City, 1949), 178.

393 Ton That Tung, *Reminiscences of a Vietnamese Surgeon* (Hanoi, 1980), 9. In his autobiography, May described Tung in the following terms: "His French culture was irreproachable, and, rare feature, he spoke, wrote, and read English as well. ... As far as I could gather, he was one of the few of his generation to take a deep interest in the cases as human problems, not merely as surgical ones. [...] I wondered if he was the man selected by destiny to receive my hands in a yet distant future the torch just placed in them," *Siam Doctor*, 188f.

394 Tung, *Reminiscences*, 28.

395 Patricia M. Pelley, *Postcolonial Vietnam: New Histories of the National Past* (Durham, 2002); and Kim N. B. Ninh, *A World Transformed: The Politics of Culture in Revolutionary Vietnam, 1945–1965* (Ann Arbor, MI, 2002).

396 David G. Marr, *Vietnam: State, War, and Revolution* (Berkeley, CA, 2013); Stein Tonnesson, *Vietnam 1946: How the War Began* (Berkeley, CA, 2010); Mark Atwood Lawrence and Fredrik Logevall, eds., *The First Vietnam War: Colonial Conflict and Cold War Crisis* (Cambridge, MA, 2007); and Quiang Zhai, *China and Vietnam Wars, 1950–1975* (Chapel Hill, 2000).

397 Tung, *Reminiscences*, 30–2.

398 Fredrik Logevall, *Ambers of War: The Fall of an Empire and the Making of America's Vietnam* (New York, 2012); Mark Atwood Lawrence, *Assuming the Burden: Europe and the American Commitment to War in Vietnam* (Berkeley, CA, 2005); Edward Miller, *Misalliance: Ngo Dinh Diem, the United States, and the Fate of South Vietnam* (Cambridge, MA, 2013); and Mark Philip Bradley, *Imagining Vietnam and America: The Making of Postcolonial Vietnam, 1919–1950* (Chapel Hill, NC, 2002).

399 STEM – Indochina, "Report of Public Health Section. Prepared for Southeast Asia Conference of Public Health Programs, Bangkok, Thailand. August 6–11, 1951," NARA RG 469, Records of the US Foreign Assistance Agencies, 1948–1961: Mission to Vietnam, Box 2.

400 "Some Suggested Guiding Principles for the Production and Utilization of Audio-Visual Aids for Health Education and Promotion in Southeast Asia" (August 6, 1951), and Gerald F. Winfield, "The Use of Audio-Visual Aids in the Development of Community Saturation Educational Campaigns in Support of Health Work in SEA" (August 1, 1951), both in NARA, RG 469. Box 2. This community development program depended on coordinating the work of the STEM teams with that of the other U.S. agencies active in Vietnam, such as the U.S. Technical Cooperation Agency and the U.S. Information Service, and with the WHO and UNICEF.

401 "Some Suggested Guiding Principles..." See also Nick Cullather, "The Target Is the People: Representations of the Village in Modernization and U.-S. National Security Doctrine," *Cultural Politics* 2 (March 2006), 29–48.

402 "Some Suggested Guiding Principles..."

403 Geneviève de Galard, *The Angel of Dien Bien Phu. The Sole French Woman at the Decisive Battle in Vietnam*, tr. Isabelle Surcouf Toms (Annapolis, MD, 2010), citations 116, 119. She described the French who served at Dien Bien Phu not as colonizers frantically trying to hold on to the remnants of their empire, but as allies of the Vietnamese, who were locked in an "atrocious civil war in which Communist ideological propaganda was supported by a relentless use of terror." See also Ted Morgan, *Valley of Death. The Tragedy at Dien Bien Phu That Led America into the Vietnam War* (New York, 2010), 495; and Christopher Goscha, "Hell in a Very Small Place: Cold War and Decolonisation in the Assault on the Vietnamese Body at Dien Bien Phu," *European Journal of East Asian Studies* 9, 2 (2010), 201–23.

404 On Lansdale's role in the Philippines, see Alfred McCoy, *Policing America's Empire. The United States, the Philippines, and the Rise of the Surveillance State* (Madison, WI, 2009), 377f, 382f; and Jonathan Nashel, *Edward Lansdale's Cold War* (Amherst, MA, 2005).

405 Ilya V. Gaiduk, *Confronting Vietnam: Soviet Policy toward the Indochina Conflict, 1954–1963* (Stanford, CA, 2003), 50.

406 For a recent interpretation of the Conference based on declassified Vietnamese documents, see Pierre Asselin, "The Democratic Republic of Vietnam and the 1954 Geneva Conference: A Revisionist Critique," *Cold War History* 11, 2 (May 2011), 155–95.

407 Ronald B. Frankum, Jr., *Operation Passage to Freedom. The United States Navy in Vietnam, 1954–1955* (Lubbock, TX, 2007), 28.

408 James T. Fisher, *Dr. America. The Lives of Thomas A. Dooley, 1927–1961* (Amherst, MA, 1997), 69ff. William J. Lederer, a friend of Lansdale, played a key role in enabling Dooley's writings to reach a mass audience, first in *Reader's Digest* and then in book form. For more on the use of books as propaganda weapons, see Amanda Laugesen, "Books for the World: American Book Programs in the Developing World, 1948–1968," Greg Barnhisel and Catherine Turner, eds., *Pressing the Fight: Print, Propaganda, and the Cold War* (Amherst, MA, 2010), 126–44.

409 Thomas A. Dooley, *Deliver Us from Evil: The Story of Vietnam's Flight to Freedom* (New York, 1956), 101.

410 Fisher, *Dr. America*, 53ff. In his book, Dooley described Vietnamese refugees as a "stinking mass of humanity... [and a] miserable and diseased people." Dooley's low opinion of the refugees he encountered there did not receive as much publicity as his screeds against communism.

411 Lederer and Burdick, "Salute to Deeds of Non-Ugly Americans," *Life* (December 7, 1959), 148–63, cited in Fisher, *Dr. America*, 178. In *The Ugly American*, Colonel Hillandale was modeled on Lansdale, Fisher, *Dr. America*, 177.

412 Dooley to his mother (September 1954), cited in Fisher, *Dr. America*, 38, 40.

413 Thomas L. Ahern Jr., *Vietnam Declassified. The CIA and Counterinsurgency* (Louisville, KY, 2010), and Lansdale, *In the Midst of Wars* (New York, 1972).

414 Fisher, *Dr. America*, 135.

415 Miguel A. Bernad, *Adventure in Viet-Nam. The Story of Operation Brotherhood 1954–1957* (Manila, 1974), 31f. See also Joseph G. Morgan, *The Vietnam Lobby: The American Friends of Vietnam, 1955–1975* (Chapel Hill, NC, 1997).

416 Bernad, *Adventure in Viet-Nam*, 135–6. In July 1955, Marion Dix filmed a documentary on Operation Brotherhood, which was widely shown in the United States.

417 Bernad, *Adventure in Viet-Nam*, 60f., 191, 206. Operation Brotherhood staff also lobbied other Asian countries to join, and Taiwan, Hong Kong, Japan, Thailand, and Malaya-Singapore actually participated, *ibid.*, 291–318.

418 *Ibid.*, 71f., 237f., 322ff., citation 237.

419 Health and Sanitation Division, USOM to Dinh Quang Chieu, Administrator General, U.S. Economic Aid (February, 3, 1955), NARA RG 469. Box 11.

420 Lansdale to Chief, Medical Division, USOM (March 7, 1955), NARA RG 469. Box 11.

421 Richard W. Lindholm, ed., *Viet-Nam: The First Five Years* (East Lansing, MI, 1959). In South Vietnam, the WHO conducted BCG vaccination, malaria control, yaws eradication, maternal and child health, and nurse training programs, often in conjunction with UNICEF. One of the highest profile products of the U.S.-led multilateral medical aid project was the construction of the high-rise Children's Hospital in Saigon. Arthur Edward Brown, *A Public Health Odyssey* (Norwich, 2005), 171, 219.

422 Bernad, *Adventure in Viet-Nam*, 55.

423 Letter from Brown (February 1, 1956), cited in *A Public Health Odyssey*, 201.

424 South Korea had already been admitted to the WHO in August 1949, and South Vietnam, Laos, and Cambodia were all admitted in 1950. Taiwan retained its seat in the UN and the WHO as the legitimate representative of China (until 1971). Mongolia and North Korea were admitted to the WHO in 1962 and 1973, respectively.

425 Pierre Brocheux, *Ho Chi Minh: A Biography* (Cambridge, 2007), 145. Although Moscow recognized the DRV in January 1950, the Soviets did not open an embassy in Hanoi until September 1954.

426 China recognized the DRV on January 18, 1950. Qiang Zhai, *China and the Vietnam Wars, 1950–1975* (Chapel Hill, NC, 2000); and Mari Olsen, *Soviet-Vietnam Relations and the Role of China, 1949–64* (London, 2006).

427 Nianqun Yang, "Disease Prevention, Social Mobilization and Spatial Politics: The Anti-Germ Warfare Incident of 1952 and the 'Patriotic Health Campaign'," *The Chinese Historical Review* 11:2 (Fall 2004), 155–82. On mass health campaigns during the Nationalist era, see Chieko Nakajima, "Health and Hygiene in Mass Mobilization: Hygiene Campaigns in Shanghai, 1920–1945," *Twentieth-Century China* 34:1 (November 2008), 42–72.

428 Ruth Rogaski, *Hygienic Modernity: Meanings of Health and Disease in Treaty-Port China* (Berkeley, 2004); and Rogaski, "Nature, Annihilation, and Modernity: China's Korean War Germ-Warfare Experience Reconsidered," *Journal of Asian Studies* 61:2 (May 2002), 381–415.

429 "Öffentlicher Gesundheitsdienst in Vietnam," *Viet-Nam Bulletin* (September 5, 1955), in PAAA, MfAA/A8340.

430 Christopher Goscha, "A 'Total War' of Decolonization? Social Mobilization and State-Building in Communist Vietnam (1949–54), *War & Society* 31, 2 (August 2012), 136–62.

431 "Öffentlicher Gesundheitsdienst in Vietnam." See also Deputy Health Minister Dr. Pham Ngo Thach, "Das Gesundheitswesen in der DRV" (February 16, 1956), and Gottfried Molwitz, report on a study visit to North Vietnam (March 15, 1962), both in PAAA, MfAA/A8586.

432 Tung, *Reminiscences*, 64. To commemorate the victory at Dien Bien Phu, a hospital was christened "7 May 1954 (No. 1 Surgical Station)," *Ibid.*, 50. In the early 1970s the U.S. bombing of Hanoi destroyed many of the healthcare facilities that had been built with the aid of socialist countries in the second half of the 1950s.

433 In South Vietnam U.S. medical education officers at the USAID mission worked on revising the medical school curriculum beginning 1956. From 1960–62 May served as consultant to USAID in this matter. C. H. William Ruhe, *Saigon Medical School: An Experiment in International Medical Education* (Chicago, 1988), 29.

434 "Das Gesundheitswesen in der DRV" (February 16, 1956), PAAA, MfAA/A8340. See also *News Bulletin* (October 8, 1957, November 8, 1957, January 29, 1958, and February 1, 1958), all in PAAA, MfAA/A8340.

435 "Gründung eines fernöstlichen medizinischen Forschungsinstituts," *News Bulletin* (August 8, 1957), in PAAA, MfAA/A8340. For more on these research centers, see *Bulletin de l'emission en langue française* (May 5, and May 9, 1957) and *News Bulletin* (May 22, 1957, August 8, 1957, December 26, 1957).

436 GDR Embassy in Hanoi, Note (October 14, 1955), PAAA, MfAA/A8311. They also provided funds to equip school chemistry labs and a gymnasium, and the FDJ also sent backpacks, photo albums, and books.

437 Engelhardt, Comments on Kirsch's manuscript (March 16, 1957 [actually 1958]), PAAA, MfAA/A8421.

438 *News Bulletin* (October 8, and November 8, 1957), PAAA, MfAA/A8340.

439 Thach, "Das Gesundheitswesen in der DRV."

440 "Gründung eines Malaria-Instituts," *News Bulletin* (May 22, 1957), PAAA, MfAA/A 8340; note from MfAA to MfG (November 20, 1958), PAAA, MfAA/A8421; and GDR Embassy in Hanoi to MfAA (March 17, 1959), PAAA, MfAA/A8408. In 1957, the Vietnamese established the country's first institute for the scientific study of malaria, and the first international anti-malaria conference held in the country took place in August 1958. By the mid-1960s, malaria had virtually disappeared in North Vietnam, only to resurface with the U.S. bombing of neighboring Laos, which brought anti-malaria efforts there to a halt. Werner Holzer, *Bei den Erben Ho Tschi Minhs. Menschen und Gesellschaft in Nordvietnam* (Munich, 1971), 64.

441 Richard Kirsch, *Moskitos, Bambus und Bananen* (Berlin, 1962), 79.

442 *Ibid.*, 76–8.

443 Health Minister Steidle to State Secretary Handke (June 6, 1956), PAAA, MfAA/A8340. See also Handke to Steidle (May 18, 1956), and MfAA to GDR Embassy Hanoi (July 31, 1956). East Germany also imported opiates and various addictive stimulants from Hanoi and sent scientists there to conduct research on Vietnamese medicinal plants and tropical diseases. See the correspondence between the MfG, the MfAA, and the German embassy in Hanoi in June, July, October, November 1956 in PAAA, MfAA/A8340.

444 Embassy Hanoi to MfAA (November 6, 1957), PAAA, MfAA/A8409.

445 Embassy Hanoi (no recipient, no date), PAAA, MfAA/A8409.

446 Embassy Hanoi to MfAA (October 27, 1958), PAAA, MfAA/A8409.

447 Kittler to MfAA (October 3, 1958), and Wolfgang Bethmann, Report (October 1958), PAAA, MfAA/ A8409.

448 Wolfgang Bethmann, radio talk (October 6, 1958), PAAA, MfAA/A8409.

449 Bethmann,"Gesundheitsschutz und medizinische Aufklärung," lecture at Hanoi University (October 11, 1958), PAAA, MfAA/A8409.

450 Bethmann to Foreign Ministry (December 16, 1958), PAAA, MfAA/A8409.

451 Kirsch, *Moskitos, Bambus und Bananen*, 32, 48, 49.

452 *Ibid.*, 118

453 "Bemerkungen zu Kirsch 'Als Arzt in Südostasien'" (July 18, 1958), PAAA, MfAA/A8421.

454 One of the chapters is strangely entitled "Arbeit macht Freunde."

455 Tung, *Reminiscences*, 55. See also Anne Raffin, "Postcolonial Vietnam: hybrid modernity," *Postcolonial Studies*, 11, 3 (2008), 329–44.

456 *News Bulletin* (April 28, 1957 and May 18, 1957), PAAA, MfAA/A8340.

457 Although the evidence is not entirely clear, the Viet-Duc Friendship Hospital may have been the first to open; however, it is certain that the Soviet Red Cross Hospital opened in January 1958, and the Vietnamese-Soviet Friendship Hospital opened in December 1958. *News Bulletin* (January 29, and February 1, 1958), PAAA, MfAA/A8340, and Embassy Hanoi, Bericht (September 9, 1958), PAAA, MfAA/A8421.

458 Kirsch, "Reisebericht" (July 13, 1959), PAAA, MfAA/A8408.

459 Nicholas Khoo, *Collateral Damage: Sino-Soviet Rivalry and the Termination of the Sino-Vietnamese Alliance* (New York, 2011); Gaiduk, *Confronting Vietnam*; and Jan S. Prybyla, "Soviet and Chinese Economic Competition within the Communist World," *Soviet Studies* 15:4 (April 1964), 46–73. The first half of the 1960s represented the nadir of Soviet influence, and the zenith of Chinese influence, in North Vietnam.

460 The Great Leap Forward relied on the permanent ideological mobilization (and the de facto forced labor) of the population, harsh political discipline, new agricultural techniques, the forced development of small-scale rural industry, and collectivization of agriculture to push the nation toward production targets that were utterly unrealistic. Although this program was redolent of the first Soviet five-year plan, it diverged sharply from the commitment to highly centralized economic planning and the reliance on heavy industry as the motor of socialist development that had characterized Soviet economic policy since the mid-1930s.

461 Pierre Asselin, *Hanoi's Road to the Vietnam War* (Berkeley, CA, 2013); Francois Guillemot, "Death and Suffering at First Hazand: Youth Shock Brigades during the Vietnam War (1950–1975)," *Journal of Vietnamese Studies* 4, 3 (2009), 17–60; and John Prados, *The Blood Road: The Ho Chi Minh Trail and the Vietnam War* (New York, 1998).

462 CIA, "Current Intelligence Staff Study. North Vietnam and Sino-Soviet Relations" (ESAU XVIII-62) (www.foia.cia.gov/CPE/ESAU/esau-17.pdf; accessed June 9, 2012). See also Brocheux, *Ho Chi Minh*, 152–160; and Martin Grossheim, "'Revisionism' in the Democratic Republic of Vietnam: New Evidence from the East German Archives," *CWH* 5:4 (November 2005), 451–77.

463 Between 1956 and 1959, the Phu Doan Hospital trained over 100 surgeons, many of whom went on to serve as directors of provincial hospitals. Kirsch, *Moskitos, Bambus und Bananen*, 131.

464 One of the predictable results of this shift was a sharp drop in the export of medicine and medical equipment to North Vietnam, Kirsch, "Reisebericht" (July 13, 1959), PAAA, MfAA/A8408. This political disaffection cut both ways; the North Vietnamese cadres and students who were studying in the Soviet Union and Eastern Europe were recalled and subjected to political reeducation as soon as they arrived in Hanoi. See Martin Grossheim, "'Revisionism' in the Democratic Republic of Vietnam: New Evidence form the East German Archives," *CWH* 5:4 (November 2005), 451–77.

465 "Hanoi Mass Rally Welcomes Korean Government Delegation," *Everlasting Friendship Between Korean, Chinese and Vietnamese Peoples. Documents*

on Goodwill Visits of the D.P.R.K. Government Delegation to China and Viet-Nam (Pyongyang, 1959), 219.

466 Connelly, *A Diplomatic Revolution*, 69. See also Martin Evans, *Algeria: France's Undeclared War* (Oxford, 2012); and Martin Thomas, "France Accused: French North Africa before the United Nations, 1952–1962," *CEH* 10:1 (2001), 91–121.

467 Central Intelligence Agency, "National Intelligence Service. Algeria. Section 54. Public Order and Safety" (June 1960); and Neil MacMaster, "Identifying 'Terrorists' in Paris: A Police Experiment with IBM Machines during the Algerian War," *French Politics, Culture & Society* 28:3 (Winter 2010), 23–45.

468 These tactics, which were widely condemned in international law, were dramatized by the Italian filmmaker Gillo Pontecorvo in *The Battle for Algiers*. On the concept of revolutionary war, see Peter Paret, *French Revolutionary Warfare from Indochina to Algeria* (New York, 1964); and Mathias Grégor, *Galula in Algeria: Counterinsurgency Practice versus Theory* (Westport, 2011). See also Martin S. Alexander, Martin Evans, and J.F.V. Keiger, eds., *The Algerian War and the French Army, 1954–62: Experiences, Images, and Testimonies* (New York, 2002).

469 Herbert Georges Beckh, "Auszug aus einem Bericht über einen Besuch von Herrn Herbert Georges Beckh am 23.7.1957," PAAA, MfAA/A13579.

470 Amelia Lyons, *The Civilizing Mission in the Metropole: Algerian Families and the French Welfare State during Decolonization* (Stanford, 2013); Neil MacMaster, *Burning the Veil. The Algerian War and the 'Emancipation' of Muslim Women, 1954–62* (Manchester, 2008); and Stephan Malinowski, "Modernisierungskriege: Militärische Gewalt und koloniale Modernisierung im Algerienkrieg (1954–1962)," *AfS* 48 (2008), 213–48.

471 The citation is from Connelly, *A Diplomatic Revolution*, 48. See also Fabian Klose, *Menschenrechte im Schatten kolonialer Gewalt* (Oldenbourg, 2009) (English translation published in 2013 as *Human Rights in the Shadow of Colonial Violence: The Wars of Independence in Kenya and Algeria*); Jim House and Neil MacMaster, eds., *Paris 1961: Algerians, State Terror, and Memory* (Oxford, 2006); and William B. Cohen, "The Algerian War and the Revision of France's Overseas Mission," *FCH* 4 (2003), 227–39. See also Todd Shepard, *The Invention of Decolonization: The Algerian War and the Remaking of France* (Ithaca, NY, 2008).

472 The real challenge for the ICRC, according to one high-ranking ICRC official, was the French insistence on the full legality of its own policing action against the Algerians and that the Geneva Conventions did not apply to the Algerian rebels. An abridged report on the visit of Herbert Georges Beckh, a delegate of the ICRC, to the DRK headquarters in Dresden on July 23, 1957. PAAA, MfAA/A13579. By 1958, however, other international organizations had begun to provide assistance to Algerian refugees.

473 Jabhat al-Tahrir al-Qawmi, *Answer to Mr. Guy Mollet, Prime Minister of France* (Cairo, 1957), 6, 10ff.; and Jabhat al-Tahrir al-Qawmi, *Genocide in Algeria: A Note Presented to the Delegations to the United Nations, Eleventh Session of the General Assembly* (Cairo, 1957).

474 Peter Gatrell, *Free World? The Campaign to Save the World's Refugees, 1956–1963* (Cambridge, 2011), 49–57; Françoise Perret, "ICRC Operations in Hungary and the Middle East in 1956," *IRRC*, No. 313 (August, 1996), 412–37; and Zoltan Csillag, *Data about the Activity of the International Committee of the Red Cross and the Hungarian Red Cross in 1956–1957* (Budapest, 1992). On the history of the ICRC, see David P. Forsythe, *The Humanitarians: The International Committee of the Red Cross* (Cambridge, 2005).

475 Laron, *Origins of the Suez Crisis*; and William Roger Louis and Roger Owen, eds., *Suez 1956: The Crisis and Its Consequences* (Oxford, 1989).

476 Perret, "ICRC operations in Hungary and the Middle East in 1956," and Anup Singh, "Political Report," in *Afro-Asian Peoples Conference (26 December 1957 – 1st January 1958). Principal Reports Submitted to the Conference* (Cairo, 1958), 14.

477 The ARC's mission also included "propaganda service" to inform the "civilized world" about the French crime of "barbarism" against Algerians. Omar Boukli-Hacène to DRK (February 2, 1957), PAAA, MfAA/A13579. See also MfAA to Handelsvertretung in Cairo (March 19, 1957), PAAA, MfAA/A13579.

478 ARC to DRK (June 15, 1957), PAAA, MfAA/A13579. Boumediene, the deputy secretary-general of the ARC, expressed his skepticism that the ICRC could protect East German aid goods–especially medicines–from being seized by the French. See report (October 15, 1957), PAAA, MfAA/A13579.

479 Omar Boukli-Hacène to DRK (February 2, 1957), PAAA, MfAA/A13579.

480 S. A. Dange, *Die Aufgaben der Gewerkschaften im Kampf gegen den Kolonialismus. 4. Weltgeserkschaftskongreß, Leipzig, 4.-15. Oktober 1957* (Berlin, 1958); and Report (October 15, 1957), PAAA, MfAA/ A13579. The constitutive meeting of the the International Trade Union Committee for Solidarity with Algerian Workers and the Algerian People was held in September 1958. Both the vice president (Fella Hamouda) and the deputy secretary-general (Dr. Bensmaine Boumediene) of the ARC visited East Germany in October 1957. The following spring, the UGTA contacted the trade unions in East Germany and the other Eastern European countries to request material assistance and technical training for Algerian workers, and by 1962 about 1,000 Algerians had received such training in socialist countries. Arnold Fraleigh, *The Algerian Revolution and the International Community* (Washington, DC, 1969), II:410, 422–7.

481 According to Bensmaine Boumediene, Deputy Secretary-General of the ARC, cited in "Bericht über den Empfang der Gäste des Algerischen Roten Halbmondes" (October 15, 1957), PAAA, MfAA/A13579. The numbers of Algerian refugees differed widely from those given by the French government and the International Red Cross.

482 The Tunisian and Moroccan Red Crescent Societies began to take part in refugee relief operations in, respectively, March and the end of 1958 under the guidance of the Red Cross League's delegation. Françoise Perret and François Bugnion, "Between Insurgents and Government: The International Committee of the Red Cross's Action in the Algerian War (1954–1962)," *IRRC*, 93, 883 (September 2011), 725.

483 "Humanitarian Aid to the Victims of Internal Conflicts. Meeting of a Commission of Experts in Geneva," *IRRC* (February 1963), 79–91.

484 A. Rørholt, "Report on Mission to Morocco and Tunisia" (December 1958), (www.unhcr.org/4417e74b2.html; accessed June 28, 2012). In Morocco, aid to Algerian refugees was initially coordinated by *Entr'Aide Nationale*, an umbrella organization of Moslem welfare societies. Politically, Morocco was more radical than Tunisia and did not ask for UNHCR aid for Algerian refugees until October 1958, almost a year and half after the Tunisian appeal. During this time, Egypt was a chief donor for Algerian refugees in Morocco. In contrast, Tunisia refused to accept relief goods from Egypt. However it did accept wheat and dried milk from the U.S. Surplus Commodities Program for refugee relief and allow the National Catholic Welfare Conference to operate in the country. Cecilia Ruthström-Ruin, *Beyond Europe: The Globalisation of Refugee Aid* (Lund, 1993), 189.

485 UNHCR, *The State of the World's Refugees 2000*, 89; "Auszug aus einem Bericht über einen Besuch von Herrn Herbert Georges Beckh am 23.7.1957," PAAA, MfAA/A13579; and "Account of the International Committee's Action in Algeria: January 1955-June 1962," *IRRC* 18 (September 1962), 482–87.

486 Ruthstrom-Ruin, *Beyond Europe*, 145, 151ff, 175. More generally, see Yahia H. Zoubir, "The United States, the Soviet Union and Decolonization of the Maghreb, 1945–62," *Middle Eastern Studies* 31:1 (January, 1995), 58–84; Zoubir, "U.S. and Soviet Policies towards France's Struggle with Anticolonial Nationalism in North Africa," *Canadian Journal of History* 30:3 (December, 1995), 439–66; Martin Thomas, "Defending a Lost Cause? France and the United States Vision of Imperial Rule in French North Africa, 1945–1956," *DH* 26:2 (2002), 215–47; and Irwin M. Wall, *France, the United States and the Algerian War* (Berkeley, 2001). During the Hungarian refugee crisis, the United States had succeeded in fronting the UNHCR for the U.S. anti-Communist mobilization of the international community.

487 "Appeal from the International Red Cross. International Aid to Algerian Refugees" (December 12, 1957), PAAA, MfAA/A13579. The Appeal stated that about 40,000 Algerian refugees were in the Oujda area in Morocco, and the rest were in Tunisia. The 19th International Conference of the Red Cross met in New Delhi from 28 October to 7 November. A joint appeal for Algerian refugees in Morocco and Tunisia was made by the ICRC and the League on December 12. See also Perret and Bugnion, "Between Insurgents and Government," 727; and Bugnion, "The International Conference of the Red Cross and Red Crescent: Challenges, Key Issues and Achievements," *IRRC*, 91, 876 (December 2009), 675–712, citations 704.

488 The Algerians also scored minor points in the propaganda war by adhering to the Geneva Conventions in more punctilious manner than the French. In October 1958, the FLN turned over four French prisoners to the Algerian Red Crescent, which then released them to the ICRC; by the end of 1959, a total of 71 French prisoners had been freed. Major newspapers in both France and the United States published interviews with the French soldiers, who all

explained that their Algerian captors had treated them fairly and provided necessary medical care, and in the fall of 1958 the Algerian provisional government stated that it would welcome any international initiatives aimed at securing the application of the Geneva Conventions to the Algerian conflict. "Account of the International Committee's Action in Algeria January: 1955 – June 1962," *IRRC* (September 1962), 484; and Jabhat al-Tahrir al-Qawmi, *White Paper on the Application of the Geneva Conventions of 1949 to the French-Algerian Conflict* (Cairo, 1960), especially 31ff.

489 The conference invited representatives of liberation movements from countries that were still fighting for their independence. Not surprisingly, the speeches and resolutions adopted there struck a more radical anti-imperialist tone than had been the case at Bandung two years before.

490 "The Algerian Problem: Report by Aiah Hasan (Algeria)," *Afro-Asian Peoples' Solidarity Conference. Cairo, December 26, 1957 – January 1, 1958* (Moscow, 1958), 108–28.

491 "Resolution on Algeria," *Afro-Asian Peoples' Solidarity Conference*, 235.

492 *El Moudjahid* 21:1 (April 1, 1958).

493 The DRK submitted protests to ICRC and the LRC, to the Tunisian Red Crescent. DRK vice president, Weitbrecht, to Henry W. Dunning (February 7, 1958), Weitbrecht to Léopold Boissier (February 17, 1958), and Weitbrecht to R. Gallopin (February 13, 1958), all in PAAA, MfAA/A13579.

494 Jeffrey S. Ahlman, "The Algerian Question in Nkrumah's Ghana, 1958–1960: Debating 'Violence' and 'Nonviolence' in African Decolonization," *Africa Today* 57:2 (Winter 2010), 67–83, citation 74. From the late 1950s until his death in December 1961, Frantz Fanon served as the emissary of the Algerian provisional government. Kevin K. Gaines, *American Africans in Ghana: Black Expatriates and the Civil Rights Era* (Chapel Hill, NC, 2006), 92; and Alice Cherki, *Frantz Fanon: A Portrait* (Ithaca, NY, 2006).

495 See Article 10 of the "Resolution on Imperialism und Colonialism," in *Die afro-asiatische Soliaritätsbewegung: Dokumente* (Berlin, 1968), 303.

496 Ruthström-Ruin, *Beyond Europe*, 175f.

497 Ulrich Lappenküper, *Die deutsch-französischen Beziehungen 1949–1963. Von der "Erbfeindschaft" zur "Entente elementaire"* (Oldenburg, 2001); Klaus-Jürgen Muller, "Aspekte des Deutsch-Französischen Verhältnisses während des Algerien-Krieges," *Revue d'Allemagne et des pays de langue allemande* 31:3–4 (1999), 509–32; and Jean-Paul Cahn, "Bedrohung für die deutsch-französischen Beziehungen? Die Bundesrepublik Deutschland und der Algerienkrieg," in Christiane Kohser-Spohn and Frank Renken, eds., *Trauma Algerienkrieg: Zur Geschichte und Aufarbeitung eines tabuisierten Konflikts* (Frankfurt a.M., 2006), 227–44.

498 In return, the Red Hand, a counterterrorist organization created by the French intelligence service, tried to assassinate both these arms suppliers and FLN operatives in West Germany. See "Der Tod Kommt mit der Post," *Der Spiegel*, Nr. 10–13/1960 (March 2, 9, 16, and 23, 1960); and Thomas Scheffler, *Die SPD und der Algerienkrieg 1954–1962* (Berlin, 1995), 46f.

499 See the documentary film by Ute Bönnen und Gerald Endres, *Der Algerienkrieg: Kampf an vielen Fronten* (ARTE/SWR, 1998).

500 Von Nostitz, *Algerisches Tagebuch 1960–1962* (Düsseldorf, 1971), 86.

501 Claus Leggewie, *Kofferträger. Das Algerien-Projekt der Linken im Ade-
nauer-Deutschland* (Berlin, 1989), 31; and Friedrich Keller, *Solidarität der
österreichischen Linken mit der algerischen Widerstandsbewegung* (Dissertation, University of Amsterdam, 2010), 217.

502 The term *porteurs de valises* was coined by Jean-Paul Sartre. See Marie-Pierre
Ulloa, *Francis Jeanson: A Dissident Intellectual from the French Resistance
to the Algerian War*, tr. Jane Marie Todd (Palo Alto, CA, 2007).

503 Eckard Michels, *Deutsche in der Fremdenlegion 1870–1965: Mythen und
Realitäten* (Schöningh, 1999).

504 Leggewie, *Kofferträger*, 101. One of the key figures here was Winfried Müller,
who was also known by his nom de guerre, Si Mustapha. Müller had moved
from East to West Berlin in 1954. In 1955, his first contact with FLN was
made in Paris; in the fall of 1956, he left for Morocco where he received
military training at a National Liberation Army training camp. Müller was
fluent in Arabic and converted to Islam. After Algeria won its independence,
Müller became Algerian citizen and state secretary in the Algerian government
cabinet. Müller's story was publicized by Bernt Engelmann in "Wer desertiert,
muss 'Alemani' rufen: Die Flucht aus der Fremdenlegion," *Der Spiegel*, Nr. 36/
1959 (September 2, 1959); "Disposition für die Besprechung" (November
28,1960), PAAA, MfAA/B3010; Keller, *Solidarität der österreichischen Linken*, 207; and Klaus Polkehn, "Die Mission des Si Mustapha – ein Deutscher
kämpft für Algerien," *Comparativ* 16:2 (2006), 30–45.

505 "Warum 'Freies Algerien'?" *Freies Algerien* 1:1 (September 1958), cited in
Leggewie, *Kofferträger*, 117. Wischnewski was the first editor. The group
also sponsored traveling exhibitions on Algeria that the group dispatched to
several larger cities in West Germany in order to raise public awareness
about the war.

506 In 1959, a small number of West German union activists established the
Algerian Aid Committee, although its membership expanded substantially
when the major welfare organizations, church groups, and youth groups
joined the organization. However, the German Federation of Trade Unions
did not endorse aid for Algeria until September 1959. At its national convention that year, these union activists called on the leadership to follow
"imperative of solidarity" by assisting some 2,000 Algerian workers with
occupational training and job placement. Scheffler, *Die SPD und der Algerienkrieg*, 67ff.; and Leggewie, *Kofferträger*, 172–5.

507 In September 1958, a press conference at the SPD House in Hamburg offered
Ait Ahcène, an unofficial FLN representative who operated out of the Tunisian embassy in Bonn, an opportunity to present the FLN position. Sabah
Bouhsini, *Die Rolle Nordafrikas (Marokko, Algerien, Tunesien) in den
deutsch-französischen Beziehungen von 1950 bis 1962* (Aachen, 2000),
214–5. See also Hellmut Kalbitzer, *Entwicklungsländer und Weltmächte*
(Frankfurt a.M., 1961).

508 Keller, *Solidarität der österreichischen Linken*, 68f.

509 "Ein Zwischenfall," *Kölnische Rundschau* (November 27, 1958), cited in
Die Protokolle des CDU-Bundesvorstands 1957–1961, Nr. 7 (November 27,

1958), 272. Afterwards, Adenauer complained about the incident and attacked Wischnewski personally.

510 Leggewie, *Kofferträger*, 73.

511 Völker Schlöndorff made his film debut in 1960 with a short film *Wen kümmert's* (*Wacht am Rhein*) on the Algerian problem. During these years such leftist publications as *Das Argument* and *Konkret* began to cover the conflict. Leggewie, *Kofferträger*, 82. See also Holger Nehring, *Life Before Death: West European Protests against Nuclear Weapons and the Cold War* (Oxford, 2011).

512 Curiously, the Congo crisis of 1960–1 did not arouse as much passion and concern among West German youth as the Algerian war.

513 Leggewie, *Kofferträger*, 68, 31.

514 When top officials of the ARC visited the DRK in October 1957, Boumediene told that "the true Germany for the Algerians" was "the Germany in the East," DRK, Bericht (October 15, 1957), in PAAA, MfAA/A13579.

515 N. Macmaster, *Burning the Veil*, 69, 98ff, 331ff. By the end of 1957, however, the ALN demilitarized these female army nurses, many of whom were evacuated across the border to Morocco and Tunisia.

516 Alistair Horne, *A Savage War of Peace* (London, 2002), 399.

517 ARC to DRK (September 5 and November 23, 1957), Ludwig to Omar Boukli-Hacene (September 21, 1957), DRK to MfAA (December 13, 1957), DRK, Bericht (January 6, 1958), and DRK to ICRC (February 13, 1958), all in PAAA, MfAA/A13579.

518 Kiesewetter to Zachmann (April 1, 1957), PAAA, MfAA/A13579. The DRK had kept the ICRC informed about its aid to the ARC in the hope that the ICRC would be willing to intervene if the aid were confiscated by the French. For almost a half year after the first shipment, in contrast, the LRC was not informed about East German aid to Algeria. Ludwig to Herbert Warnke (November 21, 1957), Zachmann to deputy foreign minister Schwab (November 28, 1957), DRK to MfAA (December 13, 1957), all in PAAA, MfAA/A13579.

519 ARC to DRK (September 5, 1957), PAAA, MfAA/A13579; and FDGB, "Betreuung schwerbeschädigter algerischer Kämpfer" (2.12.1958), and "In der DDR befindliche Verwundete und andere Beschädigte" (undated), both in BAB, DY 34/8344.

520 FDGB to General Union of Algerian Workers (December 27, 1960), and Sekretariatsvorlage, "Betrifft: Solidaritätsgeschenke für die UGTA und Abholung von 50 verwundete Freiheitskämpfern in die DDR" (September 17, 1960), both in BAB, DY 34/8344.

521 Hans Dreher, "Fraternal Solidarity with the People of Algeria," *Alles für Deine Gesundheit*, Nr. 3/1959, along with the accompanying pictures. A similar coupling of health, humanitarian aid, and the virtues of socialism can be found in a 1963 issue of a popular women's magazine *Für Dich* in which the victims of Western aggression were Cuba and the Cubans instead of the Algerians. See "Herzoperation rettete das Leben," *Für Dich*, Nr. 22/1963.

522　See the correspondence between the president of the German Red Cross and the Algerian Red Crescent (January 31 and March 4, 1958), both in PAAA, MfAA/A13579.

523　Robert Schulz, "Über Grundsätze sozialistischer Politik der Deutschen Demokratischen Republik gegenüber Afrika," *Geschichte und Geschichtsbild Afrikas. Beiträge der Arbeitstagung für Neuere und Neueste Geschichte Afrikas am 17. und 18. April 1959 in Leipzig* (Berlin, 1960), 167f.

524　Lothar Killmer, *Freiheitstrommel von Accra* (Berlin, 1962), 84f.; and "Die DDR grüßt Afrika," *ND* (April 15, 1959), cited in Schulz, "Über Grundsätze sozialistischer Politik," 175.

525　Ilona Schleicher, "Elemente entwicklungspolitischer Zusammenarbeit in der Tätigkeit von FDGB und FDJ," in Hans-Jörg Bücking, ed., *Entwicklungspolitische Zusammenarbeit in der Bundesrepublik Deutschland und der DDR* (Berlin, 1998), 114.

526　"The Guidelines for the Activity of the Working Group 'Fight against Colonialism'," cited in Patrice G. Poutrus, "'Teure Genossen'. Die 'politischen Emigranten' als 'Fremde' im Alltag der DDR-Gesellshaft," in Christian Müller and Patrice G. Poutrus, eds., *Ankunft – Alltag – Ausreise. Migration und interkulturelle Begegnung in der DDR-Gesellschaft* (Cologne, 2005), 253, emphasis added.

527　Ausschuß für Deutsche Einheit, *Bonn an der Seite der Kolonialmächte: Die Beteiligung an der Aggression im Nahen Osten enthüllt die imperialistischen Ziele der Bundesrepublik* (Berlin, 1958); and *Bonn – Feind der Völker Asiens und Afrikas: Eine Dokumentation über die Kolonialpolitik der Adenauer-Regierung* (Berlin, 1960)

528　DRK, Bericht (January 6, 1958), and DRK Präsidium, Nachtrag zum Bericht (October 21, 1957), both in PAAA MfAA/A13579.

529　Initially, information on the Algerian war was available only in French. However, beginning in 1958 a number of West Germans undertook to translate this literature into German. In 1958, *Die Folter. La question. Mit Geleitworten von Jean-Paul Sartre und Eugen Kogon* (Munich, 1958) was published in German. Because the Federal Republic banned what it called East German propaganda, such material had to be smuggled into West Germany, where it was an important source of information for those who could not read French. See the recollections of Klaus Vack in Werner Balsen and Karl Rössel, *Hoch die Internationale Solidarität: zur Geschichte der Dritte-Welt-Bewegung in der Bundesrepublik* (Cologne, 1986), 75. Two of the more important translations include Jabhat al-Tahrir al-Qawmi, *Das Algerische Volk und seine Revolution* (Cairo, 1956), and Jabhat al-Tahrir al-Qawmi, *Kolonialistische Unterdrückung und Kriegsverbrechen* (Cairo, 1957).

530　Heinz Odermann, *Wellen mit tausend Klängen. Geschichten rund um den Erdball in Sendungen des Auslandsrundfunks der DDR Radio Berlin International* (Berlin, 2003), 177–90. The SED asked the producer of the Algeria program to include propaganda against West German militarism. *Radio Berlin International* began in the fall of 1958 a weekly broadcasting for legionnaires in North Africa.

531 Roy Armes, "From State Production to Cinema d'Auteur in Algeria," in Josef Gugler, ed., *Film in the Middle East and North Africa: Creative Dissidence* (Austin, 2011), 294. See also Guy Austin, "Representing the Algerian War in Algerian Cinema," *French Studies* 61:2 (April 2007), 182–95; and Jim Dingeman, "'You cannot continually inflict': Interview with Saadi Yacef," *Framework* 49:2 (Fall 2008), 48–64. The DEFA and the state television broadcaster (*Deutscher Fernsehfunk*) also produced films on Algerian refugees and orphans in Morocco and Tunisia, including *Ahmed weine nicht* and *Sorah und Ali*. MfAA, Übersicht (October 3, 1961), PAAA, MfAA/A13579.

532 In 1958, the army film unit was incorporated into the Provisional Government and was renamed *Service du Cinéma National*. See Viola Shafik, *Arab Cinema. History and Cultural Identity* (Cairo, 1998), 18.

533 MfAA, "Übersicht" (October 3, 1961), Fritz Stude, "Aktenvermerk über einige Besuche beim Algerischen Befreiungskomitee in der Zeit vom 25.1. – 28.1.58." (January 30, 1958), and MfAA, "Hilfe für das algerische Volk" (February 7, 1962), all in PAAA, MfAA/A13579.

534 Natalya Vince, "Transgressing Boundaries: Gender, Race, Religion, and 'Françaises Musulmanes' during the Algerian War of Independence," *FHS* 33:3 (Summer 2010), 455. DEFA also synchronized a documentary produced in Egypt on Djamilla Buharid, a female militant (shown in *The Battle of Algiers*) whom the French had tortured and sentenced to death. Übersicht (October 3, 1961), PAAA, MfAA/A13579

535 In 1957, DEFA produced a short film, *Der Weg nach drüben*, which recounted the changing fortunes of the protagonist Rudi Frädrich, who moved to West Germany, joined the Foreign Legion, and was eventually killed in Algeria.

536 A shorter version of the film was broadcast in East Germany less than a week after the erection of the Berlin Wall. In West Germany Ernst Neuback, who himself had served as a legionnaire in North Africa, produced the German-Italian thriller *Die rote Hand*. In the film, which was released in October 1960, the villains and terrorists were Cubans and Asians, rather than the French. See "Rote Hand – Gelbe Gefahr," *Der Spiegel* Nr. 34/1960 (August 17, 1960).

537 Übersicht (July 13, 1962), PAAA, MfAA/A13579.

538 Werner Holzer, *Das Nackte Antlitz Afrikas* (Frankfurt a.M., 1961), 31

539 Deputy Foreign Minister Stibi to Leiter der Abt. Internationale Organisationen (April 30, 1962), PAAA, MfAA A13579. More than 100 Algerians studied in East Germany on state fellowships. MfAA, "Hilfe für das algerische Volk" (February 7, 1962), PAAA, MfAA/A13579.

540 Chadly Zouiten to Weitbrecht (January 19, 1961), PAAA, MfAA/A13579.

541 "Übersicht" (July 30, 1964), and "Übersicht" (October 3, 1961), both in PAAA, MfAA/A13579.

542 Ludwig to Ben Bahmet Hadj (October 28, 1961), and Breitfeld, Vice President of the DRK, to Ben Bahmed (May 15, 1962), both in PAAA, MfAA/A13579. The DEFA also synchronized a documentary produced in Egypt on Djamilla Buharid.

543 Deputy finance minister to Horst Brasch (December 2, 1961), and "Schwerverwundete Algerische Patrioten in der DDR eingetroffen," *ADN-Information* (December 7, 1961), both in PAAA, MfAA/A13579. The Finance Ministry agreed to pay for 23 Algerian patients to fly from Rabat to Berlin thorough Prague.

544 Cited in Leggewie, *Kofferträger*, 171.

545 Poutrus, "'Teure Genossen'," 248. Although expectations of such East German generosity may have tempted some Algerians to decamp for the socialist state, individual Algerians did not have the final say-so over whether they would be permitted to seek refuge in East Germany.

546 The amounts were over one million marks, each in 1958 and 1959. DRK, "Hilfeleistungen an den Algerischen Roten Halbmond in Tunis: Gesamtspenden des Bundesvorstandes FDGB" (June 1, 1960), PAAA, MfAA/A13579. After the establishment of the Solidarity Committee, it also contributed to the funds.

547 "Hilfe für die jungen unabhängigen Nationalstaaten und Befreiungsbewegungen" (March 17, 1961), PAAA, MfAA/A13579.

548 "Apologists of Neo-Colonialism: Comment on the Open Letter of the Central Committee of the CPSU" (October 22, 1963). www.marxists.org/subject/china/documents/polemic/neocolon.htm (accessed August 8, 2010). After the failure of Franco-Soviet summit in the spring of 1960, the Soviets began to more actively support the FLN, and in October 1960 the Soviet Union recognized the Algerian Provisional Government. Zoubir, "The United States, the Soviet Union and Decolonization of the Maghreb," and Zoubir, "U.S. and Soviet Policies towards France's Struggle with Anticolonial Nationalism in North Africa."

549 The ICRC had been informed about East German aid to the ARC from the beginning, largely because the DRK hoped that the ICRC would intervene should aid goods be confiscated by the French authorities on the way to the ARC. As a cautionary measure, however, the DRK waited long enough until informing the ICRC, so that aid goods could be safely shipped unnoticed. DRK to MfAA (June 1, 1960), and *ADN-Information* (July 22, 1960), both in PAAA, MfAA/A13579.

550 MfAA, "Übersicht" (July 13, 1962), PAAA, MfAA/A13579.

551 Poutrus, "'Teure Genossen'," 249–50. About 200 Algerians received basic vocational training in East Germany. See Ilona Schleicher, "Elemente entwicklungspolitischer Zusammenarbeit in der Tätigkeit von FDGB und FDJ," in Hans-Jörg Bücking, ed., *Entwicklungspolitische Zusammenarbeit in der Bundesrepublik Deutschland und der DDR* (Berlin, 1998), 112.

552 "Leipziger Berufsschüler helfen Algerischen Kindern," *ADN-Information* (January 28, 1961), and MfAA to ZKdSED (February 10, 1961), PAAA, MfAA/A13579.

553 In 1958, East Germany agreed to provide Egypt with long-term credits, to be delivered in forms of the textile plant equipments, spindles, and technical expertise that Egypt needed to modernize the textile industry. As a form of repayment, in turn, Egypt agreed to export to East Germany the mass

products from the textile mill, and soon over one-third of Egypt's cotton export went to East Germany. PAAA, B58-IIIB1–353. "The Sino-Soviet Economic Offensive through June 1962," and "Facts and Figures" IA 12:19 (1973), 116; K. Illgen, *op.cit.*, 227–8; and Dorothy Miller, "United Arab Republic and the Two Germanies" (September 24, 1962), HU OSA 300–8–3:24–5–52

554 Vorstand des FDGB, "Sekretariatsvorlage" (September 17, 1960), BAB, DY34/8344.

555 The FDGB acquired its second vacation ship, the *Fritz Heckert*, in April 1961. In early 1962, the ship sailed to North Africa, where 26 East Germans defected to the West. For more, see "DDR-Luxusline: Auf den Traumschiffen des Sozialismus," *Die Welt* (January 20, 2011) www.welt.de/reise/nah/art icle12257076/Auf-den-Traumschiffen-des-Sozialismus.html

556 In an interview with *Märkische Volksstimme*, cited in *ADN-Information* (January 7, 1961), PAAA, MfAA/A13579.

557 "Übersicht" (July 13, 1962), and "Bericht für das Komitee der DDR für Solidarität mit den Völkern Afrikas" (November 26, 1962), both in PAAA, MfAA/A13579. From 1957 to independence of Algeria in 1962, it was 5.4 million marks, if medical care, training, and scholarships were excluded.

558 MfAA to FDGB Bundesvorstand (November 14, 1960), PAAA, MfAA/A13579.

559 The first official contribution from the Adenauer government was a DM 200,000 donation to the UNHCR in 1960. See AA to the president of the West German Red Cross Hans Ritter von Lex (September 1962), PAAA, B85/289. In early 1961 the Foreign Ministry contributed 150,000 marks through the West German Red Cross; see the letter (January 23, 1962), PAAA, B92/182.

560 UN Information Service, A Joint UNHCR-Red Cross Press Release (June 20, 1962), and ambassador in Tunis to Bonn (July 16, 1962), PAAA, B85/289.

561 Charles R. Shrader, *The First Helicopter War. Logistics and Mobility in Algeria, 1954–1962* (Westport, CT, 1999), 170.

562 Von Nostitz, *Algerisches Tagebuch*, 199, 237f., citation 199. In 1965 Ben Bella would in turn be deposed by Boumédienne.

563 Wilhelm Schilling, Report (January 3, 1963), and Richter to AA (January 11 and February 7, 1963), both in PAAA, B92/408.

564 Von Nostiz, *Algerisches Tagebuch*, 96.

565 Schilling, Report (January 3, 1963), PAAA, B92/408.

566 Piero Gleijeses, "Cuba's First Venture in Africa: Algeria, 1961–1965," *Journal of Latin American Studies* 28:1 (February 1996), 165. The first team consisted of 29 doctors (including three women), 3 dentists, 15 nurses, and 8 medical technicians. The second team included 24 doctors, 4 dentists, 24 nurses, and 9 medical technicians.

567 Berner and Zimmering, "Bericht über den Besuch einer Delegation des Präsidiums des Deutschen Roten Kreuzes beim Algerischen Roten Halbmond in der Zeit vom 13. – 21. Mai 1963," PAAA, MfAA/A13582.

568 Ambassador Richter to AA (August 24, 1963), PAAA, B92/408.

569 Weitbrecht, "Bericht über die Delegationsreise nach Tunisien in der Zeit vom 22. Juni bis 7. Juli 1962," PAAA, MfAA/A12708, and Dr. Berner and Zimmering, "Bericht über den Besuch einer Delegation des Präsidiums des Deutschen Roten Kreuzes beim Algerischen Roten Halbmond in der Zeit zom 13.-21. Mai 1963," PAAA, MfAA/A13582.

570 Simons to Schwab (December 27, 1962), PAAA, MfAA/A13582.

571 Richter to AA (January 11, 1963), PAAA, B92/408. The Algerian health ministry asked the Adenauer government to either provide orthopedic care to a group of 20 disabled veterans, or to modernize the prosthetic workshop in Algier.

572 German embassy to AA (March 28 & 29, 1963), the complaint by the nurse Ruth P. (January 29, 1963), and other related materials in PAAA, B92/408.

573 See the notes of the investigation by Legationsrat Zimmermann (February 11, 1963), PAAA, B92/408. The man even stole one volume of a five-volume edition of Schiller, whose pages he used as toilet paper.

574 Foreign Minister Otto Winzer to Ben Bella (May 2, 1963), PAAA, MfAA/A13582.

575 "Direktive für die Delegation des DRK... zur Realisierung der dem Algerischen Roten Halbmond angebotenen poliklinischen Einrichtung" (n.d., but summer 1963), PAAA, MfAA/A12708, and "Direktive für das weitere Vorgehen bei der Übergabe einer Poliklinik-Einrichtung als Geschenk" (October 21, 1963), PAAA, MfAA/A13582.

576 See the extensive correspondence on the matter in PAAA, MfAA/A13582. The citation is from Präsidium DRK, "Vorlage an das Sekretariat des ZK der SED" (April 3, 1963).

577 Stude, Note (January 25, 1964), PAAA, MfAA/A13582.

578 Reichardt to Handelsvertretung in Algerien (April 9, 1964), PAAA, MfAA/A13582.

579 "Congo: Analytical Chronology,"19, in Lise Namikas and Sergey Mazov, eds., *CWIHP Conference Reader. Compiled for the International Conference Congo Crisis, 1960–1961, Washington D.C., 23–24 September 2004.*

580 United Nations Operations in the Congo. *Hearing before the Subcommittee on International Organizations and Movements of the Committee on Foreign Affairs, House of Representatives, 7, 14, 22.*

581 *United Nations Operations in the Congo: Hearing, 7.*

582 State Department, Bureau of Intelligence and Research. "Intelligence Report no. 8335" (August, 31, 1960), cited in *CWIHP Conference Reader.*

583 BRD embassy in Léopoldville to AA (April 25, 61), PAAA B34/255; and "Congo: Analytical Chronology," 17.

584 State Department, "Intelligence Report no. 8335."

585 Khrushchev to Lumumba (August 5, 1960), cited in *CWIHP Conference Reader.*

586 State Department, "Intelligence Report no. 8335." Most of the wheat arriving on the first ship was not unloaded because the Congolese did not have any way to mill it. The wheat was going to be sent to Dakar, Senegal, for

processing, and it was expected that it would return to the Congo at the end of August.

587 "Congo: Analytical Chronology," 39.

588 "Congo: Analytical Chronology," 51–58; and Erwin A. Schmidl, *Blaue Helme, Rotes Kreuz. Das österreichische UN-Sanitätskontingent im Kongo 1960 bis 1963* (Innsbruck, 1995), 81–2. By April 1961, about 2,000 Belgian "technicians" had returned to the Congo.

589 International News Release (July 26 1960), and League, Circular No. 131 (July 29, 1960), all in ARCL, 22/1/2. The report concluded that there were sufficient Red Cross medical personnel in the country to staff the main provincial and district hospitals even if the remaining 100 Belgian physicians were to leave. See also Brown, *A Public Health Odyssey*, 342. Brown served as deputy chief of the WHO Mission in the Congo from 1962 to 1964.

590 Press Communiqués 1960–40 (July 24, 1960), 1960–41 (July 26, 1960), 1960–42 (July 28, 1960), ARCL, 22/1/2.

591 Report No. 4 de l'OMS (August 27, 1960), cited in letter from Gallopin (ICRC) to Henry W. Dunning, Secretary General of the Red Cross League (September 12, 1960), International News Release (July 28 1960), and Press Communiqués 1960–43 (July 30, 1960), all in ARCL, 22/1/2. See also ICRC and LRCS, *Congo Medical Relief* (Geneva, 1961).

592 Dr. Glyn Davies to McLennan (February 28, 1961), and Dr. L. G. Sarkis to W. S. Stanburty (April 19, 1961), in ARCL, 22/1/2.

593 Schmidl, *Blaue Helme, Rotes Kreuz*, citation 171.

594 Weitbrecht, "Informatorischer Vorbericht über den Einsatz der Ärzte-und Schwesterngruppe" of the East German Red Cross (September 1960), BAB, DC20/2182.

595 Wolf Weitbrecht, *Kongo: Arzt unter heissem Himmel* (Berlin, 1964), 68.

596 BRD medical team to the DRK in Bonn (September 1, 1960), ARCL, 22/1/2. In the meantime, the district governor in Goma pleaded with them to remain and work in the hospital there. In the end, only two of the West German doctors traveled on to Lubero, while Hasselmann worked in Goma.

597 Drs. Benz and Gert Willich to the DRK in Bonn (September 26, 1960), and Telex from the Red Cross League to German Red Cross in Bonn (October 20, 1960), both in ARCL 22/1/2.

598 West German medical team to German Red Cross (August 24, 1960), ARCL, 22/1/2.

599 West German medical team to German Red Cross (September 1, 1960), ARCL, 22/1/2.

600 Weitbrecht, *Kongo*. The East German television program, *Aktuelle Kamera*, broadcast as story about the East German medical team.

601 Weitbrecht, *Kongo*, 19.

602 Foreign Office to ambassador in Léopoldville (June 13, 1960), PAAA, B34/166.

603 For example, when the East German anesthesiologist came down with a life-threatening illness, a West German doctor accompanied him on the

emergency flight back to Berlin, and both groups also appear to have respected the knowledge and dedication of the other. See the telegrams between Léopoldville, Geneva, Bonn, and East Berlin (November 10, 12, and 15, 1960), ARCL, 22/1/2.

604 Weitbrecht, *Kongo*, 79, 63.

605 Ludwig to the LRC (October 13 and November 18, 1960), and Henrik Beer to Ludwig (November 8, 1960), all in ARCL, 22/1/2. Among the East Germans sent to the Congo was A. K. Schmaus, who had headed the East German medical team in Hanoi for a year.

606 According to Pierre Mulele, Minister of Education and Arts in the Gizenga government, in his talk with Deputy Foreign Minister of the USSR V. V. Kuznetsov on March 18, 1961, in *CWIHP Conference Reader*.

607 "Congo: Analytical Chronology," 57–60, citation 58.

608 Glyn Davies to C. McLennan (February 28, 1961), ARCL, 22/1/2.

609 Cable (January 26, 1961), and LRC and the ICRC to the Red Cross National Societies (March 23, 1961), both in ARCL, 22/1/2.

610 Czech ambassador to the Soviet Union, and Gamal Abdel Nasser to the Soviet Deputy Foreign Minister Semenov on January 31, 1961, both in *CWIHP Conference Reader*.

611 Pierre Mulele in his talk with Deputy Foreign Minister of the USSR V. V. Kuznetsov on March 18, 1961, in *CWIHP Conference Reader*.

612 Henrik Beer, "Special Report on New Relief Problems in the Congo" (June 5, 1961), ARCL, 22/1/2.

613 Henrik Beer to John A. MacAulay (April 4, 1961), ARCL, 22/1/2..

614 Press Communique No. 1961–18 (April 28, 1961) and No. 1961–22 (May 29, 1961), boh in ARCL, 22/1/2.

615 Edward McWhinney, "Declaration on the Granting of Independence to Colonial Countries and Peoples," United Nations, Office of Legal Affairs, Audiovisual Library of International Law (untreaty.un.org/cod/avl/ha/dicc/dicc.html; accessed July 6, 2012).

616 *Middle East Records* 2 (1961), 52.

617 *United Nations Operations in the Congo: Hearing*, 10.

618 Khrushchev, "For New Victories of the World Communist Movement" (January 6, 1961), a report delivered to the CPSU Central Committee, in *Hearing before the Subcommittee to Investigate the Administration of the Internal Security Act and Internal Security Laws, 87th Congress, 1st Session* (June 10, 1961), Appendix III. In response, U.S. Defense Secretary Robert McNamara declared that the United States was "ready to fight in the 'Twilight Zone' between combat and political subversion," Open Society Archives. Radio Free Europe Munich, Research and Evaluation Department, "Wars of Liberation" (February 22, 1962), (www.osaarchivum.org/files/holdings/300/8/3/text/96-1-258.shtml; accessed July 6, 2012).

619 *Middle East Record* 2 (1961), 638.

620 George M. Houser, "At Cairo: Africa Today" (April 1961)

621 The Soviet Union also invited delegations from Guinea, Ghana, and Mali to address the 22nd Congress of the CPSU in 1961; and in the early 1960s,

Khrushchev presented the Lenin Peace Prize to the presidents of Guinea, Ghana, and Mali (Sékou Touré, Kwame Nkruhma, and Modibo Keita, respectively). Michael Radu and Arthur Jay Klinghoffer, *The Dynamics of Soviet Policy in Sub-Saharan Africa* (New York, 1991), 2.

622 The Gizenga government had already asked the East German government for assistance in December 1960 and again in January 1961.

623 "Anlage Nr. 1 zum Protokoll Nr. 7/61 der Sitzung des Politbüros des ZK" (February 14, 1961), in *CWIHP Conference Reader*.

624 ICRC and the LRC, *Congo Medical Relief* (Geneva, 1961), 25.

625 Cited in "Congo: Analytical Chronology," 67.

626 "Congo: Analytical Chronology," 67.

627 Hans-Georg Schleicher, "Afrika in der Außenpolitik der DDR," in Ulrich van der Hyden, Ilona Schleicher, and Hans-Georg Schleicher, eds., *Die DDR und Afrika. Zwischen Klassenkampf und neuem Denken* (Münster, 1993), 10–30, citation 15.

628 Kristin Roth-Ey, *Moscow Prime Time: How the Soviet Union Built the Media Empire That Lost the Cultural Cold War* (Ithaca, NY, 2011); Ruth Oldenziel and Karin Zachmann, eds., *Cold War Kitchen: Americanization, Technology, and European Users* (Cambridge, MA, 2009); Greg Castillo, *Cold War on the Home Front. The Soft Power of Midcentury Design* (Minneapolis, MN, 2010); Tony Shaw, *Hollywood's Cold War* (Edinburgh, 2007); Rana Mitter and Patrick Major, eds., *Across the Blocs: Cold War Cultural and Social History* (Santa Rosa, CA, 2004); Caute, *The Dancer Defects*; Yale Richmond, *Cultural Exchange and the Cold War,* and the special issue of *CWH* 9:4 (November 2009) on the Cold War in Film. See also Magnusdottir, "'Be Careful in America, Premier Khrushchev!'"; Krisztina Fehérváry, "American Kitchens, Luxury Bathrooms, and the Search for a 'Normal' Life in Postsocialist Hungary," *Ethnos* 17:3 (2002), 369–400; and Hixson, *Parting the Curtain.*

629 Susan E. Reid, "Who Will Beat Whom? Soviet Popular Reception of the American National Exhibition in Moscow, 1959," *Kritika* 9:4 (Fall 2008), 855–904, citation 860.

630 Jessica Reinisch, "A New Beginning? German Medical and Political Traditions in the Aftermath of the Second World War," *Minerva* 45 (2007), 241–257; Gabriele Moser, *Im Interesse der Volksgesundheit: Sozialhygiene und öffentliches Gesundheitswesen in der Weimarer Republik und der frühen SBZ/DDR* (Bad Homburg, 2003); Anna-Sabine Ernst, *"Die beste Prophylaxe ist der Sozialismus": Ärzte und medizinische Hochschullehrer in der SBZ/DDR* (Münster, 1997); and Wolfgang Woelk and Jörg Vögele, eds., *Geschichte der Gesundheitspolitik in Deutschland. Von der Weimarer Republik bis in die Frühgeschichte der "doppelten Staatsgründung"* (Berlin, 2002).

631 L. Beuthner, Petition (August 4, 1961), BAB, DQ1/6017.

632 Larry Frohman, "The Right to Health and Social Citizenship in Germany, 1848–1918," in Frank Huisman and Harry Oosterhuis, eds., *Health and Citizenship. Political Cultures of Health in Britain, the Netherlands, and Germany* (London, 2014), 123–40.

633 Cited in Ernst, *"Die beste Prophylaxe ist der Sozialismus,"* 25. On the making of the East German health system, see Anita Rausch, Lothar Rohland, and Horst Spaar, eds., *Das Gesundheitswesen der DDR: Eine historische Bilanz für zukünftige Gesundheitspolitik* (Berlin, 1999); Horst Spaar, ed., *Das Gesundheitswesen zwischen Gründung der DDR und erster Gesellschaftskrise, 1949–1953* (Berlin, 1996); and Spaar, ed., *Das Gesundheitswesen der DDR zwischen neuem Kurs und der Schließung der Staatsgrenze, 1953–1961* (Berlin, 1998).

634 These included the labor law, laws on maternal and child protection and women's rights, and the decree on social insurance.

635 While §87 of the 1961 labor code proclaimed that, "as an expression of concern for man, the preservation and promotion of health and creative power is a principle of socialist society," §88 made it clear that "every laboring person is obligated, in the interest of preserving his or her own health and in the interest of society, to participate in the continuous improvement of measures for the protection of health and labor."

636 Rudolf Neumann, "Helfer des Arztes: Populär-medizinische Aufklärung," *DG* 5:11 (November 1959), 12–3.

637 Walter Ulbricht, *Der Kampf um den Frieden* (Berlin, 1958), 124 and 122, cited in Dietrich Mühlberg, "Sexualität und ostdeutscher Alltag," *Mitteilungen aus der kulturwissenschaftlichen Forschung* 18 (August 1995), 12.

638 "Erziehung zu gesunden Lebensgewohnheiten ist eine gesellschaftliche Aufgabe," *Alles für Deine Gesundheit* 3 (1961), 2.

639 Rolf Thränhardt (October 11, 1961), BAB, DQ1/6017.

640 Spengler to Walther Brauer (July 21, 1962), BAB, DQ1/6017.

641 Young-sun Hong, "Cigarette Butts and the Building of Socialism in East Germany," *Central European History* 35:3 (October, 2002), 327–44.

642 K. Böhm and R. Dörge, *Unsere Welt von Morgen* (Berlin, 1960), cited in *Geschichte der DDR. Informationen zur politischen Bildung* (1991), Nr. 2, 33.

643 Neumann, "Helfer des Arztes."

644 Minutes (January 15, 1957), and Jähnig, "Rechenschaftsbericht" (February 13, 1957), both in BAB, DQ1/1680/1.

645 "Tote werden lebendig," *DG* 5:11 (1959), 6–7.

646 In contrast, reports on West Germany complained that so much money was being spent on the arms race that relatively little was left for healthcare. Michael Gehring, "Herunter mit der Maske: Zu den Erscheinungen des Klassenkampfes im westdeutschen Krankenversicherungswesen," *DG* 5:5 (May 1959), 10–1.

647 Many East Germans regard the decade 1961–71 as the golden age of the German Democratic Republic. See Ina Merkel, *Utopie und Bedürfnis: Die Geschichte der Konsumkultur in der DDR* (Cologne, 1999), 326. On the development of the East German economy, see André Steiner, *The Plans That Failed: An Economic History of the GDR* (New York, 2010).

648 Thränhardt, "Eine gesunde Lebensweise ist das Ziel," *Alles für Deine Gesundheit* 5 (1961), 1.

649 Cited in *75 Jahre Deutsches Hygiene-Museum in der DDR* (Dresden, 1987), 35.

650 Thränhardt, "Eine gesunde Lebensweise ist das Ziel."

651 Spaar, ed., *Das Gesundheitswesen der DDR*, 41–3.

652 Werner Ludwig, "Aktuelle Probleme der Organisation der Gesundheitserziehung in der Deutschen Demokratischen Republik," *Das Deutsche Gesundheitswesen* 17:12 (March 22, 1962), 497–500.

653 On the museum itself, see Ursula Kowark, *Die Geschichte des Deutschen Hygiene-Museums in der DDR von 1945 bis zur Gegenwart* (Dissertation, Medizinische Akademie "Carl Gustav Carus," 1986); and Hendrik Behling, *Das anatomische Labor am Deutschen Hygiene-Museum Dresden* (Dissertation, Technische Universität, Dresden, 1996).

654 H.G. Beyer, "The 'Internationale Hygiene Ausstellung, Dresden, 1911'," *Military Surgeon* 30:2 (February 1912), 125–62; Susanne Roeßiger, "In aller Munde – das Deutsche Hygiene Museum," in Martin Roth, Manfred Scheske, and H.-C. Täubrich, eds., *In aller Munde. Einhundert Jahre Odol* (Ostfildern, 1993), 56; and Eike Reichardt, *Health, "Race,' and Empire: Popular-Scientific Spectacles and National Identity in Imperial Germany, 1871–1914* (Raleigh, NC, 2008).

655 Rosmarie Beier and Martin Roth, eds., *Der gläserne Mensch: eine Sensation* (Stuttgart, 1990), 57. The title of the lecture that Lingner delivered in 1912 on the occasion of his receipt of an honorary doctorate in Bern was "Man as a Prototype of Organization," and he later coined the term "human economy" (*Menschenökonomie*).

656 On the pedagogical and representational strategies employed to reach audiences of limited literacy, see Larry Frohman "Prevention, Welfare and Citizenship: The War on Tuberculosis and Infant Mortality in Germany, 1900–1930," *CEH* 39:3 (September 2006), 431–81, especially 449ff.; and Christine Brecht and Sybilla Nikolow, "Displaying the Invisible: *Volkskrankheiten* on Exhibition in Imperial Germany," *Studies in the History and Philosophy of Science* 31:4 (2000), 511–30.

657 Bruno Gebhard, "Art and Science in a Health Museum," *Bulletin of the Medical Library Association* 33:1 (January 1945), 39–49, citation 44–45; Klaus Vogel, ed., *Das Deutsche Hygiene-Museum Dresden 1911–1990* (Dresden, 2003); and Beier and Roth, eds., *Der Gläserne Mensch*. The Transparent Woman was first produced in 1936.

658 Beier and Roth, eds., *Der gläserne Mensch*, citations 65.

659 According to Gebhard, for the 50–60 million people who viewed the Transparent Man between 1930 and 1945, it was like seeing their own insides, which, for the majority, had remained invisible and mysterious. Gebhard, "Art and Science in a Health Museum," 45. Gebhard was the curator of the Hygiene Museum (1927–35) and later the first director of the Cleveland Health Museum.

660 Rolf Pfeiffer, "Hygiene-Museum und Gläserne Wesen," ADHM, Z/Bd. 16.

661 This enabled Seiring to secure from the Soviet military administration the funding needed to begin clearing the rubble in preparation for rebuilding the museum. Seiring to Zhukov (September 17, 1945), cited in U. Kowark, *Die Geschichte des Deutschen Hygiene-Museums*, 103, and *75 Jahre Deutsches Hygiene-Museum in der DDR*, 29. See also Ludwig Stephan,

Das Dresdner Hygiene-Museum in der Zeit des deutschen Faschismus, 1933–1945 (Dissertation, Medizinische Akademie "Carl Gustav Carus," 1986).

662 Linser, Report (May 12, 1949), BAB, DQ1/3627.

663 Seiring feared that depriving the museum of its independence would squander the international reputation that the museum had built up before the war and make it difficult to resume connections with hygienic institutions in other countries. In addition, the Germans were able to convince the Soviets that such a move would limit the museum's influence to the Soviet zone and prevent it from reaching out to the country as a whole. Seiring to Paul Konitzer (March 1, 1946), BAB, DQ1/3627.

664 The Cologne museum was jointly managed by the city, state, and federal government. In 1967 the museum became the Bundeszentrale für gesundheitliche Aufklärung.

665 Klaus Vogel, "The Transparent Man," in Robert Bud, Bernard Finn, and Helmuth Trischler, eds., *Manifesting Medicine: Bodies and Machines* (Amsterdam, 1999), 52.

666 Sefrin, "Erziehung zu gesunden Lebensgewohnheiten ist eine gesellschaftliche Aufgabe," MfG, Sektor Recht to Interior Ministry (May 15, 1951), BAB, DQ1/3626; "Bericht über die dokumentarische Prüfung des DHM durch das Ministerium für Finanzen" (December 1949), BAB, DQ1/2529, G. Schrödel, "Die gläserne Eva. Zum 50. Jahrestag des Hygiene-Museums, Dresden," *Alles Für Deine Gesundheit* (1961), and Hans Biock, "Niedergang und Neubeginn," *Sächsisches Tageblatt* (May 20, 1961).

667 Rolf Pfeiffer, "Hygiene-Museum und Gläserne Wesen," ADHM, Z/Bd. 16.

668 Biock, "Niedergang und Neubeginn."

669 MfG State Secretary Jenny Matern to Trade Minister Handke (May 11, 1951), and Friedeberger to Matern (October 14, 1952), BAB, DQ1/4443.

670 Kunkel, "Bericht über die Industrieausstellung der DDR in China" (n.d., 1953) (n.d.) BAB, DQ1/4443; and "Die ersten Jahre in Peking. Ein Gespräch mit Ingeborg König," in Joachim Krüger, ed., *Beiträge zur Geschichte der Beziehungen der DDR und der VR China* (Münster, 2002), 26–27.

671 Schrödel, "Die gläserne Eva."

672 Schrödel, "Nationale Hygiene-Ausstellung 1961," *Alles für Deine Gesundheit* (1961), Nr. 1, 1. On the 1961 Dresden exhibition, see "Entdeckung des Homo sapiens," ADHM, Z/Bd.13. The continuity of the Eurocentric representation of health and civilization in the Hygiene Museum was finally broken in 1999 with the exhibition, *Der Neue Mensch*, which reflected a more critical attitude toward European modernity. This shift was reflected in the subtitle of the exhibition: "Obsession of the 20th Century." See Nicola Lepp, Martin Roth, and Klaus Vogel, eds., *Der Neue Mensch. Obsession des 20. Jahrhunderts* (Ostfildern, 1999).

673 While this first Egyptian agreement had been limited to trade alone, in 1955 the Egyptians signed a second, longer-term trade agreement, which also elevated the East German trade mission in Cairo to a consulate, called for the opening of an Egyptian trade mission in East Berlin, and opened the door to more extensive cultural contacts between the two countries. After

the signing of this agreement, the Society for Cultural Connections with Foreign Countries sponsored visits to Egypt by a number of East German scientists, students, artists, and athletic teams. Wolfgang G. Schwanitz, *Deutsche in Nahost 1946–1955. Sozialgeschichte nach Akten und Interviews* (Habilitationsschrift, Otto-Suhr Institut, Freie Universität Berlin, 1995), 236ff.

674 Sven Olaf Berggötz, *Nahostpolitik in der Ära Adenauer. Möglichkeiten und Grenzen, 1949–1963* (Düsseldorf, 1998), 206ff.

675 BMW to AA (March 22, 1954), AA, Note (March 18, 1954), West German embassy in Cairo to AA (March 19 and March 25, 1954); and AA, Note (May 21, 1954), all in PAAA, B66/33. Sebastian Haffner suggested that the trade war between the two German states had reached a provisional climax in Cairo and that it appeared that East Germany was winning the competition for both technology exports and the diplomatic sympathies of the Third World because no political strings, such as the Hallstein doctrine, were attached to agreements it concluded. Haffner, "Handelskrieg zwischen zwei Deutschlands," *Hindustan Times* (February 6, 1956), cited in Schwanitz, *Deutsche in Nahost*, 303.

676 Pawelke to AA (March 30, 1954), PAAA, B66/33.

677 Friedeberger to Steidle (12/29/1953), ADHM, 54/29; and Kunkel to DHG (May 19, 1954) on his trip to Cairo, BAB, DQ1/4765.

678 Steidle to Egyptian Health Minister Nour El-Din Taraf (March 23, 1956), Taraf to Steidle (April 1956), and Steidle to Handke (June 2, 1956), all in PAAA, MfAA/B1902.

679 Steidle to Schwab (January 5, 1957), PAAA, MfAA/B1902.

680 Treitschke to Simons (March 10, 1957), PAAA, MfAA/B1902.

681 Steidle to Schwab (January 5, 1957), PAAA, MfAA/B1902.

682 Stude to MfAA (January 19, 1957), Marten to Jacob (February 6, 1957), and Stude's report on his meeting with Taraf on January 22, 1957, all in PAAA, MfAA/B 1902.

683 Kunkel, Note (December 18, 1957), ADHM, 57/28. This gift was paid for by solidarity contributions of the East German people at the time of the Suez Crisis. See Otto Kunkel to Kroll (April 24, 1962), BAB, DQ1/3073. During the Suez crisis East Germany was able to open the office of the Plenipotentiary of the Government of the German Democratic Republic to the Arab States.

684 Stude to Simons (February 17, 1957), PAAA, MfAA/B1902.

685 See William Randolph Hearst, *How Russia Is Winning the Peace* (n.p., 1958).

686 "Bald in aller Munde: Die erste 'Gläserne Kuh'," *Sächsische Zeitung* (January 19, 1959); and the picture of Heidi in *Rhein-Neckar-Zeitung* (December 22, 1959).

687 Martin Wörner, "Made in Germany – Made in GDR," in Haus der Geschichte der BRD, ed., *Krauts – Fritz – Piefkes...? Deutschland von außen* (Bouvier, 1999), 74–81, citation 81. Otto Grotewohl had an unofficial meeting with Nehru during his visit to India in January 1959. Johannes H. Voigt, *Die Indienpolitik der DDR: Von den Anfängen bis zur Anerkennung*

(1952–1972) (Cologne, 2008); and Herbert Fischer, "Entwicklung der staatlichen und gesellschaftlichen Beziehungen DDR – Indien," in Joachim Heidrich, ed., *DDR – Indien: Partner auf Zeit* (Münster, 1998), 24–52.

688 Herbert Baensch to Damme (January 7, 1960), ADHM, RB/1, Bd. 2.

689 Rolf Pfeiffer, "Verdacht um Heidi. Hygiene-Museum und Gläserne Wesen. 2. Akt," ADHM, Z/Bd16; and J. Kiesewalter, "Bericht über die Malaria-Ausstellung in Mali," PAAA, MfAA/ A16734.

690 Willi Lehmann to DHM (July 18, 1957), BAB, DQ1/4690.

691 Letters from North Korea, ADHM, 57/30.

692 *Ibid.*

693 Brown, *A Public Health Odyssey*, 220.

694 Schedlich and Hochmuth, Report, PAAA, MfAA/ A16202; and W. A. Spengler, Bericht, PAAA, MfAA/A10014.

695 D. O. Hasenbring, "Report on Field Visit to Cambodia, 22–26 January 1963," WHO WPR/ADHS/FR/5, Rev. 1 (July 24, 1963); and H.M.C. Poortman, "Report on a Field Visit to Cambodia, 16–25 March 1966," WHO WPR/MCH/FR/38 (April 11, 1966).

696 Stude to Engel (December 13, 1961), PAAA, MfAA/A16765; and "Bericht über die Reise nach Kambodscha," (December 13, 1963), ADHM, RB 3/ Bd. 6..

697 Wandel (deputy foreign minister) to Friedeberger (October 3, 1962), PAAA, MfAA/A16765.

698 Kittler to Gunnert (March 23, 1963), PAAA, MfAA/A16765.

699 "Bericht über die Reise nach Kambodscha vom 10.10 bis 11.11.1963," PAAA, MfAA/A16765.

700 Minutes (October 1, 1958), BAB, DQ1/3072.

701 Bischof, Note (September 19, 1958), BAB, DQ1/3072. The director of the Department of International Relations at the Health Ministry lamented the "totally inadequate promotional and information materials on the East German health system in foreign languages." Kroll to Schrödel (Director, DHM) (June 10, 1960), BAB, DQ1/3072.

702 Keune to Friedeberger (October 20, 1961), BAB, DQ1/3073; and Kroll to Otto Kunkel (Acting Director, DHM) (August 19, 1963), BAB, DQ1/3072.

703 Mali and Zanzibar cultural exchange agreements with East Germany in 1962 and 1964, respectively.

704 "Bericht über die Ergebnisse der Reise einer Regierungsdelegation der DDR in die afrikanischen Republiken Ghana, Guinea und Mali" (May 12–June 5, 1964), BAB, DQ1/4217.

705 "Verordnung über den Verantwortungsbereich...," BAB, DQ1/2016.

706 Discussion among officials from MfAA, MfG, and DHM (November 30, 1959), ADHM, RB 3/Bd. 5; and "Abschlußbericht über die Malaria-Ausstellung in Conakry," and "Bericht über Durchführung der Antimalaria ausstellung in Conakry, Republik Guinea, both in ADHM, RB 1/Bd. 2.

707 Donald R. Johnson and Roy F. Fritz, "Postage Stamps Portray a World United Against Malaria" (August 30, 1963), WHO WHO/Mal/411; and "Malaria Eradication Postage Stamps. Final Report by the Director General" (May 20, 1964), WHO EB34/19.

708 "Plan für die Malaria-Ausstellung" (October 4, 1962), BAB, DQ1/3702; and Paul Wandel to Sefrin (October 9, 1962), BAB, DQ1/3702. The secretary of the Subcommittee of International Exhibition at the Cultural Affairs department of the Foreign Ministry suggested that the Hygiene Museum improve the mass propaganda effects of the exhibition. Becher to Kroll (August 24, 1962), BAB, DQ1/3702.

709 Herbert Landmann, "Im Kampf gegen die Malaria. DDR-Ausstellung in Guinea," *Neue Zeit* (1962); "Freundschaftsbrücke nach Afrika. DDR-Lehrschau in Conakry (Guinea) helft Malaria bekämpfen: Lob für das Deutsche Hygiene-Museum," *ND* (February 17, 1963); and Landmann, "Guinea. Auf Neuen Wegen. Gedanken zur Antimalaria-Ausstellung der DDR in Conakry," unidentified clipping in ADHM, Z/Bd. 7.

710 "Direktive des MfG der DDR für Herrn Medizinalrat Dr. Landmann..." (October 10, 1962), BAB, DQ1/3702.

711 Sefrin to Willi Stoph (February 7, 1963), BAB, DQ1/3702.

712 Trade Mission in Conakry, "Massnahmeplan" (no date), BAB, DQ1/3702.

713 "Freundschaftsbrücke nach Afrika;" "Im Kampf gegen die Malaria;" and "Die Malariastation im Landesinnern" *National-Zeitung* (May 28, 1961).

714 Sefrin to Burmeister (September 1963), BAB, DQ1/3072.

715 Egon Damme (Technical Director, DHM) to MfG (August 12, 1961), BAB, DQ1/3072. In 1961, the Hygiene Museum signed a contract to produce anatomical teaching materials for 281 schools in Cuba. "Niedergang und Neubeginn," *Sächsisches Tageblatt* (May 20, 1961).

716 Reif to Buhlert (October 9, 1964), BAB, DQ1/2016.

717 Friede, "Abschlußbericht" (October 31, 1967), ADHM, Z/Bd. 20.

718 For more on history of Third World workers and students in East Germany, see Almut Riedel, *Erfahrungen algerischer Arbeitsmigranten in der DDR: '...hatten noch Chancen, ehrlich!'"* (Opladen, 1994); Michael Feige, *Vietnamesische Studenten und Arbeiter in der DDR und ihre Beobachtung durch das MfS* (Magdeburg, 1999); Sandra Gruner-Domić, *Kubanische Arbeitsmigration in die DDR 1978–1989. Das Arbeitsabkommen Kuba-DDR und dessen Realisierung* (Berlin, 1997); Andreas Müggenburg, *Die ausländischen Vertragsarbeitnehmer in der ehemaligen DDR: Darstellung und Dokumentation* (Berlin, 1996); and Marianne Krüger-Potratz, *Anderssein gab es nicht: Ausländer und Minderheiten in der DDR* (Münster, 1991). More recent scholarship includes Annegret Schüle, "'Proletarischer Internationalismus' oder 'ökonomischer Vorteil für die DDR'? Mosambikanische, angolanische und vietnamesische Arbeitskräfte im VEB Leipziger Baumwollspinnerei (1980–1989)," *AfS* 42 (2002), 191–210; Jan Behrends, T. Lindenberger, and Patrice G. Poutrus, eds., *Fremde und Fremd-Sein in der DDR. Zu historischen Ursachen der Fremdenfeindlichkeit in Ostdeutschland* (Berlin, 2003); Karin Weiss and Mike Dennis, eds., *Erfolg in der Nische? Die Vietnamesen in der DDR und in Ostdeutschland* (Münster, 2005); and Damian Mac Con Uladh, *Guests of the Socialist Nation? Foreign Students and Workers in the GDR, 1949–1990* (Dissertation, University College London, 2005).

719 In 1960, there were about 22,000 foreign students and 8,000 trainees in West Germany, although they will not be dealt with here. Of these students,

68 percent were considered colored; 8,000 came from Asia (including 2,863 from Iran, 1,767 from the United Arab Republic) and Africa. Over half of these students were studying medicine. "Über 21000 ausländische Studenten: Statistik der Auslandsstelle des Deutschen Bundesstudentenrings," *Bulletin*, No. 94 (May 19, 1960), 928; "Auslandsstudenten," *DPA* (January 29, 1960); "Farbige Studenten sollen in Wohnheimen unterkommen," *DPA* (February 4, 1960); and Brentano, *Sten. Ber.* 118. Sitzung (June 23, 1960), 6881.

720 On North Korea, Eva-Maria Elsner and Lothar Elsner, *Zwischen Nationalismus und Internationalismus. Über Ausländer und Ausländerpolitik in der DDR 1949–1990* (Rostock, 1994), 18; and on North Vietnam, Mirjam Freytag, *Die "Moritzburger" in Vietnam. Lebenswege nach einem Schul- und Ausbildungsaufenthalt in der DDR* (Frankfurt a.M, 1998), 46f., as well as Foreign Ministry to Solidarity Committee (October 12, 1956), PAAA, MfAA/A8404. Eleven Nigerians who had come to East Germany to attend the 1951 World Festival of Youth in Berlin were not able to return home, and the East German government arranged their study at Leipzig University. Mac Con Uladh, *Guests of the socialist nation?* 41.

721 Rayk Einax, "Im Dienste außenpolitischer Interessen. Ausländische Studierende in der DDR am Beispiel Jenas," *Die Hochschule* 1 (2008), 162–83. On the 1980s, Andrea Schmelz, "Bildungsmigration und Interkulturalität. Ausländische Studierende aus afrikanischen und asiatischen Ländern in Ostdeutschland vor und nach 1989," *Deutschland Archiv* 38 (2005), 84–92. See also Mac Con Uladh, *Guests of the Socialist Nation?*

722 Solidaritätskomitee der DDR, *40 Jahre Deutsche Demokratische Republik – 40 Jahre antiimperialistische Solidarität* (Berlin 1989), 45. See also Ewa P. Müller, "Ausländische Studierende in der DDR," *Osteuropa und die Dritte Welt. OstEuropaForum* Nr. 75 (Hamburg, 1989), 101–9. The first regulation of the vocational training of foreigners in East Germany was issued in May 1958. See Hans von Oettingen, *Studium bei Fremden* (Berlin, 1958), which was published by the State Secretariat for Higher and Vocational Education. A few years later, the West German Federal Ministry for the Inner-German Questions published an account by an Indian student, who had studied in East Germany, but who had then left for the West. See Vijoy Batra, *Studium bei Freunden? Das Ausländerstudium an den Universitäten der Sowietzone* (Bonn, 1962).

723 "Konzeption zur weiteren Entwicklung der Aus-und Weiterbildung. Entwurf" (November 1973), BAB, DQ1/10467.

724 Correspondence between MfG and the Quedlinburg school (June 10, 1964 and July 6, 1964), BAB, DQ1/6480. In 1965, the Quedlinburg school was renamed the Ausbildungsstätte für ausländische Bürger. Heyme, "Stellungnahme" (November 17, 1968), BAB, DQ1/10467. I have been unable to locate the archives of the Medizinische Fachschule Dorothea Christiane Erxleben in Quedlinburg.

725 For example, *Freie Presse Karl-Marx-Stadt* (February 20, 1965), BAB, DQ1/6481. The Health Ministry instructed all of the teaching hospitals where these Third World trainees studied to organize and train them as a "separate group"

apart from the German students. Quedlinburg school, Report (November 9, 1961), BAB, DQ1/1767; and Charlotte Sohr to medical school at the district hospital Dresden-Friedrichstadt (April 30, 1965), BAB, DQ1/6480.

726 Minutes of the congress held from October 23–25, 1962, BAB, DQ1/2016; and "Medizin kennt keine Grenzen," *DG*, Nr. 5 (1962), 150–151.

727 Staatliche Plankommission to MfG (December 4, 1961); and MfG, Sektor mid-level medical occupations to MfG, Sektor press (January 4, 1962), BAB, DQ1/5074.

728 "Aktenvermerk über Beratung am 10.5.1962," BAB, DQ1/5074.

729 Horst Quaeschning, Zentralvorstand Gewerkschaft Gesundheitswesen, "Präsidiumsvorlage über die Aufgaben der Vorstände und Leitungen der Gewerkschaft Gesundheitswesen zur Arbeit mit den in Gesundheitseinrichtungen arbeitenden und studierenden ausländischen Bürgern" (May 22, 1962), and "Aktennotiz betr. Aussprache in Bezug auf die Ausbildung junger afrikanischer und asiatischer Ausländer zu mittleren medizinischen Kadern" (December 4, 1961), BAB, DQ1/3073.

730 By 1963, the number of physicians and auxiliary health workers from non-socialist Third World countries increased to 44 and 77, respectively, while a total of about 300 medical students from those countries studied in East Germany. Verlag Volk und Gesundheit, "Einige Aspekte der Entwicklung des sozialistischen Gesundheitswesen in der DDR" (1964), BAB, DQ1/2016. The actual number must be much larger because those who were invited by other official agencies, especially the FDGB, were often not included in the statistics. MfG, "Bericht über bisher durchgeführte und geplante Maßnahmen im Gesundheitswesen gegenüber ökonomisch-schwachentwickelten Ländern," (December 5, 1962), BAB, DQ1/3073.

731 According to 1963 statistics compiled by the Health Ministry, through July 1962 only 17 doctors, 21 nurses, and 1 technician had been sent abroad as part of these aid programs. This number, however, includes the medical teams sent to the Congo in 1960–1, BAB, DQ1/3073.

732 ZKdSED, Abteilung Gesundheitspolitik, "Information für Hager" (December 7, 1959), BAB, DY/30/IV2/19/64. On the acute shortage of nurses, see Parteisekretär Hofer at the Hufeland Hospital Berlin-Buch to Abteilung Gesundheitspolitik beim ZKdSED (November 23, 1959); Abteilung Gesundheitspolitik beim ZKdSED, "Vorschläge zum Schwesternproblem" (June 2, 1961); and "Zur Arbeitskräftesituation (Pflegepersonal) in den Berliner Krankenhäusern" (June 2, 1961), all in BAB, DY/30/IV2/19/64. See also "Bericht über die Versammlung in der Charite, in welcher über Probleme der Lage der Schwestern diskutiert wurde" (April 16, 1956), BAB, DQ1/4845.

733 "Der Arzt als 'Diener des Sozialismus'...," *Ärztliche Mitteilungen* Nr. 30/1961 (August 26, 1961) in BAB, DQ1/2491.

734 Spaar, ed., *Das Gesundheitswesen der DDR zwischen neuem Kurs*, 33–34, 37, and Ernst, *"Die beste Prophylaxe ist der Sozialismus,"* 54.

735 MfG, "Bericht über bisher durchgeführte und geplante Maßnahmen im Gesundheitswesen gegenüber ökonomisch-schwachentwickelten Ländern (December 5, 1962), BAB, DQ1/3073.

736 Freideberger, "Maßnahmeplan für Kontake und kulturell Vereinbarungen mit antiimperialistischen Ländern" (no date, but early 1960), BAB, DQ1/5074.

737 Medical School Quedlinburg, Report (November 9, 1961), BAB, DQ1/1767.

738 Dr. Somine Dolo to MfG (September 8, 1961), BAB, DQ1/1767.

739 Nimtz, Note (September 25, 1961 and October 12, 1961); Sohr to State Secretary Jahnke (October 13, 1961), Minutes (November 16, 1961), East German trade mission in Mali to MfAA (December 8, 1961), Sandau, "Bericht über eine Unterredung mit den Studenten aus Mali betreff ihrer Ausbildung" (January 13, 1962), Habedank to MfG (January 22, 1962), all in BAB, DQ1/1767. For the perspective of one Malinese student, see "Protokoll über die am 23. Januar 1962 stattgefundene Aussprache," and "Bericht über Dienstreise am 27 November 1962 nach Quedlinburg," both in BAB, DQ1/1767.

740 Kranhold to Sohr (October 29, 1962), and Zentralvorstand der Gewerkschaft Gesundheitswesen, FDGB to State Secretariat for Higher Education (October 10, 1961), both in BAB, DQ1/1767. Even if the East Germans had designed an appropriate course of study, it is unlikely that the trainees would have been able to learn much because the foreign language textbook that the students were supposed to use was unavailable.

741 Habedank to MfG (January 22, 1962), BAB, DQ1/1767.

742 Foreign Ministry of Republic Mali to East German trade mission (April 19, 1962), BAB, DQ1/1767; and Gross to MfAA (December 8, 1961), PAAA, MfAA/A14429. The secretary of the Mali National Workers Union also spoke with these students when he visited East Germany in 1961, and when he returned to Bamako he, too, complained to the East German trade mission about the "overall insufficiency" of the program.

743 Note (July 19, 1962), PAAA, MfAA/A14429.

744 Nimtz, Report (August 22, 1962), BAB, DQ1/6481.

745 Nimtz, Report (January 21, 1963), Sohr to the African Solidarity Committee (October 30, 1963), the Dessau District Hospital to Nimtz (October 11, 1963), and Nimtz, notes (January 21, 1963, and February 21, 1964), all in BAB, DQ1/6481.

746 Correspondence between Hama and Sohr in 1965, BAB, DQ1/6481.

747 State Secretary Michael Gehring to director of the Dessau Hospital (January 25, 1965), BAB, DQ1/6481. On top of all of this, there were also frictions outside the workplace, and two Nigeriens living in a local house were forced to move out after a conflict with the landlady. Sohr, Note (October 12, 1962), BAB, DQ1/6481.

748 Staatliche Plankommission to MfAA (June 19, 1964), and Prof. Ludwig Renn, Chair of the Solidarity Committee with Cuba, to Cuban Health Minister José Machado Ventura (August 12, 1963), both in PAAA, MfAA/A3382.

749 "Hallo, Ruprecht! Hast du auch wirklich an alle gedacht?" (unidentified newspaper clipping; no date, but around December 17, 1964). In 1964, the exhibit "Anatomy and Physiology," which was organized by the Dresden Hygiene Museum, had run in Havana, and following thereon a small number of Cuban physicians had traveled to East Germany for specialized training.

"Direktive für die Delegation des Ministeriums für Gesundheitswesen der DDR in die Republik Kuba" (March 26 and April 11, 1964), and "Protokoll über die Beratungen der Delegation der DDR mit Vertretern des Ministeriums für Gesundheitswesen der Republik Kuba" (May 6, 1964), all in PAAA, MfAA/A16820.

750 Nimtz, Note (October 2, 1965), BAB, DQ1/5980.

751 John Iliffe, *East African Doctors. A History of the Modern Profession* (Cambridge, 1998), 118ff.

752 Jan Behrends, Dennis Kuck, and Patrice Poutrus, "Historische Ursachen der Fremdenfeindlichkeit in den Neuen Bundesländern," *Aus Politik und Zeitgeschichte* B39/2000 (September 22, 2000), 15–21.

753 Report (November 9, 1961), Nimtz, Note (October 3, 1962), and Sohr to Kranhold (October 23, 1962), all in BAB, DQ1/1767.

754 Seeländer to MfG (September 29, 1966), BAB, DQ1/6480.

755 For more on her experiences in Berlin and Quedlinburg, see the materials in BAB, DQ1/1767, especially Nimtz, Note (undated, but March 1961, May 5, 1961, and October 3, 1961).

756 Haferkorn, Evaluation (November 1, 1963), BAB, DQ1/1767.

757 Diarra to MfG (October 12, 1963), BAB, DQ1/1767.

758 "Konzeption zur weiteren Entwicklung der Aus-und Weiterbildung von Bürgern aus Entwicklungsländern im Gesundheits-und Sozialwesen" (November 1973), BAB, DQ1/10467.

759 Gladys Nzimande to MfG (January 6, 1969), BAB, DQ1/6481.

760 German officials often mentioned this issue. For example, see Nimtz, Note (October 12, 1961), and Report (November 9, 1961), both in BAB, DQ1/1767.

761 Letter to MfG (November 4, 1965), BAB, DQ1/6480.

762 Correspondence between Frenz and Nimtz (April 29 and May 24, 1965), BAB, DQ1/6480.

763 Seiler to Sohr (July 14, 1967), BAB, DQ1/5981.

764 Sohr to Muhamed Shaame (May 17, 1967), BAB, DQ1/5981.

765 Muhamed Shamme to MfG (May 1, 1967), Shamme to Sohr (June 21, 1967 and July 3, 1967), Hamed Khamfer to Sohr (June 23, 1967, July 14, 1967, and August 25, 1967), and Sohr to Hamed Khamfer (September 7, 1967), all in BAB, DQ1/5981.

766 MfG, "Aktenvermerk betr. Zusammenarbeit mit der Liga für Völkerfreundschaft" (July 1, 1963), BAB, DQ1/3073.

767 Konrad Jarausch, "Care and Coercion. The GDR as Welfare Dictatorship," in Konrad Jarausch, ed., *Dictatorship as Experience. Towards a Socio-Cultural History of the GDR* (New York, 1999), 47–69.

768 Many of the evaluations showed racial prejudice, and the Foreign Ministry recommended that the evaluators to be more careful in their choice of words for fear of offending Malinese officials. Fritsch to Kroll (February 15, 1963), PAAA, MfAA/A14429.

769 Oleg Kharkhordin, *The Collective and the Individual in Russia* (Berkeley, 1999) is a sophisticated study of this phenomenon in the Soviet context.

770 "Präsidiumsvorlage..." (May 22, 1962), BAB, DQ1/3073.

771 Quedlinburg medical school to Afro-Asian Solidarity Committee (October 9, 1969), BAB, DQ1/10470.

772 Werner Hering to Mecklinger (October 24, 1969), and Mecklinger to Hering (undated, but November 1969), both in BAB, DQ1/10470.

773 Haas to MfG (October 18, 1971), BAB, DQ1/10470.

774 College for Health and Social Work in Potsdam, "Beurteilung zum Abschluß des Praktikums" (July 1973), BAB, DQ1/10470.

775 Mehwald to MfG (October 14, 1974), as well as "Antrag auf Exmatrikulation" (June 17, 1975) submitted to the ZKdSED, Department International Relations, and FDJ-Leitung and FDJ-Sekretär Rosenthal, "Stellungnahme zur Lehrerpersönlichkeit von Cora N" (no date, but June 1975), all in BAB, DQ1/10470.

776 FDJ-Leitung and FDJ-Sekretär Rosenthal, "Stellungnahme zur Lehrerpersönlichkeit von Cora N." (no date, but June 1975), BAB, DQ1/10470.

777 District hospital Dresden-Friedrichstadt, "Einschätzung der Schwester Cora N." (May 14, 1976), BAB, DQ1/10470.

778 "Beurteilung der Studentin Cora B. N." (May 27, 1976), BAB, DQ1/10470. See also Dr. Fezile Mpendu to Mehwald (May 27, 1976), Collective of Station 36 at the Dresden-Friedrichstadt Hospital, "Einschätzung der Schwester Cora N." (May 14, 1976), Mehwald to Health Ministry (November 24, 1975), and Mehwald to ZKdSED (July 7, 1976), all in BAB, DQ1/10470.

779 Mehwald to Cora (July 21, 1976), BAB, DQ1/10470.

780 Cora N. to the Quedlinburg medical school (July 15, 1977), BAB, DQ1/10470.

781 Finance minister to foreign minister Schröder (Oct. 2, 1964), PAAA, B58-IIIB1/388

782 Letter from Sādjadi (no date), and the letter from the German embassy in Iran to the Foreign Office in Bonn (October 8, 1957), both in PAAA B92/103.

783 Röken to the Foreign Office (November 11, 1957), PAAA, B92/103.

784 Von Bismarck-Osten to Bundesärztekammer (November 28, 1957), PAAA, B92/103.

785 Dirk van Laak, *Imperiale Infrastruktur: Deutsche Planungen für eine Erschließung Afrikas 1880 bis 1960* (Paderborn, 2004), 242f; and Lewis Pyenson, *Cultural Imperialism and Exact Sciences: German Expansion Overseas 1900–1930* (New York, 1985). On medicine, see Erich Mannweiler, *Geschichte des Instituts für Schiffs-und Tropenkrankheiten in Hamburg, 1900 bis 1945* (Hamburg, 1998); Johannes W. Grüntzig and Heinz Mehlhorn, *Expeditionen ins Reich der Seuchen: Medizinische Himmelfahrtskommandos der deutschen Kaiser-und Kolonialzeit* (Heidelberg, 2005); Grüntzig and Mehlhorn, *Robert Koch: Seuchenjäger und Nobelpreisträger* (Heidelberg, 2010); and Hiroyuki Isobe, *Medizin und Kolonialgesellschaft: Die Bekämpfung der Schlafkrankheit in den deutschen "Schutzgebieten" vor dem Ersten Weltkrieg* (Berlin, 2009).

786 In 1921/23, the Foreign Office had sponsored an expedition to Rhodesia and the Congo to test the sleeping sickness medicine *Germanin*, and a documentary film on the project was released in 1943. Stephan Besser,

"Germanin. Pharmazeutische Signaturen des deutschen (Post)Kolonialismus," in Alexander Honold and Oliver Simons, *Kolonialismus als Kultur: Literatur, Medien, Wissenschaft in der deutschen Gründerzeit des Fremden* (Tübingen, 2002), 167–95. See also Kurt Düwell, *Deutschlands Auswärtige Kulturpolitik 1918–1932: Grundlinien und Dokumente* (Cologne, 1976), especially 178–80.

787 Röken to the Red Cross League in Geneva (September 27, 1950), ADRK, 1641/1, "Deutsche Aerzte in Iran," *Darmstädter Echo* (February 2, 1951), and Walter Burkart, "1947–1997: Bundesärztekammer im Wandeln (XV). Die Auslandsbeziehungen der Bundesärztekammer," *DÄ* 94:42 (October 17, 1997), A2724 – 2730.

788 Schubart, *Ärztin im Dschungel von Sumatra* (Mühlacker, 1995), 13.

789 Schumann fled to East Germany in 1951 after the authorities issued an arrest warrant for him. After serving as a ship's doctor for three years, he found employment as a hospital director in Khartoum. In 1962, when his identity became known, he fled to Ghana and worked there until his extradition to West Germany in 1966. Hans Werner Richter, "Die Auslieferung," in H.W. Richter, *Reisen durch meine Zeit: Lebensgeschichten* (Munich, 1989), 87–114; and Werner Kilian, *Die Hallstein-Doktrin. Der diplomatische Krieg zwischen der BRD und der DDR, 1955–1973* (Berlin, 2001), 79.

790 Buddeberg to AA, Ref. 110 (November 12, 1954), and Pamperrien, Note (no date, but presumably 1954), both in PAAA, B92/38.

791 AA circular to overseas diplomatic and consular representatives (November 3, 1952), PAAA, B92/38. The hospitals in Istanbul and Tehran both received substantial subsidies in the 1950s. AA to Minister of Finance (December 19, 1959), PAAA, B92/14.

792 The German Institute for Medical Mission in Tübingen sent 68 (39 male and 29 female) physicians and 136 nurses abroad in mid-1950s. Samuel Müller, ed., *Ärzte Helfen in Aller Welt. Das Buch der Ärztlichen Mission* (Stuttgart, 1957), 11. For more on West German missionary doctors in Africa, see Johanna Davis-Ziegler, *Heimat unter dem Kreuz des Südens: Erinnerungen einer Missionsärztin in Simbabwe* (Würzburg, 2004); and Elisabeth Knoche, *Mais lacht noch auf dem Feuer: Als Ärztin 1954–1984 in Äthiopien notiert* (Erlangen, 1985).

793 P. Eugen Prucker to AA (February 8, 1957), PAAA, B92/100.

794 Deutsches Rotes Kreuz Schwesternschaft "Übersee" to AA (April 20, 1957), PAAA, B92/101.

795 Consulate Porto Alegre to AA (May 12, 1958), PAAA, B92/135.

796 Letters from the German embassy in Rio to AA (December 10, 1951, and January 12, 1952), PAAA, B92/38.

797 Circular from Foreign Office to missions abroad (March 3, 1958), PAAA, B92/135. Emphasis added.

798 AA to foreign missions, "Einrichtungen und Leistungen der deutschen christlichen Missionsgesellschaften im Ausland."

799 The government grant application form asked these agencies to provide the number and position of the personnel in three categories: German, non-native, and native. However, Catholic authorities argued for an even

more flexible definition of Germanness. Excerpt from a letter from the Catholic Missionsrat to AA, cited in AA to embassy in Dar es Salaam (January 30, 1963), PAAA, B92/322.

800 Wilhelm Bernhard to AA (June 9, 1961), and embassy Accra to AA (July 19, 1961), both in PAAA, B92/586. The hospital received DM 60,000 from the West German government.

801 Consulate Curitiba to AA (May 23, 1958), PAAA, B92/135.

802 K.W. Körner, "Das deutsche Hospital in Buenos Aires braucht Hilfe. Bundesregierung sagt 2 Millionen Mark zu; Westdeutsche Industrie soll zum Neubau beisteuern," *SZ* (February 19, 1960). To justify the German character of the hospital, the embassy explained that all 68 doctors and 180 nurses were either Germans or of German origin and that all employees had to speak German. To preserve the hospital's German character, there was an informal rule that at least 80 percent of the members of the Krankenhaus-Verein had to be German. Dr. Flachskampf to von Bismarck-Osten, Auszeichnung betr. Deutsche Krankenhaus Buenos Aires (June 15, 1960), PAAA, B92/244.

803 German embassy in Santiago to AA (December 17, 1952), PAAA, B92/38. also the letter from Schwester Edburgis, Oberin at Hospital San Jose in Puerto Varas, Chile, to Adenauer (September 14, 1954), PAAA, B92/38. Another good example of such definitional sleight-of-hand can be found in the history of West German assistance to the Mission Hospital Bambuli in northern Tanganyika. See Consulate General Nairobi to AA (September 11, 1958), PAAA, B92/135; Otto Walter, "Quarterly Report on the Progress from July 1964 to September 1964, Bethel-Mission, Report on Spending of the Grants" (October 27, 1964), and embassy in Tanzania to Foreign Office (July 28, 1964), both in PAAA, B92/322.

804 Konrad Jarausch and Hannes Siegrist, eds., *Amerikanisierung und Sowjetisierung in Deutschland 1945–1970* (Frankfurt, 1997).

805 Andreas Wenger, "Der lange Weg zur Stabilität: Kennedy, Chruschtschow und das gemeinsame Interesse der Supemächte am Staus quo in Europa," *VJZ* 46 (1998), 69–99.

806 Wallerstein, "What Cold War in Asia? An Interpretative Essay," 15–24, citation 20.

807 Urban Vahsen, *Eurafrikanische Entwicklungskooperation: Die Assoziierungspolitik der EWG gegenüber dem subsaharischen Afrika in den 1960er Jahren* (Stuttgart, 2010); and Thomas Moser, *Europäische Integration, Dekolonisation, Eurafrika* (Baden-Baden, 2000).

808 Jonathan Gosnell, "France, Empire, Europe: Out of Africa?" *Comparative Studies of South Asia, Africa and the Middle East* 26:2 (2006), 203–12; and Bo Stråth, ed., *Europe and the Other and Europe as the Other*. See also Ulrike von Hirschhausen and Kiran Klaus Patel, "Europeanization in History: An Introduction," in Martin Conway and Patel, eds., *Europeanization in the Twentieth Century* (Basingstoke, 2010), 3–27.

809 Mary Nolan, *The Transatlantic Century: Europe and America, 1890–2010* (Cambridge, 2012), 193–203; and Charles S. Maier, *Among Empires: American Ascendancy and Its Predecessors* (Cambridge, MA, 2006), 206–28.

810 Ralph Dietl, "Suez 1956: A European Intervention?" *JCH* 43:2 (2008), 259–78, citation 273.

811 Peo Hansen, "In the name of Europe," *Race & Class* 45:3 (2004), 49–62. See also Wolfgang Schmale, "Before Self-Reflexivity: Imperialism and Colonialism in the Early Discourses of European Integration," in Menno Spiering and Michael Wintle, eds., *European Identity and the Second World War* (New York, 2011), 186–201; Necati Polat, "European Integration as Colonial Discourse," *Review of International Studies* 37:3 (2011), 1–18; Catherine Schenk, "Decolonization and European Economic Integration: The Free Trade Area Negotiations, 1956–58," *The Journal of Imperial and Commonwealth History* 28 (September 1996), 444–6; and Tony Judt, "The Past Is Another Country: Myth and Memory in Postwar Europe," *Daedalus* 121 (1992), 83–118.

812 Frank Scipper and Johan Schot, "Infrastructural Europeanism, or the Project of Building Europe on Infrastructures: An Introduction," *History and Technology* 27:3 (September 2011), 245–64; and Alexander Gall, *Das Atlantropa-Projekt. Die Geschichte einer gescheiterten Vision: Hermann Sörgel und die Absenkung des Mittelmeers* (Frankfurt a.M., 1998).

813 Liliana Ellena, "Political Imagination, Sexuality and Love in the Eurafrican Debate," *European Review of History* 11:2 (2004), 241–72; Gisela Graichen and Horst Gründer, *Deutsche Kolonien: Traum und Trauma* (Berlin, 2005), 381f.; and Christian Rogowski, "'Heraus mit unsere Kolonien!' Die Kolonialrevisionismus der Weimarer Republik," Birthe Kundrus, ed., *Phantasiereich. Zur Kulturgeschichte des deutschen Kolonialismus* (Frankfurt, 2003).

814 David H. Slavin, "French Colonial Film before and after Itto: From Berber Myth to Race War," *FHS* 21:1 (Winter 1998), 144–55; and Jost Hermand, *Old Dreams of a New Reich: Volkish Utopias and National Socialism* (Bloomington, N, 1992). These cosmic racial struggles against the colored world provided the leitmotif for numerous novels and films, including Stanislaus Bialkowski, *Der Radiumkrieg* (1937), Stanislaus Bialkowski, *Krieg im All* (1935), Hans-Joachim Flechtner, *Front gegen Europa* (1935), and Heinrich Nebel, *Die farbige Front: Hinter den Kulissen der Weltpolitik* (1936).

815 Matthias Schmitt, *Kolonien Für Deutschland* (1939), Dietrich Westermann, *Afrika als europäische Aufgabe* (Berlin, 1941); Van Laak, *Imperiale Infrastruktur*, 243–48; and Karsten Linne, "The 'New Labour Policy' in Nazi Colonial Planning for Africa," *International Review of Social History* 49 (2004), 197–224. See also Wahrhold Drascher, *Die Vorherrschaft der Weissen Rasse: Die Ausbreitung des Abendländischen Lebensbereiches auf die überseeischen Erdteile* (Stuttgart, 1936).

816 Rainer Sprengel, "Geopolitik und Nationalsozialismus: Ende einer deutschen Fehlentwicklung oder fehlgeleiteter Diskurs?" in Irene Diekmann, Peter Krüger, and Julius H. Schoeps, eds., *Geopolitik: Grenzgänge im Zeitgeist*, Vol. 1 (Potsdam, 2000), 147–68; and van Laak, *Imperiale Infrastruktur*, 190ff., 231.

817 Heinz-Dietrich Ortlieb, *Europas Aufgabe in Afrika* (Hamburg, 1950); Anton Zischka, *Afrika: Europas Gemeinschaftsaufgabe Nr. 1* (Oldenburg, 1951); Gustav-Adolf Gedat, *Europas Zukunft liegt in Afrika* (Stuttgart, 1954); Hermann Sörgel, *Atlantropa: Wesenszüge eines Projekts* (Stuttgart, 1948);

Erwin Richter, "Afrika wird wichtig. Die Bedeutung des schwarzen Erdteils für Wirtschaft und Rüstung der Atlantikpaktmächte," *Rheinischer Merkur* (April 25, 1952); Hans Ulrich von Wagenheim, "Afrika – Eine europäische Aufgabe," *Der Volkswirt* (1950, Nr. 47): 14–17; Drascher, *Schuld der Weissen? Die Spätzeit des Kolonialismus* (Tübingen:, 1960); and Thomas Oppermann, "'Eurafrika'– Idee und Wirklichkeit," *Europa-Archiv*, Folge 23 (1960), 695–706.

818 Zischka, *Afrika*, 247.

819 Van Laak, *Imperiale Infrastruktur*, 363f.

820 Johannes Paulmann, *Die Haltung der Zurückhaltung: auswärtige Selbstdarstellungen nach 1945 und die Suche nach einem erneuerten Selbstverständnis in der Bundesrepublik* (Bremen, 2006), and Paulmann, "Representation without Emulation: German Cultural Diplomacy in Search of Integration and Self-Assurance during the Adenauer Era," *German Politics and Society* 25:2 (Summer 2007), 168–200. See also Helga Haftendorn, *Deutsche Außenpolitik zwischen Selbstbeschränkung und Selbstbehauptung, 1945–2000* (Munich, 2001), Michael Creswell and Marc Trachtenberg, "France and the German Question, 1945–1955," *Journal of Cold War Studies* 5:3 (2003), 5–28; and Jarausch and Siegrist, eds., *Amerikanisierung und Sowjetisierung in Deutschland*.

821 Karsten Rudolph, *Wirtschaftsdiplomatie im Kalten Krieg. Die Ostpolitik der westdeutschen Großindustrie 1945–1991* (Frankfurt a.M., 2004), 11–34, citation 20. See also Bernhard Löffler, *Soziale Marktwirtschaft und administrative Praxis: Das Bundeswirtschaftsministerium unter Ludwig Erhard* (Stuttgart, 2002); and S. Jonathan Wiesen, *West German Industry and the Challenge of the Nazi Past, 1945–1955* (Chapel Hill, NC, 2001). On the convergence of interests between industry and diplomacy in the Middle East, see Sven Olaf Berggötz, *Nahostpolitik in der Ära Adenauer: Möglichkeiten und Grenzen 1949–1963* (Düsseldorf, 1998), 141ff.

822 Cited in Jürgen Dennert, *Entwicklungshilfe geplant oder verwaltet?* (Bielefeld, 1968), 13.

823 According to one report, German industry received additional orders worth almost 8 billion marks between 1953 and 1957 due to technical assistance funded from the federal budget. *Der Volkswirt*, No. 29 (1958), Supplement, 33, cited in N. Arkadyev, "West German Neo-Colonialism in Asia," *IA* 9:4 (April 1963), 78.

824 The society published the bi-monthly journal *Afrika Heute*.

825 Berggötz, *Nahostpolitik*, 142f., 155. Krupp had worked with other German companies in Turkey and Persia before the war, and DEMAG had also had a stake in the Helwan iron and steel plant in Egypt.

826 Louis Kraft, "The French Sahara and Its Mineral Wealth," *IA*, 36:2 (April 1960) 197–205; A.M. Stahmer, "Deutsche bohren in Syrien nach Erdöl: Neue Perspektiven für die international Zusammenarbeit bei der Erdölgewinnung in Nahost," *Die Welt* (December 8, 1956). The West German position in the Middle East also benefited from the fact that, when British and French petroleum engineers withdrew during the Suez crisis, the employees of the *Deutsche Erdöl AG* remained at their jobs. This may have helped the company win the

right to explore for oil in Libya in the fall of 1958. Joachim Joesten, "In Libyen gehen die Lampen an: Bedeutende Olfunde – Chancen für deutsche Unternehmen," *Die Zeit* (October 9, 1959). The *Deutscher Ausschuss für Fragen der Erschließung der Sahara* was established in February 1957.

827   Joesten, "In Libyen gehen die Lampen an"; Berggötz, *Nahostpolitik*, 139. See also "Zusammenarbeit mit entwicklungsfähigen Ländern" (April 24, 1956), BAK B136/2519.

828   "Syrien-Risiko nicht überschätzen," *Die Zeit* (June 27, 1957). See also Maurice Moyal, "The Need for Co-operation in the Sahara," *African Affairs* 58:233 (October 1959), 329–33; Abah Bouhsini, *Die Rolle Nordarfikas (Marokko, Algerien, Tunesien) in den deutsch-französischen Beziehungen von 1950 bis 1962* (Aachen, 2000), 225–7; and Raymond G. Stokes, *Opting for Oil: The Political Economy of Technological Change in the West German Chemical Industry, 1945–1961* (Cambridge, 2006).

829   J. Etinger, *Bonn greift nach Afrika* (Berlin, 1961), 72ff.

830   Georg Gerster, *Sahara. Desert of Destiny*, tr. Stewart Thomson (New York, 1961), 185; and J. Etinger, *Bonn greift nach Afrika* (Berlin, 1961), 70ff.

831   I. Chelnokov, "Algeria and France's 'Allies'," *IA* 7:6 (1961), 90–2; and M. Voslensky, "Is France Following Bonn's Path?" *Current Digest of the Russian Press* 11:12 (April 22, 1959), 30–1.

832   Gordon Martel, "Decolonization after Suez: Retreat or Rationalisation?" *Australian Journal of Politics and History* 46:3 (2000), 403–17; Rolf Pfeiffer, "Ein erfolgreiches Kapitel bundesdeutscher Aussenpolitik: Die Adenauer-Regierung und die Suez-Krise von 1956," *Historische Mitteilungen* 13, 1 (2000), 213–32. See also Alexander Keese, "A Culture of Panic: 'Communist' Scapegoats and Decolonization in French West Africa and French Polynesia (1945–1957)," *FCH* 9 (2008), 131–46.

833   Vahsen, *Eurafrikanische Entwicklungskooperation*; and Moser, *Europäische Integration*.

834   One British official described the associational mechanism as simply "the continuation of French colonialism supported by German funds," Martel, "Decolonization after Suez: Retreat or Rationalisation?" 409. See also Ulf Engel, *Die Afrikapolitik der Bundesrepublik Deutschland 1949–1999: Rollen und Identitäten* (Münster, 2000), 236; Louis Sicking, "A Colonial Echo: France and the Colonial Dimension of the European Economic Community," *FCH* 5 (2004), 207–28; and J. Schot and T. Misa, "Inventing Europe: Technology and the Hidden Integration of Europe," *History and Technology* 21 (2005), 1–19.

835   *Sten. Ber.*, 2.Wahlperiode, 208. Sitzung (May 9, 1957), 12004-6; and Moser, *Europäische Integration*, 378–9.

836   Cited in Bouhsini, *Die Rolle Nordafrikas*, 224f.

837   Cited in Hans Magnus Enzensberger, "Algerien ist überall" (1961). The text is included in W. Balsen and K. Rössel, *Hoch die Internationale Solidarität* (Cologne, 1986), 73.

838   *Sten. Ber.*, 2.Wahlperiode, 208. Sitzung (May 9, 1957), 12012-13.

839   J. J. van der Lee, "The European Common Market and Africa," *The World Today* 16:9 (September 1960), 370–6, citation 375.

840 Rolf Itaaliander, *Schwarze Haut im Roten Griff* (Düsseldorf, 1962); Fritz
Schatten, *Afrika – Schwarz oder Rot* (Munich, 1961); Klaus Mehnert, *Asien,
Moskau und Wir* (Stuttgart, 1959); and Eberhard Stahn, *Der Kommunismus
in Afrika* (Leer, 1965).

841 *Sten. Ber.*, 3. Wahlperiode, 3. Sitzung (October 29, 1957), 25.

842 *Sten. Ber.*, 3. Wahlperiode, 4. Sitzung (November 5, 1957), 54. Gerstenmaier
maintained that West Germany's help to Africa would ease "the stormy
transformation" there and ultimately serve "the salvation of the world."
See his foreword to Otto Schmidt, *Afrika im Aufbruch: Tagebuch einer Reise
durch Belgisch-Kongo und Cameroun* (Köln, 1960), 5. Together, six parlia-
mentarians, including Schmidt (CDU), and the Secretary General of the
German Africa Society toured the Belgian Congo and Cameroon in August
and September 1959.

843 Moser, *Europäische Integration*, 378–79.

844 *Ibid.*, 391–93, 457.

845 "Frankreichs Zeit in Afrika ist abgelaufen," *Der Spiegel* (January 28, 1959).

846 Moser, *Europäische Integration*, 397. The East Germans denounced the
Common Market as a form of "collective colonialism" and "customs union
of monopolies," *Ibid.* See also Paul Friedländer and Hartmut Schilling,
*Kolonialmacht Westdeutschland: Zum Wesen, zu den Besonderheiten und
Methoden des westdeutschen Neokolonialismus* (Berlin, 1962); and Schil-
ling, *EWG-Schatten über Afrika: Zum kollektiven Kolonialismus der EWG*
(Berlin, 1963).

847 On criticism of this official policy of restraint in Africa, see Erik Verg, *Das
Afrika der Afrikaner* (Stuttgart, 1960), 18.

848 Memorandum from the foreign minister (May 16, 1960), cited in Engel, *Die
Afrikapolitik der Bundesrepublik*, 244.

849 Cited in Engel, *Die Afrikapolitik der Bundesrepublik*, 40. This claim circulated
widely in the Third World in the 1950s and early 1960s. For example, see
"Eine versäumte Gelegenheit? Deutsche Hilfe für entwicklungsfähige Länder
nicht ausreichend," *Die Welt* (January 4, 1957); and Otto Uhlmann, *Afrikaner
im Westerwald* (Hangelar bei Bonn, 1963). Later scholars have dismissed this
claim as a form of colonial amnesia. See Volker M. Langbehn, ed., *German
Colonialism, Visual Culture, and Modern Memory* (London, 2010); Sandra
Maß, *Weiße Helden, schwarze Krieger: Zur Geschichte kolonialer Männlichkeit in Deutschland 1918–1964* (Cologne, 2006); Monika Albrecht, "(Post-)
Colonial Amnesia? German Debates on Colonialism and Decolonization in
the Post-war Era," and Dennis Laumann, "Narratives of a 'Model Colony':
German Togoland in Written and Oral Histories," both in Michael Perraudin
and Jürgen Zimmerer, eds., *German Colonialism and National Identity*
(London, 2011), 187–96 and 278–9; and Helma Lutz and Kathrin Gawarecki,
eds., *Kolonialismus und Erinnerungskultur* (Münster, 2005).

850 Hasso von Etzdorf to ambassador Brückner in Pretoria (May 24, 1961),
cited in Albrecht Hagemann, "Bonn und die Apartheid in Südafrika,"
VJZ 43:4 (October 1995), 679–706, citation 685. See also Albrecht
Hagemann, "Bonn und die Apartheid in Südafrika: Eine Denkschrift des
Deutschen Botschafters Rudolf Hozhausen aus dem Jahr 1954," *VJZ* 43: 4

(October 1995), 679–706; and Heinz Gollwitz, *Die Gelbe Gefahr* (Göttingen, 1962).

851 Citations from speeches by Gerstenmaier and Erhard in *Afrika-Informationsdienst*, No. 20 (November 4, 1960), 250–2 and 255–7, respectively.

852 "Deutsches Messeschiff fährt nach Afrika" *Stuttgarter Nachrichten* (November 19, 1960), BAK, B102/94776.

853 A bilateral agreement enabled some 50 Ghanaian students and trainees to travel to East Germany in 1959. All of these programs were codified by a January 4, 1960 resolution approved by the SED Central Committee. See Hans-Georg Schleicher, "Entwicklungszusammenarbeit und Aussenpolitik der DDR: Das Beispiel Afrika," in Bücking, ed., *Entwicklungspolitische Zusammenarbeit*, 95–110, especially 99.

854 William Roger Louis and Roger Owen, *A Revolutionary Year: The Middle East in 1958* (London, 2002); Elizabeth Schmidt, *Cold War and Decolonization in Guinea, 1946–1958* (Athens, OH, 2007); and Jay Straker, *Youth, Nationalism, and the Guinean Revolution* (Bloomington, IN, 2009).

855 William Attwood, *The Reds and the Blacks. A Personal Adventure* (New York, 1967), 21.

856 East Germany also agreed to purchase (at a price well below market) the newly harvested banana crop, which had been left piled at the docks when the French refused to honor their import agreement. John H. Morrow, *First American Ambassador to Guinea* (New Brunswick, 1968), 125.

857 Lothar Killmer, *Freiheitstrommel von Accra* (Berlin, 1962), 31, 34.

858 Morrow, *First American Ambassador*, 131.

859 Felix Brahm, *Wissenschaft und Dekolonisation: Paradigmenwechsel und institutioneller Wandel in der akademischen Beschäftigung mit Afrika in Deutschland und Frankreich, 1930–1970* (Stuttgart, 2010).

860 W. E. B. Du Bois also sent a written contribution. The conference papers were published as *Geschichte und Geschichtsbild Afrikas; Beiträge der Arbeitstagung für Neuere und Neueste Geschichte Afrikas am 17. und 18. April 1959 in Leipzig* (Berlin, 1960), which appeared as the first two volumes in the series *Studien zur Kolonialgeschichte und Geschichte der nationalen und kolonialen Befreiungsbewegung* (Berlin, 1960). This series published the fruits of the institute's research on German colonialism in East Africa, Southwest Africa, and China. A 1961 conference dealt with the question of neocolonialism and the two German states.

861 Ulrich van der Heyden, *Die Afrikawissenschaften in der DDR: Eine akademische Disziplin zwischen Exotik und Exempel* (Münster, 1999), and Thea Büttner, "The Development of African Historical Studies in East Germany. An Outline and Selected Bibliography," *History in Africa* 19 (1992), 133–46.

862 See Markov, "Zur universalgeschichtlichen Einordnung des afrikanischen Freiheitskampfes," in *Geschichte und Geschichtsbild Afrikas*, especially 22.

863 Ralph A. Austen, "African Studies in East Germany," *The Journal of Modern African Studies* 2:2 (July 1964), 289–90. East German historians began to publish works drawn from the German colonial archives. See, for example, Walther Manshard, "Deutsche Afrika-Gesellschaft," *The Journal*

of Modern African Studies 3:4 (December 1965), 607–8. All of these policies compared favorably to developments in West Germany, which as late as 1964 still had no interdisciplinary African studies program at the university level. See Brahm, *Wissenschaft und Dekolonisation*, 219–243.

864 Reimbold, "Note" on German traveling exhibition through West Africa (November 29, 1960), BAK, B102/94776.

865 Peter Scholz to AA (August 29, 1963), PAAA, B34/468.

866 Ausstellungs-und Messe-Ausschuss der Deutschen Wirtschaft e.V., "Report on the German Traveling Exhibition in West Africa from Conakry to Lagos" (April 11, 1962), PAAA, B68/143; "Comments" by the participants in the mobile exhibition in West Africa (n.d.), BAK, B102/ 94777; and "Deutsche Wanderausstellung Zentral-Ostafrika 1963," BAK, B102/94784. The phrase "propaganda safaris" is taken from "Preußens Gloria," *Der Spiegel* (September 9, 1964).

867 Peter Tornow to Commerce Ministry (August 3, 1962), BAK, B102/94777; Scholz, Note (December 19, 1963), PAAA, B34/468; and the notes by Amsberg and Török (both September 6, 1963), PAAA, B68/318.

868 Török, Notes (September 6, 1963), PAAA, B68/318; Scholz, "Versuch einer kritischen Wertung der Deutschen Wanderausstellung Ost-Zentralafrika 1963" (December 8, 1963), PAAA B34/468; and "Preußens Gloria," *Der Spiegel*.

869 Doering (embassy in Cameroon) to AA (May 4, 1962), PAAA, B68/189c; Amsberg, Note (September 6, 1963), PAAA, B68/318; and Gemünd, Note (January 31, 1964), BAK, B102/94784. The locals – both indigenous and European expatriates – complained that the German march music made it appear as if the German military had invaded the place.

870 "Wagen, 'Entwicklungshilfe'" (March 25, 1963), PAAA, 68/143.

871 Scholz to Gemünd (October 5, 1963), Sarrazin to AA (October 26, 1963), and Scholz, Note (October 7, 1963), all in PAAA, B34/468.

872 "German Fair. P.R. mistakes," *Reporter* (September 21, 1963), PAAA, B34/ 468.

873 H. Walter, Landwirtschaftliche Schule Hohenheim to Deutsche Forschungsgemeinschaft (October 2, 1963), PAAA, B34/468.

874 Herbert Schroeder to AA (December 4, 1963), PAAA, B34/525; and "Preußens Gloria," *Der Spiegel*.

875 Informationsmaterial for Sendung für Afrika (Bonn, October 25, 1963), and Sarrazin to AA (October 26, 1963), both in PAAA, B34/468.

876 *Sunday News* (October 20, 1963), cited in Scholz, "Versuch einer kritischen Wertung der deutschen Wanderausstellung Ost-Zentralafrika 1963" (December 8, 1963), PAAA, B34/468.

877 Cited in "Preußens Gloria," *Der Spiegel*.

878 Christian Brockdorff, "Die schlimmsten Jahre ihres Lebens: Studenten aus Entwicklungsländern berichten über ihre Erfahrungen in der Bundesrepublik," *Vorwärts* (February 26, 1960). In September 1962, the Berlin Industry Exhibition organized a special Africa exhibition entitled "Partner of Progress."

879 On the cultural representation of Africa, see Rosemarie K. Lester, *Trivialneger: Das Bild des Schwarzen im westdeutschen Illustriertenroman* (Stuttgart, 1982); and Kum'a Ndumbe III, *Was Will Bonn in Afrika? Zur Afrikapolitik der Bundesrepublik Deutschland* (Pfaffenweiler, 1992).

880 Annette Weinke, "The German-German Rivalry and the Prosecution of Nazi War Criminals during the Cold War, 1958–1965," in Nathan Stoltzfus and Henry Friedlander, eds., *Nazi Crimes and the Law* (Cambridge, 2008), 151–72; Timothy R. Vogt, *Denazification in Soviet-occupied Germany: Brandenburg, 1945–1948* (Cambridge, MA, 2000), 175; and Jürgen Danyel, "Die unbescholtene Macht. Zum antifaschistischen Selbstverständnis der ostdeutschen Eliten," in Peter Hübner, ed., *Eliten im Sozialismus. Beiträge zur Sozialgeschichte der DDR* (Cologne, 1999).

881 Cited in "West Germany: The Adipose Society," *Time* (July 19, 1963).

882 "East Germany: They Have Given up Hope," *Time* (December 6, 1963); and "West Germany: Brunnhilde Reshaped," *Time* (May 8, 1964),

883 Erhard, "Hilfe für Entwicklungsländer. Die politische, wirtschaftliche und soziale Problematik," *Die Zeit* Nr. 49/1957. See also Hubertus von Tobien, *Die Methoden des sowjetischen Imperialismus: ein Beitrag zur Parole der Koexistenz*, 2nd ed. (Bonn, 1958); Klaus Billerbeck, *Die Auslandshilfe des Ostblocks für die Entwicklungsländer* (Hamburg, 1960); and Eberhard Stahn, *Der Kommunismus in Afrika* (Leer, 1965).

884 "The Sino-Soviet Economic Offensive through June 1962," PAAA, B58-IIIB1–353; "Facts and Figures," *International Affairs* 12:19 (1973), 116; and Dorothy Miller, "United Arab Republic and the Two Germanies" (September 24, 1962), HU OSA 300-8-3:24-5-52.

885 See also *Boten der Freundschaft. Eine Kamera begleitet Minister Präsident Otto Grotewohl durch den Nahen und Fernen Osten* (Berlin, 1959); and Hans-Peter Osten, *Wandlungen am Nil. Die staatliche und wirtschaftliche Entwicklung der ägyptischen Region der VAR* (Berlin, 1959).

886 "In Kairo sitzt der Russe," *Der Spiegel* (January 14, 1959), 19–20.

887 *Ibid.*

888 *Die Protokolle des Bundesvorstandes der CDU 1953–1957*, Nr. 16 (September 20, 1956), 1027f.

889 "Der Elefant," *Der Spiegel*, Nr. 12/1960 (March 16, 1960), 15–23.

890 Social Democrat Hans Jürgen Wischnewski, who toured Ghana, Guinea, and Togo in summer 1960, witnessed firsthand the "uncanny" initiatives of East Germany in the region, as well as the resources that they were devoted to development aid. He concluded that "we have to pay more attention to Africa," *Parlamentarisch-Politischer Pressedienst* (September 5,1960), BAK B102, Nr. 94776. Wischnewski also noted the East Germans were paying for 117 Guineans to study in that country, while West Germany was only sponsoring 4 Guinean students. See also *Bericht über die Afrika-Reise der Hamburger Delegation* (Hamburg, 1961).

891 *Sten. Ber.* 3. Wahlperiode, 118. Sitzung (June 22, 1960), 6821, 6823.

892 Wolfgang Rieger, "Wirtschaftswunder für farbige Völker," *Deutschland und die Entwicklungsländer* (Hamburg, 1961); Kurt Hesse, *Entwicklungsländer und Entwicklungshilfen an der Wende des Kolonialzeitalters* (Berlin, 1962);

Heinz-Dietrich Ortlieb, *Was wird aus Afrika? Rassismus, Neo-Kolonialismus, Entwicklungshilfe* (Zürich, 1976); Louis Barcata, *Schreie aus dem Dschungel: Africa – Aufstieg oder Untergang* (Stuttgart, 1961); Fritz Neumark, *Materielle und psychologische Probleme in den Entwicklungsländern* (Bad Homburg, 1961); and Albert von Haller, *Die Letzten wollen die Ersten sein: der Westen und die Revolution der farbigen Völker* (Stuttgart, 1963).

893 *Sten. Ber.* 3. Wahlperiod, 108. Sitzung (April 6, 1960), 50. The same motif can be found in a speech by Erhard in *Afrika-Informationsdienst*, No. 20 (November 4, 1960), 255–7.

894 Joint letter from ministers of economics and foreign affairs to Adenauer (August 1961), BAK, B102/47309; Fritz W. Meyer, "Entwicklungshilfe und Wirtschaftsordnung," in Ordo, 12 (1960/61), 279–303; and Albert Hunold, ed., *Entwicklungsländer. Wahn und Wirklichkeit* (Erlenbach-Zürich, 1961); and Matthias Schmitt, *A "Marshall Plan" for the Developing Countries* (Stuttgart-Degerloch, 1960). His 1939 book, *Kolonien Für Deutschland*, was an unapologetic claim to German colonialism. In the Bundesrepublik, he was considered as an expert on development aid to the Third World. See Schmitt, *Entwicklungsländer als weltwirtschaftliche Aufgabe* (Berlin, 1959); *Partnerschaft Mit Entwicklungsländern*, 2nd. ed. (Stuttgart-Degerloch, 1960); *Die befreite Welt: Vom Kolonialsystem zur Partnerschaft* (Baden-Baden, 1962); and *Entwicklungshilfe als Unternehmerische Aufgaben* (Frankfurt a.M., 1965). For more on the Ordoliberals, see Dieter Plewhe, "The Origins of the Neoliberal Economic Development Discourse," in Philip Mirowski and Dieter Plehwe, eds., *The Road from Mont Pelerin: The Making of Neoliberal Thought Collective* (Cambridge, MA, 2009), 238–79.

895 Hubertus Büschel, "In Afrika helfen: Akteure westdeutscher 'Entwicklungshilfe' und ostdeutscher 'Solidarität' 1955–1975," *AfS* 48 (2008), 333–65; Bastian Hein, *Die Westdeutschen und die Dritte Welt* (Munich, 2005); Hendrik Grote, "Von der Entwicklungshilfe zur Entwicklungspolitik: Voraussetzungen, Strukturen und Mentalitäten der bundesdeutschen Entwicklungshilfe 1949–1961," *Vorgänge* 43:2 (2004), 24–35; Brigitte H. Schulz, *Development Policy in the Cold War Era: The Two Germanies and Sub-Saharan Africa, 1960–1985* (Münster, 1995); and Hans-Joachim Spanger and Lothar Brock, eds., *Die beiden deutschen Staaten in der Dritten Welt: Die Entwicklungspolitik der DDR – eine Herausforderung für die Bundesrepublik Deutschland?* (Opladen, 1987).

896 "Chefbesprechung" (September 22, 1958), and Vermerk, "Ressortbesprechung" (September 8, 1958), both in BAK, B102/13759.

897 Appendix 3 to the letter from three ministries to the State Secretary of the Bundeskanzleramt (December 30, 1961), PAAA, B58-IIIB1/388. See also Ludger Westrick, "Die deutsche Entwicklungshilfe," *Bulletin*, Nr. 212 (November 11, 1961), 1985–90. In 1961, a total of 37 developing countries received development aid, with Syria topping the list, followed by Pakistan, Liberia, Iran, Brazil, and Egypt. Kabinetvorlage (November 15, 1961),

BAK, B102/52069. The leading German Ordoliberals, including Erhard, Müller-Armack, and Fritz Baade, also established a research institute for development economics. See BMW to the Interministerial Committee (January 11, 1961) and Baade, "Plan für ein Institut für wirtschaftliche Grundlagenforschung über Probleme der Entwicklungsländer," both in BAK, B102/52068.

898 Memorandum for a meeting of Interministerieller Ausschuss für Fragen der Entwicklungspolitik (December 18, 1961), BAK, B102/52069.

899 Scheel, "Möglichkeiten einer aktiven Entwicklungspolitik: Konstituierung des entwicklungspolitischen Beirats...," *Bulletin*, Nr. 103 (June 15, 1963). In 1962 the government established a development policy advisory council, whose members included representatives from the political parties, industry, labor, the churches, and academia.

900 Heide-Irene Schmidt, "Pushed to the Front: The Foreign Assistance Policy of the Federal Republic of Germany, 1958–1971," *CEH* 12:4 (2003), 473–507.

901 Jim Tomlinson, "The Commonwealth, the Balance of Payments and the Politics of International Poverty: British Aid Policy, 1958–1971," and Gérard Bossuat, "French Development Aid and Co-operation under de Gaulle," both in *CEH* 12:4 (2003), 413–29, 431–56.

902 "Gedanken zu einer Konzeption der Aussenpolitik und der Entwicklungshilfe in der neutralen Welt" (undated), BAK, B136/2924. In 1962, the United States asked Scheel to identify those regions in the underdeveloped world where West Germany would be willing to assume a leading role among the Western powers in the provision of development aid and pressured West Germany to play a larger role in Africa, where military aid was just as important as development programs. Scheel and Knappstein to Bonn, (September 27, 1962); and Prof. Otto Donner, Note on Scheel meeting at the State Department, U.S. Treasury, and the World Bank (Oct. 2, 1962), both in BAK, B102/52069. The problem was that, while military aid to such countries as Nigeria, Guinea, Somalia, and Tanganyika might have been important in strengthening relations to these countries and thus preempting such aid from the communist bloc, it ran the risk of worsening relations with those countries, whose relations to the beneficiaries of such aid were unfriendly if not outright hostile (such as Ethiopia, in the case of Somalia). Steltzer, Memorandum on the current affairs in Africa (Fall, 1963), PAAA, B34/463.

903 Lorenz M. Lüthi, *The Sino-Soviet Split: Cold War in the Communist World* (Princeton, NJ, 2008); John C. Ausland, *Kennedy, Khrushchev, and the Berlin-Cuba Crisis* (Oslo, 1996); Wenger, "Der Lange Weg Zur Stabilität," Jeremy Friedman, "Soviet Policy in the Developing World and the Chinese Challenge in the 1960s," *CWH* 10:2 (May 2010), 247–72; and Kara Stibora Fulcher, "A Sustainable Position? The United States, the Federal Republic, and the Ossification of Allied Policy on Germany, 1958–1962," *DH* 26:2 (Spring 2002), 283–307.

904 Eggers, "Ergebnisprotokoll" (December 21, 1963), PAAA, B58-IIIB1/336.

905 A similar request was made for South Vietnam. Alexander Troche, *"Berlin wird am Mekong verteidgt"*.

906 Referat I B3, "Diskussionsvorlage betr. Arbeitssitzung mit Aussenminister Kamona" (May 5, 1964), and Pauls, Betr. "Besondere Entwicklungshilfe für Tanganyika/Sansibar" (May 12, 1964), both PAAA, B34/511. See also Ulf Engel and Hans-Georg Schleicher, *Die beiden deutschen Staaten in Afrika: Zwischen Konkurrenz und Koexistez 1949–1990* (Hamburg, 1998), 233ff.

907 The West Germans were concerned about their reputation in sub-Saharan Africa for other reasons as well. Political crises notwithstanding, West Germans continued to vacation in Tanganyika with 1,500 West Germans going on safari in the country in early 1964 alone. Many Tanganyikans, however, had read newspaper accounts of racial discrimination in West Germany, including a widely circulated report that a Berlin restaurant had refused to serve four Tanganyikan trainees. Of much greater concern, however, was continuing West German support for white settler regimes in southern Africa. For example, after returning from a fact-finding trip to Portugal and Angola, Bundestag vice president and chair of the defense committee Richard Jaeger (CSU) told a reporter that "the colonial states brought order and stability to Africa for the first time... Chaos breaks out everywhere Europe yields." Jaeger predicted that "so-called sovereign Africa" would disappear into chaos within a decade due to the inability of these countries to govern themselves, and he urged the Salazar government to hold on to its colonies. "Tanganjika mit München verbunden," *SZ* (February 25, 1964); Ambassador Schroeder to Foreign Office, "Haltung der tanganjikischen Presse gegenüber der Bundesrepublik" (January 18, 1964), PAAA, B34/523; *Münchener Abendzeitung* (September 15, 1960); and Ilizwe Lasizwe, "Westdeutscher Neokolonialismus in Afrika," *Internationale Politik* 335 (March 20, 1964), PAAA, B34/557.

908 Daniel Gerlach, *Die doppelte Front: Die Bundesrepublik Deutschlands und der Nahostkonflikt, 1967–1973* (Berlin, 2006); and Alexander Troche, *Ulbricht und die Dritte Welt. Ost-Berlins "Kampf" gegen die Bonner "Alleinvertretungsanmaßung"* (Erlangen, 1996). See also Massimiliano Trentin, *Engineers of Modern Development: East German Experts in Ba'thist Syria, 1965–1972* (CLEUP, 2010); and Trentin, "Modernization as State Building: The Two Germanies in Syria, 1963–1972," *DH* 33:3 (2009), 487–505.

909 On this and the following, see Christian Jetzlsperger, "Die Emanzipation der Entwicklungspolitik von der Hallstein-Doktrin. Die Krise der deutschen Nahostpolitik von 1965, die Entwicklungspolitik, und der Ost-West Konflikt," *Historisches Jahrbuch* 121 (2001), 320–66. Egypt was the fifth largest recipient of West German aid (after India, Pakistan, Syria, and Afghanistan).

910 "Entwicklungshilfe," *Der Spiegel*, Nr. 49/1964 (December 2), 47–65, illustration 65.

911 Pauls, "Aufzeichnung Betr.: Verhältnis von Außen-und Entwicklungspolitik" (December 16, 1964), PAAA, B68/319. See also Pauls, "Außenpolitik und Entwicklungshilfe," *Außenpolitik* 6 (1965), 375–88.

912 The need to preserve the connection between development aid and reunification meant that such aid would have to be provided strictly on a bilateral basis because any aid given through multilateral programs would make it

impossible to determine whether the beneficiary country truly stood shoulder to shoulder with the West Germans on the issue that mattered most to them.

913 "Kurzprotokoll über gemeinsame Sitzung des IAE mit dem Beirat des AGE am 14. Mai 1965," BAK, B102/47307, and "Vermerk, Betr.: Entwicklungspolitik" (May 26, 1965), BAK, B102/52071. See also Scheel, *Konturen einer Neuen Welt: Schwierigkeiten, Ernüchterung und Chancen der Industrieländer* (Düsseldorf, 1965).

914 Praß to Erhard, "Betr.: Entwicklungshilfe" (March 20, 1965), BAK, B136/2924.

915 Minister of Finance to AA, "Betr.: Die internationalen Konferenzen der Entwicklungsländer und die Deutschlandfrage" (October 2, 1964), PAAA, B58-IIIB1.

916 Schroeder to other ministers, "Betr.: Die internationalen Konferenzen der Entwicklungsländer und die Deutschlandfrage" (September 4, 1964), and Lanwer, "Betr.: Entwurf einer Antwort des Herrn Minister…" (October 30, 1964), both in AAA, B58-IIIB1.

917 "Gedanken zu einer Konzeption der Aussenpolitik und der Entwicklungshilfe in der neutralen Welt" (undated), BAK, B136/2924. The document carries the notation "from representative Fritz," but the signature is illegible, and it is not clear whether Fritz is the actual author. From 1964 on, Fritz was the curator of the Deutsche Stiftung für Entwicklungsländer. For an account of China's focus on selected countries in sub-Saharan Africa (initially the four states of Guinea, Mali, Ghana, and Somalia – to which Kenya, Tanganyika, and Zanzibar were added in 1964). See Note (June 26, 1964), PAAA, B68/319.

918 On the diplomatic dimensions of the Hallstein doctrine, see William Glenn Gray, *Germany's Cold War. The Global Campaign to Isolate East Germany, 1949–1969* (Chapel Hill, NC, 2003).

919 West German embassy in New Delhi to the Foreign Office (August 31, 1970), PAAA, B85/ 2196, and "Inderinnen für europäischer Klöster. Sklavenhandel unter christlichem Zeichen? – Heikle Situation für den Vatikan," *Badische Zeitung* (August 24, 1970).

920 Report from the Consulate General in Hong Kong (September 1, 1970), PAAA, B85/2196.

921 Interview with Lee Su-kil by Wolfgang Zwietasch, *Kölner Stadt-Anzeiger* (undated). Private archive of Lee Su-kil.

922 "Die Bundesrepublik – Ein Unterentwickeltes Land," *Der Spiegel*, Nr. 36/1961, 32ff., Nr. 37, 52ff., Nr. 38, 62ff., and Nr. 39, 48ff., citations from 32–35 of the first article.

923 These advancements in medical technology also began to attract men to into the profession, which resulted in an increase in the percentage of male nurses from 6.6 percent in 1950 to 8.9 percent in 1961 and 12.9 percent in 1970. Susanne Kreutzer, *Vom "Liebesdienst" zum modernen Frauenberuf: Die Reform der Krankenpflege nach 1945* (Frankfurt, 2005), 29. According to Kreutzer (26), the work week for nurses was reduced from 54 to 51 hours in 1958, to 48 hours in 1960, and to 40 hours in 1974. *Ibid.*, 26.

924 Rudolf Bernhardt, "Die ausländische Arbeitskräfte in den deutschen Krankenhäusern," *Das Krankenhaus* 11 (1966), 446. According to a 1962 Hessian survey, the patient–nurse ratio was twice as high as it should have been.
Schell to Hessisches Ministerium für Arbeit, Soziales und Gesundheit (February 12, 1963), HHStA, 2047/251.

925 "25000 Ordensfrauen fehlen in Deutschland," *Neue Presse* (September 29,
1962). In 1962, the University Hospital in Würzburg was forced to close
three of its four gynecology wards (with 85 beds) because the lack of younger
recruits forced a nursing order to withdraw 36 of its members, "Eine
Frauenklinik fast geschlossen," *FAZ* (December 31, 1962).

926 Kreutzer, *Vom "Liebesdienst" zum modernen Frauenberuf*, 257ff., and
"Samariterinnen für Halbe Tage," *FAZ* (December 9, 1961).

927 BAA to BAS (October 20, 1966), and "In der BRD beschäftigte ausländische
Arbeitnehmer in der Krankenpflege," both in BAK, B149/22407.

928 Eichinger to Mutterhaus der Dominikanerinnen in Arenberg (March 30,
1965), AdCV, 380.40.030. Fasz.1; Maria A. Lücker to Hüssler, the Secretary
General of the Caritasverband (January 9, 1964), AdCV, 389.9n. Fasz. 2;
and Dr. Sicha/Labor Ministry to Tacke (April 19, 1961), Tacke to Labor
Ministry (April 28, 1961), and Labor Ministry, "Ausbildung von Arbeit-
skräften aus südostasiatischen Staaten" (July 1962), all in BAK, B149/6246,
as well as Kurt Schmidtke to Korean labor attaché in Bonn (May 16, 1968).
Shortly after Tacke's death in 2008, some of his papers (including this last
letter) were given to the author; the remainder are in the possession of
Tacke's son Volker. Tacke also approached the Korean government with a
proposal to recruit an additional 2,000–3,000 young Koreans. Labor Ministry to Tacke (April 19, 1961), German embassy in Seoul to Foreign Office
(September 25, 1961), both in BAK, B149/6246; and Gesellschaft zur Förderung und Betreuung asiatischer Studenten to the Foreign Minister (July 22,
1966), PAAA, B85/1319.

929 Elisabeth Bieberich to the Catholic Bureau Bonn (October 20, 1970), and
"Schwestern-Schülerinnen schlecht behandelt?" unidentified newspaper clip-
ping, both in AdCV, 389.9n, Fasz. 1. During this period a small number of
African women also came to West Germany. See "Zwischenbericht zur
Frage: Mädchen aus Übersee in deutschen caritativen Anstalten" (February
8, 1967), AdCV, 104 and 107, Fasz. 6.

930 Memorandum on the guidelines governing the employment of the non-
European workers (June 12, 1962), BAK, B149/22407.

931 Minutes of the AK meeting (November 27, 1964), BAK, B149/22428.

932 Around 1970, the number of nurses leaving for North America and West
Germany was just about equal to the total number of annual graduates from
the country's nursing schools. German embassy in Manila to AA (May 19,
1972), BAK, B119/6753.

933 The relative qualifications of German nurses and those from the Philippines
and Korea were a frequent topic of discussion. In contrast to German nurses,
nurses in the Philippines and Korea had to have graduated from high school,
rather than only elementary or middle school, and their four-year education
included the relevant life sciences, physics and chemistry, as well as

psychology, sociology, math, and both English and Spanish. According to a German embassy report, the Philippine curriculum was more comprehensive and more challenging than that of German nursing schools, and Filipina nurses were generally more educated than licensed nurses in Germany. For all of these reasons, the Philippine government would not recognize the training of German nurses as equivalent to their own registered nurses. Botschaft Manila an das Auswärtige Amt, "Betr.: Anerkennung von philippinischen 'Registered Nurses',") (April 5, 1968), BAK, B189/35644.

934 German embassy in Manila to AA, "Betr.: Beschäftigung philippinischer Krankenschwestern in Deutschland" (August, 26, 1965), BAS to AA, "Betr.: Beschäftigung philippinischer Krankenschwestern in der Bundesrepublik" (November 2, 1965), and the associated correspondence in BAK, B189/35644.

935 German embassy in Manila to AA, "Betr.: Beschäftigung philippinischer Krankenschwestern in Deutschland" (June 3, 1966), "Aktennotiz über ein Gespräch mit Vertretern der philippinischen Botschaft und des Catholic Travel Center...am 9. Oktober 1970;" and Hessische Krankenhausgesellschaft to LA Hessen (November 20, 1970), BAK, B119/6753. There were also suspicions that the Philippines Nursing Association was also profiting financially from its intermediary role.

936 Bernhardt to Käfferbitz (February 22, 1966), BAK, B149/22428.

937 "Präsident der BAA an den Präsidenten des LA Baden-Württemberg, Betr.: Anwerbung koreanischen bzw. philipinischen Krankenpflegepersonal" (August 17, 1967), BAK, B119/6752. The Australian and Canadian governments had experienced similar frustrations in their own negotiations with the Philippine government.

938 BAS to Oberin Elster (October 23, 1968), BAK, B119/6752.

939 Philippines Department of Labor (April 26, 1972), BAK, B119/6753.

940 DKG to BAS (October 10, 1972), "Ergebnisprotokoll der Besprechung am 19. Dezember 1972," BAK, B119/6753, and "Ergebnisprotokoll der Besprechung am 28. Dezember 1972," ADKGRP.

941 German embassy in Manila (May 25, 1973), BAK, B149/67446.

942 German embassy in Manila to AA (November, 14, 1974), BAK, B149/67446.

943 The following is drawn primarily from AdCV, 389.9n Fasz. 1, 187.50.0843 Fasz. 2, and, on Keralese nurses in Germany, AdCV, 380.40/125.50 Fasz. 1, and correspondence between the Baden-Württemberg government and the Baden-Württemberg branch of the DKG from August 1962 to November 1962, PAAA, B189/35644.

944 "Inder in der Bundesrepublik Deutschland" (May 1973), AdCV, 187.50.0843, Fasz. 2, and "A Service Project for Indians Abroad" (1972), AdCV, 187.50.0843, Fasz.2.

945 "Nirmala-Verpflichtung," AdCV, 389.9n, Fasz. 2.

946 "Niederschrift über die Arbeitskonferenz zum Thema 'Mädchen aus Übersee'" (February 22, 1967), AdCV, 204.15.030 Fasz. 1.

947 "Supreme Council for National Reconstruction, Republic of Korea," BAK, B149/6246, Bd. 1.

948 Park to Adenauer (November 6, 1961), BAK, B136/3264.

949 Gerstenmaier to Erhard (July 16, 1964), BAK, B136, Nr. 6264. Gerstenmaier, who visited Korea, brought Park's book back with him, had it translated into German, and sent a copy to Erhard. The German manuscript can be found in BAK, B136/6264.

950 Note (December 12, 1961), and "Besprechung mit koreanischer Wirtschafts-delegation im BMW" (December 11, 1961), both in BAK, B149/6246; and Bünger to Foreign Office (November 3, 1961), BAK, B102/102233.

951 Dahnen, Note (April 25, 1963), and BAS to AA (May 9, 1963), both in BAK, B149/6246. See also Korean Economic Planning Board, "Status as of June 26, 1964 of economic and technical cooperation between FRG and ROK and proposal for further cooperation" (June 26, 1964), BAK, B213/8749. From 1963 to 1980, about 8,000 Koreans worked as miners in West Germany. For more, see Cornelius Nestler-Tremel and Ulrike Tremel, *Im Schatten des Lebens: Südkoreaner im Steinkohlebergbau von Nordrhein-Westfalen* (Heidelberg, 1985), 1.

952 The International Human Rights League of Korea to chancellor (December 21, 1964), PAAA, B85/1319.

953 Hsinhua News Agency, "Slave Trade in South Korea" (October 6, 1964), BAK, B149/22428.

954 "Report Asked on Miners' Strike in Germany," *Korea Times* (April 11, 1965), BAK, B149/ 22428.

955 Ehman, "Vermerk betr. Delegationsverhandlungen mit Südkorea" (November 9 and 24, 1964), "Vermerk betr. Besuch des koreanischen Wirtschaft-ministers" (November, 25, 1964), and Report on Korean-German meetings to discuss bilateral treaties (December 4, 1964), all in BAK, B213/8749.

956 Dahnen's Vermerk (April 25, 1963), BAK, B149/6246.

957 Kreutzer, *Vom "Liebesdienst" zum modernen Frauenberuf*, 245ff.

958 Bernhardt, "Die ausländische Arbeitskräfte in den deutschen Krankenhäusern," 451. This article also noted that, at the time, the state labor office of North Rhine-Westphalia reported that 661 hospitals and 641 nursing homes for the elderly were unable to fill positions for 4,887 nurses, 1,239 nurse aides, and 3,353 female housekeepers.

959 Lee Sukil, *Building a Bridge between Han River and the Rhine* (Seoul, 1997, in Korean), 103–7.

960 Schultheis to Hessian Labor Ministry (August 2, 1965), BAK, B149/22428, and Schultheis to Choon Soo Lee (August 2, 1965), PAAA, B85/1319.

961 Bundesanstalt to Diakonische Werk – Innere Mission und Hilfswerk der ev. Kirche in Deutschland (January 23, 1967), BAK, B149/22428.

962 Note (March 17, 1966), BAK, B149/22428. According to the January 1967 statistics from the Bundesanstalt für Arbeitsvermittlung und Arbeitslo-senversicherung, in the health sector alone the total of 1,746 South Koreans were working in West Germany, including 1,495 nurses and nurse aides. As of June 1966, out of the total 3048 South Koreans working in West Germany, 2,084 were miners, while the majority of 820 females was employed in nursing; The number of students was 225. Cited in "Als

Bergleute, Krankenschwestern und Studenten: Die Koreaner in der Bundesrepublik," *FAZ* (July 20, 1967).

963 "Urgent Steps Asked to Halt Nurse-Drain," *The Korea Times* (September 14, 1966).

964 Bundesanstalt to Labor Ministry (April 29, 1966), and Note (March 17, 1966), both in BAK, B149/22428. It appears that during this time the hospital association reached an agreement with the Korean government regarding qualifications and recruitment procedures.

965 German embassy in Seoul to Foreign Office (August 6, 1966), PAAA, B85/1319.

966 Edeltrud Weist to Foreign Office (August 22, 1966), BAK, B213/11962.

967 Paul S. Crane, "Thoughts of the Times," *The Korea Times* (March 30, 1969).

968 German embassy in Manila (August 11, 1967), German embassy in Seoul to Foreign Office (February 15, 1968), and Labor Ministry to Gerstenmaier (April 2, 1968), all in BAK, B149/22429. See also Dorothea Sich, "Zu schade, um Lücken zu füllen. Mit der Anwerbung koreanischer Schwestern entsteht eine moralische Verpflichtung und eine Chance für wirkungsvolle Entwicklungshilfe," *DÄ*, 1971, Nr. 36 (September 16), 2551–7.

969 Note (December 12, 1966), and Rheinland-Pfalz Ministry of the Interior to Federal Interior Minister (December 8, 1966), both in BAK, B149/22428.

970 Gerstenmaier to Labor Minister (April 12, 1967), and Gerstenmaier to Development Minister Wischnewski (June 12, 1967), both in BAK, B213/11962.

971 Minutes of the AK meeting (November 11, 1966), BAK, B149/22428.

972 For example, the KCIA summoned the head of the nursing department at the Ministry of Health and Social Affairs to their offices, slapped her around a bit, and threatened her with criminal charges. "Special Orders from the Korean Central Intelligence Agency," *World News Paper* (March 20, 1986, in Korean).

973 Ferring to AA (June 2, 1966), BAK, B149/22428, as well as other materials in this file.

974 AA to Labor Minister (February 28, 1967), and letter from BAS (March 23, 1967), both in BAK, B149/22428.

975 The kidnappings received widespread press coverage and left substantial documentation in many state archives. For the former, see "Affären," *Der Spiegel*, Nr. 29/1967 (July 10); "Die höflichen Entführer," *Stern* (July 1967, exact date unknown); "Energische Bonner Schritt in Seoul?" *SZ* (July 13, 1967); "Seoul läßt fünf Entführte frei," *Die Welt* (July 13, 1967); "Auch ein deutscher Geheimdienst wird verdächtigt," *FAZ* (July 18, 1967); and "Die Verschleppungs-Affäre kommt vor den Bundestag," *Rhein-Main-Presse* (July 19, 1967).

976 In January 1968, the Korean government's anti-communist hysteria was further heightened when a squad of North Korean soldiers infiltrated into the South and nearly succeeded in assassinating Park. The fate of these kidnapped Koreans was pushed further into the background when the

North Koreans seized the U.S. spy ship Pueblo two days after the attack on Park.

977 BAA, Memorandum (July 2, 1970), and BAA to Labor Minister (July 15, 1969), both in BAK, B149/22408.

978 Irmgard Nölkensmeier, "Information über die Situation von asiatischen Arbeitnehmern und Arbeitnehmerinnen in deutschen Krankenhäusern" (January 1972), AdCV, 3291.024, Fasz. 6.

979 Weidenbörner, Vermerk (December 2, 1969), Weidenbörner to Korean embassy (December 1969), and Weidenbörner, Vermerk (April 1970), all in BAK, B149/22429. KODCO and the German Hospital Association exchanged a "Note of Understanding" in June 1970.

980 Weidenbörner, Note (August 25, 1970), BAK, B149/22429; and German embassy to AA (March 8, 1971), PAAA, B85/1511. There were, however, reservations on the German side about the employment of women who had less training and knowledge than those licensed nurses who had been recruited up to that point. See Reinhard Rörig to DKG (August 12, 1981), ADKGRP.

981 The DKG wanted to import 2,000 Korean nurse aides in 1971, and the Korean government offered 2,500 nurse aides for 1972 and 3,000 for 1973. The German embassy in Seoul to AA (March 8, 1971), PAAA B85/1511. In June 1972, about 8,000 South Koreans were working in West Germany, including about 5,000 females. BAS, Ref. 314 to Ref. 102 (April 10, 1973), BAK, B213/11962. In the winter of 1971/72, the DKG signed an agreement with the Indonesian government to recruit 320 nurses and aides from that country, and by 1974 the idea of a similar agreement with India was being considered. Labor Minister to AA, "Betr.: Vermittlung indonesischen Krankenpflegepersonals" (November 14, 1973), PAAA, B85/1263; and General consulate Bombay to German embassy in Delhi, "Betr.: Beschäftigung indischen Krankenpflegepersonals" (August 12, 1974), PAAA, B85/1262.

982 "Koreanische Krankenpflegekräfte für deutsche Krankenhäuser" (undated, and with attachments), AdCV, 204.15.030, Fasz. 1, which also contains the final regulations governing the employment of licensed Korean nurses and nurse aides in German hospitals, which was signed by the Korean Labor Ministry in July 1971. However, Caritasverband officials noted that, although many families had "sold their last cow and their last bit of land" to pay for training as a nurses aide, the demand for such persons on the part of German hospitals was far below the maximums specified in the agreement, and there was some suspicion that German hospitals were recruiting Filipinas because the per person costs were lower. See "Bericht über die Besprechungen..." (September 1973), AdCV, 20415.030, Fasz. 1.

983 Axel Sparten, "Letzte Hilfe für Krankenhäuser sind Asien und die dritte Welt," *Welt am Sonntag* (July 27, 1969).

984 "Kurzprotokoll über das Ergebnis der Beratungen zwischen d. DKGt und der KODCO..." (July/August 1974), PAAA, B85/1147.

985 Note (December 10, 1971), BAK, B149/22432.

986 "Schwestern im schillernden Hanpok," *FAZ* (no date) in Lee's possession. See also "Willkommen für 128 koreanische Krankenschwestern," *Mitteilungen der Stadtverwaltung Frankfurt a.M.* (February 5, 1966).

987 "Zarte Hand und Mandelaugen," "Immer vergnügt und hilfsbereit," "Immer nur lächeln...," "Mandelaugen unter weißen Häubchen," "Exotisches im Römer," "Schwestern im schillernden Hanpok," unidentified stories in Lee's collection of newspaper clippings relating to the recruitment of Korean nurses. The *FAZ* (May 6, 1966) took the opportunity to bemoan the decline of the service ethic at home, cited in Bernhardt, "Die ausländische Arbeitskräfte in den deutschen Krankenhäusern," 445–52, citation 447.

988 "Weitere Hilfe aus Seoul," *Neue Presse* (March 8, 1966).

989 Note (March 17, 1966), BAK, B149/22428.

990 "'Confident with Technique.' Our Nurses in West Germany," in *Jungang Ilbo* (January 14, 1966); *Physicians' Newspaper* (November 22, 1965); and unidentified clipping (1966), all [in Korean] in the possession of Lee.

991 Yoo Do-jin, *Die Situation koreanischer Krankenpflegekräfte in der Bundesrepublik Deutschland und ihre sozialpädagogischen Probleme* (Dissertation, Kiel, 1975), 131ff; and Yun-Chong Shim, *Aspekte der Sozio-Kulturellen Einordnung Koreanischer Krankenpflegekräfte in Deutschland* (Dissertation, Heidelberg, 1973), 12. Much of our knowledge of the aspirations and experiences of the first groups of nurses to travel from Korea to West Germany is based on these two dissertations. Shim's work was based on interviews with 152 Korean women working at 12 hospitals and homes in the Rhine-Main-Neckar area, and Yoo surveyed 541 nurses and aides and 309 German physicians and nursing staff.

992 "With Full Excitement to West Germany," *The Sunday News* (January 30, 1966).

993 Cited in Shim, *Aspekte der Sozio-Kulturellen Einordnung*, 62. Another Korean nurse complained that their German colleagues and superiors treated them like "ignorant barbarians," *Ibid.*, 55.

994 Besprechung betreffend Arbeitskräfte und Auszubildende aus Übersee in Deutschland (April 2, 1965), AdCV, 380.40.030, Fasz. 1. The German word for nurse is Krankenschwester, and the meaning of this sentence pivoted on the distinctions, which were made in English in the original, between the elevated status of nuns or "sisters" and the work expected of "nurses."

995 Mädchen aus Übersee (October 26, 1966), AdCV, 380.40.030, Fasz. 1.

996 "Besprechung betreffend Arbeitskräfte und Auszubildende aus Übersee in Deutschland" (April 2, 1965), AdCV, 380.40.030, Fasz. 1. It seemed to many people that these problems could have been avoided if these young women had completed their basic nursing studies before coming to Germany and if Catholic orders would only bring to Germany girls who had already begun their novitiate. Although this idea was widely discussed as early as 1966, it was not put into practice until 1971. For an early analysis of this issue, see "Niederschrift über die Arbeitskonferenz zum Thema 'Mädchen aus Übersee'" (February 22, 1967), AdCV, 20415.030, Fasz. 1.

997 Yoo, *Die Situation koreanischer Krankenpflegekräfte*, 209

998 Young-ja Kim (Peters), "Bericht über die Tätigkeit vom 1. März bis 30. Juni 1972," AdCV, 380.40.025, Fasz. 3.

999 In 1981, 39,961 Korean women held nursing certificates. Of these, 15,161 were employed in Korea and 7,341 overseas, leaving approximately 19,000 of these women who were not employed in their area of training. In addition, approximately 3,500 women were graduating from Korean nursing schools each year. Korean Ministry of Health and Social Affairs to KODCO (July 14, 1981), ADKGRP.

1000 According to Shim, 39.4 percent of the respondents gave saving "a lot of money for future plans" as the main reason, 26.3 percent the opportunity for further education, and 23.6 percent the chance to experience European culture and living. Shim, *Aspekte der Sozio-Kulturellen Einordnung*, 23.

1001 *Chosun Ilbo* (April 28, 1966), and *Kyonghyang Sinmun* (April 28, 1965).

1002 Shim, *Aspekte der Sozio-Kulturellen Einordnung*, 16.

1003 *Ibid.*, 24.

1004 *Ibid.*, 169.

1005 *Ibid.*, 16.

1006 Yoo, *Die Situation koreanischer Krankenpflegekräfte*, 177.

1007 Heike Berner, Sun-ju Choi, and KFG, eds., *Zuhause. Erzählungen von deutschen Koranerinnen* (Berlin, 2006), 32.

1008 Shim, *Aspekte der Sozio-Kulturellen Einordnung*, 20–1.

1009 Yoo, *Die Situation koreanischer Krankenpflegekräfte*, 178.

1010 *Ibid.*, 195.

1011 "Heimat in der Fremde, Fremde in der Heimat," *Hessische Rundfunk* (1974).

1012 *Ibid.*, 211. Over one-third of nurses and aides saw little connection between their work and their training, only 15–22 percent believed that their work was linked to their profession, and the remainder fell in the middle.

1013 *Ibid.*, 208.

1014 *Ibid.*, 215. To their credit, the German hospitals were aware that Asian nurses were more susceptible to tuberculosis and tried to avoid assigning them to sanatoria and hospital contagious disease wards.

1015 Shim, *Aspekte der Sozio-Kulturellen Einordnung*, 62.

1016 *Ibid.*, 43. A Caritasverband survey – whose title itself is revealing – came to similar conclusions regarding the overly strict treatment of Korean nurses by their supervisors and the unequal assignment of duties. "Teamarbeit in der Krankenpflege: Befehlsempfänger oder Partner" (1974), AdCV, 380.40.026, Fasz. 01. However, this same report also noted that Koreans did not always understand or appreciate German *Sachlichkeit* and that they were much more sensitive to what Germans accepted as normal forms of discipline and criticism.

1017 Yoo, *Die Situation koreanischer Krankenpflegekräfte*, 207.

1018 Shim, *Aspekte der Sozio-Kulturellen Einordnung*, 47. See also Yoo, *Die Situation koreanischer Krankenpflegekräfte*, 225.

1019 Berner, Choi, and KFG, ed., *Zuhause*, 85.

1020 Shim, *Aspekte der Sozio-Kulturellen Einordnung*, 80–1.

1021 Yoo, *Die Situation koreanischer Krankenpflegekräfte*, 206.

1022 Shim, *Aspekte der Sozio-Kulturellen Einordnung*, 79, 66. According to Shim (79ff.), three-quarters of these accusations of discrimination were directly related to unequal treatment in the workplace in ways other than, and in addition to, the disproportionate assignment to unpleasant, difficult, unskilled duties; the remainder related to a more intangible sense of not being respected or wanted.

1023 *Ibid.*, 74.

1024 *Ibid.*, 80.

1025 "Wochenendtagung für koreanische Schwestern..." (July 9, 1972), AdCV, 380.41.025, Fasz. 4.

1026 Yoo, *Die Situation koreanischer Krankenpflegekräfte*, 225.

1027 *Ibid.*, 113.

1028 Lee, *Building a Bridge between Han River and the Rhine*, 150–54.

1029 Bundesanstalt to Labor Minister (June 30, 1969), BAK B149/22429.

1030 Yoo, *Die Situation koreanischer Krankenpflegekräfte*, 308f. The Germans had a different explanation for the tendency of Korean nurses to retreat into their rooms. According to a report by the Caritasverband, getting out into the world required both linguistic skills and German friends to help them become familiar with their surroundings – the implication being that these women lacked both. On the other hand, the report also noted that part of the problem stemmed from the fact that the Koreans did not really have a concept of leisure time because of the way that household activities were organized in Korea. "Bewältigung der Freizeit: Einsatz rund um die Uhr oder 40-Stunden-Woche," AdCV, 380.40.026, Fasz. 01.

1031 Shim, *Aspekte der Sozio-Kulturellen Einordnung*, 95.

1032 *Zu Hause*, 84. Peters also thought that the failure to make even the slightest effort to make them feel welcome, at least on their first day, was revealing about their attitudes toward the Koreans.

1033 Yoo, *Die Situation koreanischer Krankenpflegekräfte*, 263.

1034 *Ibid.*, 263.

1035 "Beschäftigung koreanischer Arbeitnehmer in der Bundesrepublik Deutschland" (February 7, 1973), PAAA, B85/1268. In addition, there were 600–700 Korean men working and receiving advanced training in metal working trades on the basis of agreements between German and Korean firms.

1036 The Korean government itself was primarily interested in the foreign exchange earned by these men and had given little thought to what these men would do once they returned to Korea. By the early 1970s, however, the German Development Ministry had set up programs to provide training for returning miners in skilled trades other than mining and to help them establish their own small businesses. Bundesministerium für wirtschaftliche Zusammenarbeit, "Zwischenbericht, Betr.: Förderung der Rückkehr und beruflichen Wiedereingliederung von Arbeitnehmern aus Entwicklungsländern" (September 20, 1974), PAAA, B85/1268. For an analysis of this issue (with respect to nurses, rather than miners), see "Manuskript eines Referates von Samuel Lee" (February 4, 1975), PAAA, B85/1268.

1037 According to one survey, 40 percent of the Korean women were against premarital sex; 28 percent believed that premarital sex was acceptable if one planned to marry the man; and the remaining 32 percent deemed such activity more generally acceptable. Yoo, *Die Situation koreanischer Krankenpflegekräfte*, 331, 336.

1038 Shim, *Aspekte der Sozio-Kulturellen Einordnung*, 115.

1039 Cited in Abt. I to Abt. II, "Betr.: Förderung der Sozialstrukturhilfe in Entwicklungsländern" (April 17, 1968), BAK, B149/22430.

1040 This shift in immigration and labor policy also had cultural and political roots that antedated, and that were separate from, the economic crisis. See Marcel Berlinghoff, *Das Ende der "Gastarbeit." Europäische Anwerbestopps 1970–1974* (Schöningh, 2013).

1041 BAS, "Betr.: Einsetzung einer Arbeitsgruppe durch das Kabinette am 12. Februar 1975" (March 10, 1975), BAK, B189/24140. In June 1975, the cabinet decided to draft a comprehensive immigration policy that would take into account a variety of considerations.

1042 Bundesminister für Arbeit und Sozialordnung to the Deutsche Krankenhausgesellschaft (August 14, 1975), ADKGRP. This decision not to recruit married nurses formalized a decision that had already been taken in early 1973. In addition to the problems of familial separation and the general tightening of the labor market, this decision was based on the fact that issuing work permits for these men would violate the policy against recruiting unskilled workers from outside Europe. This decision not to recruit married women was rescinded a year later. Circular from Foreign Office to selected embassies in Asia (August 5, 1976), PAAA, B85/1268.

1043 Nölkensmeier, "Situation der asiatischen Krankenpflegekräfte" (May 10, 1976), 380.40.026, Fasz. 1. The trend was similar for the Philippines, and only a scattering of Indian women were still finding work in Germany. For an overview of the state measures taken to reduce the number of Asian nurses, see "Kurzprotokoll. Regionalkonferenz asiatischen Sozialdienstes" (August 5, 1977) in the same folder.

1044 Fendrich, Note (September 10, 1982), and Note (April 25, 1979), BAK B149/59670.

1045 *Informationen des Deuschen Caritasverbandes*, 3/1978, AdCV, 221.212.026, Fasz. 1.

1046 *Ibid.*

1047 At the same time, the Caritasverband decided to establish an advising center in Seoul to help returning nurses negotiate their reentry into Korean society; the center also set up a Friendship Club as a mutual support group for these women. See "Projektentwurf. Einrichtung einer Beratungsstelle in Korea für die aus der Bundesrepublik zurückkehrenden Koreanerinnen" (April 2, 1975), and "Bericht über den Verlauf der Korea-Reise..." (1975), both in AdCV, 380.40.026, Fasz. 1. On the problems faced by the women who returned, see "Beratungsstelle für zurückkehrende Krankenschwestern in Seoul/Korea" (June 1977), AdCV, 187.50.0843, Fasz. 8; Yonsei Medical Center, "An Exploratory Study on Employment Status and Problems of

Readjustment of Korean Nurses and Nurses' Aids Returned from Germany" (1976), and "Yongdong Hospital Project, Ergänzungsbericht (1): Beruflicher und sozialer Wiedereingliederungsplan für die koreanischen Krankenschwestern, die aus der BRD zurückkommen," both in AdCV, 187.50.0843, Fasz. 9.

1048 Yoo Jung-sook, *Koreanische Immigranten in Deutschland: Interessenvertretung und Selbstorg"anisation* (Hamburg, 1996), 208ff.

1049 KFG, ed., *Dokumentation* (no place, 1979), and Berner, Choi, and KFG, eds., *Zuhause*, 10–6. Indian nurses also protested against Germany's labor policy. See the resolution (May 16, 1977) signed by V. Mandapthil and A. Oommen and, on the integration problems facing returning Indians, "Gedanken zur heutigen Situation der Inder in der Bundesrepublik," both in AdCV 187.50.0843, Fasz. 9.

1050 Deutsche Krankenhausgesellschaft, "Betr.: Beschäftigung koreanischer Krankenpflegekräfte" (March 28, 1978), in ADKGRP. See also BAS an den Präsidenten des Deutschen Bundestages (May 5, 1978), AdCV, 380.40.024, Fasz. 2. See also KFG, ed., *Dokumentation*, 24f.

1051 KFG, ed., *Dokumentation*, 13.

1052 Berner, Choi, and KFG, eds., *Zuhause*, 18–19.

1053 Ibid., 18.

1054 Ibid., 19–20.

1055 Ibid. n, 99.

1056 Berner, Choi, and KFG, eds., *Zuhause*, 23, 25.

1057 See Pheng Cheah, *Inhuman Conditions. On Cosmopolitanism and Human Rights* (Cambridge, MA, 2006), chapter 6.

1058 Tani E. Barlow, "Asian Women in Reregionalization," *Positions* 15:2 (2007), 285–319, citation 290.

1059 Berner, Choi, and KFG, eds., *Zuhause*, 40.

1060 Heike Berner and Sun-ju Choi, "Einleitung" in *Zuhause*, 15f.

1061 "Fortieth Anniversary," *Urishinmun* (May 27, 2006, in Korean).

1062 Ryan M. Irwin, "A Wind of Change? White Redoubt and the Postcolonial Moment, 1960–1963," *DH* 33:5 (November 2009), 897–925, as well as John Daniel, "Racism, the Cold War and South Africa's Regional Security Strategies 1948–1990," and Sue Onslow, "The Cold War in Southern Africa: White Power, Black Nationalism and External Intervention," both in Sue Onslow, ed., *Cold War in South Africa: White Power, Black Liberation* (London, 2009), 35–54 and 9–34. See also Thomas J. Noer, *Cold War and Black Liberation: The United States and White Rule in Africa, 1948–1968* (Columbia, MO, 1985).

1063 Sergey Radchenko, *Two Suns in the Heavens: The Sino-Soviet Struggle for Supremacy, 1962–1967* (Palo Alto, CA, 2009); and Lüthi, *The Sino-Soviet Split*.

1064 George T. Yu, *China and Tanzania: A Study in Cooperative Interaction* (Berkeley, CA, 1970), 46f. It was known that the Soviet charges for technical services (including personnel) often made up about 25–30 percent of total Soviet expenditures for a project. Ghana and Mali complained about high costs for technical services. CIA, "Difficulties encountered by less developed countries in their economic relations with the Soviet Union" (March 13, 1967), ORR/S-2219 (www.foia.ucia.gov; accessed July 18, 2010).

1065 Baichun Zhang, Jiuchun Zhang, and Fang Yao, "Technology Transfer from the Soviet Union to the People's Republic of China 1949–1966," *Comparative Technology Transfer and Society* 4:2 (August 2006), 105–71, and Prybyla, "Soviet and Chinese Economic Competition within the Communist World."

1066 Kasuka S. Mutukwa, *Politics of the Tanzania-Zambia Rail Project* (Washington, DC, 1977), citation 145.

1067 On Chinese aid policy, see Deborah Brautigam, "China's Foreign Aid in Africa: What Do We Know?" in Robert I. Rotberg, ed., *China into Africa: Trade, Aid, and Influence* (Washington, DC, 2008), 197–216; Emmanuel John Hevi, *The Dragon's Embrace: The Chinese Communists and Africa* (New York, 1966); Zbigniew Brezinski, ed., *Africa and the Communist World* (Palo Alto, CA, 1963); Vidya Prakash Dutt, *China and the World: An Analysis of Communist China's Foreign Policy* (New York, 1964); John K. Cooley, *East Wind over Africa: Red China's African Offensive* (New York, 1965); and Alaba Ogunsanwo, *China's Policy in Africa, 1958–1971* (London, 1974).

1068 China's Eight Principles for Economic Aid and Technical Assistance to Other Countries (January 1964), (english.gov.cn/official/2011-04/21/content_1849913_10.htm; accessed July 8, 2012).

1069 CIA, "The New Look in Chinese Communist Aid to Sub-Saharan Africa" (September 1968) (www.foia.ucia.gov; accessed July 18, 2010).

1070 Ernesto Che Guevara, *The African Dream: The Diaries of the Revolutionary War in the Congo* (New York, 2001); Edward George, *The Cuban Intervention in Angola, 1965–1991* (London, 2005); and Piero Gleijeses, *Conflicting Missions. Havana, Washington, and Africa, 1959–1976* (Chapel Hill, NC, 2002).

1071 Deutsches Institut für Zeitgeschichte, ed., *Dokumente: Die afro-asiatische Solidaritätsbewegung* (Berlin, 1968), 250.

1072 Lederer and Burdick, *The Ugly American*. A German translation appeared in 1959 under the title *Der häßliche Amerikaner* (Hamburg: Nannen).

1073 Von Radow to AA (January 11, 1960), PAAA, B 92/103.

1074 See, for example, the letter from the mission chief in Niger to AA complaining about the incompetence and indolence of the physicians and nurses who had been sent to the country to treat the local population and train local nurses. He warned that such poor representatives of the West German people were dissipating the goodwill of their hosts. Neubert to AA (March 4, 1964), and the telegrams from Neubert (February 25, March 18, and May 5, 1964), all in PAAA, B68/270.

1075 Trident Press, 1965.

1076 Cited in Lawrence H. Fuchs, *"Those Peculiar Americans": The Peace Corps and American National Character* (New York, 1967), 33.

1077 Cited in "The New Americans," in *The Volunteer* 1:2 (February 1962), 4.

1078 Fritz Fischer, *Making Them Like Us. Peace Corps Volunteers in the 1960s* (Washington, DC, 1998), 7.

1079 Cited in Elizabeth Cobbs Hoffman, "Diplomatic History and the Meaning of Life: Toward a Global American History," *DH* 21:4 (Fall 1997), 510.

1080 Aluko, "Ghana's Foreign Policy," 87. Nkruma, however, insisted on paying the salaries of these young men and women in order to avoid the stigma of charity and dependency. As Ghana moved closer to the socialist countries, the government came to view Peace Corps volunteers as CIA spies and to regard English language instruction as a tool for colonizing local culture.

1081 Segey Mazov, "Soviet Policy in West Africa: An Episode of the Cold War, 1956–1964," in Maxim Matusevich, ed., *Africa in Russia. Russia in Africa. Three Centuries of Encounters* (Trenton, NJ, 2007), 306.

1082 Hoffman, *All You Need Is Love. The Peace Corps and the Spirit of the 1960s* (Cambridge, MA, 1998), 103.

1083 Holbik and Myers, *West German Foreign Aid 1956–1966*, 78–81. Both *Arbeitsgemeinschaft für Entwicklungshilfe*, the umbrella organization of West German Catholic aid groups and its evangelical counterpart, *Weltfriedensdienst*, also trained and sent voluntary aid workers overseas since their establishment in 1959. See Hans Eich and Hans Frevert, eds., *Freunde in aller Welt* (Baden-Baden, 1963).

1084 Martha Biondi, *To Stand and Fight. The Struggle for Civil Rights in Postwar New York City* (Cambridge, MA, 2002), 164. Nikhil Singh and Kevin Boyle have both argued that Cold War anti-Communism broke the alliance between the struggle against white supremacy and class oppression that had been forged in the 1930s. Singh, *Black Is a Country. Race and the Unfinished Struggle for Democracy* (Cambridge, MA, 2004); and Boyle, "Labor, the Left, and the Long Civil Rights Movement," *SH* 30 (2005), 366–72.

1085 Henry Görschler, *Rassen, Rassen "theorie" und imperialistische Politik* (Berlin, 1961); Wolfgang Schüler, *"Apartheid" regiert Südafrika* (Berlin, 1961); and Günter Schabowski, *Bei Freunnden im freien Afrika. Mit der FDGB-Delegation in Guinea und Ghana* (Leizpig, 1960)

1086 Ambassador Schroeder, "Haltung der Tanganjikischen Presse gegenüber der Bundesrepublik" (January 18, 1964), PAAA, B34/523.

1087 Werner Richter, German-African Society of the GDR, *Newsletter* (October 2, 1963), PAAA, B34/526.

1088 *Griff nach der Weltmacht. Die Kriegszielpolitik der kaiserlichen Deutschland 1914–1918* (Düsseldorf, 1961; English translation New York, 1967).

1089 See the replies to the Foreign Office circular from most sub-Saharan countries in PAAA, B34/557.

1090 Tanzanian foreign minister, Aide Memoire (December 18, 1964), and ambassador Schroeder to AA (December 18, 1964), both in PAAA, B34/523.

1091 The materials employed such provocative statements as "Cyclone-B experts supply toxic agents" and "Bonn mercenaries to South Vietnam." West Germany pressured Nyerere to confiscate these materials. Cited in

Independent Information Center, ed., *Vietnam Legion? A New Communist Defamation Campaign. A Document* (London, 1965).

1092 *The Neo-colonialism of the West German Federal Republic: A Documentation* (Berlin, 1965).

1093 Kilian, *Die Hallstein-Doktrin*, 192, 219f.

1094 Modibo Keita in *Die afro-asiatische Solidaritätsbewegung: Dokumente*, 253.

1095 "China Predicts Rebels in Congo will Follow Path of Vietcong," *NYT* (June 25, 1964), 11.

1096 Richard Beeston, "Tanzania: Haven of Intrigue," *Daily Telegraph* (November 23, 1964).

1097 John Kent, *America, the UN and Decolonisation: Cold War Conflict in the Congo* (London), 189–92, citation 189. See also David N. Gibbs, *The Political Economy of Third World Intervention: Mines, Money, and U.S. Policy in the Congo Crisis* (Chicago, 1991); Lise Namikas, *Battleground Africa: Cold War in the Congo, 1960–1965* (Palo Alto, CA, 2013); and Georges Nzongola-Ntalaja, *The Congo from Leopold to Kabila: A People's History* (London, 2002).

1098 Kent, *America, the UN and Decolonisation*, 171–74.

1099 CIA, "The Situation in the Congo," *Weekly Report* (November 10, 1964).

1100 St. Charles Drake, letter to the editor, *NYT* (October 10, 1964), "Six Negro Leaders Ask Shift on Africa," *NYT* (November 29, 1964), and Inez Smith Reid, "Congo's Rebel Movement; Former Resident Sees Existence of Large Popular Following," *NYT* (December 8, 1964).

1101 *Die afro-asiatische Solidaritätsbewegung: Dokumente*, 253f.

1102 Schröder to AA (November 26, 1964), PAAA, B34/526.

1103 "Dr. King Advocates Congo Withdrawal," *NYT* (December 14, 1964).

1104 Sam Pope Brewer, "Mali, in U.N., Assails U.S.-Belgian Rescue Mission in Congo," *NYT* (December 11, 1964); and Lloyd Garrison, "Tshombe's Village Epic; Congolese Premier Employs Drama to Gain a Triumph from a Defeat October 20," *NYT* (October 20, 1964).

1105 The following is based on CIA, Directorate of Intelligence, "U.S. Aid to Countries Aiding Congo Rebels" (December 15, 1964). This document also cites an Algerian representative criticizing the "imperialists' gun-boat expeditions and scorched earth policies" as well as the "racialist mentality" that placed different values on the lives of blacks and whites. The Ghanaian foreign minister explained that "Africa has to know whether the UN can guarantee small states against imperialist appetites… In international law the US was no more entitled to intervene in the Congo than Ghana would be to intervene in the US South to protect the lives of Afro-Americans."

1106 CIA, "US Aid to Countries Aiding Congo Rebels," (December 15, 1964).

1107 *Ibid.*

1108 "French Veterans to Fight in Congo: 150 Mercenaries Awaited to Bolster Tshombe Forces," *NYT* (March 6, 1965); and Kent, *America, the UN and Decolonisation*, 233, fn. 4. See also "Congo Expanding Mercenary Army," *NYT* (December 4, 1964); "More Europeans Joining Congo Mercenary

Force" *NYT* (January 19, 1965); "Tshombe's Mercenaries," *NYT* (August 30, 1964); and "Mercenary Unit Is Ready to Fight Rebels in Congo," *NYT* (August 25, 1964).

1109 William Galvez, *Che in Africa: Che Guevara's Congo Diary* (Melbourne, 1999).

1110 John C. Ausland, *Kennedy, Khrushchev, and the Berlin-Cuba Crisis* (Oslo and Boston, 1996); and Hedrick Smith, "Moscow Said to Offer Aid for Congo Rebel Airlift," *NYT* (December 7, 1964).

1111 See the exchange between Zinn and Schröder (December 7, 1964 and January 1, 1965), PAAA, B34/561.

1112 FRG Embassy to Foreign Office (August 22, 1964), PAAA, B34/526.

1113 North Atlantic Council, Committee on Information and Cultural Relations (March 16, 1964), PAAA, B34/561.

1114 Cited in Helen-Louise Hunter, *Zanzibar. The Hundred Days Revolution* (Santa Barbara, CA, 2010), 74.

1115 Schröder to AA (October 1, 1964), PAAA, B34/561.

1116 "Beiträge für die Besprechungen Staatssekretär Lahr mit Herrn Rocherau von der EWG-Kommission" (July 17, 1964), PAAA, B34/559. Conversely, in early May 1964 East German officials in Zanzibar met with Nyerere, demanded full recognition for East Germany, and departed infuriated when Nyerere refused. West German diplomats reported that Karume was considering making recognition a condition for unification with Tanganyika. Telegram from Schroeder to AA (May 4, 1964), and Embassy Dar es Salaam to AA (May 9, 1964), both in PAAA, B68/319.

1117 Hermann Wentker, *Außenpolitik in engen Grenzen. Die DDR im internationalen System 1949–1989* (Munich, 2007), 296; and Bundesamt für Verfassungsschutz to AA (August 13, 1964), PAAA, B534/511.

1118 Schröder to AA (October 14, 1964), PAAA, B34/511; and Hunter, *Zanzibar*, 82. This book was a reworking of a later declassified study that Hunter originally prepared for the CIA, where she was employed at the time as an analyst. The wife of president Karume also traveled to East Berlin for medical treatment. "Frau Karume zu Gast," *ND* (April 14, 1964); and Schröder to AA (March 26, 1964), PAAA, B34/510.

1119 Hermann Wentker, *Außenpolitik in engen Grenzen*, 294; and Schröder to AA (September 22, 1964), PAAA, B34/511.

1120 MfAA, "Zur Realisierung der DDR-Objekte in Sansibar"(undated but early 1965), BAB, DQ1/5171.

1121 West German embassy to AA (August 21, 1964), PAAA, B34/511.

1122 ADN correspondent Heiner Appelt, "Haus der Freundschaft Sansibar-DDR," *ND* (September 18, 1964), PAAA, B34/511.

1123 Garth Andrew Myers, *Verandahs of Power. Colonialism and Space in Urban Africa* (Syracuse, 2003), 100–3.

1124 Although this project was originally scheduled to be completed by the summer of 1964, work was not finished until 1967.

1125 Cited in Esmond Bradley Martin, *Zanzibar. Tradition and Revolution* (London, 1978), 65. In addition, many properties in Stone Town were confiscated and distributed to poor Africans.

1126 "Shipment of Cement from East Germany," *East African Standard* (Nairobi) (July 20, 1964), "Karume Reaffirms Friendship," *The Nationalist* (July 29, 1964), and "Isle Thanks Ship," *Tanganyika Standard* (July 29, 1964), all in PAAA, B34/510.

1127 Schröder to AA (March 26, 1964), PAAA, B34/510.

1128 "Isle Flats Begin," *Tanganyika Standard* (August 18, 1964), PAAA, B34/510.

1129 Myers, *Verandahs of Power*, 79, 82.

1130 Thomas Burgess, *Race, Revolution, and the Struggle for Human Rights in Zanzibar. The Memoirs of Ali Sultan Issa and Seif Sharif Hamed* (Athens, 2009), 94; Burgess, *Youth and the Revolution: Mobility and Discipline in Zanzibar, 1950–80* (Dissertation, Indiana University, 2001), 288–9; and Burgess, "The Young Pioneers and the Rituals of Citizenship in Revolutionary Zanzibar," *Africa Today* (April 2005), 3–29.

1131 Schröder to AA (April 11, 1964), PAAA, B34/511.

1132 "Haus der Freundschaft Sansibar-DDR," *ND* (September 18, 1964), PAAA, B34/511. The western press reported gleefully on all of problems that plagued the project.

1133 *ND* (July 30, 1964), PAAA, B34/511.

1134 Heiner Appet, "Helle Häuser verdrängen Slums in Sansibar," *ND* (August 23, 1964).

1135 Myers, *Reconstructing Ng'ambo*, 289–91, 362, 369.

1136 Their first deployments overseas were to Mali in July 1964 and to Algeria in August 1964. Over half of the costs were borne by the Solidarity Committee. Ilona Schleicher, "Elemente entwicklungspolitischer Zusammenarbeit in der Tätigkeit von FDGB und FDJ," Hans-Jörg Bücking, ed., *Entwicklungspolitische Zusammenarbeit in der Bundesrepublik Deutschland und der DDR* (Berlin, 1998), 111–38, especially 122–9.

1137 Myers, *Reconstructing Ng'ambo*, 355f.

1138 "Sachsen im Busch," *Der Spiegel* (November 18, 1964).

1139 "Aufzeichnung betr. besondere Entwicklungshilfsmaßnahmen für Tanganjika/Sansibar" (May 5, 1964), PAAA, B34/525; Török, "Betr. Ressortbesprechung" (May 22, 1964), and Pauls to Schröder (May 20 1964), both in PAAA, B34/511. The total cost of the projects to which the East Germans had committed themselves was approximately 30 million marks, AA (May 4, 1964), PAAA, B68/319.

1140 Schröder to AA (March 26, 1964), Dufner, Note (April 6, 1964), Sachs, Note (April 29, 1964), and Sachs to Ministerium für Wohnungswesen, Städtebau und Raumordnung (September 17, 1964), all in PAAA, B34/525; and "Gesprächspunkte für Unterredung Herrn Dg IB mit Aussenminister Kambona am 22.5.64," PAAA, B34/523.

1141 "Aufzeichnung betr. besondere Entwicklungshilfe für Tanganjika/Sansibar" (May 6, 1964), PAAA, B34/525.

1142 "Dank für deutsche Wohnbauhilfe in Tanganjika" (no date, but 1964), PAAA, B34/525.

1143 Schröder to AA (September 19, 1964), PAAA, B58-III B1.

1144 Schmidt to Regierungsdirektor Barth of the Hessisches Staatsministerium für Wirtschaft und Verkehr (June 22, 1964), PAAA, B34/511.

1145 Fritz Rudolph and Percy Stulz, *Jambo, Afrika! DDR-Afrika-Expedition zwischen Kongo und Sansibar* (Leipzig, 1970), 265, 277.

1146 Schröder to AA (October 8, 1964), PAAA, B34/525.

1147 Only a handful of Britons were allowed to stay. Don Petterson, *Revolution in Zanzibar . An American's Cold War Tale* (Boulder, CO, 2002), 183.

1148 Although the East Germans and the Chinese worked together well at first, frictions soon arose. Hermann Herwig to MfG (November 12, 1964), and Stein to Foreign Trade Ministry (November 9, 1964), both in PAAA, MfAA/A15073. On public health and medical care in pre-revolutionary Tanganyika and Zanzibar, see Meredeth Turshen, *The Political Ecology of Disease in Tanzania* (New Brunswick, 1984); Ann Beck, *Medicine, Tradition, and Development in Kenya and Tanzania 1920–1970* (Crossroads Press, 1981); and Fr. Severino Zuccelli, *Medical Development in Tanganyika* (no place, 1963).

1149 Zanzibari Health Ministry to the East German embassy (October 6, 1964), and "Halbesjahresbericht der Medizinischen Schule in Zanzibar" (March 3, 1965), both PAAA, MfAA/A15073.

1150 Fritsch to Kiesewetter (September 7, 1964), PAAA, MfAA/A15073.

1151 "Arbeitsordnung für die vom Ministerium für Gesundheit der DDR zur medizinischen Hilfeleistung in das Ausland delegierten medizinischen Kader" (July 1, 1968), PAAA, MfAA/C773/71; Stein to MfG (January 26, 65), and Krause to Radvanyi (April 3, 1965), both in PAAA, MfAA/A15073.

1152 "Bericht über Doris F." (April 5, 1965), PAAA, MfAA/ A15073.

1153 Hermann Kohl to Krause (June 5, 1967), PAAA, MfAA/ C344.

1154 Vizekonsul Köhn to Krause (October 27, 1967), and Generalkonsul Gottfried Lessing to Merkel (December 19, 1967), both in PAAA, MfAA/C351.

1155 Charles R. Swift, *Dar Days: The Early Years of Tanzania* (Lanham, MD, 2002), 94.

1156 Kohl to Buhlert (October 17, 1968), PAAA, MfAA/C773/71.

1157 Günter Franke, Quartalsbericht II/69 (July 3, 1969), PAAA, MfAA/C773/71.

1158 Consul Dr. Siegfried Büttner to AA (December 16, 1967), PAAA, MfAA/ C773/71.

1159 Klaus Schröder, Report (July 2, 1969), PAAA, MfAA/C773/71.

1160 Swift, *Dar Days*, 93. Issa hoped that the temporary halt to the import of medicine and vaccines would provide a better overview of the actual needs of the country.

1161 Burgess, *Race, Revolution, and the Struggle for Human Rights in Zanzibar*, 128f.

1162 *Ibid.*, 106–7.

1163 Yu, *China and Tanzania*, 35.

1164 Mutukwa, *Politics of the Tanzania-Zambia Railproject*; and Jamie Monson, *Africa's Freedom Railway. How a Chinese Development Project Changed Lives and Livelihoods in Tanzania* (Bloomington, IN, 2009).

1165 Cited in Swift, *Dar Days*, 112–113.

1166 Yu, *China and Tanzania*, 71. In March 1968, the major local newspaper praised Chinese doctors for their success in training Zanzibari physicians and for treating them as equals, instead of acting like their superiors, as was the case with other foreigners, that is, the Soviets. Vizekonsul Junghanns, Vermerk (March 27, 1968), and *Sunday News* (March 17, 1968), both in PAAA, MfAA/C773/71.

1167 Turshen, *The Political Ecology of Disease in Tanzania*, 146, n. 6.

1168 Ursula Rheintrock to Health Ministry (October 8, 1968), PAAA, MfAA/C773/71.

1169 Mutukwa, *Politics of the Tanzania-Zambia Railproject*, 169.

1170 Junghanns, Note (March 27, 1968), PAAA, MfAA/C773/71.

1171 *Ibid.*

1172 Dr. Ernst Marré, Berichterstattung über den Aufenthalt in Tansania – Pemba (January 1969), PAAA, MfAA/C773/71.

1173 Vice-consul Hollender, Note (May 21, 1970), PAAA, MfAA/B280/74.

1174 Hollender, Note (April 24, 1970), and Vice-consul Hollender, Note (May 21, 1970), both in PAAA, MfAA/B280/74.

1175 Hollender, Note (May 21, 1970), PAAA, MfAA/B280/74.

1176 Hollender, Note (July 8, 1970), PAAA, MfAA/B280/74.

1177 Antoinette Burton, "Who Needs the Nation? Interrogating 'British' History," *Journal of Historical Sociology* 10:3 (September 1997), 14.

1178 Joyce Appleby, "The Power of History," *AHR* 103:1 (1998), 10.

1179 Arif Dirlik, "Modernity as History: Post-revolutionary China, Globalization and the Question of Modernity," *SH* 27:1 (January 2002), 21.

1180 Beck and Grande, *Das kosmopolitische Europa* (Frankfurt am Main, 2004), 81.

1181 Aiwha Ong, *Flexible Citizenship. The Cultural Logics of Transnationality* (Durham, NC, 1999).

1182 Thomas Bender, *A Nation among Nations: America's Place in World History* (New York, 2006), 296.

1183 Trentin, "Modernization as State Building," 487–506; Corinna R. Unger, "Industrialization or Agrarian Reform? West German Modernization Policies in India in the 1950s and 1960s," *Journal of Modern European History* 8:1 (2010), 47–65; and Bastian Hein, *Die Westdeutschen und die Dritte Welt. Entwicklungspolitik und Entwicklungsdienste zwischen Reform und Revolte 1959–1974* (Munich, 2009). On the postwar West German industrial fairs, see Christiane Fritsche, *Schaufenster des"-Wirtschaftswunders" und Brückenschlag nach Osten. Westdeutsche Industriemessen und Messebeteiligungen im Kalten Krieg (1946–1973)* (Munich, 2008).

1184 For recent literature, see Rita Chin, Heide Fehrenbach, Atina Grossman, and Geoff Eley, eds., *After the Nazi Racial State: Difference and Democracy in Postfascist Germany* (Ann Arbor, MI, 2009); Oguntoye Opitz and Schultz, eds., *Showing Our Colors: Afro-German Women Speak Out* (Amherst, MA, 1990); Heide Fehrenbach, *Race After Hitler: Black Occupation Children in Postwar Germany and America* (Princeton, NJ, 2005); Maureen Maisha Eggers, Grada Kilomba, Peggy Piesche, and Susan Arndt, eds., *Mythen, Masken und Subjekte: kritische Weißseinsforschung in Deutschland* (Münster, 2005); Maria Höhn, *GIs and Fräuleins: The German-American Encounter in 1950s West Germany* (Raleigh, NC, 2002). See also Niels Seibert, *Vergessene Proteste: Internationalismus und Antirassismus 1964–1983* (Münster, 2008); Quinn Slobodian, "Dissident Guests: Afro-Asian Students and Transnational Activism in the West German Protest Movement," in Wendy Pojmann, ed., *Migration and Activism in Europe Since 1945* (New York, 2008); Sandra Maß, *Weiße Helden, schwarze Krieger. Zur Geschichte kolonialer Männlichkeit in Deutschland 1918–1964* (Vienna, 2006); and Timothy L. Schroer, *Recasting Race after World War II: Germans and African Americans in American-Occupied Germany* (Boulder, CO, 2007).

1185 Schleicher, "Spurensuch im Süden Afrikas. Die Zusammenarbeit mit den Befreiungsbewegungen wirkt nach," in Thomas Kunze and Thomas Vogel, eds., *Ostalgie international. Erinnerungen an die DDR von Nicaragua bis Vietnam* (Berlin, 2010), 55.

1186 The title of a book by Schleicher's wife Ilona, which focuses on the gap between the "desires of the heart and the political calculus" of the East German state, reveals a bit more self-awareness in this respect. See Schleicher, *Zwischen Herzenswunsch und politischem Kalkül: DDR-Solidarität mit dem Befreiungskampf im südlichen Afrika* (Berlin, 1998).

Index